"The *Routledge International Handbook of Therapeutic Stories and Storytelling* illustrates the potential of stories to heal and transform, having helped humans for thousands of years to make meaning, endure difficulty and face the unknown. Stretching across countries and cultures, valued storytellers, therapists, artists and academics get together to document the power of stories. The book comprises of compelling accounts tracing stories' development in history, their impact on human brain and emotionality and their diverse use in various clinical, health, educational and social contexts around the globe. It also addresses the challenges and the opportunities humankind is facing now, looking at how stories can support and shape our collective response to Covid 19."

– **Elena Boukouvala,** *Dramatherapist, Psychologist, Performance Activist, Founder of Play Perform Learn Grow (PPLG) Conference, Dramatherapy Faculty Epineio Institute (Greece), Faculty East Side Institute (USA) and PhD Sociology Researcher Open University (UK).*

"This guidebook is invaluable for therapeutic workers everywhere. Crammed with creative courage, it provides a treasure map to rugged byways of inspirational empathy and dynamic healing wisdom."

– **Nancy Mellon** *taught storytelling as a healing art worldwide for many years. Her books are translated into several languages. See www.healingstory.com.*

"This collection of international voices weaves together anthropology, ethnography, personal and cultural histories, traditional stories, neuroscience and clinical theory and practice. They speak the language of story, creating a narrative of the therapeutic use of story from varied perspectives, as if from a cast of favourite and new characters ranging from the academic to the clinician to the storyteller. The handbook is an invaluable resource for experienced therapists, students and anyone interested in the field."

– **Roulla Demetriou** *is a dramatherapist, supervisor and a Lecturer on the MA Dramatherapy at Anglia Ruskin University. Former editor of BADth's Journal, Dramatherapy.*

ROUTLEDGE INTERNATIONAL HANDBOOK OF THERAPEUTIC STORIES AND STORYTELLING

The *Routledge International Handbook of Therapeutic Stories and Storytelling* is a unique book that explores stories from educational, community, social, health, therapeutic and therapy perspectives, acknowledging a range of diverse social and cultural views in which stories are used and written by esteemed storytellers, artists, therapists and academics from around the globe.

The book is divided into five main parts that examine different approaches and contexts for therapeutic stories and storytelling. The collected authors explore storytelling as a response to the Covid-19 pandemic, in education, social and community settings, and in health and therapeutic contexts. The final part offers an International Story Anthology written by co-editor Sharon Jacksties and a final story by Katja Gorečan.

This book is of enormous importance to psychotherapists and related mental health professionals, as well as academics, storytellers, teachers, people working in special educational needs, and all those with an interest in storytelling and its applied value.

Clive Holmwood is a Dramatherapist with 25 years' experience, and an Associate Professor in the Department of Therapeutic Arts at the University of Derby, where he lectures and researches in Dramatherapy and in the areas of play and Creative Arts Health and Wellbeing. He has written extensively on Dramatherapy, Play and Education, his most recent work being the co-edited *Routledge International Handbook of Play, Therapeutic Play and Play Therapy* with Sue Jennings in 2021.

Sue Jennings is Professor of Play, a lifetime award from the European Federation of Dramatherapy, and Distinguished Scholar at the University of the Witwatersrand. She has pioneered Dramatherapy and Neuro-Dramatic-Play for many years both in the UK and overseas and has written over 50 books on Group Work, Trauma and Play and Dramatherapy.

Sharon Jacksties is a qualified Dramatherapist and psychiatric nurse with a career as a mental health practitioner in hospitals and social services settings. A professional storyteller for 30 years, her practice includes performance, applied and community storytelling. She is FEST's (Federation of European Storytelling Organisations) first ambassador to the UK, has a teaching practice here and abroad, and has written 3 collections of traditional stories published by The History Press.

The Routledge International Handbook Series

The Routledge International Handbook of Forensic Psychology in Secure Settings
Edited by Jane L. Ireland, Carol A. Ireland, Martin Fisher, Neil Gredecki

The Routledge International Handbook of Critical Positive Psychology
Edited by Nicholas J. L. Brown, Tim Lomas, Francisco Jose Eiroa-Orosa

The Routledge International Handbook of Sexual Addiction
Edited by Thaddeus Birchard, Joanna Benfield

The Routledge International Handbook of Self-Control in Health and Well-Being
Edited by Denise de Ridder, Marieke Adriaanse, Kentaro Fujita

The Routledge International Handbook of Psychosocial Epidemiology
Edited by Mika Kivimaki, David G. Batty, Ichiro Kawachi, Andrew Steptoe

The Routledge International Handbook of Human Aggression
Current Issues and Perspectives
Edited by Jane L. Ireland, Philip Birch, Carol A. Ireland

The Routledge International Handbook of Jungian Film Studies
Edited by Luke Hockley

The Routledge International Handbook of Discrimination, Prejudice and Stereotyping
Edited by Cristian Tileagă, Martha Augoustinos and Kevin Durrheim

The Routledge Handbook of Public Health and the Community
Edited by Ben Y.F. Fong and Martin C.S. Wong

The Routledge International Handbook of Perinatal Mental Health Disorders
Edited by Amy Wenzel

The Routledge International Handbook of Community Psychology
Facing Global Crises with Hope
Edited by Carolyn Kagan, Jacqui Akhurst, Jaime Alfaro, Rebecca Lawthom, Michael Richards, and Alba Zambrano

ROUTLEDGE INTERNATIONAL HANDBOOK OF THERAPEUTIC STORIES AND STORYTELLING

Edited by Clive Holmwood, Sue Jennings and Sharon Jacksties

LONDON AND NEW YORK

First published 2022
by Routledge
2 Park Square, Milton Park, Abingdon, Oxon OX14 4RN

and by Routledge
605 Third Avenue, New York, NY 10158

Routledge is an imprint of the Taylor & Francis Group, an informa business

© 2022 selection and editorial matter, Clive Holmwood, Sue Jennings and Sharon Jacksties; individual chapters, the contributors

The right of Clive Holmwood, Sue Jennings and Sharon Jacksties to be identified as the authors of the editorial material, and of the authors for their individual chapters, has been asserted in accordance with sections 77 and 78 of the Copyright, Designs and Patents Act 1988.

All rights reserved. No part of this book may be reprinted or reproduced or utilised in any form or by any electronic, mechanical, or other means, now known or hereafter invented, including photocopying and recording, or in any information storage or retrieval system, without permission in writing from the publishers.

Trademark notice: Product or corporate names may be trademarks or registered trademarks, and are used only for identification and explanation without intent to infringe.

British Library Cataloguing-in-Publication Data
A catalogue record for this book is available from the British Library

Library of Congress Cataloging-in-Publication Data
A catalog record has been requested for this book

ISBN: 978-0-367-63370-7 (hbk)
ISBN: 978-1-032-19634-3 (pbk)
ISBN: 978-1-003-11889-3 (ebk)

DOI: 10.4324/9781003118893

Typeset in Bembo
by Newgen Publishing UK

We dedicate this book to all the health, social care and key workers who kept the world going during the time of the coronavirus pandemic. And to all teachers, classroom assistants and everyone in education who managed to keep things going for our little ones and young people. We thank you for your commitment, dedication and sacrifice. We hope that storytelling, in all its shapes and forms, gives you support and stimulus in your work and play.

CONTENTS

List of figures — xiv
List of tables — xvi
List of contributors — xvii
Foreword by Paul Animbom Ngong — xxvi
Acknowledgements — xxix

Introduction — 1
Clive Holmwood

PART I
Covid-19: a storied response — 5
Introduction 5

1 Making a story out of a crisis – a response to Covid-19: a dramatic perspective — 7
  Clive Holmwood

2 The stories of Siddhartha and Captain Tom: lifetimes apart but connecting us together — 12
  Drew Bird

3 Doorways to The Deathlands: the imaginal seeing of story — 19
  Mary Smail

4 Storytelling for disability in Covid-19 — 30
  Aurora Piaggesi, Giulia Bini, Silvia Carpi, Barbara Parrini and Stefania Bargagna

5 Don't let corona become our only story   43
   Arjen Barel

PART II
Stories & therapeutic texts   45
   Introduction 45

6 Through the Fairy Door … to the Land of Stories: a journey through your imagination   47
   Sue Jennings

7 Through the looking glass: six pitfalls in story-work   58
   Alida Gersie

8 Structuring the therapist's role: an exploration of Sophocles' play *King Oedipus*   73
   Marina Jenkyns

9 Oral storytelling is not dead: she's just gone to slip into something more comfortable …   83
   Steve Stickley

10 Shakespeare unbarr'd   91
   Rowan Mackenzie

11 Healing through the Mahabharata   101
   Kavita Arora *in conversation with* Raghu Ananthanarayanan

12 *We're going on a Bear Hunt*: neuro-dramatic play, multi-sensory informed storytelling approaches to working with children under five   111
   Clive Holmwood

13 Myth – drama – narrative – performance   120
   Stelios Krasanakis

14 Creativity and power in Sicilian spirit: the stories of Giufà, The Wise and The Fool   130
   Salvo Pitruzzella

PART III
Stories & therapeutic texts in educational, social and community contexts   139
   Introduction 139

15	The use of storytelling as a pedagogic tool in the English language classroom *Sarah Telfer*	141
16	Callers and hearers: song, orality, orature and aurality in African theatre performance *Vincent Meyburgh, Ntombifuthi Mkhasibe, and Joce Engelbrecht*	152
17	Beyond the happy ever afters: how stories in a local English theatre can have a therapeutic impact on their audiences *Richard Vergette*	156
18	The Cypriot story *Seniha Naşit Gürçağ*	164
19	A personal journey to *The Clever Mountain Girl* *Lenka Fisherová and Ilona Labuťová*	170
20	Changing the world through stories of change: the work of OpenStoryTellers 2004–2019 *Nicola Grove, Alice Parsley, Clemma Lewis and Robin Meader*	179
21	From isolation to integration and advocacy: healing and empowerment through storytelling *Lani Peterson*	191
22	Seeking a common ground: storytelling and social healing *Inger Lise Oelrich*	204
23	'Janare' and '*caporaballi*': the magic and splendour of Irpinia through stories of witches, dance leaders and sacred pigs *Josephine F. Discepolo Ahmadi*	212
24	Adapting oral tales for the moral transformation of the developing child and youths: adapting *Yomandene and the Stubborn Son* from tale to play *Victor Jong Taku*	231

PART IV
Stories & therapeutic texts in health and therapy contexts **241**
  Introduction   241

Contents

25 The Body Politic: an account of my therapeutic storytelling practice with torture survivors and their families 243
    Sharon Jacksties

26 I believe in unicorns … 254
    Silviana Bonadei

27 Clay stories, crafting spirit and soul 261
    Lynne Souter-Anderson

28 'Metamyth Therapy through the Arts in Museums'©: a personal journey through story 270
    Thalia Valeta

29 Stories in crisis and traumatic situations 275
    Mooli Lahad

30 The laying on of ears 287
    Mary Louise Chown

31 Storytelling and play: how storytelling and play can be used therapeutically with people with a learning disability 296
    Jem Dick

32 A trans-cultural perspective on life story therapy with adoptive foster and kinship families, using the "Theatre of Attachment" model 304
    Joan Moore

33 Fostering storytellers: helping foster carers to build attachments and enhance emotional literacy through stories and oral storytelling 316
    Steve Killick

34 The power of storytelling for people living with dementia 326
    Alice Liddell Allen

35 Exploring the dynamics of story in dementia research: storytelling constructs that support people with dementia to share their experiences of what it means to live with dementia 337
    Alison Ward

36 Zen stories to inspire imagination in a client with vascular dementia 350
    Ravindra Ranasinha

PART V
Stories   **363**

37 An international story anthology   365
    Sharon Jacksties
    Red Hat, Green Hat (East Africa)   365
    Amina and the Silent City (Iraq)   366
    Chasing the Sun (Native American tradition)   371
    The Snake and the King's Dream (Caucasus)   372
    The Best Hunters (West Africa)   374
    The Worst Potter (China)   376
    The Shadow of Shame (Korea)   379

38 Everything that we can remember: how to create a safe environment
    through a poetic story – an introduction to *Forest of Lost Memories*   382
    Alenka Vidrih

39 The Forest of Lost Memories©   384
    Katja Gorečan

Afterword   *396*
    Sharon Jacksties
Appendix   *398*
Index   *409*

FIGURES

0.1	The three-legged stool	2
4.1	Average score of "Well-being" subscale of HCP survey	35
4.2	Average score of "Work" subscale of HCP survey	36
4.3	Average score of "Patient's family" subscale of HCP survey	37
4.4	Average score of "Well-being" subscale of parents' survey	38
4.5	Average score of "Family" subscale of parents' survey	38
4.6	Average score of "Relate IRC" subscale of parents' survey	40
6.1	Closed Fairy Door in a tree	53
6.2	Through the Fairy Door	54
6.3	Moose and Mouse	56
12.1	Annie placing the characters on the sand	116
12.2	Annie placing the figures in the puddle of water	116
12.3	Annie blobbing wet sand onto the bear	117
15.1	'Model'	147
23.1	Photograph by Silvano Ruffini (*A Woman*)	213
23.2	Irpinia: photo by Pasquale Bimonte (*Sotto o' campanero*; 'Under the bell tower')	213
23.3	Irpinia: historical centre of Castelvetere sul Calore	215
23.4	Carnival 1	217
23.5	Carnival 2	219
23.6	The *caporaballo*	220
23.7	*La mietitura* (the harvest)	223
23.8	Photo by Angelo Sullo (*La sarcena*)	224
23.9	The old woman	225
23.10	The fire	227

Figures

29.1	Modern trauma	276
29.2	Re-narrated traumatic story	285
34.1	Domains of wellbeing	327
39.1	Forest of Lost Memories	394

TABLES

4.1	Study group	32
12.1	Developmental themes	112
12.2	Multi-sensory storytelling	118
26.1	EPR summary for one group using *I believe in Unicorns*	258
26.2	EPR summary for a group using *I believe in Unicorns*	259

CONTRIBUTORS

Editors

Clive Holmwood (UK), PhD, is a Dramatherapist with 25 years' experience, and an Associate Professor in the Department of Therapeutic Arts at the University of Derby, where he lectures and researches in Dramatherapy and in the areas of play and Creative Arts Health and Wellbeing. He gained his PhD in Education from the University of Warwick, which was subsequently published by Routledge in 2014 as *Drama Education and Dramatherapy*. He is also the co-editor of the *Routledge International Handbook of Dramatherapy* with Sue Jennings published in 2016 and *Learning as a Creative and Developmental Process in Higher Education* published by Routledge in 2019. His most recent book is the co-edited *Routledge International Handbook of Play, Therapeutic Play and Play Therapy* with Sue Jennings published in 2021. He is an NDP (Neuro-Dramatic Play) Practitioner and Trainer and runs his own private practice – Creative Solutions Therapy Ltd. He has known and has collaborated with Sue Jennings for 20 years.

Sue Jennings (UK), PhD, is Professor of Play, a lifetime award from the European Federation of Dramatherapy and Distinguished Scholar, University of the Witwatersrand. She has pioneered Dramatherapy and Neuro-Dramatic-Play for many years both in the UK and overseas. Her doctoral fieldwork was carried out with the Temiars, a tribal people who inhabit the rain forest of Malaysia. She spent 18 months living in the forest, together with her three children. She has kept in continuous contact with the tribal villages and with the children she helped to deliver as assistant village midwife. Recently her focus has been writing for young children with the stories of Moose and Mouse. There is an emphasis on empathy, attachment, diversity and curiosity. These books are also recommended for children on the spectrum. Sue has written over 50 books on group work, trauma and play and Dramatherapy, and many have been translated into Korean, Chinese, Hebrew, Russian, Norwegian, Swedish, Italian and Greek. Her passion is Shakespeare, especially *A Midsummer Night's Dream,* which she explores constantly in her work.

Sharon Jacksties (UK), post Grad Dip DTh, BA (Hons), RPN, trained as a dramatherapist and psychiatric nurse and practiced in the health and social service settings. This led to a performing arts degree and on to the discovery of oral storytelling at the beginning of its revival in Britain. A professional storyteller for 30 years, her practice includes performance, applied and community storytelling. She also teaches storytelling as a performance art and as a medium for wellbeing and therapeutic change in applied contexts, in the UK and abroad. A regular tutor at Halsway Manor, Britain's only residential centre for the traditional arts, she has written 3 collections of traditional stories published by The History Press. She is currently assisting FEST – Federation for European Storytelling organisations – in a pilot project for which she is England's FEST ambassador, promoting links between storytelling organisations and developing a role for advocacy in the field of oral narrative literature.

Authors

Raghu Ananthanarayanan (India) is a post-Graduate Engineer from IIT Madras. Raghu has delved deeply into Yoga and Behavioural Sciences to develop a unique approach to personal unfolding and organizational transformation. He has devoted almost four decades to transforming organizational cultures across the spectrum from grass roots developmental organizations to modern industrial organizations. He has developed a unique methodology called "Totally Aligned Organization" and a model called the "Tensegrity Mandala" that brings together his understanding of Yoga, Human Processes and Manufacturing Systems. He has pioneered the use of vernacular theatre and the Mahabharata in experiential learning. He is a direct disciple of Yogachaarya Krishnamaachaarya & TKV Desikachar. He also has the benefit of a long apprenticeship with Prof. Pulin K. Garg (IIM Ahmedabad).

Kavita Arora (India) is a practicing Child and Adolescent Psychiatrist and Co-Founder of the organisation Children First Mental Health institute, located in New Delhi, India (www.childrenfirstindia.com). While her education has been in the modern medicine version of Psychiatry and Psychology (MBBS, MD Psychiatry in India, followed by a CCST –UK), her upbringing and influences have been located and rooted in Indian culture. Stories, storytelling, the arts, and humour all hold a deep fascination and she attempts constantly to build bridges within her culture and acquired knowledge. She also works actively in the field of early intervention services for children who are differently wired. She has experienced and been influenced by the Mahabharata Immersion experience. She is also pursuing her diploma in Neuro-Dramatic Play.

Arjen Barel (Netherlands) is director and trainer at the Storytelling Centre and artistic director/producer at Storytelling \ Theater Lab. He developed the Share to Connect method to put applied storytelling on the map worldwide. He recently worked in Morocco, Palestine, Lithuania, Slovenia, Great Britain and Hungary. He is involved in performances as a dramaturg, director or writer.

Stefania Bargagna (Italy), MD, has been head of Istituto di Riabilitazione di Calambrone (IRC) at IRCCS Stella Maris since 2019. She has worked there as a Child Neuropsychiatrist since 1988. Responsible for several research projects on early treated hypothyroidism, Alzheimer's disease in Down syndrome and on the effects and molecular mechanisms of early intervention in Down syndrome, Intellectual disabilities, Educational and Psychological Strategies. She is particularly oriented to rehabilitation programs for psychopathology of learning disorders. She is also co-founder and President of Eppursimuove, a non-profit organization working to implement sport and exercise in rehabilitation programmes for both children and adults.

List of contributors

Giulia Bini (Italy) is a young psychologist, who graduated with honours from the University of Padua in July 2019. In the same year she did an internship at the IRCCS Stella Maris and then continued to collaborate on some research projects. She is passionate about childhood neurodevelopmental disorders and works with the aim of improving the quality of life for children, and family and professionals who care for them.

Drew Bird (UK), PhD, is Senior Lecturer in Dramatherapy at the University of Derby. A member of the Health and Care Professions Council (HCPC) and the British Association of Dramatherapists (BADth), and a fellow of the Academy of Higher Education. Drew is the Editor of the *Dramatherapy Journal*. He is also a lecturer at The University of Melbourne.

Silviana Bonadei (Switzerland) is of Swiss and Italian descent. She graduated in 1985 from the Institute of Social Studies in Geneva as a special educator. She has always been interested in working with children and adolescents with differences. Silviana volunteered for 6 months in Scotland in a homeless shelter for children and adolescents in difficulty, following this working in a homeless shelter in Switzerland for 10 years with groups and providing family sessions on a regular basis. Living with them helped her to develop her interest in play and other sensory and group activities. She has worked in this field for 45 years with children with neurological and developmental difficulties, especially children on the autistic spectrum. For the last 20 years she has developed services for a Penang Malaysia-based NGO dealing with Mental Health issues and providing one to one and group sessions from toddlers until adolescence and is part of the multi-disciplinary team of the Penang General Hospital, providing support to schools and families. Her work relating to NDP, EPR and ToR has always been part of her activities.

Silvia Carpi (Italy) is a teacher. She attended the University of Florence, where she was recognized as one of the best six students to graduate in 2016. She has been working as a professional educator at IRCCS Stella Maris since 2016, using the Early Start Denver Model and paying particular attention to relationships with families.

Mary Louise Chown (Canada), BFA, BEd. BA, has been taken into hospitals and palliative care wards, and into the world of mediation and conflict resolution by her work. She has travelled extensively in Manitoba, across Canada, and overseas, gathering stories and sharing her favourite ones. All things are possible in this world, and often true stories are stranger than fiction. Mary Louise is a trained teacher, artist, and mediator, and was the first Storyteller-in-Residence at the Winnipeg Public Library. She has co-founded Magic of One Storytelling Concerts and Braveheart Storytellers, as well as The Manitoba Storytelling Guild (http://manitobastorytelling.org/) and is the current artistic director of the Magic of One Concert series, which is continuing through a series of Fringe Performances and House Concerts.

Jem Dick (UK) is a Person-Centred Counsellor with 30 years' experience working therapeutically with a multi-media approach with people with learning disabilities. Integrating the Rogerian Counselling with Nind and Hewett's Intensive Interaction and Natalie Roger's Expressive Arts Therapy, he has also added a range of other techniques, including his own approaches of 'Expressive Sounds', applied clowning and storytelling. He has developed many effective ways of aiding people with communication difficulties. His therapeutic work is informed by his being a practicing artist in many art forms.

List of contributors

Josephine F. Discepolo Ahmadi (UK) is a psychotherapist, a dramatherapist, a supervisor and a team consultant. She has worked in a variety of NHS specialist mental health services and at present works in an NHS community Psychology Department and in private practice in Hampshire. She is a supervisor, a tutor and a marker for a variety of ACAT accredited training courses, both at Practitioner and Psychotherapy level. Has been a member of the ACAT Equality and Diversity Committee for two years and facilitated workshops at ACAT Annual Conferences. She is the UKCP representative for the Association for Cognitive Analytic Therapy. Has contributed to research projects, training programmes and staff support groups and published work on her special interest subject, the impact of social inequalities on mental and physical health.

Joce Engelbrecht (South Africa) attained a Performance Certificate from the Trinity College of London. Her career started in 2001 doing a touring production, speaking out about HIV/Aids and this catapulted her to many other theatric ventures at the Baxter Theatre, KKNK and many other festivals around the country. She was using theatre as a tool to combat social ills with Department of Education, Department of Social Development and Correctional Services. She took a break from the Arts and returned in 2010 to do a short film called *Lenteblom* with Imagen Heart Films. She then completed a Puppetry Project with UNIMA, participated in Infecting the City Festival. She was introduced to Medicine Theatre with CAST, a theatre group from Georgia USA, and did a performance at a Summit for the CCD, USA. In 2014 she had an opportunity to hone in on her puppetry and facilitating skills as she joined The Jungle Theatre Company in Top Dog and more recently A Dog's Life, adding to her love for children's theatre and she now has a new appreciation for animal welfare. In 2019 she was invited to write and direct a new work for Jungle Theatre Company. It is called *Mantis and the Bee*.

Lenka Fisherová (Czech Republic) is a psychologist, special pedagogue, lecturer (workshop leader), actress and dramatherapist, and a founder member of the Association of Dramatherapists of the Czech Republic. She has long been engaged in projects focused on using drama for educational and therapeutic purposes. She is a member of The Bear Educational Theatre and an associate artist of the Prague Shakespeare Company. The main topics she focused on during her latest studies were: "The Boundaries between drama in education and drama in therapy and "Work with a story".

Alida Gersie (UK), PhD, is a writer and senior consultant in the arts therapies and applied arts. She has held innovative leadership positions in arts education, family action and community development and was for many years Director of Studies of the Postgraduate Arts Therapies at the University of Hertfordshire, UK. In the late 1970s Alida pioneered a narrative approach to improving individual and social resilience. This method is now used in over 40 countries. She has lectured at universities worldwide, served on several boards and is the author of acclaimed (translated) books including *Storymaking in Education and Therapy* (with Nancy King), *Dramatic Approaches of Brief Therapy, Storymaking in Bereavement, Reflections on Therapeutic Storymaking: the use of stories in groups* and *Earthtales: Storytelling in Times of Change*.

Katja Gorečan (Slovenia) received a Bachelor's degree in Comparative Literature and Literary Theory from the University in Ljubljana and a Master's Degree in Dramaturgy from the Academy for Theatre, Direction, Film, and Television, also in Ljubljana. She took part in a creative writing course, specializing in dramatics. This resulted in the creation of her one-act drama *Seven Girl's Questions*. In 2012 her second poetry collection *The Sorrows of Young Hana* was nominated for the Jenko Award, the highest poetry award in Slovenia, and was selected in the Biennale of Young Artists from Mediterranean Europe. In 2017, her choreo-poem *One Night Some Girls Somewhere Are Dying* was published by the House of Poetry Poetikon. She is a current MA student of Art Therapy in the Faculty of Education at the University of Ljubljana, Slovenia.

Nicola Grove (UK) was an English teacher, then a speech and language therapist. She left her job as a lecturer at City University to set up the charity OpenStoryTellers, and now practises as a freelance trainer, researcher, writer and storyteller. She is an honorary senior lecturer at the Tizard Centre, University of Kent. www.drnicolagrove.com

Marina Jenkyns (UK) has been involved in the practice and training of dramatherapy for many years both in the UK and abroad. She initially read English at the University of Cambridge, taught English and Drama in schools and then Higher Education. She combined her subsequent training in dramatherapy with an additional training in process consultancy at the Tavistock Clinic and engaged in long-term psychoanalytic psychotherapy. She also has considerable experience as a director of plays. These influences inform this chapter. She writes poetry and short stories and, now retired from therapy practice, is focusing her energies on playwriting. She has contributed to several books on dramatherapy and clinical supervision. Her own book, *The Play's the Thing: exploring text in drama and therapy*, was published by Routledge in 1996.

Steve Killick (UK), BSc(Hons) DClinPsych, was a Consultant Clinical Psychologist in the NHS for many years and now works in independent practise as both a psychologist and storyteller. He is Visiting Fellow at the George Ewart Evans Centre for Storytelling at The University of South Wales and has written several books and papers, many focussing on the links between emotional literacy and storytelling. He is on the Board of Directors of Beyond the Border International Storytelling Festival in Wales and was Storyteller-in-residence for the 2017 Storytelling and Health Conference in Swansea. He has also worked with The Fostering Network and Barnardo's in projects exploring the use of storytelling for children who are looked after and has developed a project for schools using storytelling to develop emotional literacy called 'Feelings are Funny Things.'

Stelios Krasanakis (Greece) is a Psychiatrist, Psychotherapist-Dramatherapist and Theatre Director. Founder of the "Institute of Dramatherapy AEON", in 1994, offering educational training and treatment in dramatherapy and in Expressive Arts Therapy with Dr Avi Goren-Bar. He lectures in Dramatherapy in the National and Kapodistrian University of Athens. Member of the board of directors of the Greek Psychiatric Association, founding member of the European Federation of Dramatherapy (EFD) and member of the board of directors. Founding member of the World Alliance of Dramatherapy (WADth). International member of the British Association of Dramatherapists (Badth). Director of more than 20 theatrical performances, founder and art director of Festival of Naxos. He has published many articles in books, scientific journals and in psychiatric reviews.

Ilona Labuťová (Czech Republic) is a special pedagogue, dramatherapist, lecturer, founder member and executive member of the Association of Dramatherapists Czech Republic. She has long been engaged in dramatherapy work with people with learning difficulties and disabilities and children with specific educational needs. Co-founder of UJETO Theater and non-profit organization Teatralie, which focuses on the creation and implementation of educational activities on the use of theatre in education, socially oriented projects and therapies.

Mooli Lahad (Israel), PhD, PhD, is the founder of Dramatherapy in Israel and former head of the MA in Dramatherapy at Tel Hai College. A senior medical psychologist, Dramatherapist, Bibliotherapist. Author and co-author of 35 books, Founder and president of the International Community Stress Prevention Center Kiryat Shmona, Israel.

Clemma Lewis (UK) joined Openstorytellers as part of a peer mentor project supporting people with profound disabilities to tell their own stories. She is married and lives in Somerset.

Alice Liddell Allen (UK) is a dramatherapist and storyteller. She works with older people living with dementia in groups or one-to-one in care homes and day centres. Over recent years she has developed a model of dramatherapy using a sensory approach with repetition, ritual and rhythm, which includes storytelling, music and singing that encourages the most connection, communication and joy with the aim of leaving her clients with warm feelings and a contented demeanour.

Rowan Mackenzie (UK), PhD, worked on Creating Space for Shakespeare: non-traditional and applied theatre settings, including working with people with mental health issues, learning disabilities, those within the criminal justice system and other marginalised groups as part of her doctoral research. She is also a prison practitioner in various UK prisons using Shakespeare to deliver workshops as well as longer-term projects where she works on adapting, rehearsing and performing Shakespeare.

Robin Meader (UK) was a founder member of Openstorytellers. He lives in Somerset and runs his own business as an artist and graphic facilitator, on commissions for organisations such as NHS England.

Vincent Meyburgh (South Africa) obtained a Performers Diploma from the University of Cape Town in 1993. He is the Artistic Director & Founder of Jungle Theatre Company and started this non-profit organization in 1995. This organization uses folktales and theatre for social transformation. Over the years Vincent has written, directed and performed theatre works based on South African folktales. In 2010 as part of a theatre training he directed the development of a play called ***River of Life*** based on an isiXhosa folktale passed on through the oral tradition. Since then he has developed scripts for Jungle Theatre Company called ***The Magic Shell, When Lion Had Wings*** and ***Python and the Qunube Tree***, all based on South African folktales. In 2016, the play ***When Lion Had Wings*** was published by the South African Publisher Junkets. In 2019 an illustrated children's book called ***Python and the Qunube Tree*** was designed and self-published by Jungle Theatre Company.

Ntombifuthi Mkhasibe (South Africa) is originally from Durban, currently living in Simonstown Da Gama Park, and obtained a National Diploma in Drama Studies at the Durban University of Technology. Ntombifuthi has been involved in many theatre productions before joining Jungle Theatre Company, having taught Zulu Dances called Iziqonqwane. She is a song writer, composer, choreographer, singer and an actress who joined Jungle Theatre Company in April 2009 to further her dreams and career and to learn more about the industry and to develop her skills in the process.

List of contributors

Joan Moore (UK), PhD, is a freelance Dramatherapist and Play Therapist with foster and adoptive families, applying her "Theatre of Attachment" model of life history therapy, mainly in the child's family home. Joan's doctoral study at Leeds Beckett University is on the use of narrative and drama to support permanent placements. She supervises creative arts therapists. Her publications include: Moore J. (2021) *Developing Secure Attachment Through Play*, Routledge; Moore J. (2020) *Therapeutic Stories for Foster, Adoptive and Kinship Families*, Routledge, Moore J. (2019) *A Narrative-Dramatic Approach to Children's Life Story with Foster, Adoptive and Kinship Families: using the 'Theatre of Attachment' model*, Moore J. (2014) *Emotional Problem Solving using Stories Drama and Play*, Hinton House; Moore J. (2012) *Once upon a time…stories and drama to use in direct work with adopted and foster children*, BAAF; and Corrigan and Moore, (2011) *Listening to Children's Wishes and Feelings*, BAAF. She also peer reviewed articles in *Dramatherapy*, official Journal of the British Association of Dramatherapists, *Journal of Adoption and Fostering*, and has chapters in S Jennings, ed. (2009) *Dramatherapy and Social Theatre*, Routledge and R. Rose ed. (2017) *Innovative Therapeutic Life History Work*.

Seniha Naşit Gürçağ (Cyprus) is a Turkish Cypriot counselling psychologist and psychotherapist working in private practice. She is a certificated systemic couple family therapist, child-centred play therapist, filial therapist, neuro-dramatic-play specialist and an assistant trainer. She mostly works with children, couples and families with the integration of family and play approaches.

Inger Lise Oelrich (Sweden) is a Theatre director & Educator using storytelling and creativity as a path of development through existential questions that unite us all. She runs trainings on Healing Story, organizes symposia and has founded the ALBA Peace Project. Connecting with nature, and strengthening what is uniquely human in us, is a lodestar of her work. Her latest book is *THE NEW STORY: Storytelling as a Pathway to Peace*. www.thenewstory.nu and www.storytellingforlife.com.

Barbara Parrini (Italy) is a developmental psychologist and family therapist. She has worked at IRCCS since 1998 dealing with the rehabilitation of severe neurodevelopmental disorders, in particular autistic spectrum disorders. She is a certified therapist of the DIR model. She also specializes in counselling for parents, family and individuals in therapy from a relational systemic perspective.

Alice Parsley (UK) is a member of Openstorytellers and lives in Somerset. She was the company's researcher on a project with Bristol University History Department, funded by the Heritage Lottery Fund and the Brigstow Institute, to discover and perform the story of Fanny Fust, an 18th Century heiress with learning disabilities.

Lani Peterson (USA) is a psychologist, coach, public speaker and professional storyteller. She has extensive experience working with individuals, groups and organizations in the areas of leadership, emotional intelligence, personal and team development. Drawing on her background in narrative therapy and healing through story, Lani works with both individuals and groups specializing in the exploration of story as a medium for personal growth, connection and social change.

Aurora Piaggesi (Italy) is a storyteller, creative producer and Storytelling coach working with narrative since 2016. She graduated in Cinema, Visual Arts and Entertainment and specialized in Writing for Visual Media and TV and Film Production. Since 2010 she has applied her knowledge and skills in Visual Storytelling within healthcare systems. She has led several workshops for the IRCCS Stella Maris and other public and private organizations. In 2018 her project "Living With Chronic Wounds", a transmedia series on patients' and professionals' perspective on the burden of dealing with chronic wounds and chronic pathologies, was endorsed by the European Wound Management Association. Her research on the application of Storytelling in Communication in Healthcare has started as a consequence of this project, in the late months of 2019.

Salvo Pitruzzella (Italy) is Dramatherapy course leader at the Arts Therapies Centre, Lecco, and Professor of Arts Education at the Fine Arts Academy of Palermo. Member of the Executive Board of the EFD (European Federation of Dramatherapy). He is the author and editor of many books and articles on dramatherapy, arts education and creativity studies, including *Drama, Creativity and Intersubjectivity. The Roots of Change in Dramatherapy* (Routledge, 2016).

Ravindra Ranasinha (Sri Lanka) is a dramaturge, dramatherapist, counsellor, teacher, researcher, author and a social activist from Sri Lanka. He is one of Sri Lanka's pioneers in the world of dramatherapy, and is the President of Association for Dramatherapists, in Sri Lanka. His books *Dramatherapy in Sri Lanka* (2013), *How Schools Abuse and Fail Children: Dramatherapy to Heal Emotionally Traumatized School Children in Sri Lanka*, (2014) and *Creative Arts Therapies for Autistic Children* (2015) are the first literature in dramatherapy in Sri Lanka. Ravindra is the Founder Director of the Dramatherapy Certification Programme, in Sri Lanka, initiated in 2015 as a collaborative effort with Family Planning Association and approved by Tertiary and Vocational Education Commission in Sri Lanka. Ravindra is also the Research Director, Research Centre for Dramatherapy, Colombo. He works extensively with trauma victims in schools, prisons and war-ravaged areas in the country. Ravindra works as a social activist for 'Friends of Tibet' global network and is also an Advisor to 'Centre for Social and Political Art' (CSPA), India.

Mary Smail (UK) is a Dramatherapist, trained in the Sesame Approach and a psychotherapist. She was the Director of the Sesame Institute charity for 20 years and the Myths/Fairy tale lecturer on the MA Drama and Movement Therapy (Sesame). She co-edited *Dramatherapy with Myth and Fairytale*, and presently works in private practice under the name Soul Works UK www.marysmailsoulworks.co.uk. Her passion and road map for life are the stories.

Lynne Souter-Anderson (UK) is a Fellow of the National Counselling Society, a BACP Senior Accredited Therapist, accredited Senior Supervisor with PTUK and registered Consultant Sandplay Therapist with the AST. As founder of the Clay Therapy Community, in 2012 Lynne established a pioneering clay therapy training in the United Kingdom. Her private practice is in Cambridgeshire, UK, where she offers psychotherapy for children, adolescents, adults, couples and families, clinical supervision and consultancy work. Her expertise in the field of clay therapy, the creative arts and sandplay therapy is acknowledged through invitations to present training and conference workshops across the globe. Lynne has thirty years of experience in this field and is author of *Touching Clay, Touching What? The Use of Clay in Therapy* (2010), *Making Meaning: Clay Therapy with Children and Adolescents* (2015) and *Seeking Shelter, Seeking Safety. Clay Therapy with Families and Groups* (2019).

List of contributors

Steve Stickley (UK) was co-founder of Footprints Theatre Company in 1978 and served as its Artistic Director until its cessation in 2018. Footprints focused mainly upon primary education and produced Theatre-in-Education Programmes, curriculum drama projects, shows, INSET training, and storytelling initiatives throughout the East Midlands, UK and internationally. He currently serves on the Board of the Society for Storytelling (www.sfs.org.uk).

Victor Jong Taku (Cameroon) holds a PhD in African Literature, and specializes in orature, drama and theatre arts. He is a playwright and an adapting artist of folk tales to plays, film scripts and comic strips. He is also an advocate of environmental protection and a peace crusader. He is presently a Senior Lecturer and Head of the Performing and Visual Arts Department, Faculty of Arts at the University of Buea, Cameroon. He has written and directed twenty-four radio plays currently being broadcast over Cameroon Radio and Television (CRTV) amongst which *Red Marks, Bus Love, Green Bond* and *The Leopard's Skin* have been adapted for the stage.

Sarah Telfer PhD (UK) is an Associate TIRI (Teaching Intensive Research Informed) Professor in Education at the University of Bolton. She is an experienced educational leader and teacher educator with a background in: Drama; English for Speakers of Other Languages (ESOL) and Literacy. She is currently lead for Initial Teacher Education (ITE) 14+ pathways and lectures on the Master's in Education and Doctorate in Education programmes at the University of Bolton, where she is a university TIRI teaching award winner. Sarah's specialist area of academic research is the use of stories in teaching and learning and interaction in the ESOL and literacy classroom by embedding Drama, Creative writing and Literature into English language teaching. Her specialist areas of research focus on the use of anecdotal storytelling to promote engagement and interaction in the classroom.

Thalia Valeta (Greece), BA, MA, HPC reg, is a psychotherapist/dramatherapist and the founder and director of "Metamyth"© Therapy through the Arts, a psychological method which she practices with people who have epilepsy and other organic, neurological and psychiatric disorders in hospitals. She is also running programmes of "Metamyth" Therapy through the Arts in Museums © internationally.

Richard Vergette (UK) is a teacher and playwright. His play *American Justice* played in The Arts Theatre in 2013 and *Dancing through the Shadows*, the first play in a trilogy of Hull plays, played at Hull Truck in 2015. With the playwright Nick Lane, he adapted David Mark's best-selling crime novel *Dark Winter*, which played to capacity houses at Hull Truck Theatre in March and November 2018.

Alenka Vidrih (Slovenia) is Assistant Professor in the Faculty of Education at the University of Ljubljana, Slovenia. She is head of the Creative Arts Therapy Programme and teaches on Performing Arts in the Department of Preschool Education, Primary School Education and in Special Education. Her research interests are Performance Skills in Health and Relational Pedagogy. Currently, she's part of the National research on Creativity and Gifted Education. As an artist, she performs and is involved in theatre direction. As a researcher she regularly presents in the international conference circuit.

Alison Ward (UK) is an Associate Professor at the University of Northampton with a particular interest in dementia, creative engagement and wellbeing. Alison is a founding member of the Forget Me Nots dementia social group and a certified TimeSlips storytelling facilitator.

FOREWORD

Storytelling is a major activity of human communication; it is an age-old tradition, used in many ways by different societies at different moments. Storytelling and stories can be entertaining, therapeutic and educative. The practice is a distinct form of performance but is also to be found integrated into other forms of performance. More recently it has moved in different directions with arts practitioners to produce works that are embedded in health, community or therapeutic interventions. When performed, stories can convey an opinion or seek one from the listener, illustrate a concept, establish a bond of belonging between listener and storyteller, inform about the world or entertain or change. This is all considered important in human existence as it comprises an experience shared by all humankind.

To tell stories is to affirm one's existence. No human being exists without a story. Each day, we all listen to and tell different stories in order to accomplish a desire or meet a request. In this process, there is a risk of mingling with the storyteller's own personal story without the intention of doing so. Some of the stories told are imaginary; others are fairy tales, myths or folk tales; and others are inspired from real life. Whichever, the audience to whom the story is told, listens, participates and contributes to the creative process in a co-creative manner, which results in a lived experience that can only be manifested in storytelling.

I remember when I was a little boy, my father would put me by his side and start narrating how life was when he was growing up. He told me of the ordeal they went through, trekking from Cameroon to Nigeria to sell "kola nuts" (the fruit of the kola tree scientifically known as *Cola acuminata* and *Cola nitida*, typically common to West/Central Africa), after which they would eventually buy other products to come and sell in Cameroon (then West Cameroon). In the process of telling these stories, he would sit by the fireside, sometimes while roasting corn. He would then use the illustrations from these stories to instil in me the spirit of hard work and bravery. Although he did not actually say "son, you have to be brave, hardworking and determined to make it in life," I could sense it in the way he told the stories. Filled with metaphors, these stories related to my situation in a way that I felt was purposefully designed for me. This creative spirit to tell stories that appeal to the listener permits storytelling to be used as an art form, in health interventions, and also as therapy in order to create individual change and growth.

Foreword

As if in a quest to corroborate this claim, Clive Holmwood, Sue Jennings and Sharon Jacksties' *Routledge International Handbook of Therapeutic Stories and Storytelling* is like the old saying a 'stitch in time' – stories are a way of dealing with difficulties before they become real problems. This book perfectly fits the context of arts, arts in health and creative arts therapies in that, through the cross-section of chapters, it touches on every single function of storytelling. It is intercontinental, with contributors from all the continents; this is clear proof of the editors' 'clairvoyance' in ensuring that people of all races, regions and disciplines find material in this book. Coming as the third publication in a series of Routledge International Handbooks – the other two being the *Routledge International Handbooks on Dramatherapy* and *Play, Therapeutic Play and Play Therapy* – this book is fascinating in the way it harnesses our day-to-day realities as seen from the storytelling perspective.

It is divided into five parts, each created around a particular theme, with chapters from renowned world-class scholars on aspects of stories and storytelling. The first part is dedicated to COVID-19 stories. As timely and appropriate as this is, the part sets the ball rolling by handling issues that arose during COVID-19. It opens with Clive Holmwood's perspective of creating a story out of COVID-19 and ends with Arjen Barel's quest for us not to make corona our *only* story. This part ties perfectly into the current situation (whilst writing during the pandemic), thereby creating an awareness of the importance of using stories in all circumstances for communication and therapeutic purposes.

With this premise set, Part II delves into stories and therapeutic texts. Here, Sue Jennings begins looking at fairy tales, myth drama and narrative, without neglecting the healing effects of Mahabharata or the great Sicilian stories; this part is a blend of western and non-western storytelling traditions. In the same way that each person has a beginning and will have an end, a person's stories do not exist separately or on their own but are related to the stories of others. This relationship between stories is what Pitruzzella strongly affirms, creates new meaning. In this view, there is a fictional meeting with the other, as fiction is the field used in the experimentation of identifying who a person truly is. Each person has within them the ability to bring about change. This is the quest of therapeutic stories and texts.

Part III paints a picture of how stories can be used in educational, community and social settings for general therapeutic purposes. This somehow connects with Part IV, which examines stories and therapeutic texts in a health and therapy context. These two parts provide great evidence to an understanding of the healing function of stories. Storytelling or the stories themselves are aimed at enhancing a sense of education, community and wellbeing. There is a clear exploration of the use of storytelling, therapeutic texts and stories in the service of community, in the widest sense of the term. This is all well considered in this International Handbook, which ends with an anthology of stories by Sharon Jacksties who concentrates on providing a range of international stories which have served in her therapeutic practice. Finally, finishing with a moving story about memory loss by Katja Gorečan.

This Routledge International Handbook provides a deeper understanding of the different contexts and settings in which stories are, can and should be used. It is evident in this book that stories provide consolation and encouragement to continue the search for answers to our human condition. Stories and storytelling are instruments for understanding our physical and emotional, psychological and spiritual health in more relevant ways, and are highly therapeutic.

In most stories, the protagonist often displays wit, patience and the courage that is needed to overcome life's obstacles. When the listener or reader identifies with the protagonist, they can learn to confront their own loneliness and fears. The characters in these stories act within a credible structure yet without the limitations of reality. They explore alternatives in action until they find an answer or a suitable way out of the situation they find themselves thrust into.

Foreword

The stories and therapeutic stories and ideas around them presented in this international handbook tell the underlying truth of human existence. Fantasies are created to establish a sense of safety, particularly when exploring and undergoing dangerous and personal transformations. This makes us understand the necessity of stories and storytelling to confirm their function as tools that should be used in the arts, arts in health and therapy. No matter what the context or location, professional or amateur settings, scholars or practitioners, teachers or students, this is a highly recommended international handbook that meets and serves the purpose of edu-info-tainment and therapy.

Paul Animbom Ngong, Ph.D.
Associate Professor of Therapeutic Communication,
Theatre and Film Studies, The University of Bamenda, Cameroon,
And Copenhagen, Denmark.

ACKNOWLEDGEMENTS

We would like to thank Routledge Publishers, and especially Alexis O'Brien for your help and support, especially during the final editing process. We would like to acknowledge the support and dedication of all our authors from around the world who contributed to this book during the most unprecedented times during the coronavirus pandemic. Special thanks go to the translator of Chapter 38, Rudi Filipčič. We would also like to acknowledge those authors and storytellers who were unable to contribute due to loss, bereavement or other personal circumstances. Finally, not forgetting as Arjen Barel says in Chapter 5 – we all hope that Corona will not become our only story.

Cover artwork by Lis Dobb-Sandi, (2013), *Midsummer Night's Dream Forest and Faeries*. Lis, silk artist and watercolourist, specialises in works containing hidden animals (and faeries) having enduring interest and appeal.

INTRODUCTION

When Sue Jennings first asked me to co-edit the *Routledge International Handbook of Dramatherapy* in 2015, she had a vision. A vision of three books on drama, play and stories. I remember that Sue described these three 'art forms' as being absolutely central to anyone involved in working creatively, therapeutically or in a therapy context within the creative and expressive arts. Whether work was in a community context, education, social justice, arts in health, arts therapies or any other diverse contexts drama, play and story were being used in, they were essential ingredients. They were the building blocks, the flour, eggs and sugar which created the cake. Each art form, and I include play and storytelling here as art forms, provided a safe boundary in which work could occur.

As importantly Sue reminded me that the three disciplines were also like a three-legged stool. This kind of seat has always been known to be the most safe and stable of any seat due to the way it connects with the ground. Not only is it grounded in such a safe way, using three legs, the strongest form of connection to the ground, but each leg is equidistant to the other. They remain exactly the same distance from each other, which is also why it is so stable and strong. No one leg is any less or more important than the other two. However, the moment one is removed the stool would collapse immediately (see Figure 0.1).

The distance between each leg is also very important, not just because it adds stability and strength, but because it allows the three legs to remain in sight of each other so they can offer mutual support and influence. Each leg offers not only stability but influence and mutual support. One cannot 'act' out a drama without it being playful, 'playing a part.' The moment we act out a part we tell a story. The moment we begin to play, the play contains drama *and* story. We cannot tell a story without it having elements of playfulness and drama in the way that it is told. Everything that we do in our lives from the moment we wake until we go to bed is both a story and a drama and is played out. It could be argued that story is the flour that offers the raising agent to the eggs and sugar of the cake. They cannot be separated; each is absolutely essential and relies on and has a relationship with the other. I have always believed that each of these art forms drama, play and story are are not only therapeutic but educational and that the two are interlinked (Holmwood: 2014).

Having published the *Routledge International Handbook of Dramatherapy* in 2016 and the *Routledge International Handbook of Play, Therapeutic Play and Play Therapy* in 2021, we complete

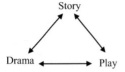

Figure 0.1 The three-legged stool

the 'stool', or cake, with the *International Handbook of Therapeutic Stories and Storytelling*. Sue and I are also very indebted to and welcome Sharon Jacksties (2012, 2018, 2020) onto the editorial team. Sharon brings a wealth of knowledge and experience as an internationally renowned storyteller, and like Sue Jennings and myself is well published in the field of stories and storytelling.

Stories, like drama and play, have occurred since man first existed. Mooli Lahad describes in Chapter 29 how the very first stories were told millennia ago; they were drawn on walls in caves by our ancient predecessors as a way of documenting their lives, as a way of beginning to understand the world in which they lived. Images of animals they relied on to survive, or pictures of their successful hunt. To this day stories are used in the very same way. Alida Gersie describes so accurately that:

> When our life is complex, which it is more often than not, we hope to find within the story images relevant to our own predicament, hoping maybe against hope, that an answer to our problem might *dwell* within the story…
>
> *(Gersie:1992:15)*

A story, however, is not a story until it is *told*, and the telling of the story is central to this process.

As with the other two international handbooks, we have been keen to involve stories from as many different cultures, countries, societies and contexts as possible. We have endeavoured to place them firstly into four broad themes. As a response to the global Covid-19 pandemic, we offer chapters on stories that in some way relate to this global phenomenon, how we use stories to make sense of what at times has seemed the unfathomable. We then offer three parts, stories and therapeutic texts, stories and therapeutic texts in educational, social and community contexts, and then stories and therapeutic texts in health and therapy contexts.

Stories are so practical and can be used in so many different ways, so finally we offer in Part V a series of story resources. Sharon Jacksties offers a range of seven specific stories that she uses within therapeutic contexts based on her many years of practice. This is followed by an example of a therapeutic story as told by Katja Gorečan in relation to memory loss and dementia.

Wherever, whoever and however stories are used and told, they are and will continue to be *essential* for humankind to make sense of the world in which we live and the relationships we have with the people and world around us, to better aid all of us as we travel on our own 'story' through life. This is particularly so now more than ever as we live in such uncertain and unpredictable times with the after-effects of Covid and general world unrest for a whole generation to come.

Introduction

On a personal note, I offer my huge appreciation for being able to share this journey with, and am indebted to, my fellow editors Sue and Sharon, for their knowledge, skill, wisdom and tenacity in the creation of this story the… *Routledge International Handbook of Therapeutic Stories and Storytelling*.

Clive Holmwood PhD
Associate Professor
Therapeutic Arts
University of Derby

References

Gersie, A. (1992). *Earthtales: storytelling in Times of Change*. London: Green Print.
Holmwood, C. (2014). *Drama Education and Dramatherapy: Exploring the Space Between Disciplines*. London: Routledge.
Jacksties, S. (2018). *Somerset Folk Tales for Children*. Cheltenham: History Press.
Jacksties, S. (2012). *Somerset Folk Tales*. Cheltenham: History Press.
Jacksties, S. (2020). *Animal Folk Tales of Britain and Ireland*. Cheltenham: History Press.
Jennings, S., Holmwood, C. (Eds.) (2016). *Routledge International Handbook of Dramatherapy*. London: Routledge.
Jennings, S., Holmwood, C. (Eds.) (2021) *Routledge International Handbook of Play, Therapeutic Play, and Play Therapy*. London: Routledge.

PART I

Covid-19

A storied response

Introduction

As you might imagine, this section was never expected or considered when the book was originally conceived. No one could have predicted that what at first seemed to be an inconsequential flu-like illness in a city in China would turn into a world-wide pandemic, infecting millions and killing hundreds of thousands. No one expected the international lockdowns that occurred across the globe in 2020 into 2021.

This part of the volume developed organically out of the writings of various contributors; it was not asked for or required, but was a storied response. Stories are influenced by the world around us and the world is influenced by the stories it hears. We therefore begin this volume by offering a small selection of responses to the pandemic, partly as a tribute to the many professionals around the world who have fought valiantly against this disease and to the many who have lost their lives and the families they leave behind.

Clive Holmwood begins by sharing his personal experiences during the early part of the lockdown in the UK in the spring of 2020, with all the uncertainties it created, and considers it from a dramatic storied perspective. This is followed by Drew Bird's comparison of the stories of Siddhartha and Captain Tom in Chapter 2. Captain Tom became a folk hero in the UK in 2020 by doing 100 laps of his garden by his 100th birthday, hoping to raise a few thousand pounds. He eventually raised millions for the UK Health Service, was knighted by the Queen and became a symbol of the National Health Service's fighting spirit. Mary Smail then compares her imaginal world of 'The Deathlands' to our experiences of Covid-19. Following this Aurora Piaggesi and colleagues share their ground-breaking research of storytelling during Covid-19. Their story is particularly apt, coming from Italy, which the world focussed on as an early hot spot during the unfolding of the pandemic in the spring of 2020. Finally, in Chapter 5, we finish with a short thoughtful piece from Arjen Barel in The Netherlands, who considers that the coronavirus should not be our only story. And as we write this introduction at the end of 2020 and the beginning of 2021, with coronavirus vaccines beginning to be rolled out, we sincerely hope that the coronavirus will not be our *only* story.

1
MAKING A STORY OUT OF A CRISIS – A RESPONSE TO COVID-19

A dramatic perspective

Clive Holmwood

Introduction

As an academic and practitioner part of my role is to write academic articles and books, besides carrying out research. My personal escape from this academic rigour has often been zombie apocalypse and disaster novels and movies. Action adventures where individuals or small groups of survivors move cautiously through urban landscapes decimated by disaster; empty streets and empty shops, that show the last remnants of a society that once existed. Recently I have begun to live, and still live, the reality of these fantasy dramas, in a way neither I, nor anyone else, could have expected.

Setting the drama – the dramatic context

The skies above my house are clear of all the vapour trails of aeroplanes in the spring sky; almost all air travel has ceased. Streets are eerily quiet, with almost no cars on the road, especially in the evenings when the eerie silence is deafening. The UK government has announced unprecedented billion-pound bail-outs for companies and workers as millions stay at home. Our Prime Minister, after delivering daily addresses to the nation from 10 Downing Street, went into self-isolation and narrowly escaped with his life after spending two weeks in hospital in intensive care. This is surely the plot and storyline for a zombie apocalypse movie or novel; but it's not, it was my current reality in the spring of 2020. We were reeling to make sense of what it meant as the semblance of normal society lurched towards fear and anxiety. The perfect setting for a drama or dramatic story.

The meanings of drama

Elam (2001) suggests that drama is a form of fiction or narrative created for theatrical representation, although he differentiates more specifically between 'drama' and its more formal representation 'theatre'. Theatre is a more formal depiction of what takes place between performer and spectator, usually in a specific venue set aside for theatrical events. Drama is therefore a more fluid and flexible narrative – it can happen anywhere and is less reliant on the actor–audience relationship or the theatrical auditorium. Traditionally the meaning of the word drama is derived from the Greek word '"drao", which designates the performance of a ritual' (Csapo & Miller 2007 pg. 121), literally meaning a thing done or performed. Therefore, any action or movement could be considered 'dramatic'.

The pioneering dramatherapist and progressive drama educator Peter Slade (1954) considered the notion of drama from a child's playful, creative, developmental and improvisational perspective. Whilst Jennings describes the notion of *dramatic truth,* (being) *like poetic truth … another type of truth*' (italics original) (1992 pg. 19). When we enter a playful dramatic space, we enter a heightened world which contains its own innate truth, tells its own stories and is separate to that of the real world story. Jennings also sees drama more as a form of ritual as described by Victor Turner (1982) – spaces that are transitional and liminal, that are in the real world but set apart from it. I would argue these spaces are much less well defined than the more traditional theatre spaces that separate actor from audience and can happen anywhere.

From a dramatherapy perspective the drama 'is' the therapy (Jones 1996). The act of doing drama is therapeutic in its very nature and could be seen to link to the Aristotelian notion of the purging of emotion or 'catharsis' (Janko 1987), being a central process for any audience watching a dramatic act when we 'do' an act of drama. We have the potential to purge our emotions or feelings through watching the dramatic act. Story and all its forms such as fairy tale, myth and legend are also central to this drama/therapeutic dichotomy and can be seen to hold the structure in which a dramatic event and cathartic experiences can unfold. Pearson et al. (2013) consider that myths contain and evoke strong feelings and memories which in some sense allow us to find ways of coping with our current situation, similar to the Jungian notion of the 'Collective Unconscious' which I will also consider later.

The dramatic world of Covid-19

Elam describes the notion of the actualisation of the dramatic world, suggesting that we access dramatic worlds in a conceptual way. 'Possible worlds are *realized* when our actual world changes so as to become them' (2001 pg. 99). He describes this notion of the transformation of the here and now into some kind of other worldly state – 'the dramatic' – suggesting that some worlds are 'explicitly remote and others which are presented as *hypothetically actual* constructs' (italics original) (2001 pg. 99). Like the zombie novels I read in my leisure time – the novel, the words on the page, in my view, act as distance between reality and fantasy. This new dramatic world of coronavirus is not hypothetical – it is a reality, and we might struggle to distance ourselves so easily from it.

What followed, in reality, over the coming weeks in the spring of 2020, as the virus spread in lightning dramatic form, was a series of intertwined stories neither I nor anyone else had fully processed. We were being encouraged to work from home. As we moved into March the government suggested that we should not have mass meetings, not go to pubs, sporting events or concerts. The notion of working from home and social distancing were being considered. March 18th 2020 became my final day at university. All schools, colleges and universities closed on Friday March 20th, despite the government insisting 48 hours earlier it was not on the agenda. This distanced 'drama' had now changed as my world changed. I was no longer seeing a drama or dramatic story from afar, I was no longer reading a zombie apocalypse novel, I was a leading protagonist in my own actualised apocalyptical drama. It is therefore difficult to connect to emotions from an Aristotelean cathartic point of view, as that requires some element of distance so we can witness the drama and emotionally respond to it, as if we were an audience. As protagonist in this dramatic story, there is no time to stop, think or feel. This appears to make sense from what I heard anecdotally from others in my various Skype and Zoom conversations. So many people kept saying they could not comprehend, think or make sense of the current situation. There was no dramatic distance, so we couldn't.

The drama of story, destructiveness, reductionism & isolationism

The story unfolded further as I, as a protagonist, had to begin to work from home. One of my first online seminars to students was on the notion of destructiveness (Dokter et al. 2011). Students were confused, anxious about the impact of lockdown on their ability to complete their studies, their college placements and the impact upon their future careers. It is interesting that I was drawn to myth as a way of beginning to make sense of our situation, as Pearson et al argued earlier. Dokter et al explore in their opening chapter the notion of Freud's death instinct – Thanatos (2011 pg. 11), who in Greek mythology was considered the god of death and destructiveness. We were all inadvertently being drawn into a classic dramatic story of life and death, without having the distance or space to respond fully to the emotions created. In reality people were literally fighting for lives in hospitals.

Jung, whose work is very pertinent to many in the arts therapies world, was particularly interested in the notion of dreams. The uncertainty of the world around us was almost a lived drama conveyed through a nightmare. Jung said prophetically:

> To a quite terrifying degree we are threatened by wars and revolutions which are nothing other than psychic epidemics. At any moment several millions of human beings may be smitten with a new madness and then we shall have another World War or devastating revolution.
> (Jung CW10 1964: para 71 in Dokter et al. 2011 pg. 16)

From a dramatherapy perspective, one could argue this is Jung's 'Collective Unconscious' at its most literal and dramatic – an unseen virus spreading throughout the very DNA of all humankind, that was completely unknown to us till a few months earlier, had no antidote and could be deadly. Yet it has come from us and is part of us. I could offer no certainty to my students about our current or future circumstances. I could only acknowledge the new landscape in which we were *all* currently living and admitted I had no answers, why should I? We all had to live and learn from the uncertainty of living in a 'not knowing' state that we as therapists have to inhabit with our clients on a regular basis; and hope the meaning will eventually emerge out of the chaos.

One could argue from a reductionist and isolationist perspective that much of our understanding of the Covid-19 pandemic is gained from TV. We have witnessed the drama of the British government giving daily briefings. Usually the Prime Minister (or other senior government Minister) at an embossed dais, or dais with buzz words on them such as 'stay alert', flanked dramatically on either side by the Chief Medical Officer and an expert professor. The very mechanism of television is reductionist, a rectangular flat screen, on the wall or in the corner of a room, distances us somewhat from the reality of the situation; and is also the same place where we watch fictionalised dramas in our home. The sombre wooden panels of Downing Street, the UK government crests on the daises, the union jack behind the 'stay at home' slogans, and the sullen tones of the speakers, could almost be mistaken for a scene from a Shakespearean tragedy; an oration of a king or prince. It reminded us of Jennings' notion of drama as a form of ritual, at 5pm each day the country stopped to listen, as if expectantly awaiting the next episode of a historical TV drama, or a scene from a Shakespeare play.

Elam discusses two essential ingredients that make the drama: the 'situation', the place or setting, and the 'context of utterance' (2001 pg. 25), the relationship between the speaker and audience. This could be seen in more theatrical terms with the politicians as actors and TV viewers as (sic) audience. However this is not a pretence, an acted play – it is real. Unlike a theatrical event we are further removed by the distractions of other people and objects in our own living rooms, where we might, ironically, regularly suspend our own disbelief with fictionalised dramas. Despite the 'high drama' of the daily broadcasts and the formal 'set' or dais and crest and slogans of the government office on display, and the earnest Minister talking directly to camera, it is not surprising that we could be forgiven for seeing this as a fictionalised drama or story.

Conclusion or 'dramatic irony'?

I was first introduced to the notion of 'dramatic irony' as an undergraduate drama student many years ago. Dramatic irony requires that the audience has a greater awareness of what is happening in the life of the character than the character does themself. Shakespeare's *Romeo and Juliet* is a classic example. At the end of the play Romeo discovers Juliet's supposedly dead body, and takes poison, not knowing as we the audience do, she is only asleep. We witness, as an audience, the moment when Romeo tragically and needlessly takes the poison. She then wakes as he dies and takes the same poison herself by kissing his lips. The fourth wall prevents us from climbing onto the stage to stop Romeo from taking the poison. The distance between audience and characters allows us to process the powerful feelings.

I am aware of the dramatic irony in writing this article. You as reader (may) have a much clearer idea of how this dramatic story of Covid-19 finishes than I do as writer. You will be reading this chapter some months or years after it has been written. You will know, through time and space, or at least have a much greater idea how this dramatic story concludes. Some have suggested it may change our way of life and how we see the world forever. That it changes our views and shifts our thinking on travel, work, the economy and the environment in profound ways. Others suggest more pessimistically that things will return to normal, to the way things have always been, and that we will have learnt nothing. You as reader will have at least processed the story much more than I can at this moment of writing. I like the protagonist in a dystopian movie await the next scene. You as reader have already watched the movie and left the theatre.

Epitaph

Queen Elizbeth the Second made a direct address to the British people, asking us to remain stoic and resolute; she ended her TV address by saying that one day, we would be with our friends and family again, one day we would all 'meet again'. I can only hope this is true for all of us wherever we live.

The Queen always uses her words wisely. The words 'meet again', it was noted by many, were taken from a famous World War 2 song sung by the forces sweetheart Vera Lynn, 'We'll meet again, don't know where, don't know when, but we know we'll meet again some sunny day'. Sadly Vera Lynn died during the Covid outbreak, not from Covid but from old age – she was 103 years old.

The Queen surely understood the power of story, that powerful stories and messages conveyed in song that comforted the nation in bygone eras can also come back and support us now, as they are part of *our* collective unconscious. There can be no greater testament to the power of story if it can be used by the UK Monarch as a way of not only connecting our shared history, when it comforted a generation in war, but also connecting those generations and being a comfort us in our hour of need.

References

Csapo, E., Miller, M.C. (2007) *The Origins of Theatre in Ancient Greece and Beyond: From Ritual to Drama.* Cambridge: Cambridge University Press.

Dokter, D., Holloway, P., Seebohm, H. (2011) *Dramatherapy & Destructiveness – Creating the Evidence Base, Playing with Thanatos.* London: Routledge.

Elam, K. (2001) *The Semiotics of Theatre and Drama.* London: Routledge.

Janko, R. (Translator) (1987) *Poetics 1 with Tractatus Coislinianus.* Cambridge (USA): Hackett Publishing Company.

Jennings, S. (1992) *Dramatherapy with Families, Groups and Individuals.* London: JKP.

Jennings, S. (1995) *Theatre, Ritual, and Transformation: The Senoi Temiars.* London: Routledge.

Jones, P. (1996) *Drama as Therapy: Theatre as Living.* London: Bruner Routledge.

Pearson, J., Smail, M., Watts, P. (2013) *Dramatherapy with Myth and Fairytale – The Golden Stories of Sesame.* London: JKP.

Slade, P. (1954) *Child Drama.* London: University of London Press.

Turner, V. (1982) *From Ritual to Theatre: The Human Seriousness of Play.* New York: PAJ Books.

2
THE STORIES OF SIDDHARTHA AND CAPTAIN TOM

Lifetimes apart but connecting us together

Drew Bird

This chapter will explore how stories during the Covid-19 pandemic offered the potential to help us re-connect with our human nature. Through the lens of a biblical parable and the story of the Buddha I will draw out parallels with the story of 'Captain Tom' and why this story during the pandemic crisis seemed to capture the imagination of the world. I will explore how personal stories can give us strength because of their imaginative capacity to help us to connect with others, conveying a truth that story can make accessible. I will consider how story can help bring balance to an over-emphasis on the intellect alone and restore us to emotional health through connecting with our existential nature and vulnerability.

Whilst changes in the way we communicate over the last 20 years have been influenced by advances in technology, the internet and the onset of social media have not diminished the need to share and tell stories. The famous anthropologist Gregory Bateson, when asked the question how will we know when computers have taken over world, responded saying, *When we ask a question of the computer and it responds by saying, 'let me tell you a story'*. Sharing stories is central to being human and is part of our human makeup, conveying the multi-faceted dimensions of human experience. Stories communicate on many different levels that engage not just our intellect alone, but our senses and emotions. Stories appeal to our imagination and our capacity and need to connect not only with ourselves but with one another (Paramananda, 2015).

In the spirit of storytelling, I want to begin by sharing a story and parable from the bible to set the scene of this chapter. It is the story of a farmer who went out to sow his seed in a field. As he was scattering the seed some of it was eaten up by birds, some seed fell on rocky ground without much soil and quickly withered away as there was no root. Other seeds fell amongst thorns, which grew but were choked by the weeds. However, some seed fell on fertile soil that produced a crop much larger than what was sown. Whilst I am not a Christian, I can appreciate how the parable has universal implications because it conveys a truth that is not culture-bound.

I am struck in the story of the sower how the seeds need fertile soil for them to grow. The seed is dependent on specific conditions in order to thrive and yield. For me seeds are like stories that are dependent on particular conditions for the story to have greatest impact. Hearing the right story at different times in my life offers the potential to act as a guide and friend when I have felt lost and confused. Like the seed in fertile soil the right story is able to take root and offer a new perspective on a situation or a problem. The story might act like a good friend one seeks out for advice, for another perspective to illuminate one's thinking. Hearing the right story in difficult times can be like being rescued from a sinking ship. Stories can change our lives and help us find direction and re-orientate our thinking. In a time of crisis, a story might help reveal options or choices we never knew we had. The right story at a particular time might change our relationship with the concern, problem or challenge we face (Jones, 2007). Stories can be like oracles, much like the priestess in ancient Greece offered people wise but mysterious advice from the Gods. Stories can offer their wisdom when we are receptive and ready, in the same spirit of the saying, when the student is ready the teacher will appear.

Stories have a mythic or archetypal theme, have universal appeal and can convey many truths and interpretations that are not bound to a single and literal interpretation. Mythic stories address the existential crisis of what it is to be human and are not culture-bound – much like Shakespeare's plays, which are still relevant today four hundred years later all over the world. Joseph Campbell (2009) considered how the role of myth helps us to integrate and widen our responsibility in society by taking a perspective that goes beyond the self. May (1991, p. 86) considers myth a way of a 'breaking through of greater meaning' and 'working out the problem (of being human) on a higher level of integration'. Myth helps us 'access our roots' and the 'ground plan of our being' (Watts, 1996, p. 27). Jung believed people become neurotic when their spiritual horizons were too low because they were cut off from the roots of their being (Watts, 1996, p. 26). Campbell further considered myth as putting us back in accordance 'with nature' due to our tendency towards separation (Cousineau, 2003, p. 7). A separation that is all the more apparent in the technological age with the advancement of consumerism, where wants of the ego can be satisfied with a click of a button. Myth thus helps us to get in touch with the repressed, unconscious and archaic urges, fears and longings (May, 1991). Hillman (1990) considers how anything that we give value to has the potential to be archetypal and help widen, enrich and deepen our understanding of being human. Myth helps us get in touch with the lost or repressed parts of ourselves by appealing to our imagination so that we can connect with a universal perspective of being alive. A perspective that is beyond the limits of ego as it connects us to others.

Mythical stories transcend time and culture and can still speak to us thousands of years later like Jesus' parables because they still convey something of our human nature. The story of Siddhartha and his first steps on the journey that would culminate in him becoming the Buddha is about 2500 years old and captures all the attributes of the myth of the hero. Siddhartha was wealthy and lived in a palace he was forbidden to leave by his parents, who feared he would become a wandering wise man based on a prophesy they had received in his earlier life. However, Siddhartha, so the story goes, managed to leave the secure confines of the palace and in doing so met four sights – the sights of an old person, a sick person and a dead person and, finally, a wise man who appeared calm and serene amongst the crowds and noise. The four sights had quite an impact on the 29-year-old Siddhartha, so much so that he made an oath to become a holy man. In the dark of night, he left the palace, leaving behind his wife, son and parents and all the familiar comforts and security he had known. Thus, the first and most important step of Siddhartha's journey to seeking truth.

I have had a fascination for this story since the first time I heard it about 25 years ago, in particular the act of leaving his family behind and beginning his search, culminating in him becoming the Buddha. The story resonates with the hero's journey, which always begins with separation from the familiar (Campbell, 2008). In English the word 'familiar' means either belonging to the family, or more often, something we're used to (Online Etymology Dictionary, 2021). The hero's journey thus begins with leaving behind all that we are used to and facing trials that help to resource and strengthen their resolve before they reach their goal.

I am deliberately using the word 'familiar' here to reduce the likelihood of the story being taken too literally. Siddhartha had to leave all that was familiar, his comforts and habitual ways of being that had the potential to hold him back and stop him growing and evolving into a wise man. And like Siddhartha we too can take refuge in our comforts and secure little homes with our televisions, laptops and burglar alarms that can protect us from the bigger and more frightening world out there.

The story of Siddhartha has helped to guide my thinking and understanding during the uncertain times across the world with the arrival of the pandemic crisis and Covid-19. Countries across the globe took different measures in order to curtail the spread of the virus by reducing social contact and instructed people to stay at home. From March to June 2020 in the U.K. people were working from home remotely, schools were closed, pubs and cafés closed and only supermarkets were open to provide food. There was no sport, no theatre and no holidays as the country maintained social distancing. For months the main road outside my house was free from the usual thick traffic and a 'quiet' descended over the neighbourhood. As a consequence of shutdown, the world's economy is in decline as unemployment has soared and reliance on the state grown significantly. Life as we know it has changed, perhaps forever. Even as I write now and the lockdown restrictions are being slowly relaxed, we do not know what the future is going to look like. We are in the midst of uncertainty and unpredictability, challenging the familiar and secure world we took for granted. We are amidst an existential crisis, that is forcing us to think differently about an existence we had taken for granted.

Three or four weeks into lockdown and shut away into my home the news was challenging to listen to as infection rates and deaths rose in the U.K. and around the world. The news abounded with stories of sickness and death and the importance of protecting the vulnerable. The first three sights of the aging process, sickness and death witnessed by Siddhartha had come to visit and weren't going away. In the comfort of my own home the risk of contracting a virus where there was no known cure was real and frightening. I was confronted with the reality of death, that myself or loved ones and friends were at risk of catching the virus. Habitual stories I tell myself in order to rescue myself from the fears of death (Yalom, 1980) didn't seem to keep at bay the growing existential anxiety. As a consequence of being more in touch with the impermanence of life I was more in contact with my vulnerability as a human, aware how fragile the human condition is. Yet I also felt connected with others. I didn't feel so alone as I connected with others all over the world who were also facing the same existential threat brought on by the Covid-19 story. I was struck how each in our different cultural ways were all part of this unprecedented story as millions, possibly billions, were confined to their homes and socially isolated. At the time it felt the Covid-19 story helped us to get in touch with our lost vulnerability, particularly those of us living in the western world who can immerse ourselves in consumerism, creating the illusion we are in control of our lives. All the façades we can hide behind to shield ourselves from our vulnerability were no longer there. It felt like we were more in contact with our existential nature, a nature that we often do not want to acknowledge (Yalom, 1980).

Despite all the more challenging stories there were also stories of cooperation. Hospitals being built in a matter of weeks to house thousands of Covid-19 patients needing more medical and intensive care and support. There seemed to be a harmonious spirit in the U.K. and willingness to understand and work together in unprecedented ways that rekindled the wartime cooperation of the world wars. There was an influx of stories of kindness and gratitude and thanks to medical staff at hospitals caring for the sick and frontline staff keeping shops stocked with food. I spent time collecting these moving stories in a notebook as they not only connected me to others but also greatly moved me. There were stories such as a man playing his violin in the streets as a tribute to health care workers in Liverpool; a 90-year-old woman climbing the stairs of her home to the equivalent of a Highland mountain (2398 feet) to raise money for the National Health Service (NHS); local neighbourhoods shopping for the old and vulnerable who were too at risk of infection to shop for themselves; and New York's ritziest hotels offering overworked medical staff five-star treatment for free. There was another story of selflessness of an Italian Priest who died of Covid-19, preferring to donate to a younger patient the ventilator he was offered to keep him alive. But there was one story that stood out, that captured the imagination not only of the U.K. but the world.

The story of Captain Tom Moore, who approaching his 100th birthday embarked on completing 100 laps of his garden with his Zimmer frame to raise £1000 for the NHS in the U.K. to deal with the Covid-19 pandemic. In June 2020 his total fundraising figure stood at 36 million pounds. Captain Tom Moore's story and spirit inspired others to give generously to his cause. His story was shared on television, radio and the internet across the world. A 99-year-old man became the figurehead for a nation in crisis and fear.

What was it about Captain Tom Moore's story that fuelled so much interest and generosity? I believe it was a story that connected with people and gave them strength in the face of adversity to face the challenges ahead. The story had the potential to bring us together. His story captured the imagination of senior public figures, who bestowed on him an honorary colonelship, a knighthood and an RAF aircraft flypast to celebrate his fundraising achievement. The story became a beacon of hope in uncertain times. Yalom and Leszcz (2005) explore the importance of the instillation of hope as one of 11 therapeutic factors in group psychotherapy and how it is necessary for believing that change is possible. Witnessing Captain Tom's challenge and small victory celebrated offered a light in the dark times. His story connected with members of the public, collectively pulling a nation together. Captain Tom's story had universal appeal because I believe it helped us glimpse our humanity, vulnerability and strength through the action of an old, frail and vulnerable man. In a time of crisis, the story helped to motivate and gather financial resources to meet the collective challenge in the early weeks of lockdown. Captain Tom became a heroic figure to pin our hopes upon and help us face the pandemic. The unprecedented response to Captain Tom's story reminded me of the seed that fell on fertile ground and was able to take root and grow. People responded to the story with such generosity because it resonated with them at a time when they could connect with it and find meaning and strength from his own unique challenges.

Salas (2003) considers how we are made to create stories in order to make sense of our lives. We are built to share stories and construct meaning through stories (Salas, 2011) as a fundamental need to communicate something that has happened to us. We need stories for our emotional health and to find our place in the world. Stories that help deepen our understanding of being human have potential to be archetypal and mythic (Hillman, 1990). Stories from complete strangers can help to connect and motivate us to navigate the chaos and confusion that can beset our lives at different times. Stories help us connect to others due to their universal and autobiographical nature (Moustakas, 1990). Captain Tom's story helped us realise we are not alone or separate, but connected (Bird, 2017). The sharing of personal stories in public spaces helps us to counter the 'destructive belief' that we are alone (Nash and Rowe, 2000).

The sharing of stories can help to reinforce and build a sense of community and togetherness (Bird, 2017) and help us realise we are not as separate and independent as we think. In truth we are more interconnected than we realise. Holding on to the belief that I am separate is like cutting me off from my roots and from nature itself, life and death. The pandemic has helped us get in touch with our human nature and vulnerability as a species. We will all get sick, all age and all die at some point in our lifetime. The way we normally live our lives has shielded us to some extent from the reality that nothing lasts forever. Hillman (2015) argues we are not separate from nature because we are nature, but we think of ourselves as being separate, believing that we are in control. I am not in control of my life as much as I think I am because conditions outside of my control can change and impact on me. Hillman (2015) argues that humanity is so inflated with its own superiority that it has lost touch with its own reality. Whilst intellectually we know we will age, get ill and die, we do not necessarily resonate with this emotionally. There is a gap between our intellectual understanding and our emotional reality (Sangharakshita, 2009). Story helps to engage the senses and emotions and is a powerful way for 'imaginatively engaging with knowledge' and making our experience more real and personal (Beatty et al., 2008; Egan, 2005, p. 2; Lindqvist, 2003). The sensory nature of stories can help us find emotional equivalents to intellectual understanding, so we are more congruent with our existential vulnerable nature.

I found daily reports and updates about Covid-19 informed my intellectual understanding, and in themselves they were important, but it was the stories about other people like me in different places around the world that stirred my emotions and helped me face the reality of the pandemic crisis. It was through stories that I felt connected to myself and others. Through the vehicle of personal stories, I was engaged at a deeper level, making the pandemic feel more real. Personal stories helped me much like a friend and gave me strength to face the situation, whilst news reports alone did not help me realise this so profoundly. Whereas news reports left me somewhat distant from myself, personal stories helped stir my emotions. Personal stories and their universal implications gave me the courage to realise my own fears about Covid-19 because I was not alone – others around the globe were also facing a similar reality. At times I felt a part of this evolving universal story, much like poet Shelley's notion that we were all part of one developing poem.

Through the growing pandemic I felt less separation between myself and others because I was less preoccupied by own concerns. Stories in the press and on television also seemed to suggest a new altruistic spirit spreading through the country and the world. It felt like the pandemic crisis helped us think more universally. Stories have the potential to help us return to our soul, a poetic expression used by James Hillman (1992) for the Psyche, igniting our imagination that connects us to others. Hillman considered how the dominance of the intellect can cut us from our imagination, narrowing our view of the world due to its tendency to be over literal. Stories offer us ways to see new possibilities. The honest stories of others are what people connect to because they are employing an emotional truth (Gaimon, 2019). Stories helped me connect with the more painful experience that I had felt cut off from because of the shared experience of others. Yalom and Leszcz (2005) consider how universality within group psychotherapy can help us resonate with others' experience that can validate our personal experience. The stories of the challenges others were experiencing in the pandemic conveyed a truth and helped to activate my own altruistic desire to support others.

Truth resonates with us; whether this is conveyed through the story of Siddhartha or through direct experience or through the magic of a novel, poem, play or film, it captures our imagination so we can connect with our truth (Gaimon, 2019). We do not need to believe in the accuracy of the earlier story of Siddhartha's sneaking out of the palace in the night leaving his family behind. The purpose of the story is to capture our imagination about human nature and that we will get old, sick and die. The story helps us realise this more deeply through emotions the story evokes in us.

The story of Kisa Gotami, who struggled to believe that her son was dead, is a story that also conveys a truth that resonates with our impermanent human nature. Racked with grief Kisa Gotami was unable to accept the loss of her son despite the villagers' attempt to console her. Eventually a village elder suggested she approach the Buddha. The Buddha said he could help her. All she needed to do was to bring him a mustard seed from a home where nobody had died. Kisa Gotami asked around the village. All were willing to give her a mustard seed, but none had been spared the death of a loved one in their home. We do not know how long Kisa Gotami continued asking round the village for a mustard seed, but eventually she was able to accept death happens to all and accept that her son was dead. She returned to the Buddha with her new knowledge and became one of his disciples. I imagine that Kisa Gotami realised that death is a universal truth and came to recognise that grief is not personal but part of the way of life. I like to believe that she came to realise this truth because she was able to connect with the losses others in the village had had. She was not alone. In a similar way stories of loss during the pandemic helped offer the potential to connect with our loss. Stories of the loss of loved ones, loss of jobs, loss of financial stability, loss of predictability and loss of our liberty were emerging from across the world helping us to re-connect with our fragile and vulnerable nature and what it is to be human and alive.

For Siddhartha to begin his journey to becoming a sage he chose to leave the familiar behind him. In some ways the global spread of the pandemic has forced us to leave behind the familiar or 'normal' and re-orientate us towards a 'new normal'. We have not chosen the path we are on, but we are learning to adapt to it, as evidenced by some of the stories of generosity I have shared as people take on the responsibility of finding ways to support one another. The story of Captain Tom epitomized this as he embarked on a challenging and heroic journey to raise funds to support those sick with Covid-19. There was something mythic about his story, causing such unprecedented responses of generosity across the world. For a moment the new normal was full of stories of kindness and selflessness as we tried to navigate the uncertain and unfamiliar times we found ourselves in. There were also the stories that we never heard – neighbours looking out for one another and small acts of kindness that the times have prompted. I believe the pandemic crisis has helped us re-connect with our vulnerability as a species and what it is to be human. We were confronted with the realisation that we had lived under an inflated illusion and that we are in control. In these difficult times we heard stories of the indelible human spirit reaching out to help and connect us with others in new and extraordinary ways. Yet, as we now start to come out of the restrictions of lockdown in the U.K., the mood seems to be changing. Stories that evidenced the human spirit seem to have been replaced with the familiar bitter stories and political in-fighting that seem to quash something inside me. I find myself yearning for the community spirit that had risen above this, if only for a few months at the peak of lockdown. So soon after the peak of the crisis, have we once more lost touch with our nature and the fragile species that we really are?

References

Beatty, R., Bedford, J., Both, P., Eld, J., Goitom, M., Heinrichs, L., Moran-Bonilla, L., Massoud, M., Van Ngo, H., Pyrch, T., Rogerson, M., Sitter, K., Speaker, C. E., and Unrau, M. (2008) Recording Action Research in the Classroom: Singing with the Chickadees, *Educational Action Research*, 16(3), pp. 335–344.

Bird, D. (2017) Playback Theatre, Autoethnography and Generosity, *Dramatherapy* 38(1), pp. 32–42.

Campbell, J. (2008) *The Hero with a Thousand Faces*, Third Edition, Navato, California: New World Library.

Campbell, J. (2009) *The Celebration of the Life*. Audio Series One, Volume One: Mythology and the Individual. 1.1., Joseph Campbell Foundation.

Cousineau, P. (2003) *Once and Future Myths: The Power of Ancient Stories in Our Lives*, York Beach, ME: Conari Press.

Egan, K., (2005) *An Imaginative Approach to Teaching*, San Francisco: Jossey – Bass.

Gaiman, N. (2019) *Neil Gaiman Teaches the Art of Storytelling* [vodcast] Available at: www.masterclass.com/classes/neil-gaiman-teaches-the-art-of-storytelling [Accessed 30 June 2020]

Hillman, J. (1990) *The Essential James Hillman: A Blue Fire*, London: Routledge.

Hillman, J. (1992) *Re-visioning Psychology*, Reissue Edition, New York: HarperPerennial

Hillman, J. (2015) *James Hillman on Changing the Object of Your Desire*. [online] YouTube. Available at: www.youtube.com/watch?v=rFa0X06hLOU [Accessed 30 June 2020]

Jones, P., (2007) *Drama as Therapy: Theory, Practice and Research*, London: Routledge.

Lindqvist, G., (2003) Vygotsky's Theory of Creativity, *Creativity Research Journal*, 15(2), pp. 245–251.

May, R. (1991) *The Cry for Myth,* New York: Souvenir Press (E&A) Ltd.

Moustakas, C. (1990) *Heuristic Research: Design, Methodology, and Applications,* London: Sage.

Nash, S., and Rowe, N. (2000) Safety, Danger and Playback Theatre, *Dramatherapy,* 22(3), pp. 18–20.

Online Etymology Dictionary (2021) [Online] Available at: www.etymonline.com [Accessed 18 October 2021]

Paramananda (2015) Hillman, Archetypal Psychology and Buddhism. Available at: www.freebuddhistaudio.com/audio/details?num=LOC2528 [Accessed: 30 June 2020]

Salas, J. (2003) *Improvising Real Life: Personal Story in Playback Theatre*, Third Edition, New Platz, New York: Tusitala.

Salas, J. (2011) Tedxsit *Everyone Has A Story*. [online] YouTube. Available at: https://youtu.be/R-UtiROCm6E [Accessed 30 June 2020].

Sangharakshita, U. (2009) *The Essential Sangharakshita: A Half Century of Writings from the Founder of the Friends of the Western Buddhist Order,* Karen Stout (ed), Somerville, MA: Wisdom Publications.

Watts, P. (1996) *Working with Myth and Story,* In *Discovering the Self through Drama and Movement: The Sesame Approach,* Jenny Pearson (ed), London: Jessica Kingsley, pp. 27–33.

Yalom, I. (1980) *Existential Psychotherapy*, London: Basic Books.

Yalom, I. D., and Leszcz, M. (2005) *The Theory and Practice of Group Psychotherapy*, Fifth Edition, New York: Basic Books.

3
DOORWAYS TO THE DEATHLANDS
The imaginal seeing of story

Mary Smail

Introduction

Once upon a time, there was an old, witchy wise woman who had magic.
One day a young woman called on her.
"What are you seeking?" asked the old one.
"I want to know as you do." said the girl. "I want to bring through magic."
The witchy wise woman looked inside the girl, seeing that everything she needed was deep within.
The only thing was, the girl did not trust it.

"Come inside," said the witch.
And this was the first lesson.

"Words are not enough to teach you."
And this became the second lesson.

"There is not much time."
And this was the third lesson.

Then the witch decreed,
"You are ready now. Now you can know."

And, the young woman, delighted, was ready to move on.[1]

This chapter intends to explore the places where therapist and client need to attend the witchy wise woman's lessons, by coming inside, moving beyond words, making good use of time and being ready to work in the currency of a 'magical-logos' that is beyond what is known or fully understood. It will look at how story offers a doorway, through which we can see into the silenced and paralysed places we enter when mortality interrupts life, and we dis-locate into the unvisited, imaginative realm that I call 'The Deathlands'. This place is generally avoided because of the tough questions travellers are called upon to answer there. How do we come to

DOI: 10.4324/9781003118893-5

terms with a medical diagnosis which unexpectedly disrupts our assumed immortality and our lifeline begins to ebb away? What happens to us when our life with a loved one becomes time-limited and days are now short? How in therapy can a pin-prick of meaning cradle the terror, loss and grief people find themselves in when death has visited, and everything familiar has vanished? How do we hold fast when Covid-19 sweeps the world with destruction, breaking death taboo and installing a lockdown call to stay within the secrets of the home ground, not run away but find solace there?

The chapter will be in a story form, relying on as few references as possible. Story needs occasional opportunities to reveal itself in its own terms through an in-the-moment potency which requires imaginative attention, uninterrupted by an obligation to literature review or citation. It will start by giving a context for story and ritual being vital soul-wise portals which guide us during any process of death. It will introduce the metaphor of a country called The Deathlands made up of four shires, each with an entry point or doorway through which people pass when they lose someone, or they themselves become terminally ill. It will then look at the kind of story that is played out in these days of Coronavirus, happening during the writing of this chapter, and the energy of Grace that is simultaneously present. A traditional story will follow each description of The Deathland shires, intended to amplify the imaginary, created story, with the time-tested, magical wisdom of an ancient myth from the tradition of different world cultures.

Story as lower education

People turn to story through cinema and theatre, seeking a liminal place to be entertained, nourished or amused beyond the limitations of the everyday story. Watching a play or a film brings distance and offers our stressed or weary individual situations respite; it is somewhere else to go. In times of trouble, when we need help, the containment of myths and fairy tales beckons to us, offering wisdom perceived differently through the eyes of images. The stories lead us round brick walls and signpost us through swamps. They give us wings when we need to fly, and, if we know how to listen, they tell of beings, creatures, and spirits that can guide our journey onwards, even when conditions are ultimately dire and hope for a positive outcome is out of reach. In times when the terror of Covid-19 stalks and stops us in our tracks, a story can touch our soul within. The extreme situation remains as dangerous, but there is an inner spiritual seeing to guide us through.

Story language is user-friendly and alluring, it brings out emotion, and provides a compass for the human predicament, reassuring the hearer that the path we find ourselves on has been walked before, we are not alone, and there is a map. When we reach for help, the stories provide a non-religious, ritual space, each offering a profound perspective, beyond the rigorous regimentation of the directing left-brain, where the goal is to verify, demonstrate, and quantify. Rumi, the poet, speaks of this when he says there are two kinds of intelligence:

> *one acquired, as a child in school memorises facts and concepts…With such intelligence, you rise in the world…There is another kind, one already completed and preserved inside you. This second knowing is a fountainhead from within you, moving out.*[2]

Story knowing relies on 'fountainhead' right-brain intelligence, and the willingness to attend to deep, non-verbal, symbolic material through imagination. It often arrives as an undressed 'Cinderella of the fire-place' epistemology who is not ready for the Ball of Dame Academia's high-towered, outcome learning. Story knowing belongs to a School of Lower Education, something that I have referred to elsewhere.[3] Lower Education deals with In-Tuition and 'In-Comes' as opposed to outcomes and result. It promotes qualitative and invisible precepts and affirms that even when nothing changes externally, soul wisdom comes through the mirror holding of a myth or fairy tale, and the soft, gentle light which Grace brings where grief and pain can be transformed.

A death ritual

When you lose someone, it is like you become an initiate. You join another club. You suddenly know what the ones who have not lost, do not know.[4]

At this point, I write personally from an intense meeting with death, through the departure of three significant people in my life, who died within the space of two years. It was a cumulative trauma that cast me into a place where I no longer recognised myself. Familiar streets and people, things that I used to enjoy, had no importance any longer. I had entered new psychological geography, refugeed into a state somewhere at the margins that I did not know. The work here was to endure the void of the ones who had gone and deal with estrangement from friends who were kindly disposed to look after me so that things could go back to normal and we could all get on with living, just as it had been.

During this time, I came across the charity Dying Matters[5] who annually hold a *Dia de Muertos*, Day of the Dead, conference in November. In this Mexican ritual, people commit a day to celebrate the return of souls who have departed, by dressing in brightly coloured costumes, representing life and death and embellishing the graves of loved ones with flowers and decorations. At the conference, we came up with reasons that prevent people from talking about death. We identified five obstacles.

- Death is taboo because we don't know what to do about it.
- A dying patient is a scientific failure: medicine is about saving a life.
- Outside a religious context, there is no teaching for young people about mortality/immortality.
- There is no funding for the promotion of death education.
- There is a lack of support for planned events and activities around death and dying, though the recent Death Café[6] movement is changing this.

Later, the evening found us setting out plates of food on brightly coloured tables for spirit visitors, and as the music of a Mexican band played lively tunes, we welcomed the dead through dance. It was as if there was a bridge, allowing a through-way. Nothing had changed, but everything was different as earth and heaven drew close, bringing our loved ones near. Of course, we could not see them, but collectively we imagined them there, and so they were emotionally present.

This moment was a pivotal one. It had been meaningful to talk earlier, but the feast with the dead ritual took us to storyland and to 'What if?' thinking – What if the rupture of death opens us so that we can see more than what is usually perceived? What if a tale readies us for our eventual disembodying transition? What if 'Something More' is waiting for us when we limp into the darkness, surrender through acceptance, and remain there for whatever Grace may bring?

Stories and ritual in The Deathlands

Within a therapeutic relationship, the strange light that death brings opens a way into a new opportunity both for client and therapist together. People come to therapy mangled, lost, and alone. With someone to accompany them in their desolation, someone who asks the right questions and who engenders confidence in the unforeseen phenomena that frequently appear in a death process, new connections to loved ones and changed responses to life slowly begin to grow. In the same way that the Mexican *Dia de Muerto* event offered a healing opportunity, so can a death-friendly, therapeutic space meet and develop an energetic relationship with what has been lost.

With this in mind, I began to consider how my therapy practice, which specialises in finding Grace opportunities within suffering, failure, death, and bereavement, could draw on story to offer space to imaginative intelligence. I set out to find traditional myths dealing with Diagnosis, the Dying Process, what I call Peripherality – things seen at the edge – and Bereavement, each an issue that clients bring to therapy. I looked for stories that represented these themes for use in the therapy relationship. Sometimes I would tell the story, and we would reflect; other times we would embody and enact. Invariably, these permitted us to speak of spiritual experiences that clients reported they had been hiding, for fear of seeming fanciful or mad. The stories normalised and validated the reality of there being gifts in a loss that come, like the animals who unexpectedly guide the way in fairy tales, and offer permission to trust the solace within and live from that place. From my work with other people, the metaphor of The Deathlands, made up of four different shires, began to form. What follows here is a story description of that land and each shire within, followed by the telling of a traditional tale which validates the place and shows something of its wisdom gifts

The four shires of The Deathlands

The Deathlands sit close to the road of life, which we all travel every day without seeing the other country close by. It has four doors leading inwards, each entering to a different shire of the one land. At the centre, there is a soft low-light Grace flame, which each shire surrounds and can access. Nobody visits these grounds until they stumble in. These are the doors.

Shire one – Diagnosis

The door to this shire can come upon you quickly. A random ache or pain, an ailment, or check-up takes you there. All has been well, then suddenly, you consult, you're scanned, you wait, then you meet with a doctor who tells you calmly what is wrong and gives it a name. That's when the door opens, and you take the first peep into The Deathlands. With luck, your diagnosis is curable, and treatment sorts you so that you can pop back out, and return to life. However, even if the visit is short, you now know there is a land of death, and through the shire of Diagnosis, you realise, you will return there one day.

Or it may be that you stay in the shire. Your time now is limited, and there is no way out. You may put up a tent in the sub-shire of palliative care, which is full of many good things, but it remains a place where you come to understand that time is shorter than you imagined. You are in the land and death is around, just like it was for Korkut.

Korkut and the Music for Death[7]

Korkut was just 16 years old when he had the dream. He dreamt that death was looking for him.

"Death can take me when I'm old," he cried and leapt on his beloved chestnut horse and cantered away. Korkut hadn't ridden far when he saw people digging a hole in the ground. "What are you digging?" he asked, "The grave of Korkut," they replied. Korkut immediately turned his horse and rode away. Eventually, he came to more people digging a hole. "What are you digging?" he asked? "The grave of Korkut," they replied. Korkut rode off quickly, but everywhere he went, there were people with spades.

Horse and man crossed lands, through all weathers, looking for a place where there was only life. "Do you know the place where Death cannot come?" Korkut asked a tree. "Birds peck and leaves fall from me. Death is here," whispered the tree. "So, Korkut asked the prairie, "Do you know the place where Death cannot come?" "Sheep graze on me, horses' hooves pound me. Death is here", said the prairie."

So, Korkut asked the mountain, "Do you know the place where Death cannot come?" "Rain lashes me, and winds howl around me. Death is here", said the mountain. So Korkut kept riding. Suddenly his horse fell to the ground, exhausted by the galloping, breathed his last and died. "Death is here," said Korkut and buried his face in the mane.

After a time Korkut cut a tree branch with his knife and carved a pear-shaped box which he covered with horse skin. He twisted hairs from the mane and tail and made them into strings and a bow. There, by the river, Korkut sang the songs of death of his much-loved horse, and as the music echoed, children drew close, men stopped working, and women put down their toil. They stood silently, listening as Korkut sang. Even Death listened, entranced by the sound, and for many years nobody died.

Eventually, Korkut became old, his hair grew white, and his back bent. "Now I am ready," he said, and placing his instrument on the ground, he allowed Death to take him. The people buried him on the riverbank and then began to sing his songs.

Korkut's grave is on the banks of the Syr Darya river in Southern Kazakhstan. It is said if you sleep there, you too will find the music, and be ready and able to respond, when Death comes.

Shire two – the Dying Process

The second door to The Deathlands can take quite a lot of opening, but if you approach it gently, it shows itself as made of soft willow wood, with a tremendously huge lock. Some people on the road of life get into bother, so they crash through this door unexpectedly, without warning or preparation. Others consider it and even plan to make it happen much too soon. For most, however, the way through is slow.

People can accompany you right up to the doorway, but only you can unlock the door. It requires your unique and personal password key, and no one else's will do. At some point, you decide to put down everything you have been carrying, leave your bags on the outside and pass right through. It will be hard to do this – leaving people you love, who don't want you to go, but it has to happen, and it can be done. It is a time for goodbyes and looking towards something, as yet unthinkable and very definitely not known. Lonebird knew about this.

Lonebird[8]

On the shores of Big Water lived Lonebird, with her mother She-Eagle and her father, Dawn-of-Day. No daughter of the tribe was as strong as she. Young braves attended her, but she didn't care for them, and it was said that her heart was frozen, as ice upon the lake.

Dawn-of-Day announced that there would be a race with all the men of the village competing for his daughter, but when he saw her upset, he said, "Do not cry, my child. Every woman will find her man". "This is not my will", she answered. And they listened to her.

Lonebird lived happily with her parents for many seasons. Eventually, they became silver-haired, and Lonebird saddened, knowing she would be left. Trees and flowers and creatures lived together, so the thought of being all alone was more than she could bear. When the day turned to shadow, she sat by the lake, while the silver moon rose. Looking at it longingly she called out. "Let me come to you. Let me not be alone, but come to you."

Great Spirit heard the cry and came close. "Is this your will?" he asked. Lonebird affirmed her wish and was carried up, taken to the half-light place where she was welcomed gently into the moon's pale arms. The next day, when her parents called her, there was no answer. She had gone.

The Chippewa people, who sit now by fading fires, no longer bright as they once were, tell her story. Although they can no longer see her, it is as if she is there. They are not alone, and neither is she, when her story is told over dwindling campfires.

Shire three – Peripherality – Edge Seeing

The third shire of The Deathlands is as close as a breath. It has an outside door opening from the road of life, but the vital door is right at the back and over to the left. It is a silver sliding hatch door made of the thinnest metal, and you will see no handle because that is placed on the other side. Most people do not account for this second door, which is understandable as it seldom opens, and when it does, you only see through into darkness. It occasionally opens from the other side, and when this happens, an orange breeze blows through the shire of Peripherality and back to the road of life, through the main door. It blows back into life, dressed as a story or a dream or a hunch carrying messages. It can reveal through synchronicities or a feeling that someone is close; all connections written in invisible ink. For those who can lean into this, who can believe it is real, there is much comfort, so long as you know the rule. You have to know that what you see is, and is not there, and trust it. This is the statute that you need to understand.

Pintalgato[9]

Pintalgato, the black kitten was not always so! His coat was once yellow with little spots, but that was before he stepped into the darkness. His mother warned him not to go beyond the edges of the day, but Pintalgato was young and curious and wanted to discover what hides under the shadow of the night. So, he disobeyed his mother and walked into the sunset to the bordering place between day and night, where the sun no longer penetrates and rules. When his mother found out what he was doing, she strictly banned it, telling him of the danger. He appeared to listen, but when she was asleep, the kitten would leap into the forbidden, beyond-light world.

It was so dark there, so dark that his eyes shone like flames. He felt sleek as he pounced on energy whirls which sped past him, all unseen, but so closely felt. At home in the dark was Pintalgato, so much so, that he stayed there for longer and longer spells. At home was the kitten, absorbing the darkness.

Days later, when he returned to light, Pintalgato discovered that his yellow coat had taken on the black velvet colour of the night. He ran to his mother, telling her what he'd done. "Who am I now, if I am no longer yellow with spots and bright as the sun?" Slowly he understood that once you have found that your eyes shine in the dark, you cannot resist it. You go there, time and time again, and this changes you. To and fro you go, seeing in the night and transformed for the day: the dark and the light co-existing together.

Shire four – Bereavement

The door into this shire of The Deathlands is unequivocally grey and misty, though sometimes if you remember to look by the beam of the low-light Grace flame, you can just see shades of violet. It is a swing-door, and you pass through it because someone else makes you. You are thrown through, without a whit of respect for your will or wellbeing, and you enter alone. You need to know this. When you are thrown through this door, you are entirely on your own, and no longer who you used to be. Not only has your loved one gone, but part of you has also gone with them. Everything that has been is no longer. The one who held part of your earth story no longer lives or tells it with you.

This shire, full of puddles, also has tiny night lamps burning. They have always been there, but now that you surrender to the darkness of despair, you have eyes to see them glowing. They seem to link to the low-light flame at the centre of The Deathlands. They shine gently, waiting for those who notice and are not extinguished by the bitter gall-water of loss that so frequently flows through this watery, grey-lined shire.

The beloved[10]

Once, there was a young warrior who lost his beloved on the eve of their wedding. Distinguished as he was in warfare, the young man was so inconsolable with the loss that he could not eat or sleep, nor could he hunt. He could only spend time at the grave of his beloved, staring into the air.

One day, he overheard elders discussing directions for travelling to the spirit world. The journey was through the forest, so he moved in that direction, but the spirit land was nowhere to be seen. Despairing, he left the woods and crossed a plain from where he could see a small hut ahead, close to a great lake. An ancient wise man who seemed to know he was coming welcomed him, saying that his beloved had passed by only one day before, on her way to the spirit world, which was an island in the lake close by, only reachable by canoe.

The warrior rushed to the shore, but the wise man stopped him. If he wanted to find his love, he must leave his body behind, continue the journey in spirit, and be sure not to speak until he was safely on the island. The old man sang magical chants over the warrior until his spirit was free. There, by the lake, among many other shades each finding their canoe, he spied his beloved, also entering a boat. As they all set out, not a word was said, nor any canoe shared, for the way to the spirit world can only be travelled alone.

Then, a terrible storm arose sweeping many canoes away. The warrior and his love crossed the water safely, and the canoes arrived at the shore of the island. For a short time, there on the shore edge, they held hands in that particular place, with time to say all that was needed.

But then a voice! "I am the Master of Life, and this is not your time. You must return to your body and retrace your steps. Do the work of your earthly life, remembering what you have learned – remembering what is beyond". The warrior listened and knew he must retrace his steps, one by one and travel back with the assurance that he would see his beloved again. Eventually, the warrior became a great chief, wise, strong and kind with compassion for those tortured by loss, because he had something good to tell them.

Grace and the killer virus

As the four shires have now been described, there is one other element common to each of them which we must visit. I want to end our Deathlands visit with the soft low-light flame at the centre and give it the name of Grace. Grace is present in each Deathland Shire when we know how to wait for it. It comes from beyond what we know, and if you are religious, you may have a divine name for this presence. Grace, however, is inclusive and does not need a title or a label. It does require you to know that it works closely with, and manifests out of, Love. You will find it at the moment when you are in the depths of terror, and something unmerited, underserved, and unexpected joins you. It may be a person, or perhaps it's an animal, or something you see when the wind blows the trees, or on the surface of water when a puddle ripples. It has no conditions, but it comes to hold us and make us more than our saddened selves. Story is full of this when it speaks of a 'happily ever after' that brings a right end to dilemma.

At this point, we need to consider a newcomer presence who has recently invested in The Deathlands. It is not a shire; perhaps it is a weather condition, or maybe it is a creature? Whatever its nature, it gathers death, dying, and bereavement into one collective experience outside common space and time and plunges us into a liminal corridor where we are neither one place or the other. Coronavirus, Covid-19 has pushed us, without invitation into Deathland literacy by destabilising, disorientating, and even destroying us. We sit at this point between what once was and what will come, not knowing for how long, nor where we will end up. Coronavirus forces us to tunnel from the old road of life, taking away our bright eyes and making us seek out the possibility of a Grace light shrine. This place has always been ever-present but goes unrecognised because of the low light conditions it preserves. We hide in our armoured pain-wound bandages, our brittle-bright narcissism, our love of purchase and greed. In our shamed vulnerability, we become visible to each other, no longer hiding. Destructive, like the Kali mother, and with the cold dispassionate death eyes of Inanna, Corona peels away our old clothes and propels us naked over the edge. With her slaughtering ways, she terrifies us into lockdown and thus changes the old order. She forces us into a new place of silence and solitude, making contemplatives or deep-seers of those who can recognise the call. She withdraws privilege of contact and takes away our touch, harassing each of us to either serve her through our service to death, or to drop down and return to the deeper resources of home ground, internalising us, making us stay inside to find source energy.

With the absence of flights and a quietening of traffic, Nature seizes the moment to repair and returns joyously, free of the damage of humankind and blessed by a virus. People learn to find other ways. We turn to the arts for expression; children create rainbow assertions of hope for a future. We develop opportunities to meet each other through virtual community choirs and a generosity of free access to music and theatre and the many offers of teaching webinars. 'Something' is being poured out as we suffer our exile from the familiar road of life, and as we realise that we are mortal and life matters. We are capable of death while being joined by Love. Through a lockdown sentence, we are forced to slow down, stay still with ourselves and change.

The great greedy beast[11]

A mother and her baby son lived in a village that had one mountain pass road which everyone used to get there. One day the sound of heavy footsteps was heard, and a great greedy beast arrived, and it was starving. It sniffed out living creatures in order to eat, so to protect themselves the mother covered herself and her child in fire ash. The creature could not smell them and passed them by. However, when they were safe, they found they were all alone. The beast had eaten everything and was lying, fast asleep, in the valley of the mountain pass.

The mother went to the stream to fetch water, but when she was away, something happened. The baby grew and grew and became stronger until he was the size of a grown man. In his hand, he held a sharp spear and a thick shield. When the mother returned, she asked him, "Where is my son?" The strong man replied, "I am your son!" He told his mother that he would go to the pass and kill the great greedy beast and despite being terrified for his safety, she agreed and let him go.

The strong man made his way to the narrow pass and climbed up onto the beast. He plunged his spear into the creature and it woke up but was trapped in the pass because it had consumed so many people. The strong man killed the beast then cut a door so that all the people and animals could escape. What tales they told about their time in the beast and the promises they had made to life, if only they were set free. The strong man was celebrated, and plans were made so that the village would never be under that danger again.

If we return to the 'What if' we spoke about earlier we might have some new questions. What if this world Pandemic is like a shrine at the centre of The Deathlands? In the old life, we were free to ignore this place, so we became superficial and selfish at best, destructive and death-avoidant. Could Corona be a collective call to the soul value of Love found at the centre of Death which has the potency to meet us and carry us through? We are invited to this shrine with its gentle light through the doorway of our terror, grief, and despair – they are the agents which lead us to wait on the Love which is always present but so often ignored. The 'Something More' that pours into our pain and transforms it through the action and presence of seeing through Grace.

Story Grace and dramatherapy

I asked a group of UK dramatherapists[12] whether they recognise the term 'Grace' in their work using story in therapy, and if so, how did they describe it. Some of the responses follow.

- Unexpected joy seemingly unrelated to what we have been working on in the room.
- Beautiful goodness. A profound and often surprising touch of Love, compassion, and aching truth at the soul level. It leaves us merely saying thank you.

- When I think about Grace, I think about a calm stillness that underpins everything else. It is dependable and holding. It is generous and listening, and it seems to come from Love. It just arrives out of enactment, and you feel it there.
- Finding Grace is like a harmonious dance with the Divine through a process of acceptance, and you know it's not just you and your patient.
- I just turn up with the story I think will fit my group, then something happens. It's the innate knowledge that Greater Being is with us ready to provide strength, love, patience, or whatever we all need. I know it doesn't come from me.
- Grace happens when you are not looking or planning – when you've forgotten yourself and you awake to find that you are plugged into the universe's will. At that moment, you feel beautifully small, perfect, and utterly blessed.
- It is very like magic. I think the kind of story dramatherapy I do has magic in it. You listen to a story, you enact it, and without knowing how, something has completely changed. That's Grace for me.

The people I asked were not from a religious background, but they each gave a place to Grace in their practice and understood that when we sit with the traumas of others and can stay with them, then healing from somewhere unexpectedly happens. This is where the stories guide when they offer the presence of helpers. They bring the notion of enabling and of magical repair from somewhere much deeper than the dilemma or obstacle that trips us up and diminishes us. This is the gift of the stories.

Final words

This writing has claimed an imaginative space for death, and through a created story and six traditional tales has invited a way of befriending what is frightening and silenced by giving it a fresh form. It has reached beyond knowledge into the soft paths of half-light seeing and has demanded that the intelligence of imagination, subjective as it may be, is substantial and imperative for healing work. Finally, it has named Grace – the presence of Love that comes from 'Somewhere Else', verified by the library of stories, which has free membership and is available for all.

Notes

1 The Three Lessons, retold by the author from an oral telling by Ingrid Harrison at an 'Evening of Story', London (2014).
2 Jalal Al Din Rumi, 'Two Kinds of Intelligence', in *The Essential Rumi*, trans., Coleman, Barks with John Moyne, A. J. Arberry, and Reynold Nicholson, New York: Harper One (2004), 178.
3 Mary Smail, 'Open Sesame and the Soul Cave' in *Routledge International Handbook of Dramatherapy*, Sue Jennings and Clive Holmwood, Abingdon: Routledge (2016), 186.
4 In conversation with Alexis Ramsden, dramatherapist (2012). Used with permission.
5 Dying Matters is a rapidly growing national coalition which aims to change public knowledge, attitudes, and behaviours towards dying, death, and bereavement.
6 The Death Café movement allows strangers to gather to eat cake, drink tea, and discuss death. Their objective is to 'increase awareness of death with a view to helping people make the most of their finite lives'.
7 Korkut and the Music of Death – an Algonquin legend, allegedly told by Grandfather Daniel Seven Hawk Eyes, abridged for enactment by Mary Smail, (2018).
8 The Woman who lives in the moon, retold by the author from an oral telling, by Ingrid Harrison at an 'Evening of Story', London (2014).

9 Pintalgato the Kitten is a traditional story from Mozambique, re-written for enactment by Mary Smail (2019).
10 An Algonquin legend allegedly told by Grandfather Daniel Seven Hawk Eye, abridged for enactment by Mary Smail (2018): www.firstpeople.us/FP-Html-Legends/TheSpiritBride-Algonquin.html
11 The great greedy beast – an African myth retold by the author from an oral telling, Crick Crack Club, London (2004).
12 Samples from the grace responses came from an informal enquiry to 20 dramatherapists who understood that it was for publication. (2018).

4
STORYTELLING FOR DISABILITY IN COVID-19

Aurora Piaggesi, Giulia Bini, Silvia Carpi, Barbara Parrini and Stefania Bargagna

Introduction

In this chapter we will describe a Storytelling and Narrative Medicine pilot study which focused on communication in therapeutic settings. The research was carried out by a group of Italian Health Care professionals (HCP) from Calambrone Institute for Rehabilitation (IRC), at the IRCCS Stella Maris Foundation, along with a group of parents of patients with disabilities. However, because of the Covid-19 outbreak in Italy, many of the participants found themselves in lockdown in their own homes with their children. To evaluate the efficacy of storytelling as a tool for emotional and communication support, we submitted to both the HCP and parents two original online surveys to get information on their current emotional state. The assessed areas were personal stress, the relationship with children and family members, and the relationship with colleagues and professionals.

Background

Narrative Medicine is a methodology for clinical settings developed by Dr. Rita Charon encouraging a holistic approach to care-giving and stimulating the person in charge of the care – what she calls "the competence to recognize, absorb, interpret and be moved by the stories of illness" (1). As Charon suggests, the narrative approach requires the HCP to answer the question: "What is important for me to know about you, now?"

The original pilot study promoted by IRC of Stella Maris Scientific Institute Foundation was planned from March 2020 onwards. It aimed at evaluating the integration of Storytelling in Narrative Medicine as a potential resource for communication among HCP and parents of children with developmental disabilities in Health Care settings.

Patients' and HCPs' storytelling becomes an essential element of contemporary medicine, because good communication and quality support increase the rate of success. Listening with more attention to the patient's story means being able to better grasp their needs, hidden inside those very stories. Consequently the successful unveiling of the right question leads to a more participative answer and the building of a treatment where patients are again the real protagonists of their care.

Storytelling is "the interactive art of using words and actions to reveal the elements and images of a story while encouraging the listener's imagination" (2).

Unfortunately, the spread of the Covid-19 pandemic from the middle of February forced all the patients and most of their parents into lockdown in their homes and led to the suspension of almost all the activities of the institute.

This exceptional "stand-by" situation made it impossible for the HCP and parents involved in the study to maintain their usual interactions. Some HCPs tried to keep in touch with their patients online. In these unexpected times, everyone had to find new ways of living their daily lives: those who were used to moving quickly had to slow down and those whose lives were rich with activities had to learn to live in stillness. Families found themselves in charge of their children for the whole duration of the day, unable to meet with other families or friends to get some help. Many times people managed to activate hidden or forgotten resources to help with scheduling or time management, but most of the time they were worried and nervous.

The restrictions a person with disabilities experienced during this time were even more severe because of the concrete health risks and the many difficulties in finding suitable activities during lockdown, not to mention logistical and practical support. A child with a disability is complex to deal with and needs the whole family to help. Generally, the mother is the only one in charge of childcare and this theory found confirmation in the low percentage of male participants. In these family contexts it is only with the support of the school system that mothers can normally delegate some responsibilities for a few hours a day. However, because of Covid-19, this source of help was unavailable. Loneliness and the sense of precariousness of human relationships in this moment in time made life and interactions more difficult. For a family dealing with disability every day, finding time for any work or leisure activity is something that, even in normal conditions, can be very hard.

Developmental Disabilities are complex conditions appearing during infancy and involving a series of functions relating to the child's interactions with others. The most common are Autistic Spectrum Disorders, Intellectual Disabilities and severe language disorders. In these conditions difficulties in communication and social interaction can be experienced, as well as emotional disregulation and behavioral problems that can lead to hyperactivity or aggressiveness. In these cases the family is usually helped by rehabilitation services and by the school system. For this help to be effective it is necessary that both the patient's family and the HCP cooperate toward the same goals, developing what is called the "Therapeutic Alliance".

IRC of Stella Maris Scientific Institute has under its treatment 160 children with a history of care over many years, because of the difficulty of their condition. Because of the long duration of the treatment relationship, a strong bond is created between the patient and the medical team – a bond that can become an ulterior support for the family and a motivation for the HCP.

With the spread of Covid-19 cutting down all everyday interactions between the patient and the HCP, practical and emotional consequences have arisen in this therapeutic alliance.

Aim

We focused on the emotional and psychological consequences that the lack of social and therapeutic interactions might have produced. We wondered whether those groups where the participants who had already undergone an education in Narrative Medicine and Storytelling techniques, despite the isolation and lack of the usual interactions within the therapeutic relationship, would be able to use this already acquired knowledge for emotional and communication support? We wondered whether, in a moment of particular personal and social distress, the narrative knowledge could have contributed toward keeping alive the communication between HCP and the patients' parents, inside the families and among the professionals' work groups?

Methods

The original study was designed in December 2019 and started in January 2020. The goal was to conduct the experiment until the end of the year. The participants had been selected and divided into four categories. Education was provided in February, and in March we had planned to start our experiment, which was stopped due to the lockdown measures brought in by the Italian government.

In April, we decided to create and give the participants a new survey (see Appendix 1). Through a quantity analysis of the answers to the online survey and a quality analysis of some written statements and diary entries the participants sent us, we aimed at evaluating if the resources gained by those who attended the educational work might have helped them better deal with their emotions in the current situation, compared to those who had not attended the education.

Participants

In the study we included 40 parents of children with an average age of nine years with a Disability of the Autistic Spectrum, an intellectual or linguistic disability and, consequently, frequent users of the Calambrone Rehabilitation Institute (IRC) of the Stella Maris Scientific Institute Foundation and 16 HCP, among them doctors, therapists, psychologists, educators, and speech therapists from the institute. Among the parents participating in the study, 80% were female. The professionals were all women. Everyone involved in the project was fully informed about the aims and procedures of the study and gave their written consent.

Participants were divided into four groups (see Table 4.1). In **Group A** both HCP and parents were to be educated in Storytelling and Narrative Medicine; in **Group B** parents underwent education while HCP did not; in **Group C** the HCP were educated while parents were not; **Group D** was the control group, where nobody changed the usual behavior.

Table 4.1 Study group

	TRAINED HCP	UNTRAINED HCP
Trained Parent (A)	**Group A**	
Trained Parent (B)		**Group B**
Untrained Parent (C)	**Group C**	
Untrained Parent (D)		**Group D**

Notes: Participants were divided into four groups, formed from the intersection of two categories of HCP and parents, trained and untrained.

In Group A both HCP and parents were to be trained in Storytelling and Narrative Medicine; in Group B parents underwent education while HCP did not; in Group C the HCP were educated while parents were not; Group D was the control group, where nobody changed their usual basic care.

Training

The training for the participants was a structured 16-hour-long workshop divided into two days. In this workshop the following topics were addressed theoretically and practically:

- How the human brain works in relation to Narrative Communication;
- Theory and practice of Narrative Medicine;
- How to practice active listening;
- How to prepare a speech using a narrative structure, with a specific focus on communications in Health Care settings;
- The key elements of oral storytelling: the use of voice, images, gestures and body language.

Following education, the parents and HCP of groups A, B and C were asked to try to apply active listening during treatments and consultations, to keep a diary of their experiences and, eventually, to record their impressions on video. HCP were also asked to write a parallel record form for each of their patients based on Rita Charon's model and collect their patients' and their parents' expectations to be considered at the end of the process.

Assessment method

To assess if this educational experience might have a positive effect on the psychological well-being of the participants, if it might have helped the relationship and the communication between the families and the HCP, we developed two original surveys (one for the parents and one for the HCP) (see Appendix 1) that would take into consideration the specifics of the current situation and the differences that might have occurred in the lives, the jobs and the habits of the people involved.

These surveys had to be answered online anonymously before the end of the first month of self-isolation.

The surveys focused on five thematic areas – two specific for the parents, two for the HCP and one in common:

- <u>Personal well-being:</u>
  We explored mood swings, anxiety, anger and insomnia, both in parents and HCP.
- <u>The HCP's attitude toward their work and their colleagues:</u>
  Most of HCP participants were not allowed to work inside the institute during lockdown. Consequently we investigated their willingness to come back to work and to meet and share work experiences with colleagues. The HCP were asked to grade their perceived efficiency and adequacy to their job, and their satisfaction about their work. It was important to consider this element, since the professionals from the IRC found themselves in the emergency having to re-structure their work and activate several strategies to keep their therapeutic goals going, despite the remote distance from their patients.
- <u>Interactions between the HCP and their patients' families:</u>
  All professionals involved in the study were asked if they had contacted the patients they could not meet in person and if they had in any way kept in touch with the families for guidance and support.

- The relationship between the parents and the children:
  Because of the unusually difficult situation in which the families were living, it was important to assess whether the parents had experienced difficulties in managing their time and activities with their children at home, or if they had felt in need of some external help.
- The relationship between the parents and the HCP:
  Not all parents brought their children to the unit where they would normally receive their treatment. Consequently we investigated if parents tried to contact the therapists and if they felt supported and guided even from afar.

Both surveys asked 32 questions in all, including some on age, gender and the personal, professional and domestic situation each participant was experiencing. To evaluate the issues previously identified, 30 questions referred to the previous three weeks, formulated around their usual tasks (3) with Likert scale response methods (from 1 to 4 and 1 to 5) in the frequency domain (Never–Always) or in the intensity domain (not at all–very much), which were then normalized into 0 to 1 range. We also added two questions that the participants had to answer by writing some sentences, to give them an opportunity to use their own words to describe their experiences (e.g. "I gave advice to my patients" or "I organized tele-rehabilitation for my patients"). At the end of the survey the participants were also asked to express themselves freely about how they felt.

Through a quantitative analysis of the answers to the online survey and a qualitative analysis of some written declarations and some diary entries the participants sent us, we aimed at evaluating if the resources gained by those who attended the training might be of concrete support in better dealing with their emotions in the current situation, in comparison to those who had not attended the training. Quantitative analyses were made with the commercial software JASP (Version 0.12.2) (4). The items with ordinal scale responses were subdivided in three subscales: "Well-being", "Work" and "Patient's family" for the HCP; "Well-being" "Family" and "Relate IRC" for parents. Mean and standard deviation were calculated. The average score of the responses at each subscale have been analyzed through a T-test made for the HCP, comparing the averages between the trained and untrained, and an ANOVA between the parent's averages, comparing the four groups.

Results

Health Care Professionals

All the professionals involved completed the questionnaires, so we have eight answers for the group of Trained HCP, and eight for the Untrained group.

Well-being: on the physical and mental health side HCP included in groups A and C appeared less prone to anger and with fewer recorded episodes of aggressiveness and nervousness. They also kept a diary (scoring 5 = always) and considered it important to express their feelings and share their experiences and stories with someone.

HCP from the groups B and D, who did not attend training, appeared to be more angry and reported a larger number of episodes of aggressiveness and nervousness, resulting in feeling more stressed.

Through a student's T-test analysis between Trained (mean: 0.702; sd: 0.094) and Untrained HCP (mean: 0.659; sd:0.073), no significant difference was found (t=1.006; df=14.0; p=0.332; Cohen's d=0.503) (see Figure 4.1).

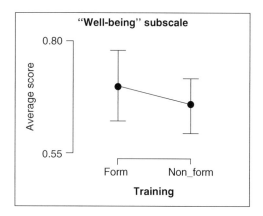

Figure 4.1 Average score of "Well-being" subscale of HCP survey

Note: Graphical representation of the averages (and confidence intervals) of the score for the "Well-being" subscale of the HCP survey. For the group of Trained HCP ("FORM") the mean is: 0.702 and standard deviation is: 0.094. For the group of Untrained HCP ("NON_FORM") the mean is: 0.659 and standard deviation is: 0.073. The student's T-test between these two groups found no significant difference (t=1.006; df=14.0; p=0.332; Cohen's d=0.503).

Regarding work and behavior toward colleagues, there was a difference among the groups. A higher percentage (60%) of educated HCP continued work activities, while only 40% of the others were working. More importantly, from the surveys it appeared that some of the HCP from these last two groups chose not to go to work even when they were allowed to do so. Those HCP who did not attend training appeared more discouraged in the way they wrote, such as the following example:

> *These are difficult times for everyone, we are in a global chaos, nothing like we are used to. We can sense fear, even if just a little, both in our patients and parents and, very often, in us professionals; it is not easy.*

They were also more critical toward the institution:

> *This emergency situation destabilized all HCP and the families of the patients. In particular, the lack of proper safety equipment generated more worries for one's self security.*

Comparing the average score on this subscale in Trained HCP (mean: 0.764; sd: 0.059) and Untrained HCP (mean: 0.679; sd: 0.095), with the student's T-test analysis showed no significant difference was found because p=0.05 (t=2.153; df=14.0; p=0.049; Cohen's d=1.077). However, looking at the data on a descriptive level, we could see that the Trained HCP had a higher average score (see Figure 4.2).

Regarding the relationships the HCP had with their patients and families, it emerged from the surveys that those among the professionals who attended training kept in touch more than those who did not, and fully understood the importance of being supportive in such a critical situation.

One HCP wrote: "*I wonder how long it will last before I will be able to have contact with my patients that is not through the internet. The families I am caring for at the moment, in my opinion have reacted well, showing many resources.*"

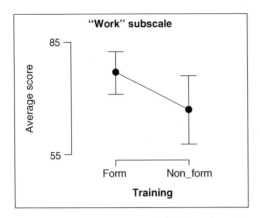

Figure 4.2 Average score of "Work" subscale of HCP survey

Note: Graphical representation of the averages (and confidence intervals) of the score for the "Work" subscale at the HCP survey. For the group of Trained HCP ("FORM") the mean is: 0.764 and standard deviation is: 0.059. For the group of Untrained HCP ("NON_FORM") the mean is: 0.679 and standard deviation is: 0.095. The student's T-test between these two groups found no significant difference (t=2.153; df=14.0; p=0.049; Cohen's d=1.077).

Educated HCP showed good introspective skills: "*I have a good relationship with the parents, to whom I kept giving indications regarding their child's problems and who I support on an emotional level. My relationship with them has always been good, hardly ever have I found unsolvable issues, I feel they take me into great consideration.*"

"*It has been harsh for our patients and often I felt I was not good enough to keep up my work to the best and I am very sorry for that.*"

Educated HCP were also more able to appreciate resilience in themselves, in their patients and in their patients' families.

"*… I believe that this experience will bring us a more respectful way of working with our patients and colleagues, because we are showing our weaknesses, our fear of the contagion and of death. We discovered our fragilities and in our job it is important, for us and for the others. We can learn from the children… to adapt, to be able to touch each other, even with gloves on. To look for each other, despite the mask.*"

HCP from groups B and D felt more lonely and nostalgic of the workplace: "*I miss my everyday life, meeting the patients and their parents, even if I tried to call them. During these weeks I also missed getting in contact with others to exchange ideas.*"

Through quantitative analysis of the average score on the "Patient's family" subscale in Trained HCP (mean:0.815; sd: 0.151) and Untrained HCP (mean: 0.665; sd: 0.200) with the student's T-test analysis no significant difference was found (t=1.696; df=14.0; p=0.112; Cohen's d=0.848) (see Figure 4.3).

Parents

Not all parents involved in the study completed the questionnaire. Therefore, we have a total of 33 answers, including nine for parents of groups A, C and D, and only six answers from parents of group B.

From a well-being perspective, the descriptive analysis of the answers showed that parents from groups A and B appeared to have a lower stress level, while parents from group D,

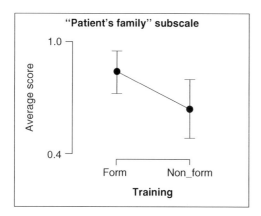

Figure 4.3 Average score of "Patient's family" subscale of HCP survey

Note: Graphical representation of the averages (and confidence intervals) of the score for the "Patient's family" subscale at the HCP survey. For the group of Trained HCP ("FORM") the mean is: 0.815 and standard deviation is: 0.151. For the group of Untrained HCP ("NON_FORM") the mean is: 0.665 and standard deviation is: 0.200. The student's T-test between these two groups found no significant difference (t=1.696; df=14.0; p=0.112; Cohen's d=0.848).

who did not attend education and who were not followed by HCP, had more frequent episodes of anxiety and insomnia.

Moreover, parents from groups A and B were also asked to apply some procedures after receiving the education, like keeping a diary and trying to conduct a conversation, keeping in mind the narrative structures. Those who were consistent with that found a way to manage their anxieties. Parents from groups C and D did not have such resources.

Quantitative analysis through ANOVA between the average score on the well-being subscale of the parents' different groups (Group A: mean: 0.645; sd: 0.066) (Group B: mean: 0.627; sd:0.118) (Group C: mean: 0.627 sd: 0.063) (Group D: mean: 0.553;sd: 0.138) showed no significant difference between groups (F= 1.475; p=0.242; η^2=0.132) (see Figure 4.4).

From their written considerations it appeared that parents who attended education were more self-reflective and more prone to sharing their insights and experiences. At the same time parents from groups C and D showed less interest in writing and sharing experiences.

With regard to the family and relationships between the parents and their children, their everyday interactions did not appear particularly different. The only exception was in the question "was it difficult living at home, these last few weeks?", from which it was possible to see that group A did not face many difficulties whereas for group D it was harder. ANOVA analysis between the average score on this subscale of the parents' different groups (Group A: mean: 0.678; sd: 0.208) (Group B: mean: 0.708; sd: 0.074) (Group C: mean: 0.678; sd: 0.115) (Group D: mean: 0.594; sd: 0.126) showed no significant difference between groups (F= 0.932; p=0.438; η^2=0.088) (see Figure 4.5)

This was also found in the written comments, where a parent from group A wrote: "*Regarding these past weeks, I felt somehow happy to stay at home with my son, without all that coming and going to therapy sessions, workshops, theatres, pools, school, etc.…*"

It was also possible to notice that educated parents (groups A and B) felt less in need of help, appearing more prepared to conceive and activate personal and, even, practical, resources: "*The past days at home with my son have been full of those things we always postponed for lack of time. We are

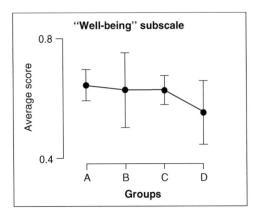

Figure 4.4 Average score of "Well-being" subscale of parents' survey

Note: Graphical representation of the averages (and confidence intervals) of the score for the "Well-being" subscale of the parents' survey. For the parents' group A (Trained parents with Trained HCP) the mean is: 0.645 and standard deviation is: 0.066. For the parents' group B (Trained parents with Untrained HCP) the mean is: 0.627 and standard deviation is: 0.118. For the parents' group C (Untrained parents with Trained HCP) the mean is: 0.627 and standard deviation is: 0.063. For the parents' group D (Untrained parents with Untrained HCP) the mean is: 0.553 and standard deviation is: 0.138. The ANOVA analysis showed no significant difference between groups (F= 1.475; p=0.242; η^2=0.132).

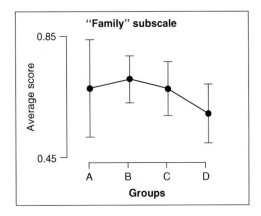

Figure 4.5 Average score of "Family" subscale of parents' survey

Note: Graphical representation of the averages (and confidence intervals) of the score for the "Family" subscale of the parents' survey. For the parents' group A (Trained parents with Trained HCP) the mean is: 0.678 and standard deviation is: 0.208. For the parents' group B (Trained parents with Untrained HCP) the mean is: 0.708 and standard deviation is: 0.074. For the parents' group C (Untrained parents with Trained HCP) the mean is: 0.678 and standard deviation is: 0.115. For the parents' group D (Untrained parents with Untrained HCP) the mean is: 0.594 and standard deviation is: 0.126. The ANOVA analysis showed no significant difference between groups (F= 0.932; p=0.438; η^2=0.088).

never bored at home, we have homework, online classes, I try to involve my children in housework, cooking, playing, going out in the garden. The days fly by very quickly."

Alternatively, parents from group C and D felt more irritable and manifested their loneliness more: *"Hard times. I can't bring my kid to the IRC and I would have preferred to keep in touch with* the HCP, even if just through video... I am struggling to keep on the goals we decided whether to use teletherapy, I don't feel able to do it, and it is not something I am inclined to do."

They also manifested more difficulties in managing their children: "*I keep her present during everyday tasks but it is really hard for me to play with her in structured activities.*" Some testimonies painted very desperate pictures: "*These days my son has shown his worst. Stereotypical screams, cries, aggressiveness (something that never happened before) and my mood has worsened or maybe we worsened together without realizing it.*"

The relationship with the professionals of the institute appeared positive in all cases, all parents seemed on good terms with everyone, but the best results were seen in group A and C, where the parents were interacting with trained HCP.

We could see it also in final considerations like: "*I strongly felt the presence and support of the HCP toward my child and us. Despite the difficult times, they kept in touch with us, supporting us and arranging meetings trying not to interrupt the therapeutic journey, and in doing so, they are enriching. We are lucky that we can count on them.*"

The help coming from the professionals was accepted well and used to ease the relationships with their child: "*Even if we can't meet in person, I feel that the professional that has my child in care is close to us, she supports us, she calls us, helping us in understanding the situation and giving us advice on how to manage our time and explain what is going on to the child. Based on my own experience, we are coping quite well.*"

Parents from group C – not educated, but followed by educated HCP – reported good feedback on their relationship with the institute and perceived support: "*It is very useful that the treatment is still going. Excellent support from IRC, the child is tranquil. These weeks have been hard, sometimes difficult. But I personally felt the closeness to the IRC, and I hope to come back there soon. My child's therapist has kept in touch and has always shown interest in helping us.*"

Where neither parents nor professionals were educated (group D), there was more nervousness as well as a certain lack of feeling; the relationship with the HCP was less good despite the positive trust toward the institute. "*I would have appreciated feedback on the treatment from the HCP, even before the lockdown, but I did not receive it. I expected more from the IRC*"

"*.... To upset my child's routine saddened me very much and it was very difficult for him... now he knows he has to stay at home... but he doesn't understand why... receiving help from IRC on how to manage and structure my son's day has helped me not to feel so discouraged and alone.*"

Also, ANOVA comparison of the four groups of parents (Group A: mean: 0.643; sd: 0.124) (Group B: mean: 0.607; sd: 0.060) (Group C: mean: 0.689 sd: 0.207) (Group D: mean: 0.579;sd: 0.221) showed no significant difference between groups (F= 0.655; p= 0.586; η^2=0.063); a large dispersion of results may reduce the possibility of results being statistically significant (see Figure 4.6).

Conclusions

None of the observed results achieved statistical significance. Our supposition is that the very small size of the sample and the great variability of the data did not allow us to find significant differences. Nevertheless, looking at the data as a whole, on a descriptive level, they indicate a positive effect of the training on both on the HCP and the parents.

The results showed how those who had attended education in Storytelling manifested less anger and frustration and tried to keep more in contact with others. Through narrative forms they expressed their emotions in their diaries, and found this particularly helpful. We also noticed that the professionals who went through the education tried to contact their patients more frequently than those who did not attend the course. We deduced that an education

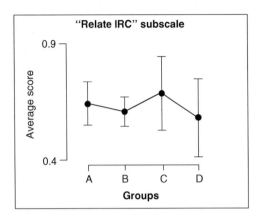

Figure 4.6 Average score of "Relate IRC" subscale of parents' survey

Note: Graphical representation of the averages (and confidence intervals) of the score for the "Relate IRC" subscale of the parents' survey. For the parents' group A (Trained parents with Trained HCP) the mean is: 0.643 and standard deviation is: 0.124. For the parents' group B (Trained parents with Untrained HCP) the mean is: 0.607 and standard deviation is: 0.060. For the parents' group C (Untrained parents with Trained HCP) the mean is: 0.689 and standard deviation is: 0.207. For the parents' group D (Untrained parents with Untrained HCP) the mean is: 0.579 and standard deviation is: 0.221. The ANOVA analysis showed no significant difference between groups (F= 0.655; p=0.586; η^2=0.063).

in Storytelling and Narrative Medicine and practicing writing and telling helped both the professionals and the parents to face a difficult psychological time during lockdown.

Among the HCP the difference in the way they evaluated their work and the relationship with the institution appeared generally stronger.

In group A, where parents learned about Storytelling and were followed by HCP educated on the same topic, there was less perceived loneliness. Parents did not feel left alone to comprehend the importance of the treatment the professionals were offering their children. In a time of global shutdown, IRC kept working, even with stronger safety measures applied. It appears that reflectiveness can help parents in understanding the importance of the confrontation with their children, and the reasons for it, during lockdown, even when it means facing fear and sadness, but they were able to share their thoughts and feelings inside the safe environment of the household.

The trained HCP tried to keep in touch more with their patients and generated a sense of satisfaction and reassurance in their parents. Parents from group B, who were trained and followed by HCP who were not, expressed more frustration, because they felt like they were being left alone, but they appeared less distraught at the general situation than group D. In group D there was perceived a lack of internal resources, and the HCP felt less responsive and more interactions were needed.

This short but effective educational intervention gave skills and knowledge to structure one's feelings and thoughts in a narrative form, equipping the participants with the resources to perceive themselves and their life experiences as the elements of the story. A story that, like any other, would include characters, antagonists, goals, conflicts and themes. Practicing observing the conflicts, showing this in their communications and cultivating different points of view, both for the parents and the HCP who received the education, gave them the chance to improve their empathy and construct their thoughts in a sequential perspective, being able to overcome the "here and now" of the current, scary and discouraging situation. The ability to put themselves in someone else's shoes, to express their feelings and frustrations through writing, allowed them the chance to first of all de-mystify and rationalize each moment and to create a new sense of what and how they were living. They were constructing a new experience starting from the act of narration itself (5). Everyone found a moment to share their thoughts and narrate their thoughts more freely, giving a sense of security and acceptance from their peers.

In other words, to cry together, confess little anecdotes, both for the HCP *and* the parents, meant they were able to listen to themselves and others. Someone else's story can help us reflect on our personal and domestic situation in a different way, whilst, if we are alone, we often persist in perceiving only our own sadness. A sense of belonging to a group can create a stronger presence even in difficult situations, like dealing with a child with disabilities or an aggressive pandemic.

HCP who could benefit from Narrative Knowledge might be able to access several emotional parachutes: finding time for themselves, listening to their emotions and giving voice to their life experiences, even when this brought anxiety and if perceived through the lenses of narration, they may have felt less heavy. This might leave room for thinking and acting toward the other, being able to cultivate a therapeutic alliance and resilience, maintaining an active critical and realistic way of thinking, that will result in a proactive and efficient outlook.

Somehow, the "narrating" professionals regained their role, choosing not to be mere "spectators" of the epidemic and life's new scenarios, but creating a sense of closeness and community with their patients. The storytelling does not mean describing reality only, but also making one's own story and being able to communicate it.

Pennebaker noticed that writing in narrative form transforms memories, motivations, emotions, sensations and thoughts in a linguistic structure with a specific time and space connotation. This allows confronting it toward a progressive change in the way we act toward ourselves, the others and the world (6). In other words, it helps give a sense to things. According to Nietzsche attributing a *why* to things helps us bear with the *how* (7). To tell through writing would allow a re-structuring of our thoughts and emotions. Pennebaker built a specific tool (Linguistic Inquiry and Word Count – LIWC) (8), to find out that those who wrote about past traumas progressively used more positive words than negative, with increasing references to causes and explanations. It appears that resilience can be linked to narration: to tell a story means to put things in order, to connect to a meaning, give facts an explanation, helping make them more acceptable in the moment they are told. Short & Casula state that "resilience puts in order the pearls of experiences of pain and joy through a thread of correlations of meanings making acceptable positive interpretations and restructuring the negative ones" (9).

Consequently we can hypothesize that parents and HCP who did not receive an education in narration could be less resilient and feel more isolated – both physically and emotionally – in the moment with their own anxiety, compared to those who received it. The parents felt abandoned to their fate and the HCP felt so overwhelmed by their emotions that they could not find quick and effective resources to give their patients the support they needed.

As a conclusion, given the limitations of the small number of participants and non-validated surveys, our results may be of limited interest. We are aware of the limitations of this study due to the small sample size, non-validated tools and the monocentric nature of the project; however, the prospective vision of the intervention and the topicality of the topic make these data useful if only to plan further larger studies, and to signal the possibility of training people in healthcare with storytelling techniques.

This chapter has therefore considered whether an education in Storytelling and Narrative Medicine might have a positive influence on psychological well-being and on the relationship between the HCP and their patients' families in a situation such as the Covid lockdown of 2020. We considered that using this kind of parallel education in Storytelling and Narrative Medicine is very helpful for the current pandemic situation and something to consider for the future when we face difficult situations in everyday practice.

References

1 Charon, R. (2006) *Narrative Medicine – Honouring the Stories of Illness*. New York: Oxford University Press.
2 The National Storytelling Network, *What is Storytelling?* Available at: https://storynet.org/what-is-storytelling/ (Accessed: 2 April 2020).
3 Chiorri, C. (2010) *Teoria e tecnica psicometrica: costruire un test psicologico*. London: McGraw-Hill.
4 JASP Team (2020) JASP (Version 0.12.2) [Computer software]. https://jasp-stats.org/
5 Frank, A.W. (1995) *The Wounded Storyteller*. Chicago and London: The University of Chicago Press.
6 Pennebaker, J.W. (2004) *Scrivi cosa ti dice il cuore. Autoriflessione e crescita personale attraverso la scrittura di sé*. Erickson.
7 Nietzsche, F. (1979) *Umano, troppo umano*. Milan: Piccola Biblioteca Adelphi.
8 Tausczik, Y.R., Pennebaker J.W. (2009) The Psychological Meaning of Words: LIWC and Computerized Text Analysis Methods. *Journal of Language and Social Psychology*, 29 (1):24–54. DOI:10.1177/0261927X09351676
9 Short, D., Casula, C.C. (2004) *Speranza e resilienza: cinque strategie psicoterapeutiche di Milton H. Erickson*. Milan, Italy: Franco Angeli Milano.

5
DON'T LET CORONA BECOME OUR ONLY STORY

Arjen Barel

What impact can the corona crisis have on our mental health? Besides the relational tensions that can arise from living on top of each other, many of us are also stuck in one negative story. It is important for our minds to keep making room for stories that are not about corona.

When corona came into our existence, the pandemic seemed to fully control the lives of everyone in Europe – and in a large part of the rest of the world. It is the topic of almost all conversations and the media continue to inform about the latest state of affairs. This is logical in the midst of a crisis, but there is a danger lurking; namely that we will fully identify with this crisis and forget which other stories also continue. In my field, where we use story sharing for personal growth and social impact, we call this the single story issue. We consciously use the word 'issue': being stuck in a single story rarely leads to something positive and usually results in victimization. This is mainly about the influence on the mental health of people whose identity has been reduced to a single story.

This happens, for example, to people with psychological or physical complaints. They often identify themselves with their problems. I regularly experience this when I give workshops to these so-called difficult target groups. As soon as they are introduced, they immediately mention the condition they are suffering from, and then put everything in the light of that condition, including the excuses for not being able to do something. Our work then consists of broadening their horizon by letting participants discover that they consist of multiple stories. By inviting them to work on those other stories as well. It is beautiful and hopeful to see how quickly people change for the better and become stronger, when they realize that it is not one story that determines their identity.

The same thing happened to the men in social isolation with whom we work in the western boroughs of Amsterdam West, part of the city that is characterized by the cultural diversity of its population, or to the LGBTQI+ in the Balkans whom we help to gain acceptance through stories. The moment these groups broaden their stories, depression, loneliness or sexual identity no longer play the only role, you see them flourish and mental resilience increases almost immediately.

Now, however, a collective single story seems to emerge. Where we know by experience what a single story does to the mental health of an individual, we are now confronted with a situation of a very large group of people who increasingly focus on one aspect. If I continue the line, I expect that this will have – and probably already has – an enormous impact on the mental well-being of a large part of the population, which will have lots of consequences.

That is why it is important to actively make room for other stories right now, in the middle of the pandemic. Memories from the past and dreams for the future. Let's share them, by asking the other person and making time to listen to them. We have plenty of that time right now. Without denying the virus and the problems that accompany it, we must continue to realize that this is only part of our existence and that there are many other things that continue to happen. This is a responsibility we have to take towards our own mental health (and resilience), just as we have to do for others. Sharing other stories and making sure people don't get stuck in that one difficult story is just as much part of caring about each other and will help us get through this crisis healthier.

PART II

Stories & therapeutic texts

Introduction

The common thread that links Part II is, as the title suggests, a focus on texts and therapeutic texts specifically. The text or story, whether it be read or told out loud, is central to story creation and is shared here from a variety of international perspectives.

Opening this section in Chapter 6, Sue Jennings uses William Shakespeare's *Midsummer Night's Dream* as her central text, linking it to a further development of her Neuro-Dramatic Play approach, which she calls 'Through the Fairy Door', a metaphor for the development of attachment-based work with children based on *The Secret Garden* by Frances Hodgson Burnett. This is followed by Alida Gersie in Chapter 7, exploring through a series of personal anecdotes and stories 'Through the Looking Glass: six pitfalls in story-work'.

Chapter 8 with Marina Jenkyns takes us firmly into classical literature with an exploration of the text of Sophocles from a dramatherapist's perspective, focussing on how the therapist might use the text in their work. Steve Stickley, seasoned English actor and storyteller, in Chapter 9 considers the role of the oral storytelling tradition, offering some wistful thoughts and narrative ideas on the practical process of telling stories. In our second visit to Shakespeare in Chapter 10, Rowan Mackenzie shares her experience of using Shakespeare within two UK prisons, one of which formed its own theatre company within the prison.

In Chapter 11 we move part way around the world to India where Kavita Arora and Raghu Ananthanarayanan consider the sacred text of the Mahabharata and its potential for healing. Returning to the UK for Chapter 12, Clive Holmwood considers the potential for attachment building in very young children using Michael Rosen's classic text *We're Going on a Bear Hunt*. Chapter 13 takes us to Greece where Stelios Krasanakis considers the use of the classic Greek myth within a dramatherapy context; he also considers how myth might be used today with examples from practice. Finally in the last chapter to Part II, we move to Italy where Salvo Pitruzzella considers the nature of 'Giufà' or 'The Fool' in his native Sicily. Here he makes some connections to his many years of therapeutic work leading and running groups using these classic stories.

6
THROUGH THE FAIRY DOOR ... TO THE LAND OF STORIES[1]

A journey through your imagination

Sue Jennings

Introduction

Stories and their dramatisation through play and drama (theatre) are at the core of human happiness, as well as the development of children, young people and adults. Stories are universally important for the health and welfare of all children. This belief is enshrined in the 'Convention of the Rights of the Child' (1989) which was adopted by the General Assembly of the United Nations (that is over thirty years ago!):

- Parties recognise the right of the child to rest and leisure, and recreational activities appropriate to the age of the child, and to participate freely in cultural life and the arts.
- Parties shall respect and promote the right of the child to participate fully in cultural and artistic life, and shall encourage the provision of appropriate and equal opportunities for cultural, artistic, recreational and leisure activity.

Stories are a part of our cultural and artistic life that belong to our individual, social and national identity, as well as our global understanding. Stories are a part of our history and ancient past (Jennings 2017), our ingrained 'historic self'. And this ancient self is both individual as well as familial and social. Storytelling influences and develops attachments, both through storytelling relationships and through the story's content itself.

Much of my therapeutic and educational work involves creating stories and listening to stories, as well as telling stories, all of which has been built into Neuro-Dramatic-Play (NDP), (Jennings 2011). NDP is a developmental paradigm that marks the early play and drama stages of young children. NDP and storytelling have grown out of my own love of stories, one of the few subjects at which I excelled at school. I also believe that most children learn in greater depth if the material is presented in story form. Many clients can access their personal issues if they communicate through a story. It may be in the first person, the third person or often a mythic person.

This chapter is therefore mainly concerned with a new system I have devised to ease our access to both creative and personal stories. It nudges our memory for stories long forgotten. It is an addition to my models, notably: 'Story Building', 'The Seven Circle Structure', 'The Story-Stones Cauldron', 'Baby Crow and other Puppet Storytelling' and 'The Story Dance'.

DOI: 10.4324/9781003118893-9

Through the Fairy Door owes some influence to a central theme in the story *The Secret Garden* by Frances Hodgson Burnett (1911, 2012). I need to acknowledge immediately the frequent racist expressions and hierarchical constructs in this story. These have been partially corrected in the film (1993) and the musical (1989/1991). Nevertheless, the story is a superb metaphor for the development of attachment and the ensuing restoration and growth of relationships. The context of the story title is that the children know that there is a garden that has been locked away for ten years. Mary starts to search for the key. There is the idea of crossing into another world, a magical world, a place of discovery, but it is also a metaphor for her making that journey into herself. Again, I am placing an emphasis on the place, 'the magic land', 'the world beyond' or any 'other-world' name we might use.

A similar structure exists in *A Midsummer Night's Dream* by Shakespeare, where various characters enter the forest and encounter chaos and confusion and change. The emphasis is on the location rather than just focussing on the individual characters. Magic lands give borders for transitions from our mundane world to other-worlds. It is said in Gaelic tradition, that the Festival of Samhain, 31 October/1 November is the time when the border between this world and the other-world is at its most transparent and people have to be careful not to fall through and become trapped in the other-world. It is a time when spirits or 'fairy folk' can also cross into this world and sometimes they decide to stay!

Another way to view 'other-world' phenomena is a consideration of trance. I write about this in some detail in my research with the tribal people, the Temiars (Jennings 1995). I think the various levels of trance bring about the same state of being as dream-like states, right-brain play and journeys into our imagination.

Scene one: stories and the brain

Neuroscience is racing ahead in new discoveries and it is only recently that researchers have identified an area that has been named as the 'The Storytelling Brain' (Gazzaniga 2016). We have known for some years that our brains have two distinguishable hemispheres, the right and left, that have quite specific functions.

Broadly speaking, the left hemisphere is for numeracy, logic, sequencing and facts, and the right hemisphere is concerned with feelings, creativity, the arts and intuition. The right hemisphere is also responsible for 'the whole picture' whereas the left is more concerned with 'the bits'; the right emphasises the group and the left, the individual.

Generally speaking, western education focusses on education for the left hemisphere more than the right. The arts are often seen as an extra or an after-school hobby; they do not have the kudos of scientific facts!

We are also more aware of important areas of the brain: the amygdala, which is a part of the limbic system, although it is often considered separately; the limbic system, often called our mammalian brain as we share it with other mammals; and the executive brain or neo-cortex. The amygdala is our 'reactive' or reptilian brain; it makes sure we eat, drink, sleep and keep warm. However, after trauma, other experiences may enter this part of the brain, and we may react to fears by flight, fight or freeze. Another reaction has been added to these three, fawn: frightened people will often try to placate their aggressor, blame themselves, comply or apologise.

The limbic system or mammalian brain is shared with all mammals. It is also referred to as the nurturing brain and is very important in the attachment process. The need for nurture was demonstrated in the research with orphans from Romania, who received no nurture-care and consequently had areas of their limbic system that did not develop (Sue Gerhardt 2014).

The neo-cortex is the area of the brain that enables higher-order thinking, is able to weigh up decisions before reacting.

I use a selection of puppets to teach children about their brains: a snake or crocodile for their amygdala, cat or cow for their nurture brain, and a boy and girl puppet for their neo-cortex. I have noticed an improvement in behaviour and self-regulation when children have understood their basic brain function.

However, there is newer research that demonstrates the influence of storytelling on the brain.

There are four main areas that we need to understand to support our case for the importance of storytelling (Jennings 2017).

Dopamine

The brain releases dopamine into the system when there is a pleasurable, emotional event. This is important because it helps us to remember the story more easily when we have been affected by it.

Therefore, we need to think about how our storytelling can always be a 'pleasurable, emotional event'. Stories that are read out like telephone directories will not engage anyone, and we can all remember the party-spoiler who tells a monotonous tale for the umpteenth time at a family get-together. The story needs to have timing and tone, vocal variation and suspense. It needs to catch our attention.

Mirror neurons

The mirror neurons feedback external happenings and actions. When these actions are pleasurable, people experience similar feelings to each other and also to the storyteller.

The most recent discovery in neuroscience is the exciting knowledge of mirror neurons. They make a huge impact on the brain of the developing child in terms of the way adults behave as well as the 'role-modelling' for family life events and the sharing of stories and performances. We share the magic moments of a story often with a collective response, just like an audience in a theatre; at its simplest: 'He's behind you' or 'Oh no he didn't!' However, it is common for people in the audience to have both an individual and a group response at the same time, whether it is comedy or tragedy.

Neural coupling

A story activates parts of the brain that allows the listener to turn the story in to their own ideas and experience. Listeners' brain activity mirrors the speaker's brain activity with a delay (Gross et al. 2010).

Extensive research has shown that our neurons 'couple' with other people's neurons during communication, and in particular during storytelling.

Cortex activity

When the brain processes facts there are two main areas that are activated. However, a well-told story can engage many areas of the brain, including motor, sensory and frontal parts of the cortex.

The importance of storytelling is shown by the fact that it involves several parts of the brain. The motor part is engaged through both our physical reactions and our gestures. We have sensory reactions such as tension, pleasure, disgust, surprise. The frontal lobes are stimulated and are involved in problem solving, memory, impulse control, language and other important functions. Collectively, our brains are involved in storytelling at several levels, which means the impact is greater.

Scene two: *The Secret Garden*

The Secret Garden was first published in 1911 and has stayed in print ever since. It is now regarded as a children's classic, recommended for young readers from nine years old; it also features in exam curricula and as a school text. Despite the racist language, referring to 'blacks' and 'natives', and the negative connotations of the 'working classes', the book is a superb example of its genre. It can be used for social discussion as well as literary study. However, it is also important as an illustration of the impact of emotional deprivation on children when there is a lack of secure attachment. The author was writing some forty years before John Bowlby was first writing and researching attachment theory. Just as Bowlby's early life experience (Van Dijken 1998) influenced his development of attachment theory, Hodgson Burnett's young life made an impact on her writing stories, initially for a living as the family lived in poverty. It is chronicled in detail in her biography (Thwaite 1974, 2007).

We are first introduced to Mary Lennox, child of socialite mother and career army father, living in colonial India with a retinue of nurses and servants. Her parents and many staff die in a cholera outbreak, and she is found, alone, by an army officer. She is sent to England, accompanying a stranger family, in order to stay with her maternal uncle in a remote manor house in the north of England. She has always been described as disagreeable, and indeed she was teased by boys who repeatedly sang:

> 'Mistress Mary, quite contrary,
> How does your garden grow?
> With silver bells and cockle shells
> And marigolds all in a row',

while they danced in a circle round her, with a particular emphasis on the first few words, 'Mistress Mary, quite contrary…'

Mary is accustomed to being on her own, servants looking after her basic needs, and has an imperious attitude towards the world. Soon she is befriended by the house-maid Martha, who relies on Mary to tell her stories about India, so that she can re-tell them to her eleven siblings. Mary is also curious for Martha to tell her stories about life beyond the manor house, as well as life within it.

Mary ventures out into the gardens, encountering the grumpy gardener, to whom she says:

> I have no friends at all. I never had. My Ayah didn't like me and I never played with anyone.
>
> *(p. 48)*

When a robin moves nearer to her, she says:

> 'Would you make friends with me?' just as if she were speaking to a person, 'Would you?' And she did not say it either in her hard, little voice or in her imperious Indian voice, but in a tone so soft and eager and coaxing… .
>
> *(p. 49)*

A journey through your imagination

The gardener is so surprised that he remarks that she is talking *like a real child* (my emphasis), rather than a sharp old woman!

The story continues:

Mary keeps meeting the delightful robin, with whom she starts to build a relationship and who eventually shows her where the key is hidden. The key that will open the door to the secret garden. This seems to be the first indication of an attachment:

Mary herself now admits that four good things have happened to her since her arrival: she understood the robin, who in turn understood her; she has run in the wind until her blood was warm; she is healthily hungry for the first time in her life; and she has found out how it feels to be sorry for someone. All of which translates into the repair of attachment in terms of a mutual trusting relationship, basic sensory awareness and the beginning of empathy. Her awareness grows and her body changes after the gift from Martha of a skipping rope.

The story continues with Mary discovering another child, Colin, who has been hidden away, and who believes he is disabled and will die soon; an opinion held by everyone in the household, including his father, Mary's uncle. Mary confronts his tempers and eventually Martha's brother Dickon and Mary coax him to come to the secret garden, where he grows in strength and health. Together they discover the importance of Magic, which they invoke with chants and rituals.

Finally, Colin's father returns home and meets his son in the garden, no longer sickly or in a wheel chair. The garden where his wife died in a tragic accident has become a garden of healing for his son.

It would be easy to be diverted at this point to consider yet more aspects of this story, such as intergenerational trauma, rhythmic and messy play, and nature-based activities. These I am writing about elsewhere (Jennings in preparation 1). Right now, I wish to emphasise two important points from this story, that underpin the method of 'Through the Fairy Door'. The first is the importance of the secret door which leads into beauty, stories and healing. The second is how attachments can be re-paired or in this case established, through nature, play and stories.

Scene three: Through the Fairy Door

'Through the Fairy Door to the Land of Stories' is a technique that is enabling to children, teenagers and adults, and helps them allow their imaginations to function. It encourages people to use the right hemisphere of their brains to create stories, rather than get stuck in a linear and logical model of beginning, middle and end. I am sure that many readers will share with me those awful moments in class where a story was required but there was an empty piece of paper in front of you! Or we were given a title and expected to write a story on the theme. And we would sit and suck our pencils and feel stuck!

I was fortunate that my love of Shakespeare was already well established, and I was able to visit the then Shakespeare Memorial Theatre. The first play that I ever saw was *A Midsummer Night's Dream*. There are personal stories about events in Stratford, too, as we visited a special café called the Hatch and had malted milk, and the Lanchester Puppet and Marionette shop, where Waldo Lanchester himself was often behind the counter. His puppet company was a leading influence on puppetry in education and I saw his marionettes in performance and was enchanted. I remember him as a fairy tale-looking person with lots of white hair and a huge white beard.

Stratford on Avon has remained my favourite place in the whole of the UK. A place where I could realise many dreams and tell many stories.

Back to the sucking of pencils, having had a little diversion through a personal story! When I was trying to write a story, I began to focus on the *how* of storytelling. I noticed that when people were telling stories, they seemed to pull phrases from the air and would repeat something in other words if they wanted to emphasise it. They would pause and wait, and sense when it was time to move on. They used their voices and gestures. Maybe this was a way of writing stories as well as telling them, instead of writing a 'lesson plan' in linear form. Ideas from here and there, what and when, now and then; and then put them into a narrative. This was the thinking behind my creation of the Seven Circle Story Structure (Jennings in preparation 2).

However, I now wanted to find a way to journey between the hemispheres of the brain. Twenty years earlier I had created the pairing of 'everyday reality and dramatic reality' (Jennings 1990) in Dramatherapy; this describes the transition between the factual left-brain hemisphere and the creative, imaginative right hemisphere, through the *corpus callosum*.

The Fairy Door that opens to the Land of Stories is a similar transition. Could the image of a closed Fairy Door in a tree allow us to make that step into our imagination? (See Figure 6.1).

Step one

Participants are invited to focus on an imagined door or to draw/paint/model their idea of a Fairy Door. Some craft shops have wooden doors that can be coloured. Cardboard can be used to cut out a door shape which is then developed with collage materials, (this way is eco-friendly as all materials can be recycled).

Step two

People are then invited to reflect on their door, and its detail. Remind participants that it is an important door that holds the way into their imagination. Do they feel ready to see what is beyond? Invite them to reflect on the expression: 'when one door closes, another opens'. Have they had a door closed to them? Remember that this door opens into the Land of Stories so there will be several stories in the landscape.

Step three

After step two, people may need to have a little pause, make notes, have a drink of water.

Invite people to close their eyes again and imagine opening the door and seeing the landscape beyond. It may change a bit and then settle into an image. The landscape contains stories, often associated with the landscape itself: a river, forest, mountains, sea, farm, meadows, desert, village, tower blocks, playground, park... Or scenes with people or animals come to mind.

Step four

You may choose to invite people to draw or paint their landscape before focussing on stories. Unless there is a story bursting to come alive and people wish to write it down immediately, painting or drawing, or modelling it in clay enables the experience to be more stable. It can also act as a memory nudge for the several stories in the landscape. I discovered that I had at least six Moose and Mouse stories to tell (Jennings 2018, 2019, 2020); you can just see the characters in Figure 6.2.

A journey through your imagination

Figure 6.1 Closed Fairy Door in a tree

Step five

People may not be ready to write down a narrative straight away. Invite them to make notes or patterns of words: objects, colours, contrasts, feelings… Then they can highlight connections, associations, contrasts.

The narrative emerges out of these connections and may need several attempts at re-shaping and refining, which are all part of the story-making process.

Figure 6.2 Through the Fairy Door

An example from my personal Fairy Door
Moose and Mouse make daisy chains

Moose and Mouse were going for a slow ambly sort of stroll. It was sunny and warm, and it felt cooler walking along the path next to the river. Occasionally there was a plop as fish were jumping from the water to try and catch flies. 'Shh' said Moose, 'Look, it is a kingfisher' and just then the flashing bright colours flew past them and dived in the water and caught a shining fish.

'I expect it is feeding a big family' said Moose, as they continued walking. Mouse thought they had encountered something really-quite-big; a kingfisher is lots bigger than a mouse.

Soon they came to the wooden bridge, 'Your turn to choose, Mouse my little friend, shall we keep going along the river path, or shall we go over the bridge today?' 'Definitely over the bridge' said Mouse, 'I love the big tree with the wide branches. And look, the grass is white with daisies'.

The two friends crossed the wooden bridge and there was the meadow that they loved; they had come here several times before. They sat under the birch tree and started gathering daisies to make daisy chains. Mouse made a very long chain and put it round Moose's neck and antlers. 'Come and look at yourself in the river' said Mouse, and they both gazed at their reflections.

'Time to go back' said Moose. 'Time to think about our next big journey, let's make it a really big journey!' (see Figure 6.3).

These are the notes to remind you of the steps in the process *before* you create the Fairy Door:

- Think about your idea of 'fairy' – something beautiful, magical, mysterious?
- Or maybe it is one of the elves, goblins or pixies? (Especially important when working with boys.)
- Imagine what your door might look like? Ornate? Simple? Celtic? Camouflaged?
- What might the landscape look like when you are through the door?
- You are making the journey into your imagination.
- That means going from the left hemisphere of your brain to your right hemisphere.
- That means crossing through the *corpus callosum*.
- Perhaps the Fairy Door is a metaphor for *corpus callosum*?

This exercise can be applied with all ages of clients and pupils, and in groups. It is also useful for parent workshops and staff training. It is a 'Fail-Safe' structure where people feel safe to explore.

Step six: closing reflections

Michael Gazzaniga (2016) is a cognitive neuroscientist with a particular interest in the right and left hemispheres of the brain. He suggests that our left hemisphere organises our memories into stories. He says that it is not only that humans *love* stories – they need them!

'What stories give us in the end is reassurance. And as childish as that may seem, that sense of security – that coherent sense of self – is essential to our survival'.

Your storytelling brain

There is a growing awareness of the importance of storytelling in education and therapy, and indeed in life itself. I have illustrated this through the recent research of neuroscientists, as well as providing a means for people to feel more confident about telling stories themselves.

Storytelling can give us new insights, different endings and an idea of the whole picture, which can be very reassuring when we get bogged down in the bits! It would seem that our brains need stories in order to bring coherence to our lives.

We forget that much of our time is spent in telling and listening to stories, in our day-to-day encounters, at the doctors' surgery, and news is relayed to us in newspapers and on television.

It is another step to share the fairy story, the myth or the legend, but all are stories. We cannot help but tell stories! And we need to remind ourselves that stories are both healing and therapeutic, as well as preventative.

Figure 6.3 Moose and Mouse

We have a storytelling brain and we need to remember to use it with ourselves as well as with others. Pomme (2006) quotes a wonderful metaphoric tale at the beginning of her book *Tales Told in Tents* which is what this chapter is all about! Just as the Bushmen of South Africa called the farmer foolish for not being to see what was in the Star Woman's Basket (Jennings 2020), again humans are being described as stupid for neglecting their stories and songs.

> *So, god made one more*
> *person and filled*
> *their brain right up to the top, with*
> *stories, songs and sparkly words.*
> *And he sent*
> *the storyteller down to*
> *earth to tell stories and to sing songs.*
> *To tell wise tales and sing wisdom back*
> *into the foolish human beings*
>   *(Pomme 2006, p.1)*

I think the image of 'sparkly words' is an appropriate ending for this chapter. I hope everyone, like Pomme, will find the sparkly words in their stories and be able to communicate them in a sparkly way!

Note

1 My thanks to the Temiar people for their endless source of inspiration.

References

Gazzaniga, M. (2016) *Your Storytelling Brain*. www.Bigthink.com (accessed July 2020).
Gerhardt, S. (2014) *Why Love Matters: How affection shapes a baby's brain*. Abingdon: Routledge.
Gross, M. et al. (2010) 'Speaker-listener neural coupling underlies successful communication', *Proceedings of National Academy of Sciences*. Princeton, NJ: Princeton University Press, pp. 14425–14430.
Hodgson Burnett, F. (1911, 2012) *The Secret Garden*. London: Vintage Classics. (Film 1993; Musical 1989, 1991).
Jennings, S. (1990) *Dramatherapy with Families, Groups and Individuals*. London: Hachette/JKP.
Jennings, S. (1995) *Theatre, Ritual and Transformation: The Senoi Temiars of Malaysia*. Abingdon: Routledge.
Jennings, S. (2011) Healthy Attachments and Neuro-Dramatic-Play. London: Jessica Kingsley Publishers.
Jennings, S. (2017) *Creative Storytelling with Children at Risk*. 2nd Edition. Abingdon: Routledge/Speechmark.
Jennings, S. (2018) *The Story of Moose and Mouse*. Wells: Close Publications.
Jennings, S. (2019) *Moose and Mouse's Big Adventure*. Wells: Close Publications.
Jennings, S. (2020) *Moose and Mouse go to Mongolia*. Wells: Close Publications.
Jennings, S. (in preparation 1) *Nature-Theatre-Play: Stories for Health and Healing*.
Jennings, S. (in preparation 2) *Creating Therapeutic Stories for Attachment and Empathy*.
Pomme, C. (2006) *Tales Told in Tents*. London: Frances Lincoln Children's Books.
Thwaite, A. (1974, 2007) *Frances Hodgson Burnett: Beyond the Secret Garden*. Stroud: Tempus Publishing.
Van Dijken, S. (1998) *John Bowlby: His Early Life – A Biographical Journey into the Roots of Attachment Theory*. London: Free Association Books.

7
THROUGH THE LOOKING GLASS
Six pitfalls in story-work

Alida Gersie

Using stories to bring about desired and desirable change may sound like an easy craft. Can't everyone tell a story? Isn't storytelling what we do naturally? In this chapter I discuss why and how things are more complex than that. I will highlight some tricky situations in my therapeutic practice with children and adults whose untold or unheard stories stuck in their throats and tied their bodies and relationships in constraining knots, thereby to uncover some key pitfalls in change-focused story-work. I bring these shadows in the wings of story-work to the fore because their unacknowledged presence often disrupts its healing potential. Once acknowledged, each pitfall can become a curative factor. But first some definitions of terms.

Definition of terms

I use the term **story-work** as a collective noun to refer to the different ways in which change-professionals with wildly different theoretical and practical orientations use stories. Through this lens story-work aims to alleviate participants' unease or suffering, to strengthen their belief in benign possibilities and to provide good-enough support to help them bring about desired and desirable change. I think that such story-work needs to do so in ways that are efficacious, cost-effective and long-lasting.

Throughout I refer to a wide range of narrative statements as **stories**. These include fictional, historical, personal, fact-based and traditional stories. This latter category comprises: myths, epics and sagas, folktales and fairy tales. The boundaries between these types of stories and between fact and fiction are of course porous.

I use the word **storymaking** to describe the interactive processes by which a teller and a listener jointly constitute the content and sense of a story. From this perspective storymaking is permeated by intricate performative, participative and interpretative dynamics. Here the word **storytelling** refers to oral storytelling – that is, storytelling that happens face to face, voice to voice and gesture to gesture. In story-work participants do both storymaking and storytelling. I presume that change-professionals introduce their clients to story-based creative techniques and facilitate the change process. During the sessions the participants, and indeed the facilitators, tend to recount a story or two.

I employ the mundane, collective nouns **change-professional** or **facilitator** to refer to teachers, health-staff, social workers, psychotherapists, counsellors, ministers and priests, mindfulness trainers, artists and organization-consultants who work with children, adults, communities, groups or organizations to facilitate a productive change in their circumstances, habits, relationships, inner-worlds or family and social dynamics. Where relevant I may describe the people a change-professional works with as **clients**, participants, patients, pupils, colleagues or simply as children or adults.

Why pitfalls

The word 'pitfall' was first recorded in the 15th century. It referred then as now to a hidden trap, something below the surface of explicit perception that can easily trip someone or an animal up as they wind their way towards somewhere. Pitfalls are by their nature hard to see, though some may hide in plain sight. Many discussions of story-work gloss over them. But as Kendall Haven points out 'misconceptions surround stories as densely and as thorn filled as the enchanted thicket surrounded and hid Sleeping Beauty's castle' (Haven 2007, p. 19). Here I discuss the pitfalls in order to unveil their thorny reality as well as their therapeutic potential. Below I will lift some to the fore.

Pitfall 1
The Streetlight Effect

On May 24, 1924 the *Boston Herald* (Massachusetts, USA) reported that the previous night a police-officer had seen a drunken man on his hands and knees 'groping about'. It was around midnight. The officer asked the man what he was up to. "I lost a two dollar bill down on Atlantic avenue," the man replied. "What's that?" the officer asked. "You lost a two dollar bill on Atlantic avenue? Then why are you hunting for it here in Copley Square?" "Because," said the man as he turned away and continued his search on his hands and knees, "the light's better up here."[1]

Now my second story.

A man is walking home late one night when he sees Nasreddin Hodja crawling on his hands and knees beneath a streetlight. He seems to be looking for something on the ground. "Nasreddin, what are you looking for?" the man asks. "My key," Nasreddin Hodja replies, "I've lost my key."

"I'll help you look," the man says and soon both men are down on their knees looking for the lost key. After a while, and not having found the key, the man says, "Tell me Nasreddin Hodja, where did you lose that key." "In the house," Nasreddin replies, "I lost it in my house…"

"Then why," the man reacts, "why are you looking for it here?"

"Because," Nasreddin Hodja patiently explains, "here there is light."[2]

There are significant differences between the urban myth and the Sufi teaching tale. While the first elicits a colloquial response of something like: "What? That's plain stupid," the second story evokes puzzlement as well as laughter. Just witness what happens when you say to yourself: "I have lost my key" or "I lost my key in my house", and you'll know one of the key differences between these stories.

I am telling both stories here for several reasons. Firstly, I want to honour the reality that change-professionals often work in complex settings with people who feel stuck. Here they try to navigate with their clients the problematic tension between both story-versions. The urban myth appeals to an all too common negative take on the problematic behaviour of troubled people. A perception which many clients have internalized. The puzzlement evoked by the Sufi teaching tale reflects the therapeutic necessity of helping clients to become aware that the search for the key to what truly matters in life, and therefore to the discovery of a better way forward, lies within the house of our self.

I further told both stories because I want to alert change-professionals and participants alike to the dangers of the so-called Streetlight Effect, which derives its name from the Nasreddin Hodja tale. The Streetlight Effect is a scientific term for the type of bias that occurs when we only look for 'what we are searching for' in the light of the theoretical and habitual understanding of practice that we are comfortable with. I call this limitation a pitfall because it curtails the therapeutic efficacy of the change-effort. In my experience the Streetlight Effect is best circumvented through the embrace of a habit of curiosity.

Pitfall 2

Unclear and underprepared for story-work

Many facilitators of story-work seem a bit lost amidst the array of definitions and theories about stories and storytelling. So are clients. I think this matters. Most would disagree with Genette's proposition that the phrase "The king died" is a story, and that if the crowd wants details, they can jolly well ask for them (Genette 1988). Neither are they comforted by Forster's earlier argument that a story needs five words (Forster 1927). Namely: "The king died of grief." They might be more impressed by the ideas of the Anglo-Indian journalist and writer Rudyard Kipling who somewhat grandiloquently announced that he kept Six Honest Men who taught him all he knew about stories and storytelling (Kipling 1902). Their names were *What* and *Why* and *When* and *How* and *Where* and *Who*. Though change-professionals rarely call these six interrogative words their Honest Men, knowingly or unwittingly they all use open-ended questions structured around these six words to make and tell a story (Gersie 1990). In this sense Genette's brusque reference to how a crowd could get a fuller story is correct. Indeed: *how, where* and *when* did that king die, of *what* did he die and *what* would happen next? A teller's answers to these queries would quickly generate a more satisfying, thickened story about the king's death and its consequences. Primarily because the story would now have a plot, complete with an initiating event, such as a challenge or conflict, one or more turning points, sometimes called the rising action, a climax, falling action and resolution. A series of events through which one or more protagonists achieve a climax (having reached or failed to reach their goal) and a resolution is generally called the plot. In many cultures, but not in all, a story's climax portends its imminent ending. And isn't that what most listeners and change-professionals want from a story: an attention-binding plot? But do they?

There are serious questions to be asked about the kind of things clients and facilitators hope to achieve through story-work (Howes 2014). Some try to encourage their clients to alter the story-map they use to interpret experiences and expectations. Others help patients in their search for a good-enough life-story. Some change-professionals mostly listen to their participants' tales. Others like to tell their clients an old or new story to offer encouragement. Some clients have joined a story-group in the hope of finding their life's meaning in a traditional story. And yet others simply long to have their stories heard. Amid this confounding array of desires for story-work, story-definitions and efficacy claims, clients can expect that change-professionals will state clearly what they might gain from story-work and what kind of stories they will work with. As part of such 'contract-setting' facilitators should be able to explain why they selected a certain technique, story or approach in preference over others. In my experience this is not always the case. I also had an important lesson to learn in this regard.

I still remember how, while on placement in a secondary school, during my early training as a dramatherapist I was wholly unable to respond effectively to such questions when Dan, a 14-year-old boy, confronted me. He attended a group for adolescent boys who played truant. It was the third session. Without much of a lead-in or story-scaffolding support, I suggested that the boys create a fictional life-story for a 68-year-old man. I complicated matters by saying said that they could draw on the life of an old man they knew as a model. "Why," Dan confronted me: "Why the hell do you want us to do that. You know nothing you… Who do you want us to talk about? I never even had a granddad. Do you want us to f…ing draw, write, talk?" He added some more swear-words, kicked a wall and shouted again "Why?" Others soon joined him. They created a pretty loud "Why" chorus. I felt scared and humiliated. For in truth, I didn't have an answer. I hadn't even done the exercise myself in preparation for the session, and like some hungry wolf-pups they could smell my uncertainty.

Just before the group started, and desperate for an idea for what to do, I had checked a drama-book and seen the exercise. There and then I told the boys the truth. They howled with dismissive laughter. Then one of the boys took pity on me. He commented that I'd at least been honest. I hadn't tried to cover my tracks. That was kind of brave, he thought. Others slowly agreed. Dan also did. I kept my voice but not my head down. Maybe if I was a bit clearer and maybe, they wondered, they could give it a go? Better than running out and getting punished for that. At this point I spoke up. I said I appreciated their willingness to give me and also the borrowed exercise-idea another chance. We still had a fair bit of time to pick up the thread of our group's work. They consented with a somewhat wry look on their boyish faces. This time I told them why I had chosen this exercise. They could now see the point of it, they said. I also showed them how they could develop a fictional character, and how to make a simply drawn life-map for that person. They began pitching in with ideas. In the remaining session-time the group created various life-maps for our fictional old man. We set them aside for use in the next session. All of us had learned some lessons. Theirs and mine hopefully were that I could make a mistake, own up to it, be forgiven, learn from it and get on. Maybe they could begin to internalize that? I can sum up my core learning in four words: prepare, repair and be honest.

Pitfall 3

Interrogative questions and unwelcome feelings

In many warm-up exercises participants are encouraged to ask each other a question to evoke a story-seed, such as 'where are you from?' or 'what brings you here?' (Jennings 2010). But do people who have only just met actually want to share this kind of storied information? Might not the very question reveal the questioner's implicit or even explicit class-consciousness or racial bias? Are the questioners prepared for the answers? I recall two occasions, one informal and one in a training situation, when the effects of the interrogative question *Where are you from?* startled both questioner and responder. These experiences made me aware that interrogative questions should carry a 'be aware' warning. Let me illustrate.

The first event happened in the mid-1970s. I was on a bus travelling towards an international work-camp organized by the United Nations Association in the UK. A tall, rough-looking man wedged himself on the little bench beside me. Looking me up and down he queried somewhat forcefully: "Where are you from then?" I answered truthfully: "The Netherlands. Arnhem." He repeated, clearly upset: "Arnhem? Not Arnhem." Then he swore. Loudly. Pointing at me, he groaned: "She's from Arnhem. Arnhem. Bloody Arnhem." "Leave her alone Liam," a woman seated a couple of benches in front of us called out. "Leave her alone. She can't help it." Turning to me she added: "It's the war love. He was there. His mates died at Arnhem. He was a prisoner. He's never got over it. I'm really sorry love." She beckoned to Liam to come and sit next to her. Before making moves to join her Liam patted my hand and mumbled "sorry", I said sorry too. I was more than a little shaken. I wanted to explain that I had come to join the work-camp to give something back but I didn't have the words. Soon the bus arrived at my destination.

At the time the term Post Traumatic Stress Disorder (PTSD) was not yet a household name. It was first included in DSM-III in 1980. But there were other names for some of its symptoms: shell shock, soldier's heart, war neurosis. Since time immemorial old stories, histories and testimony have born poignant witness to the fact that most men, women and children suffer greatly whenever they are close to humans who harm or kill humans in violent conflict, or are such humans themselves (Gersie 1994).

I was a young woman then but I could have known better. I had worked as an arts development officer in Arnhem for several years. This included some involvement in the Annual Commemoration of the Battle of Arnhem on September 17–26, 1944. I was well trained for my professional role. I also knew from personal experience the profound physical, psychological, social and environmental costs of exposure to war. My ill-thought-through answer to Liam's question re-traumatized him and agitated me. Despite my closeness to the destructive aftermath of war and despite my thorough training I had not foreseen the possibility of Liam's reaction. A decade or so later, and by then an international arts-therapies trainer, I did.

As part of their training some 2nd-year dramatherapy trainees were leading an introductory workshop for newly arrived 1st-year students. I observed the session. The new students were asked to work in small groups. Their task: tell each other a story about 'where you are from' and show what you hear in movement. I noticed that in one small group a Kinh woman from Vietnam became visibly upset. The trainee-facilitators saw it too. They quickly brought the exercise to a good end and called the group into a circle. Here we learned that some well-intended classmates had asked the woman, who I will call Jade, if she was born close to My Lai. They apparently also told her that all they really knew about Vietnam was the war and the My Lai massacre. Moreover, because they were now on the dramatherapy training programme they presumed that it was appropriate to ask her to tell them a story about this. It demonstrably was not. Jade's and their individual and intercultural learning-processes got off to a dramatic start.[3]

It is important to be aware that under normal circumstances the question *'where are you from?'* is only asked when the questioner perceives the other as an outsider, a stranger. Members of an ethnic minority, newcomers and migrants know all too well how offensive and unpleasant this question can be. Particularly because the question so often signals the questioner's racial bias and prejudicial attitude. Think about the dark, threatening underbelly of queries, such as:

- what brought you here?
- how did that happen?
- who did you come with?
- what are you up to?
- where are you going?

The conversational implicature of these questions matters (Chapman 2005). So does their private and socio-political context. In story-work the use of interrogative questions is invariably double-edged. They can indeed generate a fruitful starting point for a deeper story-exchange.

However, they can also trigger a host of very unwelcome memories, feelings and associations at a time when the safe boundaries of the therapeutic space are not yet formed. As a result, I have long since stopped using these queries during a session's warm-up phase. Suggesting instead story-invitations such as: "Please share something you noticed (saw, heard, smelled) on your way here", or "If there's a word, taste or sound you particularly like, please tell us." The development of mutual interest and concern needs creative care. It also requires interpersonal awareness. Something I lacked that day on the bus.

Over 75 years have passed since September 1944. Yet many Europeans and Americans still associate Arnhem with the Second World War, with the Allies' Operation Market Garden, with the film *A Bridge Too Far* and above all with failure and bitter loss. In 1975 I was a professional inhabitant of that town and a visitor to the UK. Liam's response taught me that I presumed too readily that my answer to an interrogative query would not unsettle the questioner. At the time I also tended to think that most people appreciated interrogative queries and that such questions did not reflect class or racial bias. These presumptions were for obvious reasons wrong and insensitive. The small-world phenomenon, also called "six degrees of separation" pertains to everyone. The six handshakes rule exists. This can be a consolation. However, when first meeting a new person this rule is also a risk. Maybe it is better to leave certain interrogative queries to a time when a good-enough relationship has been established and people are ready to volunteer the information. And by the way: Arnhem is also a city of art, architecture, music. Its northern borders overlap beautifully with those of the Dutch National Park Hoge Veluwe, an oasis of heathland, trees and inland dunes.

Pitfall 4

Neglecting a traditional story's multiple meanings

In his classic essay '*The Storyteller*' the German Jewish philosopher Walter Benjamin argues that storytellers are often imagined as people who have come from afar. And yet people also enjoy listening to a familiar person who has stayed at home, makes an honest living and is a good raconteur (Benjamin 1999, p. 84). In their archaic representations, storytellers are, Benjamin suggests, either trading seamen or local tillers of the soil. The first bring the lore of faraway places. The latter reveal the lore of the local past. Tales told by the widely travelled storyteller, he proposes, are mostly spatial and full of plausible information. By contrast, the locals' tales are mostly temporal and incline towards the miraculous. In story-work many change-professionals fit the 'raconteur' image evoked by Benjamin. Yet, they also like to tell tales from faraway places. Their stories come in many different ways.

Most facilitators like to tell a traditional story that has germinative power, is evocative and multi-interpretable, is easy to remember and spurs retelling (Gersie 1997). When giving reasons for their story-choice facilitators frequently stress the importance of overlap between their client's predicament and the story's theme. Traditional stories with archetypes (which are themes, motifs, symbols or stock characters that hold a recognisable place in a culture's consciousness) are particularly popular. So are stories with fundamental human themes, such as loss or sudden gain, the contest between good and evil, or sickness and healing. Interestingly the facilitator's knowledge about the story per se, such as its place in its specific temporal and socio-cultural context, or what various schools of interpretation have to say about it, rarely figures in discussions about the 'why and how' of their story-choice. This despite the fact that all traditional stories reflect economic and political ideologies, social constructions and ethical stances, and contain historical as well as biographical data (Cassirer 1953; Gersie et al. 2014, pp. 15–53).

I strongly believe that greater awareness of a chosen story's cultural and socio-historical context would influence how a facilitator employs it as an instrument for change in their work. Let me take a closer look at Hans Christian Andersen's well-loved literary fairy-tale *The Emperor and the Nightingale* to clarify some of what I mean. Our journey begins in Copenhagen, Denmark.

On August 15, 1843 Tivoli, a vibrant pleasure park in the centre of Copenhagen, opened its gates. It included two Chinese pavilions, a Chinese Bazaar and a Chinese-style railway station. Some weeks later Andersen wrote, in less than 24 hours, his well-known literary fairy-tale *The Emperor and the Nightingale*.

> *In the story a Chinese Emperor hears about the beautiful song of a nightingale. He orders his servants to bring one to him. A kitchen-maid leads the way. The nightingale is found. He agrees to come to the palace and sing for the Emperor who is enchanted. Some time later the Emperor of Japan sends his Chinese friend a stunningly bejewelled, mechanical nightingale. The Chinese Emperor likes its song even better, especially because he can make it sing whenever he likes. The living bird soon flies away to the forest. One day the mechanical bird stops singing. A spring has broken. Before long the Emperor misses the nightingale's song so much that he falls seriously ill. His servants once again go in search of the living nightingale. When the bird hears about the Emperor's illness he hastens back to the palace. The nightingale's song restores the Emperor to health. But when the Emperor pleads with him to stay forever, the nightingale says that he can't build his nest there. He begs the Emperor to let him go. As a bird, he says, he travels wide. He can tell the Emperor of all that's good and bad in the land. When the bird promises to return the Emperor allows him to come and go as he wants. The bird flies away.*

How lucky the fictional Emperor was and how unlucky the actual bird. Interpretations of this story in books and online overwhelmingly suggest that the story is a thinly veiled metaphor of Andersen's unrequited love for the internationally acclaimed Swedish soprano Jenny Lind. Perhaps it is. But I think that this psychological interpretation borders on being facile. I propose that the story is also about much more than that. Below I lift some of these other meanings to the fore.

At the time of Andersen's writing innumerable nightingales were captured throughout Europe for the huge trade in birds for caging in people's private homes. This despite the fact that nightingales don't thrive in cages. The nightingales that were caught for caging in spring rarely escaped the horrendous effects of their innate migratory urge. They bashed themselves to death against the bars of their cage. When the 20th century witnessed a much diminished trade in living birds for life and death in cages, the nightingale faced new threats. These included and include severe environmental loss, water scarcity, soil degradation and climate change. Since the 1960s the already much diminished nightingale population has declined further, by a shocking 90%. Then as now the European nightingale spends its spring and early summer in northern Europe and makes a perilous migratory journey and overwinters in the jungles of countries in Western Africa, such as Guinea Bissau or Sierra Leone. After its return north in April each year the male tries to establish a nesting site and to charm a female into joining him. He passionately thrills and gurgles. His song announces to her and others that he will defend their young as well as their territory. Nightingales build their nests and feed on insects in the understorey of dense woodland and shrubs. They are rarely seen. But the male is heard.

The 19th-century demise of nightingales mirrors the disappearance at the time of northern Europe's once abundant forests. When Andersen wrote his story Denmark's wooded areas had shrunk to less than 5% of its land area. Centuries of forest-conversion to agricultural land and the use of forests for pig and cattle grazing had razed both ancient and new trees to the ground.

The already severely threatened nightingales shared these scarce woodlands with outlaws, small farmers and charcoal burners who also struggled to survive. Robbing others and poaching were some of the brigands' methods of survival. They were mercilessly pursued by the absolute king's agents and where possible arrested. Around the time of Tivoli's opening many Danes eagerly awaited the outcome of a sensationalised trial of outlaws. Of the 82 people arrested, 72 received sentences that ranged from public flogging to life-time imprisonment with hard labour. A few were acquitted. Some had died in prison.

It is another pertinent fact that in the course of the 19th century more than 10% of the Danish population left its shores. Nearly everyone knew someone who had migrated, usually never to be seen again. So did Andersen. The poor migrants left in search of a better life, mostly to North America. Here the native American population suffered the extreme consequences of their and other Europeans' arrival.

In the year that Tivoli opened its door some Danish people were also breathing a sigh of relief. Between 1839 and 1842 they too had been badly affected by the first British–Chinese opium war. During this war several British ships had used the Danish flag. Not to everyone's content. The unease ended with the signing of the treaty of Nanjing in 1842. Under its terms the Qing Emperor Daoguang, whose disastrous reign was characterized by rebellion and conflict, was compelled to open so-called Treaty Ports. These facilitated more direct trade between Denmark and China. Hello to the Chinese motifs throughout the new Tivoli of 1843!

In the late 1830s the Danish king had granted the widely travelled John Georg Carstensen a five-year charter to create the Tivoli pleasure gardens. Carstensen's argument that *people who amuse themselves do not think about politics* had given the reluctant, absolute monarch a rationale for his permission. When Tivoli's Chinese-style theatre opened in 1857 the words "Shared joy with the people" were carved in big Chinese characters above its entrance. Not that the people understood what these characters meant, or what had been left out of the statement. By then Andersen's story of the Chinese Emperor and the faithful nightingale had reached a wide, international audience. Few story-listeners were aware that in Imperial Qing China all writing about the health of the Emperor was censored. The spread of palace-rumours was strictly forbidden and their originators were severely punished. Punishments ranged from beatings and exile to faraway places, to death by strangulation, beheading or slow slicing.

Andersen's readers probably also didn't realize that the earliest example of a mechanical bird dated to 350 BC when the mathematician Archytas of Tarentum invented a wooden dove that could flap its wings and fly as much as 200 meters powered by some kind of internal steam engine. Though they might have heard the phrase: if it looks like a duck, quacks like a duck, swims like a duck then it is probably a duck – words inspired by the mechanical duck that the Frenchman Jacques de Vaucanson invented in the 18th century. The first clockwork canard. In 1843 Japan was still a mystery country. That said strong trade-relations had existed for some time between Japan and the Netherlands. And yes, then as now commercial ships had international crews and sailed under another country's flag.

Andersen, like Carstensen, felt rather ambivalent about the king's patronage on which he depended. Yet he disdained social hypocrisy. Though, as Jack Zipes pointedly observes, Andersen unfortunately never bothered to ask why geniuses could not stand on their own and perhaps unite with likeminded people (Zipes 1995). Might Andersen's ambivalence about patronage inform the final sentences of this story? In the tale's original version Andersen made the nightingale tell the Emperor that he could not build a nest in the palace or live there. He therefore pleaded with the Emperor to let him come and go at will. Then he would return and sit on a spray in a tree by the window and sing of things that would make the Emperor happy and thoughtful too. And the kind of things the nightingale intended to sing about? The struggles and hard work of common folk and the contrast of their lives with that of the well-to-do. A theme that recurs again and again in Andersen's work.

In most writings about this story Carstensen's statement to his monarch that 'keeping the people amused' was a fine way to stop them thinking about politics is not mentioned. Nor is its abbreviation on Tivoli's theatre's walls. The usual re-teller's removal of Andersen's final paragraphs to this story is also rarely noted. Neither is the 19th-century trade in wild song-birds, the huge outward-migration of destitute Danish people caused by increasing landlessness and poverty, or the demise of the Danish forests where nightingales once sang.

Taking a traditional story at face value is probably one of the most tempting pitfalls change-professionals encounter. I have shared some of my knowledge about this story in order to lift just some of its socio-historical, political and environmental resonances to the fore. I could have carried on: pointing out in-story contradictions, or linking it with shared themes in contemporaneous folksongs, sermons or broadsheet-articles. Thereby to demonstrate that, as Virginia Woolf emphasized, stories are attached to life in all their corners. The questions I have are these: when change-professionals tell this story to clients would it make a difference if they knew that in the 19th century the seasonal mortality-rate of nightingales kept in cages was close to 98%, that there is at present a significant chance that the nightingale will become extinct in our life-time, that out-migration from Denmark was at an all-time high in the 1840s, or that – at the time – most migrants were unlikely ever to see their homeland and family again? And if issues such as these underpin the efficacy of story-work with this and other traditional stories: why and what and how?

Pitfall 5

Careless listening and the neglect of response-tasks

Azra attended the third session of a 10-week story-work group for adults with mental health difficulties. With her eyes closed and tightened fists she whispered: "I'll never tell my story. Nobody listens. They only want to tell their own." She then quite unexpectedly fixed me with a big, sad gaze at me and continued: "It's true, isn't it? You're the only one who listens here and that's no good." I reflected that there was a lot in what she said. Almost immediately Jack, another group-member, spoke up. Addressing Azra, he muttered: "You could ask her to help us listen. She'll have a trick up her sleeve for that." Adding dejectedly: "If we can't learn to listen, we might as well go home." Azra and Jack had a point. A crucial point. It's true – most participants in story-work want to tell stories, but more than this, most also want their stories to be heard and responded to (Gersie 1997, pp. 111–133).

All acts of verbal communication between people, of which storytelling is one, have at least three components: a sender or speaker, a message or story and a recipient or listener. From my perspective storytelling is what happens in the interplay between the teller, their story and how the listener receives it and responds to it (see also Frank 1995). The Harvard Centre for Child Development has named this crucial interactive process 'serve and return'. In story-work I call the techniques that foster 'serve and return' interactions between the participants, response-tasks (Gersie 1997, 1999 and 2014).

It is a common experience that in story-work many things can and do go amiss during this interplay. There is a terrible paradox at work in therapeutic storytelling (note the name – listening is not mentioned). As Azra stated: most tellers are keen to tell, but few listeners are keen to hear. Moreover, few facilitators attend to the yawning gap between most tellers' hopes for their stories and most listeners' responses. This despite the fact that many clients say that communication difficulties caused them to join a story-work group in the first place.

In order to provide my clients with sufficient corrective emotional experiences for their sombre interactional expectations I developed assorted 'response-tasks' (see Gersie 1997, pp. 134–153). These response-tasks are creative techniques in different arts-based modalities. Their 'doing' takes 3–5 minutes. Each task aims to strengthen a particular aspect of the participant's capacity to deeply listen to another person's story and to respond to it with a germane, creative response. These responses are then shared with the teller, thereby initiating and supporting a habit of 'serve and return' interactivity. More often than not the growth in a participant's expressive response-ability goes through a few stages.

In **Stage 1** a facilitator might aim to strengthen a participant's ability to listen for and remember, identify, copy or paraphrase something noticed in the teller's story (as in active listening), and then to share this. These response-tasks may include creative techniques such as:

- Identifying and sharing a word or phrase in the teller's story that struck the listener most;
- copying and then performing the main character (e.g. dance or gesture) as shown by the teller;
- painting a picture of one of the landscapes in the story and giving this to the teller.

In **Stage 2** a facilitator might try to broaden the listener's ability to identify and expand something that was specifically, but only very briefly, mentioned in a story. Such response-tasks aim to engage the listeners, for example, in the appreciation, extension or sharing of an idea in order to develop a specific aspect of a teller's story, such as:

- describing in some detail something that the teller had only briefly mentioned in their story (e.g. a garden, a beast, a forest, a market) and sharing this with the teller;
- identifying something that according to them gave the story-character strength, recording this in an image or a few words and then giving this to the teller;
- writing a two-line poem about this story. They might for example praise the character for surmounting or facing up to a problem or challenge, or write about what they gained from hearing the story. And again, sharing this with the teller.

In **Stage 3** a facilitator might try to increase the listener's ability to synthesize, solve or verify something specific in the story or to take it in a new direction. This might include response-tasks such as:

- creating headlines (as for a journal article) that highlight something that happened 20 years later in an important place in the story;
- creating a song about an event that took place 'next door' to the place where the story's key events occurred;
- formulating some questions for a story-character the answers to which might enrich their life.

Once more, all responses are shared with the teller, or given to them.

Response-tasks can be designed as an individual, pair, small group or as a whole group exercise. The listeners hear which particular response-task will be used before a story is told. They are reminded to do the task as soon as the story is finished. Every response-task takes the form of a creative-expressive activity of about 3–5 minutes' duration. The responses are given or shown to the teller at appropriate times during the session. After this there is ample space to reflect on the creative 'feedback' that each participant made and received.

To recap: response-tasks are formulated as interpersonal requests, such as:

- after hearing my tale please draw a symbol for something in my story that might give the main character hope;
- please show me in movement how you felt after hearing my story;
- please write a wish, or a blessing or advice for the main character.

The doing of the response-tasks scaffolds the participants' capacity for active listening as well as their ability to respond constructively and affectively to other people's stories (and thereby ultimately to their own stories). The tasks also help the teller to learn to anticipate listeners' responses, to receive them, reflect on them and in turn to respond to them. They increase their ability to do so both as an act of commitment to interaction and as a creative procedure. The process of sharing the feedback on the given and received responses helps the participants to fine-tune their communicative skills and understanding. Taken together the interactive processes of formulating, anticipating, making and sharing responses affirm the participants as alert, gifted and approachable people. It also helps the participants to hone their capacity for applied empathy. Empathy which they can both give and receive.

Pitfall 6

Ignoring the healing potential of orientational metaphors

An orientational metaphor is a metaphor that involves a spatial relationship, such as front–back, above–below, in–out (Lakoff and Johnson 1980). These metaphors, which are integral to most extended stories, matter. In the agonizing year 1933 the afore-mentioned Walter Benjamin wrote:

> Experience has fallen in value, amid a generation which from 1914 to 1918 had to experience some of the most monstrous events in the history of the world… Wasn't it noticed at the time how many people returned from the front in silence?… A generation that had gone to school in horse-drawn streetcars now stood in the open air, amid a landscape in which nothing was the same except the clouds and, at its centre, in a force field of destructive torrents and explosions, the tiny, fragile human body.
>
> *(Benjamin 1999, pp. 83–107)*

Heartrending words and images for the ominously tragic aftermath of the First World War.

It remains a wretched reality that war, joblessness, squalor, violent conflict, ill-health, lack of access to education and extreme poverty damage the lives of innumerable adults and children. It also remains an encouraging reality that countless people of goodwill try to prevent and remedy the effects of such ravages. Many facilitators of story-work are among these. As guardians of individual and social healing they stand at the cradle of hope that a better world is possible (Gersie 2017, pp. 19–43). In story-work many types of story are used to take the clients' tiny, fragile human body away from its surrounding "force field of destructive torrents and explosions" so that they can heal. Below I want to explain how attention to the sequence of orientational metaphors in a particular chant or story (to recap – these are words such as *in, out, up, down, beyond, in the midst*) can inform the facilitator's way of engaging their clients with its transformational energy. Let me illustrate.

'The First Song of Dawn Boy' is one of 161 prayer-hymns that constitute the *Mountain Chant* of the Diné (Children of God) people, perhaps better known by the name the Navajo (Washington 1887). Part of this magnificent chant contains some words and images that are familiar to many people. It reads:

> *Beauty before me,*
> > *With it I wander.*
>
> *Beauty behind me,*
> > *With it I wander.*
>
> *Beauty below me,*
> > *With it I wander.*
>
> *Beauty above me,*
> > *With it I wander.*
>
> *Beauty all around me,*
> > *With it I wander.*
>
> *In old age travelling,*
> > *With it I wander.*
>
> *On the beautiful trail I am,*
> > *With it I wander.*

In 1887, the same year that Dr. Washington Matthews translated and published 'The Mountain Chant' in the USA, Alexander Carmichael, a civil servant, travelled throughout the Highlands and Islands of Scotland in order to collect Gaelic poetry and customs. These were published in 1899 under the title *Camina Gadelica: Hymns and Incantation* (Carmichael 1900). The collection includes a hymn to the guardian angel in which a man pleads:

> *Drive from me every temptation and danger,*
> *Surround me on the sea of unrighteousness,*
> *And in the narrows, crooks and straights,*
> *Keep thou my coracle, keep it always.*
>
> *Be thou a bright flame before me,*
> *Be thou a guiding star above me,*
> *Be thou a smooth path below me,*
> *And be a kindly shepherd behind me,*
> *Today, tonight, and forever.*

What interests and moves me here is not how these beautiful chants articulate their makers' sense of profound connectivity between the human and the sacred. Others have written about such spirituality in deeply insightful ways. Instead I want to draw our attention to the particular use of orientational metaphors and their sequencing in both chants. Apart from *before and behind, below and above* and *all around*, spatial orientation words include: *on* (as in switched on or on top) and *off, in* and *out, deep* and *shallow, central* and *peripheral*.

In their chant the Diné use the following orientational progression: *before, behind, below, above,* then *all around*, thereby creating a clear sense of two intersecting axes and a forward-moving energy. The Gaelic singer, a Christian, invites our mind's eye to go from *all around* towards *before*, then to *above*, from *above* to *below* and finishes *behind*. This sequence generates only one clear axis (the top–down one) and an awareness that the past and the future can only be reached by attending to either what's above (heaven) or to what's below (hell).

Whereas the Diné singer asserts their presence on a beautiful trail where kindred dwell, the unknown Gaelic vocalist evokes a tired, lonesome stranger in a coracle at sea. Moreover, this is a sea of unrighteousness on which God's angel is begged to make a shepherding round to safeguard and surround the stranger. Diné and Gaelic people inhabit qualitatively different physical landscapes: the ancestral lands of the Diné are the great deserts of the American South West, the Gaelic people dwell on the shores of the rough North Atlantic seas in Ireland and Scotland. They cannot but relate to these worlds in physically and therefore emotionally and culturally different ways.

It may be easier to understand these energetic differences if we try to embody, through expressive movement, the sequenced directions contained in each chant. If we do so, it soon becomes clear that the sequenced directions in the Gaelic journey (which take us from all around and before towards above, below and finishes in 'that which is behind us') have a qualitative different impact on our body and spirit than those in the Diné passage (which progress from before to behind, below to above and then to all around). Whereas the Gaelic journey culminates in movements that make our body feel pulled back and in need of rest, possibly forever, the Diné passage generates a freeing joy of living. It is thus not without coincidence that the Gaelic chant closes with the tired assertion:

> *For me it is time to go home*
> *To the court of Christ, to the peace of heaven.*

In contrast, the Diné complete theirs with the revivifying:

> *On the beautiful trail I am,*
> *With it I wander.*

The progression of the orientational metaphors in both chants reveals the likelihood of the tone of their closing lines long before they emerge into the light of day or, in the Gaelic case, night's gathering gloom.

In their stimulating book *Metaphors We Live By*, Lakoff and Johnson (1980) point out that spatial orientation words make it possible to give or understand physical directions. Spatial orientation words equally convey, quite unexpectedly maybe, important things about our energetic state of body, soul and mind. My clients who lived on a no-go sink estate felt looked down on; they saw no way forward, felt left behind, while those above made them feel, in their own words "like the lowest of the low". When things started picking up (note the up) they not only had some self-respect, they knew where they were going (forwards), others now looked up to them, the stuff in the past was behind them and they didn't hang out with that crowd anymore, they had another circle of friends.

While the socio-cultural bases of spatial orientation metaphors are obvious, though by no means necessarily consistent between cultures, most experienced tellers of tales know that these metaphors are deeply rooted in actual physical experiences. They realize that for a Dutchman a sinking feeling is associated with quicksand, water, bogs and mud while the average Swiss person is more likely to associate those same words with snow, avalanches and raging meltwaters. Even though spatial metaphors work differently in different cultures and for different people (occasionally, for example, the future is behind and not in front as we customarily assume), happy is undoubtedly up.

Towards a wellspring of inspiring stories

I hope to have shown that, when neglected, the six pitfalls can seriously limit the efficacy of story-work. I have also explained that careful attention to their intrinsic complexities can turn their constraining features into healing strengths. Most children and adults who participate in story-work suffer the harsh impact of painful set-backs. Many feel anxious, sad or confused, have trouble sleeping or learning new things, are forgetful and often accident-prone. During story-work the facilitators and the clients tell, share and make stories. Especially stories that will help the client to foster mastery over intense emotions, rebuild their capacity for self-soothing and grant them practice with new ways forward. As time goes by these stories can become an inner wellspring of life-enhancing tales that lead to new cognitions, feelings and behaviour (Bruner 1986).

As we know the remembering *self* tends to rule our actions, and the rule it uses most frequently is 'how things ended'. The experiencing *self* says: "how is it now, how does it feel?" The remembering *self* says "how was it on the whole?", which mostly means: "how did it end?" Stories and storytelling enable each of us to build strong, metaphoric bridges between our experiencing and our remembering *self*. Maybe that is why so many ancient tales end with the reassuring: "*And they lived happily ever after.*" I say: 'Hope so.' And that is final.

Notes

1 1924, May 24, Boston Herald, 'Whiting's Column: Tammany Has Learned That This Is No Time for Political Bosses', Quote Page 2, Column 1, Boston, Massachusetts. (GenealogyBank) retrieved from: http://listserv.linguistlist.org, July 6, 2016.
2 Retold by Alida Gersie.
3 Identifying details have been altered to protect identity. The vignette's gist is true to life.

Bibliography

Andersen, H.C. (1980) *Tales and Stories by Hans Christian Andersen*. Seattle: University of Washington Press. Transl. Conroy, P.L., Rossell. S.H.
Benjamin, W.A. (1999) *Illuminations*. London: Pimlico. Transl. Zorn, H., pp. 83–107.
Bruner, J. (1986) *Actual Minds, Possible Worlds*. Cambridge, MA: Harvard University Press.
Carmichael, A. (1900) *Camina Gadelica: Gaelic Hymns and Invocations. Collected in the Hebrides and Western Highlands of Scotland*. Transl. Carmichael, A.
Cassirer, E. (1953) *Language & Myth*. New York: Dover Publications.
Chapman, S. (2005) *Paul Grice: Philosopher and Linguist*. Basingstoke: Palgrave.
Forster, E.M. (1927) *Aspects of the Novel*. New York: Harcourt, Brace & World.
Frank, A.W. (1995) *The Wounded Storyteller. Body, Illness, and Ethics*. Chicago: University of Chicago Press.
Genette, G. (1988) *Narrative Discourse Revisited*. Ithaca: Cornell University Press. Transl. Lewin, J.E.
Gersie, A. (1994) 'Foreword'. In: Winn, L. *Post-traumatic Stress Disorder and Dramatherapy: Treatment and Risk Reduction*. London: Jessica Kingsley Publishers, pp. ix–xiv.
Gersie, A. (1997) *Reflections on Therapeutic Storymaking: The use of stories in groups*. London: Jessica Kingsley Publishers.
Gersie, A. (1999) 'Reflections on the Role of the Listener in Reminiscence Groups.' In: Bornat, J., Chamberlayne, P., Chant, L. (Eds.) *Reminiscence: Practice, Skills and Settings*. London: Open University Press/University of East London Press, pp. 35–39.
Gersie, A. (2013) 'Foreword'. In: Pearson, J., Smail, M., Watts, P. (Eds.) *Dramatherapy with Myth and Fairytale. The Golden Stories of Sesame*. London: Jessica Kingsley Publishers, pp. 15–21.

Gersie, A. (2017) 'Wild but with Purpose. Arts Therapists and the Cry for Social Healing.' In: Hougham, R., Pitruzella, S., Scoble, S. (Ed.) *Cultural Landscapes in the Arts Therapies*. Plymouth: Plymouth University Press.

Gersie, A., King, N. (1990) *Storymaking in Education and Therapy*. London: Jessica Kingsley Publishers; Stockholm: Stockholm Institute of Education Press.

Gersie, A., Nanson, A., Schieffelin, E. (2014), 'Introduction'. In: Gersie, A., Nanson, N., Schieffelin, E. (Eds.) *Storytelling for a Greener World. Environment, Community and Storybased Learning*. Stroud: Hawthorn Press, pp. 15–53.

Haven, K.F. (2007) *Story Proof. The science behind the startling power of story*. Westport CT: Greenwood Publishing Group.

Howes, M. (2014) *Storytelling in the Moment. Exploring a contemporary verbal art in Britain and Ireland*. Gent: Academia Press.

Jennings, S. (2010) *Healthy Attachment and Neuro-Dramatic Play*. London: Jessica Kingsley Publishers.

Kipling, R. (1902) *Just So Stories for Little Children*. Download at Project Gutenberg.

Lakoff, G., Johnson, M. (1980) *Metaphors We Live By*. Chicago and London: Chicago University Press.

Washington, M. (1887) *The Mountain Chant, A Navajo Ceremony*. Fifth Annual Report of the Bureau of Ethnology to the Secretary of the Smithsonian Institution, 1883–84, Washington: Government Printing Office. pp. 379–468

Zipes, J. (1995) *Creative Storytelling: Building Community, Changing Lives*. New York: Routledge.

8
STRUCTURING THE THERAPIST'S ROLE
An exploration of Sophocles' play *King Oedipus*

Marina Jenkyns

Sophocles' play *King Oedipus* unfolds the truth of a life, a life in the context of a social and moral order. One of the greatest plays in the history of dramatic literature, it follows a man as he uncovers layer after layer of his own history to discover the truth about himself and the implications of this truth for the people around him – his family and the people he rules as King of Thebes. It follows and expounds his journey to be able, in the words of Shakespeare writing hundreds of years later, to be true to himself and not 'false to any man'; it follows the journey, step by agonizing step, of a man who must let go of the mental representations which have held him together and made him successful in the world's terms in order to find his true self. In this chapter I shall explore the role played by Tiresias and the Chorus in this tragic narrative, suggesting how it can illuminate our role as therapists and agents of change.

Psychoanalysis has often used images taken from the world of drama to give language to some of its concepts. The psychoanalyst Sandler is particularly interesting for us as dramatherapists as he conceived of the representational world as a proscenium stage; the scenes and dramas of the inner life are enacted on this stage, a stage in the mind. Dramatherapy works by the mental representations of the client being open to modification through engaging with the symbolic representations provided by the dramatic devices we use in our work: objects, toys, roles, improvisation, story, plays etc. by bringing that theatre of the mind into the actual theatre of the dramatherapy studio.

The relationship

Two people meet on the road. They decide to journey together. One is the therapist and one the client; they may travel in one another's company for a few hours, for many days or for many years. Whatever the duration, at every step of the way each offers to the other the images or mental representations of their inner worlds to nourish the task of enabling the complex and often painful business of living to be done with, at the very least less pain and confusion, and ideally with greater fulfilment, even within the limitations of disability. The task of therapy is to address the question Oedipus drives himself to confront, 'I will know who I am' and to live in the world managing the consequences and responsibilities attendant upon that knowledge. The task involves a dynamic dance between client and therapist, where there is both steadfastness and movement. It brings to my mind the seventeenth century poet John Donne's words,

> ...they are two so
> As stiffe twin compasses are two
> Thy soule the fixt foot, makes no show
> To move, but doth, if the other doe.
>
> And though it in the center sit,
> Yet when the other far doth rome,
> It leans and harkens after it,
> And grows erect as that comes home
>
> So wilt thou be to me, who must
> Like th'other foot, obliquely run;
> Thy firmness drawes my circle just,
> And makes me end, where I begunne.
> John Donne (from A Valediction Forbidding Mourning)

The therapist must hold firm and yet move within that firmness. We must be the fixed point of the compass yet leaning to catch the echoes of the client and respond with our own as they roam freely to conclude the work and find their own new life beginnings.

The process

In this process the client presents their inner world again and again and again. And we meet it with our own each time. This is the dynamic force which forms the therapeutic relationship. We have to make ourselves and our own mental processes available in the work and my own view is that, as in psychoanalysis, the dramatherapist also depends on the phenomenon of transference and counter-transference as a crucial aid to understanding the mental representations of the client, enabling us to be both a follower and guide in the therapeutic journey. How and in what way, overtly or obliquely, this is worked with will, of course, depend on the theoretical stance and style of the therapist. But it is our ongoing diagnostic tool.

Transference and counter-transference cannot exist without the phenomenon of projection and projective identification. In dramatherapy projection is crucial to our work as the mental representations of the client are explored by the ongoing process of projection and introjection in relation to a role, a character, an object and ourselves. And the cumulative effect of this engagement with projective processes, whether in psychoanalysis or dramatherapy, is that mental representations are modified.

The play

In the light of this, the dramatic relationship between Tiresias and Oedipus and that of the Chorus and Oedipus can helpfully illuminate the therapist–client relationship.

Oedipus has to dismantle the representation of who he is brick by brick, to discover his real identity. This discovery involves challenging the image he has of himself on which he has founded the identity from which he speaks at the beginning of the play; son of the king and queen of the distant kingdom of Corinth, the gifted solver of riddles, the rescuer and saviour of Thebes and the wise ruler. The Chorus and Tiresias are crucial in helping Oedipus modify this image until he arrives at a true picture of his identity – whose son he actually is and how his life has been built on false assumptions.

Oedipus and Tiresias

In therapy the withdrawal of projections is a vital part of our work, for the client to know who they are and who they are not. In *King Oedipus* the protagonist must withdraw the projections and discover and face himself. The first person who sets Oedipus on his journey is Tiresias the soothsayer. When Creon, Oedipus's brother-in law, returns from Delphi he gives the oracle's answer to the cause of the plague that is decimating Thebes, thus:

> *There is an unclean thing,*
> *Born and nursed on our soil, polluting our soil,*
> *Which must be driven away.*
> (Sophocles trans Watling 1947 p.28)

Tiresias the soothsayer is sent for to throw light on this. The Chorus describe him as, '*the prophet in whom, of all men, lives the incarnate truth*'. He is the one, therefore, who says things too close for comfort. His role as the soothsayer is to speak what he knows which other people don't know and would often prefer not to know. An unenviable task, and on this occasion his reward is to be violently rejected and abused by Oedipus. Before he tells Oedipus that it is he, the king, who is the 'cursed polluter', Oedipus addresses him thus,

> *Tiresias, we know there is nothing beyond your ken;*
> *Lore sacred and profane, all heavenly and earthly knowledge*
> *Are in your grasp.*
> (ibid. p.34)

But after Tiresias has revealed the truth Oedipus's words are somewhat different; he calls him

> *Shameless and brainless, sightless, senseless sot*
> *…pedlar of fraudulent magical tricks, with eyes*
> *Wide open for profit, but blind in prophecy.*
> (ibid. p.36)

words which are a measure of Oedipus's fear and denial. Sophocles tells us that when Tiresias is summoned he delays coming; he knows and dreads what he must say. There are times when the therapist, in order to be true to their role, will speak what the client needs to hear but does not want to hear. Such times are painful and difficult and the client may react like Oedipus, full of fury. When the defences are challenged, however gently, anger and projection can be marshalled to maintain self-representations intact. And so it is here. Tiresias is accused of plotting with his brother-in-law, Creon, against him. As therapists again and again we hear accusations when the client is engaged in negative transference; the loneliness of Tiresias's experience is surely something we can recognize, the unjust accusation, the hurtful words hurled. In our work we can experience the pain of our words and actions, made in the service of the task, being violently rejected. These reactions, born from a terror of knowing the truth, are exemplified by the dialogue between Tiresias and Oedipus. An aspect of self-knowledge is to learn the shadow side of ourselves, that which is hidden, that which we would rather remain hidden in order to preserve our self-representations. Oedipus cannot bear not to be great, the saviour, '*I have saved this land from ruin, I am content.*' In order to keep himself in this position he must denigrate Tiresias. In order to preserve his sense of being the good man he must project his 'bad' side onto Tiresias. And Tiresias must bear it in order for Oedipus to continue on his journey towards arriving at the truth of the soothsayer's words in his own way and at his own pace. Tiresias has done his job well, for he finds the chink in his king's armour through which Oedipus glimpses light.

> TIRESIAS: *Mad I may seem to you. Your parents would not think so.*
> OEDIPUS: *What's that? My parents? who then…gave me birth?*
>
> (ibid. p.38)

Tiresias's words set Oedipus on the road of discovery which will lead him to dismantle all his mental representations of who he is. In this statement he shows Oedipus a window, it whets Oedipus's appetite and he cannot resist asking his crucial question, '*Who gave me birth?*' Tiresias's words are like a good therapeutic intervention – they enable Oedipus to see the window. Then he retreats out of fear. He slams the window shut, setting up a pattern in the play. Whenever he glimpses something which will take him along the road to the truth about himself, he slams the window in anger, lashing out at Tiresias, at Creon, the Chorus, Jocasta, everyone, because he is so afraid. But his curiosity and his commitment to discovering the truth battle with his fear and his defences until finally the window is wide open and lets in the light which blinds him.

Oedipus and the Chorus

The Chorus has a different role in the play, more complex, diverse in function and subtle than that of Tiresias. In it we can see aspects of our own roles as therapists as we, like them, accompany our clients – our protagonists – on their journey. In what ways are they similar? Whilst there are other roles they play in the dramatic structure and ideas Sophocles explores in the play these are not the subject of this chapter. What I consider here are four similarities to the therapist's role.

Firstly, the Chorus is both inside and outside the main action. The Elders who comprise the Chorus are involved empathic fellow travellers with the ability to retain neutrality. From this relationship spring the other functions I shall consider: they are a container for both the action and for Oedipus, the constant reference point in the play; they bear witness and they have a mediating function.

The empathic fellow-traveller who also stands apart

The Chorus are involved yet able to think about the events of the play as they unfold. As such they are a dramatic representation of the role of the therapist. We too must be involved, our emotions must be engaged yet we must retain our ability to think and reflect. We too are both inside and outside the action; we are not part of our clients' lives outside the consulting room or studio, but we are inside their lives in the encounter we and they create together. Together we are in the business of transformation and, whilst our focus is on the client, change can only take place if we are changed by the encounter too.[1] Only our involvement can do that. The

Chorus is in tune with Oedipus. They are not detached observers. There are times in therapy when we use our intuition which brings to mind an image the client then voices, or we are about to offer our toys and objects, or our stories and plays, suggest a role, thinking that a particular choice would be relevant to the client at a particular moment; we do not speak our thought and then the client chooses that very symbol to work with. These are the times when our mental representations and those of the client meet, when we are in tune with the client at a most profound moment of sharing. We have to be in that place of empathy and in-tunement where our mental representations are available to meet those of the client.

With this in-tunement in mind let's look a little more closely at the play. The first thing to note about the Chorus is that they are not bystanders. They are Theban Elders, they are respected members of the community and they are involved. The events of the play touch them as citizens. Although they seem to stand outside the action as commentators they are in reality involved citizens who can maintain distance in order to think. They are simultaneously inside and outside the main action. When we first meet the Chorus, the third line they utter is

With fear my heart is riven, fear of what shall be told.
(ibid. p.30)

As citizens they are afraid of what will be revealed by the oracle and they set up for the audience the central emotion of fear which is the common affective thread throughout the play. Perhaps they echo one of our feelings when we meet a new client; what will this story be, what will be asked of me, will I be able to help this person, will I be able to adequately accompany them on their journey, how will I be affected, what will I learn about myself and will I be able to rise to the challenge?

After the encounter between Oedipus and Tiresias the Chorus speculate from the position of the involved commentator.

Terrible things indeed has the prophet spoken.
We cannot believe, we cannot deny; all's dark
We fear, but we cannot see, what is before us.
(ibid. p.39)

and here their fear indicates a more complex aspect of their role. First they say '*we cannot believe, we cannot deny*'; they show themselves to be capable of neutrality, they suspend judgement, just as the therapist stays with the state of not knowing. But then they say something which is startling, '*…all's dark. We fear but we cannot see, what is before us.*'

Now the Ancient Greek audience would know the story the play presents, they would know that Oedipus blinds himself and moves into a dark world where he does not know what is before him, at the end of the play. But within the structure of the play, the characters who form the Chorus do not know this. They are in the dark too. By giving them these words Sophocles heightens the sense of the unfolding tragedy. And he also strengthens the bond between Oedipus and the Elders. By using these words to represent their fears he deepens the sense that this is not just Oedipus's tragedy but all men's. Oedipus is part of a social and moral order and by binding together Oedipus and the Chorus through this symbolism of 'dark' and the fear of the unknown, the tragedy becomes the tragedy of all humanity, still relevant today. We see that they hold the wider perspective of mortality and the conflict between the forces of death and life.

> *Slay with thy golden bowl, Lycean! Slay him,*
> *Artemis, over the Lycian hills resplendent!*
> *Bacchus, our name god, golden in the dance of Maenad revelry,*
> *Thy fiery torch advance to slay the death god, the grim enemy,*
> *God whom all other gods abhor to see.*
>
> (ibid. p.39)

This is the final verse of the choric ode they speak when they first enter, invoking the gods Athena, Artemis, Bacchus and Apollo to help their city to defeat the god of death who rampages through the city beset by plague. They passionately evoke the forces of life.

As therapists we too must always hold the tension between life and death. The pull towards death which we can encounter at times of crisis in our clients' lives and in their mental states demands that we hold firm. Our role therefore requires that we face the issues of mortality within ourselves and that we are able to draw on reserves of life affirmation while being able to know our own darkness and empathize with the darkness in our clients.

We must have faith, must trust the process in which we and our client are engaged. We are aided in this as drama and play therapists because our therapeutic medium requires the involvement with creative activity. All therapy is a creative endeavour but the arts therapies employ symbolic representation in a concrete way and demand the creative, life-affirming engagement with the imagination which in itself, well-guided and supported, can be a healing force.

Like the Chorus we must wait without knowing, holding firm. We must hold the commitment. We must be the fixed foot of the compass. The Chorus never desert Oedipus. On first hearing the verdict from the oracle they say

> *I impute no blame till blame is proved.*
> (ibid. p.39)

Yet even when Oedipus proves himself to be, in his own words, '*the cursed polluter of this land*' the Chorus actually never blame him. Instead they comment on the human condition from the point of view of the involved commentator.

> *Time sees all; and now he has found you when you least expected it;*
> *Has found you and judged that marriage-mockery, bride-groom-son*
> (ibid. p.59)

The Chorus wait and they witness, they stay with not knowing. They do not ask for answers, they do not interrupt the story which unfolds before them. They exercise restraint. Theirs is a modest performance set against the passions of fear and revelation of the protagonists. As ours must be. We too have to be constant, must hold the client in the arms of our empathy and our dramatic structures, until the work is concluded. After Oedipus finally understands the inescapable truth of his birth, marriage and begetting the Chorus say,

> *And now, where is there a more heartrending story of affliction?*
> *Where a more awful swerve into the arms of torment?*
> *O Oedipus, that proud head!*
> *When the same bosom enfolded son and father,*
> *Could not the engendering clay have shouted aloud its indignation?*
> (ibid. p.59)

Their commentary shows their empathy and the pain they feel for Oedipus. They wish that his life could have been otherwise. At the end of this choric ode they show their own pain too, they voice the effect on them of their involvement with Oedipus.

I wish I had never seen you, offspring of Laius,
Yesterday my morning of light, now my night of endless darkness.
                                                          (ibid. p.59)

Anger, sorrow, pain; the feelings we too may have when the going gets tough and we doubt our own ability to make a difference. And yet by using the image of light and darkness they identify with Oedipus, for the next time we see him he has blinded himself. It is this essential empathy and support that carries the relationship between the Elders and Oedipus through to the end of the play, so that when Oedipus enters the stage having blinded himself, a broken man, he says.

Is that my true and ever faithful friend
Still at my side?
Your hand shall be the blind man's guide.
                                        (ibid. p.62)

Therapist as container

One of our most essential functions as therapists is to provide containment. The Chorus provides containment of the action of the play within the structure of a world order in which human beings are subject to the will and actions of the gods. In this role of container they are steady until the end. They arrive on stage after the desperate situation of the plague in Thebes is presented by the citizens and Priest, after Creon returns from the Oracle to tell what he has learned, that the killer of the previous king, Laius, must be found and punished, and after Oedipus vows to do all in his power to save the city. It is as though it is at this point their role begins, for it is here that the tragedy of Oedipus begins. '*I will start afresh and bring everything into the light*'. From then on they are a vital force in the play, accompanying Oedipus, holding him in the arms of their balanced words, as they bear witness to the story as it unfolds. While they are involved in the action of the play they never lose sight of human events being part of a greater, wider context. They are able to retain a perspective. One of the major factors in providing containment is their constancy in holding the drama so that it doesn't fly away in chaos. Their choric odes are a ritual which holds them, the protagonists, and us, the audience, in safety. We too have to be constant, must hold the client with the availability of our unconscious as well as our conscious selves and with our dramatic structures, until the end.

Bearing witness

One of the most important ways in which we contain and support the process of our clients is by bearing witness. We affirm their experience. We accept their mental representations while being alert to how these might be able to be modified for a more fulfilling life. We follow where the client leads and in doing so we bear witness to their experience and to every tiny change they make. One of the ways in which the Chorus provides containment is by bearing witness. In bearing witness to both the suffering of Thebes and of Oedipus they hold that involved neutrality. Involved because they are, as citizens, part of what is happening, neutral in that their minds are free to observe, to comment and thus give voice to the story being not only about Oedipus but about human experience.

When Oedipus enters having blinded himself they cry out,

> *Ah, horror beyond all bearing!*
> *Foulest disfigurement*
> *That ever I saw! O cruel*
> *Insensate agony!*
> (ibid. p.61)

These words are the expression of the raw pain they feel on seeing Oedipus blind and bleeding and broken. They give voice to the horror for both Oedipus and the audience. But then, when Oedipus speaks his own agony they reply,

> *Such suffering needs to be born*
> *Twice, once in the body and once in the soul.*
> (ibid. p.62)

Here they quickly recover themselves to support Oedipus by their witness to his suffering as part of the wider context of the human condition and, thus held, Oedipus can then reach out to them,

> *Is that my true and faithful friend*
> *Still at my side?*
> (ibid. p.62)

The mediating function

In addition to their clear dramatic mediating role, their function also shows us a symbolic representation of the way the therapist acts as mediator between different parts of the client's psyche. We know that in the therapeutic process the parts of the individual which either are unacceptable to their self-image or cannot be borne, are projected either into the therapist in the transference by means of projective identification or onto the art object. Here these projected parts can be metabolized by the therapist or expressed and contained in the art form until the client is able to modify their mental representations sufficiently to accommodate them. One of the ways I work with plays is to enable the client to take on roles which express parts of themselves of which they are not consciously aware. These aspects of themselves can then gradually be integrated. Characters in plays stand in, to use Bruce Wilshire's (1982) term, for aspects of themselves and I find it helpful to think of the drama itself working in this way too, of characters also standing in for aspects of the protagonist. In *King Oedipus* I think the Chorus stands in for parts of Oedipus which are outside his self-image. When Oedipus is defending himself in terror against what he is becoming conscious of about his identity, he lashes out against Creon. He accuses him of plotting against him; he takes refuge in a paranoid attack on the brother-in-law who is the voice of reason and loyalty. In the terror of his sense of self being demolished, he takes refuge in his role.

In these lines Creon vainly tries to convince Oedipus of his innocence.

OEDIPUS: *Still clinging to your obstinate arguments?*
CREON: *Because I know you are wrong.*

OEDIPUS: *I know I am right.*
CREON: *In your own eyes not mine.*
OEDIPUS: *You are a knave.*
CREON: *And what if you are mistaken?*
OEDIPUS: *Kings must rule.*
(ibid. p.43)

If we look at this in psychodynamic terms we see Creon speaking the words of reason that Oedipus has no access to at this time. At the same time as attacking Creon he uses Creon psychologically to hold and express the voice of reason which has abandoned him in the chaos in which he finds himself. This is something we recognize as therapists when we have to hold a part of the client which ultimately they will need to own.

The Chorus can illuminate for us modern audience the way they hold the mediating function not only between the characters, but between the split representations in Oedipus's mind. The Chorus ask

> *Is it right to cast away*
> *A friend, condemned, unheard*
> *Upon an idle word?*
(ibid. p.44)

His response to the Chorus is

> *Your voice not his has won him mercy; him I hate forever.*
(ibid. p.44)

Creon has to be the object of Oedipus's defensive rage a while longer in the play, but at least Oedipus can introject from the Chorus those parts of himself which were inaccessible and begin to find some balance. The Chorus's commitment to Oedipus, their involved-but-apart status I wrote of earlier, can enable him to move further along his terrifying journey. An important way in which they help him is that they can speak aloud the words which lie between the splits.

Conclusion

As a dramatherapist I find Sophocles's play intensely moving. I feel more keenly now for the Chorus than I did in the days I worked with students on the play before I became a dramatherapist. The Chorus are together with their king in his darkest hour and express the despair. When Oedipus enters, having blinded himself, their response after expressing their initial horror I quoted earlier is,

> *I dare not see, I am hiding*
> *My eyes, I cannot bear, I cannot bear*
> *What most I long to see;*
> *And what I long to hear,*
> *That I most dread.*
(ibid. p.62)

They long to see and hear the truth but it is unbearable. This was exactly Oedipus's position in the play. But when he had the courage to open the window and see the truth it was unbearable and he physically blinded himself to punish himself for his mental blindness. They identify with Oedipus's pain because they have that empathic relationship with him and they reflect on that pain as we do when we hold on the stage of our therapeutic work the pain and the struggles of our clients as together we grope towards the light. Like the Chorus we struggle too and hold faith even in the darkest times where the old mental representations have lost their meaning, 'old oracles are out of mind' and new representations are not yet fully formed. As T.S. Eliot wrote, '*And what you do not know is the only thing you know*' (Four Quartets p.20).

In bearing witness to Oedipus's journey the Chorus are fellow travellers in the uncertain world of human endeavour. At times they stand aside and comment on the events of the play as representations of the human condition, the uncertainty of life and the certainty of death, nowhere more so than in their final ode. But their lasting lesson to us is that they hold firm to their role whatever pain they must witness and be steadfast in the days of darkness and despair. In accompanying Oedipus they give us a model for empathy, containment and the need for suffering to have a witness and a mediator if our clients are to modify their mental representations and achieve greater well-being. And just as they, the Elders of Thebes, will not be the same after these events which have so closely touched them, so, in our therapeutic encounters, we too are changed.

Note

1 In the novel *The Other Side of You*, the analyst turned writer Salley Vickers charts this aspect of our work superbly.

Bibliography

Eliot, T.S. (1944) *Four Quartets*, London: Faber and Faber.
Donne, J. (1950) *Poems*, London: Penguin.
Jenkyns, M. (1996) *The Play's the Thing; exploring text in drama and therapy*, London: Routledge.
Sandler, J. (ed.) (1987) *Projection, Identification, Projective Identification*, London: Karnac.
Sandler, J., Dare. C. and Holder, A. (1973) *The Patient and the Analyst, London:* Allen & Unwin.
Sophocles (rep 1964) *The Theban Plays;* trans E.F Watling, London: Penguin Classics.
Sophocles (1997) *Oedipus Tyrannos;* trans Timberlake Wertenbaker, London: Faber and Faber.
Vickers, S. (2007) *The Other Side of You*, London: Harper Perennial.
Wilshire, B. (1982) *Role Playing and Identity: The Limits of Theater as Metaphor*, Bloomington: Indiana University Press.

9
ORAL STORYTELLING IS NOT DEAD

She's just gone to slip into something more comfortable ...

Steve Stickley

There seems to be a ubiquitous assumption that oral storytelling is dead. What I believe most people who subscribe to this view actually mean is, "I've really no idea what I'm talking about because I am basing my assumption upon oral storytelling as it pertains to pre-technological humans gathered around a fire with nothing else to do of an evening." The modern world, proud of its sophisticated media – all singing dancing strobing shouting pulsing flicking through millions of images per second – shoots our femme fatale through the heart believing she must be dead. But, like any good film noir mystery, as the tension mounts and heralds a dénouement, there she is in the shadows. Alive. Heart beating. Breathing. But, most of all, confounding us. No matter how stylish, intriguing and beguiling the murder mystery may seem it becomes apparent that our heroine – whether we call her Oral or Aural or, as Mickey Spillane might have it, Oriol – can never die. She will only die when all humanity has died. Oral storytelling is a way of describing who we are and she will live as long as we do. Since the Sumerians in the Fertile Crescent of Mesopotamia 6,000 years ago we humans have revered and transcribed our stories.

Meanwhile, in our recent world, within a few hours of George Floyd's tragic death, the whole population of the planet, it seemed, knew of him. We understand the role of the internet and mass communication but forget perhaps how many conversations we have had in response to something that is this shocking and this compelling. (And the mantra *Black Lives Matter* connotes a powerful story of searing historical injustice and brutality which must no longer be ignored.) But conversation is cheap and disposable to us. As we gabble our way through life we often cannot see or appreciate that we are story making the whole time. Story is our second nature and we cannot stop. Story makes us, us.

I have worked as both actor and storyteller for many years. All my working life, in fact. If I had to define the function of Story in the lives of human beings I think I would have to say it is essentially a process of revisiting the eternal triangle of Love, Death and Resurrection constantly. A narrative will, more often than not, draw us into empathising with a protagonist who eventually finds themselves in an abyss where all seems hopeless. The triumph snatched from the jaws of defeat and the subsequent restoration to new life is primal and full of potency. Over and over again we humans need reminding that new possibilities are just around the corner. But, more than that, humans have gloried in these dark dilemmas which transform into victories for thousands of years. Essentially, these are curative tales because if there is a force that can really outsmart Death, then perhaps we will yet recover. And, anyway, our predicament may be nowhere nearly as bad as the young newly married queen who has had all of her three babies thrown into a pit of snakes by her evil mother-in-law, while her twelve brothers have all been turned into ducks because of the selfishness of her true mother, and she is about to be burnt at the stake accused of murder and cannibalism and cannot defend herself because her voice has vanished as a result of a self-sacrificial promise.[1] Bad day at the office. Without Resurrection, Love and Death are doomed to travel a one-way street. With Resurrection, the dynamic is transformed and we arrive full circle, or triangle, so that life may be sustained. Eternally.

Without this there would be no Christianity, of course, and Oestra would reassert herself, seeing off the death of winter with the rebirth of spring during the equinox weekend rotating the familiar triangle to celebrate new hope. I once heard it said that Walt Disney, having created a particular formula for all his films, locked it in his safe and made it available to only to a very few people. (Ah, the glory of gossip. It conjures a potent scene as we seek collusion to establish a mutual understanding between ourselves and our listener, with whom we seek to cement friendship or intimacy. I already see Walt's famous moustache and his leather-padded, mahogany-lined office as he heads for the safe – probably hidden behind a large framed picture of his very first drawing of Mickey Mouse.) Whatever the truth, his engaging musical animation of *Jungle Book* in 1967 alerted my young mind to compare Baloo the Bear's "death experience" to the resurrection of Christ. Following the ruckus with Shere Khan, the tiger, who has been seen off for good, Mowgli walks over to Baloo's prone body, believing him to be dead. To all intents and purposes, so do we – Baloo's stillness, the mournful music, the framing and the editing tell us so. It is a tender moment of saying goodbye to a faithful, and comic, friend. Just when you think 'How can they [the filmmakers] upset us so?' Baloo comes round with a joke and all is well again.

I think I began then to make connections, realising that many stories share a similar lineage. In doing so, my adolescent brain started to find a semblance of order in an otherwise calamitous, confusing world. At that stage in life I was completely unaware that there was anything called oral storytelling, but I did know and repeat dirty jokes – as did almost everyone I knew. This was an illicit and furtive activity, of course, but I look back now and see how my storytelling skills were discovered and honed even then as I coveted an eager audience's rapt attention.

Never underestimate our listening skill as humans. Regular listeners to BBC Radio 4, for example, may be more than able to tell the subtle difference between, say, an actor playing a pig farmer talking about pig farming and a real pig farmer talking about pig farming. The timbre and register of each is different, because one acts from a read and rehearsed script while the other simply responds *ad lib*. The oral storyteller will want to hit the most suitable register at the most suitable time during a story. And most of the time the recipients won't notice the strategy because if the teller is skilful and well-practised enough, it will appear totally natural. This constitutes part of what we may consider the invisibility of oral storytelling. We sense the teller's presence and respond to their personability. We may suddenly find ourselves feeling emotions we didn't expect simply because the teller hit the right register and we didn't consciously notice it. And need I point out that I am not talking solely about storytelling with children? As I write, I am conscious of a growing movement of storytelling clubs for adults all over the UK, where I live.

Oral storytelling is open heart surgery. The teller should be fully aware of what they are doing and the skills required for the task. Full concentration is required by all those present

Oral storytelling is not dead

in the room. The teller is doing something potentially transformative and health giving, but cannot succeed if they keep their own heart closed and remote. In the same way that they need their breath to form the words, they need their heart to beat and to be felt beating. The surgeon who is half-hearted or heartless may render the patient stone dead. The task is filled with jeopardy. We do not know the outcome and lives are at stake. We focus on particulars but keep in mind the overarching progress. Everyone in the room must know what their job is, even if it is simply to watch and to feel. Some may be free to walk away but only if they can be sure that the patient will not suffer. The teller can never turn away and cannot leave until the operation is completed. We do not know the full implications of what has happened until some time later. The teller remains themselves but is always the surgeon – it is their job. Throughout the proceedings, lifeblood flows. If it stops, it can only be the teller who decides to allow that, perhaps in order to restart the flow soon after. They are always aware of signs of life. By the end of it all they may feel exhausted. By the end of it all they may feel elated – so while they are recovering, let us return to our film noir.

~

Captain Liebowitz slammed the receiver down. The Commissioner's voice still ringing in his ears, he yelled at the door before the two patrolmen could even knock on it.

"Get in here!" He lit another cigarette, turning away briefly from the two dullards who shuffled in and stood like recalcitrant schoolboys. The flame from his lighter wobbled as he knew it would. Captain Liebowitz congratulated himself on not allowing these two dolts to see his hand shaking slightly. He wheeled back round to face them; the smoke wreathed his tidy oiled hair as if it were sustaining an intimate relationship with his pomade.

"Have you any goddamn idea how many of these we have had in this last month?"

"Fifteen, Captain?" said one of the officers.

"It was a rhetorical question! I don't need your goddamn answers right now! I need you to wake up! I need this whole goddamn precinct to wake up!" Liebowitz drew heavily on the cigarette and coughed slightly as he exhaled. "That was the Commissioner and he is a worried man. The District Attorney is a worried man. The Senator is a worried man. And what do I get standing before me? Huh?"

The patrolmen glanced at each other and said nothing. A short silence made itself heard.

"That was not a rhetorical question! Answer me, you idiots!"

"Er … two worried cops?"

"No! You brainless piece of cack! I got myself two cops standing right here who don't worry enough!" Liebowitz thought about the bottle of bourbon in his drawer but decided to wait until after these dummkopfts had gone. He tried a more conciliatory tone.

"Who did this latest one say it was? Hmm?"

"Er, it said it was called …" the second cop consulted his notepad, "Utu. Yeah, that was it. Utu."

"A Sumerian sun god," said the first cop.

"Damn, that's ancient …" Liebowitz ran his fingers through his hair, some of the pomade lodged under his nails, "we've had reports of Aphrodite, Venus, Astarte, Ishtar and now Utu. This is getting serious. Next thing you know we'll be having Yahweh himself appearing. (Forgive me mama …) Every time it's the same. A woman is killed – always shot through the heart – and is then abducted by a damn god who was hitherto thought to be ethereal or invisible or what the hell ever and all we have left, every single goddamn time, is a pool of blood and nothing else except a whole load of questions! Who are these women and why is nobody reporting them missing?!"

"Because it's always the same woman, Captain …"

"How can it always be the same woman, you idiot?! Get outta my sight and file the report." They left him. Captain Liebowitz unscrewed the bottle of bourbon.

~

We call the learning of a story, learning by heart. Rote is something else, something more mechanical. The heart needs to absorb and care about the action and the characters but, ultimately, also care for those with whom the tale is shared. Stories should shoot us through the heart with their own Cupid-like arrows of intrigue and empathy. When a story is well told it involves all who hear and take part, even if it is simply by listening attentively. A story is valued highly by those who experience it together and as a species we seem to love it. But it is at that precarious stage immediately before, or as, the story begins that a slightly nervous anticipation is evident. A heightened expectation of gossip-like collusion kicks in as a story begins. Every human seems primed through social interaction to respond to another person if they think there is something important that will be imparted to them. It is then, within the first few seconds of the interaction, that we make choices. Whether to go with the teller a little longer, increment by increment, or to distance ourselves until we perhaps develop the confidence to trust them. Hence the role of humour and public vulnerability. The teller is aware that people need to make those choices early on and throughout the sharing of the story. Sometimes when I am telling a story I not only try to establish eye contact with everyone present but in those early stages of the plot development I find reasons to engage with individuals. If someone has a cough, for example, an instant choice of something like: "Now is that cough going to get any worse?" (with obvious mock annoyance); or "Are you okay? Do you need some water? I've got some here if you don't mind my slobber – oh no, maybe that's not a good idea …" (with mock revulsion). Invariably, people want to be amused because it eases the unease and there is a tacit understanding that we all need easing in together. Easy. Well, no it's not, not all the time. Inevitably, there are occasions where even beginning a story can have its problems: someone has dropped something; a light bulb is flickering or a dark cloud is gathering and a chill breeze is getting up; you yourself may have to cough or need to sneeze; someone is absorbed on a mobile device in full view; or there is a pandemic and we are all trapped in our own little fishtank on Zoom.

All of these things need turning to your advantage and, for the most part, there is an expectation from those gathered that you need to do that in order to set out the table for our story feast together.

There can be no doubt that storytelling generates and promotes community values, drawing people together and provoking interaction. But there is something else going on too. I have maintained for many years that it is possible to argue that there is no such thing as storytelling – there is only story making. What I mean by that, is when we hear a story we assimilate it into our own experience, and when we tell another person that same story we tell it from our own memory of that assimilation. As soon as the words leave our lips, or the action described by a gesture, even if they are identical to the original as we perceived it – we have made it our own. We are story making. That may seem like splitting hairs but every storyteller will tell you how they must "make the story their own". Your account of how you broke your toe when you dropped a brick on it will vary in form and content depending on whom you are telling. Your grandmother may be overly worried so you might choose to play down the effect of the injury. Your best friend may laugh at your foolishness so you might heighten your own idiocy for comic effect … and so on. In an everyday way, you are doing the same as the practised professional storyteller – you are making it your own and making choices about how you share the narrative.

Science tells us that almost all of the human body is regenerated over a period of between seven to ten years, from red blood cells every four months to the skeleton every ten years. (The exceptions seem to be our tooth enamel and the neurons in the hippocampus, which seem to evade full scientific understanding of their actual lifespan, but that's another story.) However, given that our bodily cells are constantly renewing themselves, and hippocampal neurons aside for now, it seems that the oldest part of our being could actually be our memories. We tend not to regard them as substantial as an arm or a leg and, anyway, don't memories alter with time? But so do our arms and legs. We tend to assume that memories will fade and disappear and many live their lives as if their past ceases to be important to them or to those they know. Why should we bother, then?

Our entire cellular being transforms but our memories represent the oldest aspects of our Self. When our bodies die, only the stories about us will remain in those we know and love. And what of our antecedents? What stories do we tell of them? Slowly and inexorably, tides of humanity celebrate life through storytelling. But why? Here is Dr Daniel Taylor.

> *If I can imagine nothing, I do nothing – I choose nothing – and thereby allow my life to degenerate from being a story to being a mere succession of events in a twittering world.*(1)

Dr Taylor has written extensively about myths, storytelling, and the search for meaning, wisdom, and the sacred through the tales we share. His essential message is that we become the stories we tell of ourselves. That has also been my *modus operandi* over the years as one who encourages people to engage with sharing stories.

> *In cultures where the sense of community is still strong, stories are prized as the vehicle for instruction in those things on which the life of the community depends.*(2)

Oral storytelling is not one thing. It can vary from instructional guidance to issues of identity and survival, not to mention important speculations about life and death. It may comprise a string of silly escapades or it may resound deep inside and help us realise what truly matters to us. In essence, it comes from the playful, imaginative and social heart of each unique being. That means that if you were to try to quantify its character and its approach definitively, you would need to research and to delineate almost eight billion or so separate examples individually across our planet. That's a truly Sisyphian workload.

~

Captain Liebowitz flinched again as she stepped towards him. How had she gotten into his office?

"Who the hell are you?" he still held the bourbon a few inches from his lip. He felt mechanical, inert, in need of a jump start. How was this happening? On the other side of the blinds, night traffic swished through the rain. The streetlamps splashed her face with shimmering fingers of raindrops.

"I am whoever you believe I am," she said, sitting on the edge of his desk. Liebowitz really wanted his hand to put the glass down and pick up his gun, but it wouldn't. There was something about her eyes that looked into the darkest places of his soul. She took one of his cigarettes, slotted it into her red lips and leaned towards him.

"Can you light me up?" He could almost feel her breath. Automatically he flicked the lighter and couldn't disguise his quivering hand. Did she want sex? Was that it? Sure, she was sexy … but that look in her eye. It wasn't seduction. What was it? What the hell was it?

"Tell me about your grandparents, Abe …" she whispered, the smoke swirling mostly around him rather than her, "… from before they stepped onto Riker's Island." She stared into him. Liebowitz felt himself shrink a little. That was it! It was a goddamn interrogation and he was on the receiving end for a change. No. No. There was no way he would allow her to do this. What right did she have anyhow? Abraham Liebowitz pushed himself to his feet abruptly. The bourbon soaked his paperwork. He grabbed his gun.

"Get out! Get out!" His shouts were more explosive than he had meant, as if his very soul had screamed. She fell backwards and hit the floor. Two holes in her chest bubbled up red. Rich dark red. She was stone still. All that moved was the blood. A slow motion flood of ruby ooze.

"What the hell?" Liebowitz looked at the gun, "I didn't discharge my weapon. I did not discharge my …" The room shook. An intense light turned his stare into a squint.

"I am Perun, god of your grandparents." Liebowitz froze in the thunderous wake of the voice. Perun scooped up the body and within the space of a second was gone, leaving only a pool of blood on the floor and a dazed and confused Captain of Police agog behind his desk. He knew that no-one was going to believe this. No-one. After two full minutes he slumped back into his chair, still trying to work this out.

"Best not to try …" he squeezed his eyes shut and pinched his nose, "… what in god's name …?"

~

Finally, by the time the teller has wound up the story and those of us who have been involved feel that we have got to know them fairly well, the imprint and timbre of their personality is palpable. I feel it is only right, therefore, and considering you have only had printed words to which you can respond rather than my physical presence, that as a storyteller I should end with some personal reflections and memories from my own life narrative by way of offering a personable end to this chapter. And perhaps one day if we meet you can judge whether it was successful. Hopefully, it may cause you to consider your own experiences too.

Growing up on the east coast of Norfolk in a draughty house with cold floors covered with thin lino in the days before central heating, I was often in the habit of keeping my socks on in bed. My father took exception to this and told me that if I carried on doing that my feet would go bad and turn black. I was six years old and not wishing to subject myself to this horror, nor to incur his wrath – which was usually exacted upon my elder brother, who seemed to enjoy testing the threshold of Dad's anger – I complied and climbed into bed barefoot each night haunted by the prospect of people's feet turning black and, presumably, falling off. Perhaps that was what had happened to people I saw in wheelchairs or on crutches. The idea sank deep into my subconscious and I thought little more of it. Until, aged eighteen, I went away to Yorkshire to an arts college to learn how to be an actor and to teach drama. My first-year digs were draughty and cold and my first West Riding winter found me needing to put on a jumper to go to bed. 'Oh,' I thought, 'I could keep my socks on … no, wait.' The spectre of my feet rotting sprang forth from my subconscious and I stopped in my tracks. 'Wait a minute …' Within seconds I was laughing at myself as my more scientific and biological knowledge of the world kicked in. How had I managed to sustain that deep-seated fear in the face of all I had learnt in the intervening years? I then imagined my Dad's face all those years before as he imparted to me, with utter seriousness, the dangers of sock wearing in bed. Had there been a glint in his eye? That Christmas when I returned home I described the scene of my night-time epiphany in the cold north. The person who laughed the most was Dad. And I fuelled further merriment when I pointed out to them that when I had been camping in Devon on my own the previous summer before going away to college, I had often kept my socks on as I wriggled into my sleeping bag at bedtime, reasoning that it wouldn't matter for a few nights because I would take my socks off at the beach during the day, when the sun was shining, in order to compensate. Clearly, the potent mix of my imagination coupled with my obedience to my father's cautionary advice had insinuated itself so firmly within me that it had taken on the identity of those *Facts I Know About The World*.

I had one grandfather who was nice and one grandfather who was nasty. At least, that is how it appeared to me in the uninformed brain of an infant. Grandad King would sit cross-legged in his chair, one of his big toes poking through a hole in his sock, his braces hooked over a white singlet vest, playing the mouth organ with a yellow canary sitting on his head. I remember him smiling while the gentleness in his soft voice permeated the room. Gompa was the family name given to my father's father and was synonymous with a bad-tempered growl. A large man, he had dark rings around his eyes, a sallow complexion and a small pill box hat with a tassel perched on the crown of his spiky black hair. He complained verbosely at everyone and everything as he chain-smoked. I didn't like to go too near to him.

I often tell people that I am only alive because of a twitching toe in the First World War. Aubrey Charles Walter Stickley, 'Wally' to his mates, was with seven of his army pals in the trenches awaiting orders when they were all blown up by a shell. Their bodies were dug out of the huge mound of soil and taken to the mortuary. Some time later a medical orderly happened to be passing by the corpses when the big toe on one of them moved. It was Wally's. He was taken to hospital and then back to Blighty. He lost one lung and one kidney and was no doubt plagued by guilt that, out of the eight of them that day, only he survived. Today we call it Post Traumatic Stress Disorder. In those days it wasn't called much at all, the less said the better. Ever after, his drinking became heavy and his smoking incessant. Was it any wonder? The only help I can be certain that he received was from Ruth, my grandmother. I now understand what a loving and long-suffering woman she was. Full of tenacity and strength. She is the hero who nursed her husband and raised six children. My father had a tough childhood and never spoke about it. He was forbidden to ever cry or show weakness. He was seventeen when his younger sister Vera, aged sixteen, died suddenly and he broke down and wept at her graveside as the earth thudded onto the coffin. His father never forgave him for showing such weakness. Much later in life, after my younger brother Mark died, my father was my pall-bearing partner. After we placed the coffin on the trestles in the church he turned and wept into my shoulder as I embraced him. My dad was seventy-five years old and he hadn't cried for fifty-eight years.

Every one of us has a history. It might not seem much at first glance and perhaps you are not in the habit of talking about your family's past, but perhaps you might consider asking a friend about their family history. Once the conversation starts it could easily be the case that some interesting facts and insights come to light. Our brains are quick to be enlivened by a friend's description of events and, time and again, I have witnessed people surprised by memories recalled that they previously assumed had been forgotten.

Here is some practical homework for you: take a small section from this chapter, any short section you wish, and from memory (by heart, not by rote!) tell someone else all about it. Try to repeat details and try not to leave anything out. Make it your own. And then try it again on someone else. When we speak words to each other we breathe together, our hearts beat together. When we exercise our imagination our lives are enriched and enlivened. And how we love to journey together surrounded by characters who make all the wrong choices so we know not to do the same in real life.

Storytelling is, ultimately, always about your own narrative (whatever tales you tell): your own life story; your own view of existence; your understanding of yourself and others; and of the whole universe that has shaped you. Therefore, the only way to shape ourselves is by the story we tell of ourselves, our meta-narrative – within it sit a million tantalising tales comprising the rich fabric of our being. For me, the answer to the question "What exactly is oral storytelling?" is beautifully simple and consists of only two words: *You are*.

But perhaps that penultimate sentence may have more impact if you read it again but out loud, and this time substitute the last two words with: *I am*.

Note

1 'Twelve Wild Ducks' in Angela Carter's *Fairy Tales* p 243.

References

1 Taylor, D. *Tell Me a Story – the Life-Shaping Power of Our Stories*, Bog Walk Press, (originally *The Healing Power of Stories,* Doubleday, 1996) 2001: *p.* 70.
2 Carter, A. *Angela Carter's Book of Fairy Tales*, Virago Press, 2005: *p.* 156.

10
SHAKESPEARE UNBARR'D

Rowan Mackenzie

This chapter provides an introduction to the work I do within several English prisons, using Shakespeare to help incarcerated people find ways to communicate with each other, their families and the wider world. With the dual role of being both practitioner and researcher there is a delicate balance to be struck between the competing focuses but it also enables me to develop a valuable ethnography from working with many of these people for a number of years. This chapter explores two prison projects, with very different demographics. One a local prison with a largely transient population where sessions were primarily one-off in nature and never extended beyond a matter of weeks due to turnover of inmates. The other, a theatre company which at the time of going to print has been in existence for 30 months and continues to flourish and develop within a prison in the Long Term, High Secure Estate.

Whilst there can undoubtedly be therapeutic value in telling one's own story there are circumstances when speaking another's words can give someone greater freedom to consider their engagement with the world. For some, verbalising their own narrative may be difficult if they find communication a challenge, lack the words or are unwilling or unable to discuss their personal experiences. Others may find that telling their own story reaffirms their perceived role as victim or hero without challenging them to analyse and develop a more rounded opinion on their experiences. By using someone else's story we can often free ourselves to explore issues which are important to us a little more openly and to consider how and why decisions are made in a more objective manner. This is certainly the case with the people I work with using Shakespeare in prisons.

Prisons are required to seek to progress all prisoners towards functional skills level 2 in Maths and English (equivalent to CSE Grade C or above). The latest *HM Chief Inspector of Prisons Report* rates only 59% of prisons as having a good or outstanding quality of teaching or learning, with 41% inadequate or requiring improvement (2018, p.43). The *Prison Education & Library Services Policy Framework* confirmed the requirements for encouraging all prisoners to further their education, meeting the requirements of prisoners with special educational needs, and the criteria for applying for undergraduate and postgraduate education through distance learning (2019). Rule 32 of the *Prison Rules 1999,* which continues to apply today, states that:

> reasonable facilities shall be afforded to prisoners who wish to do so to improve their education by training by distance learning, private study and recreational classes, in their spare time.
>
> *(1999, Rule 32)*

The work I do is categorised as recreational classes as it provides no formal learning outcomes and is not mapped to an approved educational curriculum (awarding bodies are centrally specified for core subjects) (2019, s.4.18).

My work is not therapy or dramatherapy; I work with the inmates to use their creativity to either explore scenes from plays or adapt, edit and perform entire plays. However, the National Research Council approved my research on the basis of exploring whether this type of programme can encourage inmates to engage with formal therapy and to consider their own behaviour, reactions and interactions through the dramatic characters with which they are engaging (2018, unpublished). The sample size for this research is necessarily small as it is only possible to work with a limited number of inmates in any project and there is also the issue of recruiting and retaining men who are interested in such sessions. My research is predominantly qualitative in nature and comprises creative outputs, edited scripts, rehearsal diaries, pre- and post-project questionnaires and feedback from those who watch the performances (other inmates, staff and families). This chapter examines the qualitative research I completed (all names are changed to protect anonymity) but the aim is not a psychological evaluation of each participant. As Smith suggested, qualitative methods are appropriate when the interest is in understanding dynamic processes or slow-moving complex events, which I identify within the context of my own work within the criminal justice system (1996, p.192). The numbers are naturally low across each establishment but collectively they build a compelling picture of the way in which the Shakespeare programmes may offer a way for the inmates to use the plays to 'enhance their confidence, transferable skills, academic work and personal development'[1] as well as being a pathway into therapy for some participants. As eminent criminologist Shadd Maruna documents, successful desisters (previous-offenders who do not reoffend) are those who have developed new life narratives; and for some of the inmates Shakespeare is a way to develop these narratives: narratives of change and positivity for the future (2001, p.42). As Michael, a prison actor, describes, this programme 'inspires us to do better, to be better and to overcome challenges'.[2]

I consider case studies from prisons with very different inmate demographics and it is relevant to understand the context in which each programme is set. The first is a category B men's prison housing many on-remand and short-sentence prisoners from the local community. It has an operational capacity of 408 and at its last inspection in January 2018 it was described by Peter Clarke (Chief Inspector of Prisons) as 'improving', although violence levels remained high (2017, p.5). The second is a category B men's prison for those serving indeterminate or life sentences, predominantly for murder. It has an operational capacity of 707 and the last inspection report in November 2017 deemed that 'it was not safe enough' due to escalating levels of violence and self-harm amongst a population where 'the clear majority present a high risk of harm to others' (2017, p.5).

Prison one

In this prison activities have mainly been one-off sessions, encouraging the men to adapt a Shakespearean scene into modern language whilst considering the themes and issues addressed. The work formed part of HMP's Talent Unlocked festival in 2017 and was awarded a grant from the City Council's 2018 Everybody's Reading Campaign. Given the transient nature of the population, as men are often released or relocated to other prisons, getting any form of continuity with the men involved in sessions proved exceptionally difficult. This naturally impacted on the extent to which they engaged with the sessions and how able they felt to open up emotionally within the group. However, even with these challenges there were instances where the men seemed to find an emotional outlet through the use of Shakespeare's language, characters and plots, as will be explored further on. My intention for each of the sessions in this prison was to choose a topic which the men would be likely to be able to easily identify with – jealousy, suspected betrayal, violent ambition, friendships, power struggles, dysfunctional families and forbidden love affairs; their engagement with the themes suggested that they identified well with the subject matter.

There were, naturally, limitations to the level of engagement when working with a new group of men who are not emotionally connected to each other or the facilitator. As Kirstine Szifris notes:

> Prison involves survival through developing a front, or a mask to live behind. But in reality, these men [have] fragile egos and complex vulnerabilities. Prison is not a place where it pays to be vulnerable.
>
> *(2019)*

This was borne out in the initial sessions and was particularly noticeable in this prison as the group changed too often to create a sense of community. However, despite this initial sense of self-imposed isolation from the others in the room, which I explore in 'Producing Space for Shakespeare' in the context of the Talent Unlocked *Othello* workshop, there remained the opportunity for the men to experience something of the therapeutic nature of engaging with Shakespeare. Each new group would start with the men actively not engaging with other inmates unless they knew them before we started, but the activities quickly got them participating in discussions with each other. When completing their post-workshop evaluations, a number of men noted changes in their self-perception, including 'empathy of viewing others past my own fixed point of view' and a realisation that 'I can challenge others from a mature point of view instead of criticism of their personality.'[3]

In early June 2018 I ran a session where we explored Macbeth and Lady Macbeth's dialogue following Duncan's murder. The eight men involved quickly engaged with the topic and split into two groups, one taking Macbeth and the other Lady Macbeth. They began to debate how to translate the text into modern language they would personally use and how the story could still be as relevant today as when it was written. Once the editing was complete we reformed into a single group and they performed a read-through, hearing the response from their counterparts for the first time. Lady Macbeth showed a decidedly 'macho' personality, goading her husband who was 'shook' and taunting him as a 'big man' with little suggestion of a loving relationship between the two of them.[4] Sadly there was insufficient time to explore their decisions about her characterisation but the group asked at the end if it would be possible to have a further session to act the scene. Thankfully, due to a supportive Governor we organised that for a few weeks later, although only half of the group remained in the prison at that time. The four men who attended paired off, with one pair rehearsing Shakespeare's text and the other the edited version. These short performances were the first time any of the men had acted and one of them particularly was reticent to do so as he was concerned about whether he would make himself look foolish. However, his slightly anxious Macbeth fitted well with the more assertive and at times aggressive Lady Macbeth of the adaptation and at the end he commented on how delighted he was that he had been brave enough to act.[5] The men became totally engrossed in creating their characters' motivation and actions, focusing on how they should use gesture and inflection to portray their role. They complained at the end about 'the little time we had to work'[6] and openly commented that they had spoken with each other between the workshops, forming bonds with other inmates over their shared experience of Shakespeare.

In contrast, the group dynamic for the *Romeo and Juliet* project differed as most of the attendees were acquainted before the sessions commenced. The project consisted of four sessions, one per week, using themes such as gang loyalty, family issues and forbidden love from the play to encourage the men to explore their own creativity. The outputs included raps, a devised performance piece, a semi-autobiographical short play about a young man's life and a number of improvised sessions. One of the men from the previous Shakespeare workshops, a peer mentor, attended the first two sessions but then explained to me that he did not want to attend the remainder as he disliked the format of these less Shakespeare-focused workshops and he did not like the raucous younger crowd who were monopolising the sessions.

However, some of the men involved used the theme of dysfunctional families to speak of their own experiences, with one commenting that 'I never dare speak in group therapy – I go to the toilet when it's my turn – but here it's different.'[7] Another went on to describe the family feud between his family and that of the mother of his own child in relation to the Montagues and Capulets. When we were discussing themes of parental control he chose to share with the group that their respective mothers had a long-running hatred so the pair kept their relationship secret until she was seven months' pregnant, fearing her family would coerce her into an abortion at an earlier stage. This level of emotional outpouring was not something I expected given the dynamic of the group but the others listened respectfully and expressed their sympathy with him as he explained how the level of interference from the families ended their relationship and made his son's formative years difficult.[8] Through the use of Shakespeare he clearly felt able to share some very personal information, which could potentially have been used to ridicule him after the sessions. I wonder if he would have been willing to share such information had he been asked direct questions about his personal life; but the narrative of the play emboldened him to articulate his own lived experiences. As Darren Henley says, 'engaging in creative activity can make a critical and positive difference to people's lives and attitudes' (2019, p.4). The seeds of this were certainly seen in Prison One; these seeds would go on to blossom more fully in the second prison.

Prison two

Whilst there are some benefits of delivering one-off workshops to pique the interest of the participants, I believed there would be more benefit from inmates having a longer-term engagement with Shakespeare's works. The opportunity to do this in a prison with men serving life sentences arose and by spring 2018 I started work recruiting a group, with the approval of the Governor and HMPPS. I chose *Macbeth* due to the relative simplicity of the plot and a view that the men would identify with the themes of power-lust, friendship, betrayal and a spiralling loss of control. The first few sessions were very challenging as the few who attended had done so only as it offered a potential alternative to the monotony of the prison regime. The men seemed unwilling to really get involved and attendance fluctuated, making it difficult to start rehearsing the much-edited script. A number of men eventually left the group for various reasons, including entering daily therapy and loss of interest. However, following some recruitment in the workshops we accrued a sustainable level of a core of eight men – the turning point for the *Macbeth* project.

During the summer this group became a cohesive whole, from an initially disparate group from multiple wings, five nationalities and with an age range spanning five decades. Where once there would be an undercurrent of hostility if one person criticised another, there came an understanding that the group were working together for collective achievement and any suggestions made were in that spirit. Throughout the period of working on this production the group became closer to each other and to me, beginning to share details of their own lives both within the prison and prior to incarceration. This was a gradual effect and I suspect partly due to the way in which we were discussing Shakespeare's characters but also partly due to the ensemble we had created. This ensemble became a more formalised structure in October 2018; following the performance of *Macbeth* the Governor announced to inmates and staff that the Shakespeare group was becoming an ongoing part of the prison regime. The men quickly asked me if we could form a theatre company and The Gallowfield Players was born, creating what I believe to be the first theatre company collectively owned by the inmates and myself. They wanted to do this to solidify the sense of community and autonomy which we had created within the rehearsal space each Friday and since then we have grown the group to maximum allowable numbers, where each has an equal voice in decisions.

The recent Prison Reform Trust Report *What do you need to do to make the best use of your time in prison?* categorised the needs of prisoners according to a prisoner's adaptation of Maslow's Hierarchy of Needs which defines three broad categories:

1. Basic needs (physiological and safety needs)
2. Psychological needs (needs relating to self-esteem, belonging and love)
3. Self-fulfilment needs (self-actualisation and achieving one's potential), (Wainwright, Harriott and Saajedi, 2019, p.4).

The Gallowfield Players contributes significantly across the latter two of these areas, providing the men with a sense of community and enhancing their self-confidence whilst at the same time encouraging them to stretch themselves in terms of creating, rehearsing and performing. The participants themselves identified benefits such as 'confidence', 'overcoming fear', 'adaptability, teamwork, cohesion and greater awareness of self', 'organisation', 'encouragement', 'writing skills' and 'the play improves our memories and keeps us mentally well'.[9] This work resonates with a number of the recommendations for change made by prisoners in this report, particularly around 'building inspiration', 'increasing a sense of ownership' and using 'creativity to support engagement, tackle isolation and build optimism', (Wainwright, Harriott and Saajedi, 2019, p.6). Michael reflected that:

> For a few short hours every week we are free; although physically we remain within the boundaries of the prison our spirits soar far above the walls and fences. This is a true sense of freedom, one that is rarely found anywhere in life, let alone within the high-security estate. It offers each of us a few brief moments of Nirvana.[10]

The men work towards a production, which in itself gives them a sense of purpose but also responsibility; but they also find ways in which to reflect their own lives and experiences through the characters they are playing.

One such example of the therapeutic nature of *Macbeth* was the impact of the 'tomorrow and tomorrow' (Shakespeare, 5.5.17–28) speech which Macbeth verbalises upon hearing of Lady Macbeth's suicide. In our performance the lines followed a blunt, short update from the Doctor that 'the Queen, my Lord, is dead',[11] which then led to the reflection on the meaninglessness of life. Malcolm applied himself diligently throughout rehearsals and was off-script weeks ahead of the performance, articulating his lines clearly and conscientiously. However, the week before the performance I asked the men to move beyond the recitation of the words and really focus on what they were saying. I had been asking them to do this for some time but with limited success, particularly for the Shakespearean lines we had retained and for the emotional speeches. Many of the men clearly felt more comfortable focusing on the humorous parts of our adaptation than the deeper, more illuminating speeches, but this was something I was keen to address ahead of the performance. This plea for them to consider the meaning of the words as they spoke them evidently impacted on Malcolm as at rehearsal the day before the performance he could not utter a word of the speech in question – he could not remember it. Even with his script in front of him he was unable to read with his usual fluency; stumbling over the words and distorting the rhythm of the speech. When we took a break he told me that the words resonated too closely with him. His anguish was visible and I asked him if he would prefer us to remove the speech altogether or offered to amend it to make it possible for myself to speak it as the late Lady Macbeth. However, he declined either option and insisted that he needed to speak the words, that to do so was important for him. He commented in the post-project feedback that 'it was easier to see the depth of his poetry when playing Macbeth than listening to any actor'.[12]

This reflective response to Macbeth's words came from an educated and cultured man who told me that he had been a regular patron of the arts prior to incarceration; however, he found more depth to the meaning when he himself was articulating the lines than hearing them from others. To such an extent that he also stated:

> I learned much about what went wrong in my index crime. I would say the therapeutic value of *Macbeth* is far greater than my nine months in the Therapeutic Community.[13]

The prison's Therapeutic Community (TC) opened 26 years ago for men who have 'long standing emotional and relationship difficulties that link to their offending' (Ross and Auty, 2018, p.59). The environment it provides is designed to foster 'communalisation, democratization, permissiveness' and is one of several such communities in the UK Prison Service (Ross and Auty, 2018, p.59). Malcolm had been a member of the community but requested to leave the programme some months before he joined the Shakespeare group. There have been many men who have successfully completed a treatment programme within the TC but he felt that it did not work for him. It was interesting that he found such powerful therapeutic benefits in the words of Macbeth and was able to relate to them in a way in which he struggled with formal therapy. Conversely, Winston joined the group in October 2018, having been an audience member for *Macbeth* and written the review for *The Grapevine*[14] but within a few months he had left as he wanted to pursue the opportunity to move onto the TC, which he has done.

Wayne is a young man who also joined after being in the audience for *Macbeth* and he threw himself into the group and rehearsals quickly as we started work on *Julius Caesar*. He has spoken openly about how the group has helped him to gain confidence and see possibilities beyond his younger life, which was heavily involved in drugs before his index offence.[15] He worked hard as Casca and despite this being his first performance he embraced the opportunities afforded to him by speaking the lines of this Roman senator. His maturity and confidence within the group have grown demonstrably within the last six months and he wrote in his rehearsal diary 'I am proud to say my identity has changed from being a Gallowfield Player'.[16] I arranged for Ben Spiller (Artistic Director, 1623 Theatre) to join a rehearsal and he commented that the group were 'so dedicated to telling the story of *Julius Caesar*'[17] and he enthused about Wayne's talent for acting. Wayne really took on board the feedback and directions in rehearsals, developing his character into a fully rounded one with a thought-out backstory connected to his own experiences in a Stanislavskian approach to the role. His desire to deliver his best possible performance was genuinely touching and he worked hard on his lines, gestures and movement to create a credible character within the narrative. He was delighted that two of his family were able to watch the performance and he wrote that:

> It was really good for my family to see me doing positive stuff because all I want to do is make my family proud and this drama performance has allowed that to happen.[18]

The performance was 'the best day [he had] ever had in prison and one of the best days in life' for the way in which it allowed him to be more than the person he had been so far in his own life.[19] His pride at introducing his family to me and the other cast members was evident. Interestingly this description of Wayne's 'best day' was also commented on by other members of the cast in their own diaries as being 'priceless'[20], demonstrating their empathy with each other; a skill enhanced, if not developed, by the work we do as The Gallowfield Players. Wayne himself is now contemplating requesting enrolment in TC as a way of helping him to deal with his previous familial issues, aid his rehabilitation and look towards a future following his release. As the *2018 Education and Employment Strategy*, states:

> Effective rehabilitation needs prisoners to engage with the opportunities in front of them, to build a different kind of life. They must be willing to commit to change, take advice, learn new skills and take opportunities to work.
>
> *(2018, p.8)*

Although Shakespeare does not lead to specific work within the prison it helps them build transferable skills such as empathy, responsibility, public speaking, teamwork and constructive criticism which may help them in the future. Their commitment is evident from the work they have put into productions. As Rosie Reynolds from the Prisoners' Education Trust commented, this group enables them to 'really utilise new skills; they seemed enthusiastic about the possibilities open to them'.[21]

The Gallowfield Players are working on their fourth production at present, albeit remotely during the COVID-19 pandemic. Their third was a hugely successful and poignant adaptation of *The Merchant of Venice* in which Shylock was ostracised not for his religion but as a man serving a life sentence whom the community fail to forgive upon his release. This was the most ambitious project to date, drawing directly on Shakespeare's narrative to crystallise and articulate the fears of the actors in terms of how they will be judged in the future by society. The choice of the thematic adaptation came from the group and the editing was carried out by them to make it resonate with their true feelings. That they felt able to tackle such an emotive topic was testimony to their development over the previous 18 months and this is sure to continue as we work together on future productions. There are so many offender behavioural programmes but perhaps for some, 'work that isn't offence focused makes them feel more than a prisoner'.[22] Michael described that 'I guess no one really understands what Drama means to me – how the freedom every Friday allows me to breathe'[23] but this freedom is so powerful in allowing him the possibility of defining a positive future for himself throughout the remainder of his sentence and upon his release. Another actor, Keith, asked me:

Why of all people and places choose us? People with the darkest of past, forever to be shunned by society, the worst of the worst in everyone's eyes.[24]

My response would be that I look not to their pasts, which cannot be altered, but to their future, which hopefully can be sculpted in a meaningful way. The narratives we take from Shakespeare and adapt, make our own resonate with humanity and it is this empathy and understanding which I hope they can take forward into the world to help them gain a place within society where they can flourish in the future, as all of these men will be returning to our communities.

Conclusion

My involvement in prisons continues to grow with the rollout of this model to a further prison, creating a theatre company called Emergency Shakespeare[25], who are currently preparing to work on their third production – an adaptation of *Othello* – and conversations under way with a number of other institutions. This appetite from the prison system to facilitate a non-traditional programme endorses the benefits to the participants and the wider prison population. The ongoing gathering of qualitative data continues to demonstrate value in using Shakespeare's narratives to explore different ways of considering and engaging with the world whilst putting on performances which are 'positive and inspirational'.[26] The engagement within an ensemble creates positive mental, emotional and physical outcomes for those involved; helping them to build confidence, transferable skills and 'a sense of community'[27] and to set aside the often prevalent 'hard-man' persona. The characters in Shakespeare enable them to look at the extremes of human behaviour a step removed from their own experiences but make those connections when they choose to do so. This work aligns closely with the current focus on reducing reoffending, encouraging purposeful rehabilitative activity and positive changes. Whilst there is no formal qualification for those involved, they speak openly of the 'family' we have created and the support it provides.[28] As Michael explains:

> There is such a magic in these plays, every time we talk about it, hold onto these moments we get the excitement, the buzz, it's addictive, it's powerful – it's what life used to be like before prison. How very different things could have been yet in every cavern there may be a diamond and this is mine. My own little precious jewel that needs to be nurtured.[29]

These are perhaps not those society believes deserve nurturing but if we are to enable them to return to society as citizens, not offenders, then there must be a counterbalance to the deprivation of liberty and humanity which prison imposes. Without such a counterbalance their world remains bleak and devoid of the concept of change, of autonomy and of hope. Perhaps Shakespeare can be the infusion of change, autonomy and hope needed by some of those incarcerated, whilst for others it may be simply a fictional escape from reality for a few hours each week. Either is a valid response, making the programmes worthwhile and so powerful for those engaging with them.

Notes

1 Learning, Skills and Employment Manager, email to myself following the performance of *Macbeth*, October 2018.

2 Michael during the post-performance speech to the Artistic Director following performance of *Julius Caesar*, 19 June 2019.
3 Feedback gathered from the workshop feedback data, 1 June 2018.
4 HMP script edit of *Macbeth*, 2:2.
5 Verbal feedback given by one of the men involved in the *Macbeth* workshop, 21 June 2018.
6 Post-workshop questionnaire, completed 21 June 2018.
7 Verbal feedback from Colin in the *Romeo and Juliet* project, September 2018.
8 *Romeo and Juliet* project, September 2018.
9 Feedback during debrief of *Julius Caesar*, Gallowfield Players, 21 June 2019.
10 Michael, *Experiencing Freedom with the High Security Estate*, March 2019 (unpublished work).
11 Rowan Mackenzie (ed.), *Macbeth*, v0.8, July 2018, unpublished script, p.12.
12 Malcolm, 'Post-project Feedback' data gathered during the debrief, October 2018.
13 Malcolm, 'Post-project Feedback'.
14 The in-prison newsletter, written and produced by inmates.
15 Conversation with Wayne at the end of a rehearsal, May 2019, where he volunteered information about his previous life experiences and his index offence.
16 Wayne's rehearsal diary, *Julius Caesar*, January–June 2019, unpublished.
17 Ben Spiller, feedback via email following a rehearsal, 10 April 2019.
18 Wayne's rehearsal diary, *Julius Caesar*.
19 Wayne's rehearsal diary, *Julius Caesar*.
20 Michael's rehearsal diary, *Julius Caesar*.
21 Rosie Reynolds, Higher Education Policy Officer, Prisoners' Education Trust, feedback emailed following *Julius Caesar*, 19 June 2019.
22 Staff feedback on *Macbeth*, October 2018.
23 Michael's rehearsal diary, *Julius Caesar*.
24 Keiths' rehearsal diary, *Julius Caesar*.
25 Governor Lubkowski requested the formation of a permanent Shakespeare group, March 2019.
26 Learning, Skills and Employment Manager, emailed feedback, June 2019.
27 Paul Johnston, Regional Lead Learning and Skills, HMPPS blog, July 2019.
28 Richard during post-*Julius Caesar* debrief, June 2019.
29 Michael's rehearsal diary, *Julius Caesar*.

References

Clarke, Peter, *HM Chief Inspector of Prisons for England and Wales: Annual Report 2017–18*. London: Her Majesty's Inspectorate of Prisons, 1 July 2018, https://assets.publishing.service.gov.uk/government/uploads/system/uploads/attachment_data/file/761589/hmi-prisons-annual-report-2017-18-revised-web.pdf

Clarke, Peter, *Report of an Unannounced Inspection of HMP Leicester, 8–19 January 2018*. London: Her Majesty's Inspectorate of Prisons, 2018, www.justiceinspectorates.gov.uk/hmiprisons/wp-content/uploads/sites/4/2018/05/HMP-Leicester-Web-2018.pdf

Clarke, Peter, *Report of an Unannounced Inspection of HMP Gartree, 13–23 November 2017*. London: Her Majesty's Inspectorate of Prisons, 2017, www.justiceinspectorates.gov.uk/hmiprisons/wp-content/uploads/sites/4/2018/03/HMP-Gartree-Web-2017.pdf

Henley, Darren, OBE, Chief Executive Arts Council, quoted in National Criminal Justice Arts Alliance 'Enhancing arts and culture in the criminal justice system: a partnership approach', 12 June 2019, www.artsincriminaljustice.org.uk/wp-content/uploads/2019/06/Enhancing-arts-and-culture-in-the-criminal-justice-system.pdf

Mackenzie, Rowan, 'Producing Space for Shakespeare', *Critical Survey: Special Edition – Applying Shakespeare: Volume 31, Number 4*, London: Berghan Journals, 2019, pp.65–76.

Maruna, Shadd, *Making Good: How Ex-Convicts Reform and Rebuild Their Lives*, Washington: American Psychological Association, 2001.

Ministry of Justice, *Prison Education & Library Services for adult prisons in England Policy Framework*, Issued 1 April 2019, https://assets.publishing.service.gov.uk/government/uploads/system/uploads/attachment_data/file/791622/prison-education-library-services-policy-framework.pdf

Ministry of Justice, *2018 Education and Employment Strategy*, May 2018, https://assets.publishing.service.gov.uk/government/uploads/system/uploads/attachment_data/file/710406/education-and-employment-strategy-2018.pdf

Ministry of Justice, *Prison Rules 1999*, www.legislation.gov.uk/uksi/1999/728/made

Ross, Gareth Edward, and Auty, Jonathan Michael, 'The Experience of Change in a Prison Therapeutic Community: an Interpretative Phenomenological Analysis', *Therapeutic Communities: The International Journal of Therapeutic Communities Volume 39, Number 1*, 2018, pp.59–70.

Shakespeare, William, *Macbeth*, ed. Kenneth Muir, London: Routledge, 1964.

Smith, J.A., 'Evolving Issues for Qualitative Psychology', in Richardson, J. (ed), *Handbook of Qualitative Research Methods for Psychology and the Social Sciences*, Leicester: Wiley-Blackwell, 1996, pp.189–201.

Szifris, Kirstine, 'How the hard man mask can affect a prisoner's sense of self', Aeon, https://aeon.co/ideas/how-the-hard-man-mask-can-affect-a-prisoners-sense-of-self, 1 May 2019.

Wainwright, Lucy, Harriott, Paula, and Saajedi, Soruche, *What do you need to make the best use of your time in prison?*, Prison Reform Trust and Prisoner Policy Network report, 9 July 2019, www.prisonreformtrust.org.uk/Portals/0/Documents/PPN/What_do_you_need_to_make_best_use_of_your_time_in_prisonlo.pdf

11
HEALING THROUGH THE MAHABHARATA

Kavita Arora in conversation with Raghu Ananthanarayanan

Setting an intention

We have written this chapter in the form of a dialogue. The Indian tradition of storytelling hands over the story from the teller to the audience, and invites the audience to actively participate in a reciprocal process. This is done by setting an intentionality that the story is theirs – i.e. is relatable to their context, and is happening within them in real time. This is regardless of content. The events of the story, while dramatic, are there for the purpose of evoking and touching the inner world of both the teller and the audience. The implicit acknowledgement is that the story as well as the act of telling it, is the conduit between the worlds inside the teller and the receiver.

We invite you, dear Reader, to proceed onwards with the intention of reading and simultaneously witnessing your own inner world.

R: Let us start by looking at **an overview of the story**.

The critical dramatis personae of the Mahabharata are the two sets of cousins: the five sons of Pandu called the Pandavas and the hundred sons of Dhritarashtra called the Kauravas. Duryodhana the eldest of the Kauravas features prominently; the others play cameo roles as the story unfolds. The Pandavas are the ones who understand the true nature of Krishna, the incarnation of Lord Vishnu on the earth. The Kauravas are blind to the sacred within and therefore cannot see Krishna for what He truly is. The story contrasts the two sets of cousins in many ways. The Pandavas are born in exile through the power of their mother Kunti to invoke the Gods. The Kauravas have a difficult birth. Their father Dhritarashtra is blind and their mother Gandhari decides to blind herself as she discovers to her shock that her husband is blind. An interesting twist is brought into the story in the form of Karna. Karna was born to Kunti before her marriage to Pandu. She abandons this very gifted child, who is brought up by a poor couple. Karna goes on to befriend Duryodhana. Draupadi the wife of the Pandavas is a very important player in the drama, as is Bhishma the uncle and elder of the clan. The contrast between the Pandavas and the Kauravas is clearly set. The saga of the fight between the two is an allegory of the two ways in which power is viewed. The

Pandavas are more self-reflective and *dharmic* (ethical). The Kauravas are acquisitive and *adharmic* (unethical). However, we must emphasise that the narrative is not a black and white depiction of the struggle for power. The humanness of the living process and the difficulty of being dharmic are reiterated at every turn of the story (1).

Within and beyond the story

K: The Mahabharata is known as a story, but why is it not just a story in the way that conventional stories go, and if it is not just a story, then what is it really?

R: No, it's not just a story at all. It is like a window. I was recently reading a paper written by Joseph Campbell where he talks about myths, being truths which are beyond time and beyond history. He says "So the popular way of interpreting the word 'myth' is 'falsehood,' whereas myths in the sense that I'm speaking of them, are final terms of wisdom – that is the wisdom of the deep mysteries of life" (2).

The word *purANa* in Sanskrit means something very similar to this. The Mahabharata (and the Ramayana, for that matter) are more *purANic* than historical. *PurANa* means *purA api navam*: *purA* means old or ancient, *navam* means new or nascent. The epic is situated in historical realities, maybe a small bit, but the whole story around it is actually speaking about the human psyche in ways that are not bound by time. So for me, they're actually archetypal situations, where archetypal figures are playing out a drama. The truth of the story is not in the content of the story itself. The truth is something you arrive at, by looking at life through the story. That is why the story is like a window.

K: A window which opens the story beyond the events being narrated. As well as a window to encourage the listener to look within and pause to connect to their inner world possibilities. This is the nature of a 'living story'. Could you please illustrate with an example?

R: Here is an example:

Take the name of Yudhisthira, an important Pandava hero. The name itself is symbolic. *A person who can be anchored and stable in chaotic and war-like situations is called yudhi (war, chaos) sthira (anchored).* So immediately it takes you away from the person and points to a more subtle reality. While I'm using the word Yudhisthira, I'm not actually speaking about a personification, I'm speaking about a whole archetypal set of possibilities.

Every person's name in the Mahabharata has this connotation. So they are transparent names, and are not just nouns. They are evocative and indicative as they are pointing to something else. If we attempt to delve deeper, the name doesn't end with the person who's being referred to. For example, Duryodhana – the Kaurava prince – is actually named **Su**yodhana at birth. *Suyodhan* means *one who thinks, who has beautiful thoughts.* No parent names their new-born child **Du**ryodhana – *one with bad thoughts!*

The story goes that he grows up in the knowledge that he is the crown prince of the kingdom. He is surprised with the entry of the Pandavas, who till then have been in exile. Suyodhana knows nothing about their existence, prior to their appearance at this point. They turn up one day and suddenly his own position as the heir apparent gets threatened. The stories tell you that at this point of time Suyodhana becomes jealous and cannot control his envy and jealousy and therefore becomes **Du**ryodhana. So the story itself is pointing to these kinds of inner possibilities.

K: So why tell it as a story? With all these seemingly hidden possibilities? Why not just talk about the lesson itself?

R: I think because a story evokes a lot of sensibilities of the person. A story is an embodied learning process whereas a moral teaching is a dogmatic process, possibly appealing to the intellect, most likely provoking fear. The moral doesn't necessarily evoke you. It doesn't touch you in a deeper inner space. And these are not logical spaces, they are pre language and logic. Like envy is not a logical thing. So it's not as though I'm feeling envious or not envious because I think about it and I logically say this is the time to be envious. There's something much, much deeper than logic, deeper than rationality that takes over. So to point to realities like this, one has to listen to stories.

Also, in Indian thought, *dharma* or ethical conduct is contextual. Only a story can bring the context, the inner dilemma and the difficulty of making ethical choices together.

K: The context of each listener at different times is also different. I can imagine that somebody gets one level or meaning when they hear it the one time, and in the same telling somebody who is listening at a slightly deeper level is getting something else out of it.

It can also mean that the same story heard at different times (by the same person) can reveal more subtle aspects or different aspects each time. It's layered in many ways and at different points in time, you may be listening more deeply than at other times.

The question in my mind that's arising then is, do we leave this to chance? Is there a process? Does the facilitator (the healer or the storyteller) make that happen? Is there a way the listener can prepare to look beyond the meaning in the first hearing? Is that the objective or intent of the storyteller and/or the telling?

R: It's a stated objective. That's very beautiful. Again, there's a story that tells you how this becomes a stated objective for writing the Mahabharata.

This story is an overarching one for all the arts being created. In all of these versions, Brahma approaches a great teacher. So for dance, he approaches Bharata, for Mahabharata he approaches Vyasa etc. The cover story is very similar. You hear it in the Mahabharata, then in the Bharata Shastra – it is the first dance drama that Bharata wrote.

Brahma says, *dharma* is not being held as it should be, so I want you to write about dance or I want you to write the Mahabharata. This person will say, why do you want me to write this? So in both cases, the answer is similar. Brahma says that human beings are full of *rasa* – i.e. their life is full of emotions. They're full of strife and so on. So the higher truth cannot be just told to them in abstract ways. Can you create a form? Can you create a story that is full of *rasa*, that is full of these deep emotions and reflects the deep churning of life, so that it will bring out what it means to make *dharmic* choices (choices where the actor, their immediate context and the larger context are enlivened simultaneously)?

Thus, the one very critical story that most of the great epics start with is the **Samudra Manthan** (the churning of the ocean), which is again an allegory of the mind being churned. Samudra, the ocean, is the symbol of life and then you have this huge mountain that's kept in the middle, which is a symbol of your own backbone, which is being churned through the outward movement and movement within. And through this churning, you understand many things about yourself. The first thing that comes out of the churning is poison. And then slowly as you work with this, you get the elixir of life.

K: It reminds me (in part) of the process of therapy in some schools of psychology. Please continue:

R: This will be a story that is told in many ways. Every temple in India will have a panel of Samudramanthan. So this theme is repeated over and over and over again. From the time you're a child, if you're growing up in that context, you've already seen many of these symbols, these images, you heard little bits of these stories from here and there, and it all starts falling together when these performances happen. So in a sense, the person who's listening to the story is not listening to it for the first time (3).

K: Yes. And that's why the resonance...

R: Absolutely.

K: The familiarity in that sense is also bringing in a deeper level of resonance. Because it's already there in some ways, in some abstract form it has already touched you at some point in time, even if you don't consciously know where exactly it touched you. So we are saying that whatever dilemmas that we find ourselves in, the encouragement or the nudging to act in a more *dharmic* way comes from these stories. So ultimately it is about self-actualisation, self-exploration, whatever it is that we want to call it in the English language.

R: I think it's two things. At one level it's got a strong healing component. At another level it is giving you a sense-making, choice-making frame because the events that are related are all events of a family. The events which are very common events. These are not great huge events. It is set in a larger context and the consequences are exaggerated and elaborated for you to understand clearly what is at stake.

So they're actually everyday events that are being talked about. See again, here, there's a certain context of storytelling that has been lost today. If you imagine, let's say a few hundred years back, a village where there's a big temple. The normal practice is this: every evening after you finish your day's work, you go to the temple. The temple architecture and the sculpture are designed in a way where common images are depicted on the boundary and in the outer wall. They're all very simple everyday images and then you're slowly drawn inward till you come to the sanctum through panels that narrate stories of various kinds. It's kind of like a gradual moving into the sanctum. After you experience the divine in you as you absorb the energy in the sanctum, you have dropped all differences that you might've experienced in the day through your role relationships. Then all the devotees go and sit in the Mandapam (a preformative space) and listen to stories being told, enacted, sung or danced. The story is how the father or mother dealt with the son or daughter, how a brother dealt with his siblings and a husband behaved with his wife. These are stories of everyday love, affection, insensitivity, hurt, envy, grief, celebration and so on. You listen to these stories, go home having that something deep within you awakened. Having also related to the stories from a quietness within you realise that being in touch with the divine energy within can inform your choice-making as you face similar kinds of problems at home (4).

The Mahabharata Immersion

K: Rituals and daily practices have changed. Indeed, the context and meaning of going to the temple no longer remains the same. How do you see it being brought into the contemporary Indian context?

R: Today when you take the story out of this context it becomes a little more difficult to reach this healing space in your mind. But if you look at where and how the story started, maybe we can then try and recreate this – which is what I'm trying to do.

Personal narratives must be evoked, a self-reflective process must be evoked, and then these Puranic stories become very, very powerful. Otherwise, my sense is people will read these stories in a very opaque way, and treat them as a nice story, but that's not what the story was meant for. That's not why it was written. That's not why Brahma said please write the story…

K: Could you speak about the context and setting of the Mahabharata Immersion process that you choreograph based on the above?

R: Modern life has alienated most of us from our inner processes and as a consequence we are often insensitive to our contexts. In the six-day Mahabharata Immersion we spend a full day helping the participants who are really "actors" being prepared to enact parts of the Mahabharata, to become sensitive to their feelings or *rasAnubhavam* (experiencing feeling qualia). I use simple exercises from traditional Indian dance and theatre to enable this inward journey.

On the second day we move into a more nuanced awareness of the inner drama. Here I use the common archetypal figures of Indian drama, which by the way is universal. These are the victim, the guardian, the friend and so on. The one archetypal figure that might be unique to Indian theatre is the meditator. Invoking the meditator within as we work further is the key to touching deep healing energies and creating the sacred space. The actors are now ready to explore interpersonal dynamics and then proceed to enact snippets of the Mahabharata. This enactment becomes the churning of one's inner space. The Daivic Pandava energies and asuric Kaurava energies and the drama they play out within each one is explored.

In other words, creating both the space as well as the process to explore has to be created as part of the immersion process. The Immersion, in its current version, is a residential workshop and participants explore this together for six days.

My experience is that without an initiation into a deeper and subtler inner realm, if you just told the story, it wouldn't have the same effect.

K: That's the power of contemplation, sharing and dialogue, isn't it? In my experience of the Mahabharata Immersion process that you choreograph, I experienced the creation of a safe space, held by the collective, which slowly deepens as the days progress. The setting of the context, I felt, was as important as the process itself. I also experienced the different layers of how storytelling is viewed and used. The use of the body, being told not to use words, listening to the story told, as well as telling it, enacting the story, all these forms seem to have a part to play in the process of understanding and self-exploration for the actor and the audience and healing thereof for all present.

Could you speak a little about the difference between enacting versus storytelling and how that informs the Immersion process?

R: With pleasure! In the Indian context if you take the Mahabharata, the way it is conducted classically in a village is very interesting. Two streams are running in parallel. There is one set of people who are telling the story through the day in a format known as "*kathakAlakshepam*" (ritual storytelling that moves between prose, poetry and song). And another set of people who are acting it out in the evenings. And the entire village will get involved in the enactment. For example, there is a village near

Chennai where every few years, the whole Mahabharata enactment goes on for 18 nights and 18 days.

On the first evening, the usual way in which it starts is Bhima (one of the Pandavas) has to defeat an *asura* (demon) called Bhakasura, and the story narrates that the Pandavas are living in a village "incognito" at the time of their exile. An *asura* is eating up the village children and one child has to be sent every week to satiate his appetite. It is the turn of the poor and old parents living next door to where the Pandavas are staying. They are in deep distress. So Kunti (Bhima's mother) hears the old couple lamenting, her heart melts and so she asks Bhima (whose strength and valour are legendary) to go and fight Bhakasura.

In this enactment, often the whole village gets involved. It is almost as though the village, in the now, is experiencing a certain sorrow for which the Pandavas have come to help them.

The process by which the actors prepare themselves is also very important. There is an elaborate ritual process where the actors paint the masks. This process of their wearing the mask is also seen as the way of invoking the hero into the here and now. Bhima enters the here and now, Bhima is not a character from then and there – he fills and embodies the actor. Bhima is fed by the villagers and the actor who is the *asura* will enter the village. The two will fight and the two warriors will chase and engage with each other through every street in the village. It is a very here and now event.

Through the day the story has been narrated and, in the evening, it is enacted. So through a lot of senses your entire understanding at an archetypal level of this event is being evoked. The way the villagers engage with the process is very revealing. In the event I witnessed, there was a catharsis, one of the elders got very agitated, "is this right for us to sacrifice our children? My children are being sacrificed to this *asura* called Dubai. All the young people are going away from the village and they're going away to Dubai. So we old people are feeling very left out and alone, this is like a Bhakasura."

K: Can we talk about any other anecdote like this to elaborate on what you said initially about the Puranas, the old and the new and the bridging of the two and how it lives, and how this enactment is in many ways inside one who's experiencing, and the person who's enacting there is a bridging of the old and the new, you're bringing out the archetypes? So to make it more relevant to somebody who's maybe new to this idea.

R: Let's take a step back. I think there's one very interesting difference between Modern Western theatre for example and this kind of Ritual village theatre that we're talking about. In the modern theatre, you have a proscenium, a raised space which belongs to the actors and another space which belongs to the audience. So there is a relationship between the audience and the actors, but it is an external relationship. The actors are out there, the audience are out here. There's a curtain that divides the two and so on. In this form of theatre, each of the characters will appear on the stage and be seen when the curtain is raised. They come into view but remain in their time and space.

In the Ritual theatre, after the actors bring down the energy of the Gods into themselves, they will look at a mirror and fully internalise the character. The space where the "*avataraNam*" – i.e. the embodiment of the Gods – happens and the space of enactment is divided by a curtain. Traditionally the curtain has seven colors, which represents time. As the enactment begins the actor/hero will come and dance behind this screen. This process is called "*prasavam*" which means "giving birth to". So these archetypal characters that have been invoked into the here and now through the actor are being born into the time and space of the audience. As the process of *prasavam* begins the actor/hero will start by singing the praises of Bhima or whoever they're representing in the past tense. They are behind the screen where they dance the birthing, push the screen, a limb will show and then a part of the head and so on. And when they finally appear from behind the screen, they will say, "I have arrived!" The entire song and the narration will change from the past tense to the here and now.

K : So in space and in time, in both dimensions there is a birth…

R : There's a birth and whatever is enacted of the Mahabharata is happening in the here and now in that space where the actor/hero and audience are one. To emphasise the relationship between the two there is the Sutradhar – "the person who holds the linking thread". They make the links by saying, look, so-and-so's behaving this, isn't this like the way one of the politicians is behaving? This is what is happening here in this enactment. Isn't this happening in your home? So there's a tying up of the divine and the profane going on constantly. The actor/hero is a signifier who points to the archetypal energies that reside in every one of us. In the theory of dance (Natya Shastra) this is called "*saddhAraNI karaNam*" – **creating the common denominator.**

The premise of healing

K : I understand the parallels between what you are doing in the Mahabharata Immersion and the ritual theatre. Through the gradual awakening of the participant-actor to their inner drama, they awaken their archetypal figures and enter the masks of the Pandava and Kaurava as it were. And how do you think that leads to healing? So I think we have to look at it from the point of view of why is this not only a performance and why is it more than a performance or more than storytelling?

R : There are two levels at which I can respond to this question. One is my own experience of what happens in the Mahabharata Immersion, week-long learning/healing laboratory I choreograph. Through a series of processes, I am first helping the spect-actors (as Augusto Boal (5) might refer to the participants of the Immersion) become sensitive to their own inner processes. By awakening to their emotional world and their own inner drama, the spect-actors of the Immersion gain insights into processes of their psyche. I then expose them to the enactment of the Ritual theatre by a traditional folk theatre group. Here the spect-actors are introduced to the whole process of enactment in the traditional ritual theatre form.

The spect-actors are now ready to engage with the whole process of invoking the archetypal energies, embodying and enacting a small piece of the Mahabharata that they are drawn to explore. After the enactment, the spect-actors enter the space and speak as and for the characters that evoked them. I call this the exploration as the alter-ego. The spect-actors are then encouraged to dialogue about the enactment in the here and now of their lives. For instance, the "disrobing of Draupadi" is a very evocative piece and this gets explored in almost every Immersion. If five out of 25 spect-actors choose to explore this episode, the others participate through the alter-ego exploration and then the dialogue opens up: how is the Draupadi's experience similar to my own experience?

What are my fears and vulnerabilities? What are my experiences of betrayal? And so on. There is deep catharsis and transformational insights get awakened while drawing these parallels.

The Mahabharata was intended to be an anti-war tale. So every critical episode narrated in Mahabharata is an inflection point where if a *dharmic* action had been taken, there would be peace and harmony. But *adharma* prevails and the narrative goes down the wrong road as it were till finally war becomes inevitable. In the village performance/storytelling, for example, I've seen individuals raise a question saying, what if so-and-so had not done this? There's an exploration of possibilities where you've got yourself into a tight situation and some wrong decisions were made. So the narrator will say, yeah, that's the *dharmic* issue, what would you like to do about it? Or the Sutradhar will say, yeah, these are possibilities, how would you like to look at it? This type of an invitation will often trigger a huge catharsis.

K : You might like to elaborate this idea a little more through the Karna story because he is a very evocative character representing the disadvantaged and the dispossessed.

R : In the village performance different parts of the 18-day performance will be funded by different sections of society. So on the *karnamoksham* day, the enactment of Karna's final battle with Arjuna (and his death and liberation) is almost always funded by the people of the lower caste. Karna in Mahabharata is like many mythical heroes in many other myths around the world. He is abandoned at birth, except that this is a story of unrelenting tragedy. He's a brilliant child born of the Sun God and abandoned by the mother (Kunti the mother of the Pandava). Karna is discovered by the Charioteer Adhiratha. He is brought up by Adhiratha and his wife Radha as their son. Karna grows up to be a great warrior, but he is continuously deprived of what is his due only because of his association with his foster parents, who belong to a low caste. Karna is therefore seen as "our hero" by the people of the lower castes and through the enactment of Karna and the whole myth retold at that point of time, the village itself kind of goes through a catharsis. There'll be people weeping for Karna, there'll be people going in hugging the dying Karna at the end. So the characters out there are not treated as separate from the audience, this whole movement between the character and the audience is happening all the time. For example, even in *kathakAlakshepam* (the traditional storytelling) when these stories are told, the movement between the "here and now" and the "then and there" is very fluid. I remember when I was very young, my grandfather would read out stories from the Ramayana and he would say, look how Sita suffered. And then he'd close the book and say, *you know what, I have also done this to your grandmother. This is what I did. And you know, I hurt her so much.* And he wouldn't say, you people shouldn't do this. He would not moralise; he would simply weep. I actually remember my grandfather weeping and saying, look, this is what I did.

Both the *kathakAlakshepam* ritual storytelling where the storyteller will go into some of these kinds of self-reflective pieces and the ritual theatre enactments become cathartic for the audience and I think these are all the processes of healing.

K : So, I think what I'm hearing is also that the person who is either telling the story or enacting it or embodying the emotions is affected. But how, for example, when you were listening to this story as a child from your grandfather and you saw this happening, how did it affect you? Because I think it's also about the transmission and the evocation in the person who is not the person enacting and is also part of the healing process, isn't it? It has stuck with you, that scene has stayed with you, but also what happened inside you during it.

R : That's right. I wouldn't say that all of us grandchildren who were listening to him were impacted the same way. In the Indian theory of dance and drama the relationship between the *rasika* (the listener who is evoked) and the *rasa* (archetypal emotions) brought forth by the actor/storyteller is critical. So if the actor touches a certain deep evocation within, the *rasika* appears when some people in the audience resonate with the same evocation. If there is no resonance of this evocation, in the Indian context there is no listening actually. There is no *rasika* and no *rasAnubhava* (experiencing the depth and subtlety of the emotion) and no shared sacred space. And I think it will impact different people at different times also depending on the reality of the listener. If you are in touch with a certain part of your hurt, let's say, then one enactment will make more sense than some other enactment. The other part will speak to you much more at some other point in time.

K : Absolutely. So the same story, the same enactment at different points in time in your own life when you're sitting in the audience and interacting as the audience may actually have a different set of impacts because you might resonate in a different way each time.

R : Many old stories in India will have this power. In the Ramayana (6), when Rama goes into the forest, he will meet many Sages. The Sage will tell him a story about a great king or a commoner in the past. So Rama is helped to reflect upon his own dilemma through listening to the story. In a sense, you're told when you're listening to my story, don't just listen to it as a story. Use it as a mirror for you to reflect for yourself. This meta message in a sense is embedded in the story.

In my understanding, many Bhagavatha Purana stories (7) (stories about Shri Krishna) will also have this. For example, if you look at the story of Krishna. At every stage of Krishna's journey, there's a story; there's a story about him as a child, Balakrishna. He's playing somewhere and he puts some dirt in his mouth. His mother Yashodha gets very concerned. She asks him to open his mouth. Krishna opens his mouth and the mother Yashodha sees the whole universe inside his mouth. There's a beautiful song about this. And then Yashodha is wonder-struck: how is this happening? And then there is a looping back into the story of how this child is actually Lord Vishnu.

And then the stories of Krishna will keep evolving. As an adolescent, he's the person who becomes the beloved of all the Gopikas and then his name becomes Navaneetachoran. *Navaneetam* means the most beautiful… I don't know what English word to use here to explain this but I shall attempt – the quintessence, the quintessential sweetness in you is Navaneetan. So Navaneetachoran is somebody who steals your heart because your heart experiences this exquisite sweetness when they are around. And that sweetness is called Madhupratekam in Yoga. The word Madhu means honey. There's the state of mind called Madhupratyekam where you feel the sweetness of life, the quintessential beauty of life.

So at one level, you're listening to the story where Krishna is called Navaneetachoran. Then the next time you hear the story, somebody will tell you that this is the deeper meaning of the word. And as you go into the same story at another level of depth, some references will be made to the fact that the yogic thought is also speaking about the same thing. So layer by layer you're drawn into the most deep philosophies, but at the surface it is just a lovely story about a boy growing up.

K: That's the power of storytelling, dialogue and enactment, isn't it? I also took away a sense of empowerment about self-exploration and healing personally. This was wonderful. Thank you.

References

1. Kamala Subramaniam; *The Mahabharata*; 2017; Bharathiya Vidya Bhavan 20th Edition.
2. Joseph Campbell; *Goddess, Mysteries of the Feminine Divine*; 2013; New World Library.
3. Bharat Gupt; *Dramatic Concepts Greek and Indian: Study in Poetics and the Natyasastra*; 2016; D.K.Printworld.
4. Sashikala Ananth; *Vaastu: A Path to Harmonious Living*; 2001; Roli Books.
5. Augusto Boal; 1985; *Theatre of the Oppressed*, trans by Charles A McBride, Maria-Odilia Leal McBride, Emily Fryer; 2000; Pluto Press.
6. Kamala Subramaniam; *The Ramayana*; 2009; Bharathiya Vidya Bhavan.
7. Kamala Subramaniam; *The Bhagavatham*; 2006; Bharathiya Vidya Bhavan.

12
WE'RE GOING ON A BEAR HUNT

Neuro-dramatic play, multi-sensory informed storytelling approaches to working with children under five

Clive Holmwood

Introduction

'Annie' (not her real name),[1] is a bright confident 20-month-old, who lives with her mom, dad, big sister, two dogs and a cat. Annie is outgoing and has no known health or medical conditions. The purpose of this chapter is to explore with Annie aspects of Neuro Dramatic Play (NDP) (Jennings 2011), in relation to story and Jennings's notion of Embodiment Project Role (EPR), from a multi-sensory informed approach, using the great children's classic *We're Going on a Bear Hunt* (Rosen & Oxenbury 1993). I will consider a range of multi-sensory ways of working using messy play, drama and rhythmic storytelling (Jennings 2011:41) in relation to Rosen's story and the potential impact that this has upon the overall personal, cognitive and social development of Annie as a 20-month-old.

Although I am a registered dramatherapist, I was not offering therapy, nor was I attempting to deal with any specific child-related issue other than supporting Annie in her general development as a young child. The work was developed from an NDP perspective, which is not in itself therapy (Jennings 2011), but also from an arts in health and wellbeing perspective (Daykin 2020). The arts and all forms of creativity including art making, dramatic play and storytelling are increasingly being acknowledged as an alternative to medicine and traditional healthcare in aiding the general physical and mental health of children and adults. Annie has no health or developmental issues, but I hoped that NDP multi-sensory play through storytelling would aid her general overall cognitive, emotional and physical development. We carried out a total of five non-directive story and play-based sessions, the first of which was in her family home with her mother; the remaining sessions took place at her grandmother's home (which she often visited), with grandmother, who she was very familiar with, and grandmother was always present at these sessions encouraging Annie.

Methodological approach and themes

The overall research methodology was an observational qualitative empirical approach (Reinke 2014). I observed Annie taking part in and responding to each session and wrote thick descriptions in my journal afterwards, with photographs taken of the play. In particular

Table 12.1 Developmental themes

Session 1: Read the story out loud.
Session 2: Read the story and add wooden figures from *Going on a Bear Hunt*.
Session 3: Read the story, add figures and dry sand tray.
Session 4: Read the story, add figures, dry sand and a little water to make wet sand.
Session 5: Read the story, add figures, and lots of water to make very wet sand.

I was interested in how dramatic and multi-sensory approaches developed from NDP could add and enhance the storytelling, thus assisting Annie with her general overall development. I devised a simple strategy to offer developmental sensory experiences through story (see Table 12.1).

Theoretical overview

As already described, there are three main overarching theoretical ideas that merge in the creation of the work with Annie, story, play/sensory (NDP) and 'arts in health' approaches.

Firstly, the notion of story. The academic and theorist Joseph Campbell spent his life deliberating the notion of story. In his seminal work *The Hero with a Thousand Faces* (1993) he considered the commonalities of plot and related them to myth and the heroic character always at the centre of every story. Booker developed these ideas further in *Seven Basic Plots* (2004), suggesting there might only be a half dozen or so basic stories in the world, told of course in many different ways. Campbell himself considered the notion of the hero's 'call to action' in *The Hero's Journey* (1990). One could argue that this is the ultimate story, the main protagonist setting out on a journey of self-discovery.

I have written about the connection between story, drama and therapy before (Holmwood 2014); Campbell himself was heavily influenced by the world of therapy, especially Carl Jung, one of the founders of psychoanalysis (Jung 2014), who was particularly interested in the concept of 'the collective unconscious' in stories, the notion that all stories held universal truths. In recent years this has been echoed by writers such as Gersie, who suggests that in troubled times 'an answer to our problem might *dwell* within the story' (1992:15) itself. Margot Sunderland (2000), a leading children's therapist, has purported the importance of story within a therapy context; as has more recently Hammel (2019), who considered the use of therapeutic stories in a wide range of therapeutic and therapy settings. However, it is important to remember in the context of this work with Annie I was not considering stories as a form of therapy; however, I need to acknowledge the overall therapeutic potential of stories to grip interest and allow the story to support her in her overall holistic development.

As already briefly discussed the second overarching theory is Jennings' Neuro Dramatic Play (NDP). It is helpful to consider it further here. Though it is often used by qualified drama and play therapists in their work, and to an extent has come out of Jennings' pioneering work in play and dramatherapy, it is not in itself therapy. NDP is a combination of a range of developmental play, dramatherapy and play therapy approaches which include multi-sensory approaches to play, including rhyme and rhythm in story, dance, drama, movement and messy play approaches which allow babies and young children to attune to the adults around them, to assist in developing positive secure attachments (Bowlby 2005). All of this has been developed by Jennings over her 50-year career.

These approaches are particularly useful for children who have had difficult or challenging early attachments and relationships with care givers and can be used in a therapy context where deep complex work is required, but it is also essential for the brain development of all children everywhere (Jennings 2011:34). Jennings also refers to the notion of 'Primary Circles' (2011:14), the circles of containment, care and attachment that establish the early bonds between a child and their primary care giver. Essential for all good early healthy attachments.

Jennings describes Embodiment, Projection, Role (EPR), one of her main theoretical developments within NDP, as a developmental paradigm that uniquely charts the progression of dramatic play from birth to seven years (2011:17). The embodiment phase is where the baby is attempting connections between itself and the real world – what is me and what is not me. This might often include tactile play and textures, leading to messy play such as sand and water. The projection phase is where the child attempts to connect and interact and manipulate objects around them – the child might endow powers and personalities onto toys and objects. The role phase, achieved by about seven, is where the child develops their own fully developed roles, characters and complex stories and narratives. It is the first two phases – embodiment and projection – that will concern us here with Annie, a child just under two.

The final theoretical model to consider here is the orientation of the work with Annie; the work is not therapy, even though I am a qualified therapist. Annie does not require specific therapy work; however, like with all children, the work is beneficial from an arts, health and wellbeing perspective. Daykin has suggested that the arts in health movement 'has grown in visibility over the last 15 years, supported by research, networking, advocacy and leadership' (2020:6). Arts and health operate in many diverse areas and largely include 'music, visual arts, dance, drama and creative writing' (2020:6). It is therefore useful to orientate using NDP in this specific context within a story-based arts in health perspective.

We're Going on a Bear Hunt – *the story*

Taking on board these three main notions of story, NDP and the creative arts, Rosen and Oxenbury's (1993) book appears to be extremely useful. From the very beginning we have the strongly defined and drawn characters of the parents, the three children and the dog on the front/rear cover, repeated on the inside title page. The story text is simple and often repeated, enabling very young children to develop language and listening skills. The necessity for an adult/caregiver to tell the story, repeating words regularly, connects with Jennings' (2011) notion of the primary circles of attention. The adult must sit closely as they tell the story. The colourful pictures and clear simple narrative of going on a bear hunt, coupled with such sounds and rhythms as 'swishy swashy', repeated three times to describe running through a field of grass, or 'splash splosh' also repeated three times for walking waist-deep in water, or the 'squelch squerch' sound of walking through wet sand/mud. The spoken phrases connect to Jennings' notion of rhythm and a playful use of words. The extended vowel and consonant sounds aid both listening and pronunciation of words for very young children. Hearing the rhythm of the sounds being repeated gives the child a chance to internally digest and, if developmentally able, verbally repeat.

The story provides an excellent framework so that NDP approaches can be developed verbally, orally, rhythmically and playfully and integrating sensory approaches, leading to developing ideas around the use of sand and water. 'The stumble trip' sounds whilst walking through the forest offer not only movement but a sense of physical balance, that can be practically tried out, and even danger. This is followed by problem-solving skills – 'we can't go over it, we can't go under it', 'we've got to go through it!' A sense of having to face the adventure and the possible dangers, playfully trying things out without the real danger – the purpose of all good play (Slade 1995). Ultimately coming face to face with the bear is the penultimate danger in the story, asking for resilience and finding ways to cope as a family/group; all this resonates with Jung's notion of the 'collective unconscious' or Gersie's notion of finding the answer within the story for how we will all survive. Rosen and Oxenbury's story is probably one of the best stories ever devised for young children at or around the pre-verbal/verbal age range, carefully constructed and perfectly suited to NDP story and multi-sensory play-based approaches.

The storytelling

I worked with Annie in her own home for session one and then in her grandma's house for the remaining sessions due to parental availability. As this is not therapy the boundaries can be looser, the nature of the work is not in-depth in the sense of working with trauma, for example, where a more neutral therapy room might be required. However, many therapists including myself are acknowledging that even therapy might need to take place in the place the child sees as most safe, their own home (Moore 2020).

Session one took place at home. I simply sat on the floor, partly due to my height, in readiness to read the story and share the pictures in the book: '*We're going on a bear Hunt*.' Annie hid behind her mother's legs at first and we thus began a game of 'peek a boo' in order to build a rapport. As I read the story I over-emphasised some of the words and phrases. There was a climbing frame in the middle of the room that became part of the story – it connected well to the telling of the 'over' and 'under' and 'through' elements of the story. At one stage Annie did stamp her feet as if she were in the woods whilst I simply sat and read her the story. As Annie was familiar with dogs, she pointed out the dog every time she saw the picture of the dog in the story; she reacted to seeing the bear with her eyes wide open. Towards the end of our 45-minute session her concentration waned. Her mother said afterwards that she felt Annie had engaged more than she might have expected her to and was chatty in her semi pre-verbal phase. Annie was just developing language and could say a small amount of words as well as making many sounds.

During session two, at her gran's house, Annie was much more receptive, more quickly and less shy. She was again fascinated by the dog and pointed to him every time his picture appeared on a page. During session two I introduced colourful wooden figures, identical to the ones drawn in the book, but slightly bigger. Every time I introduced a figure in the story, I introduced Annie to the corresponding wooden figure. Annie held the figures but did not really manipulate them. This seemed wholly appropriate as Annie was potentially on the cusp between the embodiment and projection phase of EPR (Jennings 2011).

I noticed that Annie was constantly turning the pages backwards in the book as if to get me to start from the beginning again. She would point at some of the exaggerated words as I read them out, not because she understood the written words, but because she could hear me exaggerate and repeat them 'Swishy Swashy, Swishy Swashy, Swishy Swashy'. She seemed more drawn to the pages that were in colour as opposed to the pages that were just black and white.

In session three I introduced not only the story and the wooden characters but also the dry sand tray. The sand tray is a staple technique used in much art and play therapy alongside other therapies such as dramatherapy. Kalff (1973) inspired by Jung developed a psychotherapeutic approach to using sand play using small objects and people with dry or wet sand being used, wet sand being more malleable so that it could be moulded. It is important to remember sand is used in this context with Annie in a non-psychotherapeutic multi-sensory way in order to allow her to feel, touch and explore it in a playful way with an emphasis on sensory-play and creativity from an arts in health perspective.

I began by introducing Annie to the dry sand, in a small rectangular tray[2], allowing it to fall between my fingers, she watched carefully, reluctant to join in. I placed the wooden figures in the dry sand. As I told the story she picked up the dog figure, which she had been fascinated by since the beginning, probably due to her own proximity to two lively dogs at home. She buried the dog in the sand as I told the story. I continued to exaggerate the 'swishing swashing' sounds as the characters walked through what was imaginary water, as no physical water had been introduced yet. Annie then picked up the other wooden characters and began to bury them one by one in the sand. As we got to the climax of the story with the bear chasing the characters home, she buried all the characters in the sand but the bear, which I held. Just as I told the part of the story where the family all jumped in the bed and pulled the sheets over themselves, after safely locking the bear outside, Annie buried the last family member in the sand. Annie was joining in and was beginning to manipulate the wooden figures, burying them in the sand as the characters in the story hid under the bedsheets. There was an element of synchronicity and mirroring, in the way we told the story together. Annie smiled and laughed at the excitement of the story as it came to an end. We then finished the story and placed the characters back into the cloth bag they came from whilst Annie continued to smile and laugh to herself.

At the beginning of session four I again introduced Annie to the dry sand tray. This time I took a cup of water and slowly sprinkled the water into one half of the sand tray; one half was wet, the other half remained dry. I offered the cup to Annie to do the same, but she declined. I hoped she would begin to understand and feel the difference between the sand being in two different states, dry and wet. Annie then put her hands in the wet side of the tray, lifting the sand and allowing it to fall as wet clumps. She then lifted the sand from the dry side of the tray and felt the difference as the dry sand fell through her fingers.

As I began to tell the story Annie began to pick up the wooden characters and allowed them to hop up and down on the sand. She busily began to bury the characters in the sand after listening to the story. For the first time she also began to repeat the phrase 'But I'm not scared' as I said it, and repeated it as I repeated it. As I continued to tell the story she pulled the family characters out of the sand and laid them on top of it, almost allowing the story to take on a role of its own for her (see Figure 12.1).

Annie had now entered the projection aspects of EPR and was able to manipulate the characters well. There had been several weeks between sessions three and four and her gran had pointed out that Annie's language skills had developed significantly between the two sessions. This had been very evident during the session.

What was also apparent in the session was how the notions of over and under, hiding and burying and placing the figures on the surface after burying them began to cement these constructs and notions in Annie's head, alongside her ability to copy and repeat verbal phrases. All of this is central to overall physical, social and cognitive development for a child at nearly two.

In our final session together, I made the sand very wet by pouring three large cups of water into the middle of the sand pit and created a pool of water in the centre. Annie instantly became interested in the very heavy, very wet sand, especially as it formed a puddle in the middle. I then again introduced all the wooden characters from the story; Annie laid them in the puddle (see figure 12.2) before attempting to stand them up by stabbing them into the wet sand. I then finally introduced the wooden bear character. Annie tried to stand the bear up and then laid it down in the sand and blobbed the wet sand onto the bear (see Figure 12.3).

I read the story, but it suddenly became of secondary interest to Annie. The 'splish splosh' of the original story had now been taken over by the 'splish splosh' of Annie's own real story in the cold wet sand. The sensations of the very wet cold sand seemed to take over her senses

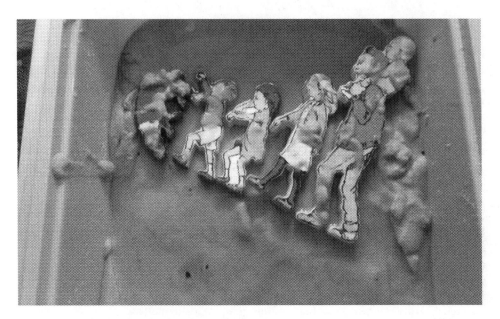

Figure 12.1 Annie placing the characters on the sand

Figure 12.2 Annie placing the figures in the puddle of water

and she continued to make her own silent stories in the sand with the wooden figures. She laid down all the wet figures next to each other in the sand. The wetter the sand the greater physical sensation and interest for Annie in the sand. I realised in this, our final session, that Annie appeared to have absorbed the story I had told over the last few sessions and was now beginning in a very simple and silent way to create her *own* story. It could be argued that at just under two Annie was teetering on the edge of the role phase of EPR (Jennings 2011). Whilst she was not

Figure 12.3 Annie blobbing wet sand onto the bear

verbally telling a story, she was in her own mind using the figures in the sand to begin to create roles and narrative. The story had been internalised and Annie was now beginning to tell her own stories inspired by the original story, the wooden figures and the physical sensations of the water and sand.

Multi-sensory storytelling

The purpose of this chapter has been to consider the notion of merging storytelling with neuro-dramatic play using multi-sensory approaches and seeing how they might not only enhance the telling of the story but enable the child to continue to develop physically, socially, cognitively and emotionally.

Annie is a bright and very well-rounded child at almost two, from a loving caring family; because of this Annie was able to make full use of all the possibilities that were given to her in relation to the experiences we shared together. Firstly, the actual telling of the story, the way the words and phrases had been broken down, and often repeated. The extended, repeated and slowed down sounds and rhythm of the storyteller, to aid listening and speaking skills such as 'S-P-L-I-S-H, S-P-L-A-S-H'. Secondly the visual images in the story, both black and white and colour. The written and visual imagery of different sensations in the story – the sand, the water, the forest, the dark cave, the size and scale of the different characters from the dog, the smallest, right up to the scary big brown bear, the largest. Thirdly the notion of the family/group of characters from within the narrative, everyone working and pulling together, with a defined leader, who is often seen carrying the smallest child. Next the wooden figures, which are exact representations of the figures in the book, including the male adult/father figure carrying the youngest child. All these characters are physically brought to life so that Annie could physically hold and manipulate the characters in the book, outside of the confined pages of the book. Finally, the introduction of dry and wet sand and the agent that moulded them together, the water.

Table 12.2 Multi-sensory storytelling

Story	NDP
The story	Provide primary circles of containment, care and attachment
The sounds of the words (storyteller)	As above but adding rhythm pace & movement
The images	Colours, patterns and shapes
Dry sand	Messy play/embodiment
Water	Messy play
Wet sand	Embodiment
Physical wooden figures	Projection
The child retelling their own story	Role and storytelling

All these multiple levels impact on the positive aspects of Annie's neurological development (Jennings 2011; Cozolino 2006), all in the guise of play without Annie even noticing. The left side of the brain which focuses on language and comprehension alongside the right side of the brain which manages creativity and abstract thought. I would argue that for a child of this age, and maybe too for all of us in order to learn, both sides of the brain need multiple stimulation, at once. This is so that we can engage both rational thought, emotion, feeling and problem-solving skills in a holistic learning experience. Hence learning is fun, and fun is about learning in a holistic and rounded way.

For story to have its full impact, it needs to be multi-sensory (see Table 12.2). Something that to an extent Rosen and Oxenbury have done extremely well in their book; as much as they could within the confines of the physical page. Introducing additional multi-sensory stimulus such as rhythm, movement, physical characters, sand and water assists in taking the story off the page and making it truly multi-sensory.

Conclusion

I acknowledge that as a piece of research, this offers limited empirical evidence as it is based on an observation of one child. Annie was well-adjusted and very bright for her age. However, in conclusion I would argue that if multi-sensory storytelling is very useful for the overall holistic development and education of a well-balanced young child such as Annie; it is even more important for children and teenagers who have had much more challenging beginnings to their lives, due to lack of secure attachment through negative parenting or other adverse childhood experiences. Some children will also have other mental health problems, learning disabilities or developmental issues alongside this. These children may need the same or similar forms of help and work, but probably in the hands of an appropriately trained and qualified practitioner such as a play, drama or art therapist where they might be offered storytelling in a multi-sensory way, as a form of therapy.

However, I would advocate here that multi-sensory NDP approaches have the potential to aid all children's holistic personal, social and educational development and I would encourage these approaches to be used throughout childhood – and possibly into adulthood too!

Epilogue

I recently spoke with 'Annie's' parents, some 18 months after I completed my sessions with her. They tell me that despite the length of time it has been for such a young child, Annie still remembers her sessions with me and on occasion can be heard to say when she is out and about '...*but I'm not scared*'.

Notes

1 Full ethical approval was applied for and given by the College of Health Care, University of Derby, Ethics Committee. Annie's parents gave full written consent for her to take part in this research project and Annie gave physical/verbal consent herself.
2 The sand tray was relatively small due to the need for it to be portable and for me to transport it.

References

Booker, C. (2004) *Seven Basic Plots – Why we tell Stories*. London: Continuum.
Bowlby, J. (2005) *A Secure Base*. London: Routledge.
Campbell, J. (1993) *The Hero with a Thousand Faces*. London: Fontana Press.
Campbell, J., Brown, S. L., Cousineau, P. (1990) *The Hero's Journey*. London: Harper & Row.
Cozolino, L. (2006) *The Neuroscience of Human Relationships*. London: Norton.
Daykin, N. (2020) *Arts, Health and Wellbeing – A critical Perspective on Research Policy and Practice*. London: Routledge Focus.
Gersie, A. (1992) *Earthtales – Storytelling in Times of Change*. London: Green Print.
Hammel, S. (2019) *Handbook of Therapeutic Storytelling: Stories and Metaphors in Psychotherapy, Child and Family Therapy, Medical Treatment, Coaching and Supervision*. London: Routledge.
Holmwood, C. (2014) *Drama Education and Dramatherapy – Exploring the Space Between Disciplines*. London: Routledge.
Jennings, S. (2011) *Healthy Attachments and Neuro Dramatic Play*. London: JKP.
Jung, K. (2014) *The Archetypes and the Collective Unconscious* (Collected Works of C.G. Jung) 2nd Edition. London: Routledge.
Kalff, D. M. (1973) Personal Communication, in Weinrib, E. L. (2004). *Images of the Self, The Sandplay Therapy Process*, pp. xi–xv. California: Temenos Press.
Moore, J. E. (2020) *Narrative and Dramatic Approaches to Children's Life Story with Foster, Adoptive and Kinship Families: Using the Theatre of Attachment Model*. London: Routledge.
Reinke, G. (2014) *Empirical Research Methods Made Quick and Easy: A Guidebook for Practitioners, Students and Researchers*. California: Gold Rush Publishing.
Rosen, M., Oxenbury, H. (1993) *We're Going on a Bear Hunt*. London: Walker Books.
Slade, P. (1995) *Child Play, its Importance for Human Development*. London: JKP.
Sunderland, M. (2000) *Using Story Telling as a Therapeutic Tool with Children*. London: Routledge.

13
MYTH – DRAMA – NARRATIVE – PERFORMANCE

Stelios Krasanakis

Introduction

Dramatherapy draws from many cultural streams and flourishes within many cognitive fields. Dramatherapy itself constitutes a landscape of the encounter of aesthetic, anthropological, psychological, sensory, neurological, creative, performative, societal, radical and other parameters at a theoretical and applied level. It is an enormous funnel, a transformative mechanism, a hybrid that hosts scientific theories, artistic trends, anthropological investigations, social behaviors, psychiatric views and psychological or educational perceptions. One scientific realm with which dramatherapy was linked from its very beginning and which might be said to have contributed to its coming into existence is mythology and this, I consider, was due to Sue Jennings' particular interest in mythology.

Personal narrative

I recall Sue's passion and enthusiasm when she spoke about the Temiar tribe and its myths, already at our first meetings back in 1986, at the beginning of the training seminars for dramatherapy in Greece. I can say I intuited the value of myths through those first inspired classes. Certainly, I had been brought up on myths since childhood and it is as if a mythical axis runs through my entire life. I was born and raised in Crete in a house built on top of King Minos' summer palace, near ancient Knossos. The place where, according to myth, lived the Minotaur and Ariadne. There, in the labyrinth, Theseus unraveled Ariadne's thread.

My childhood memories include many narrations of stories and myths, older and contemporary ones, while our house was built on top of Minos' summer palace, an edifice of many myths, real ones, less real and perhaps not real.

A palimpsest of memories, words, phrases, physical gestures, looks, smells and sounds that comprise the mythical paradise of my childhood, perhaps a personal myth-making of my own.

It is from there that I believe my subsequent love of theatre springs, as well as of psychotherapy and dramatherapy. Because what else can psychotherapy and theatre be than a myth, a play between two or more persons. I grew up in a country where the mythical was constantly present either as ancient drama and history, either that of ancient Greece which both weighs on us and also flatters our narcissism, or as the modern-day stories that reached us from World War II, the civil war or the Junta (1967–1974).

During adolescence, I began to experience the myth of sexuality searching for my own path outside the stereotypes of gender, following my desires and seeking my own private expression. It was then that I decided to shape my personal mythology through art. The arts offered me the necessary exit from daily life and the option of transforming from the position of creator, pain and lack, frustration and disappointment into works of art and creativity.

I remember introducing writing into my life, having invented an imaginary interlocutor, an alter ego, to whom I narrated my everyday in the third person, with the necessary metaphors and, also, dramatic distance. Those were my first theatrical actions and narrations, whose recipients at a later point were my parents or schoolmates. Invented stories and the creation of performances were the games of my childhood.

Gradually, these stories started to infiltrate the fairytales and myths made available to me through education, enriching and expanding their content.

When it was time to go to university, I chose medical school, with its myths of illness, healing and the paramount role of savior, as I then believed. I studied in a city with its own Balkan and Jewish myth, Thessaloniki. There, I also took up theatre studies and met up with its myths. Ancient drama, W. Shakespeare, A. Chekov, T. Williams, S. Becket, Moliere, H. Pinter and their characters started entering my life and exercising a therapeutic, cleansing function.

After my studies in drama and medical school, I was faced with the dilemma of choosing between medicine and theatre. Attending a dramatherapy seminar, "The mythical hero's journey" with Robert Landy in 1986, helped me to decide and showed me a creative life path. My studies in dramatherapy with Sue Jennings followed, under the instruction of Mooli Lahad, Steve Mitchell, Ann Catannach et al. I felt I had met my mentors in the journey with the twelve stages (Campbell) of my hero – my self. Thus, I participated in creating the first generation of dramatherapists in Greece.

After I began practicing dramatherapy, I utilized the psychotherapeutic and theatrical know-how I had acquired to create a performance-based therapy at the Drug Rehabilitation Centre of 18 Ano, where I was employed at the time. The first production was inspired by "I Die as a country", an emblematic, contemporary Greek text, a collective performance taking place in a mythical country, and the second was Tom Stoppard's well-known play *Rosencrantz and Guildenstern Are Dead,* based on Hamlet's myth. The next performance was a play that was a watershed for 20th century theatre, Samuel Becket's *Waiting for Godot.*

Gradually I started to research myths and make use of them in my therapeutic practice, aiming to shed light on the correlation of myths with psychotherapy, their role in expressing what cannot be uttered, cannot be seen, has been repressed, but also in the search for the self's unconscious conflicts and the big questions of existence. I started to excavate the ancient Greek myths, not with the spade of archaeology but with that of dramatherapy, and to discover intriguing findings that were useful and effective in my work, such as:

1. Myths are rich shells enclosing symbols of our culture.
2. Myths function as a large screen on which we may project our inner desires, fears and imaginings.
3. The processing of myths provides an ideal dramatherapy context through metaphor and aesthetic distance.
4. Myths exert a universal influence because they give expression to the unconscious.

5. Myths play an important role in the postmodern period. The success is hardly accidental of films starring the heroes of Marvel or *The Lord of the Rings, The Hobbit or Harry Potter.*
6. Myths possess an archetypal historical structure; changes can be made and different solutions suggested, but these need to be in the direction of a dramatherapy axis.

Concerning myths

As Campbell says (1990), "Myths offer the necessary structure so that man may safely 'transition' to a new 'landscape', and they frequently enact in dramatic form changes that relate to age, social position and someone's particular state of being." Jennings and Minde (1996 p.254) point out that, "The healing metaphors incorporated in myths help people hear the story they need to hear, tell the story they need to tell."

In Greek, "mythos" means a story, a plot but, for us, the term "myth" has more than one meaning. There are national myths, creation myths, myths of transition. The Greek word "mythology", according to Kereny, entails the concept not just of stories (mythoi) but of narration (to utter), a form of narrative which initially caused a resonance because it awakened the emotions when the story personally concerned the narrator and the audience. He concludes that the mythology of the Greeks must be attributed to its original means – i.e. to mythological narrative. Narrative also includes its variations, with the heroes participating each time in a different dramatic depiction or representation.

Often, an imaginary character is inserted in the representation by the author, as a link with Greek mythology. This character will deliver the prologue, introduce the protagonists and describe the costumes and scene, the look of the performance. This character, in a sense, holds the thread of the narration.

Dramatherapy takes up the thread of myths, treating them as meaningful actions, as actions which are amenable to changes and concern the majority of contemporary individuals insofar as they address the collective unconscious.

All our lives are underpinned, pervaded and traversed by a series of contradictory yet inescapable myths, we live and die mythically. Familial myths, urban, national, erotic, moral, intellectual, myths relating to the law, to vocation, power, architecture, sexuality, gender or politics. In Greece, the political myth still holds sway of the Left and the Right, though without the ideological content it once used to have. Issues of gender and alternative orientation that are increasingly coming to the fore in social debate, are to be found in the ancient myths with dual protagonists such as the Centaur, the Minotaur, Pan, Tiresias and also the story of Chryssipus and Oedipus. There are many contemporary readings of myths, and the Iliad itself, through the perspective of gender studies.

The mythologization of myth itself is one of the strongest points of modern semiotics. It is no accident that an advertisement in Athens airport with the motto "Live your myth" actually refers to a brand of beer labeled "Mythos".

Myths are situated outside the field of logic, although they invite investigative zeal and variant, often conflicting, interpretations. As has already been postulated, myths are the primary key which unlocks all of life's secret doors and answers all of its questions in a way that is magical – i.e. unconscious and symbolic. Myths are made, that is to say, from the stuff of dreams.

Myth does not belong to reality, as opposed to the fairytale. The fairytale resembles more the dream, has the same principles (symbolism, displacement, condensation, dramatization, distortion, imagery, secondary process).

Myths have a protean texture and hark back to our primal nature and predisposition. The question emerges of which necessity gave birth to them and what their meaning is. As regards their meaning, there are divergent views. Malinowski (1926 p.79) and his followers maintain that myths mean what they say, whereas the mythologists consider that behind their surface meaning, myths hide another meaning which is the one that gave rise to them. By aligning with the views favoring a determinist interpretation of myths, we miss out on the sense of performance, the narrative, the moment when the different stages emerged and on the transformations that occurred until the present day.

The one thing that is certain is that ancient myths incorporate in themselves not only their historical but also their anthropological-dramatic route.

I believe in the value of processing, reconfiguring, deconstructing myths, rather than in the myths themselves. Let us not forget that many epistemological and artistic approaches, forms and trends arrived at remarkable peaks with myths as their vehicle, creating scientific disciplines and university departments. They have travelled to destinations of paramount importance with minor transport means, such as myths, vessels of simple materials which nevertheless withstood storms and tempests.

Such disciplines are anthropology, philology, linguistics, religious studies, ethnology, art history, psychoanalysis, dramatherapy, semiotics.

It is no accident that the countries where dramatherapy spread, outside of Great Britain and the USA, were those with the richest mythology – i.e. Greece, Israel and the Scandinavian countries. In relation to Greece, although it has benefited from its rich mythology, it has also suffered irreversible damage because of its ethnocentric myths which have shaped modern-day Greeks, who consider their descent from the ancient Greeks as self-evident instead of toiling to establish, demonstrate and, above all, to actualize that continuity in the here and now. Yet, that is how it always happens: cultures first invent their myths and they construct their history afterwards. History and myth are overlapping concepts, blurred and adaptable insofar as history is easily mythologized and myth becomes even more easily historicized.

Cinema has paid particular attention to myths, especially during the periods of national socialism and socialist realism. Many anti-Semitic myths are still being screened, even in films of high artistic value. It is telling that at the time of Brexit, there is an avalanche of British films taking place in World War II, around Winston Churchill, such as *Dunkirk*, *Churchill* and *Darkest hour*.

In the sixties, Greek director Costas Gavras made the movie *Z*, while in his latest film *Adults in the room* he takes up our recent history with former minister Tsipras as his lead character. His other recent film, *Eden is West*, had as its subject the refugees and their incorporation into our country. Historical myths give birth to script ideas and inspire contemporary creators.

What, though, is the descent and origin of myth? Myths begin with the myth of earth's creation, which they not merely describe but also explain. Myth passes down from generation to generation as an intergenerational cultural heritage.

The traditions of all peoples are "the daughters of listening and narration" and by "narration" we mean myths. So, then, myths started as narration and oral tradition, with the genealogies of every tribe as their central axis, and with a particular interest in the mode of presentation. Subsequently, with the word as a vehicle, myth evolved into drama and moved from narration into performance.

We do not know when the recording started of myths, which signifies the end of the mythical period. Poetry possibly precedes history as people were still unable to engage with the written word and opted for oral culture, as Fredrich Schelling points out in *On Myths, Historical Legends and Philosophical Themes of Earliest Antiquity* (1995). He goes on to describe the childlike and innocent spirit we encounter in the ancient myths of different cultures, a fact which resonates with the initial phase of childlikeness and ignorance of every culture, when everything appears strange and exceptional.

In this period of childlikeness, imagination is the most potent psychic function.

The character of ancient myths has, therefore, the character of childlikeness and of things playful. The language of ancient myths abounds in soulful compositions, pictorial imagery and metaphoric representations. Georgousopoulos says that "Myth is one of the elements of tragic mimesis and comprises the principle and soul of tragedy" as Aristotle states in his definition (myth, logos, melos, music, chorus, scenery; 2019 p.67).

Ancient mythic heroes appear with a different psychic aspect and behavior, as is the case of Orestes in the five different tragedies where we encounter him.

During the Renaissance, there is a peaking of the fascination with myths while during the Enlightenment, myths are considered outmoded and unreliable. The toolbox of myths was considered redundant and writers chose to ignore the worn-out and commonplace use of myths. Voltaire (Ruthven, 1977 p.11) thinks that only fools pay attention to myths and Frazer (Ruthven, 1977 p.30), likewise, considers them mistaken explanations of the phenomena of life or nature.

In the ensuing period, the opposite view gains prominence – i.e. that myths are intrinsically, though enigmatically, related to literature. "Mythology and poetry are indissociable" writes Shlegel (1800 p.82) and Wallace Stevens (Ruthven, 1977 p.87) states that, "The most profound novel is Greek mythology." The view prevails that myth was converted to literature after successive "displacements" and through intermediary forms – such as legends, fairytales, folktales, songs etc.

The proponents of this view usually point out that the metaphor is structurally common in myth and literature, although these may differ in their origin.

Is, perhaps, the metaphor a condensed myth or is the myth an expanded metaphor? According to Giambattista Vico (1725–44 p.116) every metaphor is an abbreviated myth. Otto Rank (1932 p.207–31) considers myths the products of metaphors which have been interpreted to the letter.

The aim of historical myths is history and of philosophical ones theory – i.e. the exposition of a truth. Precisely this latter kind of myth is particularly useful to us in the dramatherapeutic process. Myths help in the indirect presentation of a story's truthfulness, thus making it more acceptable.

In my groups, I often tell a story which I heard from Brenda Meldrum. It is about the beauteous "Truth" which came naked down from the mountains to meet the people. She believed she would be made welcome since everyone said they wanted her and loved her. But she was disappointed to find out that doors and windows were shut in her wake and no one wished to welcome her in their home. She sat in a corner and started to weep. Then, she saw coming from afar, clad in the cloak of narrative, her sister who also went by the name of fiction. Everyone was inviting her to their home and seeking her out. Why this different attitude, she asked? Because no one can bear the naked truth, fiction answered, whereas if she wears the cloak of narrative, everyone eagerly accepts her.

The war of good and evil and the search for truth are dominant themes in most myths. At the end of the 19th century, Robert Louis Stevenson writes his own *Fables*. We find here stories with a moral lesson but also humorous ones, with mysterious and supernatural elements, where the imaginary aspect predominates and which operate beyond good and evil. Writers of the magnitude of James Joyce and Thomas Mann return to mythology to immerse their creative imagination. Mann (1987 p.34) says, "Whereas in the life of humanity, the mythical is the archaic and primal stage, in the life of the individual, it is a late and mature stage."

Myth and psyche

Thomas Mann (1987 p.46, p.33), in his 1936 lecture on Freud, says that the title could be "Freud and Myth" as "Psychology is precisely the field which is interested in myth, just as all creative works incorporate an interest in psychology". That happens because "The retroactive incursion of depth psychology into the childhood of the individual psyche is, simultaneously, the retroactive incursion into the childhood of humanity, into the primitive and the mythical."

Mythology itself is group psychotherapy in an artistic guise and, conversely, mythology could be considered a great artistic creation, a fresco that manages to showcase the deeper psychic scene, not merely the individual one but the collective and social in the broader sense. The individual mythology is synonymous with his psychology, as Carl Kerenyi (1995 p.19) points out in his emblematic work *The mythology of the Greeks*. This observation applies not only to the Greeks but to everyone, and forms the backbone of his book.

Myth is defined by H. J. Rose in the *Oxford Classical Dictionary* (1970) as a pre-scientific attempt of the imagination at interpreting a phenomenon, real or imaginary, which arouses the mythmaker's curiosity. He goes on to say that it may also be "the attempt to experience a feeling of satisfaction, rather than discomfiture, in relation to such phenomena", which is a definition rooted in psychology.

The primarily psychological approach to myths begins with S. Freud. Can you imagine what intrapsychic myths might be? Freud asks Fliess in December 1897, a mere three years prior to the publication of the Oedipus complex, and hastens to answer himself, "The vague inner perception of our own psychic make-up gives rise to illusions which naturally are projected onto the external world and particularly to the future and a world that is to come." Freud, then, is the first to speak of a psychomythology after discovering the mechanism of projection in the course of his investigation of paranoia. Five years later, the key to paranoia was found to be also the key to myths, as in *The Psychopathology of everyday life* (2013) he declares his conviction that "a large part of the mythological view of the world which extends to most contemporary religions, is none other than psychology projected onto the external world".

The work of the psychotherapist as delineated in *Totem and Taboo* (1913) is to reverse the processes so that what animism portrays as the nature of things is reassigned back to the human intellect). Freud considered the myth a deposit of unconscious processes, projections of the unconscious). In *The theme of the three caskets* he focuses on Shakespeare's inspiration from myths. Jung rejects the model of the unconscious as understood by Freud and replaces it with the personal unconscious, which at first level is amenable to Freud's theories while at a deeper level, there is the "collective unconscious" whose content is never repressed, is universal and identical in all people.

Jung initially calls the contents of the collective unconscious "archetypes", producing archetypal images which appear in myths, dreams and art – images, that is, which are universal. Jung, in other words, maintains that mythology is the collective psyche and not the individual psyche and that is why it functions psychotherapeutically, explaining to the troubled person what has been happening in their unconscious and keeping them captive. As Claude Levi-Strauss points out, it operates on the basis of a double continuum, an exterior with social and historical conjunctions and one of an interior order, dwelling in the listener's psychophysiological time.

New Mythologies

It seems prophetic of Friedrich Schlegel to demand the creation of a New Mythology in his work "Lecture on mythology" (1800). Indeed, the deeper aspects of human cognition were, as we saw, quickly sounded by Freud's depth psychology; he reached the conclusion that "our Mythology is related to the theory of the instincts".

The New Mythologies, it seems to me, work differently. They do not explain the world; they constitute the world through the dominance of the image; even the text is image. They stand in for nature and create a fictive environment of their own inside which modern people live. The New Mythologies help us understand our world and are the key for decoding society's way of operating.

In what forms does myth present itself to society today?

To the question what is a myth today, Roland Barthes gives the answer, "The myth is logos, it is a mode of signifying, a form to which we ought to give historical limits (and) everything can constitute a myth because there are limits to form, though not to essence" (1973 p.201). Yet, if it was not the word "at the beginning", then, was it maybe the thought or the action? And, if myth came to record a pre-existing ritual, then myth emerged from the ritual and not the other way round. James Frazer in *The Golden Bough* (1890–1915), for which he drew intense criticism from anthropologists as well as from Ludvich Wittgenstein, provides ample evidence to convince his reader that primitive people are deeply absorbed in nature's ritualistic processes.

Next comes the structuralist approach to myths, which gives a purely analytical explanation of myth. Levi-Strauss writes (1963 p.217), "Myth is made up by all its versions and is an open-ended process." And, he continues (1963 p.229), "The aim of the myth is to provide some rational model, capable of overcoming contradiction." Let us take into consideration how myths pass into modern drama and contemporary society and how they reach the present day through modern performances.

In these performative renditions that are part of the cycle myth–thought–society–art–body, as the contemporary high priestess of performance art Marina Abramovic says (1998 p.9), "on stage transpires not a theatrical act but, rather, a truth". Herbert Read (1938 p.178) writes that myth survives thanks to image-making and relaying.

Myths and dramatherapy

The processing of myths in dramatherapy is attuned to the new developments in the perception of myths. It takes up their dramatic aspect, ritualistic stricture, the allegories or metaphors they contain and how it all fuses together into art and therapy. Myths are amenable to the therapeutic process because we can pause the narrative and ask the participants to complete the story according to their own needs, expressing their own internal scene. The more useful aspect of myths is that of mobilizing unconscious fantasies and wishes, which are expressed in the here and now through the actions and which link real events with the mythical versions of the human situation through the aesthetic distance.

The myth "as a composite of collective representations", as Durkheim (Ruthven 1977 p.108) understands it, serves the group's dynamics and cohesion insofar as, according to Jane Harrison (1921 p.32), myth is an integral part of the psyche, a reverie of the people, just as the dream is the myth of the individual.

It appears that dramatherapy constitutes a therapeutic choice of modern people, as it represents their everyday mythologies and responds to their performative needs. Yet, the word is not compromised by the presence of the body; on the contrary, the body itself constitutes a contemporary language which is not subject to censorship. Word and body in an interminable discourse make up the mythology of modern humans, which is tantamount to their psychology.

Working with the myth of Philoctetes

I will present our mode of working by means of myths through the protocol of a workshop based on the myth of Philoctetes – a journey of exploring the landscape of the self. All three of our tragic poets, Aeschylus, Euripides and Sophocles, wrote tragedies based on the myth of Philoctetes, which we find in the *Iliad* and the *Odyssey*, but only the one by Sophocles survives. According to the myth, Philoctetes inherited from his father the kingdom of Magnesia and the alms of Hercules. Heracles had gifted them to him because Philoctetes had lit the redeeming fire for him, while he lay on the funeral pyre. According to the *Iliad*, Philoctetes followed the expedition to Troy with seven ships. A standing prophecy had it that, for Greeks to secure victory for their expedition, they needed to sacrifice at the altar of the goddess Athena on the island of Chrissi. Philoctetes was to be their guide but, on arrival, he was bitten by the temple's guardian snake. His comrades then abandoned him on the island due to the stench of his wound and his insufferable lamenting. After ten years of living there in dire conditions, his comrades came looking for him because of a prophecy by the seer Helenos that Troy would fall by the alms of Heracles and by the hand of Philoctetes. Thus, the oracle of Apollo to Telephus was fulfilled, "*the injurer will be the healer*" (Kerenyi 1995 p.575). Philoctetes was healed and then he killed Paris, thus fulfilling the prophecy. Homer believes that after the fall of Troy, Philoctetes returned to his homeland and lived there happily. Other traditions, however, have him wandering in Italy and founding several cities.

In Sophocles' tragedy, with which we will concern ourselves in a workshop, the island is uninhabited and the hero's loneliness is unbearable. The young Neoptolemos arrives, the son of Achilles, following against his own wishes the plan of Odysseus to trick Philoctetes into joining them with his bow to Troy. Philoctetes is persuaded but a new and terribly painful health crisis drives him to a stupor, forcing him to entrust his alms to Neoptolemos. When Philoctetes comes to, Neoptolemos reveals the truth and asks his consent to take him along to Troy. Philoctetes' lament makes Neoptolemos yield and return his alms, though afterwards he oscillates between his moral judgment and Odysseus' pressure to leave with the alms for Troy. He makes a last attempt to convince Philoctetes to follow them out of his own will to Troy where *supreme glory* awaits him. Faced with Philoctetes' staunch refusal, Neoptolemos decides to take him to his homeland as he wishes, but Sophocles will not overturn the myth. Hercules appears as a *deus ex machina*, reminds the tormented hero of his own trials that led to his deification and convinces him to follow them to Troy and fulfill his duty to his country.

The protocol of the process consists of eight phases and includes between twelve and twenty-four participants. This is a two-day workshop of twelve hours, six hours each day.

Phase 1: To the sound of selected music, we come together, we create a safe space. Bodily movement in space with an exploratory intent, what we seek, what we need, how much we dare, what risks we encounter, we reach the borders of physical tiredness.

Phase 2: Introduction of members, narration of the myth and its variations. Discussion on the hypothesis, mirroring, projections and reconstruction of the myth.

Phase 3: Physical work, walking in space, attempting to move as Philoctetes, Odysseus and Neoptolemos. Interaction between the members through movement in space, clashes, rebuttals and staking claims. Gradually, after experimenting with the concepts of "bow" and "injured body", we are led to the "island" and "the cave with the two entrances".

Phase 4: The group members start to experience physically and verbally the island as the place of trauma, isolation, exile and physical weakness. Depending on the number of the members, they can divide into subgroups and each group work on one of the themes that emerged in Phase 3 and present it through an action or some other creative way.

Phase 5: Each subgroup starts to present its creation.

Phase 6: Regrouping as a whole and reflecting on the process, relationships between the members of each subgroup, connection of the personal with the role we assumed.

Phase 7: A collective free action inspired by the myth's spirit and main themes. It may be a sculpture or a tableaux vivant or a visual installation.

Phase 8: Return to the group and recording of the entire experience in the form of a new myth.

Epilogue

Dramatherapy is a new therapeutic mythology and at the same time, a mythological therapy. Next to the triangle Myth–Thought–Society we may add the triangle Myth–Psyche–Society. If modern myths are the key for decoding our world, by the same key the room of the soul is opened. Therefore, myths appear to be an exceptional therapeutic tool.

Developments assure us on a daily basis that the creative axis of dramatherapy is traversed by the prevalent contemporary mythology of the pictorial, embodied word under which the mythology of modern technology also belongs.

Bibliography

Abramovic, M. (1998) *Performing body*. Milano: Charta.
Barthes, R. (1973) *Mythologies*. Athens: Greek edition Kedros.
Campbell, J. (1990) *The hero with a thousand faces*. Athens: Greek edition Iamvlichos .
Fraze, J. G. (1998) *The golden bough*. Athens: Greek edition Ekati.
Freud, S. (1997) *The theme of the three caskets*. Athens: Greek edition Agra.
Freud, S. (2013) *Psychopathologie Des Alltagslebens*. Athens: Greek edition Nikas .
Freud, S. (2016) *Totem und Taboo*. Athens: Greek edition Nikas .
Georgousopoulos, K. (2019) in *Myth and fairy tale*, p.67 Athens: Editions Nisos.
Jennings, S., Minde, A. (1996) *The masks of soul*. Athens: Greek edition Ellinika Grammata .
Jung, C. G., Kerenyi, C. (1989) *Einführung in das Wesen der Mythologie*. Athens: Greek edition Iamvlichos.
Harrison, J. (1921) *Epilegomena to the study of Greek religion, and Themis, A study of the social origins of Greek religion*. United Kingdom: Cambridge University Press.
Kerenyi, K. (1995) *Die Mythologie der Griechen*. Athens: Greek edition Estia.
Levi-Strauss C. (1963) *The structural study of myth*. New York: Structural Anthropology.
Malinovski, B. (1926) *Myth in primitive psychology*. London: Kegan Paul, Trench, Trubner & Co.
Mann, T. (1987) *Freud and the future*. Athens: Greek edition Govostis.
Rank, O. (1932) *Art and artist*. New York: WW Norton and Co.
Read, H. (1938) *Myth, dream and poem transition*. XXVII, pp.176–92.
Rose, H. J. (1970) *Oxford classical dictionary*. Oxford and New York: Oxford University Press.
Ruthven, K. K. (1977) *Myth*. Athens: Greek edition Hermes.
Schlegel, F. (1968) *Talk of mythology (1800)*. University Park & London.

Shelling, F. W. J. (1995) *Über Mythen, historische sagen und Philosopheme der ältesten Welt*. Athens: Greek edition Thimeli.
Sophocles (1992) *Philoctetes*. Athens: Greek edition Kardamitsa.
Stevenson, R. L. (1988) *Fables*. Athens: Greek edition Agra .
Vico, G. (1948) *The new science (1744)*. Ithaca, NY: Cornell University Press.
Wittgenstein, L. (1990) *Language and ritual*. Athens: Greek edition Kardamitsa.

14
CREATIVITY AND POWER IN SICILIAN SPIRIT
The stories of Giufà, The Wise and The Fool

Salvo Pitruzzella

> If the fool would persist in his folly,
> he would become wise
> *(William Blake)*

If something like archetypes do really exist, there is more than one reason to believe that the Trickster is one of them. First of all, the fact that it is present in many disguises across time and space: the Africanist Harold Scheub (2012) lists nearly 200 different names of characters from all over the world that are, more or less, related to it. Sometimes they are gods, or god-like creatures; sometimes they are talking animals; sometimes they are just human beings: whatever their personification may be, they share some features that, taken all together, describe an enticing and intriguing figure, which seems to speak directly to the hidden or buried parts of ourselves.

In the Western modern age, we can see its persistence in the Fool character, who survives in Carnival and in many figures from both theatre and literature.

In Sicily, my homeland, the traditional character embodying many aspects of the Trickster-Fool is Giufà. He is usually portrayed like a simpleton, sometimes very poor and desperate for food, but in other instances he is a lawyer or a judge. In this role, he carries into the trial his childish logic, which reveals its paradoxical wisdom, helping destitute people to attain a better justice. Therefore, notwithstanding being mocked and disdained, he serves as a symbol of the resistance of the poor against oppression, like the medieval juggler as recounted by Dario Fo.

To some extent, Giufà is a local variation of a character widespread all along the Mediterranean shores, named Guhâ in Arab countries and Nasreddin Hoca in Turkey. However, it is worth noting that in Sicily he had at least two distinguished avatars: Petru Fudduni, stonecarver and literate of the XVI century, and the street poet Peppe Schiera, who lived under Fascism. Many Giufà stories are ascribed to either of them, and sometimes vice versa. The consequence is that these stories are still alive in the memory of Sicilian people.

Tricksters and fools

When in 1912 the American anthropologist Paul Radin first listened to the stories of Wakdjůnkaga from his informer Sam Blowsnake, an old man belonging to the Sioux Winnebago tribe, he soon realized that it was something more than a local legend; indeed, he had encountered a figure that presented a deep psychological value. Wakdjůnkaga the Trickster is unpredictable, morose, mischievous, often irritatingly childish, obsessed with sensual appetites (hunger, lust), at the same time cunning and naive, wise and fool. He is a troublemaker and a chaos-triggering fellow, but he is necessary to put the world into motion. Radin showed his transcriptions to Carl Gustav Jung, who attempted an interpretation of the myth according to his model of human psyche. On the one hand, he sees it as a regressive myth: 'he is a faithful reflection of an absolutely undifferentiated human consciousness, corresponding to a psyche that has hardly left the animal level' (Jung 1972, 176). On the other hand:

> the trickster is a primitive 'cosmic' being of divine-animal nature, on the one hand superior to man because of his superhuman qualities, and on the other hand inferior to him because of his unreason and unconsciousness. He is no match for the animals either, because of his extraordinary clumsiness and lack of instinct. These defects are the marks of his human nature, which is not so well adapted to the environment as the animal's but, instead, has prospects of a much higher development of consciousness based on a considerable eagerness to learn, as is duly emphasized in the myth.
>
> *(Jung 1972, 181)*

In other words, the childishness of the trickster is a sort of invitation to 'reculer pour mieux sauter' (draw back to jump further), a regression to a primitive, undifferentiated level of consciousness, in order to enhance and expand the consciousness itself. In this backwards journey, we might become aware of some qualities concerning life itself: as Radin maintains:

> disorder belongs to the totality of life, and the spirit of this disorder is the trickster. His function in an archaic society, or rather the function of his mythology, of the tale told about him, is to add disorder to order and so make a whole.
>
> *(Radin 1988, 185)*

Meeting the trickster, we engage with an overturning of what is already known, and a challenging leaning into the unknown, because, as Scheub states:

> the trickster is outrageous. Humans move from one state to another, but the trickster's is the liminal state, the state of betwixt and between. Trickster is undifferentiated energy, ungovernable. He may appear tame, but in the next instant he shows that he is not.
>
> *(Scheub 2012, 14)*

However, as noted by Lewis Hyde, 'in spite of all their disruptive behaviour, tricksters are regularly honoured as the creators of culture' (Hyde 1998, 34), by virtue of 'a paradox that the myth asserts: that the origins, liveliness, and durability of cultures require that there be space for figures whose function is to uncover and disrupt the very things that cultures are based on' (Hyde 1998, 36). In this sense, Trickster is an agent of change: to progress, every culture needs a child to reveal that the emperor is naked. 'Trickster the culture hero is always present; his seemingly asocial actions continue to keep our world lively and give it the flexibility to endure' (Hyde, 1998, 9).

Although most of the studies on the Trickster concern non-European traditional cultures, there are many traces of them in ancient Greece, where it was embodied in many mythological figures, the most important being Hermes (the Roman Mercurius). In the Homeric *Hymn* dedicated to him, he is described as a god 'of many shifts, blandly cunning, a robber, a cattle driver, a bringer of dreams, a watcher by night, a thief at the gates, one who was soon to show forth wonderful deeds among the deathless god'. Hermes is the patron of twilight, the liminal state between day and night, and protector of thieves and deceivers, but at the same time he is invested of a very critical and delicate mission: he is the *psychopompos,* the one who escorts the dead souls in their journey to the underworld. It is singular that this attitude of crossing the threshold between life and dead is also one of the features of one of the most famous Italian masks, Pulcinella, who often deals with the Devil and other hellish creatures, and even with Death itself. The philosopher Giorgio Agamben, in his brilliant comment on Giandomenico Tiepolo's paintings of this character, writes that he 'neither belongs properly to the world of the dead or to the world of the living – he is here, irreparably here, in an unreachable elsewhere' from where he can mock both of them (Agamben 2016, 39). Being on the threshold between different worlds seems to be a relevant feature of the Trickster: he 'is a boundary-crosser … We constantly distinguish—right and wrong, sacred and profane, clean and dirty, male and female, young and old, living and dead—and in every case trickster will cross the line and confuse the distinction' (Hyde 30).

What happened to the Trickster in the Modern Age? As Tim Prenkti states: 'the trickster was once deep-rooted in European societies as well, until a combination of church and reason drove him to seek sanctuary in that last refuge of the playful, the theatre' (Prenkti 2012, 13), where we have several well-known Fools, from Shakespeare and Commedia dell'Arte to Brecht and Beckett.

The Fool keeps many of the traits of his mythological forefather, and like him, he is able to play both the stupid and the cunning, the madman and the wise man. Károly Kerényi, in his essay accompanying the joint texts of Radin and Jung, notices that this double condition of the character is well expressed in his own word in the Winnebago tale: 'My, my! Correctly, indeed, am I named Foolish One, Trickster! By their calling me thus, they have at last actually turned me into a Foolish One, a Trickster!' (Radin 1988, 27). But the most outstanding virtue of the Fool is his propensity to social criticism. Like Dario Fo's Juggler, he can sharpen his tongue like a knife to fight the oppressors. This attitude is mirrored in the situation of being an outcast: Fools 'are not seeking an authority for their position and therefore are not concerned with the discourses of power through which all human life is conducted' (Prenkti 2012, 7). The Trickster's liminality is converted into the Fool's not belonging to a precise social class or condition; therefore he can look at what is wrong in the social world with a detached eye.

In the rest of this chapter, I will explore one of the traditional Mediterranean Fool characters, Giufà, who is still alive in Sicilian folklore.

My first encounter with Giufà

'*Un fari comu a Giufà!*' (Don't act like Giufà!). I still remember the words my mother used to say when I acted in a silly or childish way (which, since I was a child, happened quite often). Sometimes, in the evening, she told me funny tales of this strange fellow, who gets into all sorts of trouble and always gets away with it. She had heard them, when she was a child, in her small village in the mountains, from my grandmother, who in turn had learned them from her mother, and so on. None of them had read them anywhere, and we can easily understand the reason why: until a few years ago, the rare editions of Sicilian fairy-tales were known only in academic circles.

The first important collection of them was issued in Leipzig, Germany, in 1870. The editor was Laura Gonzenbach, a Swiss woman who lived in a small community of German-speaking people in the city of Messina. Unfortunately, the work was not translated into Italian for many years; the first unabridged edition is only of a few years ago (Gonzenbach 1999).

Another outsider, Giuseppe Pitrè, made the next important edition five years later. He was a simple doctor 'of the poor', but he deeply loved the people he treated, and their culture too. And from the very voices of his patients Pitrè, in a few years, collected hundreds of stories, most of them from an old woman who had been his nanny. In his lifetime Pitrè succeeded in putting together a complete encyclopaedia of Sicilian folk culture, in the light of what he named 'demopsychology', which means 'psychology of the people', the forefather of what we nowadays call cultural anthropology. For a long time it was even difficult to gain access to this treasure, until, in the mid-fifties of the last century, Italo Calvino compiled his famous anthology of Italian fairy-tales, following a trend that considered the Italian folklore as the foundation of a national identity that was springing up anew from the ashes of the war. Calvino very carefully read all Pitrè's books, rewriting in Italian the ancient dialect that the Palermo doctor had attempted to restore faithfully. Being a writer of great sensitivity and balance, Calvino tried to preserve the sense of wonder, the spontaneity and the naivety of the oral narration. Today, his fairy-tales are present in most primary school books, and many children have the chance to encounter, through the mediation of the school and of the written culture, the echoes of an oral tradition a thousand years old, which seems now on the threshold of definitive extinction.

Going back to my mother, she was a primary school teacher. But in her times there were no fairy-tales in the textbooks. Instead they were crammed with rhymes and short stories conveying moral teachings, and, above all, in good Italian. Instructing everybody to speak and to write in Italian was considered an indispensable pre-requisite for redeeming the underdeveloped South, from both a moral and civil point of view. Therefore, she never spoke dialect with her pupils. It was the language of the women of the house, not even to be used with my father, if children were listening. Only sometimes, when we were alone, in the afternoon when I would sit at her feet while she was doing her needlework, or at bedtime, when she came for my goodnight kiss, would my mother speak to me in the Sicilian language. She recited poems or nursery rhymes, and told me the legends of the saints and the stories of Giufà. These stories were for me part of a warm and comfortable maternal universe, so different from the fatherly world, made of norms and principles, however complementary they are. It is interesting to notice that nearly all the sources of Pitrè (as well of Gonzenbach) were women, the first being the old blanket maker Agatuzza Messia, who had held him in her arms and maybe breastfed him. It is interesting, too, that in the stories of Giufà, his father is never mentioned.

What were those stories telling me? In order to understand, I delved into the backwaters of my memory to recall some of them. Let me try to tell you a couple. The first is called *Giufà and the piece of fabric*.

> The mother of Giufà was very poor. She had saved from her trousseau a beautiful piece of fabric, and one day she said to her son: 'Take this piece of fabric and go to the market to sell it. But don't trust people who talk too much.' So Giufà took the fabric, and went to the market, shouting: 'Tila! Tila! Cu s'accatta a bedda tila?' (Which means: 'Material! Material! Who wants to buy this beautiful piece of material?'). A man approached him, saying: 'How much do you want for it?' 'Oh, no, sir,' he

replied, 'you talk too much. My mother told me to sell it only to people of few words', and he went away, looking for another customer. But when somebody dared to ask the price, the answer was always the same: 'You talk too much.' And Giufà went on walking around all day long, looking for someone of few words. At nightfall, he found himself in a little courtyard. There were no people there, only a plaster statue. Giufà addressed the statue: 'Do you want to buy this piece of material?' Since it did not answer, he thought: 'This is a person of few words, as my mother likes.' And he put the piece of fabric onto the arms of the statue, saying: 'You can pay me tomorrow.' The following day Giufà went back to the courtyard: the statue was still there, but not so the piece of fabric. 'I've come for the money,' Giufà said. The statue did not answer. Giufà said it again and again, but it was still silent. 'Give me my money!' he shouted loudly. No answer. Then he got furious, he borrowed a spade and –bang! – on the head of the statue, which fell down and broke apart. Inside the statue, a jar full of golden coins was hidden. Giufà took them all and came back home. '*Mamà,* you were right: people of few words are the best customers.'

The second story, Giufà *and the brigands,* focuses instead on the childish and playful quality of his behaviour. Although it may look ridiculous, it is just this that protects him from danger, and leads to a happy ending.

> Giufà went into the forest to gather some firewood. He worked until dark, and then he took his heavy bundle of wood, and walked back home. He was so tired, and after a while he decided to stop and have a little rest. He felt the need to do a wee, and he looked for a tree. While urinating, he noticed that the flow on the ground was branching out into three small rivulets. So he began to play with his own pee, pretending to command it: 'You go this way; you go that way, and you turn around.' Not so far away, in a clearing, there was a bunch of brigands sharing their loot. Hearing to these words, they thought the guards were going to surround them, and they ran away. Giufà heard the noise and went to see. He found bread and meat, and he had a good feed. Then he found the loot of the brigands: gold, silver and jewels. He hid them in his bundle and brought them home to his mother. And when the people he met asked him: 'What are you carrying, Giufà?', he answered: 'Nothing, only some firewood.'

Both the stories show some aspects of children's experience that are usually condemned by adults. First, the fits of rage; second, the child's play with his own urine and excrement. In both the stories, the transgressive aspects are those that turn the negative circumstances into positive ones. If I reflect today on what my mother wanted to tell me with those stories, I seem to hear her voice saying:

> Go, my son, the world is yours. Although you are naive and childish, although you can appear hot-tempered and even obscene in your spontaneous way of expressing yourself, although you may be laughed at, you are the hero of your life.

Giufà in the Mediterranean world

What I was then oblivious of is that these stories, that for me were part of my private world, were actually shared by countless people, far beyond the time and space of my little world, and far beyond Sicily itself.

Francesca Corrao in her well-informed study on this character, writes: 'the first written report on Giufà dates from the VII century and it is from an Arabian source. The anecdotes referring to him are widespread within an area extending from the Mediterranean to China' (Corrao 2001, 135). The Arabian Giufà is named Guhâ, but he can take different names in the various regions. In Morocco he is Zha, Gawhâ in Nubia, Guhi in Persia, Djoha in Israel. In Turkey he is called Nasreddin Hoca, and it is recounted that his stories had been introduced there by Gialal ad-din Rumi, the great Persian poet and mystic of the XIII century. According to Corrao, the Arabian Guhâ acts in absurd and paradoxical ways; the Persian Guhi mocks religious orthodoxy; and the Turkish Nasreddin severely criticises social conventions.

All these aspects are present in the Sicilian Giufà, within a particular framework: from a social point of view, he is a *pariah,* a social outcast. His house is poor; he is fatherless, and he has an ambivalent relationship with his mother: sometimes she is an ally when he does his misdeeds, when she thinks she might benefit from them; more often, she harshly reproaches him, denigrates him and even deceives him. He is unfit to have a job: he is often considered not only a *babbu* (fool) but also a *foddi* (madman), because he thinks in a different way from the others, as we have seen in the two stories I have just told you. Or perhaps, like Pulcinella, he is simply too lazy to work.

However, often his naivete, which can also be considered as innocence, supports him, and helps him to overcome the obstacles. In many stories his paradoxical way of thinking, comparable to children's concrete logic, serves to defend the poor from the vexations of more rich and powerful people. Here is one:

> A poor man had bought a piece of bread at the market, but he had no more money to buy something to eat with it. There was a butcher grilling meat: how good it smelt! The poor man approached and put his piece of bread just into the smoke of the meat, to pick up its smell, and ate it quickly, enjoying his meal. The butcher said: 'You must give me money for the smoke you stole.' But when he saw that the poor man had nothing to give him, he took him to court. The lawyer was Giufà, and he addressed the judge with these words: 'Your honour, my client is willing to pay what is due.' Saying this, he took out of his pocket a silver coin, threw it on the bench so that it rebounded, and he put it quickly in his pocket again. Then, he turned to the door and went away. The butcher stopped him: 'You said that the man was going to pay me.' 'Yes', Giufà replied. 'So, where is my money?' 'For the smell of your meat, the sound of my coin is more than enough.' The judge agreed with him and the poor man was set free[1].

Giufà the fool as an avenger of the oppressed and the outcast? Let us try to analyse this aspect more in detail, looking at the way it has been preserved in Sicilian folk culture.

Some avatars of Giufà in Sicily

In the XVII century, when Sicily was under Spanish domination, a rather singular person lived in Palermo. He was a stonecarver and a poet, and even his name sounds like a legend: Petru Fudduni. (*Petra* means stone, and *Fudduni,* though it comes from a French word with a completely different meaning, is similar in sound to *foddi,* madman.) It is told that he was illiterate but that he had a prodigious memory, and that in his youth, like the old Diogenes, he had been abducted and sold as a slave by pirates, by whom at that time our seas were overrun. Some of his written poems have been conserved, one of which is dedicated to Rosalia, the patron saint of the city of Palermo, but he is still more famous as an improviser: poet laureates came to visit and challenge him, and *Mastru Petru* answered back, with a coarse wit that often bordered on obscenity, always beating his opponents. The king himself would come to discuss with him, and Fudduni looked upon him as his equal. Here's a story:

> The king, having heard about this unlearned poet who stood up to wise men and scholars, decided to go and see him. When he arrived, Fudduni was intent on his job. Abruptly, the king asked: 'Tell me, Fudduni, what is the truth?' Keeping his eye on his work, the poet answered: 'That of the lamb.' The king was astonished by the promptness of the answer and by what looked like a refined theological reference, and insisted: 'So, what is the truth of the lamb?' And Fudduni quickly replied: 'A futtuta ca cc'arresta, poviru armali'. Which is a rather unrefined way of saying: 'The fact that he always get screwed, poor beast!'

The interesting fact is that, in the collective memory, many stories of Giufà, which can be identified through a comparison with the Arabian tales, are ascribed to Petru Fudduni, and vice versa: anecdotes about the latter, easily recognisable for the modern historical setting, are attributed to Giufà. But let's go further along our road, to visit an incarnation of our character in quite recent times.

Giuseppe Schiera was born in Palermo in 1898, and there he died in 1943, a bombing victim. Although many people considered him no more than a good-for-nothing vagabond, he was very much appreciated as a street poet. On market days, he would jump over a wooden box, and improvise satirical rhymes to an audience which had gathered, who would reward him with some money, a cigarette or something to eat. It is said that during the fascist period, of which he was a fierce adversary, every time Mussolini came to visit Palermo, he was preventatively put in jail. His rhymes were of this tenor:

> U duci
> nni cunnuci
> contru u palu da luci
> (Mussolini is leading us to bang into a lamppost).

It is likely that he was not punished more severely just because he was considered a bizarre personage, half-crazy: in brief, a sort of Giufà. Can a period of little more than half a century be enough in order to make a real person become a legend? And, what is more, with no support of the mass media? I am not able to answer to this question. I can only report that I have heard not only some rhymes, often the more licentious, by Fudduni attributed to Schiera, but also anecdotes having him as protagonist, which were actually modern adaptations of stories of Giufà. What is the sense in this curious overlapping? My sensation is that it arises from the collective need to perpetuate the memory of a figure that expresses a dignity that becomes necessary in order to survive in a human way even in difficult times, in times of poverty and oppression. We must not forget that the history of Sicily goes back very far, and borders on legend, a history of endless invasions and dominions, punctuated with short revolutions, often suppressed in blood. This transpersonal dimension has always been a peculiarity of the Sicilian spirit, and it is apparent in two opposing tendencies: on one hand, giving in, sometimes with a dash of cowardice, sometimes with a caustic attitude. On the other hand, the pride and the courage to stand up against all odds, even risking one's own life. The events of the 'war against the mafia' of the nineteen-nineties have shown it once again.

Being and appearing

Having worked for many years in the psychiatric field, I find it very useful to work with stories. Exploring various kind of stories, people can experience different possibilities of existence in a safe and gentle way, achieving a sense of mastery that can be transferred to life. And the more stories are shared, the more they may be invested with meaningful feelings for the group.

A few years ago, I was running a workshop in a psychiatric day centre. I had been working with that group for a year, and we had passed through different stages together, in the beginning exploring their fantasies, and finally coming down to earth with stories of everyday life, staged with sagacity and humour and, above all, with a great sense of collaboration. After the summer holidays, problems arose in the place we were working in, so we moved into a very small church, now deconsecrated, which was built in the XVII century beside an old abbey that later became the first nucleus of the psychiatric hospital of Palermo. It was a place loaded with symbolic connotations, therefore. An ancient place, that invites us to wonder about our own roots: where do we come from, and how did we get here? It was a place within the walls of the hospital, the old 'lunatic asylum', that many of them had known from the inside, and it was felt by everybody to be an indistinct threat. The first period of this new phase of the group process was devoted to exorcising these ghosts. Gradually, the group began to loosen their initial tensions, allowing itself moments of free searching. Nonetheless, a vague sense of uneasiness was still hovering about in the group, a sort of feeling of being too small and weak before the imposing circumstances of which that place had been a witness.

One evening, seated in a circle, after a ritual of welcome, we were discussing what to do, when somebody asked: 'Does anyone know the stories of Giufà?' With great surprise, I noticed that people knew the same stories I knew, the stories my mother had told to me. The first to come out were the shorter stories, those that are told like jokes. As always, the first figure that appears is that of the simpleton, who makes us laugh at him, while at the same time keeping our distance. Then we heard the stories in which the foolishness of Giufà is revealed as wisdom. The story everybody loved the best (which someone ascribed to Fudduni), and that we decided to play, was one in which these two elements coexist.

> The king's daughter was going to get married, and his majesty had organised a great wedding feast, inviting all the people in the town. Giufà went to the palace gates, asking to get in. But the guards, seeing him so dirty and dressed in rags, blocked his way. Giufà insisted, but there was nothing to do about it: vagabonds were not admitted. Therefore Giufà went back home, had a wash and a shave and borrowed from his neighbours some clean clothes and a beautiful feathered hat. When he went back to the gates, he had no problems getting in. Inside the palace, he found a table laid with all sorts of food. Giufà approached, took a plate of spaghetti and squashed it against his chest, covering his entire jacket with the mess. Then took a bottle of red wine, and poured it into his pockets. Then he grabbed a creamy cake and smeared it down his trousers. The guests were astonished watching all these things, thinking that he was crazy, and when they got near to him to ask the reason for that bizarre behaviour, they heard him saying: 'Manciati, vistiteddi mei, ca vuatri fustivu invitati!' (Eat up, eat up, my dear little clothes, for you have been invited.)

All the group members are involved in the scene, playing the king and the queen, the princess, and all the other guests, nobles and knights. The role of Giufà is taken by Natale, a young man in his early thirties, with a severe bipolar disorder; he lives with his mother, who has never taken his disease seriously and regards him as nothing more than a slacker. When he is feeling better, Natale cares very much about his appearance, and he gets upset when he sees the beggars; he often comments: 'I would rather die young than come to that.' Gioacchino, the philosopher of the group, plays the palace guard. He is quite the opposite of Natale: he is old and he has worked all his life as a policeman. He retired when he started having serious mental disorders after being wounded in a gunfight, and being in a coma for some time. He is a well-educated person with an open and alert mind, yet he is always dressed in a slovenly way. The improvisation begins, with the guests greeting each other and beginning to enjoy the party. When Giufà comes through the door, we witness a quite paradoxical scene: Gioacchino, with his unkempt beard and a filthy scarf around his neck, calls a well-dressed and well-groomed Natale a 'tramp'. He involves the whole group in his reproach, and the group takes the challenge, playing it out in an exaggerated way, with an irresistible comic effect. Natale looks really annoyed when he goes offstage; the next part is not played but told: 'Then I had a shower and I put on clean clothes, and then I went back to the feast'. When on stage again, he gets near the table and starts acting just like the others, quietly eating and drinking. There is a suspended moment: maybe Natale has felt too involved, has not found the proper distance from the character, and has decided to change the end of the story? The group begins to be nervous. Then Natale, taking a large imaginary plate in both hands, looks us in the eyes one by one with a wide, sly smile, and with a theatrical gesture pours over his head a shower of spaghetti with tomato sauce and fried aubergines. At this point all the guests, including the guard, after a short moment of astonishment, begin to do the same. Some do it with the wine, some with the salad and some with the cakes; what until a moment ago had been an elegant banquet is transformed into something half-way between a dionysiac orgy and a potlach, the ritual in which all the saved-up riches are done away with, in order to recommence the day after, poor but renewed. It is also a great children's play, in which we can laugh at our own inhibitions and fears.

Around the foolishness of Giufà, a joyful knowledge has condensed: that we can just be as we are, whatever we are forced or condemned to appear. After the session, a patient approached me, saying: 'Do you want to know what I would like to do? I would like to continue to be mad, but just a little.'

Note

1 It is worth noting this story, with an Arabian cook as a protagonist, appears also in *Il Novellino*, a traditional collection of short stories dating to the XIII century, probably written at the intercultural court of Frederick II.

References

Agamben, G. (2016) *Pulcinella, ovvero: divertimento per li regazzi*, Nottetempo, Roma.
Calvino, I. (1956) *Fiabe Italiane*, Einaudi, Torino.
Corrao, F. (2001) *Le storie di Giufà*, Sellerio, Palermo.
Gonzenbach, L. (1999) *Fiabe Siciliane*, Donzelli, Roma.
Hyde, L. (1998) *Trickster Makes this World: Mischief, Myth, and Art*, Farrar, Strauss and Giroux, New York.
Jung, C. G. (1972) *Four Archetypes*, Routledge & Kegan Paul, London.
Pitrè, G. (2013) *Fiabe, novelle e racconti popolari siciliani*, Donzelli, Roma.
Prenkti, T. (2012) *The Fool in European Theatre. Stages of Folly*, Palgrave Macmillan, London.
Radin, P. (1988) *The Trickster. A Study in American Indian Mythology*, Schocken, New York.
Scheub, H. (2012) *Trickster and Hero: Two Characters in the Oral and Written Traditions of the World*, The University of Wisconsin Press, Madison.

PART III

Stories & therapeutic texts in educational, social and community contexts

Introduction

In Part III we consider stories and therapeutic texts in a slightly broader vein, in the context of education, and social and community settings, some of which have a therapeutic aspect to their work. Of course these broad areas share some common ground in that educational influences are not just seen in the formal classroom but reach wider into diverse international communities of vastly different social and cultural contexts.

We begin in the UK with Chapter 15 with Sarah Telfers' research into using anecdotal stories as a pedagogic tool in the classroom for those learning English. We then move to South Africa with a short chapter by Vincent Meyburgh and colleagues that explores Orature and Aurality as delivered by his community Jungle Theatre Company, which works with children and families. Staying with the theme of story in a community theatre context in Chapter 17, local actor and playwright Richard Vergette considers the importance of story and community theatre in relation to audiences in the North of England. This is then contrasted by Seniha Naşit who relates the stories of her native Cyprus in Chapter 18, offering how they might be used in the community in a therapeutic way. Similarly in Chapter 19, Lenka Fisherová and Ilona Labuťová consider practical approaches to stories from their native Czech homeland.

We move back to the UK in Chapter 20, where Nicola Grove and colleagues describes their 20 years' experience of working in the community using story with children and adults with learning disabilities. Chapter 21 considers the work of Lani Peterson and her 'Public Voice Project' (PVP) in Boston USA, where her vast experience using her PVP storytelling workshops in the community is shared with us. We follow this with social healing through community-based storywork offered by Inger Lise Oelrich in Sweden. Contrast returns in Chapter 23 with Josephine F Discepolo Ahmadi's work. Originally from Chicago she was brought up in her adopted homeland as a child in rural Irpinia in Italy. She describes her experiences of being gripped by stories of the '*caporaballo*,' who traditionally lead dances during the local festivals. Finally in Part III we move to The Cameroon, in Africa, where Victor Jong Taku considers the use of local oral tales as a way of moral transformation for children and young people.

15
THE USE OF STORYTELLING AS A PEDAGOGIC TOOL IN THE ENGLISH LANGUAGE CLASSROOM

Sarah Telfer

Introduction

There is an Indian proverb which states: Tell me a fact and I'll learn. Tell me a truth and I'll believe. But tell me a story and it will live in my heart forever. This chapter explores the practice of storytelling as a pedagogic tool in English language teaching and learning, offering an overview of its different uses. It makes reference to the use of storytelling in English language teaching with English for Speakers of Other languages (ESOL) learners. ESOL learners are often young adult or adult asylum seekers or refugees, who bring stories to the classroom in the form of life experiences from their own cultures, based on their beliefs, customs and language identity. The most effective story tasks draw on 'funds of knowledge' (Moll et al., 1992) from the learners themselves, enabling them to bring existing knowledge, skills and creativity into the classroom, taking a social practice approach to learning (Schwab, 2015). Storytelling can act as a stimulus for teachers' creativity and imagination, offering benefits and opportunities for both teachers and learners to participate in storytelling as part of classroom practice.

What is a story? What is storytelling?

The National Storytelling Network (2016) defines storytelling as an ancient art form and a valuable form of human expression, describing it as the interactive art of using words and actions to reveal the elements and images of a story while encouraging the listener's imagination. Storytelling in its basic form can be defined as the telling or writing of stories, which can take the form of oral face to face storytelling, or written stories in print or online.

The words 'story' and 'storytelling' can be found in a variety of art forms and be described in many different ways. Synonyms of the word story include: a narrative; a tale; a fable; a recital; or an account; it can be defined as a set of events or series of happenings which can be true or fictitious. A story can be a real or imagined account of events that describes experience. The terms 'story' and 'narrative' are often used interchangeably. However, some research defines a story as an 'informal' account of a lived experience, in contrast to a narrative which is a more 'structured' interpretation of story, which includes additions and omissions by the author

(Connelly and Clandinin, 1990; East and colleagues, 2010; Haigh and Hardy, 2011 cited in Drumm, 2013). Kirkpatrick et al. (2007:38, cited in Drumm, 2013) propose that 'storytelling is the individual account of an event to create a memorable picture in the mind of the listener', suggesting that storytelling lends itself well as a pedagogic tool in a classroom setting.

Storytelling as art and culture

Some practitioners discuss the 'art' of telling stories (British Council, 2014). Storytelling is the one of the oldest of arts passed down from generation to generation as a means of explaining and understanding the world. Families use stories to transmit principles, social history and cultures; they are used to entertain and to instruct, to moralise and warn, and to ensure the cultural survival of memories. New members marry into families and bring varying interpretations and historic perspectives. Fairy stories and legends are a part of every culture, in addition to love stories, adventure stories, ghost stories and religious stories, all of which can express information about different countries and cultures.

Storytelling offers opportunities to widen awareness and respect for diverse cultural backgrounds, and developing learners' schema. Linguistic scheme theory was first applied to linguistics by Bartlett (1932). He noted that when an American Indian story was told to British people, they adapted the details when retelling it to fit with their own schemata, adding in familiar frameworks and leaving out unfamiliar ones. Nair (2003) notes how stories appear to have evolved across cultures, defining a good story as one that can be taken away by its listeners and/or tellers and repeated in other conversations, contexts or cultures. Storytelling widens our awareness and understanding of our own culture as well as other cultures, offering a sense of shared belonging to a group. Collaborative storytelling tasks can be socially interactive as well as individual. They encourage students to work in cross-cultural groups on more complex tasks, encouraging a pooling of knowledge and offering multiple perspectives.

Cultural stories, fairy tales and folk stories can be used to communicate certain messages such as morals, warnings and religious beliefs. When we retell stories we adapt them to suit a different audience and context. Aspects of stories can be exaggerated for dramatic effect, the danger here being that when fact crosses over to fantasy, the story can change dramatically. When cultural stories are passed on they run the risk of being adapted and even misrepresented as the learners add their own opinions, cultural views and their own perspective to what they are trying to convey. We relay our own understanding of the story that has been told to us, which may not be honest, accurate or true to the original version. It could be argued that this is unavoidable and a part of the natural oral tradition of storytelling, as stories are passed from culture to culture. Vladimir Propp (1895–1970) in the *Morphology of the Folktale* (2010) discusses thematic approaches to storytelling based on content. He suggests that fairy stories and folktales contain common themes, events and characters and are similar in structure. Therefore, students from all nationalities, ethnicities and backgrounds are likely to recognise international structures and themes, identifying with them. Fairy stories have been easily adapted and new stories evolved by changing the sequence of events, setting, characters or narrative voice, or even changing the medium – e.g. from an oral story to a written one with words and storyboard pictures. Therefore stories are fluid, often adapted, extended, exaggerated and delivered in different forms.

The narration of stories and language learning

It is interesting to examine how the narration of stories is related to the benefits of language learning. In storytelling, narrative discourse is the presentation of an event or series of events;

events might include significant occurrences that might be linked or related to each other. Narrative storytelling skills can incorporate the practice of quite complex discourse skills such as: description, exposition (background information; setting up the story, characters, setting and problem) and persuasion (argumentation) (Rudd, 2014). Dialogue can be defined as a conversation informed by a narrative; in this way language will be used to encourage the concept of dialogue within storytelling activities, highlighting its function as a tool for seeking knowledge and consensus (Abma and Widdershoven, 2005).

Stories' narration can be told from the view of different narrative authors – for example: stories practising the use of the first person using 'I', 'me' or 'my' from the narrator's point of view; the second person usage of 'you' is common in more oral narratives e.g. 'If you would like to hear more'; or third person 'they'. These different narrative views allow students to practise different forms of narration in their productive skills (speaking or writing), or to be exposed to different narrations in their receptive skills (reading and listening) in different genres of English – for example: the third person is often used in newspaper reports to narrate external events. More advanced students could be encouraged to use multiple narrative forms in their storytelling, allowing for differentiation. Stories from lower level English classes might begin as forms of 'covert' narration, relaying more factual information without the use of speech tags when used in reported speech in a story (ibid). Story narration offers opportunities to practise a mixture of different tenses, using the simple past or reported speech to relay completed finished events, whereas dialogue or direct speech remains in the present tense, using simultaneous narration forms. The narration of religious stories or fairy stories often uses future tenses – e.g. 'the lord will come down'; psycho-narration forms in stories are used to report thoughts, feelings or sensation (ibid).

Oral narratives allow students to practise storytelling 'performance' and the relaying of physical events and body language. Labov (1972) explored the structure of oral narratives of the Black vernacular culture of inner-city New York in 'Language in the city'. He identifies that storytellers will need to go through the following processes:

- ***Abstract*** (preface, way in) – What is the story about?
- ***Orientation*** – Who was involved, when, were? Background to the story.
- ***Complicating action*** – New thing that happened.
- ***Evaluation (persuasive)*** So what? How/why interesting?
- ***Resolution/Result*** – What finally happened?
- ***Coda (back to reality)*** – Connection of story to speaker, to audience, to the here and now.

Storytelling as a stimulus for creativity and participation

Creativity has been recognised as significantly important by educational policy makers in recent years (Craft, Jeffrey and Liebling, 2001), emphasising how it offers empowerment. Simmons and Thompson (2008) discuss how creativity is often viewed by teachers as freedom from the restrictions of narrow and centralised curricula, and focused measured learning outcomes. Craft, Jeffrey and Liebling (2001) suggest that creative teaching offers teachers 'creativity of empowerment', resulting in 'effective pedagogy'. De Bono (1989) highlights the importance of developing creativity in every possible aspect and states what a great motivator creativity is when engaging the teacher's interest. Indeed it can be argued that creativity is the most important human resource of all for teachers.

It can be argued that there is a 'participatory' element to storytelling that involves both the storyteller and the audience. Professional educators need to understand each learner's 'story' based on their personal background in order to meet individual needs not just as learners but as different human beings. An individual's lived experience over time, their position in the world, their history, culture and socio-political influences, have helped to shape them into the human being they are now (Goodson and Gill, 2011).

Spiro (2007) describes storytelling as a 'sub skill of social life' during which we exchange information about imagined events and events that have really happened, inviting audience participation and sharing ideas of ideas. Effective story activities can bring the whole language learner into the classroom: experiences, feelings, memories, beliefs.

Storytelling can seek to understand the lived experiences of learners and can be used in the first class where learners are encouraged to get to know each other by exchanging personal details and information and swapping life stories. A good story requires accurate information, but crucially it needs a personal angle, combining fact and emotion together to tell an engaging story. How the story gets told depends on what needs to be communicated, who we are talking to and what medium we are using (Kenton, 2011).

With regard to ESOL learners, Mallows (2014) advocates a *'Participatory ESOL' approach* to teaching English language which draws out and builds upon the story of students' experiences to develop a shared critical understanding of the world. Bryers, Winstanley and Cooke (cited in Mallows, 2014) define a participatory ESOL classroom as one which is driven by ESOL learners' exchanges, these exchanges being always relevant and meaningful to the learners' lives.

Anecdotal stories can be used to initiate a 'participatory approach' to storytelling such as the use of personal anecdotes as story forms in the classroom. Teachers often use personal anecdotes unconsciously to help discussion along, to give examples and to encourage students to offer their own anecdotes. It can be argued that encouraging students to tell their own anecdotal stories, rather than the teacher's examples, 'offers learners the message that the language used in the classroom is theirs, not given to them to use by the teacher' (Bryers, Winstanley and Cooke, cited in Mallows, 2014).

Stories form a large part of daily communication patterns, often in the form of a longer narrative, establishing context, developing the story with description, building expectation, suspense etc. Many daily colloquial story exchanges relate to work, home and past experiences. These anecdotal stories are often repeated to other people. Teachers often start classes with anecdotal stories of what happened at the weekend and encourage learners to join in. It could be argued that anecdotal storytelling by a teacher counts as valid teacher talk time as it encourages reciprocal storytelling opportunities for students, thus promoting student talk time in the classroom; when teachers tell an anecdotal story in a shared context we are offering our learners understanding and empathy. 'Spending time talking to your learners, telling stories – as long as they are engaging – is almost certainly a good thing for their learning process' (British Council, 2014).

Heathfield (2014) discusses how retelling stories in their own words can help students build up rich mental images and story mapping techniques, which enable them to enter a vividly imagined story space. Retelling anecdotal stories to an audience in a classroom setting might focus on the use of reported speech – for example, reporting the gist of a conversation that took place in the past, allowing learners to organise speech in a way that would alert the audience to important material (Shafaei, 2012). The novelist Philip Pullman (2014) states that after nourishment, shelter and companionship, stories are the thing we need most in the world. Storytelling can offer learners an opportunity to share stories and motivate them to participate in storytelling by using activities which appeal directly to their interests and concerns, rather than as a vehicle to practise 'target language' (Cooke and Roberts, 2007). Many learners bring storytelling skills from their own cultures, based on their beliefs, customs and language identity.

Oral communication and storytelling traditions are essential in some communities where the spoken word is relied on to communicate, as access to other forms of literacy is not possible. ESOL learners learn through their own schemata. Members of communities and the wider society participate in events and practices in which they frequently use oral language, drawing on skills that are both personal to them and cultural or social in origin (Hughes, 2010:265).

Nelson (1989) states that the storytelling experience is a vehicle for enhancing understanding, both literal and inferential: motivating oral discussion; increasing and promoting interesting language usage. Storytelling can indeed be an effective teaching and learning tool to aid learners in becoming more proficient in speaking and understanding a new language, as before students can achieve proficiency in other skills such as reading and writing, oral language is one of the most important means of learning and of acquiring knowledge.

Storytelling as a pedagogic tool in the ESOL classroom

A recent research study entitled *An Investigation into the use of Storytelling as a Pedagogic Tool in the English for Speakers of Other Languages (ESOL) classroom* (Telfer, 2017) was conducted with trainee teachers training to teach in the Further Education (FE) and Skills Sector. The study analysed the reflections of trainee teachers' experiences of using storytelling as part of their teaching practice in the ESOL classroom where they were teaching teenagers and adults. The purpose was to map how storytelling was applied, modified and reflected upon by trainee teachers and how the strategy of encouraging trainee teachers to implement more untraditional approaches to their practice impacts on their professional development.

Results and findings were based on: the observations of ESOL teachers using story activities in their classroom; the teachers' reflections of using storytelling after their lessons; and the responses of ESOL learners to their teachers' use of stories in language teaching. The research analysis focused on the responses and evaluations of trainee teachers and ESOL learners on their perceptions of the effectiveness of storytelling as a pedagogic tool to enhance language and literacy skills development.

The aim of using storytelling activities in the ESOL classroom was to encourage a shared social practice through which explicit and tacit knowledge could be transmitted and identities acquired (Boje, 2001). The objectives were to explore different uses of storytelling to engage students' interest, allowing learning to take place more readily and more naturally, in a meaningful and interactive communicative context (Fitzgibbon and Wilheim, 1998).

The study was based on the supposition that storytelling can offer language practice in the safe and relaxed environment of a classroom, encouraging friendly and co-operative interaction between classmates. It was anticipated that this would lower learners' anxiety so that English language acquisition could take place more easily; that in a comfortable learning environment students would be more likely to develop language from their participation as both speakers and listeners, learning to respect the opinions of others. As a result, it was hoped that this would promote turn taking and encourage students to generate dialogue and develop ideas by listening to and telling stories from a variety of cultures, whilst identifying the similarities and differences. Trainees were encouraged to devise their own story activities and use a range of storytelling mediums in the ESOL classroom, which would enhance learner engagement and interaction and promote language communication skills, therefore developing interactional language by encouraging learners' socialisation in literacy learning. This is one of the primary goals of language learning, as learners need the ability to competently interact in social situations, by engaging in social practices – both inside and outside of the classroom. This competence is achieved through socialisation in the language classroom; interactive storytelling activities can be used to promote English literacy and language skills and engage learners in 'language socialization'.

The research study also hoped to capitalise on the multi-diverse classrooms attended by young adults and adults who bring shared life experiences and understanding of the world to the ESOL classroom from their home languages and cultures, thus providing important contextual resources for storytelling which are salient to the learners. Savvidou (2010) states that storytelling is a way of thinking about experience valuing the individual's view of the world. As storytelling is a feature of language interaction and the main focus of English language teaching is to develop learners' speaking and listening skills, it was hoped stories could be used to encourage learners to communicate effectively. The specific educational and social benefits of using storytelling with second language learners are numerous and well researched, especially with regard to children. According to Wilson (1997) including storytelling in the curriculum can improve the level of learning in all four language skills. The concept of storytelling is grounded in theories of speech communication, that is to state that storytelling is inherently dialogic, so that whenever a story is told it provokes a response (Bakhtin, 1986). It was hoped that this would be the case in the language classroom.

One of the most prevalent findings identified in the study was the successful use of anecdotal stories to engage ESOL learners and most noticeably the use of personal anecdotes by teachers to elicit empathy, raise 'schema' or tune learners into a subject area. The use of personal anecdotal stories by teachers was also seen to act as an 'appropriate modelling approach' to aid the process of language acquisition (Bandura, 1977). The use of anecdotal stories by learners was reflected in accounts of their autobiographical storytelling but was also reflected in anecdotal stories told by the teachers themselves. The use of personal anecdotal stories appeared to make the teachers 'more human'. This was also successful in eliciting 'return' stories in response from the learners themselves. Teachers reported that they learnt a lot more about the learners individually in such exchanges, describing how this process acted as a 'warmer' and 'ice breaker'. This finding links to Barton and Hamilton's (1998) Social Practice Theory, identifying how literacy is essentially an interactive social practice between people. The exchange of anecdotal stories can be viewed as an interactive social act based in the social, economic and cultural context in which ESOL learners learn.

Anecdotal stories were viewed as an effective pedagogic tool which was used effectively by both the teacher and by the learner. The use of anecdotal stories was seen to promote natural practice of communicative discourse, encouraging learners to produce incidental inductive language through stories, without the fear of making mistakes. This can be built into lesson time and should be considered worthy of pedagogic value, using learners themselves as a valuable teaching resource.

Findings also indicated that anecdotal stories can be used as an opportunity to engage learners in informal communicative discourse, examining new perspectives whilst developing language skills in a naturalistic context. The results of the study suggest that the sharing of stories offers students exposure to new realities, offering opportunities to establish a wider network of experiences, by taking a social constructivist approach to learning. This suggests that teachers should actively encourage the use of anecdotal stories in class and consider them as valid teacher talk time (TTT), using them as ice breakers and warmers to engage learners, eliciting empathy to add a more human element to the teacher–student relationship; in addition to tuning learners into topic areas, modelling examples of language structures; but also as a valid listening activity.

The research presents a strong argument for the use of anecdotal stories in all subject areas, not just ESOL and language teaching. Such stories can be used to draw learners in, frame

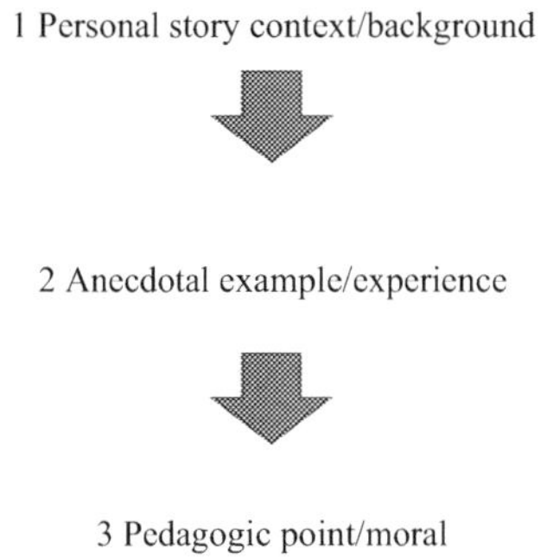

1 Personal story context/background

2 Anecdotal example/experience

3 Pedagogic point/moral

Figure 15.1 'Model'

an activity and illustrate a pedagogic point. An effective model can be seen to operate as follows: teacher sets up the background context to the story; gives an anecdotal example of what happened; follows with a pedagogic point (see Figure 15.1).

Personal anecdote stories can often follow a universally recognisable pattern, 'this is what happened to me', 'this is what I learnt from my experiences', thus informing learners. The study identified that learners respond well to such personal anecdotal stories as they add a human element to teaching and learning, indicating that the most effective story tasks were authentic so that students could attach personal meaning and experience to the story, applying it to their lives, thus suggesting that storytelling tasks in general need to be framed around 'real life' situations. Authenticity of materials, such as true stories and contextualisation of story tasks with relevance to the learners, would appear to be a key consideration when choosing story materials, as all language is inextricably linked to context (Halliday, 1973).

The study also indicated that storytelling provides good opportunities for teachers to develop professional creative autonomy. The findings indicated that trainees were able to implement storytelling creatively in a wide range of contexts with various groups of learners in different level classes. Storytelling as a pedagogical tool was used in various forms, from unplanned impromptu uses when demonstrating a grammatical or lexical point, through to pre-planned anecdotal and routine classroom uses with innovative approaches and materials designed by the trainees themselves. Key findings therefore suggested that storytelling can offer teachers opportunities to develop autonomy within the classroom, enhancing creativity, adaptability and flexibility when using storytelling tasks in teaching.

Mishra and Henriksen (2013) suggest that teachers should contemplate the use of innovative and creative methods in lessons, to meet the educational needs of the new generation. All in all, trainees demonstrated highly creative and imaginative approaches, some devising a whole lesson around storytelling and story making, utilising all four skills and collaborative learning. All materials were written and devised by the trainees themselves; resources were tailored to the context of their individual ESOL learners' needs, demonstrating an understanding of not only pedagogical skills but also of the 'aesthetic' value of stories. The trainee teachers' reflective accounts demonstrated a mostly positive impact on the implementation of storytelling on their professional development, which is mainly reflected in the components of attitudinal and intellectual change to teaching and lesson delivery, with good evidence of positive behavioural change. The key findings of the study indicated that storytelling provides opportunities for teachers to develop their creative autonomy in the ESOL classroom. It highlighted the importance of anecdotal stories in engaging learners and suggests that with careful planning and sensitive consideration of storytelling materials, stories can be used as an effective pedagogic tool in teaching and learning.

However, it also indicated that for some learners the fear of speaking publicly or making mistakes can inhibit their creativity in storytelling, suggesting that ESOL teachers need to reassure learners that mistakes are an inevitable part of learning a new language; and that the most important thing is to attempt to communicate and take part. This reassurance should form an essential part of preparing the ground when setting up a story task. This will allow the teacher to establish an open and relaxed atmosphere conducive to learning, by creating a supportive atmosphere to reduce learners' anxiety about the inclusion of peer collaboration and the scaffolding of story tasks.

The findings of this study highlight the benefits of using creative storytelling activities to develop teachers' English language teaching skills. Indeed Ofsted promotes the use of new ideas and approaches in teaching and learning, stating: 'teachers are encouraged to be innovative and creative and to try different approaches and take risks' (Ofsted, 2014:22). Simmons and Thompson (2008) discuss how creativity is often conceptualised by teachers as the liberation from the confines of a restricted curriculum. This assertion is supported by Dewey (1916), who states that teachers should be free to be 'an intelligent medium of action' in their classroom.

Morgan and Rinvolucri (1983) suggest that storytelling is the language teacher's oldest technique and the findings of this study suggest that it is one that teachers can adapt to be creative in language teaching. This research has identified that ESOL teachers, when given the freedom and opportunity to be autonomous, will use creative and innovative approaches to language teaching, using their own subject specialisms and past learning experiences as a springboard to inspiration. Therefore, it suggests teachers should be encouraged and supported in trying out new and creative storytelling techniques in their ESOL classrooms, experimenting with storytelling techniques in all four skills and tailoring their storytelling activities to develop the skills their ESOL learners need for progression and employment opportunities.

This study also suggests that perhaps more trust should be placed in trainee teachers' creative capacities to use what appeals to them in teaching and learning. Burnard and White (2008) suggest that 'creativity' or 'freedom and control' has significant implications for pedagogy and propose a 'rebalancing' in which a higher trust is placed in teachers' professional judgement. Richardson (2015) supports this, noting the importance of greater respect for the insights of teachers. Teacher reflections analysed in the study would seem to indicate that when trainee teachers are offered the opportunity to be autonomous, it results in imaginative engagement, enjoyment and more resourcefulness in teaching and learning. This research study (Telfer, 2017) identified that creative storytelling tasks can be tailored to suit an ESOL class, developing learners' wider skills in areas such as communication, presentation skills, research and collaborative team work. It can be argued that these are the 'Functional English' Skills which ESOL learners need in order to participate effectively as citizens in a new cultural society.

The findings of the study present a strong case for the use of storytelling not just in the ESOL classroom, but in all classrooms. This might be because, as Drumm (2013) suggests, the use of stories places the person at the centre; adds richer dimensions to understanding; engenders empathy; encourages reflection; and aids learning and development. Research indicates that while storytelling has been extensively used in the pedagogy of teaching young children, it has been used less so as a pedagogic tool for young adults or mature learners. This might be due to conceptions of storytelling activities being linked to pedagogy for younger learners, and therefore considered as inappropriate for adult learners. This study suggests that story activities are just as appropriate as a pedagogic tool for adult learners as for younger learners. In addition, it is important to note that many ESOL class cohorts in Further Education include a high proportion of young adults from different cultures and backgrounds, some of whom are forced to attend classes to improve their English to access other courses. This has resulted in diverse ESOL classes and more difficulty engaging learners with low levels of motivation, so ESOL teachers need to apply more creative teaching strategies when approaching language teaching to be effective.

Conclusion

This chapter suggests that storytelling activities and strategies can elicit a high level of eclecticism and creativity into pedagogy, and hence encourage the professional growth of teachers. It can be argued that storytelling can be a very effective and multidimensional pedagogic tool that covers a number of teaching and learning aspects required in not just an English language class but all classrooms, regardless of subject area. Storytelling activities can address social and personal issues that lie at the very heart of extremely diverse cohorts of classes, while simultaneously supporting communication processes that enable learners to explore, test and practise language in meaningful communicative contexts. In addition, storytelling activities can encourage learners to use more extended narrative forms in written and spoken work, thus providing excellent feedback for teachers to observe the progress and needs of their learners.

Richardson (2015) discusses the connections between narrative, nation, classrooms and values. He argues that the discussion of values by learners and their teachers through storytelling dialogue can help to promote greater respect and insights into new communities, particularly in the fields of citizenship, history and religious education, thus providing opportunities for teachers to embed so-called 'British values' within the classroom curriculum. He goes on to argue that education should develop participation skills and 'a reservoir of shared images, insights, and stories'.

Story activities not only allow both teacher and learner to establish a cultural and personal identity in the classroom, but also offer opportunity to exchange knowledge and understanding of different perspectives, this being very pertinent in multilingual language classes containing many different nationalities. Stories offer opportunities for both ESOL students and teachers to develop oral skills that have political, social and economic address, thus offering literacy emancipation, power and freedom. It could be argued there are powerful political, moral and ethical elements to storytelling. Therefore story activities can act as a rich reservoir to explore the individual values that our learners live by.

Bibliography

Abma, T.A. and Widdershoven, G.A.M. (2005) Sharing stories: narrative and dialogue in responsive nursing evaluation. *Evaluation and the Health Professions*, 28 (1), pp. 90–109.
Bakhtin, M.M. (1986) *Speech genres and other late essays*. Edited by: McGee, V.W. Texas: University of Texas Press.
Bandura, A. (1977) *Social learning theory*. Englewood Cliffs, NJ: Prentice Hall.
Bartlett, F.C. (1932) *Remembering: an experimental and social study*. Cambridge: University of Cambridge Press.
Barton, D. and Hamilton, M. (1998) *Local literacies: reading and writing in one community*. London: Routledge.
Boje, D. (2001) *Narrative methods for organizational and communication research*. London/Thousand Oaks, CA/ New Delhi: Sage University Press.
Bordine Fitzgibbon, H. and Hughes Wilheim, K. (1998) Storytelling in ESL/EFL classrooms. *TESL Reporter*, 31 (2), pp. 21–31.
British Council (2014) *Premier skills storytelling*. [Online] Available from: http://premierskillsenglish.britishcouncil.org/teachers/professional-development/storytelling [Accessed 22 November 2014].

Burnard, P. and White, J. (2008) Creativity and performativity: counterpoints in British and Australian education. *British Educational Journal*, 34 (5), pp. 667–682.

Connelly, M.F. and Clandinin, J.D. (1990) Stories of experience and narrative inquiry. *Educational Researcher*, 19 (5), pp. 2–14.

Connor, M. and Pokora, J. (2007) *Coaching and mentoring at work: developing ethical practice.* Maidenhead: Open University Press.

Craft, A., Jeffrey, B. and Liebling, M. (2001) *Creativity in education.* London: Continuum.

Cooke, M. and Roberts, C. (2007) *Developing adult teaching and learning: practitioner guides – ESOL.* Leicester/London: NIACE/NRDC.

De Bono, E. (1989) Six thinking hats. Harmondsworth: Penguin.

Dewey, J. (1916) *Democracy and education: an introduction to the philosophy of education.* (1966 edn.) New York: Free Press.

Drumm, M. (2013) *The role of personal storytelling in practice.* IRISS Insights, No 23. [Online] Available from: www.iriss.org.uk/resources/role-personal-storytelling-practice. [Accessed 20 November 2014].

East, L., Jackson, D., O'Brien, L. and Peters, K. (2010) Storytelling: an approach that can help to develop resilience. *Nurse Researcher*, 17 (3), pp. 17–25.

Goodson, I.F. and Gill, S. (2011) *Narrative pedagogy. Life history and learning.* New York: Peter Lang Publishing.

Haigh, C. and Hardy, P. (2011) Tell me a story – a conceptual exploration of storytelling in healthcare education. *Nurse Education Today*, 31, pp. 408–411.

Halliday, M.A.K. (1973) *Explorations in the functions of language.* London: Edward Arnold.

Heathfield, D. (2014) *Storytelling with our students: techniques for telling tales from around the world.* [Online] Available from: http://iatefl.britishcouncil.org/2014/sessions/2014-04-02/student-storytellers-retelling-tale-using-mental-imagery#sthash.PPyOeyru.dpuf [Accessed 30 October 2013].

Hughes, N. and Schwab, I. (2010) (eds.) Teaching adult literacy: principles and practice. Maidenhead: Open University Press.

Jeffrey, B. and Craft, A. (2004) Teaching creatively and teaching for creativity: distinctions and relationships. *Educational Studies*, 30 (1), pp. 77–87.

Kenton, N. (2011) *Telling stories: the uses and misuses of communicating for change.* [Online] Available from: www.iied.org/telling-stories-uses-misuses-communicating-for-change [Accessed 6 April 2013].

Labov, W. (1972) *Language in the inner city: studies in the Black English vernacular.* USA: University of Pennsylvania Press.

Mallows, D. (2014) *Language issues in migration and integration: perspectives from teachers and learners.* [Online] Available from: https://esol.britishcouncil.org/sites/default/files/Language_issues_migration_integration_perspectives_teachers_learners.pdf [Accessed 15 June 2019].

Mishra, P. and Henriksen, D. (2013) *A NEW approach to defining and measuring creativity: rethinking technology & creativity in the 21st Century.* [Online] Available from: http://punya.educ.msu.edu/wp-content/uploads/2013/08/tech-trends-9-13.pdf [Accessed 11 July 2014].

Moll, L., Amanti, C., Neff, D. and Gonzalez, N. (1992) Funds of knowledge for teaching: using a qualitative approach to connect homes and classrooms. *Theory Into Practice*, 31 (2), pp. 132–141.

Morgan, M. and Rinvolucri, M. (1983) *Once upon a time: using stories in the language classroom.* New York: Cambridge University Press.

Nair, R. (2003) *Narrative gravity: conversation, cognition, culture.* New York: Routledge.

National Storytelling Network (2016) *What is storytelling?* [Online] Available from: www.storynet.org/resources/whatisstorytelling.html [Accessed 26 July 2019].

Nelson, O. (1989) Storytelling: language experience for meaning making. [Online] Available from: www.jstor.org/discover/10.2307/20200160?uid=2452662975&uid=3738032&uid=2&uid=3The Reading Teacher pp360-390 [Accessed 4 June 2015]

Ofsted (2014) Teaching, learning and assessment in Further Education and Skills. [Online] Available from: www.ofsted.gov.uk/resources/teaching-learning-and-assessment-further-education-and-skills-what-works-and-why [Accessed 20 October 2014]

Propp, V. (2010) *Morphology of the folktale.* 2nd ed. Austin: University of Texas Press.

Pullman, P. (2014) *Philip Pullman* [Online] Available from: www.philip-pullman.com [Accessed 4 June 2019].

Richardson, R. (2015) British values and British identity: muddles, mixtures, and ways ahead. *London Review of Education*, 13 (2), pp. 37–48.

Rudd, D. (2014) *How are things narrated? (1) Narrating the World (II).* The University of Bolton.

Savvidou, C. (2010) Storytelling as dialogue: how teachers construct professional knowledge. *Teachers and Teaching: Theory and Practice*, 16 (6), pp. 649–664.

Schwab, I. (2015) *Training to teach adults English*. Leicester: NIACE.

Shafaei, A. (2012) Frontiers of Language and Teaching. *Proceedings of the International On Line Language Conference*. (IOLC 2011) Volume 2: Florida, USA: Brown Walker Press.

Simmons, R. and Thompson, R. (2008) Creativity and performativity: the case of Further Education. *British Educational Research Journal*, 34 (5), pp. 601–18.

Spiro, J. (2007) *Story building*. Oxford: Oxford University Press.

Telfer, S. (2017) *An Investigation into the use of Storytelling as a Pedagogic Tool in the English for Speakers of Other Languages (ESOL) classroom:* A thesis submitted in partial fulfilment of the requirements of the University of Bolton for the degree of Doctor of Education.

Wilson, J.A. (1997) *A program to develop the listening and speaking skills of children in a first grade classroom*. [Online] Available from: http://files.eric.ed.gov/fulltext/ED415566.pdf [Accessed 4 June 2014].

16
CALLERS AND HEARERS

Song, orality, orature and aurality in African theatre performance

Vincent Meyburgh, Ntombifuthi Mkhasibe, and Joce Engelbrecht

Today's South African children often grow up disconnected from their own traditions. Grannies in a township context are far from a rural lifestyle and often find it difficult to uphold the oral tradition of storytelling for children. Theatre for children, young people and families is a space in which reconnections can be made, but within modern paradigms.

Jungle Theatre Company use children's and family theatre to promote our vision of a society that is environmentally, socially and culturally conscious and active. As an award-winning, dynamic non-profit and public benefit organisation since 1995, we bridge the divide between commercial and community theatre. We create original proudly South African productions that use the mediums of multi-lingual storytelling, visual puppetry, live music and physical theatre and are accessible to all.

We often involve a narrator that directly links to the audience encouraging them to participate and tell parts of the story in English, Afrikaans and isiXhosa. Our style is still as visual and musical as possible to transcend language and hold the attention of children. This interesting dynamic between what can be narrated and what can be portrayed theatrically through visuals and sound is a dynamic we constantly play with. How much needs to be explained and how much will the children work out for themselves? How much do we leave up to the imagination?

Our natural heritage is still abundant and accessible to many regardless of class or culture. It is also more and more topical as it gets increasingly threatened. JTC draws from a traditional and modern connection between culture and nature as a back ground to developing theatre.

'Umlambo Wobomi' – River of Life

One of our plays called *Umlambo Wobomi – River of Life* (2010) is a story told to one of our actors by her grandmother. It's about a village that lives by a river that fulfils their every need. The people of the village forget to take care of the river and the fish decide to teach them a lesson by drinking up all the water. Once the villagers clean the river the fish spit all the water out and the village's livelihood is restored.

Like many stories from oral tradition the plot is simple and the story teller can improvise at length within the confines of the main plot. The story is not owned by anyone; it belongs to all humanity. However, stories from specific cultures also need to be respected. I heard of a theatre director who worked with actors on a new portrayal of a Maori myth. When they performed this myth for the elders of a rural tribe, they were very upset. The portrayal had strayed too far from the original story. I suppose in a culture that does not write stories down one needs to be rather strict on telling the originals so as not to lose the stories.

In bringing this story to the children of today and onto stage we did the following, the isiXhosa clan name Mamlambo came to light. The name means mermaid and this led to the mermaid princess, a universal archetype in our play. These universal archetypes have been kept alive in the mass media by Disney and are therefore accessible to many South Africans. At the same time the clan name Mamlambo is very specific to tribal life in the Eastern Cape and the isiXhosa culture.

A current character called ma1010 that is known in modern townships as a salesman of cheap but breakable products became the source of the litter in the river. This character became the symbol of advertising and was performed in the tone of so many advertising jingles that also are in the mass media.

The core cliché of 'My King!' accompanied by a kneeling gesture was repeated throughout the performance, much to the delight of the children. They enjoyed this repetition and started joining in every time the king was greeted in this way during the show.

When drought destroys the village the king decides that their only hope is to ask advice from the Sangoma that was previously exiled from the village. Nobody in the village dares to visit the Sangoma far off in the mountains apart from the princess. Her father gives her a necklace passed on by her great grandfather and sends her on a prophetic journey guided by her ancestors including her late mother. This necklace is symbolic of heritage being passed on. It is a tangible physical image that represents the inheritance of special talents.

The princess goes on a journey through a windy desert, a forest full of scary creatures, and climbs a slippery mountain cliff. This entire journey is portrayed with mime, sound effects and music: the protagonist imagining the environments and the other performers creating them with their voices and musical instruments. Here the descriptive element of storytelling is replaced by theatrical devices that go beyond the spoken word yet stimulate the children to imagine these environments. In creating these scenes, the actors improvised orally the descriptions of the environments and then presented them to the group. One was chosen and retold as a basis for the non- verbal communication.

The character of the Sangoma re-establishes the princess's ancestral connection to the river and its creatures. She learns to speak to the fish and finds out what their current environmental needs are and motivates the village to take action to restore the balance of nature. In the end she becomes a mermaid so that she can facilitate communication between people and river creatures for always.

This play uses the context of a tribal village affected by modern consumerism as a symbol of modern township life. How can we get involved in transforming our world by re-establishing our connection with our natural and spiritual world and accessing our own power?

Jungle Jive

Jungle Jive (2004) was a story told by a spirit of nature. This narrator gets the audience to help free a tree from a cage controlled by a robot and the tree gets planted as part of the performance.

Taking this show on tour we performed at a few schools around Hermanus during the week. We invited the children to return with their parents and friends to watch the show at the local community centre on the Saturday. When the Saturday came, we had a large crowd of children in the hall but very few parents. The excitement was very high. We waited for the children to settle down so we could start the show. There were too few adults around to help us to get the children to be quiet. We tried everything to calm them down. I had tried everything I knew and was sitting in the corner chanting a Buddhist mantra.

Eventually our evil robot character gave them a talking to and threatened to send the children out who were not giving us a chance to tell the story. This quieted them down so we started the show. After a few minutes the children started chatting amongst themselves again. We tried to carry on with the show but it became impossible and we cut the performance short. Afterwards I spoke to some of the adults who were sitting among the children. They said that the children who had already seen the show had brought their friends who had not. They were so busy telling their friends about the show that they could not quiet down.

Next time we call the children to bring their friends to an event related to the show we will get them involved in retelling it. This will be in the form of a workshop that sets up storytelling games, telling the story one sentence at a time to describe it. We will cast them as the characters and sing the songs with them again.

Many times the songs we sing in the shows are remembered by the children. When we leave they sing the songs for us and when we return they will have remembered the songs from the previous show and they will sing them for us. These songs seem to be powerful triggers for the imagination and for participation from the audience. Songs that get repeated all through the performance are learnt and children sing along. Often children will pick up on a little idiosyncrasy that is a hook for participation. The key for participation is to challenge your audience enough so they don't feel stupid but make it simple enough for them to feel confident. Start with simple small interactions like a greeting. Then make an honest comment on their reaction, e.g. 'Hello when I say hello you say hello XAM because that is my name'. React positively to whoever does respond to your interaction and build on those who are participating.

Current productions

Our latest production is called *Metamorphosis* and is almost totally non-verbal. It uses spectacular stilt costumes, drumming and mime to portray the life cycle of a butterfly. The only words in the play are sung at the very end 'We love to Play in the garden' in English and isiXhosa. This is a curtain call and it is a comment from the actors directly to the audience. This way we leave the audience with the essence of our performance in their language in the form of a song that they learn to sing and take home with them.

Our next production will bring an ancient Khoikhoi story to life as street theatre with large costumes and loud music. This kind of theatre performed at festivals aims to bring theatre-going audiences together with people on the street who are surprised and drawn into the show, as well as being accessible to all ages.

Often after our performances in schools we will call a group of 30 learners who have seen the show to a workshop that explores the themes of the story further. They sing the songs from the story, imagine and interact with the environments, become the elements, plants, animals and people.

Firstly we ask them who remembers the song from the show and sing it with them. Then we invite learners to imagine a location from the show like Boulders beach. We describe the sound of the waves, feel the warm sand and the cool water, the taste of the salt in the air, smell the penguin poo and the flowers in the trees. Ask them to see a penguin in their imagination and describe the black and white feathers, the floppy feet and flipper wings.

Explain that when you clap your hands, use shakers or drums in a rhythm you will perform a magical ritual that will turn them all into the penguins they see in their imagination. Then clap your rhythm and watch the magic happen. Invite the penguins to swim, run and eat and other activities. Shake out the penguin character. This game will encourage learners to create credible characters and give them a glimpse of the cultural ritual of transformation performed by ancient Shaman.

Then invite them to re-tell the story. In a circle each one gets a chance to tell part of the story until the facilitator points to the next one in the circle, who will continue where the previous teller stopped. Children normally need guidance with this game to remember the sequence of the plot.

Conclusion

Jungle Theatre aims to challenge the ethics and morality of imported media, and offer something more intrinsic to the cultures we are serving that both reconnects children to their communities and histories, and challenges them to see beyond their current circumstances.

References (theatre performances)

Hoerikwaggo (2014) Jungle Theatre Company.
Jungle Jive (2004) Jungle Theatre Company.
Umlambo Wobomi (River of Life) (2010) Jungle Theatre Company.

17
BEYOND THE HAPPY EVER AFTERS

How stories in a local English theatre can have a therapeutic impact on their audiences

Richard Vergette

Let's start with controversy: a playwright isn't always a storyteller. In John Yorke's definitive manual on script writing, *Into the Woods* (2014), esteemed playwrights Eugene Ionseco, Harold Pinter and Samuel Beckett don't merit so much as a mention. *Waiting for Godot* (1953) might be a work of existential genius but try serialising it so each episode ends with a cliff-hanger; you'd be better off serialising a phone book. *Godot* was famously referred to by the critic Vivian Mercier as the play in which 'Nothing happens twice'.[1] It is no less brilliant for its lack of linear plot, its circular structure essential in creating a sense of despair and repetition. Great dramas, therefore, do not always rely on great stories. Even if a story is intricate, its moments of greatest dramatic intensity may not be due to sudden or exciting plot developments. Macbeth's monologue excoriating the meaninglessness of life (*Tomorrow and Tomorrow and tomorrow, creeps in this petty pace from day to day, to the last syllable of recorded time*)[2] does not move the story on in any significant way, any more than 'To be or not to be' from *Hamlet* does. These are moments of reflection, insight and realisation that are focused on character and we, the audience, listen to them, learn from them and are moved by them. Of course, the character does not bring a halt to the story to share their reflections; we are drawn in by their reflections and self-evaluation and become concerned for their fate as the play progresses. Story isn't always the dominant dramatic ingredient!

Sometimes, however, a play might connect with an audience, at least initially, because of factors beyond either story or character. Many towns and cities during the late 20th century and early 21st century created or commissioned 'Community Plays'. These are plays which might feature a story from the city's past or might invent a new story where the city or town is the overarching backdrop to the story – i.e. the place itself becomes the major dramatic ingredient.

Director and playwright Rupert Creed lives and works in Hull and for many years was the Artistic Director of Remould Theatre Company, a community theatre company focused on regional stories and local history. Among many distinguished works, Creed devised the play *The Sea Shall Not Have Them* (1996), a community play involving literally hundreds of citizens from the town of Bridlington. The play focused on two stories of lifeboat disasters from the town's maritime past. That these stories were already well known to some of the audience enhanced the sense of engagement rather than diluted it. So too did the involvement of many local actors. The ingenious staging involved converting the interior of the town's leisure centre into a 19th century harbour, so that as the audience entered, they were immersed in that world. The sights and sounds of 19th century Bridlington Harbour were fantastically recreated, and there was more than a sense of ownership of the play by both cast and audience. Whether there is a strictly therapeutic value to seeing elements of one's community's past is debatable but the sense of pride and the impact of the tragedy were palpable. Interestingly, although the lifeboat disasters had both occurred beyond the living memory of any member of the audience or cast, all were profoundly moved; partially, of course, because the story was emotive, but talking to some audience members after the show it was because it was 'their story'.

Creed says, 'The stories have to really get under the skin of the participants and the community.'[3] Somehow the story has to fire the company's imagination and their spirit. He told me of one community play that had failed because its author had tried to focus on a story which showed the community in a less than positive light. 'This can be the problem', says Creed. 'Occasionally you find yourself leaving sections of a story out or including other sections against your better judgement as a playwright, but because it's important to the community and the community insists on it'.[4] This presents us with an interesting paradox dramatically; the better drama may not always be the better community play, if part of its purpose is to add to the sense of well-being enjoyed by the community. Therapeutically, perhaps, the play has to give its participants a boost, not make them feel embarrassed or awkward about their town's past.

This almost proprietorial instinct reinforces the notion of ownership of stories by a community and is hugely important. Sometimes, however, it may not specifically be the stories themselves that create the sense of ownership so much as the tradition of storytelling. For example, the cycles of Mystery Plays are an important part of the cultural traditions of three UK northern cities: Wakefield, York and Chester. There is also a fourth cycle named the Ludus Coventriae, identified as being from the East Midlands, although the precise town isn't known. The stories they tell, of course, are not specific to the towns from where the plays originate; they tell the Christian view of the world in a cycle of plays starting with *The Creation* and/or *The Fall of Lucifer* and culminating in *The Resurrection*.

The plays were sponsored by trades or guilds and often the guild was related to the play being sponsored; for example, from the Wakefield Cycle, the Goldsmiths sponsored *The Visit of the Magi* (possessing the right materials to provide the 'gift' props!) and the Carpenters sponsored *Noah's Ark*. These were plays where part of the community effectively made as well as performed the productions and other parts of the community watched. In an increasingly secular society, it may be thought surprising that these plays are still being performed, yet they provide the same focus and sense of pride as any community play. In the year 2000, I was one of 250 performers who took part in Mike Poulton's adaptation of the York Mystery plays staged in York Minster. Some of us were keen amateur and would-be professional actors, others were simply happy to be involved. In his programme note, director Greg Doran commented on the wide variety of motives that had brought the cast together. There were clearly some who had joined the cast for social reasons, to alleviate loneliness, to participate in a community event, to have a hobby or to meet people. Is there a therapeutic dynamic to this involvement? Yes, if by involvement in such a project, someone is meeting their emotional as well as cultural needs. However, involvement of this type is not the same as a therapeutic impact of seeing a story. Given that this production played to 30,000 people over a four-week period, presumably some of that audience were moved by the religious content of the plays, others by the spectacle and others by the language. And equally, many of those members of the audience were from way beyond the boundaries of the community of York. Good grief, we even got a few critics from London and the Radio 2 celebrity, Canon Roger Royle!

There are other examples where stories pertinent to specific communities might have wider appeal beyond that community. David Edgar's *Entertaining Strangers* (1986) started life as a community play for Dorchester written in 1985. Here, the story which Edgar alighted on was not particularly well known – indeed he was warned off making obvious choices so far as the community was concerned. In his foreword to the published edition of the play he comments:

> I also discovered that the town was definitely not interested in my writing about any of its three main claims to fame, and perhaps reasonably felt it needed a play about the bloody assizes, the Tolpuddle martyrs and/or Thomas Hardy like a hole in the head.[5]

Ultimately after a number of discussions, particularly with the play's director and fellow playwright, Anne Jellicoe, Edgar focused on the story of the Reverend Henry Moule, a fundamentalist Christian who ministered the parish of Fordington (Dorchester's slum suburb) during a cholera outbreak in the 1850s. In Edgar's play Moule, also an advocate of temperance, clashes with Sarah Eldridge, founder of Dorchester's leading brewery. The story was impeccably researched and was a successful community project. However, it found even greater and wider appeal when it was redrafted for production at the National Theatre in 1987. In redrafting the play, Edgar adds somewhat wryly that 'In reworking the play for the more modest resources on offer at the National Theatre, I've been able to develop and…deepen the relationships of the central characters, and I've allowed myself considerable leeway with their history.'[6] This supports Rupert Creed's earlier observation that when writing a Community Play the wishes of the community might hold sway over the playwright's instincts; historical accuracy is perhaps more of a major concern when the play is playing to and involving the community. When adapting the play for a wider audience, a different set of criteria might be applicable. The sense of the play being of therapeutic value to its original participants is less relevant when it becomes part of the canon of a national theatre.

Community Plays are usually a high-profile, localised theatrical event and distinct from plays that just happen to be set in specific regions but not on such a large scale. Indeed, apart from the well-funded Royal National and Royal Shakespeare companies, most theatres presenting new work limit themselves to a small number of actors. During our conversation, Rupert Creed[7] told me of a play he had written for Hull Truck Theatre (a theatre whose role in the community I shall discuss in greater detail later) which was much smaller in scale than a Community Play but which focused on a specific moment in Hull's history. Rupert was commissioned to write a play, *Every Time it Rains* (2009), which covered the story of the floods in Hull in 2007. This was a catastrophic event for the city, when on 25 June an unusually heavy rainfall resulted in extensive flooding, leading to thousands of citizens having to be evacuated from their wrecked homes. In all, 10,000 homes were damaged at a cost of 40 million pounds, all 98 schools were also damaged, local farms had their crops destroyed and one man, Michael Barnett, lost his life when he became trapped in a storm drain. When Rupert Creed, two years later in 2009, asked citizens of Hull to come forward with their 'flood stories' two of the volunteers were Michael Barnett's father – also called Michael – and Richard Clark, the police officer who was first on the scene when Michael (junior) became trapped. The situation for the company, and for Rupert in particular, couldn't have been more sensitive, as this was a tragedy which had occurred relatively recently. PC Richard Clark suffered considerable trauma after the incident and, although he was still in the police service at the time the play was written, he subsequently retired early. For both Michael (senior) and Richard, the experience of contributing to and then seeing the play had a deeply therapeutic effect in helping them come to terms with the appalling events of two years earlier. Nevertheless, that therapy involved a painful reliving of those life-changing events. Perhaps, in part, the therapy here is linked with Aristotle's notion of catharsis in tragedy, that an audience witnesses vicariously the sufferings of others and so experiences catharsis – the 'purgation of fear and pity'[8]. Only, in the case of these participants – Richard Clark and Michael Barnett – the experience is so intense and close-up as to be hardly vicarious; they are seeing themselves and their stories played out literally in front of them. Rupert had a similar experience with an earlier work, *The Northern Trawl* (1986), which told the story of the frequently hazardous voyages to the Arctic waters undertaken by the trawlermen during the heydays of Hull's fishing industry. 'One ex-trawlerman who had lost a finger in a winching incident came to see the play several times', Rupert told me. 'He always sat down stage right on the front row as close as possible to where the scene was staged which showed him losing his finger.'[9]

Hull Truck Theatre has something of a tradition of producing plays which connect the city with its past heritage. When John Godber took over the artistic directorship of Hull Truck in 1984 he discovered a company which badly needed a hit. Drawing on the city's love of Rugby League he wrote what would become his most famous play, *Up 'n' Under* (1984). Such is the city's love of rugby that legend has it that on the day when both of the local rugby league teams – Hull Kingston Rovers and Hull FC – met at the Challenge Cup final, some wag put a sign on the Clive Sullivan Way, the main road exiting the city, which read 'Last one out switch the lights off'. Presumably it was the same wag who put another sign on the same route back into the city which read 'First one home put the kettle on'! *Up 'n' Under* had a huge impact on the city and, indeed, the country as it transferred to the West End, playing at the Fortune Theatre and subsequently winning the Laurence Olivier award for Best Comedy in 1984. It tells the story of a down at heel rugby 'sevens' team and the efforts of its manager to make its players competitive enough to beat the league's best team. It's a feel-good physical comedy which never fails to leave its audience uplifted and amused. Whilst Godber is no stranger to creating hard-hitting socially gritty plays (e.g. *Salt of the Earth* (1988) and *Shafted* (2011), both plays focused on the playwright's mining background) this was a play that connected with Hull because of its sporting traditions and its rich comedy. The therapeutic value of laughter is well documented and the lift that Hull audiences felt at a time of national strife and considerable economic privation has proved memorable. Godber's work became synonymous with Hull Truck for the next 25 years.

In 2011 I was commissioned to write a one-act play for Hull Truck Theatre – *Harry's Luck*. It would be the first of four short plays whose overarching title was *Ring around the Humber*; the other three were *Dear Paul McCartney* by Morgan Sproxton, *The Storm* by Nick Lane and *Finders Keepers* by Sarah Louise Davies – all set about 25 years apart. The narrative link between the four plays is a sovereign ring passed from one generation to the next. *Harry's Luck* is set in 1941 when Harry, a jeweller, sells a ring to a young woman purchasing it for her fiancé, who is about to serve in a minesweeper (many Hull trawlers were converted into minesweepers during the Second World War). Subsequently the young woman's mother recognises the ring as the one she gave to Harry years before and the two meet once more. It is a simple tale, but the significance of the story to a Hull audience was its historical setting during the Second World War. If you ask anyone what city was the most bombed outside of London during the war, chances are they'll answer with Birmingham, Leeds, Newcastle, Manchester, Coventry or Liverpool. It's unlikely that they'll identify the correct answer, which is – Hull. In two nights during May 1941, 400 people were killed and numerous buildings destroyed in air raids. *Harry's Luck* is set during those two nights, culminating in the death of Harry during the second of the two raids. The response to the play was very positive and led me to believe that a full-length play might be warranted – a play which would delve into greater detail of the history of Hull during the Second World War and explore the impact of war on the civilian population.

It seemed something of a mystery that such a play had never been written. Ninety-five percent of houses in Hull had been either destroyed or damaged at least once, 1200 civilians had been killed and many of the city's previously famous landmark buildings were destroyed. Dozens of trawlers were converted into minesweepers, with many being sunk and trawlermens' lives lost; factories and heavy industries destroyed (the heavy industries which made Hull a target in the first place – as well as its geographical nearness to Europe). Almost literally adding insult to injury, the devastation and violence experienced by Hull was not widely known, partly because during war time reports the city was referred to merely as 'a north-east coast town' (for security reasons). However, whilst the city's sufferings may not have been widely realised beyond the city, they were well documented in an extensive archive held in the newly built History Museum.

I was concerned, too, to create a play which demonstrated an awareness of its own immediate political and historical context. A play, any play, whether it's set in the past, present or future, is always a product of its own time. During the researching and developing of the play (which would eventually be titled *Dancing through the Shadows*) the civil war in Syria and the rise of ISIS were very much in the news. The cities of Homs and Alleppo had been barrel bombed by the Syrian government and the refugee crisis from Syria into neighbouring Jordan and Lebanon was reaching the levels of humanitarian disaster. Whilst it would be unlikely for audiences to make a direct link, I wanted to create a story which reflected not only the time during which it was set but also the times in which it was written. It was important to me that the play asked the question 'what is the impact of war on the civilian population?'

Visiting Hull's History Centre in Worship Street, you realise the extent of the Second World War archive. They have tens of thousands of documents, all meticulously recorded and stored. Whilst this is a reflection of the tenacity and care of the archivist, it's also an indication of how organised the city of Hull was under the direst of circumstances.

When I started work on the play, I was clear that I didn't want to write a documentary drama. Whilst the historical context of the play had to be carefully researched and faithfully depicted, attempting to tell the story of the 'war in Hull' held little appeal. Instead I wanted to create a number of fictional but believable characters and have them tell a story which would be engaging and compelling enough to convey the reality of living in Hull at that time. To try to tell the whole story of the war in Hull would have required the resources and personnel reserved for a Community Play. Quite simply, they weren't at my disposal. The question remained, however: what story and what characters?

Among the documents I found useful were the records of each air raid, detailing the names, addresses and ages of the casualties. It should be no surprise that the age range was broad, but there was something particularly tragic when realising that a number of babies had been killed during the raids; too young, presumably for their mothers to allow them to be evacuated as so many children from Hull had been. The archivist with whom I met told me of the mental and emotional breakdowns often suffered by air raid wardens as a result of their work and both a central plot point and a central character began to emerge. The same archivist also showed me a diary written by an alderman's wife, residing in Hessle. (Although Hessle is only just outside of Hull it was never hit by a bomb once during the war). When I looked at the diary, I instinctively turned to the two days in May 1941 to discover how the most deadly and traumatic raids had affected her. Astonishingly, her chief concern was that as there had been such extensive bombing in the city, the maid had been unable to get through to the house and therefore she (the wife) had had to make her husband's lunch. Again, a plot and, in particular, a major character began to emerge.

The plot of *Dancing through the Shadows* tells the story of Tom and Sylvia. They meet on the dance floor of the Newington Hall in 1938 and 'click' but their circumstances hinder their burgeoning relationship. Tom is a bank clerk and the son of snobbish Grace and shy Gilbert from Hessle. Sylvia, on the other hand, is the daughter of widower Maurice, who lives on Hessle Road and works in the Smoke House. (The Smoke House or Fish House, as it was locally known, was where fish was treated with the orange dye to give it its smoked flavour and appearance.) Hessle Road is perhaps the most iconic and well-known road in Hull as it was at the centre of the fishing community. My mother-in-law, Shirley, was born there in 1933, the daughter of a fisherman who lost a leg in a winching accident when only 19. Shirley describes Hessle Road 'as a world within a world – a community apart'. Hessle, on the other hand, is a relatively affluent, middle-class area. As Grace says, early in the play, when discussing Sylvia's background: 'Hessle and Hessle Road, what a difference a thoroughfare makes.' Whilst I wanted to make the love between the two central characters real from the outset, it had to be clear that their differences made communication difficult – he is romantic; she is practical. The outbreak of war makes him profess love; it makes her want to live for the moment. Almost inevitably their relationship falters and for a while they neither speak to nor see each other. When Tom is evacuated from Dunkirk, in desperation his mother visits Sylvia at the Fish House to find out if she knows of his whereabouts. It's only then that Sylvia realises that Tom has asked after her constantly in his letters home to his mother. The two are eventually reunited, but the dynamic of a relationship placed under strain not just by war but by contrasting expectations continues through to the climax of the play. Ultimately, Tom is killed at D Day, leaving Sylvia pregnant. Whilst both women are heartbroken, at the end of the play Grace and Sylvia resolve to raise the baby together.

An important juncture in the play's 'journey' came a little over a year before it was produced. Nick Lane, who was the literary advisor at Hull Truck at the time, invited the Act 3 group to hear a reading of it. Act 3 is a group of over-55-year-olds – mostly retirees – who write and produce their own plays at Hull Truck under the tutelage of a professional writer (both Nick Lane and Rupert Creed have worked with them). In fact, most of the group are in their 70s and 80s so would have been children at the time the play was set. Their insight was invaluable. Whilst their contributions didn't change the storyline fundamentally, it was the touches of authenticity which characterised their ideas and had the biggest impact. It seemed a small point at the time, but one member of the group recalled that the Germans were rarely referred to as 'the Germans' or 'Nazis' but invariably as 'Jerries'. Some of them chose to write down personal recollections for me, a few of which found their way into the final draft – one example being a lady who remembered the sight of someone silently praying during an air raid in a shelter. It was this kind of detailed observation that lent the play its authenticity and enabled audiences to connect with it. What I felt at that read-through was the start of a process which would gather momentum during the run of the play the following year.

One of the reasons that Hull was successful in achieving the accolade of 'City of Culture' in 2017, with all the investment and attention that brought, was that historically it is an area of low engagement with the arts. In 2011 I remember seeing an excellent production of Arthur Miller's *The Price* at Hull Truck which had been co-produced with the Octagon Theatre, Bolton and directed by their Artistic Director, David Thacker (arguably the most celebrated UK director of the works of Arthur Miller). It was a Tuesday evening and I was one of approximately 40 people in an auditorium built for 400. People in Hull need a reason to go to the theatre – it is neither a habit nor a favoured pastime and there is no specific or regular constituency that the theatre can rely on to turn up whatever the programme of work might be. During the week that *Dancing through the Shadows* opened, the first matinee had to be cancelled because literally no bookings had been taken. This was worrying! However, as the previews gave way to press night and the start of the run, a peculiar event occurred: the prophecy of *Field of Dreams* (1989) ('People will come') started to materialise. Hull Truck staff subsequently informed me that a large section of the audience were people who'd never visited the theatre before. People felt a connection with the story because it was part of their history; a sense of ownership took root and ensured the play's commercial success. It's difficult to determine whether it was purely the play's historical setting which led to its success, but my feeling is not. It may have initiated interest, but if Mark Babych's production had not achieved the quality it did, I suspect the project would have foundered.

One evening about halfway through the run, a friend of mine was in the audience. Although from Yorkshire, she is not native to Hull. During the interval, the friendly gentleman sitting next to her suggested that if she weren't from Hull, she wouldn't be 'getting it'. My friend replied politely that she was, indeed 'getting it' and, furthermore, 'enjoying it'! Although this was an anecdote which I found amusing, it hit on an important point about topicality. In *Dancing through the Shadows,* there are many references to Hull – but not ones which require in-depth knowledge of the city. In one scene Sylvia is talking to Tom about the death of her mother when she and her younger brother, David, were children. She says that her grandmother had gently told them that 'Mam has gone to a better place. David thought she meant Beverley'. Beverley is a reasonably well-known and wealthy town in East Yorkshire, about twelve miles outside of Hull – you don't need to be from Hull to get the joke. In an earlier draft, however, instead of Beverley I used another area of Hull known as Gipsyville in Sylvia's story. My mother-in-law, explaining to me the particular character of people from Hessle Road had said, 'We even thought of people from Gipsyville as posh.' The problem with such a line is that it moves away from topicality and becomes an 'in joke'. People outside of Hull wouldn't have got the reference, so the script would descend from being engaging and relevant for an audience into corny 'playing to the gallery'. Another play I watched during City of Culture Year in 2017 relied constantly on references to the city and, in particular, the historical rivalry between the two rugby teams. Such references were accompanied by knowing looks to the audience and the whole effect was a little contrived, however well enjoyed! It was important to me that no matter how resonant the play might be with the citizens of Hull – particularly those who had lived through the war – it needed to strike a chord with those from outside the city too.

Conclusion

I began this chapter by suggesting that some dramas don't rely on story for their success but may engage an audience more through theme, character, structure or situation instead. We have seen through some of the work developed in Community Theatre how specific stories might connect an audience with drama but also how the treatment of those stories (e.g. The Mystery Plays) might be equally significant. We've also seen that plays which stage stories pertinent to specific regions may also have an appeal beyond those regions (*Entertaining Strangers* and *Up 'n' Under*). However, my conclusion on creating *Dancing through the Shadows* and having reflected on the work of others, is that there is a specific kind of therapeutic value inherent in locally depicted stories. The nature of that therapy is one of personal recollection and identification. In Rupert Creed's *Every time it Rains* and *The Northern Trawl* that recollection is intensely personal and specific as the people themselves see their lives enacted. In the instance of *Dancing through the Shadows* it was a therapy linked to experience or knowledge of a particularly traumatic time. So, in these instances, stories ARE important, very important, and the respectful treatment of them by their creators – in terms of historical accuracy, dignity and affection for one's material – is essential.

Notes

1 *Irish Times*, 18 February 1956, p.6.
2 *Macbeth,* Shakespeare, Act 5, scene 5, lines 17–28.
3 Rupert Creed interview, 27 September 2019.
4 Ibid.
5 *Entertaining Strangers,* Methuen, David Hare 1988, p.vi.
6 Ibid p.vi.
7 Rupert Creed interview, 27 September 2019.
8 Aristotle, *Poetics*, Section 1449b.
9 Rupert Creed, interview 27 September 2019.

18
THE CYPRIOT STORY

Seniha Naşit Gürçağ

In this chapter, I invite you to embark on a therapeutic journey with a story from my Mediterranean island Cyprus. Turkish and Greek Cypriots inhabit this island. There are several shared cultural aspects including stories.

Cypriot stories

Research on Cypriot stories shows that the island's historical characters from real life – like sultans, kings, viziers, Muslim preachers, priests etc. – and supernatural creatures like giants, dragons and fairies coexist in stories. These stories usually share a general theme revolving around struggles in which the good always wins and gets rewarded (İslamoğlu & Öznur 2012). Although the concept of struggle is commonly observed in many other cultures, this is a concept which particularly overlaps with the historical past of Cyprus and its people because this Mediterranean island has witnessed great struggles and wars for centuries. As recently as a generation ago, Cypriots were victims of war; experiencing uncertainty, fear, loss and displacement. Political struggles continue in the present day. Cypriot stories on confronting supernatural powers like giants and dragons, and prevailing with benevolence, are meaningful for their healing powers as well as instilling hope for the people of this geography.

I will tell you about the Cypriot character Drimmo and how he can be transformed into a therapeutic story. Drimmo's story is valued by both cultures inhabiting Cyprus. I investigated the origins and the meaning of the word "Drimmo" but I was unable to find anything in available literature. Different oral sources (one of them being Ş. Öznur, the editor of *Cypriot Stories*) state that "Drimmo" is of Latin origin, which means "tiny". Versions of Drimmo's story are found in all three major languages used on the island (Turkish, Greek and English). In all versions, the hero of the story is Drimmo, a character that defeats the invincible great giant with clever and playful plans. Only a few elements in the story vary according to culture. For example, the sultan character in the Turkish version is a priest in the Greek version and a king in the English version (İslamoğlu & Öznur 2012). The common cultural element in all three languages is halloumi, a type of cheese unique to Cyprus. Halloumi is semi-hard to hard, tight textured, elastic cheese that can be made from ovine, bovine or caprine milk (Papademas & Robinson 1998). The original texts in Turkish, English and Greek can be found in İslamoğlu and Öznur's book titled *A Comparative Analysis of Turkish Cypriot and Greek Cypriot Tales*. The story in this chapter is a mixture of all three versions. I have reworded the story to remove elements of violence and fear that may adversely affect children.

Drimmo's story

Once upon a time in Cyprus, there lived three poor and orphaned brothers. One day the siblings decided to travel in search of work. On their way, they came across a wheat field ready to be harvested. Drimmo, the youngest and smartest of the brothers, came up with the idea of asking a job from the owner of the field. The owner was a giant disguised as a human who was reputed to make sinister plans for children. The giant agreed to employ the three brothers. He asked one to cut and the other to bunch the crop. To Drimmo he said, "You are too young to work the field. I will give you a letter to take to my wife. She will give you bread and halloumi cheese for us to eat together." Smart Drimmo suspected this stranger to have sinister intentions so he decided to read the letter on the way. He realised that the sinister giant had planned to eat the children. In the letter, the giant was asking his wife to cook Drimmo for dinner. Drimmo tampered with the letter and wrote, "send us bread and halloumi with the boy". The giant was very surprised when Drimmo returned with the food. Drimmo told his brothers about the letter and the three brothers escaped the evil giant's field and started working in the land of the Sultan. Young Drimmo soon caught the attention of the Sultan and became his assistant with his smart and hardworking character.

One day the Sultan's subjects told him that this evil giant had a magic blanket. So, the Sultan started looking for someone who could bring this blanket to him. No one believed little Drimmo could steal the magic blanket from the giant but Drimmo quickly came up with a genius plan. Drimmo put lice in one pocket and fleas in the other, and then made his way to the giant's castle.

When Drimmo arrived at the castle, he opened a hole in the roof while the giant was sleeping and released the lice and fleas onto the giant's bed. The giant was soon itching all over. Before long, he was so annoyed that he threw the blanket up on the roof. Drimmo seized this opportunity. He grabbed the blanket and returned to the Sultan's Palace laughing at the giant all the way. On his arrival, he proudly presented the blanket to the Sultan.

People who disbelieved Drimmo were both surprised and jealous to hear the news. Drimmo soon gained the Sultan's trust – but the envy of some others. Those who coveted Drimmo's achievements told the Sultan that the evil giant was planning to wage a war against him. They told him that maybe Drimmo could catch the giant and bring him back alive. The Sultan had a lot of confidence in Drimmo. He asked him to capture the giant alive and promised a reward if he succeeded. Once more, Drimmo came up with a clever plan for the giant. He had a huge chest built and dressed up as an old man before setting off for the giant's castle.

Upon his arrival, he approached the giant and asked:

- "Oh Giant, have you heard of Drimmo?"

The Giant replied in an annoyed tone: "Of course I have. The things I will do if I get my hands on him!"

The "old man" continued: "Do you see this chest I am holding? I made it to capture him. He has done bad things to me. I plan to take revenge but I need your help."

- "I will certainly help you with whatever you need", said the Giant.
- "You are strong. I want you to get inside this chest to make sure it is sturdy enough, "Oh Giant," said the 'old man'. The Giant was delighted with the proposal. He left his jobs and climbed into the chest singing songs. Drimmo immediately locked the giant inside the chest. He laughed at the giant at length as he took the chest back to the Sultan. The Sultan kept his promise and granted three wishes to Drimmo.

The message of the story

Drimmo is a story of empowerment. The main theme is that solutions can be found even in very challenging conditions with self-sufficiency, confidence and creative problem-solving skills.

It can be used in cases of:

- Building on self-sufficiency and confidence
- Developing psychological resilience
- Nurturing the parent–child relationship
- Enhancing playful experiences

The story can be used for children's group and parent–child interaction practices. Stories can only be effective if they can relate to clients' own stories. Every client is different and unique, even if they are experiencing similar problems. This is why stories can be adapted in an infinite number of ways to suit the specific needs and conditions of clients. Below I will provide embodiment-projection-role applications for the story that might prove useful.

1) The story can be told from start to end.
2) The story could start at the beginning and finish at the point where Drimmo retrieves the magical blanket and presents it to the Sultan, then adding Sultan's reward and him granting three wishes.

Therapists can use their initiative in determining an approach based on the child's age and needs. I will provide some suggestions from my clinical practices:

Neuro-Dramatic-Play and its applications to the story

Dr Sue Jennings, the developer of Neuro-Dramatic-Play (NDP), defines NDP (2011) as follows:

> Neuro-Dramatic-Play (NDP) is the term used for sensory, rhythmic and dramatic playfulness that takes place between a mother and her unborn baby and newborn from conception to six months. Neuro-Dramatic-Play has a profound effect on the growth of the brain, the chemical balance of the body and the healthy attachment between infants and parents. It influences the future emotional and social maturation of the child.
>
> (p. 33)

"Neuro-Dramatic-Play is unique as it emphasises the importance of the attachment process from conception to six months" (Jennings, n.d. p. 2). NDP overlaps Dr Jennings' value-free

"Embodiment-Projection-Role (EPR)" paradigm that explains childhood dramatic development from the unborn phase of a baby up through to 7 years of age (Jennings 2012). "NDP and EPR show that dramatic play and the 'as if' are central to human development" (Jennings 2012, p. 4). EPR stages are defined by Jennings (2012) as follows:

Embodiment: Birth–12 months (everything is experienced through the body).

Projection: 13 months–3 years (toys and media beyond the body are explored).

Role: 3 years–7 years (roles and stories are developed in dramatic play).

These stages are not absolute as some children take longer than others, but all stages need to be completed for confident maturation and emotional resilience.

(p. 4)

We use NDP playfulness at our individual, parent–child, group and family practices as a healing process alone and/or with other therapeutic interventions for children, adults and even older people. Now, let us take a look at how the EPR techniques apply to the story of Drimmo in NDP group practices:

Embodiment plays: sensory and rhythmic creation of the story

- Making step sounds by hitting legs for walking scenes. Use this rhythm quietly while Drimmo secretly goes to the giant's palace and loudly together with giggles when he returns to the Sultan's place.
- Play the marimba while Drimmo is thinking or developing his plan.
- Shake the maracas whenever Drimmo completes his missions successfully.

Projection plays: creating, drawing and/or colouring the story characters

Every child can:

- Draw a picture of the characters/shape the characters from clay and/or play dough.
- Create their story setting with little creature figures if you can use a sandbox.
- Create their own magic blanket from fabrics and/collectively create a big magical blanket together.
- Create a large chest for the giant.
- Collectively create the giant.

Role playing: dramatisation of the story together with children

Children can:

- Choose their roles.[1]
- Dress up as their character.
- Make their own contributions to the story and dramatise versions of the story with the group.

NDP group exercise of the story

A group application of the story for groups of children aged 5–8 who feel anxious, insufficient and/or unable to perform due to self-sufficiency problems.

1) While telling the story incorporate certain gestures, voices and rhythms and ask children to accompany you at some points in the story.
2) Ask children to draw/create their own magic blanket and add the magical powers they need.
3) Discuss the story with children (How did Drimmo realise that the man was a giant? What would you feel if you were Drimmo? What would be your solution plan? If Drimmo had parents, what would their parents/teacher/friends say if they listened to this story? If you were Drimmo, what would you demand from the Sultan?).
4) After telling the story again while children dramatise it, ask for other participants to join in the process with the sounds and rhythms that you set.
5) As a sensory closing activity, offer children the traditional cheese and bread as a gift from Drimmo for the children in this group.

NDP parent–child exercise of the story

A parent–child interaction game can be created from the second version of the story. It could be very useful in enhancing parent–child relations and also child empowerment. Exercise application steps could be organised as follows:

1) The parent and child can listen to the story in contact with each other, in a comforting position.
2) After the story is told to the child and mother, they are asked questions about the story, such as:

   To the child: What are Drimmo's strengths? What would his parents say if they saw his achievement?
   To the mother: What is the strongest attribute of your child?
   To the child: What do your parents tell you when you achieve something?
   How did the Sultan reward Drimmo?
   To the mother: In general, how do you reward your child?
   To the child: What do you think Drimmo might wish for? What would you wish for if you were Drimmo?

3) The mother and child create their own magic blanket and assign three magic powers for it.
4) As a closing exercise the mother covers the child with their magical blanket, tells the child their own success story and then feeds the child with bread and traditional cheese served by the therapist.

It is very important to have rich creative materials that will provide different sensory experiences in these applications.

Note

1 You can get help from a co-therapist and/or volunteer to act the giant, create one with the group or use any large character for it. Because this is an empowering group for children who have self-sufficiency and confidence problems, the giant in this story is huge but dumb.

References

İslamoğlu, M. & Öznur, Ş. (Eds.) (2012). *Comparative analysis of Turkish Cypriot and Greek Cypriot tales.* [Karşılaştırmalı Kıbrıs Türk ve Rum masalları] Nicosia: Gökada Yayınları.
Papademas, P. & Robinson, Richard K. (1998). Halloumi cheese: The product and its characteristics. *International Journal of Dairy Technology*, 51(3), 98–103 doi.org/10.1111/j.1471-0307.1998.tb02646.x.
Jennings, S. (2011). *Neuro-dramatic-play and healthy attachments.* London: Jessica Kingsley Publishers.
Jennings, S. (2012). *Neuro-dramatic-play and trauma: 'towards healing and hope'.* Penang: B Braun Medical Industries.
Jennings, S. (n.d). *Neuro-dramatic-play part one: A play-book for adults of theory and practice.* Penang: Phoenix Printers Sdn, Bhd.

19
A PERSONAL JOURNEY TO *THE CLEVER MOUNTAIN GIRL*

Lenka Fisherová and Ilona Labuťová

Introduction

This chapter is conceived as a 'workshop on paper', which the reader-'participant' can use as direct inspiration for working with clients. At the same time it can be conceived as a space for the reader's own experience and a 'living' meeting with the story *The Clever Mountain Girl*, its message and some of the themes it brings up.

The authors are from different backgrounds and work in different fields. What connects them is an emphasis on the experiences of the client and the relationship of both the client and the therapist to the material and their personal journeys with it. The authors made a choice from a number of different original Czech fairy-tales that could be used in the context of dramatherapy. They asked themselves and each other which story best spoke to their own lives, their work, their life experience and their personal experience. In the end they settled on the story *The Clever Mountain Girl*.

The story of the mountain girl was first published in 1846 in a collection of national tales, by the renowned Czech writer Bozena Nemcova (1846). However, it feels contemporary, which attests to the fact that the themes of interpersonal relations and personal searching are always living and actual. This chapter should be above all an open space for the reader to have a personal experience, relating their own opinions, experience and life situation to the story. The authors were very inspired by their common teacher Dr Sue Jennings (2011), who guided them through their dramatherapy training, and whose EPR model is the main theoretical basis for this work.

We are presenting our work with this story as if it were work with a group. It can however be adapted to suit work with an individual client. The clever mountain girl was a simple girl of the people, who didn't know the etiquette of the nobility or the ways of the court. She was, however, wise, direct and very much her own person. We will move into the first person now and address the reader directly. We will be glad if you can dive into our story and together with us find your own 'Clever Mountain Girl'.

A description of the workshop
Gallery – first visit

(Recommended time: 10–15 minutes)

We will begin our journey to *The Clever Mountain Girl* with a visitor's gallery. Please enter our little dramatherapeutical Louvre. Instead of pictures, you will find the art of words: impressions, questions, riddles, quotations and sections of text. Look over the individual exhibits, and see how they affect you. Give them a chance to speak to you and try to be conscious of what feelings, thoughts, associations or memories they give rise to in you.

(Note: We leave it up to you which of the offered texts you wish to use, how to position them around the space etc. These offerings are for inspiration. The gallery may also be entered through guided imagination. It depends on the composition of the restraints etc. If you feel that, for example, pictures or sculptures related to similar themes would resonate better with your clients ... then you may decide to place them in the gallery and so activate more senses (touch, smell, hearing).

Items
Riddles

What is the sweetest thing in the world?
What is the cleverest thing in the world?
What is the richest thing in the world?

General themes and polarities

Love of others vs your personal journey/integrity
Truth/directness vs lies/deception
Justice vs injustice
Wealth vs poverty
Forgiveness

Quotes

- "The true voyage of discovery consists not of seeking new landscapes, but having new eyes." Proust (Marks 2011 pg. 139)
- "You may be disappointed if you fail, but you are doomed if you don't try." Beverly Sills (Marks 2011 pg. 24)
- "Try not to become a man of success, but rather try to become a man of value." Albert Einstein (Marks 2011 pg. 135)
- "Each player must accept the cards life deals him or her. But once they are in hand, he or she alone must decide how to play the cards in order to win the game." Voltaire (Marks 2011 pg. 54)
- "As we are liberated from our own fear, our presence automatically liberates others" Nelson Mandela (Marks 2011 pg. 54)
- "Those who bring sunshine into the lives of others, cannot keep it from themselves." Sir James M. Barrie (Marks 2011 pg. 54)

> "*Happiness is that state of consciousness which proceeds from the achievement of one's values.*" Ayn Rand (Marks 2011 pg. 55)
> "*A happy person is not a person in a certain set of circumstances, but rather a person with a certain set of attitudes.*" Hugh Downs (Marks 2011 pg. 77)
> "*Silly things do cease to be silly if they are done by sensible people in an impudent way.*" Jane Austen (Marks 2011 pg. 73)
> "*We are all born originals. Why is it so many of us die copies?*" Edward Young (Marks 2011 pg. 309)
> "*Riches may enable us to confer favours, but to confer them with propriety and grace requires a something that riches cannot give.*" Charles Caleb Colton (Marks 2011 pg. 74)
> "*I once had a sparrow alight upon my shoulder for a moment, while I was hoeing in a village garden, and I felt that I was more distinguished by that circumstance that I should have been by any epaulet I could have worn.*" Henry David Thoreau (Marks 2011 pg. 77)
> "*Life itself is the most wonderful fairytale of all.*" Hans Christian Andersen (Marks 2011 pg. 305)

Dividing into groups

(Recommended time: 15 minutes)

Choose one 'item' or place in the gallery where you would like to stand. It should be next to something which resonates and speaks to you, the item that you feel closest to.

Split into smaller groups (two to four people) either:

1. according to the item that you chose (join with others who chose the same item or who can agree that the item is close to them, that they have something in common) or
2. according to where you are in the gallery (join with those who are standing close to you)

In these groups share your individual impressions from the gallery and the position in it, or the item, that you chose. (Why did you choose it? What connects you to it? What does it mean to you?)

Reading/telling the story The Clever Mountain Girl

Now we are going to tell you the *Tale of the Clever Mountain Girl*. Everybody find a place where you feel good, sit comfortably and listen.

(Note 1: you may invite your clients to close their eyes, or even do relaxation exercises before the reading. It depends on your personal experience, the needs of your clients and the context of your work.)

(Note 2: below you will find a text with simplified version of the story ready to be read to your clients. You are of course welcome to adapt the text and present it in your own words.)

The Clever Mountain Girl

Once upon a time there were two brothers. One of them was a rich landowner, who had no children and was extremely mean. The other was a poor cottage-owner; he had one daughter, called Manka, and he was very good-natured. When the girl entered her twelfth year, he sent her to his brother to work as a goose keeper. She worked two years for her keep; after two years she got stronger and became a young lady.

The uncle promised Manka that, for her work, he would give her a young heifer instead of money. Manka agreed willingly and ran her uncle's household excellently. When, after three years of service, Manka wanted to return home to her aging father, the young heifer had become a full-grown cow and the uncle did not want to hand it over. He just made excuses and tried to dismiss her with a few coins.

However, she wasn't simple enough to accept the money. She went home to her father and with tears in her eyes told him the whole story. She wanted her father to make a complaint to the public prosecutor. The father was very angry with his unscrupulous brother; he went straight to town and registered the complaint.

The prosecutor listened and sent for the landowner. The landowner knew well that unless the prosecutor fixed it for him, he would have to hand over the heifer, and so he looked for a way to get the prosecutor on his side. The prosecutor was in a difficult situation. He did not want to anger the rich man, but the poor man had the truth on his side. So he made a clever decision. He called them individually and gave them some riddles: What is the cleverest thing in the world, what is the sweetest thing in the world and what is the richest thing in the world?

Both brothers sullenly went home. The whole way home they tried to work out what the answer could be, but neither of them could find it.

Back at home the landowner told his wife about it. If he couldn't find the answer to the three riddles he would lose.

What is the cleverest thing? What is the sweetest and what the richest? If she could guess the answers the heifer would be theirs. What could be cleverer than our black pomeranian dog, what could be sweeter than our barrel of honey, what could be richer than our chest of gold coins? The landowner was proud of his wife and the good answers that she had found. He was almost sure that the heifer would be staying with them.

The cottage-owner also went home sadly and told Manka what the prosecutor had said. "Oh, is that all? I will work it out, don't be sad; I will tell you the answer in the morning." Manka came down in the morning and said, "When the prosecutor asks you, say, the sweetest thing is sleep, the cleverest thing is an eye and the richest thing is the earth, which all things come from. But I am telling you that you mustn't say who you learnt this from."

The prosecutor called the landowner first and asked him for his answers to the riddles. He answered that nothing could be cleverer than his dog, who could sniff out and chase out everything, nothing sweeter than a barrel of honey which has stood for four years and nothing richer than his chest of gold coins. The prosecutor wasn't impressed with the answers, shrugged his shoulders and waited to see what the poor brother would come with.

He answered that the cleverest thing is an eye, which can see everything, the sweetest thing is sleep, for no matter how sad or downtrodden a man feels, when he sleeps he feels nothing and can even find joy in his sleep, and the richest thing is the earth, from which all of our riches come.

The prosecutor considered, and gave him the heifer, but only on the condition that he say who had told him such a clever answer. The cottage-owner resisted for a while, but then betrayed that it was his daughter.

"Good, so if your daughter is so clever, let her come to me, but it mustn't be by day or by night, neither clothed nor naked, and neither on foot or in a vehicle."

The father was unhappy about this, but Manka was not afraid of the conditions. At two o'clock in the morning she got up, took a very thin white woven bag and put it on. Then she put a stocking on one leg, leaving the other foot bare, and when it was three o'clock, between day and night, she sat on a goat and half walking, half riding made it to the town. The prosecutor was looking out of the window, and was already expecting the clever mountain girl. When he saw how well she had satisfied his conditions, he went out to meet her and said, "I see that you are a girl of wit; if you wish, I will make you my wife."

Manka agreed that she would gladly become the prosecutor's wife. However, she had to promise that she would never become involved in his affairs, not his legal cases or anything else or she would have to immediately return to her father. The wedding was the next day and Manka became a great lady. But she also worked hard, she was kind to all and loved her husband. Because of this everybody held her in high esteem.

One day two landowners came to the prosecutor with horses; one had a stallion and the other had a mare. When the mare had a foal there was a question who the foal belonged to. The owner of the stallion said the foal should belong to him; the owner of the mare made the argument that he had more right to the foal. And so they argued and took the case to the prosecutor. The landowner with the stallion was very rich and bribed the prosecutor and the stallion got to keep the foal.

However, the prosecutor's wife had been listening to everything from the next room, and she did not like the unjust decision of her husband. When the poor landowner went out she waved to him and asked him how could he let that stand? Who ever heard of a stallion having a foal? And so she told him what he should do to show the prosecutor that he had made a mistake, but under the condition that nobody should ever know who had given him the idea.

She told him to go out the next day around noon, take a fishing net, go up the hill and pretend to be catching fish. The prosecutor and some gentlemen would go by at this time and when they saw him they would ask what he was doing there. And he should answer them that if a stallion could have a foal, then fish could grow out of the ground. He promised and did this the following day.

"You're crazy," cried the prosecutor. "Who ever heard of fish growing on the hill?" "If a stallion can have a foal, then fish can also grow out of the ground," answered the landowner. The prosecutor stood still as a stone, then he took the landowner to one side and said "The foal is yours, but first tell me who advised you to do this." The landowner held out the best he could, but in the end he told the prosecutor.

When the prosecutor got home, he was very angry with Manka; he reminded her of her wedding promise and asked her why she had advised the landowner against his will. "Because I can't stand injustice. The poor landowner was cheated."

"It doesn't matter if you were upset or not, it was none of your business. Now go back to where you came from. However, so you can't say that I was unfair to you, you can take from this house the thing that is dearest to you."

"Thank you dear husband for this kindness, and if there is no other way, I will obey. Allow me to have dinner with you one last time, and let us make it merry as if there were no problem between us."

The prosecutor agreed. He allowed Manka to prepare a rich meal with a lot of good wine. And when she saw that her husband was a little drunk she told the servants to give him one more full glass of wine. Her husband took the wine and drank it down in one go to the health of his wife. Then, tired from the amount of wine he had drunk, he fell into a deep sleep. Manka locked up the house, the servants put her husband to bed, then they took the bed with him in it on their shoulders to her father's cottage.

The sun was high when the prosecutor woke up. He looked around, rubbed his eyes and couldn't remember what had happened. Then his wife came in through the door wearing a simple, but clean peasant dress, with a black cap on her head. "Are you still here?" he asked her. "And why wouldn't I be here? This is my home, after all." "And what am I doing here?" "Didn't you tell me that I could take the thing that is dearest to me? You are the thing that is dearest to me, so I took you." The prosecutor burst out laughing, forgave her everything and admitted that Manka was cleverer than himself. He made her prosecutor in his place. The prosecutor's wife was glad for this, and from that day on, she made all of the decisions and all was well.

(Abbreviated, adapted.)

Gallery – second visit

(Recommended time: 10–15 minutes)

Now that you know the story *The Clever Mountain Girl* and the themes which arise from it, go through the gallery and try to be aware if your perception of the exhibited items has changed and how. Do the same themes resonate, or has space opened for others? If so, which? Would you now choose a different place to stand? Where? Why?

Craft work to express your own experience

(Recommended time 20–60 minutes depending on the difficulty of the creative technique)

Think about who or what your Clever Mountain Girl is. Try to remember different life situations when you had to make a difficult decision, when you were having a difficult time, something disappointed you or deceived you, when you felt you were treated unfairly etc.

Think about who or what helped you in that situation, what inspired you, who supported you etc. Using any artistic form, create your 'Clever Mountain Girl'.

(Note: you can offer your clients various materials, which you consider suitable and inspiring for them – paint, clay, objects in the room, clients' personal items or things which you offer them: chalks, paper, material, clothes, magazines for a collage etc. An independent projective technique can be to create puppets or masks. However, these two options are both very time-consuming and you should take that into account. They are suitable techniques if you intend to work with a theme over a longer period of time.)

Work in groups II

- ➤ Share your creations and say something about your Clever Mountain Girl.
- ➤ As a group, put together a single story which contains at least some of the 'threads' of the individual stories of everybody in the group. Did you find some common ground where the stories connected?
- ➤ Create a theatre performance of this common story (you can use story-telling, pantomime, dance, music, sounds, props, etc).
- ➤ Perform the common story for the whole group.
- ➤ Reflection on the performance. (How was it to create the story in the group? What role did you choose in the story and why? How did you feel when making your presentation in front of the group? Etc.)

(Note: We leave it to you to decide whether to have the clients work in the original groups or offer the chance for meeting and sharing with other members of the larger group.)

Completion of the workshop and reflection

(Recommended time: 15 minutes)

Sit in a circle and invite the participants of the workshop to close their eyes and each, individually, to follow their own personal 'path to The Clever Mountain Girl'. They should also choose a concrete thing, an impression, experience or situation that is important for them (something that they learnt from it) and, at the same time, something which they want to take home with them and think about further.

Then invite everyone to open their eyes and say what they will take away from the programme. (For example: I am taking away 'courage', the fact that I was able to play something in front of people, even when I am shy and do not like to present myself to people.) We can have a ball of wool or string, which the participants hand around to each other whilst still holding onto their own length. This provides a visualisation of who has already spoken – it is a symbol of the connection of the group and the thread of the story which we will take home with us.

A few touches of theory

We have attempted to open a space for a meeting with the story *The Clever Mountain Girl* in such a way that you could enter the story personally, meet it and take something away from the meeting for work with your clients or for your own personal therapeutic journey. It is a space that you can expand and change in your own way. The whole chapter has therefore been conceived to be as 'practical' and 'open' as possible. However, so that our contribution doesn't stay completely without grounding or context, we will mention at least the basic theoretical background and take a look at how we put the workshop together.

There are many possible theoretical relations to this type of work and our commentary on the creation of the workshop. We will pick out just a few things which we consider to be fundamental, even without consideration of context.

In dramatherapeutic work and in consideration of this particular workshop, the following two considerations are key:

1) the person/participant/client and their experience stand in the centre of the whole programme and
2) for their journey and for the quality of the experience, it is important for them to feel safe.

In other words, whatever the reality of your work (clients, the approach and personality of the therapist, the material chosen, the way of working, the aims of the work etc) it is important to draw on the participants and focus the programme on them. Also, during personal and intimate work it is important to establish the safety of all members of the group and a relationship of trust between them and the therapist and among each other.

For this reason the following ideas and references focus mostly on how we thought about personal participation and ensuring safety, the principles we adhered to and what we would like to recommend in this respect.

Safety and intimacy in EPR

One way of achieving sensitive and safe work is with the EPR model of Dr Sue Jennings, and our workshop is based on these principles to a large degree.

EPR (Embodiment – Projection – Role) is a complex theory and we refer you to Jennings' *Healthy Attachments and Neuro Dramatic Play* (2011).

For the purposes of this chapter, we would like to look at the significance of ensuring safety during this kind of work where we meet with peoples' personal and intimate space.

In EPR we usually begin with individual work – that is, with activities which lead people to themselves (their own body, personal imagination, association, personal story etc.) We only gradually get to sharing those personal experiences with others, through working in pairs, in small groups and eventually joining the group as a whole. Presentation in front of the others (sharing in a group circle) comes later, often at the end of the whole programme. The individual's personal tale is also hidden in the shared tale from the group work. If people want to they can share their personal experiences with the larger group, but nobody is forced to do this through the nature of the programme and the scale and nature of the sharing is left up to them. This set-up supports the protection of the individual's personal boundaries and their individual timing for the dramatherapeutic journey and the individual phase of the programme.

What is good to remember during the preparation of the programme and during its realisation

For some people it can be threatening or unpleasant to create craft work, so it should be emphasised that the work need not be, and even should not be, artistically perfect – it is individual, nobody will judge it etc.

Another rule that all participants should respect is that everybody can only touch their own work. We shouldn't touch or move other peoples' work without their permission. In this way we lead them to respect the work of others and to respect its intimacy (the craft work is not just a piece of work; it is a symbol of a personal experience).

For others it can be, for various reasons, unsettling, or even threatening to have to play a role or to perform in front of others. The group members generally themselves recognise 'which path to choose' and what they are ready for, even if they are not able to express this verbally.

The opportunity to perform (in the theatrical sense of the word) should be taken as a catalyst, rather than a controlling mechanism. Each group member has a different timing, as do we ourselves. Some may not want to actively participate in certain parts of the work, want to remain 'neutral' observers – at that moment that may mean more for their future development.

We should warn the clients that they should only share what they want; if a theme is too personal, encourage them to concentrate on the pleasant aspects and positive memories (possibly things which gave them strength).

You generally have to evaluate the timing of the workshop individually, according to the group that you are working with. The times we quote should be taken as orientational. Any of the sections can be made longer or shorter according to need. You may split the workshop into several meetings. If you are going to make a mask or a puppet be sure to leave enough time. The actual process of making the items has great creative therapeutic potential.

In order for a person to meet the story personally, it is important to create space for their own associations and interpretations. That is why we placed the actual telling of the story *The Clever Mountain Girl* after the gallery of impressions. At the same time we must say that the given quotations and polarities are our own associations with the chosen story and the themes that seemed pertinent to us. If you have different associations, include them.

The final phase of the programme may be led in different ways, verbally and non-verbally. Other techniques for this phase include relaxation/calming, withdrawing from the process – stepping out of the role with a transition to 'here and now' – feedback on the process through movement, writing a diary, ritual or directed recapitulation.

A closing word

We drew the above ideas from our study of dramatherapeutic practice and from years of experience in the field of dramatherapy. However, the most relevant things in this moment and in the context of this meeting are your own experience and the reality of your work. We have aimed the workshop and the whole chapter to you and your work. So we want the conclusion to take the same course.

Before working with your own group we recommend that you answer these questions:

- Is the story *The Clever Mountain Girl* inspiring enough for you and your clients?
- What thoughts, themes and impressions occur to you when you read *The Clever Mountain Girl*?
- What themes would be relevant for the clients that you are working with?
- Could it be set up differently or adapted for your clients?

Our journey together is at an end. Just as we started with a personal invitation into our workshop, we would also like to say goodbye personally. We hope that we have managed to awaken some of the curiosity and desire to discover more that we felt as we worked with this Czech fairy-tale. Please listen to your 'Clever Mountain Girl', who knows best which questions you need to ask and which riddles you need to solve on your own journey. Have a nice trip!

With warm thanks to our translator, David Fisher, without whom this chapter could not have been written.

References

Jennings, S. (2011) *Healthy Attachments and Neuro Dramatic Play*. London: JKP.
Marks, D. (ed.) (2011) *Inspirational Quotes Ultimate Collection*. Houston: Everlasting Flames Publishing.
Němcová, B. (1846) *Národní Báchorky a Powěsti*, volume 3, W Praze: Tisk a sklad Jarosl. Pospíšila; Němcová, B. Prague: Print and stock Jarosl. Pospíšila.

20
CHANGING THE WORLD THROUGH STORIES OF CHANGE[1]

The work of OpenStoryTellers 2004–2019

Nicola Grove, Alice Parsley, Clemma Lewis and Robin Meader

"O God, Horatio, what a wounded name,
Things standing thus unknown, shall live behind me!
If thou didst ever hold me in thy heart
Absent thee from felicity a while,
And in this harsh world draw thy breath in pain
To tell my story."

Hamlet uses his dying breath to ensure that his true legacy is sustained in a world where, 500 years ago as now, reputations were made and shattered through the power of the tale. Who gets to tell the stories? What authority do they have? What if you can't tell your own story? What if the stories told about you are untrue?

These questions affect all of us, and are of course highly relevant to people on the margins of society – those who are stigmatised by race, class, gender, lack of confidence, lack of cultural capital and disability. But narratives are more than a tool for exercising control. In the words of Barbara Hardy (1968:5) "We dream in narrative, daydream in narrative, remember, anticipate, hope, despair, believe, doubt, plan, revise, criticise, construct, gossip, learn, hate, and love by narrative". Without the ability to tell our stories, our interactions with others are restricted to the transactional and the phatic, whereas a story forges links between your past and mine, and hence your future and mine.

This chapter will describe some 20 years of work with children and adults who have learning or intellectual disabilities, with a focus on the contribution they make as citizens and community storytellers. Although I (NG) am responsible for drafting the content, it is co-authored through verbatim contributions in interviews from three members of OpenStoryTellers (www.openstorytellers.org.uk).

Background

There are around 1 million adults with a registered learning disability in the UK.[2] The majority have mild or specific learning difficulties, but a significant proportion have a moderate, severe or profound intellectual disability, meaning they need support for everyday living, and are likely to have significant problems with language and communication. Around 200,000 children with a statement of learning difficulty fall into this category. Population demographics in adults are difficult to determine, but latest estimates suggest a total population in the UK of around 215,000 people, with a projected increase of around 4% over the next 10 years (Emerson & Hatton, 2016). Many will have complex needs, meaning overlapping diagnoses such as deafness, autism, epilepsy and mental health problems. Statutory support is falling, with most local authorities now only providing services to those in critical or substantial need (meaning largely those identified as having severe and profound disabilities). Only 6% of people with a severe learning disability are employed, and they are at great risk of social isolation, exclusion and prejudice.[3]

The past 30 years or so have seen great changes in life expectations for people with learning disabilities. Taking children with Down Syndrome as an example – better health care and awareness of their particular strengths and needs (for example, stronger visual than auditory memory), has meant that many more successfully attend local mainstream schools and colleges, are employed and lead independent lives (Corby, Taggart & Cousins, 2018; Kay-Raining Bird et. al., 2008; see also www.globaldownsyndrome.org). Attitudes have also shifted, towards more acceptance of the role that people with disabilities can play in our society – though they are still marginalised.[4] Access to the job market is quite restricted. Most of those with learning disabilities work in catering, horticulture, animal care and low-grade supermarket jobs, broadly a continuation of the work they carried out in traditional institutions. There has been a growth in engagement with the arts as professional, as opposed to therapeutic, endeavour: visual artists, actors, dancers and musicians, as well as bands, theatre and dance companies. Reason (2018:163) points out that this entails a shift towards public rather than private, sheltered spaces and funding, with a commensurate change in the expectations of audiences. Storytellers, however, are thinner on the ground.

OpenStoryTellers: purpose and history

Our company was formed in 2004 as a Lottery-funded initiative to develop a training course in storytelling for people with learning disabilities.[5] For three years, a group of 12–15 people met on a weekly basis, led by "tutors" comprising a speech and language therapist (NG), a professional storyteller, a musician and community arts worker, supported by a seconded member of staff from the local social services. We evolved a way of working which involved the following core elements:

- Hearing and learning traditional stories from all over the world
- Relating these to our own lives
- Story skills
- Group work

The full course materials are provided in a handbook *Learning To Tell* (Grove, 2009). In parallel we also worked with a small group of artists to create story-related images, such as a Khavad[6]; and on personal storytelling with adults with profound disabilities (Storysharing® Grove, 2014).

When the funding period ended in 2007, a small group of four storytellers continued to meet with the support of two volunteers, both speech and language therapists and storytellers.

Numerous applications were made, which finally succeeded in funding a development manager, premises and an administrator, and from these fledgling beginnings, the charity OpenStoryTellers was formed in 2009. Based in Frome, Somerset, the organisation has had tremendous support from the local community, and beside the storytelling company, runs groups, book clubs and social events.

The nature of the company

This handbook is about the therapeutic application of storytelling – and it is a real privilege to make a contribution through this chapter. However, we need to clarify in what sense the work of OpenStoryTellers is therapeutic. Traditionally, arts with people with learning disabilities are often qualified by the term "therapy", denoting some kind of intervention aimed at remediation of a problem if not always a complete cure. For example Wyndham, in an online article, suggests that:

> 'Artistic therapy is an essential tool in dealing with learning difficulties. This is an excellent way to achieve the right balance in the brain. An imbalance affects an individual's learning ability. Incorporating this creative therapy with counselling can help them achieve any skill that is lacking in conditions like conduct disorder and Autism Spectrum Disorder'.[7]

Likewise, according to the National Coalition of Creative Arts Therapies Associations, Inc. (NCCATA), the creative arts as therapy can "teach cognitive, motor, and daily living skills to people with developmental disabilities".[8]

This view of art (any art form) as therapy, delivered by professionals to individuals and groups, sits squarely within a medical paradigm which sees disability as lack of, or as disruption to, a norm. However, a learning disability is not an illness to be cured. Certainly, individuals may benefit from educational and therapeutic interventions – their life experiences may also mean that counselling or psychotherapy is appropriate – but our approach is informed principally by the social model of disability, which focuses on human and civil rights and empowerment to challenge the barriers and prejudices that dis-able people (Barnes, 2012), and by an understanding that learning disability is culturally constructed and located (Goodley, 2011). Raising awareness of the experience of learning disability is now perceived by the members as central to the purpose of the company:

> CL: *Telling stories because it's important to tell them and make our voice heard.*
> RM: *It's the history of people like us, and community awareness of telling stories. That doesn't get through to everyone.*
> AP: *To get messages across about people with disabilities, help them understand…*

At one point in our chequered history we described our mission as "changing the world through stories of change"…which is compatible with De Botton and Armstrong's claim (2013:151) that "the underlying mission of art lies in changing how we experience the world". At a UK national storytelling conference shortly after the project began, Brian Marshall, founder member of the company and later trustee, asked for Kevin Crossley Holland's reaction to his memory that the doctors had told him he would never amount to anything in his life, to which the author and storyteller memorably responded that Brian had just falsified W. H. Auden's dictum that "art changes nothing".

The benefits of storytelling are well known, both in general and in the case of people with learning disabilities (e.g. Agosto, 2013; Grove & Harwood, 2007; Koenig & Zorn, 2002, Manning, 2010). Our members value participation in the company certainly for the social and emotional benefits that this brought, but it was also obvious from the start that they are committed to the discipline and practice of storytelling as an art form in its own right – as the following comments[9] illustrate:

> *I've made more friends you know, they're all very good...and they're all friendly, they don't look at you as if you shouldn't be there you know, they all treat you as you would expect them to treat you.*
>
> (HE)

> *When I first started I felt like I was...on me own a lot, but when I went to storytelling I then felt like it's being in a great big circle, to me it feels like being in a family of professional storytellers.*
>
> (RM)

> *I can tell stories now without having to use a book, by using my imagination.*
>
> (RM)

> *Help me to listen to other stories...Helps us to get on with other people.*
>
> (FG)

> *I'd like to learn...how to improve my stories.*
>
> (RM)

In the interviews for this chapter, Parsley, Meader and Lewis likewise articulate specific personal benefits:

> CL: *Years ago I wouldn't have known how to speak up for myself whereas now I've got a voice.*
>
> RM: *Listening to (i.e. getting across) my own point of view...A lot more well balanced, and a lot more interactive keeps me more relaxed. I'm not sitting down going to sleep. Being part of a team, family, like being at home, can come out of your own little box and seeing how yourself is working out really well. Makes me feel really intelligent.*
>
> AP: *When we're in the group, having a discussion, I'm able to follow the conversation, and to ask if I don't. How it used to be, I used to lose the thread and give up, and get my book out. At that point, I couldn't express or acknowledge the problem...I suppose in a way I had to throw myself in the deep end, to get myself to wake up and change. If I hadn't joined storytelling I really don't know how I would be, or where I would be. I really don't know. Storytelling has really helped me.*

However, the purpose of the company is clear to them, and they have set themselves specific aims as storytellers[10] (and in the case of Meader, as an artist):

> AP: *To try to get to tell a story on my own. I've been in the process of doing it...I just have to push myself.* (We will return to the question of independent telling below.)
>
> CL: *To finish my own life story, write poems and publish it and get my own book. As a performer, better at my character in Fanny Fust, more precise.*

RM: *Designing a package (art and animation) to help people who are really struggling with COVID-19.*
Develop the character of Daniel Defoe, standing up for Peter like the judge stood up for Fanny.

So if the purpose of the company is not only to foreground the experiences of people with learning disabilities but also to develop skills in storytelling, what are the challenges and affordances involved?

Performance storytelling by people with learning disabilities

The traditional view of the professional storyteller is articulated by Yashinksy (2004:5):

> The fundamental experience of storytelling hasn't changed since the beginning of human history. One person speaks to a circle of listeners who give their attention. If the tale is told well, its words have the power to spark across the gap and take root in the listeners' souls.

This is the role of the storyteller as bard or shaman, with the quality of the telling (how well it is done) determined by verbal fluency. Early on in our project, we had a visit from a disabled artist practitioner, who offered us the benefit of his experience and some ideas on performance. One of his questions was why we were attempting to tackle such a demanding art form when so many of our members face some challenges in remembering, structuring and narrating stories. Similar points are made by McCaffrey (2019). Our visitor's advice was that we should consider abandoning oral narration and use mime and gesture instead.

However, although there is a popular perception that nonverbal movement and communication is a relative strength for performers with learning disabilities, this is by no means always the case. All of our storytellers were verbal communicators, none relied on sign; mime was in fact very challenging for the majority. More importantly, to negate their preferred and characteristic form of discourse would have felt profoundly disrespectful and inauthentic. We elected instead for an ethos that was collaborative, participatory, multi-modal and discursive, inviting audiences to pay close attention to the authentic voices of "experts by experience".[11] We profiled people's skills in storytelling and worked as far as we could so that tellers complemented each other, working as a team. Every contribution, however small, was valued. So, for example, when H, a rather quiet woman who lacked the confidence to tell on her own, was paired with Jane (tutor) for a Hallowe'en story, with both dressed as witches, Jane enumerated what they put into their cauldron, and H provided a forceful cackle, which functioned as the comic climax of the story.

Since those early days, many of the storytellers who have spent a long time in the company have developed the confidence and skills to tell stories solo in performance – however, the basic philosophy is that everyone has a story to tell and a unique way of putting it across which does not have to rely on the traditional model of storyteller as monologic bard. Parsley (above) articulated her personal aim as telling a story independently. We discussed this issue at some length, as she had in fact been engaged with this particular story for some time, and said frankly that she was finding the task challenging ("I just have to push myself"). Subsequently, reflecting on the power of the group, she stated:

> *The group has accepted me for me. Everyone, all of us have accepted all the others. Together we are more powerful than we are apart. I'm comfortable in the knowledge that when we're telling a*

> story, if I get lost, the others will put me back on track. I feel more comfortable, more confident, telling stories in the group than on my own.

Maybe solo narrative is a choice she wants to make – but maybe there are other avenues to pursue, such as tandem telling, using images or filmed inserts, telling through dialogue, interspersing reading original text. Such approaches blur the boundaries and challenge the orthodoxy that storytelling has to rely on oral transmission alone. In Calvert's words (2017:18) "What is at stake here is not the individual agency to determine one's own subjectivity, but the collective agency involved in negotiating meaning through performance".

Parsley later made the point that a collective ensemble does not in fact obscure or limit the contribution of the individual:

> For the audience, each of us is telling it from our own perspective even though we're members of the same group.

So where does this more collaborative aesthetic sit in the context of the art of storytelling?

The aesthetics of learning disability performance

Little has been written on learning disability narration, but the aesthetics of learning disability *theatre* are discussed in detail by Hargrave (2015), Calvert (2017) and McCaffrey (2019) *inter alia*. In brief, there is a consensus that a challenge for audiences and performers lies in the way in which a "dis-abled' identity is foregrounded and constructed. Hargrave and Calvert share the view that in a performance event there are two perspectives: "a social frame which foregrounds the performer's learning disability; and an aesthetic frame which is troubled by the appearance of learning disability" (Calvert, 2017;23). These remain in tension – there is no synthesis, but the relationship can be viewed as an intersectional, creative dynamic:

> …which investigates the aesthetic significance and innovations of learning disabled performance, while also considering cognitive impairment itself as inextricable from the aesthetics, as well as the thematic considerations and making practices of the performers. This critical approach maintains the connection between performance studies and disability studies to look at the ways in which artists with learning disabilities challenge received ideas about performance, while simultaneously reflecting on the challenges these performances present to the conventional understanding of learning disability in the social field.
>
> *(Calvert, 2017;16)*

Reason (2018) proposes five aesthetics whereby theatre making with learning disability engages an audience: universal and human (avoiding difference, celebrating shared humanity); radical (emphasising difference); identification (a radical sameness, where the audience are invited to cross the boundary and see themselves as, at times, disabled too); authentic (emphasising difference and lack of artifice – running the risk of romanticising performers as inherently naif); disruptive (foregrounding the question and occupying a space where reality and representation overlap or collide.

I posed the question about identity directly in interviews with my co-authors. "What do you want audiences to think about when they watch you performing? Is it important to be seen as storytellers with learning disabilities, or would you want them to see you just as storytellers?" Their responses show how alive they are to the conundrum:

> RM: *Well there are two choices. I want them to see, yes we have got learning disabilities but that we are also independent storytellers, an international company...When we perform I want them to see the actual person in the story, like an animation for real, seeing the characters come to life, gets the audience into that other world.*
>
> AP: *The audience to be aware we have learning disabilities, and to realise that just because we've got learning disabilities doesn't mean we can't tell stories. Accept us the way we are, as storytellers regardless of disabilities.*
>
> CL: *I'm hoping they are thinking how good we are...They know what they're actually looking at, cheer us on...Just because I've got a minor disability that doesn't make me stupid.*

Clemma is forthright – audiences can take it or leave it, she is confident in what is on offer:

> *I know what makes a good performance and if you like it, come and see it, and if not, you don't have to...we're learning.*

Their answers can't be pigeonholed into any one of the categories proposed by Reason, but they certainly incorporate the universal, the disruptive and authentic presence. The radical political challenging stance (type 3) characteristic of some learning disability theatre is not – currently – particularly prominent; and they don't talk here about the kind of boundary crossing and blurring that is critical to an identification aesthetic.

What stories do we tell?

The company continues to develop personal and group repertoires of traditional stories, with public performances and events focusing on two areas where we feel we have a unique contribution to offer: legends that feature characters with disabilities, and hidden histories.

Legends

We explore the role of legends as vehicles for exploring and challenging stereotypic representations of impairments.

For example, the group took the story of the hunchback who dances with goblins to Festival at the Edge, the UK's premier prominent storytelling gathering. In the story a hunchback is vilified for his disability by the villagers, in particular the bullying baker. He meets the goblins, and shows no fear of them, despite their "deformities". Instead he rejoices in their music and entertains them with his wonderful dancing (despite his so-called disability), for which he is rewarded with a sack of gold. Believing that his hump is his most valuable possession, the goblins keep it as security to make sure that he returns to dance for them again. The following evening, the baker visits the goblins to get a similar reward, but dances so badly that they want to get rid of him – this they do by giving him the hump. Thus the tables are turned.

This complex story carries a surface moral that those who bully and stigmatise may themselves be punished by becoming like their victims – i.e. disability as pejorative. However, the more intriguing aspect, which the group chose to highlight, is the goblins' appreciation of the protagonist's difference from other humans (who all look the same) by poetically describing his "deformed" spine as being beautiful like the twisted trunk of an aged and venerated tree. The group usually finished the telling by asking the audience whether the this newly acquired "deformity" made him behave more or less compassionately to those who were different from the norm. They also discussed the tyranny of idealised views of beauty.

One of the favourite genres of the company is "Jack" tales, found of course all over the world. In many of these stories, Jack takes the role of "simpleton", with a guileless take on life[12] and the literal interpretation of instructions that is characteristic of many individuals on the autism spectrum. For example in the English tale of "Silly Jack", he follows his mother's instructions to the letter and ends up carrying a donkey on his shoulders through the town. On the surface, we laugh at Jack, but in fact when we look deeper, the underlying problem is his mother's failure to specify precisely what she needs him to do. This fits not only with the experience of speech and language therapists, training staff to adjust their language, but also with a social model of disability, where the issue is how to change attitudes and practice of interactive partners. We had a lot of fun with "Jack's Review" – a show that imagined an annual review where professionals shook their heads over Jack's presumed incompetence as revealed in the first half of several stories, only to have their preconceptions overturned when Jack advocated for himself and showed how he was vindicated by the end of the tale.

It's evident that there are in fact very many stories that feature characters who are present with neuro-diversity (Grove et al., 2016). The telling of these tales is part of the history of disability but also the history of storytelling. Often the tales carry messages about inclusivity, though they may also reflect stigma and scapegoating. Care needs to be taken not to simply reinforce stereotypes. Thus, when we tell a story such as "The Three Sillies" we always relate it to our own experiences of doing stupid things.

Hidden histories

Unearthing and voicing untold stories of people with learning disabilities is a particular focus for the work of the company.

Peter the "Wild Boy" came to public attention through the historian Lucy Worsley, who – working with a geneticist – established that he probably had the condition Pitt Hopkins syndrome. In the 1740s, Peter was found living wild in the German forests, came to the court of George II and was something of a sensation. He never developed speech, found it hard to conform to polite expectations, was cared for at a farm in adulthood and was lost for a time when he ran away, ending up in Norwich in the public lock-up – where he nearly perished in a fire. Learning about Peter's story meant that we delved into historical records, and contemporary accounts, leading us to reflect on comparisons between then and now (Branch et al., 2018).

> RM: *The description of him as a thing in human shape says he might be an animal. Something creepy like a hunchback or werewolf.*
> KB: *It isn't very nice. It may mean that they are not treated well*
> TLS: *I think what interested them is that never seen a boy as wild as that.*
> *He is ending up as a trophy in a cabinet.*
> *I think even today people can be treated like Peter. I used to have a job in a riding stable, and I wasn't allowed to have coffee with the girls, I had to sit separately as if they didn't want to be associated with me.*
>
> (Branch et al., 2018)

More recently, C, a member working on the new production of this story said:

> It's really good the story. I like when he comes out of his shell and telling us about his life, like when he was in the dungeon. It's a little bit upsetting, but he gets through.

Her comment illustrates the importance of the story in creating empathy and a sense of resilience.

The Adventures and Misadventures of Fanny Fust coincidentally also draws on the 18thC. Fanny was a young Bristol heiress, with what would now be termed severe learning disabilities, who was abducted by a fortune hunter. Her story conforms precisely to the structure of a contemporary picaresque novel: she is entrapped by former friends, taken all over France in a desperate attempt to fund a priest who will marry her to her abductor, finally being tracked down by agents employed by her mother and returned home. A four-year court case ensued, which turned on the question – highly relevant today – of her capacity to give informed consent. This project was a collaboration with researchers from the History and English departments of Bristol University, and involved visits to local 18th C sites, learning about customs, dress, transport, legal systems, dance, art and literature. The performance was informed by our readings of epistolary novels, so we composed and read imaginary (and real) letters to help communicate the story. The culmination was the court case, where conflicting testimonies were read out and the audience invited to act as the jury to determine Fanny's capacity. Again, it was critical to locate the production in relation to our own 21stC experience. CL and NG researched news reports of young women with learning disabilities in abusive and coercive relationships. BL reflected at the end of each performance on how Fanny reminded him of a closely supervised female friend.

In both cases, careful research determined that although there were clearly features of each story which involved stigma and prejudice, in fact the people who surrounded both Peter and Fanny demonstrated affection, care and good judgement, which compares rather favourably with what happens now. We really have not come all that far in 300 years, when we are still uncovering terrible abuses in care homes, and despicable exploitation and bullying.

Touchstone stories

Asked about which stories really were the ones that convey the ethos of the company, all the co-authors mentioned our historic stories – as these are the current focus of production and rehearsal. Two others from the repertoire were selected as particularly meaningful.

Awongalema[13]

This African folk tale tells of the magic tree which gives sustenance and life when its name is spoken aloud. The animals have all forgotten the name and have to travel to discover it from the mountain spirit – however, due to their particular foibles, they all forget the name as they hurry back. Tortoise keeps asking to be nominated but is scorned and laughed at because he will be too slow…but in the end, he is the one to remember.

Lewis and Parsley both felt this had critical messages to put across.

> AP: The one that was the slowest proved that just because you're slow doesn't mean you're not able to do it.
>
> CL: The message is don't underestimate the power of a small animal, don't be cruel.

Meader's choice was *Stone Soup*, which was in fact one of the first stories we told as a group and is used in workshops to explain how the group runs. Meader also values the story for its inclusivity, thinking of its multi-sensory potential when used with people who have sensory impairments.

Stone Soup[14]

The townsfolk are fascinated by an itinerant pedlar who arrives in the market place, sets a fire, collects water, puts it in a cauldron and adds a stone. To the question "what's cooking?" comes the answer "stone soup...the most delicious soup in the world!" "Can I taste it?" "Hm let me check...not ready really, needs a certain something before I would want you trying it...I think...Carrot..." "I have a carrot, look here!" By the end of the day the soup is rich with donated produce and there is more than enough to go round. But what does he do at the end with the stone?

> *Stone soup, can get all the audience involved – it's like teaching people how to cook and how to share their food. It's really interactive; gets people sharing in their own life. The magic is, it's a stone that's brought people together to share their experiences. It's the stone, the people, the experiences.*

Meader went on to describe more broadly the importance of stories and storytelling.

> *Stories are like a time machine, about people from long ago, people from now and people from tomorrow. If you use your voice as a storyteller they can imagine inside their minds what it is like to be the person in the story...*

Stories, in other words, have to be told.

Conclusion

Finally, it's critical for me as lead author, to say something about my own learning through nearly 20 years of work with a dedicated and committed group of storytellers who have learning disabilities. That learning has been at a personal level – managing anxiety about the future and developing my own resilience with their support; at an academic professional level – testing theories about narrative by openly discussing theories as well as practical applications; political as I realise how often I still fall into traps of low expectations and lazy assumptions; and professional as I am pushed to try working outside my comfort zone of oral bardic performance telling.

I and my co-authors do endorse the view that storytelling is a therapeutic endeavour in the broad sense. Through stories we come to understand ourselves and other people, to imagine solutions to our problems, to know that our experiences are valid because they are reflected in the legends people have told for thousands of years. But including people with learning disabilities as tellers, as well as audiences, is also beneficial to society. They shift the balance of power by taking control of narratives that reflect their own experiences. They offer us new ways of listening – not always comfortable or easy, but important. By foregrounding, as we do, the collaborative, interdependent nature of telling, we challenge not only the hegemony of bardic storytelling, but a neoliberal agenda that explicitly values and privileges autonomy, independence and material achievement. Above all we are reminded that storytelling is the right and the inheritance, of us all. Stories and the experiences that give rise to them must be passed on and shared if we are to build sustainable and empowered communities. As Robin Meader says:

if we tell a thousand times, pass the story on, everyone gets a chance to tell it, not stuck in a ball going round and round and we can't tell the story.

Acknowledgements

OpenStoryTellers is a true collaboration, and we would like to pay tribute to the contributions of past and present members, staff and volunteers, with particular mention of Brian Marshall, Jem Dick, Jane Harwood and Derry Street. Vicki Ross who did so much to develop the early work of the company. More information can be found at www.openstorytellers.org.uk.

The work described in this chapter was funded by grants from numerous sources, amongst which we gratefully acknowledge The Big Lottery; the Arts Council; the Brigstow Institute, the Heritage Lottery Foundation.

Thanks to:

Dave Calvert and Matthew Reason for sharing their research with us.

Sharon Jacksties for her in-depth analysis of *The Hunchback and the Goblins*. Versions of this story can be found at www.pitt.edu/~dash/type0503.html; the Japanese legend of *The Old Man who lost his Wen* coming closest to the version told by OpenStoryTellers.

Notes

1. We dedicate this chapter to the memory of Brian Marshall (1951–2021).
2. Terms are confusing. In the US, "learning disabilities" refers to specific problems with maths, reading, writing – e.g. dyslexia. The worldwide term is "intellectual disabilities", but in the UK self-advocates prefer the term "learning disabilities".
3. https://communitydoor.org.au/service-delivery/disability/how-to-hear-me-a-resource-kit-for-working-with-people-with-intellectu-18
4. It is noteworthy that at the time of writing (May 2020), news outlets in the UK were slow to report on the impact of COVID-19 on the life chances of people with learning disabilities, and when they did so, featured reports from carers rather than from self-advocates.
5. Building on an earlier exploratory project funded by the Health Foundation www.health.org.uk
6. A box with painted scenes which opens out to tell the story in sequence, traditionally used in the Indian sub-continent by itinerant storytellers.
7. www.ldabc.ca/guest-post-can-art-therapy-help-those-with-learning-disabilities/ retrieved 23/5/20
8. www.nccata.org/research retrieved 25/5/20
9. Collected from a 2005 focus group discussion early in the history of the company.
10. References to performances are explained below.
11. www.england.nhs.uk/learning-disabilities/about/resources/caretransformed/expert-by-experience/ retrieved 25/5/20
12. It is important not to fall into the honey trap of overstatement, stereotyping people with learning disabilities as holy innocents.
13. https://spellbinders.org/story/the-awongalema-tree/ retrieved 31/5/20
14. www.learningtogive.org/sites/default/files/handouts/Story_Stone_Soup.pdf retrieved 31/5/20

References

Agosto, D. (2013). If I had three wishes: the educational and social/emotional benefits of oral storytelling. *Storytelling, Self, Society, 9*(1), 53–76.

Barnes, C. (2012). Understanding the social model of disability: past, present and future. In N. Watson & S. Vehmas (Eds.) *The Routledge Handbook of disability studies.* London: RKP, (pp. 12–29).

Branch, K., Fleet, C., Grove, N., Lumley-Smith, T. & Meader, R. (2018). What Peter means to us: researching the past and present of Peter the Wild Boy. In C. Goodey, P. McDonagh & T. Stainton (Eds.) *Intellectual disability: a conceptual history 1200–1900*. Manchester: Manchester University Press, (pp. 148–161).

Calvert, D. (2017) *Performance, learning disability and the priority of the object: A study of dialectics, dynamism and performativity in the work of learning disabled artists.* PhD thesis, University of Warwick. http://wrap.warwick.ac.uk/95588/1/WRAP_Theses_Calvert_2017.pdf. Accessed 25/5/20.

Corby, D., Taggart, L. & Cousins, W. (2018). The lived experience of people with intellectual disabilities in post-secondary or higher education. *Journal of Intellectual Disabilities,* October 9. 1744629518805603 retrieved 22/5/20

De Botton, A. & Armstrong, J. (2013). *Art as therapy*. London: Phaidon Press.

Emerson, E. & Hatton, C. (2016). *Estimating Future Need for Social Care among Adults with Learning Disabilities in England: An Update*. Available from http://webarchive.nationalarchives.gov.uk retrieved 31/5/20

Goodley, Dan (2011). *Disability Studies: an interdisciplinary introduction*. London: Sage.

Grove, N, (2007). Exploring the absence of high points in story reminiscence with carers of people with profound disabilities. *Journal of Policy and Practice in Intellectual Disabilities, 4,* 252–259.

Grove, N. (2009). *Learning to tell; a handbook for inclusive storytelling*. Kidderminster: British Institute of Learning Disabilities.

Grove, N. (2014). *The big book of storysharing*. London: Speechmark.

Grove, N. & Harwood, J. (2007). How storytelling contributes to quality of life for people with learning disabilities. *SLD Experience, 48,* 27–30.

Grove, N., Takano, M., Udo, M. & Mitsudo, Y. (2016). Heroes with a difference: Legends and personal stories with Japanese school children. *SLD Experience,* Spring 2016, 3–5.

Hardy, B. (1968). Towards a poetics of fiction: an approach through narrative. *Novel, 1,* 5–14.

Hargrave, M. (2015). *Theatres of learning disability: good, bad or plain ugly*? Basingstoke: Palgrave Macmillan.

Kay-Raining Bird, E., Cleave, P., White, D., Pike, H. & Helmkay, A. (2008). Written and oral narratives of children and adolescents with Down syndrome. *Journal of Speech, Language and Hearing Research, 51,* 436–450.

Koenig, J. & Zorn, C. (2002). Using storytelling as an approach to teaching and learning with diverse students. *Journal of Nursing Education, 41*(9), 393–399.

Manning, C. (2010), 'My memory's back!' Inclusive learning disability research using ethics, oral history and digital storytelling. *British Journal of Learning Disabilities, 38,* 160–167. doi:10.1111/j.1468-3156.2009.00567.x

McCaffrey, T. (2019). Giving voice: making theatre with actors who have learning disabilities. www.researchgate.net/publication/331561308_Giving_voice_making_theatre_with_actors_who_have_intellectual_disabilities retrieved 30/5/2020.

Reason, M. (2018). Ways of watching: Five aesthetics of learning disability theatre. In B. Hadley & D. MacDonald (Eds.) *The Routledge Handbook of disability arts, culture and media*. London: Taylor and Francis, (pp. 163–175).

Smith, N., Westcott, L. & Edmonds, J. (2018). *Experts by experience: no such word as can't and what we learnt along the way*. Sussex Partnership NHS Trust. www.bps.org.uk retrieved 31/5/2020

Yashinsky, D. (2004). *Suddenly they heard footsteps: storytelling for the 21st Century*. Toronto: Vintage Canada.

21
FROM ISOLATION TO INTEGRATION AND ADVOCACY

Healing and empowerment through storytelling

Lani Peterson

Introduction

Tall and lean with a fountain of dreads cascading from a red bandana on the top of his head, nineteen-year-old Martin exuded a nervous energy that permeated the room. Barely able to contain himself in his seat, he seemed to be struggling with whether to stay in the room or to flee. That winter evening, Martin was attending a performance sponsored by City Mission Boston's Public Voice Project (PVP). After just six sessions of working with a facilitator, a group of eight storytellers between the ages of twenty-five and eighty were daring to bring their stories of racism, violence, poverty, and homelessness to the stage. When all the presentations were done, the audience was invited to share their appreciations and ask questions of the tellers. Martin jumped to his feet and asked, "How can I get to tell MY story? Because it is killing me." He was not speaking in metaphor.

Before the evening was over, Martin had filled out the application to attend the next story workshop scheduled for March. With exuberance, he convinced the woman who had given him a ride that evening, his best friend's mother, Beverly, to sign up to take the workshop with him. When asked about his commitment to join the program, Martin made assurances that he would attend. Beverly said she would see to it that they both made it. For Beverly, it was a promise as best as she was able, to keep him alive until then.

The first PVP was launched in November of 2004 by City Mission Boston to build a speaker's bureau for formerly incarcerated men to raise public awareness about social justice issues related to incarceration, rehabilitation, and re-entry. The overall intent was to create a process that would be as helpful to the speakers as the content would be to the public forums where they were invited to tell their stories. By telling the stories of their journeys through the penal system and beyond, these men could impact policy reform while gaining increased self-awareness, confidence, and the ability to positively present themselves to prospective employers, landlords, and future colleagues. The PVP expanded over time to offer storytelling workshops to formerly incarcerated women, youth at risk, homeless men and women, and young women trying to escape a history of street-trafficking.

The workshop Martin and Beverly attended in the spring of 2013 was offered for free (subsidized by a generous grant from the Roxbury Foundation) to any resident of Roxbury, Massachusetts. The goals of the storytelling program had evolved to encompass personal development through insight into stories of self and other, public education around important social issues, and community building through shared stories. By that time, many rounds of previous observation and experimental application of theory had influenced the evolving curriculum of the storytelling workshop. As each round of the PVP evolved, facilitators became increasingly aware of the power of the story sharing process to positively impact the tellers as much as the audience.

The following chapter speaks to some of these observations and learning, integrated with various narrative theories about healing. I am tremendously grateful to participants like Martin and Beverly (names changed), who through their presence, courage, and trust helped me to better understand what happens when people come together to discover, reclaim, and share their stories. As a White, female facilitator in her late 50s leading multi-race, multi-age groups coming together to share their stories, I am continually working to be aware of my own story lens and its limited perspective. My goal is to support the emergence of the story that is wanting to be told with the aim of eliciting a "thicker story" for the sake of the participant as well as their audiences. Through this work of being witness to these stories of perseverance, courage, and growth, I am grateful for the myriad ways my own storied lens has expanded.

Overview of theoretical models that contribute to narrative healing approaches

There are many theoretical models that address narrative approaches to storytelling and its intersection with healing. There is both overlap and important information within each of these theoretical frameworks which have influenced the evolution of PVP's healing storytelling workshops.

In her book, *Trauma and Recovery; The Aftermath of Violence – From Domestic Abuse to Political Terror,* Judith Herman presents the narrative stages of healing from trauma as:

1. Establishing safety
2. Reconstructing the traumatic story
3. Restoring the connection between the survivor and their community.

Shearer-Cremean and Winkelman, authors of *Survivor Rhetoric: Negotiations and Narrativity in Abused Women's Language,* describe a related process of narrative healing. Individuals are encouraged to tell their story to move from:

1. Silence and isolation, to
2. Agency, to
3. Integration, a final stage that opens the door to advocacy and social organizing.

Finally, within the traditional story arc, there is movement from a:

1. Beginning (what things were like before something happened), to a
2. Middle (what happened), to an
3. End (what things are like now because of what happened).

Each of these models has a common progression through three main stages. There is an evolution that begins in an initial place of silence, isolation, and/or losing equilibrium. The middle stage involves using agency to work and rework a relationship to a given situation. Ultimately, the end results in a return to some form of equilibrium but changed by a renewed perspective or insight. In an ideal outcome, the change involves empowerment to engage and sustain a healthier connection to one's self, relationships, and larger community.

Many things can happen through a story exploration process. As tellers intentionally focus on developing a story to tell others, they are also hearing themselves. Walking around a story from multiple perspectives opens that story to deeper inspection and an opportunity to challenge previously held assumptions. Through sharing the story with others and feeling heard through active listening and appreciation, tellers gain deeper insight into the parts of their story that previously may have been blind spots. They have a chance to tease out places in the story where they did or didn't have control, where they relied on personal strengths or resources to meet difficult challenges, to see more clearly the ways that they coped and survived. They have the potential to move from being the victim to the hero of their story.

Doing story work within a safe and supportive community enables tellers to witness and be witnessed, to listen and feel heard. Hearing others' stories helps to normalize each teller's experience while building active listening skills and encouraging compassionate and empathic responses. Group members build respect for and responsibility towards self and other in balance through an increased focus on presence and awareness of self in relation to others.

In this way storytelling and story listening are built on emotional intelligence: knowing and sharing oneself while also getting to know and understand others. Through evolving insights and growing perspective, both are enabled to move to a stronger place.

Within our PVP workshop structure, we focus on creating safety, trust, and connection in the first stage (**Beginning**). Participants are supported to emerge out of their silence (story isolation) to join a group of fellow tellers who are also ready to share storytelling and listening in a safe space.

In the second stage (**Middle**) participants are invited to remember; to find the story that needs to be told. Exploring a story through exercises that involve multiple tellings, storytellers challenge the meaning they make of their story and their role in it. In hero's journey terms, it is facing the dragons within their story, be they external or internal. This is a process of increasing agency, moving from a passive retelling of a stuck or painful story, to an active re-working/owning of that story. The facts of the story have not changed, but a new relationship to the meaning of the story can lead to increased confidence and empowered choice to move differently into the future.

The narrative healing journey, however, is not complete until stage three **(End),** when the storyteller brings the renewed and empowering story back to their old life and steps into it in a new way. This often involves a public telling to begin the process of both integration and sustainability of the new and empowered story into the storyteller's life, family, and/or community.

Stage 1 Beginning: emerging out of isolation and silence

Many Public Voice workshops are formed around homogenous groupings with a specific focus on a related issue: formerly incarcerated, homelessness, youth at risk, women escaping the street-trafficking industry. The group depicted in this writing was generated in response to a generic flyer posted by local non-profit organizations, churches and community centres. Participants were invited to learn storytelling and public speaking skills, with the option to share their stories though PVP's social justice advocacy speaker's bureau. This outreach resulted in a group with diverse backgrounds and agendas attending this storytelling and advocacy program.

For purposes of brevity, this chapter focuses on the experiences of Martin and Beverly, who are Black. There were six other participants in the group: three White women, one other Black young adult man, and one man of Black/Hispanic/European heritage. Their racial backgrounds are important in considering the complexity of the social context of their lived experience and the courage they displayed in openly sharing their vulnerable stories first with each other and ultimately with public audiences.

Pre-interview process

Potential participants are interviewed prior to the first meeting to give them more of a sense of what the workshop will entail and to help facilitators learn more about their interest in taking it. The pre-interview questions are themselves an intervention, guiding participants to think about who they are in their story and what they hope to accomplish in exploring it and telling it to others. The pre-group interview questions explore whether the potential group member is ready, willing, able, and stable to do story work in a group format. (We asked the same questions of ourselves as group leaders before beginning this work in leading others.)

- **Ready** (Clarity of purpose): Why are you interested in taking this workshop? Is this the right time in your life to do this work? What do you hope to gain from your involvement? What do you plan to contribute?
- **Willing** (Openness to self-exploration and sharing with others): Are you willing to explore and perhaps share personal stories? Can you be thoroughly present for both yourself and others through this process of self-discovery, vulnerability, and disclosure?
- **Able** (Commitment and perseverance): Are you able to physically commit to this process, including the time and resources, as well as transportation to get to meetings? Does this program conflict with other responsibilities in your life right now? Can you make the commitment to attend all the sessions?
- **Stable** (Emotional stability): How will you manage your emotional journey if things get stirred up for you through this story sharing process? Who or what are your supports external to this group (e.g.: family, friends, mentors, therapist, clergy)? What do you see as your strongest inner resources (self-discipline, resiliency, conflict resolution skills, experience with similar challenges in the past)? What is your experience of working with people who are different from you (people whose struggles may have seemed to you to be less important or heavier than your own?) What would you need to have in place to be comfortable in this workshop experience?

The pre-interview process is designed to ensure that participants are clear about the expectations and potential demands of the group. Although they have chosen to come knowing they will be sharing personal stories, few realize what that means in terms of self-honesty, emotional vulnerability, and courage as well as possibly also awakening fear, shame, and anxiety. Similarly, they also have little idea of the potential benefits (increased self-confidence, clarity, deeper connection to self and other, pride, agency, power, freedom) that might arise should they see this process through to the end.

For this round of PVP, we interviewed ten candidates. Eight chose to participate in the group. For the purposes of this chapter, it is mostly important to know about Beverly and Martin.

Beverly is a single mother of three sons in her early-forties. She works as an administrative assistant and is active in her church. Her oldest son, seventeen-year-old William, had been murdered the previous year when he resisted a peer trying to steal the new gold necklace he had just bought with his first legitimate earnings. Over the previous year, William had been working hard to turn his life around: attending school more regularly, getting an after-school job, and trying to stay away from old friends who were putting pressure on him to follow them into gang activity.

Through a similar path of getting into trouble and out again, Martin and William had become close friends. Since William's death, Martin had been wracked with guilt that he had not been with William on the night he died, to either save him or die with him. Since William's death, Martin now spent more time in Beverly's home than in his own. Beverly had heard about the Public Voice Project and brought Martin to the open telling in their neighbourhood, hoping it might help him to hear stories of how others had struggled with adversity and survived. She had been pleased to see his interest to be part of a future training as well as his earnestness to tell his own story in a public forum. She was here for him, but after the interview process, she realized she also had a story that needed to be told.

The first night of our storytelling group, Beverly arrived a few minutes early. Martin was not with her. She said that they had talked earlier in the afternoon and he promised to meet her at the church where the workshop was being held. Throughout the evening, we kept the door open for him.

Getting comfortable

In the first few sessions of the storytelling workshop, most of the focus is on building trust and connection between group members and with staff. Gathering for the first time, participants may be feeling vulnerable or self-conscious about the stories they bring with them. The first phase, therefore, is about establishing comfort while also gently encouraging participants to take small risks in emerging out of isolation and silence. To encourage connection with others in meaningful ways through their stories, introductory exercises are built upon seemingly simple prompts. Examples include, "Tell me the story of your name," or "Tell me a story about your shoes." Although "seemingly simple," any prompt can lead to flooding or a triggered reaction, especially for those who have a history of trauma. At this early juncture, it is important to let participants know that they are in control of their story and can share as little or as much as they choose.

Establishing safety

When a group gathers for the first time, it is essential to establish a culture of safety and trust in the form of a group safety agreement. The initial introductory storytelling prompt of telling about their name or their shoes gives everyone an idea of what it feels like to share in the group. Now it would be easier to think about what they might need to have in place to feel safe enough to go deeper. As participants wrestle individually and collectively through brainstorming about what safety means to them, essential components begin to emerge. Examples from previous groups include:

- Speak only for yourself
- What's said in the room stays in the room
- Speak with honesty

- Respect one another
  - No criticizing others
  - One person talks at a time
  - Tolerate all ideas and all feelings (your own and others)
  - It's okay to cry (this was raised in a group of formerly incarcerated men who had never given themselves this permission before)
  - No violence of any kind—physical, verbal, emotional
  - Each person sets personal boundaries and limits—seek permission to ask questions or make comments on another's story
  - Judgement—own it and convey it respectfully
- Make room for everyone to share; step up to participate, step back to let others have a chance to talk as well
- Keep a focus on gratitude
- Bring a sense of humour, have fun

Some past participants have stated that creating a safety agreement together was one of the most empowering parts of the group for them. They had not previously reflected on their needs and/or felt empowered to state their wishes directly to others. Taking ownership and responsibility in both creating and maintaining a safe space to speak openly and honestly with others was the beginning of establishing enough agency to emerge from their silence or the isolated perspective that their voice is not important.

As the safety agreement is collaboratively created, we also talk about how such an agreement may still not prevent people from feeling unsafe. Two ideas have emerged over the years from these discussions:

1. There is a difference between being unsafe and being uncomfortable. We have coined the term: "Safely Uncomfortable" to describe the place we go when we challenge ourselves to step outside of our comfort zone in order to grow. Only we know when we are being too safe to grow. Likewise, only we know when we are pushing ourselves too far into a danger zone where we may get triggered. Everyone is encouraged to both challenge their old boundaries of comfort and simultaneously listen to and respect their internal cues when a story is too much or moving too fast. This can happen not only while telling one's own story but when listening to another. Together we created signals to use to let others know when we need to pause in the telling or listening to re-centre or step out for a moment.
2. Safety is not only taking preventative measures but knowing how to respond when one no longer feels safe. If someone becomes flooded or triggered, how can we care for ourselves and/or each other? In this opening session we talked about what people might do to self-calm. It can be helpful to introduce breathing and centring exercises at this early point in the workshop, that may become skills for a lifetime. Guided visualizations and mindfulness techniques have become a regular part of these workshops. A colleague once introduced me to the exercise of finding an anchor word that represents one's safe place within. Using indelible markers, participants write their anchor word on a small stone. Everyone is invited to keep their stone in their pocket to "ground" themselves when needed. I have run into participants years later who, after greeting me, pull their stone from their pocket to let me know they are still using it to bring themselves back to their calm place.

Through the first few meetings, both the participants and the workshop are in a beginning phase. Establishing a holding environment with consistency, repetition, and ritual further helps to strengthen the sense of safety and trust as members learn what to anticipate within the group structure as well as from each other. For that reason, we designed each session to unfold in the same way:

- Opening check-in
- Meditation or inner reflection to get centred
- Pause to review the previous session for thoughts or questions
- Introduce the theme or focus for this meeting
- Story work through exercises or prompts
- Debrief session with focus on new learning and questions
- Closing ritual

Check-ins

Through opening each session with a quick but storied check-in, participants are encouraged to reflect on what new experiences they have had since last meeting as well as what excites them about what might be ahead. The weekly discipline establishes the habit of looking within to reflect on the connection between experiences and emotions. Many participants have said that personal check-in has evolved into a mindfulness practice they use in between sessions. Checking in with themselves to get a reading on highs and lows has helped them to monitor habitual reactions and behaviours, and the underlying emotions that may be fuelling them. Ritual check-in also gives the message that everyone's experience is important, and the group is not started until every voice is heard.

We have found it helpful to use a metaphor structure to share highs and lows. Two different metaphors we have found work well are:

- Share a "peak" (high point), a "pit" (low point) and a "vista" (something you are looking forward to out ahead). It could be about what's happened since the last meeting, or a more general overview of what you are carrying in your mind, heart, or body as you enter the room for this session. The forward-looking part of the prompt (vista) is a gentle reminder that the current emotional state will most likely change with future events.
- Share a "rose petal" (something sweet), "thorn" (something challenging or painful), and "bud" (something you are looking forward to blooming).

Each participant gets a timed minute to share. Although people preliminarily tend to separate out their highs and lows, by the end of the workshop many people begin to see how interrelated are their highs, lows, and hoped for changes. We have also found that in the early weeks, check-ins can be superficial and protected. As the group builds trust and interest in each other, check-ins become more meaningful. It is important to time each person as they can become involved and time-consuming otherwise.

Martin never showed up for that first session. Beverly appeared to be disappointed but not surprised. Upon leaving, she affirmed that Martin genuinely wanted to be a part of this program, and she hoped that he might make it for the second session. If he came, would he still be welcome? It was agreed that he could participate as long as he could be there for week number two.

Stage 2 Middle: building agency through re-storying – listening to self and others

We are meaning-making creatures, and our human minds are involved in a constant process of rewriting our stories to fit our current reality. As new experiences occur, we respond by working to integrate the remembered self of the past with the perceived self of the present and the desired self of the future. Suffering happens when we get stuck in a thin story of cause and effect that keeps us smaller or less than we want to be. Story change work involves pausing the replay of an old story to explore it from multiple angles and perspectives. Insights, understanding, and wider possibilities for future action emerge through challenging and expanding the current meaning.

There are many ways that story change can occur. Speaking a story out loud allows the teller to hear themselves as the content moves out of the frontal lobe and re-enters through the temporal lobe. As outside listeners respond to the story with deepening responses through active listening or reflective question asking, new possibilities open for insight and understanding. Listening to others' storied answers to the same prompt allows one to normalize their experience of human suffering and/or see different ways of responding to a challenging situation or making sense of it afterwards. Exploring a story from different angles raises possibilities for meaning that may not previously have been seen. Perhaps most importantly, the very act of being in community and sharing part of yourself opens tellers and listeners alike to move out of silence and isolation. Engaging in active listening and meaningful connection is in itself a practice of agency.

Doing the work

After the first week, each session unfolds in the same manner, supporting participants to engage, build trust, and connect with each other through an expected sequence of rituals and exercises. Following check-ins and a meditative pause to help people centre and be present, the meeting moves to review the previous session and thoughts or questions that may have emerged over the course of the week. When all are settled, the current week's focus or theme is introduced and story sharing exercises begin.

On the second night of our workshop, Martin was not there again. Beverly was confused as she had spoken with him just an hour before and he said he was on his way. She appeared concerned, but it seemed that was a familiar feeling for her. An hour into the session, Martin appeared in the doorway. After an initial pause to assess the room, he planted himself in a seat in the furthest corner. When invited to participate in the current activity, he replied that he would rather just watch for a while.

The initial weeks of the workshop involve storytellers playing with multiple prompts to discover stories that may be wanting to be told. Similar to the first week, prompts begin simply and then evolve to probe more deeply. Storytellers are assured that they are always in charge of their story and free to choose how much to delve into details with any given listener.

Story exercises begin with prompts that leave room for tellers to take them in any direction or depth that they choose. Examples of early prompts include:

- Firsts: first day of school, first date, learning to drive a bike or car, attempting something new...
- A time when: I was cold, safe, angry, relieved, scared, challenged, successful, proud...
- Describe a favourite place and then tell about something that happened there
- Tell about a person who has been a mentor/teacher who helped you through something

The possibilities are endless to get people sharing stories in easy and fun ways.

Stories are shared between participants as they carefully monitor their personal boundaries and safety, testing the waters of how much to share with each new partner. This process of opening to another through story sharing is new to them and they are still vulnerable in their telling. Later there will be time for expanding dyads into triads and eventually everyone will stand in front of the whole group to tell a story.

When participants form into new dyads for the next exercise, Martin jumps up and stands next to Rodrigo, another young man of colour in his late twenties. The prompt was a simple one. Martin began by sharing a story with Rodrigo. Rodrigo leaned in to listen intently. When Martin was finished, Rodrigo quietly shared some appreciations for what he had heard.

Following a story telling, listeners are instructed to share back what they heard, responding with both their head and their hearts. From their head: the most important message I heard in the story you just shared. From their heart: how that story moved or touched me.

When the round is over, partners are invited to thank each other for both the telling and the listening in any way that feels mutually comfortable. Rodrigo gave Martin a long hug. Then everyone changes partners, and the exercise is repeated with either the same prompt or a new one. Martin does not return to his corner chair but stays in the next exercise to be the listener for another. This time, with a huge smile across his face, Martin initiates the hug afterwards to his storyteller. It is the end of week two, and Martin has finally engaged.

As participants get comfortable with story techniques and feel safer in the company of each other, the prompts can get more serious. Some examples include:

- A challenge you faced and how you met it
- A time when it felt like everything changed (it all changed when…)
- A moment when you saw things differently
- "I used to be…, but now I am…"

In the last few sessions, storytellers focus on one story that they want to develop to share with a public audience at the end of the program. It is an opportunity to explore one story deeply to see what they can learn about the story and its meaning for them. Exercises turn towards uncovering and exploring underlying messages buried within a story. Working in multiple different dyad combinations, each group member gets the opportunity to tell their story multiple times to different partners to hear the impact of the story on differing listeners/audiences.

Playing the role of story listener for each other, everyone in the group now has developed skills of appreciation and active listening to reflect what they heard as the most important messages within each other's stories. Appreciations are different from feedback. They involve listeners owning their perspective and speaking to what they appreciated about what they heard; what they were moved by or will most remember from hearing the story. It gives the storyteller insight into what is memorable, meaningful, and impactful in their stories. Through this process of mutual story sharing, all participants are normalizing their own experiences of struggle and growth as well as developing connection and empathy to others.

One of the empowering ideas conveyed within these sessions is that we can't change the facts of our stories, but we do create our own meanings and those meanings can change as we grow. Is the meaning you now hold one that sustains you and helps you in your journey forward? Or is it a meaning that constrains you, keeping you stuck or feeling like less than you are or want to be? Through challenging the meaning that one is making of a story and playing with different possibilities and outcomes, a thin story has a chance not to change but to grow. A thin story with one conclusion expands into a thicker story that holds more room for the complexities of a larger truth.

Through the last few sessions, group members' stories began to evolve. They worked together, telling and listening to each other to find the parts of their story that fit together to deliver the message they want this audience to hear.

Each week, Beverly had courageously opened herself towards revisiting the story of her son's death. Although poignant in the recounting of the facts, she told her story with a stoicism that revealed none of the underlying emotion that she was carrying or the larger message of meaning it held for her. When asked if she would be willing to work on her story at a deeper level, she hesitated but agreed.

Beverly was surprised when asked to describe William. As she drew a verbal picture of him with her words, her face began to soften. When asked about the way he talked, her voice deepened as she repeated "Love you, Ma, but give me some space." As she spoke his words, she was both laughing and weeping. When asked about how he walked or moved through space, she shared with the group that he loved to dance. As she moved her matronly body as if she were a teenage boy, William was in the room with us.

This opened Beverly to tell a story focused on more than William's death. She related with a humour tinted with frustration that he was a charmer, a big personality; someone well-liked by his peers, but sometimes attracting the wrong kind of attention. She knew that he often felt angry and confused by the cultural messages he received about who he was and what he was capable of. He had come to believe that school was a waste of time and he stopped caring about his academics. His increasing truancy led authorities to become involved, but to her relief, William slowly responded to the guidance he received from them. He had been directed to a part-time after-school job, which had given him an honest income and direction. His first purchase was a gold necklace that he wore with symbolic pride of how he now saw and held himself. The irony of William dying by defending his necklace was not lost on Beverly.

As part of the story transformation process, tellers may be prompted to think about how they want their story to unfold in the future. What might a positive next chapter look or feel like? What skills, resources or supports do they have internally or externally to make that happen? An example of this method is extending the prompt from "I used to be…, but now I am" to include "and someday I plan to be."

Beverly's story no longer ended with the night that William died. She related that she knew how much her son's friends were struggling, lost, and hurting. After the funeral, she opened her door to them. Anyone was welcome to come for a meal, or even spend the night if they needed a safe refuge. "And I mean, anyone," she stated firmly. "I suspect that William's murderer may be among the young men who have sought safety and comfort at my kitchen table. God forgive them. They are all wounded. They are all caught in a system not of their making. I will offer salves wherever I can, no questions asked."

The senselessness of William's death would have been a devastating message for Beverly to end on. Instead, Beverly introduced the audience to her charismatic and treasured son, helping them to also feel the devastating tragedy of his death. The central message in her story became how she transformed her loss and anger into a mission to support other young Black men to have a different outcome. Her story had grown from one of a grieving mother, paralyzed by anger and fear, to a champion of young Black lives and advocate for change in her neighbourhood.

Stage 3 End: social integration, advocacy, and sustainability

The healing process begins through re-authoring a thin story of shame or suffering into a thicker story with a wider perspective. Healing is solidified when a person can both maintain and gain strength from that thicker story even when returning to previous settings where the original story began. The transition to living in the thicker story begins with speaking those new truths in an open and honest way to those who may hold either a different story or different meaning to the facts of a same story.

Social integration, therefore, begins with challenging oneself to own and tell the thicker story beyond the safe circle of the group. That is the reasoning behind ending the workshop with a public storytelling event where members of family and community are invited to hear tellers share the story that they are ready to tell.

In the last week of the workshop, participants rehearse the latest version of their story as it now stands. Everyone is aware that a story is an evolving entity. The story that emerges in the dress rehearsal will resemble what they will share the following week to the public but will not be exactly the same. Memorization is a theatre performance. Storytelling is alive and shifts with each audience and telling. Our stories continue to change through our lifetime as we understand them more clearly or deeply through each new experience we have. That is where change lies and hope lives. The story we feel and know today will be different tomorrow, depending on the life we live in the interim, and the knowledge and perspective we accrue from living it. When we are open to exploring its evolving meaning for us, we allow ourselves to change and be changed by it. We are in a continual process of cocreation. As our life experiences impact us, we change ourselves as we thicken the stories of what we understand to be true in response to it.

In the last session of this workshop, one of the group members, Melody, a White woman in her early thirties, experienced a seizure while telling her story. Everyone rushed to her care and someone initiated a 911 call. At the sound of sirens, Martin raced from the room, down the stairwell and out to the curb to meet the ambulance. Through the open window we could hear Martin cursing at the medics. "Why did you take so long?" "You don't care about anyone in this neighbourhood." "You're okay to just let people here die."

Carrying a stretcher, the medics quickly and silently climbed the stairs as Martin raged beside them. Entering the room, one medic turned to Martin, telling him he had to leave the room for them to do their work safely. Martin refused but slunk into the chair in the far corner of the room. Within minutes, the paramedics stabilized Melody on a stretcher and left with sirens blazing. The rest of the group stood in shock in the now quiet room. Martin sat with his head in his hands quietly sobbing in the corner chair.

Everyone came together in a circle. With arms around each other, we did a check-in with how everyone was feeling in response to what happened. Martin had joined the circle but remained stiff and silent. By his side, Beverly spoke soothingly to him, encouraging him to share. When he remained silent, Beverly took us deeper into the story of William's death. She and Martin had later learned that William had not died immediately after being stabbed at the party. Although paramedics had arrived quickly to the crime scene, they were not allowed to enter the building until police arrived. In the five-minute interim that they waited outside, William bled to death.

As Beverly finished her last sentence, Martin's words poured out in rage. "None of this sh-t matters. Our stories don't matter. No one will ever listen anyway. This is all so fu--ed up. I'm done with this." I expected him to run from the room, but he stood still in the circle of his fellow tellers, now listeners, who continued to hold him and his words. And then group members began to respond with their heads and hearts to let him know he had been heard. "You've been through hell, man." "I feel your anger in my body." "I get why you responded tonight the way you did." "I feel your fear." As we had practiced through all our sessions, they did not try to soften his feelings, change his story, or advise him of next steps. They simply held him in his story and reflected what they heard, what touched them.

The meaning we make of any experience is impacted by all we have been through before and will unconsciously shape how we step into what is ahead. Remaining in silence or isolation while holding a painful story allows it to continue to wound us. Should we choose to tell our story to another, we have the opportunity to gain perspective. When we are held by another in our story or give ourselves a pause to reflect on the meaning we are making, we can question whether it is helpful (sustaining) or harmful (constraining) to us. Rather than react, we have the power to choose a response that leads us closer to our intentions and the future story we want to experience. Choosing our response is the foundation of agency and empowerment, both of which are at the heart of healing. Shifting our relationship to our story doesn't change the story but can change us.

The date for our community storytelling event arrived the following week. Before doors opened to the public, the group warmed up within a check-in circle to hear each other's feelings of excitement and dread as they anticipated telling their stories in a public venue. We spoke of Melody and the update that she was home and recovering. She wished everyone well. Martin was not present. Beverly had not seen him since the night of our last class.

Audience members began to arrive and fill the seats. Beverly's two younger sons, dressed in coat and tie, were already stealing the attention of the audience with their exuberant excitement. It was time to begin and Martin still was not there. As the evening's host opened the event, Martin entered through a side door, with a friend on either side. Beverly caught his eye and motioned for him to join the other storytellers up front. He hesitated, then stood and came down the aisle to take a seat next to Beverly.

One by one each storyteller stood in the front of the room to share the story that in that moment felt right to tell. They read the audience and matched their words and message to the gathered group. Beverly took her turn with a picture of William in her hands as her two little boys stood by her side. She began, "I want you to know my son, William. He was unique and beautiful and there are thousands of other vulnerable young men in danger of dying just like him."

Martin watched and waited. It was a moment of trust in himself, in us, in this process, when he finally rose to tell his story.

Martin began by talking about what had happened in class the week before and his reluctance to come tonight. He was tired and felt like nothing he could do would ever change the way things were. He felt like he had nothing left but his anger and his story and they were too intertwined to separate. But tonight, he was going to try to tell it in a way that people could hear it and get him. He went on to talk about his deep friendship with William and the grief and guilt he has lived with every day since William's death. He talked about the rage that runs just under his surface as people make assumptions about him based on his skin colour, his dress, his speech. He explained how hard it is to talk when all you want to do is explode. He talked about how much he wants to be seen and known but too often feels like no one really wants to know. He talked about how much he wants people to care.

A further transition from healing to empowerment occurs when tellers realize that their story matters to more than themselves. To enable social change to happen, others need to hear your story. This transition from discovering a story's personal meaning to seeing its relationship to larger social issues, can strengthen a teller's resolve to keep both their voice and message being heard.

Moreover, we can speak with blame or rage which distances others, or we can speak with confidence, clarity, and honest emotion that draw others into the depth, passion, or heartbreak that we are feeling. Through our stories we can deepen divisions with words that wound, or we can build allies who gain insight and compassion for our experiences and become inspired to join us in action. The way we tell our stories can lead to healing for ourselves, each other, and the communities that we share.

When the audience rose out of their seats to applaud Martin at the end of his story, he stood still and took it in. Later in the evening I looked over to see him talking animatedly to a local politician who had come to learn about his neighbourhood. Martin was no longer holding his story inside like an explosive device ready to detonate. He had found his voice and realized there was power and release in telling his story. I think many minds and lives changed that night.

We are all storytellers capable of healing and being healed through telling a story that needs to be heard. Simultaneously, we are all listeners capable of healing and being healed through opening ourselves to receive and be changed by the powerful stories within and around us. We can change ourselves and our world through the stories we choose to focus on, the meaning we make of those stories, and finally finding the courage to tell them to the people who need to hear them the most.

22
SEEKING A COMMON GROUND
Storytelling and social healing

Inger Lise Oelrich

In a light, spacious room, somewhere on the coast of the Baltic Sea outside of Stockholm, 30 people are sitting in deep concentration listening to each other speak, in Arabic. The hum and cadence of their voices rise and fall in concert, expressing worlds, landscapes and experiences under a scorching sun far away from our dark and cold Nordic winters with their high, light-filled summers. I don´t understand a word. But close by is our interpreter, Said, who is moving around quietly, picking up a word here and there, so I can have an idea of what kind of stories are turning up in the room.

I am leading a session on creativity, using storywork as a way of opening up imagination which, hopefully, can tackle the theme at hand from a broader perspective. Creative imagination is closely linked to dynamic thinking and, as we know, our thinking about a thing sends our actions into a particular direction. But if we always think in the same way about something, we probably will keep on doing the same things in relation to it. It might be wise to free ourselves a bit by jiggling the bag and mixing the cards. Storytelling and appreciative listening are an excellent way of doing this.

We are here under the auspices of the Folke Bernadotte Academy, a Swedish government authority for peace and security, who have invited the people present to discuss the oil situation in Iraq, where oil is prolific, with lots of petrodollars coming into the country but, unfortunately, these funds often flow out again without ever touching the ground, largely due to foreign investments. A large part of the population was at the time living with a lack of functioning hospitals, electricity, school buildings and other basic needs, particularly in the countryside. The question at hand can simply be expressed: Who owns the oil, the raw materials of the land?

The people present have flown in from Baghdad, and consist of various stakeholders, from government officials and local authorities to private businesses. The FBA has been supporting the growth of democratic processes in several Middle Eastern countries since 2007 by organising dialogues where a variety of voices can be heard in a more informal setting, under a different sky. I am not here as an expert on the oil question in Iraq; however, I do know something about story and how it can wake up and call out everyone's inherent humanity and wisdom, not to speak of ingenuity and radical thinking. I also know that storywork exercises strengthen the experience of human connection, creating a common ground between people who normally don't sit together and listen to each other. This is what I am up to, taking them through some different areas of freedom space. But like all things creative, results seldom come in a direct route. Lots of other things are opened up and come to the fore that are seemingly unrelated.

The storywork exercise I start out with can be done in practically any setting. People sit together in threes facing each other; the whole group is spread out across the room. I begin by saying a few words about the form and intent of what we are going to do. This is an exercise where one person speaks about a theme for three minutes, which I will announce in a moment. The other two have the task of listening without interrupting. I usually spend some time at this point talking about the art of listening and of being present. How do we listen in a friendly, interested way so the teller feels welcomed and received, no matter what they say? How do we help them feel they have all the time in the world? We are talking about a non-judgemental attitude, without interpreting or going off on tangents inwardly that have nothing to do with what the person is saying. No analysing or giving advice – just listen! I make the point that each person is responsible for what they say and how much passes over their lips; there is no group pressure. By now, everyone wants to get going and start "the game" it is time to decide who goes first. Now I give the theme: Tell the story of your name.

You can say anything you like; it doesn't have to be a full-feathered story, just speak about it from all kinds of point of view, yours, others', historically – whatever. Tell the story of your name. Freely.

And off they go, all at the same time. It actually works fine, even with many people. I remember doing this kind of exercise in Norway once, when I was giving a talk about storytelling to over a thousand kindergarten teachers in a huge hall. Each person just turned to the person next to them, nattering away.

It is interesting how speaking about your name opens up worlds about you for the listeners, while at the same time strengthening your own identity as you speak. Your name is imbued with your total life experience – it really turns out to be quite a personal affair. Besides, it is not difficult to speak about – you are the expert! After three minutes it's the next person's turn. I could continue with the same theme, but I decide to change direction a bit. Tell the story of your feet. Where have they been? What have they experienced? After all, they have carried you through your whole life – what have they felt, sensed? Cramped shoes, cool water in a brook, hot sand, hard pavement etc. Three minutes. Just speak. The others listen. By this time, they are starting to get it. Being listened to in this way reinforces your own open listening when it is your turn; in this way, each telling deepens, as the attentiveness in the group grows. Besides, being "given permission" to speak without being interrupted can be a complete novelty for some, to the point where someone might say afterwards: I have never spoken this long and been listened to like this before. Three minutes!

Finally, the third person gets their task: Tell the story of your hands. What have they done in life, touched, felt, experienced? It is a novel way of speaking about yourself, a bit quirky and exciting, and non-threatening. It can free you up to just let your voice come out, it doesn't have to turn into anything, you are just free-wheeling about something you know plenty about.

After these three short tellings, the groups come back to the full circle. How did it go? What did you experience? Was it difficult? I was really wondering how it went for them, most probably they had never done anything like this before, it is not part of traditional culture in Iraq. There was a silence.

Then responses came, one by one, in a measured way. We should do this more. We never listen like this to each other. We should go home and do this with our young people. The mood in the room was thoughtful. Then one man said, gesturing to another close by him: "My brother here and I, when we spoke about our feet, we both told about the battle of ..." It turned out they had both been in the battle, but on different sides of the mountain. A few more words were said, pointing to some mutual experience too great for words. There were slow nodding glances between the two and for a moment, the air was thick with gun smoke and screams and a wordless shared experience of the futility of war. It also spoke to the rest of us in the room and we seamlessly stepped into a shared empathy space.

Some years later, we did the same exercise at the Syrian Dialogue Meetings in Istanbul. We followed it up by using the image of the Tree as a metaphor for growth and development. Having established a form of speaking together in groups of three without interrupting, judging or analysing, a couple of these exercises were done every morning before the actual political debates and discussions took place. Building on the Tree image, we started with: What have you inherited from your culture, what have you received? What values? And step two: What would you like your children to inherit? What will you give, what values, what way of living, being? This time, we were working under the shadow of war in Syria and the people in the room represented many different parties involved. It was an attempt at dialogue before violence and I was of course wondering whether these storywork exercises would have any kind of peace-supporting effect. The clear form and intention of the exercises, the skilful leadership of the FBA combined with the power of story given space to unfold in the room, gave everyone permission to be human in the midst of the turmoil and political chaos they were in. Yes, the storywork exercises and wisdom tales did awaken a feeling of common ground for a moment, framing the political meeting in a more humane way, giving us all a little more space to breathe in.

In our storywork sessions we combine the three branches of the Storytelling Tree in a variety of ways, depending on the theme and intention of the process. They are:

- Our heritage from world culture of myths, legends, wisdom stories, wonder and folk tales, everything that is given, offering us a treasure chest of wisdom and human experience which address existential themes that speak to us all.
- Life stories, which are unique to every individual and trace the journey through life with its challenges and joys, sufferings and transformations.
- Intuitive, spontaneous storytelling created in the moment, where our healing imagination serves a need, an illness, a problem or a situation, resulting in a story, metaphor or image that can be of help in a variety of situations.

We combine stories, exercises, metaphor, reflections, conversations on the theme at hand, often with the support of singing, movement, painting and spending time in nature. Each session is a composition by the facilitator, there is no "cookbook" with recipes. To be a storyworker is to learn how to take hold of each situation and challenge anew with the help of stories and exercises that draw out the deeper wisdom and insights embedded in the themes present in the room.

Social healing is normally associated with groups of people or nations who have experienced traumatic events and move towards forgiveness and reconciliation, together and personally.

Storywork in the present context addresses the growing erosion of social cohesion and sense of belonging that are at the roots of much personal suffering, conflict and violence today.

On a global scale there is a growing focus on individuality, bringing with it the risk of people splitting off from each other and from their connection to a common whole. This individualisation is part of an evolutionary process of human consciousness moving from tribe mentality to an increasing awareness of personal self and freedom as distinct from the other. Unchecked, this leads to self-centredness, aggression, loneliness, a weakening of social skills such as tolerance and empathy, with difficulties of working together, escalating into conflicts, wars and nationalism, with an intent of excluding others who are different. Digitalization of our lives exacerbates this growing individualism in an artificial way, strengthening alienation and a confused sense of reality, bringing with it depression, meaninglessness and anxiety – all serious malaises of our times. There is a felt loss of connection, seriously weakening the basis for solving conflicts and creating viable futures together. A counter-force is needed if we are not going to go spinning off into our own isolated worlds and end up in a war against all. Where is the common ground of humanity? And how do we access it?

Social healing through storywork addresses this situation by bringing people together around existential questions, with exercises and reflections arising out of wisdom tales from world culture, life stories, intuitive telling and appreciative listening. Storywork is both an individual and group process, strengthening social cohesion and building resilience from within, using story and metaphor as a common language. Participants are encouraged to speak from the heart and out of their own reality and personal integrity. Of importance is the role of creative imagination in creating one's own life but also for stepping out of one's own isolated me-sphere: all social skills are trained in storywork, fostering an expanded moral imagination. Participants in Story Circles report increased well-being, trust and courage, including the ability to communicate, listen and tolerate diverse realities. The existential themes in fairy tales, wisdom stories and life experiences awaken a common ground of humanity that lies dormant in every human being and forms the basis for community and building future together.

Stone of Vishnu

Vishnu, the great god of ancient India, was sitting high up in the seventh heaven, looking out over the world. So beautiful was it with its hills and dales, its oceans and vast steppes that even Vishnu lost his breath for an instant. All the beings of the earth, the wild animals, the rich and lush verdant forests and the wonder of human beings, all were going about their lives, living in sublime harmony.

Vishnu smiled. In his hands he held the Stone of Wisdom, a glorious, vibrant jewel shining with the eternal truths of the universe. The god Vishnu let the precious stone glide playfully from one divine hand to the other, enjoying its many-coloured splendour. He held it up now this way, now that way. Everything changed, depending on where you looked. What a treasure to behold! Caught up by the ever-moving forms and shapes of creation, Vishnu leaned back on his heavenly couch, playing with the marvellous stone, and threw it into the air to see how it glittered and shone. Suddenly, it slipped through his hands and fell. It fell down, down.

Down through the seventh heaven it fell and through the sixth and down onwards through all the other heavens towards earth. And now it sped through the cloudy atmosphere, the clear air and blue skies, finally hitting the earth with a deafening crash. It shattered into millions of pieces. And each piece in turn broke into another million pieces. They spread out over the whole earth.

Instantly people came running from everywhere to retrieve a piece. Kings, soldiers, paupers, lovers, daughters, mothers, Queens, everybody wanted a piece of the Stone of Wisdom.

A wail rent the skies. It was the god Vishnu lamenting. So loud was his crying that it drew forth King Hanuman, wise ruler of the monkeys and noble friend of Vishnu.

"What is the matter, O Lord?" cried King Hanuman.

"Misery, misery! I have dropped the Stone of Wisdom," wailed Vishnu.

"But that is good! Very good! Then wisdom can come down to earth."

At that Vishnu wept even louder.

"No! You don't understand at all! The Stone of Wisdom has broken into millions of pieces!" cried the god.

"But surely that is very good!" said King Hanuman. "Wisdom for all!"

Now Vishnu's tears were streaming silently down his face, he could not stop them, and his eyes were glistening as he spoke.

"No, my friend. For you see, now everyone will think he has The Truth. The one and only truth, the Whole Truth."

(India traditional)

Let us now turn our eyes towards the sprawling city of Toronto with its rich culture of diversity, clearly seen in the many faces of humanity that meet you when you walk down the street.

According to the Endangered Language Alliance there, Toronto is the most linguistically diverse city in Canada with its 200+ languages, not counting a multitude of special dialects. Despite the enormous diversity in the city, it appears that getting people to talk to each other across cultures is proving difficult. I have also experienced this, when working in one of Stockholm's most culturally diverse neighbourhoods, Tensta-Rinkeby, where over 80 languages are spoken. This isolation against other influences and preservation of culture in a fixed form is potentially a problem. Small sparks of conflict can start a large forest fire elsewhere in the world. Or vice versa.

It was here in Toronto that a pioneer of the World Music movement, David Buchbinder, struck on the idea of bringing different cultures into conversation with each other through Story Circles. He coined the name Diasporic Genius and envisioned its intention as: Creating the Future from the Wisdom of the World. Diasporic Genius supports the cultural, economic and physical transformation of Toronto through creative civic engagement, using the power of story to release the wisdom inside all of us to activate a re-imagining of our communities and cities. At an early stage, David asked me to help him build up the Story Circles with my storywork methods and I have been involved with Diasporic Genius ever since. Their work falls into five main streams: Story Circles, Creativity Workshops, Seasonal Festivals, Creative Pathfinders Training and 21st Century Village Squares.

When people tell their stories connected to wisdom tales and appreciative listening, they will find their initiative, their calling, and get moving in new ways! Storywork with these intentions also helps grow social skills, such as decision-making, communication, empathy and creative thinking about old problems and much more. According to David, participants in Story Circles regularly reported that they saw the work as relieving their stress, helping them come out of depression, making their challenging lives seem not so hard, making them feel connected to each other across boundaries of culture, language, religion, gender, age, country and also helping several go back to school for further training, eventually landing a job.

I remember clearly a young woman from Pakistan having a revelation through one of the exercises, when I visited Toronto in 2012. We did a two-step exercise, starting with: Describe someone from your childhood or in your life who means something to you. This is done in pairs or small groups, three minutes uninterrupted speaking and listening each. Then comes step two: If this person you have described was a landscape, what might it look like? You have the whole world as your palette, all of nature, the elements, colours, sounds, forms, movement. If that person was a landscape, what would it look like? Describe. This is not about making up a story – all you have to do is begin to describe what you see and experience, paint with words. It turns out everyone can do this and intuitively knows what the landscape might look like. In fact, as you unfold this landscape to your listener, after a while you know exactly where you are going, for it is your own creative imagination at work, you are the authority.

When sharing in the big circle afterwards, it turned out the young woman had described a dear friend from childhood. The landscape that then turned up for her began with a rose, a beautiful fragrant rose. As the image unfolded, it turned out the rose grew in a desert and had a wonderful revitalizing effect on the drab and dreary surroundings. I can describe it like this in abstractions, but the reality of the situation was that when we listened to the story of the rose, the image itself conveyed more than a thousand words. That is the beauty of metaphor spoken with feeling and meaning. It is one of many exercises in storywork which lifts us from the literal day-to-day world of the senses to the healing power of our creative imagination. When a loved one is spoken of in this way, a blossoming of gratitude unfolds, bringing with it meaning and strengthening our feeling of being carried and helped in our childhood. A good base to touch into when working with difficult issues.

As our young woman from Pakistan finished her story, she said with starry eyes: "I have just realized, that I myself have created these images – I am thinking, not someone else through me! I am the originator of my thoughts." It became clear to us listeners that she had experienced a fundamental change in how she viewed herself and the world. She turned into the author of her own life and we all heard her loud and clear.

> Imagination is the faculty through which we make sense of the world coming towards us.
>
> *(John Keats)*

High up on the Arctic Circle lies Jokkmokk, capital of the Sami people of Sweden. Across the northern parts of Norway, Sweden, Finland and also Russia, the indigenous people of Lapland or Sami have lived a nomadic life, following the pastures of the reindeer through the year. Like other indigenous groups in the world, the Sami people were treated harshly and with disdain by the powers to be. From the end of the 1800s, young children were taken from their families and transported far away to schools which had very primitive standards of human warmth and education. They might see their families once or twice a year and were forced to speak Swedish, although they only knew their own Sami language. Their mores and culture were taken out of them.

When the children returned home after eight years, their sense of belonging had been quashed – they neither felt a part of their Sami home community nor of the newly acquired Swedish way of being.

Several generations of people had their identities severely disturbed in this way. These practices stopped in the 1960s, but to this day, the older generation still carry scars from what they experienced at those schools. To make matters worse, their stories have never been told or acknowledged until very recently, just a few years ago. Neither did I know much about this, until I was asked by the Sami Federation to go to Jokkmokk and give a storytelling workshop which would help bring out these untold stories about life at school, a long, long time ago.

I started pondering. Here was potentially a minefield of stories locked up inside for more than half a century, most probably wrapped in shame and a sense of exclusion. What could I do to create a space where these stories could be told and heard in an appreciative, warm environment? How could this happen without the risk of traumatic incidents suddenly blossoming out into the room? I did not feel competent to handle that kind of scenario, always emphasizing that this is a storytelling workshop, not a therapeutic situation. Granted, when working with stories we laugh and cry and are moved by moments in the stories, a natural expression of human behaviour. After all, we are not made of steel, are we? I also make a point of saying that everyone is responsible for themselves, and to come to me if things are getting out of hand. But now, what about all these untold stories? How to handle them?

All stories that are denied or not told exist anyway, invisibly as part of our society and our history. They leave a hole in the weave of life and their presences make themselves known by other means than letting the truth come out, surfacing as depression, illness, aggression, anger, conflict and other social malaises. The truth will out. All traditional wonder tales around the world tell us so. You can chop and hack and bury and lock up the child or woman or whatever is the expression of some wrong-doing – somewhere in the world it will begin to speak, through a horse's head, by some birds on a branch, a melody whistled through reeds or any other means. The truth has its own vitality and one day, it will come out. Interestingly enough, you can only *tell* the truth, you don't *do* a truth, you tell the truth or a lie. It is done through speaking. And therefore storytelling is an eminent way of bringing hidden stories, often difficult stories, into the light of day. I kept thinking of the Truth and Reconciliation Commission under Bishop Desmond Tutu, who travelled around South Africa after apartheid. Here it was the listening to the stories, the witnessing by the village community and the courage to speak which brought about change and a feeling of personal and social healing. The mere fact that the truth was spoken and received made a real difference to both the individual and the community as a whole. That was enough. You didn't have to do anything with it. This was about truth-telling.

I made the long journey up to Jokkmokk in February, the coldest time of the year with temperatures around -20°C, dressed in all my warmest clothes. My host drove me the last four hours through white landscapes and dark pine forests. Along the roadside were reindeer licking up road salt – it is like candy for them. We saw a couple of cars. The landscape is vast up there; I am in Lapland. We drove into Jokkmokk by evening and, famished for a meal, my host suggested we go to a local restaurant. A friendly Thai restaurant. Inside, Thai women nod, smile and make us dinner, Thai curry on the Arctic Circle. I glance out the window at the white town, snow piled 15 foot high next to the houses. Two men shuffle by, dressed in thin jackets with sneakers on, pushing an empty pram with some plastic bags. Their appearance suggests they are from Somalia. Where am I? Here I am expecting to see and meet the Sami people, but haven't seen anyone yet. Only people from the other side of the world. Ah yes, up here, far from the big cities, the local authorities have created jobs by building a refugee camp. Quite a trek from possibly Somalia to Jokkmokk. And not just on the outside, I reckon.

I bring my thoughts back to the workshop next day. I have decided to establish a common ground first, a base on which to stand when the going could get rough, approaching the stories slowly from the periphery. The aim is not to get everyone to spill their guts and tell everything. In story settings, often an image or a subtle pointer to some incident can be more than enough to express a whole spread of emotions. The point in speaking words that coalesce into what one wants to say is that in so doing, we may feel witnessed in our personal experience. In fact, the healing comes at just this point, when the speaker is able to express deeply meaningful things with choice words to a circle of attentive and well-willing listeners. We know that being seen and heard works wonders. And so I realize that the task here is to teach the participants how to listen and be a witness to a story. My idea is that once learnt here in the workshop, they can take this ability to witness each other with them and gather, when needed, to a listening of someone's story. Witnessing a story with warmth and care is a different matter to doing therapy on the person's experience. This also has its place, but it is not my area of work. I am staying with the social arts.

A group of fine people turn up on the first day of the workshop, all wondering what this will bring them. I decide to meet them with my own story of being a traveller since being a child and of how I was taken from place to place, put in several schools and how lonely I indeed felt at times. I decided that the only way to gain their trust was to bring something of myself to the circle, and not necessarily something splendid on the surface, but certainly something heroic on the inside, being a survivor of difficult circumstances. In reality, we had a lot in common. It takes courage to open up, and we managed to create warmth and a sense of inclusion and trust through the steps we took.

I started out with common ground exercises and then, slowly, we approached describing the school buildings, what they looked like. Next, an exercise on whether there was anybody at school who was a friend or helped you, and onward to little cameos of incidents with clear beginnings and ends – all in order for everyone to inwardly keep step with the process and have a container for all that was spoken. I also told some wisdom stories. Wondertales or wisdom stories are very helpful here, one can enter into a world of metaphor and mytho-poetic consciousness full of meaning and weave between worlds. Besides, those stories begin with Far Away and Long Ago – nothing to do with us.

We can relax from our own pressing matters. Slowly, but surely, we built towards the afternoon of the last day, where everyone was asked to prepare a 15-minute episode from their time at school, to share in groups of four. The mood in the room was very respectful and deeply attentive as one by one, the stories were told. And held. Probably for the first time. In our final round, it was clear that much had happened and hidden away stories had begun see the light of day, the group now knew how to hold a story and to tell it. The next day I left Jokkmokk, feeling that a journey had begun, not just for me, but also for the lovely group of Sami friends in the north.

> It takes a whole village to tell a story.
> *(Native American tradition)*

23
'JANARE' AND '*CAPORABALLI*'
The magic and splendour of Irpinia through stories of witches, dance leaders and sacred pigs

Josephine F. Discepolo Ahmadi

Introduction

We live in a world where our internal and external territory are defined by constantly shifting boundaries. The history of our planet continues to be marked by tragic migrations and experiences of mass dislocation due to oppressive regimes, wars, famine and poverty. The impact that these movements have on the life of groups and individuals generate a kaleidoscope effect; it shapes the way we understand our position in the world, it fills us with fear and anxiety as well as with compassion and curiosity. Many of us might experience serious difficulties in relation to family, nationality, geography, language and social and political identity at some point in life. When I am confronted with these difficulties, I often remind myself of a statement made by a great British writer, Kazuo Ishiguro. During an interview he said that for people like him 'home' is a place within their heart. He might have said 'within their mind' or 'within their soul', I am not sure, as I am quoting him very loosely. I could never find again a copy of the article where I read the statement which made such a powerful impression on me. Also Irvin Yalom, the American psychiatrist and novelist, describes this human condition in his book *Becoming myself* (2017). He refers to the experience of growing up as a plant without roots, to the painstaking efforts to create a personal story which encompasses all fragments of early experiences of oneself and others and to the attempt at organizing these fragments into a coherent script, into a patiently intertwined tapestry to help with making sense of the past, with generating a vision for the future and with engaging us fully with the present.

As I grow older, I realize how I have extrapolated many of the fragments for my tapestry from the stories that I used to listen to when I was a child, the dark and frightening stories told by the African American or Puerto Rican neighbours in the ghetto where I was born in Chicago, the stories of black magic used by a child from my neighbourhood to frighten me and to extort my favoured toys from me, as well as the stories told by the Italian villagers which were passed on from one generation to another. When I was six years old I moved with my mother and my brother from Chicago to Irpinia, (see Figure 23.2) an area in the south of Italy where story telling has been for centuries the natural expression of a rural society for which stories constituted a huge deposit of knowledge and were used to promote the assimilation and dissemination of community values. I believe that the stories of the oral and written tradition of Irpinia have largely contributed to shaping my cultural identity even when this process moved

Figure 23.1 Photograph by Silvano Ruffini (*A Woman*)

Figure 23.2 Irpinia: photo by Pasquale Bimonte (*Sotto o' campanero*; 'Under the bell tower')

well beyond the boundaries of Irpinia. It must be no coincidence that Giambattista Basile, who wrote the most important collection of folk tales within the European tradition, came to Irpinia in 1615 to draw up the final version of his masterpiece, a monumental collection of stories *The tale of tales* (2016).

Stories and characters

Among many, two characters from my childhood stories have been particularly influential on my development, two characters that I was often compared to. They played an important role in the tales that I was told when we were sitting around the fireplace in the evening during the long and cold winters in Irpinia (see Figure 23.1) and in shaping my personal, professional and political identity. I was a tomboy, loud and exuberant, riding my bike to remote woodlands until dark, especially in summer. Sometimes the adults in my family grew so worried that they went around the village to ask people coming back from working the land if they had seen me. There were times when they could not contain their frustration and on my return I would be told off for wandering alone in the woods like a '*janara*', the witch whose many powers included knowledge of the medicinal and magical power of herbs and natural elements and the capacity to control the storms. I suspect that I must have also looked like a witch with windswept hair, my clothes often ripped by the thorn hedgerows and with cuts to my knees.

When I stayed near the house and played outdoors with other children I often followed my wild imagination. I invented and staged with my friends all sorts of complicated and implausible stories where I could be the hero and rescue myself and others out of all sorts of dangerous situations. In the neighbourhood the ladies with the black scarfs found me both irritating and amusing. When they heard loud noises coming from outdoors they would inevitably pass comments similar to my grandmother's ones 'It is you again, of course! You are always leading the dances, aren't you, "*caporaballo*"?' The '*caporaballo*' was the character who led the dances during the complex and fascinating rituals of our traditional Carnival. Since the 50s anthropologists and ethnomusicologists coming from all over the world have been very interested into these rituals and in the passionate rhythm of the 'Tarantella of Montemarano', the music which accompanies them. These have been studied and recorded by such eminent anthropologists and ethnomusicologists as Lomax (1953), cited in Cohen (2003); De Simone and Rossi (1977); D'Agnese and Giuriati (2014).

When I was a child, my reaction to being called those names was mixed. I suspect that I quite enjoyed the attention and the tolerance that people treated me with. After all, I was 'the American child' and everybody expected me to be different with my short trousers and funny two-tone shoes. However, I soon realized that to be different was not always an advantage, especially for a child who ended up struggling to understand where she belonged.

Over a number of generations, there had been a recurrent history of emigration in my family, especially to the United States of America, to Argentina and Brazil. My father was born in a village of the Irpinia district, Castelvetere sul Calore. The name of the village translated into English is something like 'The old castle upon the river Calore'. When I was six years old, as soon as my father started to succeed with his business and social affirmation, he literally shipped me, my brother and my American mother back to Italy to live with his parents. I still remember how scared I was when I climbed the steep stone stairs to the old castle, the area where my grandparents lived and where I was going to spend five years of my childhood. I could not understand why I was surrounded by all those grey stones in the dim light of a cold autumn afternoon, welcomed by old women with long, black dresses and scarfs and by the barefoot children puzzled over the weird American children's funny shoes.

Figure 23.3 Irpinia: historical centre of Castelvetere sul Calore

Over the years I grew proud of my mixed cultural background and very interested in the richness of the culture and history of Irpinia, with its stories where ecstatic joy, salacious humour and the darkness of fear, tragedy and death find ways to be compounded.

Irpinia is a district of the Apennine Mountains around Avellino, a town in Campania, South Italy, about 50km east of Naples (See figure 23.3). At present, the extent of Irpinia matches approximately the province of Avellino.

It was the territory of the ancient Hirpini tribe. The name 'Irpinia' derives from the Oscan word 'hirpus', which means wolf, and the wolf remains Irpinia's symbol to this day. Oscan tribes and the Sabines, under demographic pressure, migrated towards this area in the 6th century BC from what is now Umbria. Oscan and Sabine tribes were part of the Samnite people and during the 3rd and the 4th century BC they fiercely fought against the Romans, who felt threatened by their wealth and power. Eventually, the Romans prevailed and Irpinia became prey to the greedy followers of Sulla, the Roman general and statesman. Over the centuries the area was subjected to a number of rulers and weakened by divisions and subdivisions. The passage from traditional pagan cults to Christianity laid the foundation for the ruling of the Normans and of the Spanish.

According to very old legends, the Irpinia and Sannio districts of Avellino and Benevento are inhabited by witches. They are called *janare*. They can be good or bad witches who can cast evil spells or remove them and perform magic rites of propitiation and exorcism to prevent dangers to themselves, to others or to crops. The transition from various pagan traditions to Christianity marked also a significant change in the way the social and healing role of the *janare* was described and understood. The *janara*, in the popular beliefs of southern Italy and in particular of the area of Benevento, is one of the many species of witches that populated the stories belonging to the tradition of the rural and peasant world.

The name could derive from *Dianara*, or 'priestess of Diana', Roman goddess of the Moon, or from the Latin *ianua*, 'door': it was precisely before the door that, according to tradition, it was necessary to place a broom, or a bag with grains of salt' to protect the house from the *janare*. The incorporeal nature of the *janare* meant that they could enter houses by penetrating under the doors, like a gust of wind, or penetrating from the windows like a slight draft. If the witch was forced to count the threads of the broom, or the grains of salt, she would have lingered until the rising of the sun, whose light seems to have been her mortal enemy. Probably the legend was born in the period of the Lombard reign over Benevento, since even if almost all the inhabitants of the city had converted to Christianity, some still secretly revered the pagan gods, in particular the goddesses Isis, Diana and Hecate whose cult is still witnessed from monuments scattered around the city.

The '*bad janara*' was considered an indeterminate female figure, half-animal and half-human. In the popular consciousness, the *janara* is not associated with the devil as she has no religious values, but only magical ones. However, she is also considered the devil's mistress, a dark figure of rural civilization who was deemed capable even of infanticide. The *janara* is a figure of the popular tradition and, like all magical beings, has an ambivalent character, positive and negative. She knows how to make remedies for various diseases through the manipulation of herbs and she can trigger or change the direction of storms. Traditionally, they were sorcerers able to perform spells and to prepare magic filters and potions capable even of procuring abortions. The *janare* were also known for the teasing they did to the peasants, tampering with their work tools, causing their supplies to rot. Some farmers assert that in the morning, going to the stable, they found sweaty horses (it is said that sometimes the same thing happened with the cows), as if they had been riding all night; sometimes the hair of their manes was gathered in numerous braids. The responsibility for these prodigies was attributed to the *janare*. In the popular imagination in the district of Benevento, under a walnut tree the *janare* used to perform a witches' Sabbath, a Dionysian ritual during which these women abandoned themselves to frenzied dances and banquets with children and dead cats. Modest Mussorgsky captured the atmosphere and the

Irpinia through stories

sensations generated by the presence of the *janare* in our culture in the symphony *A night on Mount Calvo* (the music has also been used as one of the soundtracks for the animation film *Fantasia* by Walt Disney). According to traditional accounts, the author composed the symphony during his stay in Montecalvo Irpino, hosted by the duchess Maddalena Pignatelli, the daughter of Peter Fesenko, counsellor to the Tzar Nicolas II. When we listen to the symphony

Figure 23.4 Carnival 1

we have a clear sense of the impression that the area with its traditional stories of witches and magic rituals must have made on Mussorgsky.

In this socio-economic context, a long-standing tradition based on agriculture and family self-sufficiency, the power that traditionally these women held became a destabilizing and menacing factor (Piedimonte, 2008) to the point that they started to be held responsible for deformities in children they had touched and for the damage caused to crops by storms and bad weather.

The *caporaballo* instead, the leader of the dances during our traditional Carnival, symbolizes and represents an ancient tribal authority and holds a power of a very different nature (See Figures 23.4, 23.5 and 23.6). He symbolizes a typical patriarchal figure which also acts as a guarantor of the harmony and safety of the carnival parades. He decides the routes of the parades and strives to ward off clashes and collisions between the marches. He participates in the collective happiness without losing awareness of its indispensable function, maintained over the centuries and in constant reference to the wisdom and pragmatism of the populations which have inhabited the mountains in Irpinia for centuries. They were aware that they had to subject themselves to strict rules if they wished to preserve their independence and freedom. The *caporaballo* embodies this norm by participating in the collective joy and at the same time ensuring strict adherence to the traditional rules of the community celebrating the carnival.

In Irpinia the choreography of the carnival processions is composed behind one or more *caporaballi*, in proportion to the number of figures in the masquerade which parades in the most strange, picturesque and extravagant costumes representing trades, professions and customs as well as known behaviours and characters of the territory. The carnival is a choral representation, rich in impromptu satirical and parodistic sorties in the wake of the ancient Atellan Farce. The Atellan Farce, also known as the Oscan Games, originally was an improvised masked farce that originated in Italy by 300 BC and remained popular for more than 500 years. They were meant to entertain the audience on holidays and market days. Most historians believe the name is derived from Atella, an Oscan town in Campania. The farces were written in Oscan and imported to Rome in 391 BC. The subjects and characters were decided upon just before the performance began and the performers, all men, improvised the dialogue.

These farces were already performed before the start of the Samnite wars, when the clash with the Romans was in preparation as they had already showed their threatening power. They are an irrefutable part of a lively tradition of rituals and superstitious and propitiatory practices. The fact that the Hirpini were resolute and combative people, guarding a vast territory, has always conditioned their daily life to the point that they developed frequent superstitious and devotional rites to ward off bad luck from their villages. Over the centuries, Irpinia has been the crossroad of the routes between the Tyrrhenian Sea and the Adriatic Sea, the directions through which the migratory phenomenon of nomadic peoples, marching armies or armies in disarray occurred. Irpinia became the focal point of many religious and devotional interests and the inevitable encounter with variegated cultures and customs produced a proliferation of feasts and rituals in relation to the rural cycles between winter and spring. The permanence of these rituals throughout the centuries has established a level of continuity within the communities in Irpinia. The cohesion of the Hirpini people must have been perceived as a threat, given the fury with which Roger II of Sicily in 1127 wrought on Irpinia putting it to iron and to fire.

The rites of the carnival underwent a transformation over the centuries and on the trunk of the tradition of pastoral and Dionysian agricultural rites the baroque passion is grafted, determining the fusion of the rural culture with the urban culture of the Spanish Court in Naples.

Figure 23.5 Carnival 2

While in the 16th century only the nobles were allowed to celebrate and have fun, in the 17th century the carnival became a delirium of the people favoured by the court to ingratiate the masses at least once a year (2015), offering them a break from the daily struggle with dire poverty. In this way the Spanish court brought back into fruition the old ruling strategy of the

Roman Emperors who used '*panem et circenses*' (bread and entertainment) in order to receive acclaim. In Irpinia during the carnival people can thus relive the whirling freedom of the dance with its rhythm and primitive processional imprint together with the display of the masquerade from which clearly emerges the wish for the people to be protagonists and to include the audience as protagonists as well. The Spanish court contemptuously dismissed the potential threat, the social implications and the political impact that these aspirations might have had if the proud people whom they ruled in a very oppressive way were to express these wishes beyond the dimension of the carnival rituals.

In the area of Castelvetere sul Calore and especially in Montemarano, which is 3.2km from Castelvetere, rituals have undergone a playful, circus-like and deeply evocative transfiguration. The carnival is its fulcrum and is relived as a ritual to release negative energies through the use of a powerful propitiatory and liberating music and dance, the *tarantella*. There are an infinite number of versions of the tarantella in Irpinia and throughout the south of Italy. The Tarantella in Montemarano is characterized by the syncopated rhythms of the tambourine, the large melodic phrasebook of the clarinet (originally the shawm), the harmonic modulations of the accordion (originally the hand-organ) and by the wooden clackers. De Martino in his provocative work, a classic in Italian anthropology, *The Land of Anguish* (1961), defines the Tarantella of Montemarano as different from all the others in southern Italy. 'Its unique rhythm and great capacity for involvement' is immediately recognizable according to the work of the ethnomusicologists De Simone and Rossi (1977). The main occasion in which the Tarantella of Montemarano is performed is precisely the Carnival, which begins on the 17th of January, the day of Saint Anthony the Abbot.

The *caporaballo* wears a hat with many ribbons of different colours and guides a group of four dancers who wear colourful costumes. The dancers walk the streets of the village, accompanied

Figure 23.6 The *caporaballo*

by a musical ensemble consisting of clarinet, accordion and tambourine. The *caporaballo* carries a stick as a marker of his authority to represent the fact that in ancient times the role of the *caporaballo* was usually performed by individuals who in everyday life had no power or authority within the social hierarchies of the village and were even beaten by the nobles who owned them. Carnival was the only time when they could pretend to be in charge of the stick of command and when the nobles would condescendingly allow the people to live this illusion. In *The Land of Anguish,* De Martino (1961) explores the intrinsic meaning of the phenomenon of 'tarantism' in the south of Italy, a phenomenon closely related to our rituals and to the music of the tarantella. He interprets them as a loss of the sense of self that results in one's inability to act on the world and control one's own existence. Ultimately, our rituals can be understood both as an attempt at representing how individuals and groups lose their place in history as well as an instrument of reintegration to overcome what De Martino defines as a 'crisis of presence' and regain their place in history. This approach highlights an issue which became central to the work of Foucault and cast new light on the relationship between subaltern and hegemonic cultures and challenged the definition of 'isolated' communities and peoples 'without history' (1997 esp. 340–341).

The issue of power appears to be the focus of the rituals performed during the last days of the carnival, Sunday, Monday and Shrove Tuesday, and when it resumes the following Sunday, the first of Lent, when carnival's death is represented in the afternoon. This opens with a funeral procession in which Carnival, in the form of a puppet placed in a coffin, is led through the streets of the village accompanied by his wife (a disguised man) who engages in a loud lamentation. After the theatricalized attempt of a failed surgery, Carnival dies and his will is read, a sort of ironic and satirical commentary on the life of the community over the past year. After his death, which is sanctioned by bursting a firecracker placed inside the coffin and then burning the puppet, the processional dance of the masks begins again to the rhythm of the tarantella. In Irpinia the passion for music and dance is experienced as a sort of 'disease', of a benign nature, but still a disease to which one can only succumb (De Francesco, 2012).

My story across the stories

As a child I found these stories and traditions confusing and, when someone compared me to a '*janara*', I was aware that the intention was not to compliment me for my energy and power, but to reprimand me for my repeated breaking of rules and for not meeting everyone's expectation that I finally develop into 'a good girl' who wore appropriate clothes and kept herself clean, tidy and 'composed'.

As I was eager to know more about the *janare,* the women whom I was often compared to, there were times when the old ladies in the village would speak under their breath and tell me some of the scary stories in which the *janara* was depicted as a vindictive woman who used her powers to harm and disfigure children. These stories caused me nightmares and exacerbated my fear of having something in common with them until one of the old ladies, a sweet, old woman, told me the story of a farmer who had become very poor.

> The farmer was hard working and loved his small estate where he grew corn and vegetables to feed his family and the animals. Unfortunately, for a few years adverse weather conditions had destroyed his crops and he and his family were struggling to survive. On a very dark and stormy evening he was sitting in front of the fireplace sharing the last loaf of bread with his family. He was aware that the storm was destroying his crops and that the day after he would have to witness once again the destruction of his hard work and count his losses. He was sad and could not find the

words to tell his children and his wife that he did not know where the next meal would come from, when someone knocked at the door. He was reluctant to open the door at such a late hour, but the sound of the wind blowing through the branches of the oak was so powerful that he felt sorry for the lost wayfarer. His surprise was even greater when he saw a woman with a black shawl that barely enveloped her body numbed by the cold.

He welcomed the woman in despite the bad looks that his wife was giving him and shared his bread with her. The woman ate her bread greedily, casting suspicious looks around. The man was not discouraged by the woman's attitude and offered her a place near the fireplace where she could rest until the light of dawn would make her journey easier and safer. His wife could hardly hide her disappointment for her husband's unwise invitation and went to bed keeping her children close to her for protection. She whispered to her husband that he was a fool and that he was putting his family at risk. The man shushed the woman and reassured her that he was going to stay awake and keep things under control.

Despite the man's best intentions and the rumbling of his empty stomach, he fell fast asleep and woke up only to see a black bird flying away from the kitchen window. Also the woman with the black shawl had gone and the man checked his tools to reassure himself that she had not stolen anything. He drank a sip of cold water because nothing else was available for breakfast and tried to prepare himself for the destruction that he knew was waiting for him outdoors. He was astonished when he realized that the corn plants were filled with plump cobs, the vegetable plot was filled with all sorts of delicious variety ready to be picked, and the branches of the trees in the orchard could barely hold the weight of an unprecedented quantity of fruit. He noticed that all the fields surrounding his property had been severely damaged by the storm during the night, as if an invisible force had directed the storm away from his fields. At this point he had no doubt that this was the gift of the janara whom he had hosted so kindly during the night and who had used her power to control the storm.

It was only after the sweet, old lady told me this story that I could be more accepting of being compared to a *janara*. I even started to fantasise about the possibility for me to develop a special talent of some sort and to persuade myself that sooner or later my family would appreciate that my being 'different' would not necessarily be a disappointment to them. However, to add to my family embarrassment, I continued to be totally unaware or unconcerned with the unspoken rules of the class structure in the village.

I spent most of my time wandering in the fields (see Figure 23.7) and I was intrigued by the variety of tasks that the farmers had to complete. They marked the time and the seasons of rural life and I was vaguely aware of the importance for our community of the farmers' hard work and skills. Therefore, it came naturally to me to speak with everyone and to try and get involved in their work. Sometimes I succeeded and I was thrilled when they allowed me to help with pulling water out of wells, to water the vegetable plots or to participate into removing the dried leaves from the corn cobs. I guess that they found my interest in their work quite weird and, possibly, they were also humoured by the scrupulousness with which I tried to complete the tasks entrusted to me. Perhaps, in their ancestral wisdom, they understood my feelings of loneliness and my longing to be part of a community within which I was probably a misfit.

Irpinia through stories

Figure 23.7 La mietitura (the harvest)

   There was another more prosaic advantage in my connection with the farmers – their generous sharing of delicious food! I had poliomyelitis when I was a few months old and I had been treated with old fashioned, powerful medication and force fed in order 'to heal the weakness' caused by the illness. The result was that my weakness increased as the legs affected by the epidemic ended up having to carry an obese body. When my family realized the mistakes made by far too many family doctors involved in my early care, I was put on a strict diet for the years to come and was prohibited to eat the delicious food that my grandmother so skilfully and lovingly cooked and that was such an important aspect of my family culture and of the convivial nature of Southern Italians. I remember a childhood filled with feelings of hunger and guilt on every occasion when I violated the strict rules imposed by several dieticians. Indeed, I transgressed those rules more often than I can remember and more often than my family would tolerate.
   All this happened with the complicity of our caring and compassionate neighbours and of the farmers (see Figure 23.8), who never failed to invite me to share their food when I was around. When it was time for dinner they used to call for the children who were allowed to play in the fields until late. If I was playing with them the parents never failed to invite me to share their food. It was considered very bad manners, especially for a child, to accept an invitation, but, once accepted, it was considered very inappropriate to express any dislike about the food offered. Therefore, the invitation often included an open encouragement to let the host know if I did not like their humble food, a reassurance that they would not be offended if I were to refuse it, as they assumed that I was used to more sophisticated and richer food. Needless to say, the food was delicious and served in a large terracotta platter in which we all dipped our forks sitting around a small and low table positioned in front of the fireplace. Most often the platter was filled with the most common food used by the villagers, a large quantity of green leaf wild

Figure 23.8 Photo by Angelo Sullo (*La sarcena*)

herbs parboiled and stir fried in olive oil and garlic accompanied by large pieces of unleavened flat bread made with corn flour and cooked on the terracotta 'chinco' in the fireplace.

It was heavenly delicious food for me; for my hosts it was the only food they could afford. They picked the herbs for free in the woods where they spent most days to collect the wood that they burnt in the fireplace to heat their houses and to cook their food. Whenever possible, they collected also dry branches in a large and heavy bundle, the *sarcena*. This was to be sold to make money for essential items that they could not produce themselves. Inevitably, my grandmother would show up at the door of my hosting family, catch me eating and apologize to my host for my cheeky and intrusive behaviour. If she was not too angry with me, she would make a joke to try and alleviate my anxiety and shame in front of the hosting family, but I knew that I would be severely reprimanded during our journey back home.

She stopped only when we got there and only to avoid my mother punishing me in her usual harsh way. 'You should be ashamed of yourself! Haven't you got enough to eat in your house that you have to deprive the children of this poor, hard-working people of the very little food that they have managed to put together?! Shame on you!' This was the speech that I endured in silence because I knew that she was right. She was trying to pass on to me the values which had been crucial in her life and which informed her practice when she entered other people's modest houses to care for someone or give injections to someone who was ill. Unfortunately, she did not always use such restraint! There were times when she expressed her disapproving anger much more directly by passing the sarcastic comment 'Here you are again!

Irpinia through stories

Figure 23.9 The old woman

You really are a Saint Anthony's pig!' This often happened when she caught me either helping myself at the table of someone who was really very poor or eating secretly a large, delicious piece of home baked bread with olive oil and oregano offered by a compassionate neighbour who knew that I was constantly on a diet and hungry. To be compared to a dirty pig, even if it was a sacred one, and in front of neighbours, was very humiliating for me, and I often blushed and ended up in tears.

Once a neighbour was deeply moved by my tears and tried to inspire me with a sense of pride for having been compared to a Saint Anthony's pig. 'Don't you know that Saint Anthony descended into hell and confronted the devils twice with the help of his beloved piglet?' I blew noisily my nose while glancing curiously up at the old woman who carried on with her story (see Figure 23.9).

> Many centuries ago Saint Anthony lived as a hermit in the desert together with a piglet who followed him everywhere. Every day Saint Anthony had to win against the temptations of the devil who played a great number of tricks on him. (According to the implausible anachronisms and irrationalities contained in the old woman's story, at the time there was no fire on earth and men suffered from intense cold.) After a long discussion the governors of the earth sent a delegation to Saint Anthony to beg him to procure fire to alleviate the suffering of men. The old saint was taken by a great compassion for human kind and embarked with his faithful pig in a descent into hell, where he knew that flames burned day and night. He knocked at the immense door and, when the devils saw that the visitor was the saint, their worst and most invincible enemy, they refused to allow him to enter.

In the meanwhile, the pig had managed to sneak into the diabolical place. The small animal started running around, generating great mayhem. The devils were unable to catch the pig despite the variety of powerful tricks that they tried. They had to admit to their defeat and ask Saint Anthony to return to hell and get his pig back. The hermit, who had anticipated this outcome, went back to the realm of the damned with his inseparable tau-shaped ferule stick. During his return journey with the piglet he set his stick on fire and kept the spark hidden in the hollowness of the ferule stick until he reached the earth. The first task that he attended to when he arrived was to light a large pile of wood, thus offering the first and longed-for fire to humanity (see Figure 23.10).

I remember how persuasive and caring was the woman's voice while she was telling this Catholic version of the myth of Prometheus to me, and how it alleviated my shame. After all, Saint Antony had stolen the fire from the devils, not from the gods. He needed a pig as a passport between separate worlds in order to subvert the laws regulating the passage to and from the underworld. Saint Anthony could not enter hell and have his share of 'revelation' without the sneaky pig with its greed and capacity to use any means to get what it wants. The pig found a solution to Saint Anthony's predicament because he was used to disregarding all rules and obligations except from those imposed by its hunger. The pig was a natural hermit, whilst the saint had become a hermit only when he could set himself free from the imperatives of the culture which shaped him. Thanks to its antisocial nature – its 'difference' – the pig became a perfect and essential travel companion for the saint.

However, even if it took much longer for me to develop a capacity to reflect on the role that 'difference' had played in my life, the possibility to be compared to a pig that a poor community had the religious duty to feed never prevented me from enjoying the delicious country food when it was offered. It is impossible to describe the variety of emotions that I experienced when my mother gave me a collection of books by Italo Calvino with *200 Italian Tales* (1956) as a Christmas present and I found the story of Saint Anthony's pig as the old lady had told me!

Sadly, in those years it was not unusual for young children to die because of a sudden illness or an epidemic. In Italy a national health service to offer free medical care and medication had not been introduced yet. People who lived within a subsistence economy could not afford to pay for healthcare. It was always considered a miracle when a child survived a severe illness. Since one of Saint Anthony's attributes was 'The Healer' and he was the most popular saint in the Catholic Church, often the parents of the child who had recovered vowed for the child to wear a monk tunic for a year. Also, they used to buy a piglet and fatten it up until it was time to sell it. The vow was fulfilled with the sale of the pig and the offering of the proceeds from the sale to St Anthony's church. It is easy to understand how heavy the burden was for a poor family to feed a pig for a year when they struggled to feed themselves. Therefore, the rule generally agreed on within the community was that Saint Anthony's pig had free access everywhere and that to feed it was a religious collective task and a way to give thanks to God. I remember the freedom and the respect that Saint Anthony's pig enjoyed when I was a child and how often mothers sent their children to feed it with scraps from the kitchen and with small potatoes or apples when they were beginning to rot. It was this tradition and religious ritual my grandmother referred to when she used to catch me eating here and there in the village.

In comparison with this shaming association with a sacred pig, I found the comparison with the powerful witch flattering. After all, she was a female figure with a unique knowledge of the powers of nature and beyond. I was intrigued by her ubiquity, her power to go places which

Figure 23.10 The fire

was unrelated to physical attributes or to religious obligations, but to her incorporeal nature. I found it much more flattering to be compared to the feminine entity who not only was in charge of winds and storms, but who participated of their nature. I guess that both my caring and protective grandmother and my critical, demanding and guilty father never allowed me to forget the limitations, although minimal, my disability imposed on me. Other children in the village who had been affected by the same poliomyelitis epidemic experienced much more severe limitations to their functioning. One child had to use a wheelchair and others suffered from severe learning difficulties.

However, I do not recall any feelings of gratitude expressed within my family for the fact that I had been affected only very mildly. Only much later in life, when I saw parents of disabled children for psychotherapy, did I start to make sense of the variety of feelings that they experienced and to recognize the complex dynamics that the presence of a disabled child generates within a family. The women in my family had a reputation for being beautiful, elegant, attractive and strong. It must have been very difficult, especially for my father, to accept that his daughter was an exception to the norm. This might explain why I found the identification with a powerful figure like the *janara* more flattering as it effectively compensated for my feelings of inadequacy and limited physical strength and power. At the time, I could not understand that both the *janara* and Saint Anthony's pig represented ways for our people to come to terms with the alternate cycle of life and death, of darkness and light and an attempt at developing myths and rituals in order to retain a level of control over their fears.

Only much later in life did I realize that there were similar and yet contrasting strata of meaning in the characters that I was compared to and which populated my imagination. The *caporaballo* leads the dances during our carnival and our carnival starts on the 17th of January, Saint Anthony's day. At times, I feel as if my modest personal history developed in the shadow of the confluence between the rural myths of an ancient rural civilization and the influences derived from a sumptuous and lively urban atmosphere. Apart from literally playing the *caporaballo* role by leading dance performances with other children, I was always inventing new games, building shelters with any material I could snatch – stones from the craggy cliffs, wood from the fagots, straw from the haystacks and any other material I could get from my grandmother and the neighbourhood ladies, the generous 'commari' who spoilt me and fed me. I was often surrounded by a large group of children, those who lived in the historical centre of the village, but also children who came from 'La piazza', 'Lo Portiello' or even 'La Cortina', nearby neighbourhoods. We went to school together and my reputation for inventing new games and for staging new stories rapidly spread among other pupils until I also was deprived of my illusory stick of command.

Just like it happens to any *caporaballo*, the illusion that I was generating and sharing had to come to an end. The 'commari' started to complain about the confusion caused by the growing number of children invading our neighbourhood and asked my grandmother to resolve the situation because they resented the fact that we had turned the area around the old castle into a noisy playground. I have vivid memories of long, exciting summer afternoons when it felt as if we were all together discovering the world and learning how to enjoy a sense of freedom together with an experience of being deeply connected to one another and to our surroundings. I was so proud of my capacity to initiate these experiences and I never felt offended by the comparison with the *caporaballo*. I intuitively understood the value of the capacity to bring people together that I was developing through play. In addition to this, dance had always a special place within my family culture and within the life of the village. One of my paternal grandfather's brothers migrated to Argentina and his son, Enrico Santos Discepolo, called *Discepolin*, was a well-known tango composer. He was also a playwright, a theatre and film director and was called 'the Argentinian Sartre'. He defined tango as '*sadness to dance with*'.

When my father came and visited us from Chicago for the first time after four years, we started to have parties quite frequently at my grandmother's house. Obviously, the parties included plenty of delicious food, good wine and good company, but the highlight of all parties was when the musicians that my father employed played the enthralling rhythm of the *tarantella*. The most skilful *tarantella* dancers in the village performed in front of us, capturing everyone in a collective fascination with their mysterious and magic moves, the jumps, the playful and not so subtle erotic allusions, the screams '*Ohi, chi vo' muri'!*' (Oh, we don't want to die! – We want to live forever!).

Conclusions

The very act of telling or listening to a story seems to engage us more intensely with our own human experience and to enable us to express feelings in a more vibrant way. The dilemmas that we often agonize over when we have to make a decision about telling or not telling about facts that deeply affect us, find, in storytelling, their resolution and their metaphorical representation. Stories are not only a safe repository for our deepest truths and a source of inspiration, they also generate some questions of fundamental importance.

Vinicio Capossela, one of the most intriguing contemporary artists from Irpinia, has developed his last novel around the character of a wayfarer who journeys across a surreal territory (2015). The variety of characters he meets throughout his journey ask him the same questions over and over again: 'Who are you?' 'Where do you belong?' 'What are you looking for?' The questions are repeated almost obsessively and in the repetition they depict a constant shift from the intersubjective quality of the dialogue to an intra-subjective dimension. In both cases the main character cannot find an answer. The author seems to confirm my impression that the answer to such questions can be found only through a constant and patient reconstruction of a tapestry, the complex script which I refer to at the beginning of this chapter, which we constantly look for, to try and make sense of the fragments of our human experience.

The difficulty remains that of accepting the precarious and temporal nature of these constructs and the need for us to always generate new organizing systems to incorporate new experiences, new visions. Vinicio Capossela describes the werewolf as an aspect of the self who longs for a return home, a home where he can be human again and elude his loneliness. And yet a return home becomes impossible because the notion of home is constantly transformed by our experiences and the experiences of others who are included in our external and internal landscape. At times, just like werewolves, we express the pain for this impossibility by tearing into pieces fragments of memories, or like James Joyce's Mr. Bloom, in *Ulysses*, by questioning the value of both the *topos*, the location from where one departs, and the *nostos*, the meaning and purpose of returning home.

I come from a part of the world where many powerful stories used to be told and great respect was paid to storytellers because of their capacity to transmit the values of a community from one generation to the other and give shape to their aspirations and fantasies. Both the storytellers and the stories that we almost inhaled in the magical and ancient land of the Hirpini tribes have influenced the way I continue to try and understand my place in the world and my professional role. As a psychotherapist, I have the privilege of listening to the most intimate stories of the suffering human beings who journey with me, side by side, through the therapeutic space and time. Together we try and discover the hidden power of the stories as they unfold between us while we weave a new tapestry where the rips and the embroideries both contribute to the beauty of being alive.

Acknowledgements

I am deeply indebted and sincerely grateful to Dr. Aldo De Francesco, journalist, writer, painter and '*montemaranese DOC*'; to Prof. Aniello Russo, prolific writer and researcher of the oral and written traditions of Irpinia; to Dr. Nino Lanzetta, journalist, writer and '*castelvetrese DOC*'; to Prof. Vincenzo Esposito, cultural anthropologist at the University of Salerno in Italy who introduced me to the intriguing work of Vinicio Capossela, and to the photographers Silvano Ruffini, Pasquale Bimonte, Angelo Sullo and the Associazione Culturale La Ripa who have kindly agreed for me to use their evocative photos. My unreserved gratitude goes to the editors of this book, who have been endlessly patient and supportive and who have offered me an opportunity to revisit my past and the magic that was part of it.

References

Basile, G. (1986) *Lo cunto de li cunti*. Milano: Garzanti.
Basile, G. (2016) *The Tale of Tales*. New York: Penguin Books.
Calvino, I. (1956) *Fiabe Italiane: 197*. Torino: Giulio Einaudi Editore.
Capossela, V. (2015) *Il Paese dei Coppoloni*. Milano: Feltrinelli Editore.
Cohen, R. D. (Ed.) (2003) *Alan Lomax: Selected Writings 1934–1997*. New York: Routledge: [1972]: p. 286.
D'Agnese, L., Giuriati, G. (2014) *Mascarà Mascarà me n' a Fatto 'Nnamorà*. Udine: Edizioni Nota.
De Francesco, A. (2012) *Il Novellino Montemaranese: Personaggi e Umorismo nel Paese de Lo cunto de li Cunti*. Naples, Italy: Iuppiter Edizioni.
De Francesco, A. (2015) *Festabarocca. Il Carnevale di Montemarano. Popolo, Caporabballi e Viceré*. Naples, Italy: Iuppiter Edizioni.
De Martino, E. (1961) (English translation 2005) *The Land of Remorse: A Study of Southern Italian Tarantism*. London: Free Association Books.
De Simone, R., Rossi, A. (1977) *Carnevale si Chiamava Vincenzo: Rituali di Carnevale in Campania*. Roma: De Luca Editore.
Foucault, M. (1997) "The Subject and Power," in Faubion, J. (ed.), *Essential Works of Foucault 1954–1984*, Volume 3: Power NY: New Press, esp. pp. 340–341.
Joyce, J. (2000) *Ulysses*. London: Penguin Modern Classics.
Piedimonte, A. (2008) *Nella Terra delle Janare. Viaggio nell'Irpinia Segreta, tra Leggende, Magia e Misteri*. Napoli: Edizioni Intra Moenia.
Yalom, Y. (2017) *Becoming Myself: A Psychiatrist's Memoir*. New York: Basic Books.

24
ADAPTING ORAL TALES FOR THE MORAL TRANSFORMATION OF THE DEVELOPING CHILD AND YOUTHS

Adapting *Yomandene and the Stubborn Son* from tale to play

Victor Jong Taku

Introduction

Many African communities have hitherto employed storytelling events to enforce positive character traits and development, especially amongst children and youths. One of the communities that effectively used the oral tale for the moral transformation of children and youths is the Bakweris of Buea in Cameroon. They employed *Yomandene*, a collection of animal tales narrated by the fireside by parents and elders of the community, to instill in children and youths values such as honesty, obedience, respect for parents and elders, hard work and discipline. This chapter will focus on ways and means of adapting the oral tale to incorporate issues and aspects that help to transform the original version of the tale so that it incorporates values and aspects that speak to the developing child in modern day societies. The choice of *Yomandene and the Stubborn Son* was arrived at because it contains the fear factor in the tale which proved successful in reforming children and youths not only in Buea but other communities in Cameroon and Africa in general.

Adapting oral tales

Adapting an oral tale is a process that renders the tale more useful and valuable and makes it available to new and modern outlets of information and entertainment. Adaptation for stage permits the adapting artist and the actors to reinforce pedagogic, moral and environmental values of the oral tale in an era of rapid cross-cultural exchange. The birth of a new tale could be relevant not only to the community where the tale is narrated but to other peoples and communities of the world. The oral tale is educative in nature, provides entertainment and guarantees solidarity between the narrator and the audience. The tale is also a vehicle of unity, peace and security and the transmission of valuable cultural heritage from one generation to the next. A major problem has been to guarantee the survival of these narratives in their original states and to assure their importance and value in the present context of globalization, where different cultures are finding a place not only to exhibit their strength but to dominate weaker cultures. It is against this backdrop that this study is focused on redynamizing the oral tale with a view to transforming and adapting it to stage plays not only to guarantee the preservation of the tale but to assure its transmission to a wider audience. Focus will be on the positive role played by the fear factor of *Yomandene and the Stubborn Son* in the moral transformation of children and youths in Buea and other African communities. It is in an attempt to transform the oral tale to fit new environments and address some current issues facing society that we decided to engage in the process of adaptation.

Why adapt or innovate the oral tale for moral transformation of children and youths?

The oral tale is gradually departing from its original fireside settings. Many parents in rural and urban settings are unable to create time to sit with their children and other members of their community to narrate tales that contribute to the moral, spiritual and academic development of their children and other members of society. The storytelling event that used to create an atmosphere for family members to commune during the evenings has been replaced by the television and internet. Recent development in communication has greatly affected interpersonal communication between parents and children. Today we find parents and children glued to the television screen and cellular phones for information and entertainment. The need to adapt *Yomandene and the Stubborn Son* into a play with the aid of process drama will witness the contribution of the adapting artist and the classroom teacher in formal learning environments geared towards transforming the tale to address current moral concerns. The fear factor of the selected tale has been used by many parents in Buea as a technique of instilling positive moral conduct amongst their children and also to combat deviant behavior amongst the youths. Although this practice has been considered by Jack P. Shonkoffield et al of the National Scientific Council on the Developing Child in terms of how children learn, solve problems and relate to others, many parents in Buea and other African communities still continue to invoke fear to scare their children from embarking on activities considered immoral and disrespectful. It is on this note that Shonkoffield (2007) and others affirm that all children experience fears during childhood including fear of the dark, monsters and strangers. They also affirm that these fears are normal aspects of development which are temporary in nature. In spite of the fear factor in the tale, parents in Buea have continued to exploit it to check the excesses of negative moral behavior of their children as they grow up through youthfulness and adulthood.

Adapting *Yomandene and the Stubborn Son* from tale to play

It is important to note that drama permeates different strata of the society. Bole Butake and Gilbert Doh (1988) affirm that long before the official annexation of Kamerun by the Germans in 1884/85, missionaries from the British Isles and America found drama a very effective means of communicating Christian religion to the natives through dramatizing passages from the Bible during festive occasions like Christmas, Easter and other Christian festivals. The narrator, in essence, was cautioned when he attempted to deviate from the agreed or approved trend of the tale. Therefore, the tale did not provide other outlets of expression, except otherwise approved by the audience or the community. The process of adapting *Yomandene and the Stubborn Son* from tale to play provides the adapting artist an opportunity to collaborate with parents and teachers to explore new avenues where the relevance of the tale can be seen. By taking the tale from the fireside to the stage, the adapting playwright is in essence attempting to address a wider audience, raise new issues concerning the tale, situating the tale in a wider context and exposing it to a wider audience for interpretation and analyses. To go through this process we will justify the choice of the tale, adjust the title, incorporate stage directions, adjust plot structure, propose a new storyline and incorporate dialogue.

The choice of the tale

The choice of the tale is premised on the many versions of *Yomandene* amongst the Bakweris of Buea and their relevance to the socio-cultural and moral upbringing of children and youths who lived the heydays of storytelling in Buea and her environs. Our narrator, Frida Luma, simply referred to the tale as *Yomandene* considered by Mola Mbua Ndoko as ways and wisdom of the Bakweri. These tales, according to Frida Luma, were narrated to check the excesses of young boys and girls as they grew up through the turbulent childhood to adolescence. According to Luma, the fear factor in most of the tales prevented children from disobeying their parents and elders in the community, going out at night, engaging in quarrels and fights and being generally disobedient for fear that they will be devoured by *Yomandene*, the beast. It is in this light that the tale was chosen because it presents a twist of interesting events around the exploits of two brothers who decide to confront *Yomandene*, whose presence regulates good and evil in the village where the story is set. The play is relevant to society as it teaches young people the virtues of love, kindness, forgiveness and respect of elders. It also reveals the reward reserved for children and youths who obey their parents, show love towards other members of their family and respect elders, especially the old that they come across on a daily basis. The tale is therefore relevant in the upbringing of children and the youth who are the leaders of the future.

The tale of Yomandene and the Stubborn Son

In the tale, we encounter an old man, his wife and their two sons deeply troubled by the presence of a beast in their farmland that would mysteriously cause the trees and grass cut to rejuvenate on the day following their felling and cutting respectively. The events further escalate to a crisis when the younger brother mistakenly uses the arrow of his elder brother, instead of his own, to shoot at the beast. When the ailing beast finally disappears into the bush with the arrow stuck on its body, the elder brother refuses to forgive his younger brother in spite of pleas from his parents. So the younger brother is forced to embark on a search for the arrow in the land of the beast. The story builds up from a situation of lack or disorder and mounts to a climax, with different forces intervening to restore the lack of order. The younger brother, who mistakenly misplaces this elder brother's arrow, is assisted by an old woman to recover the arrow due to the respect and assistance he showered on the old woman he met on his way. The story ends with the elder brother being punished because of his refusal to forgive his younger brother and disrespect of his parents and elders of the community.

Adjusting the title

Adjusting or modifying the title may be considered an important aspect in the process of adaptation. Depending on the choice of the audience, the setting of the play text and the mission of the adapting playwright, the title may be modified or completely changed. While moving from tale to play script, it may be relevant to change the title or modify it based on the impact you intend to achieve. With reference to the tale under study and adaptation, we decided to change the original title from *Yomandene and the Stubborn Son* to *Yomandene and the Twin Warriors*. This title does not respect the principle of brevity but it is attractive because the audience will be eager to find out what happens between the beast and the twin warriors. It also leaves the audience anxious to discover what the beast has in store not only for the twins but for humanity in general. The inclusion of twins hints at a duel, which leads the audience to expect an impending conflict. In essence the title is apt because it allows the audience to ask questions, whose answers can only be gotten after reading or watching the play. Such an atmosphere of suspense, and longing for an inevitable outcome characterized by divine justice and reward on acts of wickedness, may ultimately sustain the attention of the audience. Therefore, it is necessary to change the title from *Yomandene and the Stubborn Son* to *Yomandene and the Twin Warriors*, not only to give the tale a universal appeal but to hold the attention of the audience, who would be anxious to discover or learn what will transpire between the beast and the twin warriors.

Employing stage directions

Stage directions are useful and play a host of functions in play writing. They are instructions carefully written into the script of a play, indicating actions, movements, age, costumes of performers and other relevant production requirements that guide the play director and other artists involved in the production process. A careful handling of stage directions by the adapting artist will reveal much about setting, characterization, action, props, sound, costume, make-up and lighting.

The opening scene reveals Pa Lyonga in a small hut sitting on a wooden chair. Standing on his left is Mokosso and on his right is Sasse, his twin brother. Pa Lyonga is eating colanuts while sharpening his cutlass. Little drops of rain can be seen splashing on his calabash from a hole on the roof of his hut. Ma Lyonga, dressed in Kabba, a gown commonly worn by women in Buea and other coastal areas of Cameroon, is outside watching a pot of cocoyams on the fire.

We realized there was a need to provide a stage direction which adjusts the original opening scene of the tale to a new scene with universal appeal thus:

> In a small house. An old man, with grey hair, is sitting on a chair. Standing on his left is Pride and on his right is Humble his twin sons. The old man is eating some nuts while sharpening his machete. Little drops of rain can be seen splashing on his bowl from a hole in the roof of his house. His wife is outside stirring a pot of food on the fire.

The aforementioned is another step in the adapting process which takes the story to a global space where anybody in any part of the world can identify themselves with the characters and action. It is important to note that we can find old men in all regions of the world; props such as machetes and bowls commonly used; firesides are common, especially in rural areas all over the world; while the use of names representing human character attributes renders the characters universal. The stage directions also reveal the profession and the kind of activity of the character(s) mentioned. The old man is revealed eating nuts and sharpening his machete. The eating of nuts in most traditional African settings is usually associated with the old, who struggle to strengthen their teeth eroded by old age. His profession as a farmer is also revealed by the act of sharpening his machete.

Stage directions also reveal other characters involved in the play. The mention of Pride and Humble standing on either side of the old man introduces his two sons, whose names reveal much about their character traits. The audience can rush to the conclusion that the elder son is proud while the younger is humble. It is important to note that in most forest settlements, sons learn from the activities of their fathers. In this wise the audience will be eager to find out if their names will correspond with their character in the play. It is therefore normal to see the two boys stand and watch their father sharpening his machete.

It is also important to note that stage directions can tell the time and atmosphere of the opening or continuing action. Mention of little rain drops splashing on the bowl also reveal the weather conditions and the season of the year. Mention of his wife stirring the pot of food outside reveals the place of women in most traditional communities in Africa. She is mostly portrayed as the person who ensures that food is found on the table of her home. This is evident in the opening scene, where the old man is in the company of his two sons while his wife is cooking for her family members. While some consider this as relegating the woman to the background, the women feel it is their duty to cook food for their husbands and children. The only sound mentioned is the constant dropping and splashing of rain on the bowl. It is therefore obvious that there will sometimes be rays of sunlight penetrating through the roof of the house.

Plot structure

The tale has a deep structure which Ibrahim Kashim Tala (2013), referring to Longacre, includes expository unit, inciting moment, developing conflict, climax, denouement and conclusion. Tala points at Denise Paulme (1965) classification and structural patterns of African narratives, which include ascendancy, descendancy, cyclical, spiral, mirror-image, hour-glass and complex. The tale under study can be considered as mirror-image, involving two characters who engage in two symmetrical series of tests but with actions that are of inverse relationship to each other described in moral terms as good and bad, with the former rewarded and the later punished.

In the original tale under transformation, the protagonist is simply referred to as younger brother and the antagonist as elder brother. The younger brother is humble, kind and gifted with courage, intelligence, respect and discipline for his parents and all those he comes across in the community. These are the qualities that guide him to succeed in recovering his elder brother's arrow from the land of the beast. When he successfully returns to the village he is rewarded with a mansion and a singing bird that attracts the villagers, who lavish him with wealth. There is a turn of events when the elder brother lets out the bird from its cage and it flies into the forest. Pride, in his pride and ambition to also get rich, embarks for the forest in search of the bird. As a consequence of his greed, wickedness, unforgiving nature, lack of respect for elders, indiscipline, full of pride and foolishness, he finds himself in the land of the beast, where he meets instant death. After his death, the bird miraculously returns to the younger brother and there is feasting and celebration in the village.

Adjusting plot structure

After adjusting the title, setting and characterization, the adapting playwright may proceed with adjusting the plot or storyline. It is important to note that in the original tale, the plot or story is determined by the narrator and the expectations of the audience. In the adaptation process, the plot has been adjusted to address what the play is all about, who the main character is, what they do, who the antagonist is and what they do to enhance the plot. In this wise the adapting artist decided to name the younger brother Humble and the elder brother Pride, names symbolic of their actions and attitudes. For purposes of situating the tale within a real and modern context, the singing bird was replaced by a golden guitar and the imaginary mansion with a box of clothes and jewelry.

The adapting artist and the classroom teacher also decided to create two sub-plots. The first sub-plot begins when Humble is forced to go into the forest in search of his brother's arrow and ends when he succeeds in his quest and is rewarded by the old woman with a box of clothes, jewelry and a golden guitar. The second sub-plot begins when Pride misplaces the golden guitar and embarks on a similar path in search of it. In the original story the bird finds its way back to the village, while in the adapted story the old woman finds the guitar and returns it to Humble. The adapting artist by replacing the mansion and the bird with the box of clothes and jewelry and the golden guitar respectively is hereby placing emphasis on real items and events, rather than fantasies and things not related to the social environment.

At the beginning of the play, there is some degree of calm and serenity as the old man advises and prepares his sons for farming. When the beast's presence is announced, it is Pride who agitates and expresses his readiness to kill it. There is complication in the rising action when the beast finally makes its way into their farm. In such an atmosphere and with the urge to kill the beast, there is further complication when Humble mistakenly picks up Pride's arrow instead of his own to shoot at the beast. When Pride discovers that his arrow has gone with the wounded beast, he insists that Humble provides his original arrow. There are further complications when Humble finds his way amongst the beast's children and interacts with them. The climax is when he is about to be identified as a fake member of the beast's family then succeeds to escape with the arrow. The action falls when Humble, led by the advice and blessing of the old woman, successfully finds his way back to the village without being hurt by the beast's children. The resolution or ending of the first sub-plot is attained when Humble breaks an egg on the ground and the box of jewelry and clothes and a golden guitar miraculously appears. He is admired when he plays the guitar and attracts a lot of wealth and recognition. At this point the play may be considered to have come to an end.

The second sub-plot begins when Pride expresses envy and jealousy at Humble's quest. There is tension and complication when he misplaces Humble's golden guitar and is forced to go in search for it. Led by pride he gets himself into more difficulties when he comes in contact with the old woman and insults her. This earns him a curse of death. The critical moment or climax comes when he attempts to escape with the golden guitar, but is caught and killed by the children of the beast. Both plots merge when the old woman, through some magical means, brings back Humble's golden guitar to the village.

After arriving at the decision to either add or reduce the number of characters, the adapting artist is now ready to build the plot of the story based on the hour-glass structure. The scenes are important in unraveling the plot and dwelling on the important parts of the story. The scenes also enable the adapting playwright to represent the time of the different actions, the different locations and when they change.

Proposed storyline

Scene 1: In a little house. The old man is with his two sons, Pride and Humble, instructing them to clear the farmland for planting.

Scene 2: At Night, in a shrub. Pride and Humble are hiding to get a good glimpse of the beast that replants the portion of land they previously cleared for farming.

Adapting an oral tale to a play

Scene 3: In the presence of Old Man. Pride and Humble are reporting what they saw on the farmland.

Scene 4: In the farmland. Pride and Humble are hiding in the shrub.

They fall asleep as the beast approaches. Humble is awakened by the loud noise made by the beast. He mistakenly uses Pride's arrow to shoot the beast.

Scene 5: In Ma Lyonga's kitchen. Pride and Humble quarrel over the missing arrow. Pride wants Humble to look for his arrow while his father and mother plead in vain to convince him to forgive his younger brother.

Scene 6: Early morning. Humble sets out to search for Pride's missing arrow.

Scene 7: In the heart of the forest. Humble is woken by an old woman who promises to assist him in his search for the missing arrow. The old woman blesses and gives him an egg.

Scene 8: In the beast's village. Humble joins the villagers in mourning the beast. He is led to the beast's house by 1st villager.

Scene 9: After one week. Humble is in the company of the beast's children. He succeeds in stealing the arrow and escapes.

Scene 10: Back home. Humble hands over Pride's arrow, clears an open space and breaks the egg handed to him by the old woman. A box of jewels with nice dresses and a golden guitar appear. Pride admires the guitar, plays with it and misplaces it.

Scene 11: Back home. Humble insists on having his golden guitar. Pride proudly sets out into the bush to search for the missing guitar. Pride meets the old woman and is rude to her. He insults her and he is cursed with death.

Scene 12: In the beast's village. Pride finds the golden guitar, tries to take it by force and he is killed.

Scene 13: Back in the village. The old woman mystically returns the guitar back to Humble and there is celebration.

Creating dialogue

Creating communicable dialogue is also an important aspect in the process of adaptation. It is important to note that the original tale is void of dialogue between characters, except feedback and response by the audience or listeners while the tale is being narrated. In most cases, these words of feedback are usually not mentioned in the tale. So creating dialogue out of the tale is a creative process on the part of the adapting playwright. It is important to note that creating dialogue does not necessarily mean creating a new story. Digressions and interjections may be used to situate the play within its new and present context.

In this wise we would not expect the old man to be so grounded in the English language. This should be seen in his exchange between his two sons. The first words by the old man to his two sons reveal a lot about his state of mind and his plans and aspiration for them. Let us examine his words:

Old Man: My dear son, age is no longer on my side. I have fought two great wars before packing my bags to search for a resting place in this village, where I met your mother. Since then, she has been the flesh of my flesh, and the bone of my bones.

The old man's words are figurative and rich in imagery and symbols. When he says 'age is no longer on my side' he is personifying age and giving it human qualities to mean that he is already an old man and no longer a youth. When he goes ahead to affirm that he has fought two great wars, what comes to our mind are the First and Second World Wars, which saw the active participation of Africans, especially the Second World War. We therefore see an old man, pensive and resigned from the vagaries of war to confront farming and sedentary living.

Pride, who picks up the cue from his father, is so distant from his father's experiences. He thinks only of the farmland handed to him and his brother. In heed of his father's advice to find out the root cause of the strange happenings, Pride begins sharpening his arrows and cleaning his bow. He says:

> **Pride:** We shall fight the phenomenon, man or spirit!
> I will personally bring back its ugly head!

Dialogue is revealing of character. From his words, we do not see a calm and calculative human being. We see an aggressive and impatient youth, who thinks that violence and show of force are methods of subduing an enemy. His character contrasts that of his old father and twin brother, Humble, whose first response is to thank and acknowledge his father. All these should be seen in their speech rendition. The punctuation marks in Pride's speech indicate his strong feeling of anger. The pause in Pride's speech indicates the deep breath after the outburst of energy exercised in the first part of the sentence: 'we shall fight the phenomenon—'. The pitch rises to the word 'phenomenon' and drops in the second part of the sentence when he states '—man or spirit'. The use of punctuation marks is not only indicative of the mood of the speaker but his psychological state of mind and temperament. Another instance of Pride's hot temperedness is evident in scene two:

> **Pride:** I will shoot anything I see.
> **Humble:** Even Yomandene?
> **Pride:** (Agitated) Even Lucifer!

His courage, from the aforementioned, has no bounds. He is even prepared to challenge Lucifer, considered the leader of all evil beings in the world and an arch angel which, according to the biblical scriptures, was cast body and spirit to dwell among men on earth. From such show of excessive courage, it becomes clear that he is doomed to failure and defeat, because a spirit being like Lucifer cannot be defeated only by a shot from an arrow by a mere mortal.

Another aspect of Pride's character brought about by dialogue is his rudeness and disrespect of elders. This is seen when he encounters the old woman.

> **Pride:** Old witch! What are you doing here?
> Where are your children?
> Have they abandoned you?
> **Old Woman:** My son, you must be tired.
> There is food and water for you.

Pride's choice of words and expressions are not only insultive but disdainful. Addressing the old woman as witch and asking if her children have abandoned her brings to light the poor treatment accorded to the old, especially widows who live alone in many African communities. Most of them are victims of attacks and poor treatment, especially when something considered evil happens in their vicinity. They are usually suspected of bewitching youths and others considered prosperous amongst them. The old woman's kindness, passion and love are expressed when she sympathizes with Pride's tiredness and proposes food and water for him.

Conclusion

We have observed in the tale under adaptation that the process of moral transformation enhanced by the use of the oral tale in Buea and other African communities is meant to instill in children positive character traits relevant for growth and survival. The fear factor in *Yomandene and the Stubborn Son* discouraged many children growing up in Buea and other African communities from deviant behavior and wayward actions. It has been observed that many who listened to *Yomandene* tales grew up scared from staying out late at night, restrained from disobeying their parents, respecting elders, especially the old in the community, and assisted their parents in the farms and other household chores. We have also observed that the absence of the storytelling event, especially the narration of *Yomandene* tales that contributed to instilling positive behavior in children, has led to an upsurge in negative attitudes amongst youths like stubbornness, laziness, disrespect for parents, elders, cultural values; aspects that used to guide the moral transformation of children and youths in the distant and near past.

References

Butake, Bole and Guilbert Doho, Eds., 1988. *Theatre Camerounais/Cameroonian Theatre, Proceedings of the Symposium on Cameroon Dramaturgy and Theatre Arts*, Cameroon, Centre Camerounais de l"IIT. Bet and Co. (Pub.) Ltd.

Elaine, Aston and George Savona, 1991. *Theatre as Sign-System: A Semiotics of Text and Performance*, New York, Routledge.

Mola, Mbua Ndoko, 2012. *Wisdom and Ways of the Bakweri People*. Online, Available at: www.mbuandoko/ 2012/03/301-the-big-fight-njoh-versus-njoke-e-njuma-yamba-njoh-a-nyame-wona-njoka.html. Retrieved on 10/10/2020.

Schipper, Mineke, 1977. *Oral tradition and African theatre*. In Mineke Schipper-de Leeuw (Ed.) *African Perspectives Text and context: Methodological explorations in the field of African Literature*, 1977/1, pp. 123–134. Available at: www//openaccess.leidenuniv.nl/bitstream/handle/.../05_090_065.pdf?...1 Retrieved on 20/5/2014.

Shonkoffield, Jack P. et al., 2007. *Persistent Fear and Anxiety Can Affect Young Children's Learning and Development*, Working Paper 9, www.developingchild.havard.edu. Retrieved on 10/10/2020.

Simms, Laura, *Thinking Like a Storyteller: The Living Context*. Available at: www.laurasimms.com/ essaycontext.html. Retrieved on 25/04/2012.

Stam, Robert, 2008. *Introduction: The Theory and Practice of Adaptation*. In Robert Stam and Alessandra Raengo (Eds.) *Literature and Film: A Guide to the Theory and Practice of Film Adaptation*, Carlton, Victoria, Blackwell Publishing, pp. 1–47.

Tala, Kashim I., 2013. *Cameroon Oral Literature: An Introduction*, Kansas City, Miraclaire Academic Publications.

PART IV

Stories & therapeutic texts in health and therapy contexts

Introduction

In Part IV we consider stories and therapeutic texts specifically from a health and therapy context. Not that chapters in the previous parts of this volume haven't considered partly or wholly the notion of health and therapy in a broader context. It is difficult for stories not to have these intrinsic links throughout this book. However, here, we focus more specifically on health and therapy in a more clinical context.

We begin with Sharon Jacksties' moving and emotional account of using therapeutic stories with survivors of torture, people who had travelled to the UK from all parts of the world. She considered how stories are used in this challenging context. Sil Bonadie in Chapter 26 offers a contrast in seeing the therapeutic use and healing impact of Michael Morpurgo's *I believe in Unicorns* with children with special needs in Italy. This is followed in Chapter 27 by Lynne Souter Anderson's innovative use of clay within the context of telling stories with children in psychotherapy in the UK. Chapter 28 offers an innovative therapeutic approach to using therapeutic myth in museums in Thalia Valeta's homeland of Greece, based on her childhood fascination with history, myth and museums.

In Chapter 29, world renowned Israeli therapist Mooli Lahad, creator of the 'Six Part Story' process, introduces us to his thoughts and theories on stories in trauma, based on his significant lifetime's experience. In Chapter 30, Mary Louise Chown from Canada introduces us to her experience as a storyteller working in hospital wards and hospices. She approaches this health context from the perspective and role of an artist. In Chapter 31, Jem Dick, based in the UK, considers the use of storytelling and play in his many years of experience working with adults with learning disabilities. Remaining in the UK, Joan Moore then offers a chapter based on her doctoral research using a 'Theatre of Attachment' model as a way of considering the stories of fostered and adoptive children and their families. In a similar way in Chapter 33, Steve Killick offers his experience of using storytelling to help foster carers build their attachment and emotional literacy.

Part IV: Stories & therapeutic texts

The final three chapters of Part IV share a common and pertinent theme, an illness that affects our modern world in particular, dementia. We begin with Alice Liddell's experience of using storytelling with people with dementia, before contrasting this with Alison Ward's fascinating research around the use of storytelling with people living with dementia. Our final chapter in this part, Chapter 36, looks at the moving experience of Ravindra Ranasinha working with a client with vascular dementia.

25

THE BODY POLITIC

An account of my therapeutic storytelling practice with torture survivors and their families

Sharon Jacksties

Background

I worked as a volunteer for a charity which is now known as 'Freedom from Torture' but was then called 'The Medical Foundation for the Care of Victims of Torture and their Families'. Its staff were professionals from a multidisciplinary range of medical and therapy backgrounds. The charity was set up by a woman of unique vision, Helen Bamber OBE, who, amongst initiating other projects, was also instrumental in setting up the charity Amnesty International. During Amnesty's work it became apparent that the therapeutic/psychological needs of torture survivors, rather than only the practical and legal, were not being addressed. This was understood through contact with the increasing numbers of asylum seekers who were managing to reach the UK, along with a growing realisation that many were torture survivors.

Freedom from Torture defines torture as a political act perpetrated by or sanctioned by a government or regime. Of course other forms of torture exist, whether inflicted by individuals, families or groups. However, torture as an apparatus of the state, along with its implications for the granting of refugee status, is what concerns this organisation. It is this context, the use of torture as a political tool, that informed my practice.

At that time, interventions with this group of people, whom I now refer to as 'torture survivors' rather than 'victims', were almost non-exist. The Foundation was a trail blazer, particularly with regard to acknowledging and addressing the ongoing psychological and emotional effects of clients' experiences of torture. Apart from a small team of full-time paid staff most practitioners in the organisation were highly qualified and experienced professionals voluntarily giving their time to a cause which, due to increasing demand, would always be under-resourced. There were as yet no models for dealing with this client group, and multidisciplinary approaches were welcomed. It was mandatory for volunteer staff to participate in weekly group supervision.

A friend had suggested that I offer my services, partly due to my professional background and partly because I had time to spare, adjusting as I was to a career change after returning to London on completion of my degree. My first training was as a Registered Psychiatric Nurse, followed by a Post Graduate Diploma in Drama Therapy. This had led to my taking a performing arts degree, specialising in drama. On my return to London I discovered traditional storytelling, at the beginning of what was to become a Europe-wide revival of this art form. To my surprise, I discovered that I was also in demand as a dance practitioner and was increasingly becoming involved in a world where the physical body was revered and celebrated – a poignant contrast to the experiences of my clients.

This potted work history is relevant to my biases in the development of my practice at the Foundation as well as to the creative path it took. Prior to becoming part of its varied team, I had 2 interviews with Helen Bamber. She was particularly interested in my experience of the abusive aspects of psychiatric hospitals, which in my case occurred during my training. We had a long discussion about how institutions, at their worst, can become agents of abusive control. We spoke about how hierarchical structures can lend themselves to bullying staff into becoming controlling, punishing and abusive towards each other and the most vulnerable members of the institutions, their patients.

Ms Bamber was interested in my personal experience having led to my understanding that abuse of power can be found close to home, and that it isn't necessarily an exotic import. Coincidentally, the European Court of Human Rights was about to declare certain practices used by British armed forces in Northern Ireland as coming within the definition of torture. We discussed how we can look at abuse as a continuum: the mildest form may consist of undermining remarks, but it has the potential, in some circumstances, to become as extreme as the systematic torture of groups or populations. Another factor which undoubtedly colours my sensitivities is that I myself come from a refugee/immigrant background.

Not long after this conversation, fearful of being late, I took a cab to my second interview. I was living at the time in an area with a huge migrant Irish population, increasingly including those who did not feel safe in the North of Ireland, especially if they were from the Catholic minority. My driver was from this community and on hearing my destination spoken in my markedly 'BBC English', anger at his countrymen's situation overcame caution. For the rest of the journey I was in for some tough questioning myself. To his surprise we had nothing to argue about. I also managed to point out that the survivors I was working with were in an even worse position, being in effect stateless people – most of them not yet having received refugee status and me knowing that many of them would be turned down. The threat of forced repatriation was, for them, an ever-present background noise. As a mark of respect to those even worse off than himself, my driver refused to accept his fare. It was this conversation that led to my understanding of the additional traumas lying in wait for my clients, in the new circumstances in which they found themselves.

It soon became clear to me that the survivors were experiencing several 'layers' of suffering and difficulty, which were not only to do with persecution in their own country. Below is a rough break down of these:

- Surviving in a country which was a war zone/a failed state/had a persecuting and oppressive regime.
- Experiencing torture whilst in detention for continuous periods or when randomly taken into custody.
- The uncertainty of being able to escape those circumstances, including long dangerous journeys with the risk of being caught and returned/using the family's savings to escape/trusting the wrong people to effect an escape.
- Feeling unwelcome in the sought-after country of 'asylum'.
- Not having one's story believed after the period of silence that the process of torture imposes. Having to 'prove' one's story in an adversarial institutionalised process whilst attempting to recover from trauma.

- Possible detention in a centre – being treated like a prisoner when innocent of committing any crime.
- Living with the uncertainty about one's asylum claim's outcome – a usually prolonged process during which one is not allowed to work.
- Worrying about the fate of family and friends left behind, feelings of guilt and helplessness at being able to do nothing for them.
- Adjusting to the demands of living in a different culture/climate/learning a new language.
- Experiencing direct or indirect racism and marginalisation in a xenophobic country.

Whilst expecting people to tell me about the horrors they had escaped, I was surprised when they often spent longer talking about the added difficulties they encountered when expecting a place of refuge. Of course there could be many reasons for this – avoiding the pain of re-evoking their trauma is an obvious one. Associating me as an authority figure from this new country could have been another. Certainly it was ironic to me that people who only wanted to survive were sometimes being treated like criminals. It also showed how naïve I was in thinking that legislation and The Declaration of Human Rights could be so regularly circumvented by those who were entrusted to implement them. Our legislation ensures that the onus is on the state to prove that a crime has been committed, whereas these innocent people were being forced to prove what had happened to them.

So they had to tell their stories, and stories are not proof. One of my clients, from the Oromo people, told me that he would never be able to return to his homeland, now taken over by people of another ethnicity from a more arid, mountainous region. With a descriptive gesture and the poetic eloquence typical of his culture, he mimed picking food out of the ground. '…Why would they ever give back a country where they say you can pluck eggs from the ground?…' Without needing to say it, his gesture had shown what he meant, which was, of course, potatoes. But his body also told more of his story. Sometimes forensic evidence also bears a narrative. He had been tortured by being left to hang for hours, tied up by wires looped around his biceps. The scars he presented were fairly incontrovertible corroboratory evidence. It would have been impossible for those injuries to have been self-administered. Nevertheless, he lost his claim for asylum. What use stories then, even if they are true?

Rationale

My practice at the Foundation began with the usual one-to-one sessions. Although being listened to and being believed must have been of some benefit, I increasingly felt that there was another dimension that needed addressing. It was becoming clear to me that although my clients experienced all the psychiatric/psychological symptoms that could be expected, such as PTSD, anxiety, depression, sleeplessness, panic attacks, impotence, these were in response to circumstances that many would not have survived. Most would not have had a predisposition to, or history of, mental health problems. It was the regimes that were 'sick in the head', rather than those who had the resources, acumen, hope and good fortune to escape. Whilst going over my notes to prepare for this chapter, I see that my group co-worker had written:

> …Guzel is worried about the hallucinations she had on release from prison – she thought she was going mad. Sharon explained that it is normal for survivors to think they are going mad and to have those experiences, because the mind develops a life of

its own. It goes off to another place for survival. It's the torture which is not normal, not the survival mechanisms…

Another feature that they had in common was a sense of limbo at being separated from their culture and unassimilated in an unwelcoming or actively hostile one. It is true that companionship and support could be found with various groups from their communities, but this could also be tricky. People in exile from the same region could be on 'different sides' or mistrustful of each other – the belief that agents from their ruling regimes attended any gatherings, proliferated.

As I listened, I increasingly heard people who had lost their 'sense of place'. Their homelands were now places of anguished memories whilst evoking feelings of longing, homesickness and guilt about those they had left behind. Life in this new place presented different hardships. Where they now lived did not value those homes, cultures, customs or stories.

As I listened, I increasingly heard people whose orientation and sense of self was shaped by who they were within their families and their communities, rather than as independent identities as individuals. This made me question how, or even whether, our 'individual centred' forms of therapy were always relevant for those who felt themselves to be less of a person without the defining milieu of family and community. Maybe their lack of wellbeing was also an 'external' one – a chronic malaise due to an ailing personal and social context.

During this period I was developing my skills as a storyteller and increasing my repertoire of traditional stories from multicultural oral traditions. I came to realise that these narratives had been shaped by countless voices over generations. The reason why they had survived, in some cases for millennia, was because they reflect issues and values that transcend the passage of time and are therefore still relevant to the human condition. They were told, and to some small extent are still being told, as an acknowledgement and a celebration of community. The very act of listening together and sharing these oral tales is in itself a socially bonding process. A storyteller was often a person of esteem or authority – educator, cultural custodian and transmitter of values. In the days before modern medicine, the healers and shamans would often also be the communities' storytellers, promoting the wellbeing of all through this shared activity.

And what of the narrative content of these stories? Do some contain reflections of our dilemmas, difficulties, horrors that are too difficult sometimes even to name? To answer this rhetorical question – all the drama, the blessings and ills of human life are there to be found. Apart from their collective impact, it is certain that healers choose particular stories to tell to those who consult them about their problems.

I have been privileged enough to have listened over a period of time to an elder from the Chippewa Cree nation in Canada. He shared with us his experience and understandings of how storytelling was used in his culture and specifically with regard to his practice as a member of the storytelling lodge in his tribe. Requests for help were responded to with an appropriate story chosen for that particular individual. I remember him laughing as he described the reaction of the government authorities as their every direct question was met with a story. Fundamental to his culture is avoiding offending or insulting someone by directly telling them what they should do; the approach is always oblique. Traditional story, for First Nations people, is an ideal distancing device for guidance or for painful material to be explored, just as it can be in a therapeutic situation – as useful as the other art forms used by fellow arts and play therapists.

> …Folk tales teach the accumulated wisdom of those whose survival depends on outwitting the powerful…
>
> (Margaret Meek Spencer – Educationist)

My learning journey as a therapist with torture survivors and my professional development as a traditional performance storyteller were 2 paths that were about to join. My request to initiate a therapeutic storytelling group at the charity was warmly supported by Helen Bamber. To introduce colleagues to this new departure in my work, I invited them to a traditional storytelling session. As mentioned, we were a motley crew of multidisciplinary practitioners, and many had come from abroad as refugees. Knowing this, it was logical to surmise that some of the staff were also torture survivors. The session went very much as it would have done at any public venue until the very end of the last story:

> ...She was tied to the horse's tail and the horse was galloped through the whole of the land until not a single shred of flesh was left on her bones...

Until that moment this had always been a satisfying end for an evil woman punished for her wicked deeds, but on this occasion I met with a divided audience reaction. Staff with backgrounds not dissimilar to mine looked back at me with the placidity of satisfied closure. The rest stared with horror, reproach, some gasped, some changed colour. It was easy to distinguish between those for whom the story had been a mere fairy tale and those for whom that kind of sadistic detail was rather 'too close to home'. Then a Guatemalan colleague approached me,

> 'I never knew you spoke Spanish, Sharon. And such excellent Spanish too!'
> 'I don't speak Spanish, Juanita.'
> 'Well how did you tell all those stories in Spanish then?'
> 'I didn't tell them in Spanish Juanita.'
> 'Don't tell me you told them all in English! How come I heard everything in Spanish?'

Therapeutic storytelling group's aims and objectives

- To provide a welcoming, supportive environment for women from diverse cultures with shared experience of torture and/or family experience of torture.
- To return a sense of control and empowerment by enabling a non-hierarchical peer group way of working.
- To acknowledge the different cultural mores whereby difficulties are dealt with by a group approach, rather than by an individually focussed one-to-one process.
- To avoid reinforcing the power balance of the therapist as an authority figure in a restrictive and authoritarian host culture.
- To discover a more appropriate 'non-Western' model of good therapeutic practise.
- To enable a shared pleasure in storytelling to also become a therapeutic medium.
- To provide an opportunity to experience the sense of empowerment that being listened to affords.
- For the sharing of traditional stories in which the magical/fictional events are accepted due to the suspension of disbelief – in direct contrast to the dismissiveness shown to many torture survivors' true testimonies.
- For group members to take responsibility for the therapeutic roles of tellers and listeners to enable insight and empowerment.
- To use traditional stories from participants' respective cultures to value, celebrate and show respect for their diverse backgrounds in a host country where 'asylum' can be experienced as xenophobic and racist.

- To enable participants to re-connect to what they value from their countries and cultures despite recent memories of political upheaval, war, persecution, suffering and danger.
- To use traditional narratives as a distancing device to enable participants to share their own stories of intimate painful experiences.
- To ensure a collective presence of shared experience to hold these personal testimonies.
- To counteract one of the objectives of torture, which is to impose silence.

Practice

The group was advertised as a women's group for several reasons – the main one being that most of the charity's clients were from cultures in which the genders do not mix socially unless they are related. In a situation where sharing painful personal experiences is part of the healing process, mixed genders would have been an additional layer of constraint to revealing such intimate material. Furthermore, sexual assault and rape are frequent weapons for torturers. I couldn't be sure whether we would ever get as far as referring to these issues in a women's group – I certainly couldn't imagine doing so with men present. Men's groups were also available, including a movement group, which may have provided access for male survivors to mention this method of torture that some would likely have been subjected to.

Due to staff and clients' commitments, it was decided to meet fortnightly. Women were referred by the rest of the staff team, some continuing with their 1 to 1 therapy sessions with their referring therapist in the organisation. Partly due to the advice from another staff member, who described a support group where women shared food, this also became part of our shared practise. Most of the women loved to cook and they shared their regional dishes with pride. Another volunteer helped me to run the group. I discussed process with her, listened to her observations, chewed through various interpretations and she helped with the note taking. In theory, all of us took it in turns to bring food and a story from our own cultures. I was the exception to this, not having a background in which traditional stories were shared orally – therefore my repertoire was more eclectic. Whoever volunteered to be next session's cook and teller was given the cash for any purchases. The group rejoiced in the rather unwieldy name, 'Food for the Mouth, Feast for the Ear'.

It ran for about 2½ years, varying from as few as 3 clients to no more than 7. One referral sheet spanning 18 months shows 15 referrals. Out of these 6 joined the group; 2 attended 1 to 1 introductory sessions but elected not to join the group; 2 found full-time work; 5 did not attend or contact. The 'did not show' number may appear high, but this was consistent with attendance figures for 1 to 1 sessions throughout the organisation. Clients often had chaotic and random lives, struggling to keep up with appointments from other agencies or unable to keep track of time or dates. The small number of referrals was of greater concern. Hindsight contributes to my belief that I should have put more work into engaging colleagues in understanding this completely new therapeutic approach. This was particularly true for those from this country who were not acquainted with an oral tradition at a time when the storytelling revival was only just beginning.

The group always reacted to the stories that were heard. Sometimes they triggered reminiscences of happier times, domestic customs, family stories. Sometimes there was direct comment or discussion about the difficult issues raised in the traditional stories. Sometimes I guided the teller towards recognising the features in the story that resonated with her own circumstances, but only with those that she had already shared with the group. I tried to keep my interventions to a minimum, but on occasion I would tell a story that reflected on the discussion in hand or on issues that women raised directly. The group dynamic was varied: the women could challenge and even argue with each other, sometimes acrimoniously. This wasn't necessarily a bad thing – they had after all emerged from regimes where to be outspoken or contradictory could be a danger to life. Sometimes the atmosphere was awkwardly resistive or apathetic. These were the hardest moods for me as a therapist to address. It would have been so easy to plug the silences with a story instead of leaving space for the women to become active agents in their engagement. The most animated and even high-spirited interactions happened around comparing and contrasting participants' family and cultural backgrounds. These were brought out by sharing memories of family celebration as well as traditional stories. There seemed to be endless interest in the regional variations of the same traditional story. The strongest reactions occurred when someone suddenly realised that this was the same story she had heard from her grandmother,

'…Only in Kurdistan it was a fan, not needles…'
'…Ah yes, I see, but in Iran we only have the needles not the fan…'

These similarities and differences were endlessly picked over, sometimes across languages and the richness that their distinct nuances brought, as we interpreted for each other through English, French, Arabic, Parsee, Kurdish and Turkish. I never noticed an occasion when cultural differences were not respected. These encounters through traditional and family story were the strongest bonding mechanisms in the group – more so than the women's shared suffering. Despite the difficult sessions there was a pervading sense of acceptance and compassion.

Examples of traditional stories enabling therapeutic process

Readers may want to know more about the particular tales referred to in these contexts. The ones marked by an asterisk can be found in the anthology located towards the end of this volume.

> …Stories can provide listeners with an increasing imaginative repertoire of ways of coming to terms with their emotions, which, unlike all other aspects of their being, are full-sized from the day of their birth…
>
> *(Margaret Meek Spencer – Educationist)*

Fatima was an unhappy woman whose attempts to settle in Britain were also being undermined by her husband, who prevented their teenage daughters from participating in the social and cultural opportunities their new country had to offer. She gave the impression of 'being stuck' and described herself in these terms. She found it hard to see how she also contributed to this state of impasse. One example is how she would move heaven and earth to get appointments with specialists of one kind and another, announce her success triumphantly and then never keep those appointments.

During one session I told the story 'Red Hat Green Hat', which tells of 2 families reduced to inaction because all has been destroyed around them. Fatima had a strong reaction to this story, she cried out,

> But this is exactly where we are now in Iraq. All has been destroyed – we have destroyed everything and now we are all helpless!

Subjectively true though this statement was, I felt that my task was to enable Fatima to develop the insight to see how she had internalised this state of paralysis in herself.

Her attendance at the group was extremely haphazard and if she did appear she would often challenge the boundaries by not having her story to tell or forgetting to bring food. On one occasion when, despite what had been agreed the week before, there was no Fatima and no food, I was attempting to fill the gap by feasting our ears with a story about food – therapists get angry too! Halfway through our session, there was a knock at the door and Fatima stood there laden with food. She 'couldn't possibly stop' but didn't want us to go hungry! Dumbfounded we watched her put down the bags of food and disappear. Next session, after she had spent many weeks explaining that she 'couldn't possibly ever tell a story' she told the longest, most complex ever heard in the group, one which would have been a challenge to many professional storytellers.

The narrative of 'Amina and the Silent City' depicts loss of family, exile to a strange land, a paralysed city, the surrendering of final resources, betrayal instead of rescue, loss of identity, hopeless anonymous confinement, demeaning tasks and unexpected redemption at being able to speak of her troubles.

It was an astonishingly 'parallel' story to have chosen. It also marked a change in Fatima's commitment to the group – her attendance improved and she was more able to interact with the other members, contributing to the discussion in a less superficial way and sharing her own feelings with courage and honesty.

Guzel was an outspoken young woman who had become an activist as a university student. She had repeatedly been seized by the 'secret police' and endured periods of imprisonment which had involved sexual torture. One of the ways in which this had been perpetrated was by penetrating her body with objects. Her medical profile included fertility problems as a result – she and her husband had been trying for a baby for some time. The louder the protest, the greater the number of family members persecuted, is the normal pattern. I knew that her husband, also a student at that time, had his own experiences of being been repeatedly picked up – he may have been tortured too, but this is speculation.

Yasmin was a young unmarried mother in an uncertain relationship with the child's father. She had managed to form this liaison after escaping persecution in her own country. At the age of only 16 she had been picked up by 'security forces'. Completely sexually inexperienced, she had been gang raped. During her asylum hearing, when she had to testify to this experience, the court witnessed the assault through her eyes as she relived it in a florid episode of post-traumatic stress. So extreme were her reactions, and so traumatic were they for the assembly to witness, that the judge stopped the hearing. He reprimanded the authorities for putting her in a position in which she was forced to re-live her assault, and asylum was immediately granted. This is the first instance I or my colleagues had heard of when proceedings were halted and asylum granted due to the undeniable distress shown at the recalling of traumatic events.

The spectre of rape and sexual assault is one that stalks all dialogue about torture. Torture is an act designed to intimidate and to silence. Survivors are silenced by the guilt of knowing that they have put their families in danger – who knows which one of them will be next? They internalise the actions of others by experiencing the guilt that should belong to the perpetrators. In some cultures, the sexual discretion of women is of paramount importance. Their chastity or married fidelity is a symbolic representation of the moral integrity of entire families and communities. To admit to being raped can be seen as a threat to the reputations of many. Beyond all other methods sexual torture silences.

We were a group of women. Even in countries enjoying political stability and the rule of law, most women at some time are wary of, or have felt threatened by, the possibility of being raped.

Guzel was the first to address this subject directly when she shared with the group what her husband had told her in response to the sexual assaults she had endured. She gestured to her pelvic area, and showed how he had placed his hands above and below her pubis and said,

> This is not where you are, this is not who you are. Whatever they have done to you here is not you. You are not that person.

Not only had she now shared with the group that she had been sexually assaulted (she had previously only spoken of her infertility problems), but she had described how her relationship had survived in spite of it. She had broken the taboo of silence about this topic and the expectation that this violation could not be tolerated by a spouse. Her marriage had endured despite any revelations and with the active support of her husband. Guzel had shown that breaking silence could have positive consequences. I felt that she had given me an opening to at long last tell a story about rape.

Due to the hyper-sensitive topic with its overriding theme of oppressive physical immediacy, I deliberately chose as non 'naturalistic' story as I could, to enable distancing. This genre of story chosen is known to storytellers as a creation myth and these tales always contain the most randomly magical happenings as unlike our daily lives as can be imagined. I have chosen to entitle it 'Chasing the Sun' for this anthology. In this traditional tale a young woman is raped in the very midst of her community but in circumstances that prevent her from identifying her attacker. She decides to seek him out herself and shame him publicly. She is successful in this, but there is a huge price to pay for her courage, including the discovery that the rapist is the very person she should be most able to trust. This challenging tale of how a heroic woman takes on her abuser single-handed also raises many questions.

When the story ended there was a deep silence in the room; nobody was looking at anyone else, not to avoid eye contact, but because the group members were in a reflective state. Perhaps they were thinking of their own experiences, those of people close to them or in a broader way of this weapon that pervades society. I remained quietly vigilant whilst showing a calmness that I hoped would give the impression that I would be able to contain any reactions.

Yasmin spoke. She told us how her child's father kept telling her that she was not normal, that she couldn't feel anything during sex. How he found it hard to sustain a relationship with her due to her 'frigidity' (my terminology). How her passive sexual response was driving a wedge between them. In the context of the session, it was clear that Yasmin was referring to having been raped without actually saying so. I felt this was a huge breakthrough for Yasmin personally and for everyone in the group given the persecution that they had survived including sexual assaults, and/or the fear of them happening at any time. Moreover, Yasmin was able to speak about the after effects of this trauma – life changing and maybe insurmountable as they were; she was nevertheless no longer trapped in the uncontrollable re-living of her horrific experience. She had moved on enough to talk about the legacy of her torture. Yasmin and Guzel had not been silenced. They could refer to their experiences in a supportive group where they wouldn't be judged. Despite what they had endured, one had a child she adored and one had a marriage which had survived the kind of pressures that would have ended many.

Towards the end of my time at the charity now known as Freedom from Torture, I heard a story from a psychiatrist colleague during supervision which has preoccupied me ever since. He told the group how he had been seeing a torture survivor from Iran over a period of time and how he had been having difficulty in asking his client an awkward question. As a therapist he had the insight to know that this inability to ask had become a feature in their therapeutic dynamic. He knew that the man had worked for the secret police under the Shah's rule. The client had become a target for torture by the security forces in the new regime that had gained power immediately after the revolution. For weeks my colleague wondered whether this man had himself been a torturer when his employers were wielding the upper hand. His inability to ask this question, the enormity of its possible implications, was another example of how torture silences. How can we voice the unspeakable?

At last therapeutic integrity prevailed and the question was asked. There was silence for a while, then came the reply,

...Only when it was necessary...

There was an awkward silence in the supervision group when we heard about that chilling exchange. We were all left questioning the extent of our remit – here to support victims and survivors – but perpetrators too? It was as though my learning experience working in the organisation had come full circle. At that time various studies were emerging about how torturers are made, along with the familiar debates about whether the capacity was innate, or whether everybody has that potential given the right kind of training and context.

I recalled my early conversations with the charity's founder and how, as a very young woman during my first employment in a backward psychiatric hospital, I had discovered that institutions can become the perfect settings for nurturing and normalising abuse. I recalled, too, the conversation with the taxi driver from Northern Ireland about how torture also happens close to hand. Here was a man who no longer felt safe in his own country due to an unresolved conflict that had endured for centuries as a direct result of Ireland becoming England's first colony. This gap in my 'English' perspective was filled by an Irish colleague, who, during supervision, was rather indignant that nobody in the room was aware of that glimpse of history.

To this day I continue to think about how colonialism destabilised huge areas of the world, harvesting wealth and plucking the privileges that grow on the power tree. It is hard to quantify to what extent this legacy of exploitation has contributed to the failing states, the brutal regimes that have so opportunistically, or even inevitably, risen at the demise of colonial empires. Surely the tide of refugees, amongst them many torture survivors, is the result of these wrongs, albeit generations later, coming home to roost?

Looking elsewhere, to the exotic, with a 'not in my back yard', 'it could never happen here' perspective is to miss the point about what makes a torturer. We know it can be an insidious process, indeed the more insidious the better the success at normalising what should never happen. Even now I have friends who are in therapy because their parents forced them to attend brutal boarding schools where physical assaults were daily events. These were sanctioned as part of the 'character building' that was deemed so necessary 300 years ago to further the interests of the nation and its empire. Unsurprisingly sexual assault was also colluded with in the institutional culture that tolerated physical abuse. This behaviour is no longer legal and practices are in place to safeguard against it. However, for hundreds of years, thousands of brutalised children were desensitised into being able to perpetrate the brutality that was needed to create and maintain an empire – which could not have survived without practices now recognised as torture.

I am finishing this chapter during a resurgence of social unrest about Britain's colonial history. Statues of slave owners are being torn down, black people are being shot on the streets of America and people who are demonstrating legally are being attacked by security forces. The Black Lives Matter movement has become an international force. My work with torture survivors has been a glimpse into the harm wrought on individuals by the huge entities of political systems or failed states, all dependent on institutionally administered abuse.

But how to turn this closed circle into a spiral – the shape that allows a sense of movement whilst incorporating the tail of its past? How can we move on with those perpetrators who have become disempowered? What is our moral and ethical position towards these people? Is it ever appropriate to consider a healing process for ex-torturers? Towards the end of my 4 years working with the Medical Foundation, I heard of an acquaintance who had become very depressed. He was involved in the performance storytelling scene, but I hadn't seen him around for a while. On asking a mutual friend, I was told that he had succumbed to memories of his time working for security forces in Northern Ireland, many years previously. Times had changed, and he now had a very different perspective on the practices that he had been involved with. What he had thought of as 'doing his duty' had now come to haunt him. I still hope that one day, he will hear a traditional tale that so expertly tells of the coercion, betrayal and forgiveness that is possible when contextualised within the bigger picture, as described in 'The Snake and the King's Dream'.

On leaving my work with the Medical Foundation I was able to get government grants to run oral storytelling projects with refugees and asylum seekers. I was fortunate enough to be with a unit that was attached to a school which was in a part of London with one of the highest numbers of recent immigrants in the whole of the UK. The refugee unit and school are a model of good practice for welcoming, including and assimilating refugees, and the project was filmed for a documentary broadcast on national television.

Now that I live in a rural location I no longer have the opportunity to work with these groups. If I were asked what is the most important thing I have learned from my experience over those years, I would say that it is so important to remember, whatever the setting, the impact that a person in a position of 'authority' can have on vulnerable people. The power balance is never in favour of those seeking help. Torture is a deliberate and extreme form of abuse. As therapists, as participants in that huge endeavour called humanity, we have a duty to question where we are on that sliding scale which includes intimidation, indifference, ethics and compassion.

26
I BELIEVE IN UNICORNS …

Silviana Bonadei

Introduction

In this chapter, a group of children and young adolescents with varying abilities have participated in a program based around a story written by the children's author Michael Morpurgo. We chose *I believe in unicorns* for the space it gives to the imagination as well as for the large choice of varied characters.

Story telling adapts to all circumstances for as long as the most appropriate narrative or story is chosen. In this case we debated first the needs of the group as we knew most of the participants that attended the sessions; then we made sure that the story would be adequate. Several participants had poor self-esteem building up from an inadequacy in their respective schools and as a result tended to be bullied. Others had difficulties in coping with the syllabus due to impaired reading abilities and lastly poor social interaction skills constituted the main challenges our participants had. Some of the messages in this story matched our needs.

In *I believe in unicorns*, most of the roles could somehow be chosen by children with learning difficulties and those on the autistic spectrum. The scripts could be long, others had few lines or none at all, with humans, animals and fantasy creatures, which provided a vast choice for all our participants.

The approach

The life of a child, an adolescent or an adult with differences can be compared to the unicorn's desire to survive in a somehow hostile world, in this case flooding. Often experiences of failure erode self-esteem and bring about unhappiness about going to school or to work, as happened to Tomas, the little boy who disliked reading and preferred to follow his father fishing. His mum did not respect his desire and brought him to the library, where he slowly developed an interest in reading. Too often the bullying children experience creates fear, insecurity and self-withdrawal but if there is remedial work, they can board Noah's Ark, find a friend, enjoy learning and find help or even be "saved". One of our participants who was 9 years old received a note one day saying that it would be better for her not to be in that class she was in. How can you feel when you read such a note and you are 9 years old? This information was related by her distraught and helpless mother.

Sitting back-to-back with someone you are comfortable with or lying down and listening to a story teller brings back memories, pleasant or hurtful, wakes up fantasy, provides relaxation and allows you to detach from reality. A study by Meringoff et al. (1981) showed that a story told on the radio provided stimulation for children to create imaginative drawings. Children who listened to a story translated it into images and had more content and more details than those who watched the same story on television. The latter tended to reproduce what was seen, and therefore belonging to others and not coming from their own imagination.

The method

In our center that caters for children and adolescents with challenges, we organized *I believe in unicorns* sessions at the beginning of a school holiday, as preferred by the parents, over a period of 3 days for a total of 16 contact hours. The participants ate lunch and had their tea breaks together and that reinforced their friendship. Some free time after lunch was planned, which provided a breather for some and friendships that gradually built up over the days for others and the possibility for the organizers to observe the dynamics or individual behaviors. Some rested, others discussed or re-wrote scripts and those in need of movement played chasing games and other outdoor ball activities and those tired lay down and even slept. On the last day, after a last rehearsal and lunch, all the scenes were combined and the interested parents, siblings and friends attended the play.

Our goals were to provide the children with the opportunity to excel in areas other than the usual academic study, which is what parents and schools usually focus on. Most importantly we wanted them to enjoy a variety of activities aiming at personal and group development.

The *I believe in Unicorns* story was shortened and divided into 5 scenes and each group was composed of 3–5 children and 2 adults. Other adults were present to support any group, provided it was needed.

Our program included 20 children and adolescents, whose chronological age was between 8 and 20, but all had lower developmental ages between 6 and 14. The majority were diagnosed with a learning difficulty or were on the autistic spectrum.

Embodiment Projection Role – EPR

The daily activities were developed around 3 principles developed by Professor Sue Jennings (2011), namely Embodiment (being in tune with the body), Projection (creating with/without tools) and Role (becoming a character within a play or a story); most children are able to achieve this by the age of 7.

The overall idea of the assessment would be to highlight the strengths and weaknesses, as well as identifying the favorite mode of expression of an individual. In Embodiment, the aim was to develop and sensitize the children to their body, accept it and make use of it, in a child-centered way with some group interactions as well. The most timorous participants hesitated to engage in these activities, looking away, but as all the activities were non-directive and space was of the essence here, it was observed that most of them engaged gradually, especially in activities with more of an individual scope. They walked like an animal or like a person scared to go to the dentist, brisk walking to school or college etc. On the other hand, it appeared to be more difficult for the quieter children to measure their abilities in group activities like push and pull games or keeping beach balls in the air. Some relaxation activities at the end of the day, including a safe back massage, created unexpected reactions of touch sensitivities or, for some participants, reluctance to massage a friend – but for others an enjoyable experience to act out.

This story of *I believe in unicorns* provided endless possibilities for Projective activities. Drawing a scene of their choice, creating masks of an animal or a character, creating Noah's Ark, the decorations for their scene and making a unicorn in papier mâché were among the suggested activities. Noah's Ark came to shape using mostly cardboard and was complete with the anchor, the external door close to the waterline, the rudder and the effects of the wood planks. The library's brick wall was made of shoe boxes and the unicorn was placed on a deserved pedestal after completion. During these activities several behaviors transpired: from being at ease/relaxed and creative, to hesitating to touch, to disgusted reactions to the glue or the paint, or even not being able to create what was asked. For the masks a participant thought for a while and cut her mask to make a half-one and it paved the way for others to copy her idea. Not all participants put their masks on as it can be emotionally difficult to become another character and cover their faces with a mask.

The determination and trust in each other built up gradually in all the groups, but at times some participants had to compromise and accept that their ideas were not chosen or accepted, and meltdowns happened. Some participants with lots of ideas struggled when they were not chosen, and adults needed to intervene and moderate. Scenes, roles and scripts took shape, costumes and decorations were chosen and created. The play emerged and assimilated the themes of friendship, perseverance, discovery of stories and their power, and moreover provided a sense of accomplishment. The 2 girls who acted out the unicorn decided to create their own script. The horn of the unicorn was the most elaborate part of their costume; once completed, they practiced their part intensively but then improvised beautifully during the play.

This story also fitted adequately a large group of participants in terms of choice of characters, as it allowed the children to choose based on their interest and level of confidence. Again, without directing the children they were asked to choose what they were going to do. A girl decided to be the story teller and an adolescent helped to adjust the fitting of costumes and props in her group. Someone else said that she wanted to be organizing the actors behind the scene when we'd put it together, as she disliked acting in plays. Interestingly the librarian was one of the oldest participants and the 2 unicorns were 2 witty and chatty young girls who organized the layout of their scene.

It was interesting to follow the participants' development throughout the 3 days using Jennings' 3 developmental phases of Embodiment, Projection and Role. The most powerful example of gaining confidence was a young adolescent with severe dyslexia, agreeing to read the introduction of the story and his scene. A friend playing the librarian helped him during the rehearsals and the 2 actors complemented each other. Some children were observed to take more risks than others as they progressed in their learning path, and others offered their dexterity in creating the decorations. There was a space for each and every one!

Most of the children and adolescents could blend in their respective groups, except for a boy with sensory issues and other difficulties related to the autistic spectrum. He participated in his own way and moved all around the space but brought in his creativity by creating unexpected props related to the story. Another girl took time to adapt to the large group activities but performed better in her sub-group, where she took the role of the director and organized her peers. Others worked skillfully to prepare the props, a costume-designer "appeared", who even brought from home accessories that others wished they had.

No doubt the play represented the culmination of our sessions and everyone gave what they could, whilst perfection was not the aim. All the actors overcame their fear, and even if some needed prompting, everyone performed to their best. A truly mesmerizing, enchanting and healing story!

Evaluation

In order to evaluate the work, we observed the participants, noticing that when they performed on a regular basis, patterns emerged that allowed us to assess the goals each one of them strove for and achieved.

The first session for staff was what I called a discovery phase. It needed intense observation while the process of the 3 components (EPR) unfolded. During the assessment of a group it was necessary to have more than 1 person observing and then sharing individual observations, upon compiling the assessments. In our situation 2 adults worked together, discussing our observations before writing them down. At the end of the 3 days an analysis of the flow of the sessions would substantiate each child's development. See examples in Table 26.1.

Throughout the sessions the activities provided further information on the development of the participants. An example is the striking change in a quiet boy who came out of his shell when the group decided to create Noah's Ark with a large cardboard box. He actively played the role of the door, put up the mast and created the anchor and was able to share his ideas with his peers.

The EPR observation developed by Professor Sue Jennings assessed the 3 parts, namely Embodiment, Projection and Role, throughout the 3 days. We divided the children among the adults and we each observed 2 children throughout the 3 days (see Table 26.2). The dynamics of the group were also assessed, and we determined whether an adaptation to the initial plan was needed. For example, the boy with sensory issues needed to be allowed to detach himself from the group when he became overloaded, but knowing this allowed everyone to accept and accommodate his needs. Interestingly, when we joined all the scenes of the play, he impressed everyone by being in role and coming in at the right moment, adding his own interpretation of his role of silent narrator, considering that he had prepared signs that helped in the understanding of the story timeline in his scene.

Another change we brought was to increase the time for movement activities, as the younger ones needed it. Within the Embodiment phase, a girl who used to stay in the periphery of the activities was observed to gradually join in and she wasn't the only one. In the first day, many participants were stiff, reluctant to allow themselves to run, shout, twist and turn, but significant changes were observable by the end of day 3. Improvements were also observed in 2 siblings who seemed to be "glued" together, but slowly found their respective space and demonstrated their very individual capacities.

At the end of each day all the adults gathered for a discussion about group dynamics, individual functioning and behavioral observations and then we wrote our observations down to have an overall picture that represented each participant.

We created a rating chart of behaviors which covered, for example, playfulness, spontaneity, innovation and other determinants to provide the practitioners with an input for the base line, that could then be compared to further improvement or stagnation in the sessions (Jennings 1999).

The last document we used was the Ritual and Risk observation (Jennings 2017) as it allowed an estimation of the proportion of risk and ritual the participants took during the sessions or for determined activities. It was compiled daily at the end of each session. It is a pie chart, divided in half, whereby the practitioner evaluates the percentage of risk taken. The ritual is related to cultural activities and affirms the person's identity and replicates a scenario that is safe and that already exists. The risk establishes the level of activity, innovation and the ability to self-regulate.

Table 26.1 EPR summary for one group using *I believe in Unicorns*

NAME	DAY 1			DAY 2			DAY 3		
	E	P	R	E	P	R	E	P	R
TZYa	stiff	hesitant	none	more engaged	engaged in mask, hesitant in role	held back	participates	mask limited	better in role
TZYu	stiff	engaged	none	starts to "free" himself	engrossed	attentive and creative	participates	mask limited	at ease and in role
LXR	timorous	timorous	none	less hesitant	engrossed	at ease	not at ease in body	mask limited	at ease and in role and director
CK	hesitant	gets inspiration from others	none	"freer"	present with hesitation	integrated	smiling and participative but stiff muscles	mask limited	stiff role
MD	occasionally gets involved	sticks to facts	none	more inhibited	engaged in mask, self-engaging	acts his own ideas	engaged in solo but unable to test himself in push–pull	mask limited	participates not as a character but as props
LCY	restrained	engaged and hesitant	none	increased participation	at ease and creative	shares with partner; very engaged	relaxed	mask limited	very in role and at ease
LXY	restrained	engaged	none	jovial and participative	at ease and creative	participative and resourceful	enjoyed	mask limited	director in role

I believe in unicorns …

Table 26.2 EPR summary for a group using *I believe in Unicorns*

Name	day 1			day 2			day 3		
	E	P	R	E	P	R	E	P	R
AB	stiff	hesitant	none	more engaged	engaged in mask, hesitant in role	held back	participates	mask limited	better in role
DE	occasionally gets involved	sticks to facts	none	more inhibited	engaged in mask, self-engaging	acts his own ideas	engaged in solo but unable to do it in push-pull activities	mask limited	participates not as a character but as props
MN	restrained	engaged	none	jovial and participative	at ease and creative	participative and resourceful	enjoyed	mask limited	director and in role

Shena took risks in that she chose her costumes and props carefully, not accepting other suggestions and brought a twist of her own in the rehearsals; she made sure she kept them aside and away from other costumes. In fact, she also started to move according to how she imagined her character would do it.

Conclusion

Therapeutic stories are a powerful tool that offer a vast array of social and personal development to children, adolescents and adults, enriching their lives be it in a group or in a 1 to 1 setting. They also impart inspiration and dreams. These activities based on a story also have a formative aspect, in regard to the development of the child's personality. Using Jennings' EPR (2011) as a reference point and theoretical framework allowed a spontaneous and as much as possible a non-directive approach; the participants could get in touch with their imagination, represent or illustrate their understanding and maybe express difficulties, and they could also show what they were learning.

All over the world, populations have developed their respective stories or narratives and they bring an opportunity to be used in a therapeutic way in a determined period of time. Choosing the desired one with a scope to facilitate everyone's feelings and expressions will certainly be beneficial for the participants. Having said that, any story might resonate at any time. For we facilitators, building up a personal collection of therapeutic stories and repeated experiences is helpful for the participants we work with, and equally therapeutic for us.

References

Jennings, S. (1999) *Creative Play and Drama with Adults at Risk.* London: Routledge.
Jennings, S. (2011) *Healthy Attachments and Neuro-Dramatic Play.* London: JKP.
Jennings, S. (2017) *Creative Storytelling with Children at Risk.* London: Routledge.
Meringoff, L. et al. (1981) *How Shall You Take Your Story with or without Pictures?* Biennial meeting of the society for research on child development.

27
CLAY STORIES, CRAFTING SPIRIT AND SOUL

Lynne Souter-Anderson

This chapter begins with the idea that clay itself has its own unique story. It is a story that connects us with the planet Earth and the associated fundamental elements of air, water and fire and, of course, to all life. In his writings Jung (1995, p. 47) referred often to the prima materia – earth. Clay as a form of earth, has come to be known as the prima materia. The prima materia is known also as 'radix ipsius', meaning root of itself. How wonderous is this, the notion that it roots in itself? In this sense, earth is seen to capture, cradle and hold all the stories in the world that have ever been told, almost like a collective earth spirit, that has its own life and soul where everything draws strength from it. Viewed like this it is much like the collective unconscious considered to be the part of our unconscious mind that is genetically inherited from our ancestors and shared with all humankind. This fascinating concept is at the heart of Jungian theoretical perspectives (Jung, 1968) on the human psyche.

How did we come to be here? Children often ask. Where do you come from? Scientific and poetical minds have offered many answers to these fundamental and existential questions, with each of us adding our own imaginings to the answers. Such is the need to tell and want to share our experiences with families and friends. Creation myths across the Globe are full of fascinating stories that have captured the imagination of people historically and from all cultures, these being associated with deeply held beliefs about earth clay and the stars. Imagine the idea of earth clay and stars blending! This enigmatic thought points to magnificent things being possible in the minds of early humans and, indeed, for those of us living today.

Travelling back in time and to other places – for this is what all good stories do – we begin to reconnect with ancient wisdoms linked to the elements and, in essence, to earlier spiritual times. For you see, the land upon which we walk is the very same substance that we human beings are made from. Our roots lie within the depths of the lands and the seas that cover this planet called Earth – Mother Earth connecting us to the great story of human civilisation.

There are stories from the Indian continent that offer us an understanding and acceptance of the Great Goddess being one and the same as the Universal Mother of Mankind. Whilst in another part of the world, on the continent known as Africa there are myths handed down from generation to generation about clay pots being made and used in almost all aspects of life, such as birth and death, and those in between. We cannot help but story-tell when we create with clay. In fact, the decoration on the clay pots depicts stories of how life was lived at the time of the making and they give us a real sense of what was significant in that cultural and historical time. This means we can know something of the life cycles and yearly cycles of those that have come before us, since the decorations on the clay pots portray traditions embedded in earlier belief systems when ethereal aspects abounded.

It is no wonder that when we handle clay and really touch this earth medium, we feel so much more than just slimy clay, for the contact with it draws us in with our whole selves – such is the connection with clay. We are from the earth; we are made of earth clay and we come to realise we are part of all creation. When this happens, we discover more about ourselves metaphorically and spiritually. In describing a theoretical underpinning for what happens when we work with clay in a therapeutic setting it can be useful to refer to Souter-Anderson's Theory of Contact: Physical, Emotional, Spiritual and Metaphorical (Souter-Anderson, 2010, 2015, 2019) for a deeper explanation. Here it is sufficient to say, that 'there are many complex processes involved, since physical, physiological, biochemical, neurological, emotional and psychological aspects are simultaneously activated. A five-lens framework helps to understand the continuous oscillation of fragile but powerful connections intrinsically and intricately interlinking client and therapist as they work together in clay therapy' (Souter-Anderson, 2015, p. 7). What often happens is that as the clay is given form and shape by our hands, hitherto hidden scary worries, fears and concerns are made visible, thereby enabling the client and therapist to begin an exploration of the story that emerges from the deeper recesses of our minds.

Our hands are powerful tools that help us to communicate matters of importance. What often happens is that as the clay is given form and shape by our hands, hitherto hidden scary worries, fears and concerns are made visible, thereby enabling the client and therapist to begin an exploration of the story that emerges from the deeper recesses of our minds.

Now comes the time to tell you about three stories that children have shared when they have been moulding and modelling clay. When we hold clay, there can be an instant and an innate connection with this muddy formless mass that communicates possibilities and potentials as our imaginations are captured.

Firstly, six-years-old Cissy's story lets us know of a particular clay pot that she made, which became known as the *The Forget-me-not-pot; Not the Witch's Pot*. This is a story about a young girl beginning to know herself differently as she creates a clay cooking pot. It is almost as if the story of renewal and rebirthing was being told as a new Cissy began to emerge.

Tessiah, an eight-years-old girl named her clay story *The Enchanted Blackberry*. It is a tale offering insights into how a child harnesses her imagination to sustain herself through a mundane and dreary existence.

Finally, the story of Mack's clay creations shows how important his view was on both his own and his deceased father's afterlife and how they would be together. Mack was secure in this, his own belief of an enduring relational bond with someone he loved dearly.

Cissy's story: *The Forget-me-not-pot; Not the Witch's Pot*

As with many young children when using clay, the making of food, cooking pots and eating utensils are favourite activities. Food preparation, cooking it, then eating it are inherently significant aspects of life, for they ensure survival for self, family and friends. However, when there are many children in the home, as was the case for six-years-old Cissy, vying for attention when there are six other siblings and half-siblings was a full-time occupation since attention and time from the adults in the home was scarce.

Eating with others is important socially, with food nearly always being present during familial and societal rites of passages and throughout rituals. So it was with Cissy that towards the end of her therapeutic time she immersed herself in making clay pots. She had made many roughly shaped clay cups, bowls and plates previously but on this occasion, Cissy chanted rhythmically as if beating a drum,

I'm going to make another pot, but this is a different pot – it's going to look like a big cooking pot –

A big cooking pot, A BIG COOKING POT. A witch's cooking pot.

I forgot it's not a witch's cooking pot.

It's a big cooking pot –

With a forget-me-not –

Forget-me-not-pot

Cissy's hands had set to work modelling a big clay bowl, well big in comparison to the size of a six-year-old's hands! Whilst her mind was focused on chanting her rhyme the clay shape had become too thin. There is a myth that Yoruba potters, who live in Africa, tell on how the passage to the spiritual world, by a person who has died, should not be broken, otherwise parts of this person will reside in the 'world of broken pots, with the spirits of witches and suicides' (Witte, 1984, p. 245). Cissy somehow, instinctively, knew her clay pot needed to remain whole so that she could complete an unconsciously known ritual for she knew her pot was not to be that of a witch.

Resourcefully, she pulled more clay from another piece, then squeezed and squashed it with some force in between the palms of her two hands. Once satisfied with the thickness Cissy pressed the clay hard against the thin areas of the cooking pot that she had made. Whilst she had been doing this an idea had seemed to form in Cissy's mind for as she stood back from the clay pot it became clear, something was not quite right!

"It needs some paint on it. It has to be yellow because that's my favourite colour." Cissy told me as she smiled into my eyes. A smile from Cissy was rare so this, for certain, conveyed something special had to be taking place.

A tube of yellow paint was located, and Cissy joyfully squeezed a thick layer of yellow paint right into the centre of the cooking pot. Splosh! Standing over the pot she peered in and then moved her head around so that she could inspect the inside of the pot's walls. She then noticed there were some small blue beads in a box resting on a shelf and some blue glass gemstones nearby. Haphazardly Cissy set about pushing the beads and gemstones onto the clay pot to decorate the outside. As can be imagined this was quite a fascinating frenzied dance between Cissy's hands, and the clay, paint, beads and gemstones, seeming to all be moving together, but the cooking pot was not yet finished! Next came the request for gold and silver glitter which was liberally sprinkled over the cooking pot. And finally, Cissy needed a blue forget-me-not flower to rest on the yellow paint inside the pot. There did not appear to be a blue flower to hand and so an improvised flower was cut from a piece of blue card to complete the creation.

This cooking pot, that was not a witch's pot, was amazingly beautiful because of its child-like crafted quality. Cissy was overjoyed with her creation as I offered,

"You're right – no way could this be a witch's pot!" And Cissy gleefully exclaimed,

"It's the best pot in the whole world and it's mine! We have put magical ingredients in it together and out of it will be made a new piece of cloth that will become the new skin colour for all to see. It will be shining and bight and spectacular."

Reader, please sit for a while imagining Cissy with her forget-me-not pot before I invite you to consider your own version of what this story may have meant to Cissy, for no versions can ever be the same. Each story is unique to each of us. Story themes are often about a struggle and in the making of the big cooking pot, Cissy had struggled with the making of the cooking pot sides. By being with Cissy in her struggles I hoped I had offered a reliable and consistent therapeutic relationship that was real and secure enough, enabling her to steadily become more alive, that is to say she was awakening to whom she was becoming.

Through an alchemical process of changing the base material of clay into something spectacular, Cissy's forget-me-not pot had emerged for both of us to see. This deep connection that we have with earth clay, metaphorically could be considered as being in touch with our primal Self – our true core that reaches deep within us. When this process gets under way and, as the client 'surrenders to the clay' (Souter-Anderson, 2015, p. 190–194), we often move in and out of different states of consciousness. In this play space of potential so many levels and connections for both the client and the therapist are simultaneously at work in both their inner and outer worlds. We come to see then that transformational experiences become organically possible through the therapeutic relationship because as significant meaning comes to be understood, this new information holds the power to change our thinking about ourselves and others. Such experiences provide important opportunities for blossoming relationships.

So why might this story hold a special meaning? Well, here is a little clue. A cooking pot is a vessel and in Jungian (Kirsch, 2000, p. 253) thought the therapeutic relationship is known as the alchemical vessel – possibly a type of womb where newness may be experienced and when there may be the opportunity for a psychological rebirthing process to get under way. For sure as day follows night, we discover that when we feel seen and acknowledged by another person who is special to us, then we know we exist. This is such an alchemical process and we understand this as the idea of base psychological matter taking on a new meaning which often enlightens us, for we have been seen and appreciated and, therefore, valued.

Of course there is a further clue towards the end of Cissy's tale when she excitably tells of the magical ingredients that have gone into the cooking pot to make a cloth that will become the new skin colour for everyone to see. It will be spectacularly shining and bight.

Metaphorically and symbolically people change – children change, when we know we are accepted and loved, and this happens very naturally and irrevocably when working with clay in a safe and comfortable environment where the ambience is conducive to creating and sharing stories.

Tessiah's story: *The Enchanted Blackberry*

Tessiah, an eight-years-old girl, came from a deprived background where adverse childhood circumstances and experiences had been reported to authorities whose job it was to keep children safe. What she did not possess in material wealth she made up for with an amazing imagination. When Tessiah worked with clay her aptitude for storytelling became utterly magical.

Tessiah spent a particular therapy session making endless numbers of unremarkable spherical-like clay forms – all slightly different in shape and size. When it seemed as if she had done enough of this repetitive process, she stood back and gazed at her effort. She raised her eyes to look at me and with this she announced that she knew precisely what she intended to make. I enquired what this was going to be but was told to wait and see. So, I dutifully did this, though Tessiah's quizzical looks had me captive as to what her hands were doing with the clay. Ever mindful that the hands will tell the story through the clay I relaxed into the chair and waited.

Being dainty in her movements, Tessiah began to pile the clay spheres on top of each other in a somewhat wobbly way. Her attention intensified, though, as one clay spere toppled from the pile. Tessiah was not happy about this, exclaiming that the big blackberry she was making would be misshapen if a part of it was not there.

"Aha, a big blackberry," I wondered to myself aloud. Tessiah did not seem to mind that she had let slip what she was making.

"Yes, it's called the Enchanted Blackberry."

"Hm, hm," I exclaimed. And then as Tessiah worked to sculpt the blackberry some more she began to tell a tale which became known as *The Enchanted Blackberry Story*.

A long time ago, in the woods near a child's home, there was a place called the Enchanted Forest. When the child left her house, she went to look for magic blackberries but along her journey, there were many difficulties she had to go through. She went through sandstorms. She went through snowstorms and she knew she needed to find shelters like caves to sleep in because this child was on her own. It was a scary time for the child, but she needn't have been so worried. One morning, just as she awoke, she saw a pair of tiny, bright shiny eyes peeping from round the doorway of her shelter. (At this point Tessiah crouched to the floor and peered around a chair.) The tiny eyes belonged to a magical animal and he had brought his friends to see the child. Now the child knew she was not on her own anymore – she had friends!

After the child had got to know her new friends, she realised she was hungry so the animals with magical powers showed her where they could find some special fruit to eat. She knew in her everyday life back home that these fruits, that her new friends said were magic, were indeed blackberries. Her friends told her that if she were to eat the special fruit, she would grow wings just like them, and be able to find her way home. The child was very excited about this as she had never been on such an adventure before. She now knew that whenever she wanted to, she could find the path into this amazing forest and have her own adventure finding enchanted blackberries.

Tessiah ended the story saying confidently,

> So, you see, this blackberry is very special and magical. I know I've made it from soft clay but when it dries out it will keep its shape and I can look at it whenever I need to or want to. I will take it home so that it is always with me – forever!

Enthralled I replied,

> "That's quite a story, Tessiah."

> "Yes, did you know that blackberries are supposed to be a superfood; they have loads of goodness in them so the child in this story is looking for good things to make her strong so that when she went home she would feel different."

What a transformative experience Tessiah had been narrating. Symbolically blackberries, often known as brambles – a term referring to rough prickly bushes – have numerous meanings across cultures and myths. Noteworthy here is that in Christian art (Ferguson, 1966, p. 28), the bramble was considered as the burning bush that did not consume Moses who was written about in Exodus, the second book of the *Bible*. Blackberries have also come to be seen as a theme of spiritual neglect and certainly Tessiah's family life experiences were of difficulty and neglect, though not being consumed by this.

"My goodness," I said as we smiled in a mutually shared way that suggested an unspoken understanding.

Earlier in this chapter there was an invitation for the reader to consider their own thoughts upon hearing Cissy's clay story and now it is time to reflect on Tessiah's story. This has been a story about a young child going on a journey and needing to find shelters when encountering scary and frightening things at times. It is a story of finding friends who can share little adventures to locate new things in life that seem to offer respite from worries and troubles. It also shows how the worth of a child's imagination may be priceless in an existence that knows only dreariness, darkness and despondency. Importantly in this story there is a beacon of hope when the clay yields up a superfruit – The Enchanted Blackberry. It is worthwhile remembering that creating clay models in our own way may help us to know who we are, and what we need, at a particular time in life. We just know when we have found something of value that provides goodness and so we come to tell our stories differently.

Unconsciously and yet instinctively, Tessiah knew that by connecting with nature in a gradual and quiet way her spirit would find nourishment and be nurtured and all of this was possible through her use of imagination. Her imagination combined with the yielding qualities of the clay brought a unique way of harnessing the world of fantasy and symbolism. The sense of realness for a child, when stories, images and metaphors are used in a most natural way, enabled Tessiah to metaphorically give voice to, and let others know, what was so dull but, also how she found what was really exciting.

Mack's story: *A Royal Tomb; Afterlife and Togetherness*

Finding ways to live and to thrive are essential for a reasonable healthy passage through life. However, departing life on this Earth is especially significant too. Death and the process of dying at times can provide unexpected opportunities that paradoxically help those still living to find a how and why to live, thereby giving a purpose for being.

I had met Mack, a twelve-year-old, some fifteen months after his father had fallen ill and suddenly died. Meeting Mack for the first time, his most striking feature was the roundedness of his stooped shoulders. He appeared to be carrying the full weight of loss upon shoulders that simply were not strong enough to carry the tragic burden of losing his father. Slow to move, Mack carried an air of an extremely sad young person who had decided to shield his face from prying eyes, by almost resting his chin on his chest. The family had been told that usually after a year following a bereavement, they should begin to see signs of a young person resuming normal life. According to this information this was not so for Mack. So, for the family to receive this information only caused further worries, for to be sure, everyone responds differently to losing a close loved one.

Described as a young person who did not want to paint, Mack also said he could not draw very well, but that he would give clay a go! This was somewhat surprising since working with clay often takes a certain amount of energy to flatten, shape or sculp. Nevertheless, Mack had expressed interest in using clay and it was important to respect his choice of medium.

Taking hold of a large lump of clay Mack began bashing it down onto a wooden board. It seemed that the sleepy energy Mack had entered the room with had awoken, for the bashing of the clay got louder and louder. The more the clay was bashed, the flatter the lump appeared, and the more energised Mack became. Mack studied the flattened clay from various angles. He scooped the longest sides up by pushing his flattened palms underneath the clay, slowly raising them so that the clay edges curved upwards. It seemed Mack here experienced a flash of insight, as is often the way when becoming more engaged with the process of manipulating the malleable clay. It was almost as if the clay and Mack became merged in a purposeful manner for he appeared to feel more than just the moist pliable clay, he was seeing beyond that which his hands were creating. Mack ensured that the two long sides could stand firmly as if they were to be walls. Next, he took a craft tool and straightened the ends of the walls, so they were even in height. At this stage he seemed to remember my presence for he lifted his face and registered that I was fully engaged in tracking and watching what he was doing; I was witnessing how his hands were working with the clay.

"I need two short ends cut from the clay so I can make a box," Mack said.

I reached for more clay, which Mack took from my hands and then he began again to flatten the clay as he had done initially. When satisfied with the clay thickness he cut two smaller slabs of clay. Mack intended for these smaller shapes to fit between the long ones, thus making a box. The atmosphere in the room had felt charged with emotion but as Mack straightened himself up the intensity lessened with him saying,

"It's my Dad's coffin that I've just made and it's got to be very special. My Dad needs things in his coffin for his next life when I'll meet him again."

Enquiring solemnly and quietly I asked Mack what needed to be in the coffin for his Dad. He told me that a cricket bat and a ball were needed. After a pause, Mack said there needed to be a mug for tea drinking, but that a second one was needed too, so he could join his Dad and they would drink tea together the way they had always done after a cricket match. Mack set about making these items from clay. His hands were of a good size, yet I noticed how he crafted the items with much patience, and I commented,

"You've got lots of patience when making such small objects in clay for it is not easy to do this!"

Mack appeared to like this regaling,

"My Gran says I've got my patience from my Dad. You know my Dad was her son and she said my Grandad, who was my Dad's Dad, had lots of patience too because he used to make things from wood."

Mack went on to share how his Grandad had made him a wooden farm when he was a young boy and how he had made Mack's sister a wooden doll's house and the memories just tumbled out, of time spent together as a family. It was not too surprising that Mack was fully open to talking about his own afterlife as a time when he would be reunited with his Dad again. Mack seemed to show no fear of this. He talked in a manner that demonstrated his ongoing relationship with his Dad. This continuing bond (Klass, 1996) with the deceased males in the family was a perfect example of society more and more coming to appreciate how helpful it can be to hold on to the possibility of a sense of continuity between the past and the present, where a spiritual connection with the family ancestors is maintained and revered. When we know or have a sense of our past, we can begin to understand our present situation and time, which in turn helps us to move ahead to the future.

In essence, then, the making of the clay coffin was an opportunity for the good father–son relationship to be made stronger, providing Mack with emotional resilience during his time of grieving. Mack had shared from his heart and yet was also drawing strength from the warm relationship he had experienced with his Dad. For such a young person Mack was talking reflectively about how much he had appreciated his Dad and how lucky he had been to have such a good one because not all children are that fortunate and for that he felt immense gratitude. Mack subsequently questioned if I knew that many people understand the links between the past and the present and that it was quite normal. Through his making of the clay coffin he hinted that the clay his crafted coffin was made from had special powers and was sacred, being imbued with nostalgia and spiritual essences. Something seemed to be changing as Mack began to understand and appreciate his own thoughts and views.

At a later time Mack described his Dad as having the heart of a lion but before I could ask what he meant by this, he rushed on to say that he knew a lion was a king – king of his animal family. In his thoughts this suggested Mack's Dad had been acclaimed king of his own family; Mack therefore stated firmly he deserved the burial of a king in a royal tomb. All of this was shared in a dignified manner and with pride. I could feel the place of honour Mack's Dad had in this young person's heart. To know and be in relationship with our forebearers and ancestors, is the work of the soul. Mack was looking backwards and forwards, remembering a shared past and the dream for the future of meeting with his Dad again.

Returning to the idea of a royal tomb Mack set about using the full weight behind both of his hands to push and heave some clay into a roughly shaped pyramid. I commented how the early builders who made the pyramids in ancient Egypt must have worked incredibly hard doing such physical work to build such huge tombs. A little chuckle from Mack told me he could see what I meant in acknowledging the effort he was putting in to building the royal tomb. Part of me wanted to comment on the difference in size between the clay coffin and pyramid, though realism had no place here and to have done so would have spoilt this significant therapeutic work – anyway proportions seemed irrelevant here; paramount was the royal tomb for a precious father. This sacred work seemed hugely significant for Mack – it had been the soul's work and both of us knew this.

The child who draws such strength and warmth from a special and meaningful relationship with a father may carry emotional resilience and robustness through into adolescence and later life if the grieving process at the time of the death has been worked through. For Mack, his love for his father had come to be internalised with the clay work, helping to transmute his grief. In this way a gentle, spiritual transformation had taken place.

Reader, what is your story about Mack's clay story? What is significant for you when reading a fascinating story told through clay by a twelve-year-old adolescent with such amazing powerful foresight? Maybe you have a continuing bond with an absent friend or relative or perhaps you wish this were the case for you?

Conclusion

The Earth is our Mother, the clay is her substance – her body which is full of life-sustaining energy not just physically but psychologically and spiritually also. If we are to stay in relationship with ourselves and others, we need to stay connected with the prima materia.

We need to maintain our continuing bond with our Earth for the emotional well-being of all humanity. The three clay stories in this chapter have illuminated vividly the connections of our hands with earth clay, and how in turn, we come to know our soul's desires. All of this metaphorically unfolds as sacred alchemical journeys get under way. Cissy's cloth that emerged from the clay cooking pot when many ingredients were mixed together was to be a new skin colour for everyone to see. When we know we are seen, we know we exist, and this was her story of awakening to whom she was becoming in a new coloured skin. Whilst the Enchanted Blackberry tale that Tessiah spoke of as she formed her clay blackberry beautifully illuminated a child's imaginative powers of lifting herself from the everyday dreariness of a deprived background.

Remember the stories of old that have shared myths about how the Earth is imbued with special healing energies for it is a living organism. Yet Mack's present-day story also showed that when the clay and his hands connected, he began to see beyond what he was creating and hinted that the clay his Dad's coffin was being made with was a sacred medium – this being the work of the soul. These healing properties seem to be experienced when touching, holding and working with clay. As we do so, our stories connected to the clay appear to help us to let go of hurtful experiences and pain, simply because Mother Earth is within us too: we have a continuing bond with our planet, Earth.

References

Ferguson, G. (1966). *Signs & Symbols in Christian Art: With Illustrations from Paintings of the Renaissance*. London: Oxford University Press.
Jung, C.J. (1968). *The Archetypes and the Collective Unconscious*. London: Routledge & Kegan Paul.
Jung, C.J. (1995). *Jung on Alchemy*. Schwartz-Salant, N. (Ed.). London: Routledge.
Kirsch, T.B. (2000). *The Jungians – A Comparative & Historical Perspective*. Hove: Routledge.
Klass, D. (1996). *Continuing Bonds: New Understandings of Grief*. London: Routledge.
Souter-Anderson, L. (2010). *Touching Clay, Touching What? The Use of Clay in Therapy*. Dorset: Archive Publishing.
Souter-Anderson, L. (2015). *Making Meaning, Clay Therapy with Children and Adolescents*. Buckingham: Hinton House.
Souter-Anderson, L. (2019). *Seeking Shelter, Seeking Safety. Clay Therapy with Families and Groups*. Dorset: Archive Publishing.
Whitte, H. (1984). *Yoruba Symbolism of the Earth*. PhD Thesis, Netherlands: State University of Groningen.

28
'METAMYTH THERAPY THROUGH THE ARTS IN MUSEUMS'©
A personal journey through story

Thalia Valeta

Introduction

This is a story about a dramatherapist, Thalia, who liked museums from a young age. She lived in the old part of the city of Athens and under the hill of the Acropolis. She has visited many museums around the world and felt happy and peaceful when she was in there. Later when she became an actress and a dramatherapist she created a psychological method 'Metamyth: Therapy through the Arts in the Museum'© with which she could help people who came to the museum to be happy too. Not just the people, though – the museum itself began to shine when the people were there as if it was saying 'thank you for making me alive; I am grateful!!'

My story

I always liked museums. At the age of six when I had already begun to fall asleep whilst watching ancient Greek plays in the ancient theatres with my parents, I heard someone say how unbelievable it was 'that people who live in Athens had never been to see the Acropolis.' So this had to be fixed and we went to the Acropolis on a Sunday soon after that.

We lived in Plaka, where I was born, between the Anglican Church and the hill of the Acropolis. Both these points and the area between them marked my neighbourhood; these were my cultural references, but also defined my everyday life. This environment was to allow me to develop and unfold as a magical cloth full of turns and surprises.

Climbing up the rock of the Acropolis was a laborious experience, because it took so long and was very hot. Every step was a step into mythology and history connecting the past to a meaningful present. My imagination was connecting the past and the present and working them into the unknown crevices of my psyche; all of this I experienced for the first time, as a six-years-old girl.

Undoubtedly all ancient Greek sights are an open museum and an invitation to marvel at nature; I was provoked as a child by temples dedicated to different kinds of gods, male and female, many known for popular stories around them. There were also statues, weapons, utility objects, and ornaments made with aesthetic fancy. I still recall that I could consciously forget myself when I was there collecting my thoughts, mourning for all that was past but not lost, where past and present were not in strict chronological sequence.

Allowing feelings to reveal themselves and creative imagination to enrich the days of my life, I felt I could start to pull together the structure that was called self. On my return home I was calm, I felt complete and confident, even happy. This is when I began to play games, games where I was a doctor, an ambassador, an actress, or Cinderella; this allowed me on occasion to begin to understand myself better and know who I really was.

At the same time I was learning French, 'Civilisation Francaise' and 'Histoire de France.' I loved the sound of the French language and my teachers. I also felt reassured by the support of my father (it was his idea that I learnt French), when I did not understand some grammar issues because I was so young. The French was the door to modern art, novels, music, film, romance, and their application in real life. This took me to the Louvre Museum in Paris where between the Impressionists, the Maoists, the Existentialists, and Les Gitanes (my French cigarettes), in May 66, I also met the Victory (Niki) of Samothaki, the ancient Greek statue, displayed in the Louvre since 1884. She stood on a pedestal, lit by yellow light. She looked like an angel, a woman, and a goddess and I felt 'fear and pity.' I felt 'Catharsis,' a purge of emotions, what Aristotle (1995) would have described as being part of an ancient Greek Tragedy. On my way back, bare foot by the river Seine, I was feeling some kind of freedom inside, that everything was possible, and the same feeling of wholeness and calm which I had felt before. The Ashmolean Museum, the world's first university art museum, in Oxford, also reminded me of this feelings of catharsis; it received its first collection in 1677, called 'The Cabinet of Curiosities'. It also reminded me of home, because I, too, had a box with loved objects which I kept at home.

Many years went by and I have visited many, many, museums in many countries, big and small, private and public, all very important to me. I am still looking for opportunities to see exhibitions, of modern art, paintings, or sculpture, that would be of interest, permanent collections of historical or scientific importance. I love to drop into a museum in the centre of a city, or go and take a special trip to find one; on one occasion I was even taken up the mountain by a lovely creature, an elephant to get there!

I feel that works of art displayed either in the most beautiful and effective way, or just placed in the museums for conservation, are telling me stories about the place, the past, the present, and the future; I see museums as homes of history and culture.

Museum means 'the shelter of the muses' in Greek, but apart from that, for me it had become, what Winnicott (2005) would have described as my 'transitional space', between my inner and outer worlds, in which primary creativity (illusion) can exist and develop. Here, for me, time stops, art can be lived as an experience, in a timeless unending moment, my moment of catharsis.

The development of 'Metamyth in Museums'©

I invented the word 'Metamyth'© from the Greek language and its meaning is the centre of the work. Etymologically the prefix 'meta' means 'after' in modern Greek and 'with' in ancient Greek. Together with the word 'myth' it means 'with the myth and after the myth'. I made up the word 'Metamyth'© because I see that from the moment a person enters therapy the togetherness of the therapist with the client creates a myth of its own. The meaning of the word 'Metamyth'© expresses the companionship and togetherness of the patient and therapist to create a relationship of trust and openness, a myth, which then, meta, will lead to another way of being of the patient and the therapist.

Therefore 'Metamyth'© has to do with time, with how things have been before, during and after. It also means the story, the myth of every person's life during the time it is lived and after the events for which they are concerned.

I had already created the psychological approach 'Metamyth©/Dramatherapy', a branch of 'Metamyth'© (Valeta 2000, 2009, 2017) which I practice with people who have organic neurological and psychiatric disorders in a hospital. This approach links creativity and clinical perspectives promoting reflexivity. It is a psychological treatment that has drawn upon Arts-based approaches and Dramatherapy (Jennings 2004), a mind/body approach and a neuro-biological method used in psychology and therapy. It is influenced by Humanistic Jungian and Existential psychotherapies and it is psychoanalytically oriented. 'Metamyth'© is both a therapy and an art form and has a poetic basis which contributes to the thinking and practice of therapy. It makes use of all the arts and draws from the historic use of the connection of the arts and healing. It can be described as an attitude to the world around us, seeking to connect to the bigger picture of our own life stories, like stepping stones underpinning the biography of our lives.

In my internship in the museum and my research, I became involved in an inner dialogue with literary personalities, poets, and philosophers who have been concerned in how to make sense of history and culture in the magical place where time and space intersect – the poet Paul Valery (1928), the writer Marcel Proust (1913) and the philosopher Foucault (1967). For me they became debates in which the works of art are no longer conscious, objective and absolute notions, but exist only in my internal perception, the perception that I as an observer have of them. At the same time the empty rooms of the museum are extensions of the studio where the artist created their works of art, bringing the observer nearer to the internal world of the artist. Foucault's museums like Heterotopias – meaning in Greek a place that is other – are real places which stand outside the known, but are intrinsic and necessary.

I felt moved by the interconnectedness of all these different components and responded to what felt like a 'calling.' My work was to be about beginning and coordinating a dialogue between art and emotional feelings, memories, thoughts, and the experiences of the participants. As a metaphor inspired by the psychoanalytic theory and practice I proposed that the museum space is a liminal or transitional space (Winnicott 2005) where a person feels safe enough and powerful enough for both individual creativity and cultural activity to emerge.

I theorised that the visitor/participant is the subject (client), the object is the work of art (painting, sculpture, music, theatre architecture). The purpose of 'Metamyth'© for the museum practitioner is to guide or facilitate the subject, who trusts the practitioner to hold the process with the group, who witness as a Chorus. I think of the works of art, artists/curators, the visitors, and myself (therapist/director), in the quiet rooms of the museum being like a theatrical production being performed on a stage, where everything is alive and a new experience is born. The feeling of wholeness, the urge for creativity and enlightenment that I have experienced is always there and alive.

This is how 'Metamyth Therapy through the Arts in Museums'© was conceived and delivered within a museum context. Myself as director connecting the visitors to the art work. The developmental process was a journey, a process of discovery through making connections between visitor and art work, where ideas were revealed or uncovered. This experience was influenced by my own research and development in the fields of the Arts Therapies and Dramatherapy, Cultural Studies, Philosophy, Psychoanalytic theories, Mind and Body approaches, as well as my personal involvement in the Arts and Culture in the Museums.

The inspiration and practice of 'Metamyth in Museums'©

'Metamyth Therapy through the Arts in the Museums'© is a branch of 'Metamyth'© that has a cultural, artistic, and psychosocial aspect which links to history and aesthetics, philosophy and the arts, including museums, galleries, music, and culture. These ideas can be underpinned by a wealth of knowledge from these traditions in the arts and culture. My idea is to include my experience in the museums as an in between space or transitional space which Winnicott (2005) described as being full of potentiality and authenticity. In my psychological method 'Metamyth'© in the Museums I share the joy that I felt in the museum space with other people; this was upper most in my mind and heart. I borrow this expression of potential space from Winnicott consciously knowing the weight it carries in our therapeutic work, it feels appropriate when considering the transitional or liminal spaces I work in in establishing 'Metamyth Therapy through the Arts in the Museums'©.

The work started from within with awe and wonder. I read a lot and practiced a lot to give my method a form and a structure that could be delivered within the museum context. Steeped in the tradition of ancient Greek theatre and mythology it is not surprising that I have become increasingly inspired by the legacy of my own culture. As both an actor and a dramatherapist I know that the ancient knowledge is important in contemporary therapy and art. My ideas have further developed by living in other cultures and experiencing alternative therapeutic and artistic forms.

I have been inspired by and have adopted Aristotle's qualitative and quantitative elements of tragedy in my practice. In a 'Metamyth in Museums'© session firstly comes the plot (Mythos), that is the way the therapist/director conceptualises, dreams, and plans the work. Then comes an introduction (the Prologue), focusing on the theme of the work with a warm up. The main part (Episodia), is when visiting the exhibition the participants play and think (Dianoia), speak (lexis), and sing or move in their own rhythm (Melos), and choice of participation or style of presentation (opsis). After the main part (Episodia), the group returns to base (Exodos). The Choric song is when the group shares feelings, thoughts, impressions, comments, after the work.

The first time I had presented my work in a private gallery (2001), it felt like it was the work that I always had in my mind and heart to do. Following that I proposed to include 'Metamyth Therapy through the Arts in Museums'©, in the National Museum of Modern Art and the Art and Industry Museum at St Etienne, in a wonderful exhibition called 'The Island Never Found' (2002), then at The Macedonian Museum of Contemporary Art in the permanent collection in Thessaloniki and also at the museum of Fine Arts and Music in Athens.

Conclusion

'Metamyth'© brings focus and quality of attention to self, others, and the cultural context of museums. This can enable a journey of increasing awareness, facilitating, co-producing, and researching meanings, value, and purpose in historical contexts. People can bring their challenges to the intersubjective process building relationships with the works of art and discerning their significance for the individual's personal lived experience. In this work one finds the most authentic and creative aspects of our personal and communal existence, including artistic, scientific, religious, and cultural expression. Most of all one feels alive, and finds joy while the museum opens its doors to offer and receive people in gratitude.

Having shared the context of my biographical story I hope this brings the text of 'Metamyth in Museums'© to life for the reader. The aim of my work is to promote healing and has produced a range of therapeutic outcomes for people over the last 10 years that I have been practicing 'Metamyth (Valeta 2010/2019) Therapy through the Arts in the Museums'© internationally. The six-years-old girl inside me is cheering.

Thank you for listening.

References

Aristotle (1995) *Poetics*, trans. Philip H. Vellacott. London: Harvard University Press.
Foucault, M. (1984) 'Of Other Spaces, Heterotopias'. *Architecture, Movement, Continuity*, no 5: 46–49.
Jennings, S. (2004) *The Handbook of Dramatherapy*. London. Routledge.
Proust, M. (1977) *On Art and Literature*, trans. Sylvia Townsend Warner. Boston, Massachusetts: Da Capo Press.
Valery, P. (1964) *Selected Writings of Paul Valery*. New York: New Directions.
Valeta, T. (2017) "Metamyth"©/Dramatherapy" in: *The Epilepsy Book: A Companion for Patients*, pp. 127–135. London Springer International Publishing.
Valeta, T. (2010/2019) "Metamyth"© Therapy through the Arts in Museums, Programmes in video personal archives.
Valeta, T. (2009) "Metamyth" in: *The Potential of Dramatherapy in the Treatment of Epilepsy*, pp. 35–57. MA Thesis, University of Derby.
Valeta, T. (2000) "Metamyth"© and its Application in Everyday Life. Lecture Neurolinguistic Programming course, Regents College London.
Winnicott, D. W. (2005) *Playing and reality*. New York: Routledge.

29
STORIES IN CRISIS AND TRAUMATIC SITUATIONS

Mooli Lahad

I would like to open this chapter with an argument against the known "Maslow principle" (Maslow 1954). In his master work on the hierarchy of needs Maslow used the terms Physiological, Safety, Belongingness and Love, Esteem, Self-Actualization and Self-Transcendence needs to describe the pattern that human motivations generally move through. At the bottom of the hierarchy he placed the physiological needs that are the physical requirements for human survival and at the top Self-actualization. This level of need refers to a person's full potential and the realization of that potential and includes creativity and spontaneity.

Well I wish to argue that creativity is a basic need and without it humans can't survive.

My argument goes back about 45,000 years ago when homo sapiens started to create stories and documented them in huge murals in caves, such as the cave drawings of *Lascaux* France, *Altamira* Spain and more.

Let's examine the facts. Forty-five thousand years ago fire was very scarce, precious and holy. It was very difficult to light it, it was protection against beasts, it was used for cooking, light and to protect against vicious animals and it was scarce.

Rest was extremely important for these people, who were searching all day for food, protecting themselves, and the time to rest shouldn't be missed for "unimportant" activities such as leisure and drawing.

Now in order to draw so many images one has to take the sacred fire to the distant deep cave, to spend hours inside and to get the group approval to use the fire as in those days you couldn't just disappear.

So if art-form and expression is at the top of the hierarchy how can we explain that in times when survival was the name of the game, humans dedicated scarce resource, time and energy on something so remote from their "daily needs?" My conclusion is that the need to express themselves was so fundamental that without it their life couldn't go on; therefore I argue that Art is a basic need.

How is it connected to trauma, fear of survival?

Well we don't exactly know what the purpose of this act was. We can guess that by drawing the animals, people assumed control of these animals. It is obvious that the animals were frightening as they were bigger, stronger, quicker than men. So by capturing them on the wall they experienced mastery. It could also be a way to rehearse for the hunting, as a sort of a preparatory ritual so that the hunters transcend into "fantastic reality" (Lahad and Leykin 2012) and prepare themselves emotionally to withstand the fear of the encounter and get symbolic strength. The third option (out of many more) could be a tribal ritual of "telling the story" of victory or of some kind of ritual of passage. If we examine all of the above the common denominator is of course managing Fear.

Indeed life was full of fears. One can't assume that today's fears are the same but certainly there were so many frightening things. The moment the homo sapiens started to be able to tell stories, whether verbal or symbolic, they were able to start to tell themselves stories to make sense of the world, "understand" it and reduce or control their fears. They could express their happy as well as sad moments, loss and longing. Stories about the big powers (wind, rain, storm etc.) the disappearance of the sun, sudden droughts or floods, the creation and the creators.

With stories they made sense and helped themselves to meet the unavoidable pain of grief pain and trauma.

Thus stories, storymaking and storytelling were and still are the way we make sense, the way we heal ourselves.

How did the "storytelling ape" become the ruler of this planet?

For a long time people believed that homo sapiens is the evolution of the Neanderthal man (see Figure 29.1). However, this is not the fact. In reality some 100,000 years ago there were at least six types of human; none had any more significance than any other animal on the planet. However, something happened about 70,000 years ago in one species: the homo sapiens developed the ability to talk, not just with signs but with words and later on some

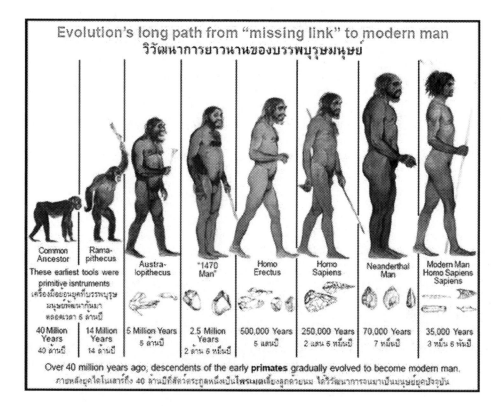

Figure 29.1 Modern trauma

35 to 40,000 years ago it was able to tell stories to the next generation and inherit acquired knowledge unlike the instinctual communication of birds or dolphins (such as birds' knowledge to build nests). Despite the fact that the homo sapiens was smaller and weaker than the Neanderthal, they managed to win the war against much stronger but non-speaking species and extinguish the last of the Neanderthals some 30,000 years ago. What made the storytelling animal stronger? It is in fact the ability to tell stories, to tell where good food is, how to build things, myth and creation stories, and more than anything to transmit this knowledge to the next generation and plan for the future.

Already in 1893 Breuer and Freud described trauma as a main cause for human suffering that wasn't processed or worked out through natural processing. Freud's way to help his client to work through trauma can be seen as metaphoric story about urges and unconscious needs using mythology to help make sense of such traumata (for example, the myth of Oedipus). In modern times, since the decision of the American Psychiatric Association to redefine trauma as Post-traumatic Stress Disorder (1980), trauma was disassociated from neurosis (up until then it was known as Traumatic Neurosis and Fright Neurosis), and became the outcome of an external, unusual event – that the person has experienced an event that is outside the range of usual human experience and that would be markedly distressing to almost anyone.

With time this definition has changed drastically and it is now, DSM 5 (2013), "exposure to actual or threatened death, serious injury or sexual violation." But what is Trauma? Many view it as a story frozen in time in the memory of the victim, activating the person through various reminders as if the event is happening now, causing them severe distress and a multitude of symptoms. When most people are exposed to traumatic events they tell and retell the story many times until the story, sad and frightening as it may be, becomes part of their narrative. But the person who develops PTSD will, as much as they can, avoid retelling, revisiting that traumatic memory, hoping that this avoidance will rescue them from it. For the PTSD patient remembering the story is connected with an immense sense of danger and helplessness and the fear of impending death whether physical ("I'll die if I tell this") or emotional ("I will go crazy if I tell it"). This fear of re-narrating the story is the basis for almost all the Evidence Based Treatments' (EBT) inclusion of the traumatic story re-narration as a central part of the methods.

There are many theories why this part is crucial for the healing process; some are more cognitive (Foa et al. 2010), suggesting that the reconstruction of memory in a cohesive way enables control of the frontal cortex on the fear/emotional arousal. Other narrative models suggest that there is no "true story" and encourage the client to add possible elements that could have made the story more bearable or possible for them (Onyut et al. 2005). Suggesting that as it is "the" story that makes the client's life unbearable and it is not necessarily the "true" story as it was in reality but the way the client remembers or interprets what happened, it is within the client's ability to create a new story that bears meaning or possible positive outcomes.

The Chinese traditional way to deal with nightmares was somewhat similar and of course was used for centuries before the narrative method was developed. In this traditional healing the client with nightmares was asked (in daytime) to reinvent a more desirable outcome to their dream, re-narrate it with the healer and instruct themselves to dream this new dream the next night.

Dreamcatcher is another example of how stories can help to remedy fears. It originated with the Ojibwe people, who have an ancient legend about the origin of the dreamcatcher. Storytellers speak of the Spider Woman, known as Asibikaashi; she took care of the children and the people on the land. Eventually, the Ojibwe Nation spread to the corners of North America and it became difficult for Asibikaashi to reach all the children. So the mothers and grandmothers would weave magical webs for the children, using willow hoops and sinew, or cordage made from plants. The dreamcatchers would filter out all bad dreams and only allow good thoughts to enter our mind. Once the sun rises, all bad dreams just disappear (Densmore 1929).

Indeed, we need stories as "maps" to understand the world, to make sense of all the various quests that our inner heroes are travelling through. It is when we accompany the fictitious hero in fairy tales that we fear with them and for them, we travel through the most frightening obstacles and pits and we go out the other end to feel relieved. If we were hungry for one such story, why would so many of them remain with the same pattern? In his memorable book *The Hero with a Thousand Faces* Campbell (1968) suggests that these various stories are the way the human mind makes sense of this impossible world and the psyche's quest for sense, meaning and reassurance.

Is there a clear biological need for stories?

Gottschall (2012) in his book *The Story Telling Animal* suggests that:

> Fiction is a powerful and ancient virtual reality technology that simulates the big dilemmas of human life. When we pick up a book or turn on the TV—whoosh!—we are teleported into a parallel universe. We identify so closely with the struggles of the protagonists that we don't just sympathize with them; we strongly empathize with them. We *feel* their happiness and desire and fear; our brains rev up as though what is happening to them is actually happening to us. RAT advocates say that dreams are highly emotional because the limbic system and the amygdala—both of which are linked to emotion—happen to be aroused during REM sleep.
>
> *(p. 178)*

Talking about the brain need for comprehensive structure he suggests "Our hunger for meaningful patterns translates into a hunger for story" (p.240).

So far, I have tried to explain the deep meaning of stories in helping us to make sense of this world and to work through difficulties.

Let us now go into practice.

How do we use stories to help children and adults in times of distress or following traumatic incident?

The prevention model

Ayalon and Lahad (2000) pioneered the use of bibliotherapy for the education system in Israel as early as 1980. Their three books all to do with preventive work for school-age children and youth concentrated on "Life". The first, *Life on the Edge*, addressed issues of stress prevention, living in distressful situations, making the world safer and more pleasant for children living on the border. The second, *Your Life Ahead*, was dedicated to adolescents' life crisis, search for identity, friends and separation and, more than that, suicide prevention. The third book, *On life and Death*, focused on death education, helping adults to deal with life and death questions of children and youth looking at the various cycles of life and facing loss. Their model known as the BASIC PH model (Lahad 1997) looked at the stories as an opportunity to work through these very loaded subjects, using the story as a basis for multiple exploration through arts, relaxation, movement, music and of course drama.

I wish to share with you two of the stories.

The first exemplifies the freedom to stay in pain and the second an option to bring some hope.

Let's examine one story.

The Big Wave

(Based on Pearl S. Buck.)

Goals:

- To confront the finality of death.
- To learn about the process of mourning and recovery.

Stand in a circle with eyes closed. Listen to the story. Let your body move to the music and the story.

To the coach/trainer:

Play some soft background music. Then start the guided visualisation:

You are walking on the beach, feeling the soft sand and the cool water under your feet…

There is a small cloud on the horizon. You are playing in the water…

(Stop the music).

Suddenly the wind changes. The sky is covered with stormy, black clouds. The wind shrieks., big waves are rising from the sea., you start running to the shore… escaping from the wind, from the sand flying in your face, from the rain and the storm…

Finally you find a small shelter where you can hide and be safe. Slowly you calm down…

To the participant:

Use crayons and paper. Draw your feelings. Write your image in one sentence or word at the bottom of the page. Sit in a circle and listen to the story.

To the coach/trainer:

Read the story to the participants.
From: *The Big Wave* **by** Pearl S. Buck

> Jai is a ten-year-old Japanese boy who lives with his parents and brothers in a little fishing village on the coast. While he was visiting his good friend Keno, who lived on the top of a hill, a storm brewed up at sea and giant waves hit the coast and washed the whole village away into the sea. All Jai's family members were drowned.
>
> Keno and his father were sitting waiting for Jai to wake up. "I don't think that Jai can ever be happy again", said Keno sadly.
>
> "Yes, the day will come when he will be happy", said his father, "because life is always stronger than death. When Jai wakes up, he will feel that he can never be happy again. He will cry and cry, and we must let him cry. But then, he cannot cry without stopping. After a few days, he will not cry all the time and his crying will become less and less. He will sit sad and silent. We must let him be sad and we mustn't force him to speak. We must do what we have to do and we must live our lives as before. And the time will come that Jay will feel hungry. He will taste the food that our mother

cooks, something particularly tasty, and he will start to feel better inside. He will no longer cry in the day, just at night. We must let him cry at night, all this time his body will renew its strength. The blood flowing in his arteries, his growing bones and his mind thinking new thoughts once more will all bring him back to life".

"He will never be able to forget his mother and father and brothers", cried Keno.

"He will never be able to; neither should he ever forget them", explained his father. "Just as he lived with them when they were still alive, so he will live with them after their death. With time, their death will seem to be part of his life. He will cry no more, he will carry them in his memories and thoughts, he is of their flesh and blood and, as long as he lives, they will live in him. The great wave came and left, the sun shines once again, the birds are singing and the flowers are blooming. Look at the sea now!"

Keno looked out through the door and saw the sea, smooth and shimmering and the skies were blue once again. A few clouds on the horizon were the only evidence of what had gone before, apart from the desolate coastline.

"How cruel it is, that the skies are so bright and the sea is so calm", said Keno.

But his father shook his head. "Not so, it is a wonderful thing that after the storm, the sea becomes calm once more and the sky is as blue as ever. Neither the ocean nor the sea made the great storm".

"Who did make it, then?" asked Keno. Tears streamed down his cheeks because there were so many things beyond his comprehension. His father saw the tears and understood their meaning.

"Oh, no-one knows who makes the bad storms", his father replied. "All we know is that they happen and, when they do, we must stand up to them with courage and strength and once they go, feel how wonderful life is. Every day of life is of much greater value than before the storm".

To the participants:

- Choose five sentences you remember from the story and write them down.
- Write a letter to Jai, which he will read on waking up from his sleep.
- Continue the story: "Jai woke up and…"
- Sit down in groups of five and show each other your chosen sentences, read the letters and the ending of the story.

Story as an intervention with crisis intervention team

Humpty Dumpty, the saviour myth or understanding the compelling urges to put all the pieces together again

Humpty Dumpty sat on a wall.
Humpty Dumpty had a great fall.
All the King's horses and all the King's men
Could not put Humpty together again.
(Carol 1872)

In my book *Creative supervision* (Lahad 2000), I described my work with a psychosocial crisis intervention team that was exposed over and over again to horrendous images of destruction and dismembered bodies. Their work with the bereaved families slowly, slowly led to losing their ability for empathy and getting very weak. The term that we use for it is "compassion fatigue". That is when helpers are emotionally involved and wish to do everything they can for the victims, much beyond the "required" protocol and get emotionally and physically affected by this closeness to the victims' stories and pain. This example shows how a poem from a children's book can be a great opening for distressing issues and help people work through their painful story.

I met these nine helpers a few days after they had been involved in a disaster. This was their third incident in the past five months. All of them have been through CISD (Critical Incident Stress Debriefing is a specific, 7-phase, small group, supportive crisis intervention process; Mitchell and Everly (2001)) sessions, but the group showed signs of fatalism, tiredness and apathy. Some were in constant contact with individuals and families from previous disasters even though it was not their official role. Some were manifesting anger and discomfort, but all were very dedicated to their role as helpers and continued to report at any incident. I was offered three sessions of crisis supervision with them.

The atmosphere at the start of our meeting was a combination of "He [me, the supervisor] will solve all our problems" and "What can really be done? – it is a hopeless situation". I immediately registered in my head the parallel processes between them and their clients moving on the scale between despair and omnipotence.

In the first session (see details in the book) I was using movement, sounds and very little words.

The next session was opened by reading Humpty Dumpty. They all knew it, but did not connect it to their experience. The purpose of bringing the poem (a distancing technique) was to look into their need to put all the pieces together, how frustrating and impossible a task this is, and to allow the expression of their anger towards the "King" who in their minds expected them to put Humpty together again.

They were now encouraged to take different roles and experiment with different inner and outer dialogues. For most of them it was the first time they realized the impossible role they were putting themselves in, the need to fix things for others, their fantasy of replacing the irreplaceable and the enormous pressure this puts on them. The "King" was demystified and there followed heavy attacks and expressions of anger and frustrations toward the "King" who expects so much of them. The last part of the session was a guided imagery leading to a meeting with Humpty Dumpty and sharing with him "what I can and what I can't do for him". Sharing these thoughts in the form of a letter was the end of the session.

A healing story

One type of story we can use with groups who suffer from long-term depression, loss of hope and the feeling that darkness engulfs them are "the healing stories".

These stories directly address the feeling of despair, magnifying its sensory aspects by focusing on senses rather than many words, and whilst acknowledging the pain and anguish they lead their listeners to look for a new option.

I recently used one such story with a group of homeless people in Japan after the March 2011 tsunami and nuclear disaster.

Here is this African story that I heard a while ago from Alida Gersie.

Mooli Lahad

The animals in the forest: an African tale

Retold by Mooli Lahad

A long time ago the whole world was in total darkness. For a long time all the animals had lived in the forest in complete darkness.

However, one day a sound appeared in the forest and this sound was light.

This sound was all around with many tones and voices. Most of the animals did not know what it meant as they never heard it before.

Some old animals remembered vaguely something back in their childhood that their forefathers mentioned as Light.

A handful of very, very old animals remembered that when they were very young there was something called "light" but they also did not fully recall what it was.

Still, one day a sound appeared in the forest and this sound was light.

And so with this sound all the animals started to walk, crawl, fly, jump etc., to the clearing in the forest and sit in circles and the sound light was heard everywhere.

When they all sat down suddenly they did not know what to do and there was a complete silence.

Then a big animal said loudly: "I am going to look for the light." Off it went; one day passed, two days passed, three days and after a week the animal came back tired and wounded, but it didn't find the light. The animals were rather upset but before anything happened a much bigger animal in a much louder voice said: "I am going to look for the light."

Off it went; one week passed, two weeks passed, three weeks and after a month, the animal came back, wounded and tired and blind. But it didn't find the light.

The animals were very sad and they lost hope somehow. But just as they were about to go back to their places in the forest, a broken shy voice was heard from behind. The soft voice: "I am going to look for the light."

Now I invite you all to answer the following 10 questions. You can do it in the form of a story or as answers to the questions. You will have about 15 minutes.

1 Who is the animal that speaks last? How old? How big?
2 What does it know about light and from where?
3 Why is it going to search for the light? Why now?
4 Does it make any preparations?
5 When does it leave?
6 What is the first obstacle on its way?
7 What can help it?
8 What is the second obstacle on its way?
9 Who can help it?
10 What happens at the end? Does it find light and what does it do about it?

When you finish writing you may draw an image of the scene you liked the most.

- Please re-read your story to yourself and mark all the words/terms/sentences that you liked.
- Now sit in groups of four and each of you will tell the story of the animal you chose.
- When the others listen they need to choose one or two sentences they liked the most from each story and write them down.
- Let all members read their story.
- At the very end choose one story that will be retold to the whole group.

The use of storymaking in psychotrauma

As early as 1999 I started to investigate the power of imagination when dealing with psychotrauma. I soon realized a few things. That people suffering from PTSD do not play, that they stay on guard to prevent any memory of the tragic story from reappearing, spending their life in a jail of avoidance, numbing and fears and that despite the fact that they don't see themselves as imaginative, and thus don't want to use imagination, they are in fact the masters of powerful negative imagination. The entrapped past in their mind intrudes into their life almost always unexpectedly, causing them to relive it "as if" it is happening now. Thus, I thought, maybe if we teach them positive or at least neutral-potential imagining we can help them be more playful and less incarcerated or confined in the horrific past.

In 2003 when I read the meta-analysis of Ozer and her colleague about dissociation as the prime early predicting factor of PTSD, I was perplexed, because so many of my clients told me that the moment of bliss of "psyche saving" for them were the moments during the horrible incident or recurrent torments that they felt safe/saved.

I later worked with my then PhD. student Nira Kaplansky and studied the phenomena of Near Death Experience (NDE) (see Lahad and Doron 2010). We discovered that people who "transcend into fantastic reality" and tell themselves somewhat dissociative stories of out of body experience, floating, light, tunnels and meeting with figures, although conforming to the "at risk group" of Ozer et al. (2003) don't meet the expected 70% level of PTSD but… have NO PTSD at all. We also discovered that these people, when compared to patients with PTSD, had been involved during childhood in a multitude of extramural activities much higher on all aspects than their PTSD counterparts. Significant differences were found between the NDE and the PTSD samples in the following activities: Books Reading, Writing, Swimming, Playing an Instrument, Drawing, Crafts, Story Telling and Ballet. The NDE sample was significantly more intensively involved in these activities than the PTSD sample.

Based on these findings we concluded that perhaps the re-narration of the story in a "realistic way" may not be sufficient to bring the playful mode and the artistic position of the client and we developed a new model known as SEE FAR CBT (Lahad and Doron 2010).

During the re-narration phase, the client chooses several cards representing the traumatic event and is encouraged to observe the cards and then to narrate the story. In the sequel, the client is asked to choose and remove the cards they "wish to" exclude, or to reorder the sequence of cards, and retell the story. This helps them to experiment with possibilities, to "play" with alternatives and to gain control over their story. Last, the client is instructed to add new "as if" cards to the array. These cards should represent things or people which, if the client had had them during the incident, could have assisted them, without the "as if" cards changing or erasing the outcome of the incident.

We argued that in our method re-arranging the narrative by means of the therapeutic cards is likely to stimulate simultaneously visual cortex (the images) and emotional memory (the association that goes along with the personal choice of specific cards) whilst making contact with the prefrontal cortex (through the verbalization of the perceived images). Another unique component of the SEE FAR CBT protocol is the sense of empowerment achieved via the suggestion to remove cards and check the outcome on the narrative and, taking this even further, the instruction to experiment with potent play by adding the "as if" or "if only" cards. These cards enable the client to recount the story with helpful elements in so far as the outcome does not change.

We suggest that the observation of the visual sequence creates a competing positive visual stimulus that directly affects the visual cortex and is encoded as an alternative "memory" to the traumatic one, or at least a more flexible succession of segments of the event. Based on our argument that, in fact, PTSD clients are "experts" in fantasizing or in imagining, we suggest that it is possible that they may be able to capitalize on this "expertise" and that we can train them to use alternative fantastic solutions.

The observer position is unique to this treatment. In none of the other effective psychotrauma protocols does the client observe their traumatic story as a distant, observable story. It is the distancing within the art-form which both contains the experience and allows it to be seen from many perspectives. In aesthetic distancing "the 'in-between' or 'liminal' state allows the individual to look at the situation through identification and distancing at the same time" (Tselikas-Portman 1999, p.9).

Aesthetic distance, according to Landy (1996) is the midpoint that is a balance of affect and cognition; "an ideal state in which one is able to think feelingly and feel without the fear of being overwhelmed with passion" (p. 48). The positive impact of being an "audience in your own drama/trauma" has been described by Grinberger (2005) in her research on Holocaust survivors. The effect of aesthetic distance (Landy 1996), redefined by us as observing one's own traumatic story as it unfolds through projective/associative cards, makes it possible for the client to master control, and reduce arousal as the story is "out there" and is less oppressive. This contributes to the sensation of empowering and thus influences the process that helps the change of the helpless position of the PTSD client from a victim to a victor.

We suggest that the protocol assists the client to slowly learn to play by using the cards (see Figure 29.2) and Fantastic Reality and thus diminishes the debilitating influence of the rigid haunting and especially reduces the need to be in an "on guard position." The adoption of safe and secure places allows traumatized clients to re-experience and master their pain through metaphoric milieus.

We suggest that the ability to play that the client gradually acquires during the course of treatment, by means of using the cards and experiencing Fantastic Reality, reduces the frequency of the invasive memories. The idea of Fantastic Reality as a realm of the "as if," an imaginary space where anything is possible, together with aesthetic distancing, creates a safe and protected place where the sufferer can on the one hand re-experience their pain but also control it by means of a metaphoric environment.

This chapter was an overview of what stories are, why they are and how they can help in "impossible" situations.

I wish to conclude by referring to the burning question: will humans continue to use stories in the era of virtual reality? One can argue that the "readymade" games, films, internet interactions, social media are the "end" of the Story. I would argue that all of these are just new ways for the mind and for people to find meaning to get confirmation and, although they

Figure 29.2 Re-narrated traumatic story

might be different from the old-time stories, the myths, the plots, the emotions and the search for meaning are there.

But … Time will tell.

References

American Psychiatric Association (1980) *The Diagnostic and Statistical Manual of Mental Disorders*, Third Edition (DSM-III).
American Psychiatric Association (2013) Diagnostic and Statistical Manual of Mental Disorders (DSM-5®), American Psychiatric Pub.
Ayalon, O., and Lahad, M. (2000) *Life on the Edge*, Haifa: Nord Publishers.
Buck, S.P. (1931) *The Wave*, NY: John Day Company.
Campbell, J. (1968) *The Hero with a Thousand Faces*, Princeton: Princeton University Press.
Carol, L. (1872) *Through the Looking Glass*, London: Macmillan.
Densmore, F. (1929, 1979) *Chippewa Customs*, St. Paul: Minnesota Historical Society Press.
Doidge, N. (2016) *The Brain's Way of Healing: Remarkable Discoveries and Recoveries from the Frontiers of Neuroplasticity*, NY: Penguin Books.
Elliott, J.W., with Dalziel, G. and Dalziel, E. (1870) *Mother Goose's Nursery Rhymes and Nursery Songs Set to Music*, NY: McLoughlin Bros.
Foa, E.B., Keane, T.M., Friedman, M.J., and Cohen, J.A. (Eds.) (2010) Effective treatments for PTSD: Practice Guidelines from the International Society for Traumatic Stress Studies, New York: Guilford Press.
Freud, S., and Breuer, J. (1937, 2004) *Studies in Hysteria*. Translated by Nicola Luckhurst, London: Penguin Books.
Gottschall, J. (2012) *The Story Telling Animal: How Stories Make Us Human*, Boston: Houghton Mifflin Harcourt.
Grinberger, I. (2005) *The Therapeutic qualities of the process of Re-narrating life stories with holocaust survivors*, Thesis submitted in partial fulfilment for the degree of PhD, School of Human and Life Sciences, Roehampton University, University of Surrey.
Lahad, M. (1997) The story as a guide to metaphoric processes. In: S. Jennings (Ed.), *Dramatherapy theory and practice*, Vol. 3, London: Routledge, pp. 31–42.

Lahad, M. (1999) Supervision of crisis intervention teams: The myth of the savior. In: E. Tselikas-Portmann (Ed.), *Supervision and Dramatherapy*, London: Jessica Kingsley Publishers, pp. 136–154.

Lahad, M. (2000) *Creative Supervision*, London: Jessica Kingsley Publishers.

Lahad, M., and Doron, M. (2010) *SEE FAR CBT: beyond Cognitive Behavior Therapy. Protocol for treatment of Post-Traumatic Stress Disorder*, Amsterdam: IOS Press.

Lahad, M., Farhi, M., Leykin, D., and Kaplansky, N. (2010) Preliminary study of a new integrative approach in treating post traumatic stress disorder: SEE FAR CBT, *The Arts in Psychotherapy*, 37: 391–399.

Lahad, M., and Leykin, D. (2012) The healing potential of imagination in the treatment of psychotrauma: an alternative explanation for the effectiveness of the treatment of PTSD using Fantastic Reality. In: S.A. Lee and D.M. Edget (Eds.), *Cognitive Behavioral Therapy, Application Methods and Outcomes*, NY: Nova, pp. 71–93.

Landy, R. (1996) *Essays in Drama Therapy: The Double Life*, London, UK: Jessica Kingsley Publishers.

Maslow, A.H. (1954) *Motivation and personality*, NY: Harpers.

Minnen, v-A., and Foa, E.B. (2006) The effect of imaginal exposure length on outcome of treatment for PTSD, *Journal of Traumatic Stress*, 19, 4: 427–438.

Mitchell, J.T., and Everly, G.S. (2001) *Critical Incident Stress Debriefing: An Operations Manual for CISD, Defusing and Other Group Crisis Intervention Services*, Sussex: Chevron Pub Corp.

Onyut, P.L., Neuner, F., Schauer, E., Ertl, V., Odenwald, M., Schauer, M., and Elbert, T. (2005) Narrative Exposure Therapy as a treatment for child war survivors with posttraumatic stress disorder: two case reports and a pilot study in an African refugee settlement, *BMC Psychiatry*, 5,7. https://europepmc.org/article/MED/15691374#free-full-text

Ozer, E.J., Best, S.R., Lipsey, T.L., and Weiss, D.S. (2003) Predictors of post-traumatic stress disorder and symptoms in adults: a meta-analysis, *Psychological Bulletin*, 129: 52–71.

Suggate, S.P., and Martzog, P. (2020) Screen-time influences children's mental imagery performance, *Developmental Science*, DOI: 10,1111/desc.12978.

Tselikas-Portman, E. (Ed.) (1999) *Supervision and Dramatherapy*, London: Jessica Kingsley Pub.

Valkenburg, P., and Beentjes, J.W.J. (1997) Children's creative imagination in response to radio and television stories, *Journal of Communication*, 47: 21–38.

Valkenburg, P., and van der Voort, T.H.A. (1994) Influence of TV on daydreaming and creative imagination: a review of research, *Psychological Bulletin*, 116: 316–339.

30
THE LAYING ON OF EARS

Mary Louise Chown

In this chapter, I will describe some of my experiences as a visiting storyteller in hospital wards, hospices, and palliative care centres. As a trained artist, with no medical role in healthcare, my task was to respond to the whole person, helping them to stay engaged with life, while preparing for their death. Storytelling in healthcare settings differs from performance-based storytelling, and many tellers may not know how to share stories with people who are very ill. In healthcare, the focus is on the patient, not on the prowess of the storyteller. My chapter is meant to be a practical guide for storytellers, describing activities and choices that are especially meaningful in healthcare. Sections of selected folktales and parts of some patients' stories and conversations will be included, to illustrate how narrative can link our experiences with those of others, helping to place them in a mythological, or even sacred context. There will be reflection on the importance of non-medical engagement of patients with metaphor, imagery, and archetypal symbols, springing from our deepest selves, and often easing physical pain and discomfort in many situations.

The opportunity to work as a visiting artist in healthcare settings was created by Manitoba Artists in Healthcare, now called Artists in Healthcare Manitoba. AIHM is an organization that sends artists working in various media into a variety of healthcare centres. In addition to working in hospice and palliative care settings, my connection with AIHM led to several storytelling workshops and presentations for clients of Cancer Care Manitoba, and Hospice and Palliative Care Manitoba. Finally it led to a book of my experiences.[1]

It has been a privilege to enter into the lives of those who are ill or dying, and to hear their stories and those of their families and the staff who care for them. I am not medically trained, nor am I a therapist, psychiatrist, or chaplain. I am a trained teacher, a trained artist, and a storyteller. My explorations over the last thirty years have centred on storytelling as an art form and as a way of encouraging a sense of community among people of all ages.

I also want to emphasize that I was a paid artist, the funding coming either from an arts grant or the hospital in question. Volunteer visitors were greatly appreciated, but their role had more limitations. As a paid part-time worker, I was able to build a relationship with nurses, doctors, and spiritual care providers. I was invited to attend regular Rounds Meetings and asked for my input. My role as a working artist was taken seriously. My feedback was asked for and staff often suggested which patient they would like me to spend time with. I truly felt part of the healthcare team when I did this work.

To begin, a general word about stories

Stories are heard in the deep heart's core and answer the burning questions, which we all have. Who are we? Where did we come from? Who do we love? What have we forgotten that is important to remember? Why is there goodness and evil in the world? Why is there something rather than nothing? The answers, which are the most meaningful, come, in the end, from deep within our own selves. Our entire lives are narratives and we develop our own private meanings for the events in our lives by subconsciously ordering them into story form. Often, events are understood as isolated happenings at a specific time, and then perceived as part of the whole later on. It has been a fascinating process to explore the affinity between storytelling and personal experience, consciously linking the two together using the themes and motifs found in myth and folktale. These two worlds can co-exist, much like interior and exterior space, each informing the other. Our stories must be held in our waking consciousness from time to time so that we can redefine and reinvent ourselves and discover where we fit in the "real" (or "outer") world. So, storytelling is both an art form and a way of sharing among people of all ages. Shaun McNiff writes, "Whenever illness is associated with loss of soul, the arts emerge spontaneously as remedies, soul medicine".[2] Art is a great leveller. Anyone can participate regardless of economic class, education, ethnicity, or ability. When we hear a story, we understand what it means for us alone, and that's the only important result. It doesn't matter how someone else interprets the story. We get what we need from the story. Storytelling in hospice and palliative care requires no props, or extra equipment, just our voice and our willingness to be present.

Transitional storytelling

The type of storytelling I am describing in this chapter can be called "transitional storytelling". I am telling and listening to stories for the transition between life and death, as the patients in palliative care are very near the next stage in their lives. They may not see this as storytelling because often what they say comes out in short anecdotes or comments, and I see my role as one of helping them process or reflect on their experiences: helping them to stay engaged with life while preparing for their death. Transitional storytelling can give form and voice to experience. The actual telling, relating, and listening to life stories can restore meaning to people. I also think that I help them uncover or remember their own wisdom.

I loved the phrase "the laying on of ears" when I first came across it in an article written by Bronna Romanoff and Barbara Thompson.[3] What a wonderful metaphor, evoking an image of truly listening and caring, because of its similarity to the better-known phrase. Because of my non-medical background, all I was required to do as a storyteller was to sit at a patient's bedside and listen. What a privilege to be with people as they struggled with their illness or approached their dying. I visited with many patients and learned how to listen to, and simply be with, those who were nearing the end of their lives on this earth. Sometimes our time together began with the words of a folktale chosen especially for them, while at other times the patient wanted to talk about themselves to someone who had no agenda, other than to listen.

There is no "one way" to tell a story

One patient, whom I shall call Agnes, was an elderly woman who lived alone and was suddenly admitted to the palliative care ward without warning. I visited her several times and our conversations ranged over many topics with seemingly little connection, much like Alice's conversations with the Red Queen and the White Rabbit in *Through the Looking Glass*. She was too frail to go home, and was waiting for a place in a small hospice. She had very few visitors but her memory and imagination were still very active. Whenever I think of her, the poem from *Through the Looking Glass* comes to mind:

> The time has come the walrus said, to speak of many things ... of shoes and ships and sealing wax, of cabbages and kings.[4]

Just like Alice, my patient Agnes had abruptly found herself, without warning, in a different place, with no prospect of returning home. She badly needed to talk about the things of ordinary life and once remarked to me that "If I didn't talk about things I would be howling. But it's better to talk". So I allowed myself to simply show up at her bedside, relaxed and fully open to whatever she wanted to say, her own words inspiring my choice of stories to tell her. I knew that whatever folktale I chose would contain at least one motif that connected with her rambling speech. One day, she mentioned that she would like some of her beef broth, the way she used to make it at home, and she told me her recipe. On my next visit I told her one version of the well-known folktale, "Stone Soup", about a traveller who is able to make the most delicious soup from an ordinary stone.[5] My time spent with Agnes illustrates that there is no one way of storytelling. Sometimes you have to tease out responses and visit several times if that is possible, and sometimes you just listen and the words come pouring out. Stories you might tell will come from your own repertoire. Some will be stories you care deeply about. Some will be stories that you search for and learn in response to what you learn from your patient. Just one motif in a story may be what initially connects with what you know about a patient and allows you to choose a story from your repertoire. The story of Stone Soup has of course the motif of making something out of nothing, but it also has motifs of hunger, clever trickery, and generous sharing of limited resources.

Functions of storytelling

Often it's impossible to delineate each separate function of transitional storytelling, because any given interaction with a patient or family member can cover more than one aspect and have more than one result, just like our stories, both traditional and personal, are multi-layered, containing many motifs. Here are some of the many reasons to tell each other stories in hospice and palliative care settings.

- To help patients prepare for death and to help those who are survivors to go on living.
- To help us remember what is important to remember: to define who we are and where we come from.
- To help us experience the wholeness of life and knowledge rather than its separateness.
- To open up our worlds and make it possible for each of us to talk about our lives more deeply.
- To entertain each other.
- To engage the deep part of our brain that only speaks in images, where words are not as important.

Note that I use the terms "we" and "us", because you as a visiting storyteller will experience many of the same outcomes as the patients you visit. Your life will be enriched along with theirs. All of the points written above can be summed up in one sentence:

> I tell stories and listen to stories to accompany people; to be with them where they are.

Picture two canoes paddling on the river. They meet up and draw alongside each other for a while, holding onto the gunwales while they greet each other, give out information on what to expect downstream, tell who they are and where they have come from. When they part they may say goodbye and wish each other a good trip. Stories are like this. They accompany us on our journey: come alongside for a while or remain with us for a lifetime. They link our experiences with those of others, helping to place them in a mythological or even sacred context. Stories give form and voice to patients' experiences, helping them to remember their own wisdom. Stories help to hold and store memories. Stories can even help patients and their families prepare for death. When a patient or their family hears a story, it causes them to reflect on their own lives and be reassured that they are not alone in what they are experiencing.

Linking our experiences

Transitional storytelling can link our experiences with those of others, helping to place them in a mythological or even sacred context. The story of "The White Stone" illustrates this. It began when I told a Russian folktale, "The Frog Wife", about a princess who was under a spell where she had to take the form of a frog until certain things transpired.[6] The frog princess in the story is the clever one who makes everything right in the end. A group of elderly patients were gathered in a small alcove on their ward and one of them, Mrs. G., remarked after that men are as clever as women, though in different ways. She went on to tell me about her husband and all the things he built, and then she told me a story about a white stone that began like this:

> My mother had a white stone that she kept all her life. A small white stone. I remember seeing it. It's gone now, but I can tell you a story about it…

She was so pleased when I brought her the written version of her story and gave me permission to tell others the story of The White Stone.

I told the story to Sophia, a woman in the palliative care ward of another hospital, who was deeply sad and had lived a hard life, which included escaping to Canada after WW11 with only her two children and nothing else. When she heard the story of The White Stone, she commented:

> It must have been a happy marriage for her to keep the stone. People who are hiding or who are on the run from bombs don't keep very much.

I visited another woman on that same ward and also told her the story of The White Stone. Marilyn was close to death and was almost transparent. After I finished the story, she said to me, "I like that. They must have loved each other". I had brought with me that day a small pouch with stones inside and I took one out and placed it in her hand. Perhaps it was that story of the white stone that prompted her to speak out about what was in her heart, but this is what happened next. I was thinking that she was tired and I should leave, because her sister was also there visiting, when she murmured, "I'm afraid".

She was holding the stone in her hand and had placed that hand underneath the coverlet. She said to her sister,

> "I don't want to let it go."
> "You mean the stone?" asked her sister.
> "Yes. I have to tell you… . I need to … I don't want to give it away."

I asked her,

> "Are you afraid of letting go yourself?"
> "Yes!" she whispered.
> "You can keep it for as long as you like." I assured her.
> Her sister added, "See, you can keep this and you don't have to give it up until you're ready."

The last thing she said to me before I left her room that day was:

> "I have to give up my place on the water. I have to stand up and give up my spot on the water."

She died a few days later. Stone and water are archetypal images connecting to a deeper part of ourselves. These images were the only way that Marilyn could express her deep emotions. Words alone can be insufficient, but images and metaphor run deep. This is the great gift that the arts can bring to life situations. Ordinary objects such as a smooth stone or running water can become sacred.

Listener responses

Responses will vary when you are telling stories at the bedside of palliative care patients. Many patients cannot give too much reaction to hearing a story, so don't expect one. Others may want to comment on the story, saying it reminds them of something or other. You can always be sure that the patient is listening. The human voice and the human face are endlessly interesting and comforting to look at and hear. One woman named Dorothy, to whom my book is dedicated, always had a comment to make after the story was over. She would say,

> "Some people are greedy, never satisfied" or "When I was growing up, I was always told that good things come in small packages".

Once, I told "Maybe Good, Maybe Bad" to a trio of patients gathered for lunch in the hospice dining room.[7] It's a story from China about a farmer and his son who have a magnificent stallion. Their fortunes keep changing throughout the story, with the father repeating his opinion after each event that happened to them that it may be good or bad, but it was too soon to tell. All three told me that they enjoyed the story. They said that it could have happened in real life, when you think something's bad and then it turns out all right. One patient rose from the table and began walking slowly back to his room, pushing his walker in front of him. As he passed by where I was standing, he paused, turned to look at me, and said, "Those Chinese really knew what they were talking about".

Often I would listen to a patient's life story over the course of several visits and then I would read it back to them as a "once upon a time" story. One man, only known as J.D., whom I visited told me he didn't want to hear any stories and he didn't have anything interesting to say. He was in constant pain and moved continually from bed to chair to standing. Our visits were short but little by little he revealed things about himself and his life. I kept notes of where he was born, where his parents came from, where he worked, and I filled in details from researching his cultural background. I decided to put all the information I had into a story form and read it to him on my next visit. My story began at the beginning:

> Long ago a baby boy was born. His parents gave him a name when he was baptized, but he was never called by that name. For he was known to this day as J.D., short for Jedduzza, which means "little bird" in the Sicilian language…

As I read J.D. his own story he covered his face with one of his hands and he wept. Thinking I had needlessly upset him, I stopped reading, but he signalled for me to keep on talking by waving his hand at me in an imperious way and commanding me to keep reading. When I reached the part about meeting his wife and read:

> "Whether or not it was love at first sight, I don't know"…
> He blurted out, "You never asked me!"

Aha, I thought. Now I knew where we would start the next time I came. But when I returned the next time, he had died. I was distressed with the fear that I had unduly upset him, but the nursing staff reassured me, saying that it was a good thing that he heard his own story being told and that he wept, because he was a lonely man whose only relative was his wife, who was herself ill and unable to visit.

Another very ill patient, Sophia, whom I mentioned earlier, told me on my first visit that,

> You might be interested in my story, but no one else is.

She had a very unfriendly manner and an aura of deep gloom surrounded her. The nursing staff was well aware of this and asked me if I would visit her. I assured her that I wanted to hear her story and made sure she could watch as I wrote down her every word. She began, as a storyteller would:

> My life is like a fairy tale. I was born in the old country and I grew up poor. I was often hungry and I walked barefoot in the snow…

The words poured out of her. It was a story of war, survival, and immigration to a new country. I merely had to write her words down. I returned the next day and read out the text of her story. She gave it her approval and I left it with her. By contrast, when J.D. told me snippets here and there about himself, I was the gatherer, storing up his words and later weaving them into a story full of special births, dreams, and hard struggles. I recount these stories because it illustrates how much this man and this woman needed someone to witness the shining threads of their lives: to be reassured that their existence was important. The perfect time for storytelling is when the soul is open and vulnerable.

Dorothy, whom I wrote about earlier, grew up in Trinidad. She loved to hear the story of "The Magic Fish" and asked me to tell it again and again.[8] She was often visited by one of her sisters. All three women loved to hear stories. When I told The Magic Fish for the first time, they blurted out comments along the way, such as, "My god what does that woman want now!", causing me to say, "Yes that's exactly what the fish was thinking!"

Later that week, I sat with Dorothy and her sister in front of the fireplace in the living room area of the hospice. And after I greeted them and sat down, Dorothy's sister said to me, "I've been thinking, you know, about stories; they may seem magical, but there is a little bit of something in each story to teach. Stories teach you something".

Once Dorothy's sister told me the following story about Anansi:

> He's African, Anansi, and we call him Brer Nancy in Trinidad. He's tricky, always getting into trouble.
> Once he was caught red-handed and he cried out, "I'm guilty. Do anything you want with me except one thing."
> "We're going to grab you round the neck and choke you!" they said.
> "That's fine, do anything you want except one thing."
> They kept saying what they would do, and Brer Nancy keeps agreeing and pleading until they finally ask, "What is this one thing?"
> "Oh, please don't throw me in the briar patch!"
> "Well, maybe that's what we should do, if Brer Nancy is so afraid of it."
> So they throw him in the briar patch and off he goes.

Towards the end of her life, Dorothy didn't remember the stories that I told her, yet I still told them, because the nurses encouraged me to continue, since they had noticed that Dorothy relaxed and felt calm when she heard my stories. The only one she remembered from one visit to the next was The Magic Fish. On those last days of her life, she lay very still, her eyes fixed on my face, saying nothing.

Choosing stories

The spare words of most folktales, honed through centuries of telling, rely on the listener to fill in meaning. The interpretation of any story is based on the listener's life experience, just as the telling comes from deep within the storyteller's life. Folktales can join our experiences with those of others; they can help place them in a mythological or even sacred context where ordinary events can be seen as extraordinary, even universal. We are all in this life on earth meant to live life to the fullest, in all of its meanings and interpretations. This is where art steps in. I choose my stories based on how patients speak about their situations and their lives; or, if this information isn't available to me, then I try to imagine what sort of story they might like to hear. I have found that, when I know little about the patient, a short folktale is the best place to start. In addition to the folktales already mentioned, everyone I visited also enjoyed hearing the story of "The Old Woman Who Cheated Death",[9] "Elijah and the Wish",[10] and "The Magic Drum".[11] All storytellers have a number of potentially suitable stories in their repertoire like these.

Know that between our birth and death lie all manner of tales, seemingly disparate, but actually closely related to one another. Life continually revisits earlier times, while at the same time, everything we experience is part of who we are today. A well-told story presents us with two realities: an outer one of action, of the sequence of events; and an inner one of meaning, of what is really going on. It is the listener who ultimately decides what the story means, because a skilled teller only implies possible meanings. When you are choosing a story to tell in a palliative care situation, know that your listener may find the meaning you intended, based on the thought and planning you gave to the situation before you entered that patient's room. Or they may not. Be confident that if the story has a deep meaning for you, you will convey that to your listener through your voice and body language. Trust that they, in turn, will discover their own meanings.

Some stories I told were chosen purely for their ability to entertain and divert. "Caps for Sale". originally from India, is a hilarious tale of a pedlar selling caps, having them stolen by a tree full of moneys, and eventually retrieving them.[12] I told my version of Caps for Sale to a young woman in the final stages of brain cancer. She was quite fearful and was having trouble remaining calm. She always enjoyed a short, simple, or funny story, and then she would be able to have a restful nap afterward. In some cases I merely told about a story. There was one man I was asked to visit who told me he wasn't interested in hearing a story. He assured me he was going to be going home soon, where his wife would look after him. The doctors had mentioned at the Rounds Meeting that he was close to death and required too much care for his wife to manage at home. They thought some storytelling would help him. When he asked me what kinds of stories I told, I saw my opportunity. I decided to tell him about Gilgamesh.[13]

"It's probably the oldest written story in the world", I said.

This intrigued him and he asked me what it was about. His attention sharpened when I began to say that Gilgamesh was a king of ancient times who wanted to live forever and who travelled beyond the edge of the known world to find the plant of immortality. My contract was over shortly after that and I never knew what became of him. I do know that simply talking about stories was a way of being with this particular patient, allowing him to remain in his own place of comfort.

Of course, the interpretation of any story is based on the listener's life experience. This became apparent whenever there was a chance to have a conversation after a story. It is as if when we hear a story, we have already travelled a similar landscape in our own lives and so we can follow along as the story is told. A good story also has an element of surprise, a twist in events that gives it magic for the listener and teller. Whenever I told "Kytna's Story", my listeners invariably remarked on how strange, yet satisfying it was.[14] In the story, which comes from the Chukchi people of Siberia, Kytna sets out to rescue her daughter from the wolves who have taken her, and her daughter has gone for so long that she has become a wolf herself. Her mother must also take on the shape of a wolf in order to bring her home.

The importance of metaphor and imagery

I cannot stress enough the importance of non-medical engagement of patients with metaphor, imagery, and archetypal symbols, springing from our deepest selves, and often easing physical pain and discomfort in many situations. Images run deeper in our subconscious than words. As a working artist this is what I can offer and what is familiar to me in every aspect of my work. Every folktale, epic, and myth contains metaphors and archetypal symbols. Caves, mountains, streams, birds, storms, and sunsets evoke one's own memories of these elements. The listener becomes the old woman, the silly young man, the clever girl, the monkey, or any one of the many characters that we come across in the stories. We simply cannot follow a narrative if we can't imagine the characters that people it. I remember one woman suffering from cancer telling the nurse who came with her afternoon medication that,

> I don't need anything right now. I'm listening to a story, and it's taking my pain away.

Oral storytelling is an expressive art, which demands a personal and creative response, even from one who is weakened through illness. Listening to a story requires imagination and concentration, as visual and textural clues are not there to tell one how to respond. One must dig deep into the unconscious level of being and this is actually surprisingly easy to do. It requires no words. We meet this part of our being every time we dream. Creative thinking and self-expression are nurtured through storytelling. Sometimes the most helpful thing one can do is tell a story.

Last words

Once we recognize the imagination as something powerful within ourselves, we are able, ultimately, to live life more fully at any point in our life. This is also true of those patients in palliative care, if they are open to what is happening to them. Some aren't, like the man whom I told about Gilgamesh, but often we can help someone in the last stages of their life by telling them a story, and being present to listen to whatever they have to say. A story can help to open up that imagery part of our brains and encourage us to make connections with the characters and settings in the story. It's a neutral thing we offer when we tell a story. It's about the listener and yet it's not about the listener. It never directly points a finger. Rather it can be considered a gift. For the patient or family member, the very act of telling a story can change the way an event is perceived, and can alter the way one feels. Telling another person about an event or illness can transform it, reducing its potential to linger in the mind as a great burden. One is no longer the victim of circumstances beyond their control.

Notes

1. Chown, Mary Louise, *Now I Know the World is Round: Stories at the End of Life*, Winnipeg: A Ladyslipper Art Book, Art Bookbindery, 2011.
2. McNiff, Shaun, *Art as Medicine: Creating a Therapy of the Imagination*. Boston and London: Shambhala Publications, 1992.
3. Romanoff, Bronna D., and Thompson, Barbara E., "Meaning Construction in palliative Care: The Use of Narrative, Ritual, and the Expressive Arts", *The American Journal of Hospice and Palliative Care Medicine* 24(4): 309–316.
4. Carroll, Lewis. *Through the Looking Glass and What Alice Found There*. New York: Morrow, 1993.
5. A version of "Stone Soup" can be found in Cole, Joanna, "The Old Woman and the Tramp." *Best Loved Folktales of the World*. New York: Doubleday, 1989.
6. My telling of the Frog Wife has developed over many years and after reading many versions. A version can be found in Baugh, Tad R. "The Frog Tsarevna". *Russian Folktales*. San Rafael, CA: Leswing Press, 1973.
7. Li, Yao-Wen, and Kendall, Carol. "Maybe Good, Maybe Bad". *Sweet and Sour: Tales from China*. New York: Clarion Books, 1980. [And see also "From Bad to Good to Bad to Good" in the same volume].
8. "The Magic Fish" has many variants all over the world. Another version can be found in Zipes, Jack, trans. "The Fisherman and His Wife", *The Complete fairytales of the Brothers Grimm*, vol 1. Toronto, New York, London, Sydney, Auckland: Bantam Books, 1987.
9. A version of "The Old Woman Who Cheated Death" can be found in Ragan, Kathleen, ed. "Death and the Old Woman". *Outfoxing Fear: Folktales from Around the World*. New York, London: W.W. Norton and Co., 2006.
10. Yolen, Jane, ed. "Elijah and the Wish", *Gray Heroes: Elder Tales from Around the World*. New York, London, Melbourne, Toronto, Auckland: Penguin Books, 1999.
11. Metayer, Maurice, trans. "The Magic Drum." *Tales from the Igloo*. Edmonton: Hurtig Publishers, 1972.
12. Slobodkina, Esphyr, *Caps for Sale: A Tale of a Peddler, Some Monkeys and their Monkey Business*, HarperCollins Publishers CA, 2015.
13. Mitchell, Stephen, *Gilgamesh: New English Version*, New York: Free Press, 2004
14. Van Deusen, Kira, "How Old Woman Kytna Brought her Daughter Home" in A. Cox and D. Albert, eds. The Healing Heart: Communities. Gabriola Island, British Columbia. New Society Publishers, 200.

31
STORYTELLING AND PLAY
How storytelling and play can be used therapeutically with people with a learning disability

Jem Dick

We all have our stories, things that happened to us, or people we know. There are also the wider stories about people we have never met, but who interest us. Then there is fiction: traditional stories and folk tales, authored fiction in many genres, plays, soap operas and so forth. Story and music may be the oldest forms of communication. Even in the animal kingdom some creatures will make up stories. A subservient monkey who finds a titbit on the ground that would be taken from them by a more dominant monkey may make the alarm cry for snake, thus sending the rest of the troupe up into the trees so they can enjoy their prize in peace.

Our earliest ancestors would have told the stories of successful hunts, thus passing on the knowledge to future generations. There would also have been stories about who was mating with whom, and who cheated on whom.

With stories we learn about our world. From anticipation games with pre-verbal infants to stories that teach us about our cultural and social mores. Stories have always been used for teaching, as well as entertainment.

A Chippewa Cree tribal elder said that the quickest way to shut him up is to ask for a story. He said that stories came out of conversation or teaching. He told me that the commander of the reservation had said to his grandfather, "You people drive me nuts – I ask a simple question and I either get a grunt or a two-hour story." All these forms of story are actually our stories. They all deal with the human condition (even if they are about mice, elves or five-dimensional plasma beings from the Andromeda Galaxy).

Some stories may be outside our own experience, but can teach us about the experience of others, thus strengthening our empathy. We all need our stories to be heard, we need to know that our lives are valid and are of value and interest to others. If we have a learning disability and communication difficulties, then telling our own stories and understanding others' stories may be difficult for us. What will make the effort of understanding stories worthwhile? Our lives are full of stories because they are enjoyable to tell and to hear. That is the answer: make it fun. It may be that an individual with learning disabilities has felt marginalised, and has low self-esteem. Their locus of evaluation is placed in the parents, carers or staff around them.

They can seem like nice people, biddable, they will always give the answers they think you want to hear. This is a terrible story. There are many like it.

We can use an understanding of story to help people to change their stories.

In the case studies below, I have changed names and any identifying details, because these stories are personal to the individuals in them. There are many case studies here, because if we are looking at story, what better way to demonstrate it, than with people's stories. Also, as each individual's needs are different, a range of case studies can best illustrate my multi-disciplinary approach. Case studies can make the writer sound very clever. We generally illustrate our points with the interventions that were successful. I ask the reader to bear in mind that in attempting to find an effective intervention for an individual, we may have to try several approaches before we hit on the right one: if we don't make mistakes, we don't make anything.

Case study 1

Jim is a man of about forty who has Downs Syndrome. He does not talk, but he makes expressive sounds and uses some rudimentary sign language. He joined a music group I was running at a day centre for adults with learning disabilities.

At first he would join in, smiling and having a go on various instruments that were on offer. Never any trouble, always willing to join in, that was 'Good Old Jim.' Then one day he picked up a pair of drumsticks and started beating violently on a huge horizontal drum. He was shouting. He looked angry. I started playing power chords on my guitar and singing, "I'M SO ANGRY. I'M VERY, VERY ANGRY…!!" Jim's playing and shouting intensified. This behaviour went on for about eight of our weekly sessions. After about four weeks the manager of his group home said to me, "You have to stop doing this music with Jim. He keeps getting angry and shouting, sometimes in the street or the shops."

I thanked the manager for coming to me and I explained that what was coming from Jim was a reaction to some awful thing that had happened to him at some time in the past. I said:

> He needs to work through his hurt. It is my job as a Creative Therapist to help him do that, and it is your job as a provider of social care to help Jim to understand that there are places where it is appropriate to let off steam, and places that it isn't. We all need to get things off our chest sometimes, and we are lucky enough to be able to moan into a sympathetic ear. At last Jim has found a way to express his difficult feelings. We should both help him with that.

Fortunately Jim's house manager was able to see my point, and instructed his staff to follow my advice. During my music session, some eight weeks after Jim's first outburst he suddenly started crying and beating the drum softly. I changed my guitar playing to a minor key and sang, "I'm so sad, I'm so unhappy…" This went on for another two weeks and then Jim smiled and started doing the signs for 'holiday' and 'boat.' I improvised a song about going on holiday in a boat upon the water, and how it made me feel happy and peaceful. We will never know the details of Jim's story. We don't need to. He told us all that was important about it – something horrible made him furious, he was so badly hurt, but there had been a happy time on a boat. And now he felt better. Another thing that got better was Jim's ability to say "No" to things he didn't want. Isn't that a happy ending?

So there is a story from someone with a profound learning disability. We know the emotional narrative of Jim's story, but not the details. Those details are Jim's, not ours; the important thing is that he was able to retell his story in a way that was relevant to him, and he knew that I heard what he was saying and I empathized and stood beside him through that difficult journey. As any good therapist would. Jim became more self-actualized and his delightful personality became richer. A year after the above intervention Jim presented with a new difficulty.

A traditional or authored story can be a powerful way of addressing our real issues in a safe way. If we know that the protagonists and the events in a story are not real, we can approach our own problems at our own pace, keeping control of the distance between the fiction and our own realities through the filtered safety of the story. Let us visit Jim again, a year after the intervention above.

Case study 2

One day Jim came into the day centre in great distress. He was tearful, making traumatised vocalisations and miming a stabbing motion with his hand. I talked to his supported living and day centre staff and was told that he gets terribly worked up when he sees violence on television. This is something I have seen often with people with learning disabilities; they can find it difficult to understand the difference between events in real life and those in a story.

I got access to a video camera, VHS player, television, a large plastic sheet and a squeezy bottle of red paint. Jim liked to indulge in gentle play fighting, a sort of seated tag. When playing this game when Jim tagged me I would pantomime being terribly hurt, but with a big smile on my face; Jim would laugh at this. When this pattern was established I instigated a tag game over the plastic sheet. When Jim tagged me I said "Ow, ow, ow!" and squirted the red paint from the arm he had tagged and said, still smiling, "look, Jim, you've made me bleed!" As he was familiar with the squeezy paint he laughed.

Jim loved police officers; we had one visit the centre once and Jim was thrilled when the policeman let him wear his helmet. I then filmed a drama with the service users at the day centre. The story was where an old lady had her bag snatched by a robber who ran off with it. Jim as the policeman apprehended the thief, taking the bag from him and banging him over the head with it. The bag was very soft, so we dubbed on a loud thump in postproduction. Jim was delighted with the film. I then showed Jim the scene from *Monty Python and the Holy Grail* where King Arthur fights with the Black Knight and cuts off his limbs one by one as ridiculous amounts of 'blood' gush from his severed limbs. As this was happening I squirted the red paint from the bottle again, saying, "How much red paint did they use when they filmed that, Jim?" Jim got it. I was able to advise the residential staff of my intervention so they could refer to it when Jim was watching violence on TV.

To help someone change an ingrained or unhappy story they have developed about themselves may need a careful choice of medium or media, depending on what they present with. Here are two examples of this flexible approach.

Case study 3

Patsy was pre-verbal and had severe autism. She would happily join in with a music session most of the time, but could suddenly start making repetitive, stressed vocalisations: "aaagh, AAAGH, AAAGH…" This would build to a crescendo until she started to strike herself in the face with her fist. This behaviour obviously had to be modified. I tried various approaches, none of which worked, until I took a risk and mirrored her vocalisations. I slipped my "aaagh"s in between hers, building to a tremendous releasing sigh: "Aaahhhhhh." Sometimes Patsy would stop in surprise and look at me, if she hadn't gone too far in winding herself up. I was learning the subtleties of her vocalisations and adapting my interventions in response. After several months Patsy gradually started to copy the releasing "Aaaah"s I was making and eventually learned this way to change how her story ended into one of finding peace, rather than self-harm.

Case study 4

Another approach in a different medium I developed was with Baz, a man who went regularly to a day centre.

Baz never interacted with anyone at the centre or joined in any of the activities; he just sat down and looked through an Argos catalogue. The staff there were at a loss as to what to do with him. I worked with him one to one in a quiet room away from the general hubbub of the centre. At first I just sat next to him and watched as he leafed through the catalogue. I noticed that he would occasionally stop turning the pages and look at a particular item. I pointed to what I thought he was looking at and say, "Are you looking at that one?" This carried on for a few weeks, and gradually Baz started to point at things he was interested in in the book. I would point to them too, and then draw them on a piece of paper.

One day Baz looked quizzically at me. I pointed to his face and drew his expression. Baz's eye contact became more frequent, and each time I saw a different expression on his face, I pointed to it and drew it. If he repeated an expression I had already drawn I would point to the drawing of it I had already made.

The outcome was that when Baz came in in the morning I would ask how he was feeling and show him a laminated sheet of all the drawings I had made of his various expressions and he would study it at length and then point to between one and three expressions. I made copies of this sheet of expressions and gave them to the members of staff at the centre. They started using them, and so Baz was drawn into the life of the centre, no longer suffering the isolation he had experienced before.

One of the stories that people with learning disabilities commonly tell themselves is that they are less than the able people around them. Some staff working in this area also tell themselves that they are less than others, and go into working with people with learning disabilities to feel superior in this situation. This is the shadow side of care as this attitude can engender abusive behaviour by staff towards people in their care.

Case study 5

Once, a few years ago, when I was running a disco for adults with learning disabilities, I noticed a member of staff sitting at a table with the people from the home she worked in. I noticed her because she had just slapped a woman with severe learning disabilities around the face. I immediately went up to this member of staff and said, "What do you think you are doing?" She said, "She was really annoying me and getting on my nerves, so I slapped her."

I said, "This woman you just slapped has a learning disability; you do not. It is your responsibility to care for these people, not assault them."

She said, "Yes, but I..." I interrupted, "There is no 'Yes but'; you have just committed common assault. I could have you arrested. I am not going to do that, but I will be informing your manager of what you have done. This is unacceptable behaviour; I do not allow it here and your manager does not allow it either."

That young staff member was sacked immediately.

Having fun is a serious business

People with learning disabilities will often be unable to stand up for themselves. They may feel inadequate or even stupid. They may have been told this many times. I have noticed that they are delighted when staff also do something silly. (Let's face it; we all do silly things now and then.)

Clowning can be a great leveller. When I am working with my guitar I will often slide it on its strap onto my back to free my arms. From there I will, when I feel it is appropriate, pantomime: "AAh! Where's my guitar? Someone has taken my guitar! …Have you got my guitar?!" Someone invariably says, "It's behind you!" I spin round, one way then another, saying, "I can't see it!" Sometimes someone will pull my guitar round to the front; I act surprised and delighted and put it in the playing position, but with the strings towards me and the back facing out. I try to play it, and say, "The strings have gone, have you eaten the strings?" This is improvised according to people's responses.

I also sometimes use a swanee whistle. This is very effective with people with profound learning disabilities. With the swanee whistle you can imitate all the prosody and affect of speech. It is a good tool for clowning. For example, I make a long falling tone with an element of relief as I slowly sit down. Just before I reach the seat (which may be one of the clients) I shoot up with a loud fast rising note of shock, then rub my backside, looking round to see what 'bit' me. This usually elicits gales of laughter from the people with learning disabilities and staff alike – again it is a great leveller.

Being guided by the person or people with learning disabilities themselves is essential. As in all good therapeutic practice, the client is the expert. The special skills we need to bring to this are those of being able to notice and understand the slightest nuances of reaction. Sometimes it can help by asking the people most closely involved with the individual for their interpretations of observed behaviours. Bearing in mind that interpretations by anyone will of necessity be subjective.

Play as a safe model for exploring life's challenges

If someone finds certain things in life difficult – for example, they are extremely shy, or find transitions like going into a different room difficult – a game can be made of the challenging situation. What we need to do is find a way of adding a fun or distracting element to the challenging situation. Sometimes a gently playful commentary can help to ground the distress.

Case study 6

When working in a school for children with autism, a year three class of about eight children came in; one of them sat on a chair and put his jacket over his head. I gleaned his name from the teacher talking to him, so I started to sing:

> "Simon is in a new room.
> There is a man he hasn't seen before
> But it's safe inside Simon's jacket
> Simon knows the inside of his jacket"

(At this point Simon peered at me briefly from under his jacket.)

> "Simon just looked at the man
> The man is singing what is happening now."

And Simon just looked out from his jacket again
And I smiled at him...

Simon's curiosity overcame the challenges of being in a new room with a stranger in it, and he slowly emerged from under his jacket like a shy tortoise.

After the session the teacher said that Simon always found transitions difficult, and that that was the quickest by far.

The teacher was so delighted she continued to use this technique with Simon. Sometimes modelling a behavioural intervention is the most effective way of passing it on to staff, carers or other adults supporting an individual.

With this in mind, here is another case study.

Case study 7

Doreen was an elderly woman with learning disabilities. She had a good vocabulary, and a good sense of humour. She was, however very over-sensitive to the slightest suspicion of criticism or teasing. She would burst into tears at the merest suggestion of criticism or sleight. An example of this was with another service user who would always mime a monkey to anyone eating a banana; another was if you said, "Come on, slowcoach, or we'll be late." She believed she was less than others and that is why the friendly banter hurt so much. Her friends, who did the bantering, did not mean to hurt her – it was just friendly joshing.

I developed a programme of positive reinforcement whenever Doreen did or said anything good, encouraging her peers to join in. I then developed an intervention of acclimatising teasing. First making the banter so ridiculous that Doreen couldn't help but see the funny side. An example of this was that as Doreen was so small and thin, I would stand well back when she came past saying, "Look out here comes the terrible giant!" or, "Look at the state of us – we're like a herd of hippopotamuses!" I would also include others in the joshing so Doreen would see them laughing and not being offended, therefore modelling the friendly nature of the exchanges. Over about six months Doreen learned to enjoy friendly banter, and even join in with it. The story she was now telling herself was that she was among equals who valued who she was and what she did.

For some people with a learning disability some form of fiction or entertainment can become extremely important or defining for them. Somehow the stories they see can externalise their fears, aspirations or tastes. We can work with these stories to develop a good rapport, and to increase their feeling of self-worth.

Case study 8

Charles, a man with Downs Syndrome who was pre-verbal but had some rudimentary signing, adored Laurel and Hardy. He would laugh at their slapstick, and also loved it if something went wrong in the real world – for example if I dropped something or broke a guitar string. His sign for Laurel and Hardy was scratching the top of his head in the style of Stan Laurel and he would do this when he wanted me to sing the song, *The Blue Ridge Mountains of Virginia* for him. I would struggle Oliver Hardy-wise to put up my music stand and get the music on it as it kept collapsing.

Charles would laugh and laugh. We developed a great rapport, and sometimes he would do the silly dance from *Way Out West*, which I would join in with. He also responded well to the clowning I mentioned earlier. When the care staff also laughed at our antics, Charles responded by smiling more and aiming his performance at the staff audience. By his feeling part of the whole interaction in the room, the convention of carers and those being cared for was broken down for everyone, enabling Charles to feel an equal part of this interaction. This clearly enhanced his sense of self-worth now that he had become a giver as well as a receiver.

This can work well with verbally able people as well. They will often really like a particular TV programme, film etc. which we can work with.

Case study 9

As I mentioned above, as therapists we will make mistakes – we are human after all. Mistakes can be good things, though. At the very least we have ticked an item off a list of things to try, and have got one step nearer to finding the right way forward. Mistakes can also lead us into new territories and new discoveries.

I was working in a large day centre for adults with learning disabilities. There were about thirty members of staff running programmes and projects with the service users. All the staff were very motivated and we had a weekly meeting where we would share our successes and so develop best practice together.

I was running a film and drama session where I would discuss with the group what they wanted to make a film about on that day. As they came up with ideas I would draw simple illustrations of each scene on a sheet of A4 paper and tack them on the wall, moving them around and pointing out gaps in the narrative. This built up a storyboard that everyone could follow. This proved to be a very effective and inclusive approach.

One morning the group decided to make a film based on a popular soap opera about a casualty department in a hospital. Someone said that they would fall off a ladder, another was going to burn their arm, another would be knocked down by a car…and so it went on. I was getting frantic, saying, "If everyone is just having accidents, where is the story?"

At tea break I reflected on the problem, and realised that I had become too fixed on my storyboard system, and when we returned after the break I apologised to the group and asked if they wanted to keep trying with the storyboard or should we just start filming? They chose the latter, and as we filmed they improvised a perfectly acceptable story.

When I shared my mistake at the next staff meeting, it opened the floodgates and suddenly all the staff felt that it was alright to talk about their failures as well as their successes. My mistake had changed the culture of the entire centre for the better.

Case study 10

I have worked for many years with the charity, OpenStoryTellers, founded by Dr. Nicola Grove. I teach adults with learning disabilities to tell stories.

We have worked with traditional material, especially stories that deal with difference, marginalisation and disability, with personal stories and with historical stories about people with learning disabilities. The transformational power of learning to tell a story is profound.

A man called Sam joined the storytelling group I was running, wanting to learn the art of storytelling. He had trouble listening, he was easily distracted and would listen to music on headphones much of the time. He therefore was not able to develop an understanding of what storytelling was, and was becoming quite stressed about that.

He came in one day and was talking about how exciting the latest James Bond film was and how he loved the car chases. I asked him what the best car chase sequence in the film was, and when he told me I asked him to describe it. He did so in graphic detail. I said, "You described that chase really well, I felt I could see it happening before me – that is exactly what storytelling is!" He was delighted. He also loved the *Lord of the Rings* and *Hobbit* films, so I found some traditional stories with elves, wizards and dragons in them.

His engagement led to committed involvement and the development of an impressive range of performance skills. Now a fine storyteller, he is appreciated by audiences in many settings, including mainstream venues.

I have worked for the OpenStoryTellers charity since its inception in 2004, teaching adults with learning disabilities to become storytellers. We have performed in learning disabled communities, elderly care settings, schools, mainstream venues including international storytelling festivals, theatres and conferences.

I have seen the traditional stories we work with create powerful transformations in people, akin to the transformations portrayed in the traditional stories we tell.

Nearly all the stories we tell deal with issues of disability, difference and marginalisation. One example is a story from the Arthurian cycle, 'Gareth of Orkney.' In that story the youngest of four royal sons wants to join his father and brothers in Camelot. He doesn't want to be made a knight by default, so disguises himself, takes the most menial job in the kitchens for a year, then goes out, defeats four giant knights and rescues a maiden. He is knighted and marries the maiden. 'The most menial jobs' are generally the only ones people with learning disabilities are given. This is a story that affirms that we can all grow to be the best we can be.

One of the learning disabled storytellers in the group summed up the effects of learning to be a storyteller much better than I could: "I used to feel like a book on the shelf that nobody ever took down and read. Now I can tell stories, people can see who I really am, not just my disability." In the storytelling group we play many games that develop people's skills as storytellers. Examples of these are miming a scene from a story so the rest of the group can guess it; copying facial expressions; making up a group story, each person telling a small bit; and more challengingly, telling three 'facts' about yourself where the others have to guess which is the only true one.

Working with these wonderful people with learning disabilities for the last thirty years has been a privilege. I have learned so much from their sometimes unfettered expressions of how they are feeling and who they are. It is easy to forget that just as someone with, perhaps, no legs or no sight may be a world class musician, so the people that can't think as fast as us may have, for example, a sensitivity and emotional intelligence that can teach us a great deal.

32
A TRANS-CULTURAL PERSPECTIVE ON LIFE STORY THERAPY WITH ADOPTIVE FOSTER AND KINSHIP FAMILIES, USING THE "THEATRE OF ATTACHMENT" MODEL

Joan Moore

Introduction

The United Nations Convention on the Rights of the Child (Articles 8.1, 9.3 and 9.4) specifies the right of children separated from their birth parents to be given information about themselves and their families of origin, a right endorsed by the National Institute for Health and Care Excellence (NICE) in 2014. In 2015 the UK government introduced the Adoption Support Fund, which recognises that therapeutic life story work can positively affect the stability of adoptive placements. This Fund expanded to include children and young people subject to Special Guardianship and those who are internationally adopted. Yet although Wilkinson and Bowyer (2017, p.57) assert that life story work enables children in care to develop a clearer sense of their identity, in social policy research, as McMurray et al. (2010) have noted, identity as a developmental process and outcome is often subordinated in favour of more tangible outcomes such as educational achievement. McCulloch and Mathura (2019) point out that, "little evidence exists regarding therapeutic interventions with maltreated children who are removed from their birth families and then adopted". These authors report success with their neurodevelopmental and sequential approach, which incorporates therapeutic life story work and supports the parents as well as the child.

In this chapter the author reflects on a PhD study of "Theatre of Attachment", a therapeutic intervention undertaken with adoptive and foster families, whose children had been removed from their birth families and in many cases had multiple experiences of care. The study involved 17 parents and 14 children aged 6–9 years, of varying ethnicity. Intervention is carried out in the family home, where the children feel safer. Perry (2012, 10) remarks that, "without a life story, a child is adrift, disconnected and vulnerable". Hence the main focus is on the children's life story as a means of facilitating secure attachment where past trauma and the children's propensity for self-blame had made this problematic. An important task is to raise the parents' empathy for the children and their birth parents. I find that this is most effectively achieved by sharing the contextualised story with parents prior to starting work with the children. So often I hear parents say, "Why didn't anyone explain this to us before? If only we had realised what they'd been through we'd have understood [their problems] so much better!" even though in most cases they were given the documents detailing the life history before the children were placed with them.

The children's experiences

Howe (2005) illustrates records on children in public care, which reveal why the most serially traumatised need to be safe before they can begin to heal. Children who have experienced caregiving to be highly unreliable are prone to transferring patterns of behaviour from the abusive environment into their new situation (Schofield & Beek, 2014). Their attempts to get their new parents to reject them indicate their underlying assumption that they are unworthy of care. Poor social skills cause them to misread social cues. They sense disappointment from caregivers, who long for reciprocity but find affection from them to be unforthcoming or indiscriminate.

Trauma and safety

Porges' (2015) Polyvagal theory has proved influential in explaining why traumatised children live in constant fear of abandonment. The home setting is therefore considered especially important to ensure sufficient safety to engage children for whom the impediments of poor self-esteem, lacking a sense of belonging, expectation of rejection and of being moved on, add to their emotional fragility. As advised by Perry and Szalavitz (2008), I find foster and adoptive parents almost invariably need help to recognise when their children are functioning emotionally at a younger age and to address their needs with that age in mind. Key challenges are helping parents to recognise the child's fear states so that their perspectives can be reconstructed and new alliances formed. Paramount to securing attachment is enabling the child's sense of belonging. Adult survivors of trauma discovered through exploring their life experiences that their fears and anxieties were constituted by their relationships and environment rather than by something innately wrong with them (Rosenthal, 2003; Etherington, 2009). Similarly, therapeutically processing events of their life helps to release children from damaging self-blame. Of course, they need adults to help them to process painful memories.

An important aspect of helping the families to understand the children's fears is the tailoring of intervention to individual need. This requires recognition of attachment styles and their influence on family relationships.

Attachment and culture

Attachment theory is a formulation for interpreting learned patterns of insecure behaviour, such as avoidance and ambivalence, which transfer into new relationships. As a western concept, it is criticised for taking too little account of non-western cultural contexts, or of subtle variations within cultures, personality or peer influence (Rushton, 2010; Levine & New, 2008). Indeed Lancy (2008) challenges the very idea that young children depend solely on a primary attachment figure. Since a multiplicity of interlocking factors makes it difficult to separate out the various influences of personality, temperament, culture and heritage, poverty, disability and substance misuse, attachment theory invites assumptions that may be wrong. Emphasising the prominence of dramatic action in attachment relationships, Jennings (2011, 23) points out a need to ensure "the embedding of the child's culture is available through a continuation of the dramatic development and process within social groups".

Culture and identity

Inevitably, our self-esteem and self-belief are affected by the context in which we are raised, the way we define identity and culture being subject to change in each context and generation (Gergen, 2009; Music, 2010, 2014). Just as inevitably, parents' attitudes have an impact on their children. Each culture has its own rules and understandings for acknowledging emotion. The culture of the Fulani in West Africa, for example, discourages the praising of children, and expression of all emotions (Montgomery, 2009, 57). In western culture it is frowned on for parents to ignore their children. Children's play is also affected by attitudes to gender – not least adults' toleration of boys' cheek and aggression whilst letting them off the domestic chores they expect of girls.

Adoptive and foster parents' attempts to gain emotional closeness with their children are easily thwarted by fear-based behaviours they experience to be rejecting. The culture of the birth family may be very different to the one the children are now experiencing. I encounter children accustomed to greater freedom railing against the rules and restrictions imposed by new parents to keep them safe. Some parents have confessed to me that the difference in their child's physical appearance was making it harder to feel an emotional connection to the child. A lack of emotional connection affects both them and their child's ability to correctly interpret non-verbal signals. For example, one parent experienced the child's eye rolling as criticism and rejection of them.

Whilst attachment theory recognises the concept of shame as a protective factor, Caw and Sebba (2014) point out that it may be something to avoid at all costs in cultures where eye contact is viewed as disrespectful – or where the conventions of saying "thank you" are not considered necessary for showing gratitude. Children who have never learned the social etiquette of table manners, picking up their litter or saying "please" and "thank you" can feel harshly judged for this social ineptitude. When the children's heritage differs from their caregivers', misunderstanding and mutual mistrust can arise. It is incumbent on the practitioner to learn about the mores and expectations of the families being served, and to contextualise the life story appropriately.

In Moore (2020) I refer to studies of ethology, neuroscience and anthropology, which reveal that the pleasure derived from play has long facilitated human survival and mental health. Indeed, the presence of play in all cultures is cited extensively in research (Music, 2010; Lancy, 2008). I find that explaining play's role in evolution (e.g. to provide practice for relationships) encourages these parents to reflect more empathetically on the sources of their children's problems. Particular sensitivity is needed to support parents who are unfamiliar with play and children who are delayed in emotional development.

A humanistic approach

Humanism respects each individual. Adoptive and foster parents who feel rejected by their child may interpret the expression of rage as malicious, or the child's retreat as intent to avoid them. They require help to appreciate the sheer effort their traumatised child is making, but the parents also need to be respected for their efforts. The children, too, need to experience empathy and compassion in order to learn to trust and attach safely. But emotions are expressed differently within different cultures. Moreover, children are rarely able to explain their fear-based reactions, especially when stemming from pre-verbal or traumatic memory (Perry & Hambrick, 2008). The benefit of creative arts is their facilitation of relaxation. The safety of fictional distance mirrors the nurturing mother–infant relationship that abused children missed.

Rationale for focus on the life story

Children's dependence on stories about their birth family for sense of self and security is noted (Moore, 2012; 2020; Rose, 2012, 2017). The loss of these stories leaves children confused about who they are and where they came from. Some wish they had been born to the adoptive parent, perhaps to avoid the humiliation of having been given away. As Weber and Haen (2005, p.233) advise, the practitioner's task is to reframe their negative beliefs about why they are being raised in this family; I find, along with Marin, Bohanek and Fivush (2008), that this is most effectively achieved by helping the parents to make sense of what had happened to their children.

Rebuilding identity through story

Identity develops initially from our family relationships, through the stories we hear and those we construct about ourselves (Moore, 2012). These stories build on our beliefs, intentions, purposes, hopes, ambitions, values, mores, dreams, visions and commitment to particular ways of living. In a therapeutic context, as Bruner et al., (1976, 3) observe, "Storytelling performs the dual cultural functions of making the strange familiar and ourselves private and distinctive". The creating of stories (both fictional and from real life), applying the "Storying Spiral" (Moore, 2019, 2020), is central to the Theatre of Attachment approach.

In the course of creative play children learn something new and possible about their capacities. Stories are also an effective way to validate the culture the child was born into. Still, as Killick (2014, 46) notes, cultural obstacles can get in the way of using stories therapeutically. A story created by a child may present as a re-enactment of other fiction, its psychological relevance obscure to the parent, who thinks the child is merely copying something they've seen. They ask me, "How do we know they're not making things up?" Yet if children relate to a theme they instinctively connect with, their extracting from other fictions need not invalidate their story. I find that children, like adults, are often drawn to stories which somehow illustrate their real-life experience. The practitioner can encourage the child to find a satisfying ending whereby the brave protagonist resolves their dilemmas and enjoys a satisfactory outcome.

Emotional expression

An emphasis of Theatre of Attachment practice is on noticing and responding sensitively to non-verbal interactions, their importance noted by Olsen-Morrison (2017, 174) in his observations of work with survivors of trauma. It is not always easy to accurately interpret non-verbal feelings and experience. After all we do not always express our thoughts and feelings and may not wish to disclose our reasons for this. Certainly, young children often express themselves more adroitly through action that is more expressive than mere words. What is unspoken or unsayable such as fear, silence or tears is as important as what is said. That said, emotions are expressed differently in different cultures, so caution needs to be exercised in their interpretation.

This emphasises the importance for practitioners to be familiar with cultural forms of expression being used by the families they are helping. A benefit of creating stories with the children is that the themes that repeatedly arise from the stories often reveal the children's pre-occupations and fears, thereby informing the attendant adults of the kind of reassurance the child needs.

Ritual and ceremony

In the transitional process between birth family, temporary foster home and permanent family, children can be left with a sense of existing in society's margins, particularly if experiencing a different culture. Rituals and ceremonies can be a valuable means of integrating children into a new family and culture. Rituals, after all, carry a message of order, continuity and prediction. Theatre has its traditional rituals to ease transition between the play and everyday reality, such as the rise and fall of the stage curtain that reminds us we will survive the experience however frightening the place of "make-believe" might be (Jennings, 1995). The combining of rituals and ceremonies can be deeply meaningful (Van Gennep, 1960; Turner, 1969). In Theatre of Attachment practice, trees, water and candles serve as symbols of strength, love, endurance and identity (Moore, 2012, 2020). Ceremonious rituals, with lighted candles for example, enable a dramatic sharing of memories and feelings. Such experience calms the children's fear of being overcome by their feelings or others' reaction to them.

Applying the Theatre of Attachment model

The co-creation and dramatisation of life stories begins with the collaborative telling of a mutually agreed narrative of the child's history that combines the information from official files with the child's memories. These narratives both from real life and fictional representations of it are processed in dramatic play. The presence of the adoptive (and foster) parents as participants in play enables the children to recreate their identity as heroic survivors. Costumes and other sensory materials invite the children to try out new ways of being and resolve issues impeding their relationships (Moore, 2012, 2020).

Case example: Joel aged 13

Joel's ethnicity is Black Caribbean (father)/White Irish (mother). His birth parents met in a hostel for young people with mental illness. The birth father's ethnicity was not confirmed since Joel's mother kept changing the information she gave. A DNA test indicated some White European ancestry but Joel has sickle cell traits and his skin and hair suggest African/Caribbean heritage.

Case history

Joel's birth mother having been abused throughout her childhood had acute mental ill health and addiction to illegal drugs and alcohol. Joel was removed when he was 5 days old to the foster care of a Black Caribbean family. At 10 months old he was placed with his adoptive parents, the mother White British and father, Malaysian-Eurasian. This father began to drink heavily and left the family when Joel was 7 years old. Following their divorce the couple communicated through solicitors or through Joel, who regularly spent time with his father. When Joel began to ask why he was adopted, his father alleged that he, Joel, had been conceived from rape. He was still drinking and as a lawyer, had high expectations, which Joel struggled to meet so began to see less of his father. The history indicates that foetal alcohol intake was likely to be affecting Joel, who was behind his age group and suffered bullying until he was moved to another school. As he became more insistent to know about the circumstances of his birth family and how he came to be adopted, Joel and his mother were referred for 10 hours of life story therapy.

Reaction to life story

On inspecting the life map I had drawn of houses Joel had lived in, he added his friend's house and a garage where they played. The map became the backdrop for enacting scenes from his life story. Joel engaged in this process with immense enthusiasm. He had many questions about his mother's circumstances (of childhood abuse) her subsequent actions and decisions. All his questions and my answers were recorded in Joel's book along with his stories, memories and thoughts about it. We talked about why it had not been possible to establish his paternity. Joel guessed that his birth father described himself as Caucasian, and suspected this was from a desire to fit in. He went on to talk of his feelings towards his adoptive mother's partners and friends.

The following week we replayed Joel's life story via a game, in which water represents love that flows until blocked by pain. Joel made clay figures of his birth parents, which he thumped for not having realised the implications of what they were doing. Supported by his mother's acceptance of his feelings Joel realised that his birth dad, at the age of 16, would have been far too immature to be willing to admit responsibility for having made Joel's birth mother pregnant. Joel then made another clay figure, which he thumped to punish the man who hurt his birth mother when she was a vulnerable child.

In the final session, a ceremony was held as a means of saying goodbye to the past. Each lighted candle represented a person in Joel's life. Invited to speak to the candles. Joel found himself unable to think of anything to say to his "birth parent" candles other than "Hello". We talked about the legacy these parents had given him – a life, the ability to jump on the trampoline, run, swim, learn at school and his propensity to be kind to others. We agreed it was a shame they had to let someone else bring up their child. His adoptive mum remarked that raising Joel had made her life worthwhile. Joel lit candles for the foster family and thanked them for having looked after him. More candles were lit for the adoptive family. Joel told his mother that he really loved her and wished his father could be more open, less inclined to create conflict. Joel then lit candles for friends, relatives and a (dead) pet dog he still misses. He enjoyed a nurturing activity of decorating biscuits, which we shared out.

Themes emerging from play

Rules: Having arranged toy figures in the sand tray Joel created a story on the themes of what young people of his age group are or are not allowed to do.

Rebirth: From making clay figures, Joel developed a story about changing relationships, betrayal, death and subsequent rebirth. This is a common theme for adopted children, whereby the characters must "die" – be disposed of – in order to contrive rebirth and renewal and start afresh.

Black v White: In one story that Joel enacted, rival gangs learn to appreciate each other's differences. The hero's obtaining the services of a professional doctor to mend his team presented as a metaphor for the therapeutic process.

Trust v mistrust: In Joel's story "Solving Problems" he explored how to establish trustworthiness of others and how to rate the calibre of friendships.

Strength v weakness: Play with puppets led to a story set in the jungle, where creatures competed at somersaulting, flips etc. This led to spontaneous demonstration of Joel's skills on the trampoline. Joel drew several superhero figures, which presented as symbols of the power he craves for himself.

Survival: In Joel's story, superheroes enjoy Parkour (activities of running, jumping and somersaults) and survive danger. We listed the superhero characteristics he most admired – of being realistic, aware of who and what is around and behind you, also of helping anyone in difficulty.

Safety: Following a row in which Joel's father had backed him against his mother (thereby undermining her authority), I invited Joel to create a "safe space" to keep in mind when he felt under stress. Joel chose from a selection of fabrics to create what he described as a fort for "The Purple Hand Gang" and was really pleased with it. He told me he identified with the character Horrid Henry, who is naughty, mischievous and resourceful.

Stuck: Joel created a story about God's wish to control his pet dog, Goddess, to whom he gave the gift of speech. In this story, Goddess soon forgets the gift and just barks. God then tries to use the dog as a horse and they both die. James decided the moral of the story was "Don't try to use your dog as a horse". The story presented as a processing of Joel's relationship with his adoptive father and of accommodating to different rules that he found tricky to navigate. Joel declared his reluctance to stay at his father's any longer than the agreed time, but his father often asked him to stay an extra night. His dad being easily offended made it hard for Joel to express his preference to be at home with his mum. I encouraged Joel to practice assertiveness and recognise his entitlement to and responsibility for his way of thinking. Joel thought of things to say like, "Actually I'm a teenager now and I've made my decision".

Development

Joel engaged with immense enthusiasm in exploring his life story and using creative play to address the various conflicts preoccupying him. Supported by his mother, he was able to be open about how he was feeling both to her, her partners and his father. Joel examined his peers' motivations for behaving in particular ways and his own need to understand these motivations in order to sustain friendships. During the course of the intervention Joel was very proud to gain an award from his new school for his efforts in every subject. The process of storytelling enabled him to find ways to manage conflict and gain more confidence in his creativity, problem-solving abilities and his right to his opinions. Joel stated that he better understood his life story and felt the storytelling and plays had helped him reconcile to his identity as an adoptee.

Evaluation

Joel's mother attended every session. She was emotionally supportive, helping him to ask questions and ensuring he understood our answers. She displayed flexibility in encouraging Joel to develop his ideas in play. In their evaluation Joel's mother felt the life story therapy had been especially helpful for clarifying the reasons for their having chosen Joel, who had come to terms with his status as an adoptee. Joel's self-esteem improved and both of them expressed their appreciation of the life story folder with its collection of his stories. The therapy reinforced his adoptive mother's confidence in parenting Joel and Joel's capacity to take responsibility and be more independent.

Case example: Layla, aged 10

Background

Layla has a White English mother and Black Caribbean father. He had no relationship with Layla, having been only briefly involved with her mother. Addicted to hard drugs, her mother had frequently been in prison. At birth, Layla suffered drug withdrawal and spent her early weeks in an incubator. At 3 weeks of age, she was taken from hospital to a (White English) foster carer. Layla had an older (White English) half-sister, who lived with their maternal grandparents. These grandparents decided they were too old to take on another child. Layla had grown up convinced that her (White) birth mother and grandparents had given her up because she was "Black", despite her adoptive parents' attempts to reassure her that this had not been the case

Layla's adoptive family had multiple heritages. The mother's ethnicity was African-Caribbean and father's Caucasian-Chinese and African-Caribbean (with Caucasian appearance). Living in a predominantly White English area, they had 2 sons aged 4 and 6 years at the time they adopted Layla aged 9 months. Three years later they had another son. At the time of the life story intervention, the sons were aged 16, 14 and 7 years. The goal was to secure Layla's placement. Ten hours of direct work took place weekly with Layla and her mother, and a few more hours with her siblings and parents.

Presenting issues

The 3 main problems that prompted referral were:

(1) Layla's behaviour towards 2 of her brothers, and with younger children, which was perceived as sexualised and causing the family to feel isolated;
(2) Layla's intense jealousy of her younger brother;
(3) Layla's unwillingness to talk to her parents, which made it difficult for them to understand her needs.

It transpired that Layla's behaviour towards the other children was merely that of a curious 4-year-old who wanted to know what private parts look like. As it seemed likely that the arrival of her youngest brother, who was favoured by the parents, had confirmed for Layla that she was no longer "good enough" I met with each of the brothers separately to help them understand Layla's history, her anxieties and struggling self-esteem. This enabled them to recognise their sister's feelings of estrangement. In response they increased their efforts to involve her in their activities and Layla soon felt more included.

Layla's adoptive mother was initially reserved and somewhat wary. Sharing my own encounter of intolerance (for my English accent, when I was living in Scotland) encouraged her to openly share inhibiting experiences of everyday racism, such as of being stared at threateningly, being followed by security officers round stores and frequently ignored in the checkout queue. This mother confessed that she felt threatened by the expression in Layla's eyes. Possibly it reminded her subconsciously of the racist humiliation that she encountered so regularly. She had trained her children to "rise above" racial taunts and sensed that Layla had been feeling left out. The mother's growing recognition of the value of creative play for enabling Layla to process her feelings brought them closer and enhanced their relationship.

Reaction to the life history

Layla's adoptive mother was present throughout the intervention. We began with play and towards the end of the first session I read the life history to explain the facts in her files. Layla remarked that hearing this made her feel "much better" as if "something had changed". She expressed regret at not having believed her adoptive parents' previous explanations. Each week the life story was explored via various techniques. It started with a life map of places Layla had lived and was followed by the water game (described above). Although Layla was sad that her birth mother was addicted to drugs, she expressed relief that her mum had wanted to keep her baby and just not been capable of this. Layla began to speculate that her (birth) mother and grandmother were still yearning to see her. To explore her assumptions and fantasies and help her gain a better understanding, we held a play of the life story. I took the roles of birth mother and grandmother. The adoptive mother acted as nurse, neighbour and social worker. Layla took the roles of police officer and judge. Her adoptive mother and I guided Layla as to the conversations likely to have taken place. In her role as judge, Layla interviewed (me as) her birth mother and grandmother and gained answers to the questions preoccupying her.

Themes arising in creative play

Whilst it was important to encourage Layla to learn about her history, I started by inviting imaginative play with the sand tray and toy figures, in order to explore her perceptions and take notice of which coping strategies she relied on. Layla told a story of a farmer "learning her lesson". It began with the farmer disguising herself as a vet so she could exchange her animals for better ones owned by her kindly, successful neighbour. (This metaphor indicated Layla's view of herself as the "impostor" in her family, in which everyone else was more deserving than her. The dishonest farmer's admission of guilt seemed to symbolise Layla's sense of self-blame). The story ends with the richer neighbour inviting the farmer to collaborate, share stock. Their becoming friends suggested Layla's wish to be better integrated in her family.

Layla developed stories, which revealed her anxiety about being perceived as predatory and as having un-containable impulses. As Cyrulnik (2010) observes, children repress feelings to avoid the disapproval they expect. Creating clay figures of the adoptive family led to a story about a family adventure. Yet Layla needed lots of persuasion to find any heroic role to represent her. Encouragingly, she eventually decided she had the ability to "calm everyone down". Layla's positive identification with such a maternal role indicated her desire to model on her adoptive mother. She moved on to creating collages. Her adoptive mother recognised that having interested adults "hang on" the child's every word replicated the early attachment dance (Stern, 1985), which provides infants with a valuable sense of self-worth.

Outcome

From the start of this intervention Layla was appropriate in her interactions with her brothers. She began to play with them and to show self-assurance. Layla also began to talk to her mother when she had worrying feelings. She joined a cricket team and attended a holiday camp. On return to school after the summer holiday, Layla's enhanced self-confidence led her to join 3 special interest groups and sign up for a residential trip. Her adoptive parents declared feeling far more competent in their parenting of her. Layla's self-perception changed from feeling unloved and excluded to feeling wanted and entitled to membership of her adoptive family, who now felt more closely bonded. Enjoying the variety of materials for play alongside the exploration of her life history empowered Layla to find new ways of being and responding.

Conclusions

Eleven themes emerged from the PhD on this practice (Moore, 2018), as follows:

(1) Reframing the children's life story reduces propensity for self-blame;
(2) Theatre and rituals to replicate mother–infant attachment dances;
(3) Use of role – to practice new, healthier ways of being;
(4) Safety – of the home setting and of fictional distance;
(5) Sensory experience – to supplement missed nurture;
(6) Joy in transformation, which enhances children's self-belief;
(7) Play as practice for life and to provide enjoyment;
(8) Collaboration with parents and involved practitioners;
(9) Repetition to rebuild neural pathways;
(10) Role-modelling empathy to model ways of being in relationships;
(11) Creating stories enables positive reconstruction of identity.

An important aspect of the practitioner's use of self is that of flexibility, which involves taking the role of stage manager to control the boundaries of play – for example, deciding when to move it forward; supporting participants as needed. On feeling listened to, valued, respected and appreciated, participants become more compassionate and self-reflective. The fictional context of play lends the privacy to achieve these goals by reducing the fear of failure. I am reminded of Jennings' (1994) observation that, "Healing comes about when communication with 'other'…is a culmination of our dramatic imagination and performance structures within dramatic reality" (p. xxviii).

For Joel and Layla's families, among many others, heritage was just one dimension of a complex prism of issues of which the practitioner needs to be aware without being overly distracted from addressing the whole picture. Play, stories, rituals and ceremonies served to validate both their past and present experience. The creative activities proved effective for helping vulnerable children to become more integrated into the culture and ways of being of their adoptive families and to thereby build stronger, more positive identities as they gained self-confidence and the all-important sense of belonging.

References

Bruner, J., Jolly, A., and Sylva, K. (1976) *Play – its Role in Development and Evolution*, New York, Basic Books.
Caw, J., and Sebba, J. (2014) *Team Parenting for Children in Foster Care; A Model for Integrated Therapeutic Care*, London, Jessica Kingley.
Cyrulnik, B. (2010) *The Whispering of Ghosts: Trauma and Resilience*, New York, Other Press.
Etherington K. (2009) Life story research: A relevant methodology for counsellors and psychotherapists. *Counselling and Psychotherapy Research: Linking research with practice* 9, p. 4. https://onlinelibrary.wiley.com/doi/abs/10.1080/14733140902975282

Gergen, K. (2009) *An Invitation to Social Construction*, California: Sage.
Howe, D. (2005) *Child Abuse and Neglect: Attachment Development and Intervention*, Basingstoke: Palgrave Macmillan.
Jennings S. (1994) *Theatre, Ritual and Transformation: The Senoi Temiars*, London, Routledge.
Jennings S. (1995) *Dramatherapy with Children and Adolescents*, London, Jessica Kingsley.
Jennings, S. (2011) *Healthy Attachments and Neurodramatic Play*, London, Jessica Kingsley.
Killick S. (2014) A play on words: helping foster carers build attachments and create meaning through storytelling, *Child and Family Clinical Psychology Review*, The British Psychological Society, 2: pp. 45–52.
Lancy, D. (2008) *The Anthropology of Childhood: Cherubs, Chattels and Changelings*, Cambridge: Cambridge University Press.
Levine, P., and New, R. (eds) (2008) *Anthropology and Child Development: A Cross-Cultural Reader*, Oxford: Blackwell Publishing.
Marin, K. A., Bohanek, J. G., and Fivush, R. (2008) Positive effects of talking about the negative: Family narratives of negative experiences and preadolescents' perceived competence, *Journal of Research on Adolescence*, 18: pp. 573–593.
McCulloch, E., and Mathura, A. (2019) A comparison between a Neuro-Physiological Psychotherapy (NPP) Treatment group and a control group for children adopted from care: support for a neurodevelopmentally informed approach to therapeutic intervention with maltreated children, *Child Abuse and Neglect*, 97: November 2019, https://doi.org/10.1016/j.chiabu.2019.104128.
McMurray, I., Connolly, H., Preston-Shoot, M., and Wigley, V. (2010) Shards of the old looking glass: Restoring the significance of identity in promoting positive outcomes for looked-after children, child and family, *Social Work*, 16, 2: pp. 210–218.
Montgomery, H. (2009) *An Introduction to Childhood: Anthropological Perspectives on Children's Lives*, Chichester, Wiley Blackwell.
Moore J. (2012) *Once upon a Time…Stories and Drama to Use in Direct Work with Adopted and Fostered Children*, London: BAAF.
Moore, J. (2018) *Story and Drama with Adoptive and Foster Families in their home*, Unpublished PhD, Leeds Beckett University.
Moore, J. (2019) "The Storying Spiral": A narrative dramatic approach to life story therapy with adoptive/foster families and traumatised children, *International Journal of Play*, 8, 3: pp. 1–15.
Moore, J. (2020) *Narrative and Dramatic Approaches to Children's Life Story with Adoptive, Foster and Kinship Families*, London, Routledge.
Music, G. (2010) *Nurturing Natures: Attachment and Children's Emotional, Sociocultural and Brain Development*, East Sussex, Routledge.
Music, G. (2014) *The Good Life: Wellbeing and the New Science of Altruism, Selfishness and Immorality*, East Sussex, Routledge.
Olsen-Morrison, D. (2017) Integrative play therapy with adults with complex trauma: A developmentally-informed approach, *International Journal of Play Therapy*, 26, 3: pp.172–183.
Perry, B. D. (2012) Introduction to R. Rose, *Life Story Therapy with Traumatised Children*, London, Jessica Kingsley, p. 10.
Perry, B. D., and Hambrick, E. P. (2008) The neurosequential model of therapeutics, *Fall*, 17, 3: pp. 39–43, [Online]. Available at: https://eric.ed.gov [Accessed 20.09.17].
Perry, B. D., and Szalavitz, M. (2008 ed.) *The Boy Who Was Raised as a Dog and Other Tales from a Child Psychiatrist's Notebook: What Traumatised Children Can Teach Us About Love, Loss and Healing*, New York: Basic Books.
Porges, S. W. (2015) Making the world safe for our children: Down regulating defence and up-regulating social engagement to "optimise" the human experience, *Children Australia*, 40, 2: pp. 114–123.
Rose, R. (2012) *Life Story Therapy with Traumatised Children*, London: Jessica Kingsley.
Rose, R. (ed.) (2017), Foreword by D. D. Gray, *Innovative Therapeutic Life Story Work: Developing Trauma-informed Practice for Working with Children, Adolescents and Young Adults*, London: Jessica Kingsley.
Rosenthal, G. (2003) The healing effects of storytelling: On the curative effects of storytelling in the context of research and counselling, *Qualitative Inquiry*, 9, 6: pp. 915–933.
Rushton, A. (2010) Thinking on developmental psychology in fostering and adoption, *Adoption & Fostering; BAAF*, 34: pp. 38–43.
Schofield, G., and Beek, M. (2014) *The Secure Base Model: Promoting Attachment in Foster Care and Adoption*, London: BAAF.
Stern, D. (1985) *The Interpersonal World of the Infant*, New York, Basic Books.

Turner, V. (1969) *The Ritual Process, Structure and Anti-structure*, London: Penguin.
UNICEF (1991) *United Nations Convention on the Rights of the Child*, Svenska: UNICEF, Kommitten.
Van Gennep (1960) *The Rites of Passage*, London: Routledge.
Weber, C., and Haen, A. (2005) *Clinical Applications of Drama Therapy in Child and Adolescent treatment*, Hove: Brunner-Routledge.
Wilkinson, J., and Bowyer, S. (2017) *The impacts of abuse and neglect on children; and comparisons of different placement options: Evidence review*, Department for Education (DfE) March 2017.

33
FOSTERING STORYTELLERS
Helping foster carers to build attachments and enhance emotional literacy through stories and oral storytelling

Steve Killick

Introduction

Using stories is well established in the area of working with foster carers and children who are looked after and this is mainly in two defined areas; Life Story Work, which is often used with Children Looked After (CLA) to help give them a clearer picture of their past and help them understand the impact of what has happened in the past upon their present, and Therapeutic Story Making, where stories are constructed to help children deal with trauma, understand themselves or boost their self-image and understanding through coherent and sensitive narratives. Both these applications are important and powerful interventions but storytelling, particularly oral storytelling, has a lot more to offer, especially to foster carers seeking to build relationships and a positive learning environment for the children in their care. Both Life Story Work and Therapeutic Story Work lie, on the whole, within the domain of work that professionals such as social workers and therapists carry out. This, however, omits the role that foster carers can play. Storytelling is an activity that is easily available for foster carers to carry out, involves minimal cost and can be adapted for all ages. It has the benefits of helping build both safety and playfulness between foster carers and CLA and also is a natural tool for learning, especially about feelings – an area which is often difficult for children who have experienced developmental trauma.

It is generally accepted that CLA tend to achieve poorer educational outcomes (Berridge, 2012; Social Exclusion Unit, 2003) due to multiple factors such as adverse impacts of trauma, placement instability, mental health needs and time out of school. To help address these situations there has been therapeutic emphasis on relational aspects based on attachment theory and development. Also, there has been interest in how creative arts and cultural experiences can contribute to emotional health and wellbeing and help young children who have experienced care achieve better outcomes (Department for Education and Skills, 2006). Given this background there was a clear rationale for helping foster carers realise that storytelling could be an important way of building relationships by creating a space for carer and child (or children) to enjoy spontaneous storytelling. Many foster carers, of course, regularly use storytelling but often do not appreciate the full benefits that storytelling brings. A need was identified in Wales, UK to help support foster carers in gaining a deeper understanding of the importance of creating strong attachments, and for understanding the impact of early experience on later development and how to help it. It was proposed that training in storytelling could help meet this need. This led to a series of one-day workshops, initially supported by the Fostering Network and later by several other organisations, to encourage foster carers to use stories and storytelling to build relationships and assist learning.

The rationale for this made a distinction between stories and storytelling. Stories are, of course, attractive to children and easily engage their interest. They also appeal to adults, often in the form of written fiction and drama on TV, cinema or stage. Engaging with and enjoying stories in their various forms is a universal human behaviour (Oatley, 2011) and they are social artefacts often carrying important cultural values. Oral storytelling – that is, one person relating a story to another or others in a 'live' context – is an age-old way of communicating stories which is always unique, interactive and communal and it is to this type of storytelling that this chapter refers, as opposed to reading stories aloud. However, storytelling is now often seen as a more trivial activity perhaps better suited to younger children. Although it might be valued for the pleasure it gives it might be seen as a lesser form of communication than reading, although the storytelling revival has challenged this view. There is a renewed interest in oral storytelling, particularly traditional storytelling in performance, academia and health and education over the last 30 years.

As a psychologist and storyteller, I had been interested in how stories and storytelling could play a role in developing emotional literacy in schools (Thomas & Killick, 2007) and how it can build attachments and facilitate learning in families (Frude & Killick, 2011). Lacher, Nichols and May (2012) had developed interventions using narratives and story making to help parents of adopted children form stronger and closer relationships with children and use stories to help them overcome trauma and feel wanted. Although a powerful model it also demanded commitment and intensive training. The opportunities for the latter especially are difficult for foster carers, who have many demands on their time, and there are competitive demands on training requirements.

A rationale for a series of workshops for foster carers to explore and encourage the use of storytelling was developed. These workshops have now been run all over the UK to encourage the frequent use of stories and storytelling in foster care situations. This chapter describes the ethos and values of the intervention, exploring the areas of the 'the tale, the telling and the talk' and examples of the content of the workshops. Finally some of the outcomes of the workshops and the foster carers experiences are described.

The underlying values – safety and playfulness

The ethos and values of the workshops were that storytelling should be a daily part of life at home, featuring both personal and fantastical stories, and they should be shared in a way that encapsulates both playfulness and safety. These aspects of safety and playfulness are fundamental to secure attachment, where the child has a secure base from which to go out and explore the wider world, often through play, and in so doing build skills, developing competence and mastery. The child also has a safe place to return should the world become threatening or unsafe. In the storytelling place the emphasis is not on fixing or remediating of problems but on a joyful, interactive and spontaneous experience that enhances relationships and positive emotions. Like play, it is done not for an outcome but for its own sake. But also, like play, engaging in it brings many beneficial effects. Storytelling has 'general' benefits such as developing listening skills, vocabulary, imagination, memory and emotional understanding. It provides the opportunity for scaffolding around learning and a positive interactional experience. These benefits accrue when storytelling is a frequent activity, as opposed to a one-off or exceptional event. General effects might be seen in contrast to the 'specific' effects of hearing a story that makes someone think or feel differently, such as is intended in a 'therapeutic story'. Perhaps, the greatest benefit would be that if children heard enough stories they would become storytellers themselves through having something to say and learning how to say it. The confidence gained through this would further increase their confidence that they have something to say and also in finding their own voice. Indeed, there were many reports of children hearing stories and going on to tell those stories with other family members, especially younger children.

The gains of these frequent playful storytelling events have a paradoxical effect. As noted, the nature of play is something done for its own sake yet it is essential for healthy child development. It enables the child to develop skills and a sense of mastery. It also allows the child to understand the world by manipulating and testing it in the imaginative domain. When an adult structures play, and telling a story and interacting around the story is a form of structured play, it gives permission for the child to explore the world. Storytelling is an imaginary playroom and stories increase the child's stock of knowledge about the world (Frude & Killick, 2011). Stories also contain darkness and negative thoughts, actions and emotions. These can be examined and possibly resolved, safely aided by the adult's experience and care for the child. One of the powerful reasons for storytelling to all children is that it can help them understand difficult emotional categories such as sadness, anxiety and anger and begin to learn strategies for dealing with them. A child who feels safe and secure can experience something fearful in a story as exciting. They are also learning about the feelings and strategies for dealing with them. If you have no understanding of difficult emotions then managing them is harder. Children who may have experienced developmental trauma or inadequate adult support may lack a basic emotional vocabulary or rapidly dysregulate. An adult when telling is able to modify and moderate the emotional intensity of the story, thus helping to keep it safe. The playfulness of storytelling contributes to the safety and the spirit is 'being there to have fun together'. Safety is also created through the narrative structure of beginning, middle and (mostly happy) endings, as well as through the attachment relationship with the presence of an adult able to keep the child's emotional state in mind and regulate their own emotions. Indeed, it provides an opportunity for the co-regulation of emotions where the adult can gently 'scaffold' the child's emotional experience through empathy and naming of the emotion.

Stories also work through metaphor; an ogre, dragon or wolf can symbolise all sorts of powers or difficulties which can also be outwitted, out-fought, defeated or transformed. Storytelling can work through subconscious or symbolic processes.

A model was developed which helped foster carers understand how storytelling can be useful to children – particularly those with attachment difficulties. This model categorised three elements of the storytelling activity that could benefit children with attachment difficulties; this was the content of the 'tale' or story, the process of 'telling' directly (as opposed to the story being read by the child or adult) and the 'talk' or interaction that might take place before, during and after a story. This analysis of 'the tale, the telling and the talk' became known as the 'Talen' model as this old Anglo-Saxon word was the etymological root of the three terms. As these three aspects of storytelling were central to the workshops they are discussed in more detail now.

The tale – content

A story can be delivered in many ways; it can be told face to face, it can be read or watched on a screen. A story is a structured narrative that usually concerns the tackling of some kind of difficulty facing a protagonist. A story can be an account of actual events such as personal, family or community histories. This definition also includes children's literature. It might include stories made up and created by children and adults in play together. All these types of stories were valued and special emphasis was given to traditional stories – stories that have emerged from continually telling and retelling– as they have particular benefits. What distinguishes these stories from other types of narrative is, as well as the narrative structure of beginning, middle and end, the emotional and metaphorical richness they contain. Stories are packed full of image, symbol and metaphor and are invariably concerned with human relationships and overcoming some difficulty or achieving a need – for instance defeating the 'threat' of a monster, finding a partner in life or a more 'everyday' story of dealing with a difficult person. Part of the appeal of stories is that they engage us emotionally (Oatley, 2011) and a story will often feature several emotional moments such as fear, sadness, anger and happiness in various degrees. Oatley described this as a process of experiencing emotions in response to a story in which we engaged as 'affect attunement' and also noted that in a sense the story is a 'simulacrum' in that we are not experiencing the emotion in reality. For instance, if a loved character in a story dies, we do not experience actual grief, but our emotional responses are simulated and its similarity to the actual experience helps us to understand it better. It may of course reflect our own experiences and bring them to mind. Stories are a natural way of communicating about human experience and learning about the nature of emotion, thinking especially of our internal dialogue, motivation and intention, choices, actions and consequences. That stories so easily make sense of these aspects of our experience, are so essential for understanding ourselves and others, makes them helpful for children in learning the domains of emotional literacy, awareness and regulation of emotion, motivation, empathy and social skills. To help foster carers reflect on these themes, we would explore stories such as *Harry Potter* or the Grimms' version of *Cinderella*, as how these apparently fantastical stories also explicitly talk about abusive family relationships, bullying, anger and loss. The fantasy element of these stories gives a degree of distance which can serve to make it safer to engage in the stories.

The following exercises are examples of activities used in workshops to help foster carers think about the content of the stories in terms of emotions, themes and messages implicit or explicit in the story. As the areas of content, process and reflection often overlapped, the exercises often can be used for exploring other areas also.

Your favourite movie or book

This was often used as an ice breaker or introduction game and involved asking participants to introduce themselves by telling the group about a film or book that has a particular resonance or meaning for them. It might just be something they enjoy a lot or turn to at a particular time. It may be something that is important now or at any stage of their lives including childhood. This exercise sets the tone for the day.

Listening to a story

A traditional story is told and then explored by the listeners in pairs and the group as a whole. This exercise gives participants the chance to experience listening to a tale as an adult – something that most may not have experienced. They are then asked to reflect in pairs on what went through their minds as they listened, how they reacted to the story and what emotional moments they noticed – what pulled them into the story and what may have pushed them out. Major points to emerge from this exercise are how the mind is very active in listening to the story and stimulates visual pictures in response to the story and searches for meaning. Interesting group discussions typically emerge. Some foster carers seek out stories that have particular meanings or morals, such as 'don't steal' or 'don't play with fire'. However, we emphasise not using stories because they have a particular moralistic message. This can be perceived as another form of control – rather, tell many stories and let listeners find their own meanings, which they may or may not want to share.

We have used many stories but found stories like *The Snow-Tiger's Whisker* (adapted from Estes, 1992, and Cabral, 1994) to be very useful in helping foster carers grasp some of the emotional struggles children might face. The latter story tells of a young boy whose mother dies; his father looks after him but remarries. Now there are three in the house and the boy has a 'new mother' he feels confused, angry at the new arrival and at his father. The mother tries to care for him but the boy rejects her. After she tries to make him eat he pushes her away, which leads to a quest to repair the relationship. This story is explored with reference to how it articulates the different emotions of loss, grief, fear of new relationships and power between parents and children. The story articulates these emotions and offers the opportunity for them to be explored, if the child chooses.

Childhood memories of stories

If the group has established a degree of safety it can be a powerful exercise to ask participants to silently reflect on their own experiences of stories and storytelling from their own childhood. This might be books they enjoyed or experiences of being told stories. Experiences are then reflected on in small groups, then brought to the large group to share. This exercise can bring powerful stories of childhood and the role of stories as being a place of sanctuary and escape from reality or how figures and incidents in stories can evoke powerful emotions. It often helps participants' awareness of how powerful stories can be. It can also bring memories of family members and who was telling stories, which moves into the interpersonal aspects of storytelling.

The telling – the process

If stories, particularly written ones, help those who engage with them to learn about thoughts, feelings and the world about them, these benefits are likely to be increased dramatically when the transmission is interactive. Zipes (1995) argued that just listening to stories developed children's oral and cognitive skills. By telling stories, especially in ways that are dynamic and spontaneous, where the teller can modulate and moderate their telling depending on the listeners' engagement, listeners will have an increased effect of affect attunement. The teller can directly engage with the listener, checking for understanding and helping assist learning. Storytelling can be a pleasurable time together where both parties can enjoy the story. The child can join in both verbally and physically with refrains and actions. Most importantly, the adult can intensify the experience depending on the mainly non-verbal feedback from the child, such as laughter, smiling and eye-contact. Here storytelling can be clearly seen as an attachment-building behaviour. As the adult and child or children experience the story together, they are engaging in an 'intersubjective' experience where affect attunement and shared attention to the story and shared intention – usually enjoyment – are naturally and easily taking place (Killick & Boffey, 2012). The intersubjective elements of affect attunement, shared attention and intention are a key relationship-building skill that works across the age range, including adolescents

(Hughes, 2009a). As well as enhancing positive experiences these intersubjective experiences help develop language and feelings of self-worth. It is of value to all children, but of great benefit to children who have experienced developmental trauma and may have missed some of these crucial early developmental experiences.

Storytelling in families is often associated with bedtimes, where it is naturally associated with calming and helping the chid to sleep. This is one example of how stories can help with soothing and calming and is an opportunity for co-regulation of feelings (Gersie, 1992). But other opportunities can also be created: over mealtimes, car journeys, walks or the creation of special environments like dens or a regular time and place for stories. These are all times for the telling of stories or related activities such as singing, poetry or visualisations. In the participation and improvisation of stories more visual clues can be given around emotions. For instance, facial expression and tone of voice and the heightened prosody and gesture make emotional expression easier for the child and allow the adult to assess and respond to the child's emotional understanding. The telling is an improvisation with an attitude of playfulness and humour which children can respond to from their own level. There is evidence that reading stories aloud to children develops the attachment relationship (Blake & Maiese, 2008); however, this is not always appropriate with older children and teenagers. Oral storytelling can be adapted to any ages, including adolescents, who are often intrigued by the 'adult' content of fairy tales and other stories.

The following exercises explore storytelling experiences and develop skills in interactive storytelling.

Story swap

The group is divided into two and each sub-group is then told a different story. The group then learns the story using visualising and gestures that emphasise the improvisational and interactive nature of the stories. Short traditional tales such as *The Talking Tortoise* and *The Cracked Pot* that are easy to learn are used. Each person then finds a partner from the other group and they exchange stories. At the end they are encouraged to give each other positive feedback about their partner's telling, followed by a group discussion of how the stories can be used. The process is described more fully in Thomas and Killick (2007). A development from this is to have foster carers tell stories from a short text and participants are given a booklet with a number of easy to learn stories.

How was your day?

This is a group discussion that looks at the power of everyday personal stories. The example of how asking the question 'How was your day?' to children about their school day often leads to brief non-informative answers being given such as 'good' or 'fine'. This is contrasted with a carer telling a short anecdote from their day where they faced an obstacle or difficulty, particularly where they may have felt a difficult emotion. This often leads to the child telling an incident from their day, demonstrating the reciprocal nature of storytelling. Several carers have found this technique has had dramatic effects in how they talked with their children. The importance of remembering special or interesting events that have happened or significant family stories is discussed, and foster carers often have powerful examples of this. We also discuss and demonstrate how these stories can be co-constructed and told together and this is linked to the ideas of rich reminiscing (Reese, 2013) and story sharing (Grove, 2014).

Creating storytelling places

We discuss how storytelling can take place in many different environments and contexts. Bedtimes are obvious examples but often need consideration to make them safe for child and carer, and often the goal then is to settle rather than excite or engage the child. Situations like walks, car journeys, mealtimes, setting a special time or place such as making a den for storytelling are all opportunities for a shared storytelling experience. One foster carer gave an example that he had learnt from his father: at certain times he would produce his keyring and say each key represented a story and a child could choose one key and get that story. Also ideas such as riddles or objects could be used to prompt a story.

Visualisation – the mind's eye

Participants take a comfortable position where they can close their eyes and have to imagine a guided tour through their own house or a house they grew up in. This is an exercise to encourage visualisation and imagination skills. Visualisation is seen as a key skill in both telling and listening to stories, which can develop cognitive and memory skills in children and assist problem solving skills. Visualisation is seen as a key tool in 'The Storyteller's Toolkit'.

The talk – shared reflection and interaction

Storytelling is not a one-way activity with one person doing all the talking and another passively listening, but is a highly interactive experience that can sometimes even be slightly chaotic. A story can come out of a conversation and be reflected upon and discussed afterwards. Most importantly the story can be paused and discussed. The storyteller can ask questions such as 'What do you think they were feeling?', or the child can give opinions or ask questions. These opportunities for thinking and reflecting together are seen as critical to the process. We stress there are no right or wrong answers that the child can give, but these conversations are an opportunity for thinking. We emphasise that a story should not be told to make a child think in a certain way; rather, it is an opportunity for thinking.

These storytelling encounters enable the adult to take an attitude of safety, warmth and approval towards the child and we encourage foster carers to practise Playfulness, Acceptance, Curiosity and Empathy (PACE) during these times. The PACE approach, developed by Dan Hughes (2009b), echoes positive early interactions between carer and child. It can be used as an approach to help children who may have experienced early maltreatment to help build a stronger relationship with the carer, and develop emotional regulation and a more positive sense of self. It can play an essential part in helping the child manage their own behaviour. The storytelling context allows an opportunity to use these skills where behaviour is not a central concern. As already stated playfulness is a central feature of the storytelling experience and is characterised by rhythms, movements, laughter and fun. Both adult and child enjoy the story together and the adult also conveys the enjoyment of the child.

The child's responses, particularly emotional responses, can all be accepted. Storytelling offers a great opportunity to explore the feelings, thoughts, motivations and behaviours of the characters, which allows distance from talking about our own experiences. Of course, our perceptions are personal, of value, and need to be respected, as do personal reactions to the stories. There is no right or wrong way of understanding a story; it is our most personal responses that need acceptance, and in that acceptance the child experiences their viewpoints and their own self as validated and of value. The PACE approach is increasingly being taught to foster carers in the UK and using storytelling has been an effective way of introducing or reinforcing the approach and is central to its use.

Many of the previous exercises involve conversation stimulated by a story. These exercises develop this further.

Tell a story and watch what happens

'Tell a story and watch what happens' is a key principle that takes the carer away from having a predetermined outcome or expectation of what will happen during or after a story. Examples are discussed of child comments or actions to a story and then how a PACE attitude can help the carer respond.

Pair reflections

At any point a story may paused and participants asked to reflect on how they are responding to the story; emotional moments can be explored, which can lead to a discussion about the emotion itself and to what things the listeners have reacted, both positively and negatively, most strongly. What has the story said about family relationships? Pausing and reflecting on the story works best with longer stories with strong themes. The Grimm Brothers' version of *Cinderella* is often used with an emphasis on family relationships, bullying, loss, anger and grief. Themes that have emerged in discussions have included gender roles, happy endings, dealing with loss and death and advantages and disadvantages of clearly moral stories.

Dealing with disclosures

Child protection and safeguarding issues have not infrequently emerged in story times where children have disclosed something of their own troubled experience, often in response to a story. It is important to consider how to respond calmly and helpfully. Clearly following safeguarding procedures is important and there needs to be good communication with Social Services. Lacher et al. (2012) describe a number of ways that carers respond in a way that emphasises their care and connection to a child. For instance, to a child who described being left alone without food or supervision, a carer might say something like, 'If I had been with you, I would not have let that happen to you'. There are many sensitive issues and the importance of supervision and support for the carer here is important for safeguarding, as is using such incidents in ways that are helpful and therapeutic for the child.

Discussion

The workshops received positive feedback, both immediately afterwards and at follow-up. Participants were mostly self-selecting so may have been favourably disposed to such an approach. Many felt this work encouraged or rejuvenated work they were already doing and gave them ideas about more that they could do with it. It was generally seen as more therapeutic than much of their other training. There were many reports of children enjoying these times, one foster carer declaring that they 'had never felt so close' to the child in their care than when storytelling together. Male foster carers particularly felt that it gave them a specific role. There were reports of children going on to tell others, especially younger children, the stories they had heard. Two stories that emerged particularly demonstrated how telling stories made an impact. One carer described telling a child who had a troubled relationship with her birth mother the story of Rapunzel, a girl imprisoned in a tower by an over-protective and controlling witch. The child made the story central to her play and wanted the carer to act out the role of the witch. Positive and negative feelings emerged towards the mother/witch over several weeks before the child's interest in the story dissipated. A re-assessment by a therapist felt the girl had changed her ambivalent feelings towards her mother significantly over this period, possibly because of these storytelling play encounters. Another carer reported that a boy struggling with the transition to secondary school repeatedly watched the movie *How to Train your Dragon*. The carer noticed that the protagonist's difficulties of exclusion from peer group echoed the child's own. The carer introduced the book and storytelling around this, to help the child talk more about difficulties at school. The carer then felt that his relationship with the boy became close and he became more of a mentor and support.

More formal evaluation would certainly help support carers reports. Interest in the workshops led to storytelling skills being included in the 'Skills to Foster' training manual for all new foster carers (Fostering Network, 2014) and a web-based guide to storytelling for foster carers (Killick & Boffey, 2012). There are also many ways the intervention could be developed to help carers use storytelling sessions to integrate more approaches that could be helpful for the child. These would include using storytelling to help with language acquisition for the many CLA with speech delay, and could be based on the story-sharing technique developed by Nicola Grove (2014). Using rhythm and repetition and other physical activities could also be developed to help sensory processing and emotion regulation. As well as developing a basic emotional awareness, therapeutic strategies such as mindfulness could also be incorporated. There are then many possible ways of developing storytelling from a basic space for playfulness and safety between carer and child to incorporate many therapeutic activities. However, at its heart, the storytelling sessions remain an interactive space with direct human contact and this may be their most powerful therapeutic aspect. Such face-to-face and eye-to-eye contact remains a stark antidote to the many hours of screen time that is such a feature of many children's lives.

Acknowledgements: With thanks to Maria Boffey and the Fostering Network, Barnardo's and Prue Thimbleby and The Storytelling for Health International Conference, 2017, for their support of this project.

References

Berridge, D. (2012). Educating young people in care: What have we learned? *Children and Youth Services Review* 34, 6, 1171–1175.
Blake, J. & Maiese, N. (2008). No fairytale… The benefits of a bedtime story. *The Psychologist* 21, 5, 386–388.
Bombèr, L. M. (2007). *Inside I'm Hurting: Practical Strategies for Supporting Children*. Worth Pub.
Cabrel, L. (1994). The Lion's Whisker. In: *Ready-to-Tell Tales*. Eds. Holt, D. & Mooney, B. August House.
Department for Education and Skills (2006) *Care Matters: Transforming the Lives of Children and Young People in Care*. Norwich: HM Government.
Estes, C. P. (1992). *Women Who Run with the Wolves*. Rider.
Fostering Network, The (2014). *The Skills to Foster – Complete Course Pack*. The Fostering Network.
Frude, N. & Killick, S. (2011). Family storytelling and the attachment relationship. *Psychodynamic Practice* 17, 4, 441–455.
Gersie, A. (1992). *Earthtales – Storytelling in Times of Change*. Green Print.
Golding, K. (2014). *Using Stories to Build Bridges with Traumatized Children*. JKP.
Grove, N. (2014). *The Big Book of Storysharing*. Speechmark.
Hughes, D. (2009b). *Principles of Attachment-Focused Parenting: Effective Strategies to Care for Children*. Norton Pub.
Hughes, D. (2009a). Principles of attachment and intersubjectivity – still relevant in relating to teenagers. In Perry, A. (Ed) *Teenagers and Attachment – Helping Adolescents Engage with Life and Learning*. Worth Pub.

Killick, S., & Boffey, M. (2012). *Building Relationships Through Storytelling: A Foster Carer's Guide to Attachment and Stories.* The Fostering Network www.thefosteringnetwork.org.uk/sites/www.fostering.net/files/content/building-relationships-through-storytelling-31-10-12.pdf (Accessed 21 September 2019).

Lacher, D. Nicholls, T. Nicholls, M. & May, J. (2012). *Connecting with Kids through Stories – Using Narratives to Facilitate Attachment in Adopted Children.* JKP.

Oatley, K. (2011). *Such Stuff as Dreams – The Psychology of Fiction.* Wiley-Blackwell.

Reese, E. (2013). *Tell Me a Story – Sharing Stories to Enrich Your Child's World.* Oxford Publishing.

Social Exclusion Unit (2003). *A Better Education for Children in Care.* SEU. [online]. Available at: https://webarchive.nationalarchives.gov.uk/+/http:/www.cabinetoffice.gov.uk/media/cabinetoffice/social_exclusion_task_force/assets/publications_1997_to_2006/abefcic_summary_2.pdf (Accessed 27 August 2019).

Thomas, T. & Killick, S. (2007). *Telling Tales as Emotional Literacy.* EPS.

Zipes, J. (1995) *Creative Storytelling – Building Community, Changing Lives.* Routledge.

34
THE POWER OF STORYTELLING FOR PEOPLE LIVING WITH DEMENTIA

Alice Liddell Allen

Storytelling has a magical power to break the ice and to get people talking by stimulating imaginations and triggering memories.

I have been lucky enough to attend a couple of residential storytelling courses run by Sharon Jacksties, who has a wealth of experience and stories as well as giving me some very helpful counsel to help me to hone my storytelling skills. I have used many of her *Somerset Folk Tales* (2012) in Somerset care homes.

For the last couple of years I became part of Sharon's storytelling team. I went into care homes on a weekly basis over a twelve-week period to tell stories to older people in dementia units as well as to older people without dementia. Our aims were to tell stories that would stimulate responses from the residents and to encourage individuals to tell their stories.

As well as a storyteller I am by profession a dramatherapist and I have been going into care homes and day centres for the last eight years to run sessions with groups or one-to-one with older people living with dementia and the main activity of a session is always a story.

When I first started with this client group I wondered how on earth dramatherapy/storytelling was going to work with a group of people whose short-term memory was very weak and in some cases completely eroded. Some were in wheelchairs; there were people who seemed to sleep all the time and others who had varying levels of anxiety. At the onset I would often despair at the lack of response even though I had planned the sessions carefully to meet the needs of my clients.

I soon learned that a response could be as little as the slightest move of the hand, a fleeting smile, nod of the head or transitory sparkle in an eye and my observation antenna grew ever lengthier to try to spot these infinitesimal reactions. I found the group responded to sensory stimuli such as a basket of autumn leaves, or strong-smelling spices. Song lyrics or poems also triggered word-perfect recitation, often led by an apparently non-verbal member. There was definitely something here that I could work with and develop and that's when the model of dramatherapy for older people with dementia began to evolve. This model always includes storytelling.

I became convinced that repetition and keeping themes simple and familiar were the absolute key. This helped the group or individual to feel secure within the structure that was

Storytelling for people with dementia

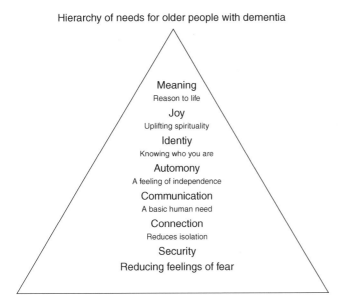

Figure 34.1 Domains of wellbeing

repeated each week. Familiarity of activities increased trust and confidence and with constant encouragement helped them to tell their own stories.

This model for clients with dementia had the properties to make connections with lost memories, facilitate feelings of belonging, wellbeing and individual identity and best of all encouraged communication that helps to reduce feelings of isolation and I realised that storytelling played a big part in this.

As a dramatherapist I always use a 'person-centred' approach (Kitwood and Benson 1995) – in other words I adopt an individualised approach whether it is within a group or one-to-one. Taken from Brooker (2016) I try to value all human lives regardless of age or cognitive ability and recognise the uniqueness of each individual. In addition, I acknowledge that it is important to provide a social environment that supports psychological needs.

My aims are to meet the needs of all and to help me do this I devised the Seven Domains of Wellbeing for older people based on 'Maslow's Hierarchy of Needs' (see Figure 34.1).

Starting at the bottom they are:

- *Security:* A feeling of being safe and contained is essential for all but particularly for older people with dementia, reducing feelings of fear.
- *Connection:* Isolation and loneliness contribute to depression and many older people live on their own, so connection with others helps to reduce these feelings.
- *Communication:* From the moment we are born we are looking to communicate with our mothers or primary carer with eye contact and facial expressions.
- *Autonomy:* All our adult lives we have been independent and used to making decisions; moving into a care home, decisions are made for us and we no longer have independence.
- *Identity:* As human beings we all need to have a solid knowledge of our identities for healthy levels of self-esteem and confidence.

- *Joy:* All of humanity needs some joy and laughter in their lives and can increase endorphins and the feeling of wellbeing.
- *Meaning: A Reason to be alive* is having a sense of wellbeing and feeling that we have some worth.

Approaches I use to achieve the above

To start the session I pass a drum around the circle. Inviting individuals to do a spontaneous beat on the drum gives them a chance to be creative and autonomous. Furthermore, by echoing their beat it gives them the sense of being valued by another. This not only is a ritual that gives the signal that a 'dramatherapy/storytelling session' is about to begin but it provides an opportunity for a wonderful form of communication, particularly for those whose speech has been affected by dementia and the recall of so many words expunged. It offers an opportunity for eye contact and to create a dialogue through the medium of *call and response;* it reinforces and acknowledges an individual's identity, so often masked by dementia. I repeat the drumming at the end of each session to signal the closing of the session. I have found that the repetition of signals at the beginning and end of sessions builds up a memory of sorts, which I describe as a 'recollection' rather than a memory.

Repetition, ritual and rhythm are the mainstay of my sessions (Booker 2011). As with the repetition of signals, repetition of activities means the group members become familiar with the activities and this takes away any fear or threat that they might feel. Fear, for people living with dementia, of not being able to cope or of being asked to do more than is within their physical or cognitive abilities, is an overriding emotion.

Rituals are all part of the rhythm of life. Our daily rituals are simple things like having breakfast, cleaning our teeth and catching the bus to work. With mobile phones and earphones we are able to listen to our favourite music when travelling to and fro, providing an external rhythm to top up our internal rhythms. These rituals establish a sense of comfort and stability in knowing what is coming next. Dementia strips a person of the rhythm of life. So by creating external rhythms we help to restore the internal body rhythms (Jennings 1995).

To increase energy levels in the group I encourage group integration and connection. I always use a balloon for this because of the lightness and ease of batting it around the circle; it not only creates joy but it gets arms and the upper body moving as well and this in turn stimulates the brain through increased blood flow. The balloon activity never fails to create fun and laughter. Only once have I had any negative response to using a balloon, when a lady called Millie angrily shouted out, "This is too childish!" But even she could not resist joining in when the balloon came her way! Sometimes staff or visiting relatives see it as childish but my reply to this criticism is that rather than being childish we are being playful. As we become adults we lose the capacity for play. We become inhibited, self-conscious and worry about what other people will think about us. So activities like the balloon batting provide the opportunity to become playful and playfulness opens up the imagination, creates laughter and fun and lifts the spirits! In addition, I also use a softball football to exercise legs and feet.

Storytelling sessions

The aims I have for outcomes from my sessions are to:

- *Reduce feelings of isolation*
- *Create connection and communication*

- *Increase self-esteem and confidence*
- *Restore identity*
- *Encourage group integration*
- *Create a sense of fun*
- *Encourage the telling of their own stories*
- *Generate feelings of wellbeing*

I introduce the theme of the story with a 'bridging' activity. This usually involves introducing some sensory objects connected to the story, which are handed around for smelling, tasting, seeing and touching. Only after this activity do I start the story.

At the end of the story, to help process the content and any emotions from within the story that might resonate, and depending on the cognitive levels of the group, I invite them to take on a role of a character from the story and offer an array of hats and colourful scarves with which they can 'dress up' to help them become their chosen character. Not everyone wants to do this but there will always be a small handful that will. It is wonderful to watch the interaction between them as they take on the roles and are able to express those difficult emotions at a distance. So not only does this part of the session summon processing but it encourages connection and communication.

At this stage I might invite everyone to make a group 'one word per line' poem from words expressing the emotions that the story has brought up.

After the role-play, it is important to make sure that anyone who has taken on a role is asked to remove the dressing-up items and return to being 'themselves.' So to de-role I might get them to say their name or to make eye contact with me to make sure they have not been left with any anguish associated with being in-role. If possible, I will ask them how they felt being in-role.

We then move on to a winding-down activity; this might be a song, connecting everyone with a circular line of colourful, chiffon scarves knotted together. Each person holds a piece of scarf and moves their arms in time to the music copying my movements. This results in sensing the pressure from their neighbours, thereby gaining a feeling of togetherness and encouraging a glance in the direction of their neighbour to make eye contact. To ring the changes the scarves can be taken across the room creating a sort of spider's web, as opposed to a line going around the circle. This urges eye contact with people opposite as well as the neighbour. As a winding-down activity it leaves everyone with a sense of belonging or being part of a group, which in turn fosters wellbeing.

Examples of stories I have used

For people with more advanced dementia it is important to find stories that are simple but not childish and folk tales usually fit the bill. I find stories where I can introduce interaction and I will spend some time before starting the story rehearsing the actions and/or songs with the group.

The following story is from *The Singing Sack* by Helen East (1989) and it's called 'The Lonely Mermaid.' I have told this story many times to people with dementia. It has a theme of being taken away from your natural environment and a theme of loneliness and depression.

After a short warm-up, to prepare everyone for the story, I take around some sensory objects such as some fishing net, an antique wooden fishing reel and a squashy fish, some blue floaty fabric to represent the waves and a fisherman's hat.

It is a short story but during the story there will be much interaction and a repeated, very simple song, which I will teach the group beforehand. I have adapted the song to repeat the same words several times and while we sing we do the actions of pulling bracken.

While I am telling the story I will move around inside the circle and do actions such as a weaving hand for the fishes' tail and a heaving action to pull in the fishing net so as to create a focal point.

'The Lonely Mermaid' (re-told by Alice Liddell Allen)

Once there was a fisherman who lived on a very remote island off the very northern coast of Scotland. One day when he was out fishing he threw his net out waited a while and started to haul it back in. It seemed much heavier than usual. With a final huge effort he pulled the net close to the boat and in it he saw the most beautiful woman he had ever seen and he fell instantly in love with her. As he drew the net into the boat he saw that instead of legs she had a fishes' tail. In spite of her desperate pleas to return her to the sea he couldn't let her go because he was so deeply in love with her. When he took her home he made her remove her fishes' tail, which he hid deep inside his barn at the back of the house so that she would never be able to find it and return to the ocean.

He married her and she bore him two beautiful boys. On the island the women's work was to pull bracken, for they were unable to grow corn on the island, which meant there was no straw to make beds for the animals or the humans.

The mermaid too had to pull bracken and every day she would sit on a hillock feeling lonely and looking longingly at the sea and while she worked she would sing:

> I'm so lonely pulling bracken
> Pulling bracken, pulling bracken,
> I'm so lonely pulling bracken early
> Pulling bracken, pulling bracken
> Pulling bracken early.

Life went on like this for a couple of years and the mermaid was very lonely and sad until one day her youngest son was playing in the barn and found the fishes' tail. He came running in to tell his mother, who was overjoyed to see it. She put it on and immediately returned to the sea.

When the fisherman returned home he was very sad to find that she had gone and he went down to the edge of the water and called and called for her to come back to him. He could see her way out in the water sitting on a rock and singing the song:

> I'm so lonely pulling bracken
> Pulling bracken, pulling bracken,
> I'm so lonely pulling bracken early
> Pulling bracken, pulling bracken
> Pulling bracken early.

She swam over to him and beckoned to him and he dived into the water and joined her and they swam away together.

You might be wondering what became of their sons but they had a kindly grandmother who continued to look after them until they were adult.

It was said that they married and had children of their own and that they all walked like mermaids, a little bit like the walk of a seal, and this was even said of the next generation as well!

§

At the end of the story we sing the song once again and I ask the group to think about what it feels like to be lonely and sad and to make a sound or do an action that represents that feeling. As we go around the circle I invite the rest of the group to copy that sound or action.

We then shake off the lonely and sad feeling by shaking our hands and feet and throwing the feelings into the middle of the circle.

Most of the group joins in the actions and some will be more likely to if they have support from a member of staff sitting next to them. When asking for an action or sound, if someone has dropped off into a sound sleep then I go onto the next person, or if I sense that it would cause confusion or distress I will just go up to that person and touch their arm gently, making eye contact, and move onto the next person.

Then we sing a happy familiar song and to close the session I go around the circle and invite people to do a beat on the drum. This also serves as an opportunity to make sure no one has been left with any bad feelings from the story.

Another story I use from *The Singing Sack* is 'Quilla Bung.'

This is a story with the theme of belonging to a group, connectedness and communication. Again this is a short story but with many actions and a repeated song with a simple tune, all of which I teach the group before I start telling the story. To prepare the group for the story I take around a basket of different soft and fluffy feathers, which I have collected over time while out walking my dog. I invite each group member to choose a feather and once everyone has a feather I encourage them to take their feather to their face and softly wipe the feather across their cheek. Then I invite them to turn to a neighbour and softly touch their neighbour's hand. This usually makes people laugh and encourages contact with others. Then I start the story.

'Quilla Bung' (re-told by Alice Liddell Allen)

Many years ago in a distant country there was an old couple who lived in a small cottage. Their sons had left home many years before so there was no one to bring home food and they were very poor and had little to eat. One day the wife looked in the cupboard and cried out to her husband that there was nothing left for their supper that day.

So the husband got down his big gun from above the door and he went out to find something to shoot for supper.

As he was walking along he heard singing coming from the sky above.

> Lalee lu come quilla, come quilla
> Bung, bung, bung quilla bung.

As the sound became louder and clearer, he looked up and there was a flock of geese about to fly over him. He quickly put his shotgun up to his shoulder, aimed, and BANG! The goose he had hit came spiralling down, singing the song all the time.

> Lalee lu come quilla, come quilla
> Bung, bung, bung quilla bung.

He picked it up and took it back to his wife to prepare and cook for their supper. The wife was delighted and took the goose into the kitchen, where she started to pluck out the feathers. As she did so each feather flew up and out of the open window and the goose continued to sing the song.

She laid the plucked goose in a large roasting pan and put it in to her oven and even when she shut the oven door she could hear the muffled sound of,

> Lalee lu come quilla, come quilla
> Bung, bung, bung quilla bung.

An hour or two later the goose was cooked and the wife took it out of the oven and laid it on a carving board for her husband to carve. He began to sharpen his knife on a stone and was about to plunge the knife into the flesh of the goose when once again from outside the kitchen window he heard,

> Lalee lu, come quilla, come quilla,
> Bung, bung, bung quilla bung

The rest of the flock of geese flew in through the kitchen window and each goose had a white feather in its beak and one by one they placed a feather into the skin of the goose on the table. They surrounded the goose on the plate, picked him up and flew out of the window with him.

The husband and wife were left sitting at the table holding a knife and fork over empty plates, their mouths open in astonishment and listening to the sound of the song becoming fainter and fainter as the geese flew up into the sky and over the mountains into the distance singing:

> Lalee lu, come quilla, come quilla,
> Bung, bung, bung quilla bung.

§

We sing the song over and over, getting quieter and quieter.

After a short pause, I ask the group to look around the circle and make eye contact with someone else and to do an action to show a sense of belonging to the 'Storyshare' group. On one occasion a lady threw her arms open wide, another gentleman waved and someone else laughed and did a flapping action with his arms.

There are many people who have lived on a farm in Somerset and known hard times so this story generates stories from them about owning guns and shooting rabbits and pigeons for the pot.

To wind down I invite them to pick up their feathers and blow them into the centre of the circle; this creates laughter and joy.

I hand out some long ostrich feathers and play a song, inviting everyone to wave their feathers in time to the music and sing. We then have closure with a beat on the drum around the circle.

For pure fun and enjoyment the trickster story of 'Spider Drummer,' also from *The Singing Sack*, is a story full of mischief, music and humour.

As a bridge to prepare for the story I take in some things related to the story such as a toy spider and web and party hats and blowers. I make it interactive by inviting everyone to choose a percussion instrument from my basket such as maracas, shakers and small drums. We practise shaking and playing the instruments to the music, which I play from my iPad and each time the music is played during the story everyone shakes or beats their instrument in time to the beat of the music.

'Spider drummer' (re-told by Alice Liddell Allen)

In the days when animals could talk there was a spider musician who lived in a village with his large family. There was going to be a wedding in the village and for any party or celebration Spider was invited to play music. He was a wonderful musician, for you see he was able to play a different instrument on each of his eight legs.

However, the villagers decided that because Spider and his family always ate up all of the food at parties they would not invite him to this party.

Well, you know how it is with secrets, they always manage somehow to leak out. Spider got to hear that he was not welcome at the wedding party and he was furious. "I'm always invited to parties; who will play the music?" He thought indignantly. He decided he was going to get his revenge.

On the day of the wedding he called his family together and told them they were going to play a trick on the wedding guests. He instructed them to hide in the bushes on the banks of the river. It needs to be said here that in those days there was no running water in the village so the villagers had to collect water from the river.

At the party site the preparations had begun. The cooks needed water to start preparing the feast, so a young girl was sent down to fetch water from the river. She took a bucket and as she began to scoop up some water, loud music began to play. It was so alluring she immediately dropped the bucket and began to dance. She danced and danced and couldn't stop. Back at the wedding site the cooks were wondering why the girl had not returned with the water, so they sent down a boy to find out what she was up to. When the boy reached the river bank he saw the girl lying on the grass and he went up to her and asked her why she had not brought the water back. She told him how she had heard music and danced until she was so exhausted she collapsed on the ground. The boy told her she was lying and that she was just being lazy. He took the bucket and began to fill it and immediately the music started and the boy started to dance wildly and unable to stop. When the boy didn't return with the water, either, more people were sent down to see what was happening and one by one the same thing happened. Eventually, the main chef went herself but what do you think happened? ... Yes, you are right, the music started and she started to dance and everyone who had come down to the river to collect water couldn't stop dancing.

At last they came to their senses and someone said, "We need to start thinking here; who would be doing this to us?" "There is only one person who can play music like that." And they guessed it was Spider.

They called his name and he came out of the bushes and when they asked him why he was playing this trick on them, he replied. "Because you didn't invite me to the wedding and I will only stop if you allow me and my family to come to the wedding." The wedding guests had no choice but to agree, but they told him that he could come as long as he promised he would not eat up all of the food as he usually did. Spider refused, so they had to let him and his family come to the wedding anyway and guess what? ...

Spider and his family did eat up all of the food! But it was a jolly good party because the wedding guests danced to Spider's music until the early hours of the morning.

§

Spider's music is lively and loud, which raises the levels of energy and I try to encourage people to use their voices as well with the odd 'Whoop.' It is a story that keeps everyone awake!

At the end of the story I throw out the idea of feeling 'left out' and quite often people come up with a story from their childhood of feeling left out at school. I've heard other stories about feeling left out in families because of a big age gap and older siblings were allowed to do things they were too young to do.

With a familiar song and ritual drumbeat from everyone I close the session.

For older people with not such advanced dementia, my favourite stories are from *Storymaking and Creative Groupwork with Older People* by Paula Crimmens (1998).

I try to find a balance of stories, which have male and female main characters. However, the following story 'Yaaba' is a story about a female central character who is being unappreciated and misunderstood, which is something we have all experienced at some point in our lives and resonates with most people, male and female.

Before I tell the story I invite everyone to touch, feel and smell the objects in the basket, which come into the story, such as a black woollen shawl, a pestle and mortar with herbs and a pottery pitcher for carrying water. This not only gives a sensory experience but it also prepares people for the story ahead and creates lots of chat and reminiscences.

Yaaba (re-told by Alice Liddell Allen)

A long time ago in a distant country there was an old woman who lived by herself on the edge of the village. Her name was Yaaba and she was a herbalist. The villagers thought that she was a witch and the children who were sent to collect water from the well near where she lived would call her names and throw things at her.

One day a young woman found that her baby had a high fever. She waited until her husband had gone to work, for she feared he would be angry. She slipped the baby under her cloak and hurried to Yaaba's cottage. Yaaba took one look at the baby and she fetched her pestle and mortar to pound herbs to a paste, which she spread over the baby's forehead. She told the mother to sit by her fire and wait. A few hours later the baby's fever had gone and the young mother was delighted and thanked Yaaba and took her baby home.

When her husband returned from work she did not dare to tell him that she had taken their baby to Yaaba.

A few years later the baby had grown into a strong and healthy young boy and when he was sent to collect water from the well, instead of taunting Yaaba like the other children, he would talk to her and help her carry her water to her hut. They became friends and the young boy would often secretly go to Yaaba's hut to chat with her.

The following year there was a terrible drought and water shortage. The word went round the village that this was the work of Yaaba. Everyone was jealously hording water.

The young boy had not seen Yaaba for a couple of days and was worried about her, so he knocked on her door but there was no reply. He pushed the door open slowly and there he saw Yaaba lying on her bed, very sick. He rushed over to her and asked what he could do and she told him she needed a drink of water. The boy ran home as fast as he could, gathered a little food together and reached up to take the last pitcher of water from the top shelf.

When his father returned from work, a neighbour told him that he had seen his son walking in the direction of Yaaba's hut with a pitcher of water. He was furious to hear that his son had taken the last of their water for Yaaba. He gathered together some of the villagers and started out towards Yaaba's hut carrying sticks.

On the way they met the boy returning from Yaaba's and the father grabbed hold of his son and said, "Why did you take the last of our water to that witch?" He was about to start beating the boy when his mother stepped in and said, "Our son would not be alive if it was not for

Yaaba curing him when he was a tiny baby. We owe her everything!" She continued to tell the story about Yaaba using her herbal paste to reduce their baby son's raging fever.

At that moment a shout went up from a man at the back of the crowd and he was pointing to the sky; Yaaba was forgotten. Everyone looked up and there was a huge black cloud which began to drop fat drops of rain on their upward turned faces.

Everyone raced home to collect all the containers they possessed to collect as much rain as possible.

When the rain stopped the whole village had a celebration and they invited Yaaba. From that time on the villagers changed their view of Yaaba and she was included in the village community. The father allowed his wife and son to visit her whenever they liked. They even moved Yaaba's hut closer to the centre of the village so she could have more visitors and everyone gave her the respect she deserved.

§

When the story is finished I invite comments from the group about any part of the story that has stood out for them and ask them to think of one word to describe the feeling for that part of the story. With sticky notes and pens each person writes down a word and a one-word-per-line poem is created.

On a flip chart we arrange the words in the order that the group would like them to be read.

Below you will see a poem created by a group from listening to the story and as you will see it has captured the essence of the story.

Yaaba,
Lonely,
Sad,
Sick,
Boy,
Good boy,
Water,
Angry,
Rain,
Sunshine,
River.

Before closure we sing a familiar song like *Singing in The Rain* connected by the chiffon scarves with encouragement to acknowledge the neighbour on either side even if it is only to feel the tug on the scarf as it is pulled from side to side in time to the music.

With a drumbeat around the circle the storytelling session is closed.

From the experience I have had working with those living with dementia and the reading I have done around the research into dementia care I would like to close this chapter with the guidelines I use when working with any group or individual living with dementia.

Golden guidelines – person-centred

- To give 100% of your attention to that person.
- Remember that contradicting can trigger a distressed reaction.
- Be with that person in their world and above all take into account that the person with dementia has a history of individual values and beliefs.
- Change the phrase 'challenging behaviour' to 'distressed reaction.'

- Caution around asking questions that can sometimes cause confusion and distress.
- Tolerate and embrace repetitiveness.

References

Booker, M., 2011, *Developmental Drama: Dramatherapy Approaches for People with Profound or Severe Multiple Disabilities, Including Sensory Impairment*. Jessica Kingsley, London, Philadelphia.

Brooker, D., and Latham, I., 2016, *Person-Centred Dementia Care; Making Services Better with the VIPS Framework*. Second Edition. Jessica Kingsley, London.

Crimmens, P., 1998, *Storytelling and Creative Group Work with Older People*. Jessica Kingsley, London Philadelphia.

East, H., 1989, *The Singing Sack: 28 Song-stories from around the World*. A & C Black, London.

Jacksties, S., 2012, *Somerset Folk Tales*. The History Press, Gloucestershire, UK.

Jennings, S., 1995, *Theatre Ritual and Transformation*, Routledge, Oxford.

Killick, J., 2015, *Dementia Positive; For Everyone Wishing to Improve the Lives of Those with Dementia*. Luath Press, Edinburgh.

Kitwood, T., and Benson, S. (Eds.), 1995, *The New Culture of Dementia Care*. Hawker Publications, London.

Marshall, K., 2013, *Puppetry in Dementia Care; Connecting through Creativity and Joy*. Jessica Kingsley Publishers, London, Philadelphia.

Rodenburg, P., 2009, *Presence; How to Use Positive Energy for Success*. Penguin, London.

35
EXPLORING THE DYNAMICS OF STORY IN DEMENTIA RESEARCH

Storytelling constructs that support people with dementia to share their experiences of what it means to live with dementia

Alison Ward

Introduction

Stories are an essential part of being human, they tap into our cognitive processing, supporting what we see, hear, and how we engage and experience with what is being told to us (Kottler, 2014). Stories also act as a way to remember who we are, helping us to learn and grow (Rich, 2014; Moon, 2010), and to make sense of our lived experience (Kottler, 2014). Stories can be particularly relevant when working with people with dementia, as they encourage us to use our brains, draw on our long-term memory, help to make sense of the present and adapt to changing situations (Kottler, 2014). They can also support a connection to the self, enhancing our sense of who we are as an individual, something that can be challenging when the memory is fading, and personal stories can be forgotten (Schweitzer and Bruce, 2008; Basting, 2011). This chapter will look at a study that used storytelling and photography as a way to learn about people with dementia's experiences of attending a lifelong learning service in Denmark. The focus will be on the use of storytelling methods and how constructs of storytelling can be used in a research context with people with dementia, in a way that can provide a collaborative approach to support what it means to live with dementia. This chapter will consider the way story can be woven through discussions, as well as presented in a traditional linear format. It will also explore those stories that are repeated and how story is not just personal but can also be shared by a group of people. Techniques were identified that can support a person with dementia to share their stories, and encourage others to listen and engage in the telling. By drawing on traditional story techniques, this chapter will demonstrate ways we can support a person with dementia to share what it means to live with this condition and to learn about their experiences. This in turn provides a richer understanding of the experience of dementia, how best to provide support to those living with the condition, and ways of encouraging positive verbal and non-verbal communication.

Setting for the study

This study took place in a unique setting of a school of lifelong learning for people with dementia. The school was, at the time of the study, the only one of its kind and was delivered in Northern Jutland, Denmark. The concept of the school is to provide access to lifelong learning that could support cognition, decision making, and everyday activities and provide a social outlet for those attending. The school delivers teaching in cognitive activities, music, art, woodwork, history, and a range of topic areas depending on the needs and interests of those attending (Ward et al., 2018; Ward, 2019). Since I first visited the school in 2014, it has grown with eight new sites now in Denmark, one in Norway, and one in the UK. On my first visit I found the lifelong learning model presented a new approach to providing support for people with dementia and I was interested in exploring what the experience was for those who attended and what it meant to them to be students with dementia at this school. Drawing on current thinking for working with people with dementia (Basting, 2009; Murphy et al., 2015), the study was designed as a creative qualitative study, using a mixture of photography and storytelling. Ten people with dementia took part in the study, five male, five female (I will refer to them as students as this was the identity they took on, and how I engaged with them at the school). Each was provided with a camera and asked to take photographs of activities, objects, and people at the school and in their home life. These photographs were then incorporated into discussions across four weekly sessions, where we met in two groups to talk through the photographs, and what they signified in terms of being at the school. Storytelling techniques were used to support the sharing of their experiences, including reminiscence, narrative approaches, and storyboards. From our discussions, a rich picture emerged not of only what it meant to attend the school, but also providing an insight into what it means to be a citizen of Denmark and to live with dementia. Throughout this chapter I will include extracts from the discussions we had to illustrate the use of story. All names are presented as pseudonyms to protect the identity of the participants.

The constructs of storytelling

An interesting starting point for this chapter is to consider what the constructs of story and storytelling are. The traditional construct of a story would be that it has a beginning, a middle, and an end, or as Kottler (2014, p. 22) suggests, an introduction, a conflict, and a resolution. When working with people with dementia, it is not always possible for them to share stories in this linear format; rather, stories may emerge over time and conversations that require piecing together (Overcash, 2003). I have heard stories from people with dementia described as akin to a 'jazz riff' (Jacobus, 2018), sometimes abstract, but recognisable as a story. Due to the impact of dementia on memory and language, following or sharing a story in a traditional format can be challenging (Stenhouse et al., 2013). Therefore, what emerges can often be 'degrees' of a story and while narratives may be 'broken' (Hydén, 2011, p. 346), due to the impact of the dementia, people with dementia are able to share and follow stories.

Stories can come in many different formats (oral, visual, and written), but there are key components that make a story. Stories, it is suggested, should share an experience, use characters and events, have tension, and have a final outcome (Kottler, 2014). There are many reasons why we share stories – we do this to entertain, to teach or pass on knowledge, and to share something about ourselves and our identities (Rich, 2014). From working with the two groups in this present study, I found that the following factors were key components of storytelling: the use of humour; body language; active listening; metaphor; narrative scaffolding; and characterisation. Either in isolation or together, these factors worked to support a person with dementia to engage in the storytelling process.

Often, we talk about feeling connected in a story, having a sense of being part of it or emotionally engaged. Working on this study, I found that understanding how to bring a story to life in a way which engages those listening emerged as an important finding. This related to the way story was told, both verbally and non-verbally though gesture, eye-contact, and tone of voice. Emphasising the non-verbal aspects of storytelling is important when working with people with dementia as language can be a challenge (Hydén and Antelius, 2011; Hydén, 2013), and therefore non-verbal cues may support communication (Cute et al., 2013).

Several of the students had a very natural style of engaging their audience, particularly Emma and Kurt. In talking about his home life, Kurt was observed to use the photographs alongside his narrative and made eye-contact with the other students. He drew in the group by asking them for help to tell his story – for example, to recall the name of a flower. The other students became part of the retelling and seemed to have a greater connection to the story, something Hydén (2011) refers to as 'narrative scaffolding' (p. 339), whereby the listener becomes a collaborator within the narrative by supporting the teller through prompts and feedback. Teller and listener therefore co-construct the narrative. Hydén considers this particularly important for people with dementia, who may find telling a story complex given potential problems with language or memory. Scaffolding becomes a central part of supporting the person to be an active storyteller. Hydén used this term in reference to carers supporting people with dementia, but here, the students were seen to support each other, helping to recall words or ask questions, for example:

KURT: [Pointing to a photograph of a group of people sitting around a garden table] This picture is the last picture we took, it has that story that this is not what we do every day. This is a Saturday and these two lovely people… they just live beside us and they have just put their, what is it called?
EMMA: To sell?
KURT: What?
EMMA: You said to…
KURT: Oh, to sell, yes, yes. Their house.
EMMA: Yes, that was also.
KURT: They have put it on for sale.

Emma was also very expressive, using movement and gesture to act out elements of her story, and creating layers within the story through pauses and laughter. In telling her story of how she beat a Danish chess champion, Emma took on the character of the chess player, demonstrating how he reacted, and brought the story to life.

EMMA: Both of the boys could play chess, so they were very good. But they also taught me and I have won over a Danish chess champion. He almost sat an hour [leans over on desk as if concentrating] and said, I think he said it 20 times, I do not understand this! And I didn't say a word. I thought he had to sit with it and get through it. Yes, I have to admit, you have won. Yes, I said yes, I have!

Emma tells her story in a linear fashion, using the key components of story that Kottler (2014) identified: an introduction, a conflict, and a resolution. Emma introduces the story by talking of learning to play chess from her sons, she sets up the conflict through her win over a chess champion, and finds resolution in the outcome with the champion accepting his loss and remaining friends with Emma. Her tale draws in the listener through her characterisation of the chess champion's emotions of trying to accept his defeat (she enacted the moment, showing his frustrations and disbelief), and by telling a good story. Kottler (2014, p. 206) suggests that truly transformational stories are those where the storyteller has a 'dramatic' performance; this, he says, helps the listener to feel special as the teller puts effort into the dramatic telling of the story, using voices, movement, and energy to create the story – all of which Emma demonstrates. You can see this in Emma's story as she recreates the drama of the chess game. Emma ends on a moral tale of the importance of friendships (see the extract below). Hers is a story told in a more 'classic' retelling with good physicality and characterisation and follows a linear format – although it also required prompting and input from the audience, emphasising the importance of narrative scaffolding in the development of story.

> EMMA: But he was very nice and we had a good relationship afterwards. We worked through it and we found each other again, in a good way. A game does not ruin a friendship.

On listening to Emma's story, we cannot be sure how much is an embellished interpretation of what actually occurred. At the time I took her story as the truth of her experience. This exemplifies Kearney's (1997) argument that stories are a product of both fact and fiction, with embellishment made through the retelling of our memories. Kottler (2014, p. 189) suggests that all stories are untrue, to some degree, as the facts are adapted to suit our audience and our reason for the telling. This is not always a deliberate act and is often done to protect ourselves, with the stories often taken on as truth by the teller. The truth of the story is perhaps less important than what the story is telling us. This embellishment, Kearney suggests, is what makes the story come to life and provides the story with 'plot, composition, character, point-of-view', without which narratives would be dry and difficult to relate to, and it is this complex interplay between fact and fiction which 'makes us see, feel and live it as if we were there' (p. 190). The dynamics of story allow for this merging of fact and fiction (Overcash, 2003) and support the way story can be used by people with dementia to share their experiences. Emma's dramatic retelling evidences the importance of how a story is told, her approach drawing in the other students, who seemed to enjoy watching Emma, turning their chairs towards her and asking questions, demonstrating that it is the sharing, being heard, and being understood that is important (Kottler, 2014) – something that people with dementia do not always experience. Whether embellished or not, Emma's telling was engaging. People with dementia can find empowerment through storytelling when people do not try to correct or 'reality-orientate' the individual (Heggestad and Slettebø, 2015, p. 2327). It therefore does not matter whether the tale is fact, fiction, or a mixture – the fact that they are sharing a story and expressing themselves is important (Gridley et al., 2016).

Active listening

Storytelling is a collaborative process between a teller and an audience, and it is from this collaboration that meaning is co-created (Abma, 2003; Kottler, 2014; National Storytelling Network, 2016). The power to communicate with people who listen and who give time to a person with dementia has been explored by Alsawy et al. (2020), who emphasise that active listening, empathising, and being present in conversations promote positive engagement. One of the aspects I was interested in exploring through my research with the students with dementia at the lifelong learning service was to understand the cues that can support active listening and being present.

I observed the students with dementia participated by being active listeners. Listening was observed in the students through their body language – they were seen to lean forward, nod, and react to what was being said. The students also asked questions to seek clarity or to gather further details of the narrative, evidencing that they were listening and engaged. Hydén (2011) argues that the to and fro between teller and listener – of telling, acknowledging, or asking questions – is a crucial part of the collaborative convention of storytelling. Where there is mutual understanding this convention can support the telling of stories.

Listening was also supported by the storyteller, whose narrative style could equally engage or disengage. Theresa was observed to have been aware of her listeners. She used eye-contact and turned to face individuals when she spoke. This was particularly evidenced during a talk about the German occupation of Denmark during World War II. Theresa told of her experience of being a child at the time, and shared her fear of having German soldiers in her town. She was seen to turn towards her audience as a way to include them in the conversation, and told her story with changes in tone, emotion, and physical displays for emphasis – much as Emma had done. This collaboration between teller and listener is a way of 'monitoring' each other's engagement and understanding (Hydén, 2011, p. 340). By facing her audience, Theresa could monitor how her story was being received, while they in turn were in a position to nod and acknowledge Theresa, showing they were listening.

Both I and my co-facilitator also used a number of active listening techniques (National Health Service, 2017) to show we were focused on the students. This was more challenging for me when listening to the narratives in Danish – and having to wait for their translation to English; however, the focus on non-verbal communication became essential here, and is particularly important when working with people who may have difficulties with language. For example, mirroring emotional responses (smiling/laughing), maintaining eye-contact, and turning to face the student who was speaking. Another technique we used was to repeat back what students had said, as a way of validating their contribution, showing that we had been listening and were person-centred in our approach (Kitwood, 1997; Basting, 2011). This also acted as a way to ensure the group had heard what was said and to act as reminders of the narratives being shared. This develops upon Stenhouse et al. (2013), who recommend this technique when using story with people with dementia as a way to remember and keep the thread of stories. It is also important to note what Gridley et al. (2016) discuss in facilitating lifestory work, that this should be done with an open and non-judgemental approach so that the person's story is validated rather than criticised, something echoed by Alsawy et al. (2020), who identified the negative aspects of communication were in not treating people as equals, judging, and avoiding any interactions.

Public and private stories

I found that the students tended to share personal or public stories; these could merge from one to the other as members of the group shared their interest in what was being told. Having shared their narratives this was one way to engage the group and encourage the students to share their experiences, be this through discussions of national heritage and culture or universal interests such as sport and food. Finding a common topic between the members of the group helped to engage them in what was being discussed. One of the students, Bent, tended to steer the conversation away from his personal life. In the stories of home life, he chose to share a narrative about his summer cottage and where it is situated, keeping to factual rather than emotional comments (e.g. directions to his cottage).

His narrative could have remained quite impersonal and dry, but the group joined in and turned it into a story about the rivalry between two villages, enabling other members of the group to share their experiences of these villages and of their summer cottages. Bent created a group narrative, moving it away from any personal details. More than being a product of his dementia, I feel that this was more revealing about Bent as an individual, something that story can enable, bringing a lens onto a person's identity and character (Rich, 2014), and showed him as a private person. The benefit of storytelling allows for this style of narrative, and for individuals to choose their level of engagement and disclosure. Bent's lack of information on personal issues was in sharp contrast to the other students, who all talked about family and friends. Bent made a choice not to discuss anything too personal with the group and his choice was respected by both students and facilitators, who did not push for more information.

> BENT: If you come to [village name 1] and then you go farther out then you get to [village name 2], and those in [village name 2] are dangerous!
> THERESA: Yes! [Laugh]
> BENT: That's where they steal the hubcaps before you get through the town…
> THERESA: …I think I know it like this. We live by [place name] and those from [village name 2] where some are a little bit violent.
> BENT: You normally say the good, the bad, and the ugly, from [village name 1]!
> THERESA: Yes exactly, I have heard that too!

In contrast to Bent's narrative, Helena's was very personal and intimate, talking about her daughter. She spoke with emotion, pride, and love, and it was clear what it meant to Helena to be close to her daughter.

> FACILITATOR: You sound very proud of your daughter.
> HELENA: I am in love with her, I am. And she has such a nice guy and that means a lot and he comes as much as she.

Helena had an honesty to her narrative and was very expressive, her emotions came through clearly and she was not worried about showing these. Scheidt's (2015) study of older people sharing life stories suggests that honesty comes with trust, and Helena showed great trust in the group through her personal narrative. However, on reviewing the transcripts, the other students had little engagement with Helena – they listened but did not ask many questions and it was predominantly a conversation between Helena and the facilitators.

This identification of the private and public stories furthers Frohlich's (2004) discussion that story can be derived from an individual perspective and a shared narrative and that both have equal importance. The stories told by the students seemed to enhance their social bonds and identity as: students; Danish citizens; and people with dementia. Joint narratives, or public stories, had a way of engaging the students, while the personal and more individual stories could both engage and disengage depending on the interest shown by the other students and the way the story was told. Furthermore, the joint narratives told by the students were co-constructed with members of the group contributing to their development, something that may be considered central to the role of storytelling (Hydén and Antelius, 2011).

During a story about World War II, Helena tried to be part of Theresa and Bent's recollections of occupied Denmark, talking about her parents and her summer cottage as a way to connect to a narrative to which she had no personal experience. Similarly, Johan did this through interjections with historical facts. While this story had elements of a group story, it was largely reminiscences by Theresa and Bent:

THERESA: … and [the] beach was also German. They occupied the beach and the hills behind where they had barracks out and it was like. Yeah, yeah.

HELENA: Our parents have suffered there.

THERESA: It was so unsafe. … I remember…I had a sister who lived down there and I can remember if I should go down visiting my sister then it was something about mother can you. [Leans forward, raises her voice and gestures with her arms.] Then my mother said can you then get going because you have to be there before it gets dark and it was because the Germans were there out in the hills.

What became clear in this story was the way story had a greater connection when it was collaborative and more public so that everyone could feel included. This is not to say that the private stories were not important but that within a group setting, the stories where more students could input seemed to generate greater engagement and interest. Drumm (2013) cautions against the marginalisation of voice in a group setting, stating the power of story is to give voice to experiences regardless of personal stance. Drumm adds that if the listener does not find a personal connection to the story, it can act to disengage. This identifies the need for careful facilitation of story within research to ensure that each participant has a voice and that everyone's opinions are valued. Reminiscences and culturally relevant stories can have a way of strengthening interest in group stories, and help to provide cohesion to the group (Kottler, 2014). This collaboration between storytellers also shows how working together can lead to a successful story (Hydén, 2011).

Those stories that make us, us

I became aware during my time with the students that their stories were being repeated and were not always shared as examples of their experience of being at the lifelong learning service, but rather were examples of stories that we tell about our lives. Kottler (2014) talks about people having 'seminal stories' (p. 199) they tell about their experiences, ones that have had an impact and say something about us as individuals and our history. Scott (2019) also found that when working with people with dementia, repetition is a part of the story process. She describes the use of repetition as a way to connect with others and to create meaning, something that becomes more prevalent as the dementia progresses. The storytelling process in this study exemplified this and provided a way to understand the experiences of living with dementia – particularly in seeing the students' responses to these repeated stories, as they were observed to listen to and engage in these as if they were heard for the first time. The clearest example of this is Emma's story of winning against a chess champion. I visited the lifelong learning service prior to starting the study, spending time in the classroom and meeting the students. During one of these visits, I spent time with Emma and she told me about winning against a chess champion. So, when she told this story in the session, I became aware that this was not a story prompted by the study, but was her story, and one she thrived on telling. The first mention was during our second session together, when we talked about the games the students play in class; this prompted Emma to talk about chess. Emma then retold this story during each successive session.

What was particularly interesting was the way the other students reacted to Emma sharing the story. They did not stop her to say they had heard the story before, but responded each time with interest, asking questions and getting involved. They may have been experiencing the story as new, due to their dementia, but I had a feeling that it was familiar to most of the students. They gave the perfect response when a person with dementia is repeating the same story and engaged with Emma in the retelling and seemed to enjoy her enjoyment in sharing the story (see extract below). Goldsilver and Gruneir (2001) discuss how people with dementia attending a support group were forgiving and accepting of each other's dementia, often finding humour in their forgetfulness. Capstick and Ludwin (2015) consider the repeated stories people with dementia share are metaphors for their current lives and situation, suggesting that these might provide a more holistic way of working with people with dementia, and helping them to have a greater sense of self-identity and agency (p. 162).

PETER: Oh impressive!
FACILITATOR: Yeah.
KATHERINE: It must be something to win over a Danish chess champion…
EMMA: I sat half an hour and said, 'I do not understand'.
KURT: Yeah.

This develops upon what Connelly and Clandinin (1990, p. 2) call 'storied lives' – that our lives consist of stories that are told and retold as we progress through life. Ryan and Martin (2011) consider these stories as integral to who we are as individuals and our sense of belonging. The connection to self is important in the telling of these repeated narratives, especially for people with dementia, whose diagnosis brings changes to the external world, and biologically and psychologically within the individual (Ryan and Martin, 2011). The way in which we respond to these stories was exemplified by the students, who provided valuable learning on listening to and treating repeated stories as brand new.

Dementia narratives

The narrative of dementia emerged naturally out of our conversations and interactions during the project; it was not a topic that I asked about directly. The students often expressed what it meant to live with dementia, voluntarily, verbally, through gestures and facial expressions. The students expressed their frustrations with their dementia, of the loss they had experienced and how they were coping. They were very open about its impact and used descriptive language and metaphor to emphasise their meaning. Their honest discussions develop our understanding of what it means to live with dementia.

An exchange between Bent and Helena about Helena's daughter revealed that dementia feels like a dusty place in their brains, something that hasn't been used for a while and is lying dormant. Castaño (2020) suggests that metaphors are an important way for us to understand and to share challenging experiences; they help to make these relatable, familiar, and tangible. The use of metaphor offers a way to see into the 'window' of an individual's experience and world view (Castaño, 2020, p. 116). The metaphor Helen and Bent use is powerful and demonstrates the frustration a person with dementia must experience trying to access those parts of the brain that are becoming 'dusty'. This metaphor provides a way for us, as the listener, to understand better what it means to live with dementia, and makes the complexity of dementia more tangible to comprehend.

> HELENA: She [daughter] goes on [name] school. They use each other there. She is clever and her brain is functioning so it is good, she is not like her mother.
> BENT: Have you got her brain dusted?
> HELENA: It is not necessary to dust anything off.

Problems with memory were evident in both groups. The students were observed to struggle to find a word or would openly say relying on their memory was challenging. Both Kurt and Gudrun commented on this, Gudrun saying that it feels as if 'everything is in slow motion when you are as us'; she also explained how difficult it could be to learn new things, while Kurt simply said 'that is what we have trouble with – remembering'. Theresa also talked of the benefits of being at the lifelong learning service, saying it was like going into a 'lost memory book', feeling as if she was being 'confirmed' and finding things that had been 'forgotten'.

During one session, Johan explained what it meant to get a diagnosis of dementia. Over the course of the conversation, Johan explained that a diagnosis can lead to overprotection by those around you, limiting what you do. As a result, it can be increasingly difficult to leave the house. For Johan, the benefits of going to the lifelong learning service were in increased confidence and experiencing something positive. The following extracts are taken over the course of a 10–15min conversation, which weaved in and out about his experience of living with dementia and emerged out of a discussion about the challenges of attending the service. Johan's use of the doorstep metaphor is particularly expressive in helping the listener to understand what it means to live with dementia.

> JOHAN: It is also a challenge just to get out of your house, to get out… The longer time you go the more difficult it gets to get over the doorstep, the higher it gets, so you can't get over it. I have said that for many years… It is but when you get diagnosed it is like being totally alone and somebody is protecting you and now you should just sit down and clean the house then mow the lawn and the day goes with that. And the ones that are staying at home are just waiting for the husband or wife to get home and tell a little bit about what is happening… I have told you that, it is about now you are having a good time when you are here and you are feeling good when you go home but it can happen that some problems occur when you go home but you have had some good experiences… Because it is good times, good moments that you collect, everything does not matter.

The dementia narratives tended to focus on issues of loss, be this loss of memory, access to language, or the loss of ability to leave the house. In an analysis of autobiographies by people with dementia Page and Keady (2010) found loss to be a central theme across the books, particularly related to a loss of identity. This was not necessarily a central theme from the students, whose sense of loss related to activities of daily living, although Johan's story is more closely associated with the loss of self through overprotection and reduced confidence. What Johan expressed, however, is that he wanted to be part of society and wanted to develop and learn. This sense that the 'self' is not lost through the diagnosis has also been evidenced in poems by people with dementia, who retain their 'human values, skills, capabilities and needs'

(Clark-McGhee and Castro, 2015, p. 24). This is also shown through the students' humour, support for each other, and ability to express their reminiscences and feelings.

Story is reported as a therapeutic approach to sharing experiences of an illness; it can be an objective way of discussing and coming to terms with a condition (Overcash, 2003; Gucciardi et al., 2016). The creative approach provides a sense of distance from the illness in which to verbalise the impact and feelings it may bring (Taylor, 2003; Prendergast and Saxton, 2013). The narratives of dementia were perhaps a way for the students to come to terms with their diagnosis and not feeling alone in their experiences.

Disengaging voice

I have so far talked of the positive ways in which story engaged the group and helped them to share their stories, especially working collaboratively in a group. However, this was not always the case and on a number of occasions, the group could become disengaged from what was being told. Being judged, or criticised, and not given space or supported to have a voice in the process were key factors in this process (Hydén, 2011; Wiersma, 2011; Gridley et al., 2016). As an example, Gudrun was sharing her thoughts on how the group could create a group poem, and her suggestions were interrupted and talked over by two other students. I observed Gudrun assent and for a while she did not engage in the discussion or offer further suggestions. Moments like this were difficult to facilitate, as trying to act in the best interests of the group and of the individuals is challenging and, in this situation, it resulted in Gudrun disengaging.

In another example, Katherine explained where she lived, and Gudrun interrupted, talking about her own experiences and making assertions about Katherine's town, even arguing about the size of the town. As facilitators, we intervened, supporting Katherine, who was showing signs of agitation from the exchange, and trying to recognise Katherine as the authority on her town. On the second occasion, Gudrun challenged Katherine's assessment of the distance from the town to city centre. Kurt intervened to confirm that Katherine was correct, at which point Gudrun accepted she may have been mistaken. On both occasions, Gudrun had incorrectly made a statement about Katherine's town, upsetting Katherine. These interruptions challenge the person telling the story and rather than furthering the discussion alter the flow of the narrative, breaking the conventions of storytelling and working in contrast to the scaffolding and collaboration which Hydén (2011) identifies as successful markers for storytelling.

Misunderstandings or the impact of an individual's dementia could also inhibit participation. As an example, Helena asked Johan his age and he responded with a dismissive answer. Helena looked upset and turned away from Johan. On reviewing this exchange, I do not feel that Johan meant to insult or dismiss Helena, but rather that he did not want, or know how, to answer the question. Age can be a difficult thing for a person with dementia to remember. It can also be difficult for a person with dementia to respond to factual questions. Greater engagement was found when questions were asked about experiences or that focused on emotional responses. These examples show the importance of asking appropriate questions with people with dementia to minimise uncertainty and to help people to stay engaged in the story process.

Conclusion

This chapter explored the constructs of storytelling that can support a person with dementia to share their experiences and have a voice in the research process. Story provides a flexible format that enables an individual to choose and take ownership of what they share and how, and what they say about themselves (Karlsson et al., 2014). Having this choice is important for people with dementia, who can be marginalised and often feel that they are not heard and not able to share their feelings and experiences with others.

However, story can be challenging as it is reliant on language, something that is affected by a diagnosis of dementia. People with dementia may also find it challenging to remember what has been told and may repeat words, sentences, or stories. The tradition of a beginning, middle, and end is not always possible for a person with dementia to follow. As has been discussed, the stories told by the students did not necessarily follow this linear format. However, they did have elements of character, plot, tension, and resolution, all key aspects of story (Kottler, 2014) – for example, Emma's characterisation of the chess champion. This finding has implications for working with people with dementia in research as the narrative method may need to emerge across discussions and be brought together, as was Johan's description of being diagnosed with dementia. Techniques within the sessions to support narrative are also important in supporting people to have a voice and share their experiences. As discussed, being an active listener and supporting the co-construction of the story through questions and personal examples can help the teller. This is particularly important when working in a group as the participants should be encouraged to support each other in this co-construction so that the story remains that of the participants rather than the researcher. The distinction of the group or the personal story is also important to consider, as shared narratives brought greater engagement across the group, and enabled stronger bonds through shared understandings of their culture, heritage, and their dementia. The collaborative nature of story (Hydén, 2011) emerged strongly as a way of encouraging voice, and facilitation of the process became integral to the success of the story. The focus on language can make this a challenging research tool with people with dementia; however, the use of gesture, tone of voice, eye-contact, and use of metaphor enhance the way a story is told and make it more engaging for those listening.

References

Abma, T.A. (2003). Learning by telling, storytelling workshops as an organisational learning intervention. *Management Learning*, 34(4), pp. 221–240.

Alsawy, S., Tai, S., McEvoy, P. and Mansell, W. (2020). 'It's nice to think somebody's listening to me instead of saying "oh shut up"'. People with dementia reflect on what makes communication good and meaningful. *Journal of Psychiatric Mental Health Nursing*, 27, pp. 151–161. https://doi-org.ezproxy.northampton.ac.uk/10.1111/jpm.12559

Basting, A.D. (2009). *Forget memory: Creating better lives for people with dementia*. Baltimore: The Johns Hopkins University Press.

Basting, A.D. (2011). *TimeSlips training manual: Creative storytelling with people with dementia*. Wisconsin-Milwaukee: University of Wisconsin Milwaukee Centre on Age and Community.

Capstick, A. and Ludwin, L. (2015). Place memory and dementia: findings from participatory film-making in long-term social care. *Health & Place*, 34, pp. 157–163.

Castaño, E. (2020). Discourse analysis as a tool for uncovering the lived experience of dementia: metaphor framing and well-being in early-onset dementia narratives. *Discourse & Communication*, 14(2), pp. 115–132. https://doi.org/10.1177/1750481319890385

Clark-McGhee, K. and Castro, M. (2015). A narrative analysis of poetry written from the words of people given a diagnosis of dementia. *Dementia*, 14(1), pp. 9–26.

Connelly, F.M. and Clandinin, D.J. (1990). Stories of experience and narrative inquiry. *Educational Researcher*, 19, pp. 2–14.

Cute, A., Pring, T., Cocks, N., Cruice, M., Best, W. and Marshall, J. (2013). Enhancing communication through gesture and naming therapy. *Journal of Speech, Language, and Hearing Research*, 56(1), pp. 337–351.

Drumm, M. (2013). *The role of personal storytelling in practice. Insights 23*. London: Institute for Research and Innovation in Social Services.

Frohlich, D.M. (2004). *Audiophotography – Bringing photos to life with sounds*. London: Kulwer Academic Publishers.

Goldsilver, P.M. and Gruneir, M.R.B. (2001). Early stage dementia group: an innovative model of support for individuals in the early stages of dementia. *American Journal of Alzheimer's Disease and Other Dementias*, 16(2), pp. 109–114.

Gridley, K., Brooks, J.C., Birks, Y.G., Baxter, K. and Parker, G. (2016). *Improving care for people with dementia: Development and initial feasibility study for evaluation of life story work in dementia care (final report)*. York University, York: Health Services and Delivery Research.

Gucciardi, E., Jean-Pierre, N., Karam, G. and Sidani, S. (2016). Designing and delivering facilitated storytelling interventions for chronic disease self-management: a scoping review. *BMC Health Services Research*, 16(249), pp.1–13.

Heggestad, A.K.T. and Slettebø, A. (2015). How individuals with dementia in nursing homes maintain their dignity through life storytelling – a case study. *Journal of Clinical Nursing*, 24, pp. 2323–2330. doi: 10.1111/jocn.12837.

Hydén, L-C. (2011). Narrative collaboration and scaffolding in dementia. *Journal of Aging Studies*, 25, pp. 339–347.

Hydén, L-C. (2013). Storytelling in dementia: embodiment as a resource. *Dementia*, 12(3), pp. 359–367.

Hydén, L-C. and Antelius, E. (2011). Communicative disability and stories: towards an embodied conception of narratives. *Health*, 6(15), pp. 588–603.

Jacobus, S. (2018). Evaluation of work images to inspire imaginary life stories. In: *TimeSlips Webinar*, 18th January 2018.

Karlsson, E., Sävenstedt, S., Axelsson, K. and Zingmark, K. (2014). Stories about life narrated by people with Alzheimer's disease. *Journal of Advanced Nursing*, 70(12), pp. 2791–2799.

Kearney, R. (1997). The crisis of narrative in contemporary culture. *Metaphilosophy*, 28(3), pp. 183–195.

Kitwood, T. (1997). *Dementia reconsidered: The person comes first*. Buckingham: Open University Press.

Kottler, J. (2014). *Stories we've heard, stories we've told. Life-changing narratives in therapy and everyday life*. Oxford: Oxford University Press.

Moon, J. (2010). *Using story in higher education and professional development*. Oxfordshire: Routledge.

Murphy, K., Jordan, F., Hunter, A., Cooney, A. and Casey, D. (2015). Articulating the strategies for maximising the inclusion of people with dementia in qualitative research studies. *Dementia*, 14(6), pp. 800–824.

National Health Service (2017). *Communicating with someone with dementia* [online]. Available at: www.nhs.uk/conditions/dementia/communication-and-dementia/ [Accessed 2 Feb. 2018].

National Storytelling Network (2016). *What is storytelling?* [online]. Available at: www.storynet.org/resources/whatisstorytelling.html [Accessed 8 Oct. 2016].

Overcash, J.A. (2003). Narrative research: a review of methodology and relevance to clinical practice. *Critical Reviews in Oncology/Hematology*, 48, pp. 179–184.

Page, S. and Keady, J. (2010). Sharing stories: A meta-ethnographic analysis of 12 autobiographies written by people with dementia between 1989 and 2007. *Ageing & Society*, 30, pp. 511–526.

Prendergast, M. and Saxton, J. (2013). *Applied drama: A facilitator's handbook for working in community*. Bristol: Intellect.

Rich, R. (2014). Storied identities: Identity formation and the life story. *University of Sussex Journal of Contemporary History*, 15, pp. 1–16.

Ryan, E.B. and Martin, L.S. (2011). Using narrative arts to foster personhood in dementia. In: P. Backhaus, ed., *Communication in elderly care cross-cultural perspectives*. London: Bloomsbury, pp. 193–217.

Scheidt, R.J. (2015). The elders: everyone is a story. *The Gerontologist*, 55(2), pp. 330–331.

Schweitzer, P. and Bruce, E. (2008). *Remembering yesterday, caring today: Reminiscence in dementia care: a guide to good practice*. London: Jessica Kingsley Publishers.

Scott, J-A. (2019). The visceral remains: revealing the human desire for performance through personal narratives of Alzheimer's Disease. *Text and Performance Quarterly*, 39(2), pp. 116–134. doi: 10.1080/10462937.2019.1595116.

Stenhouse, R., Tait, J., Hardy, P. and Sumner, T. (2013). Dangling conversations: reflections on the process of creating digital stories during a workshop with people with early-stage dementia. *Journal of Psychiatric and Mental Health Nursing*, 20, pp. 134–141.

Taylor, P. (2003). *Applied theatre: Creating transformative encounters in the community*. Portsmouth: Heinemann.

Ward, A. (2019). *Understanding photography and storytelling with people with early-stage dementia to understand their lived experience and enable them to tell their stories*. University of Northampton.

Ward, A., Sorensen, K.A., Kousgaard, H., Schack Thoft, D. and Parkes, J. (2018). Going back to school – An opportunity for lifelong learning for people with dementia in Denmark (Innovative Practice). *Dementia*. doi.org/10.1177/1471301218763190.

Wiersma, E.C. (2011). Using photovoice with people with early-stage Alzheimer's disease: A discussion of methodology. *Dementia*, 10(22), pp. 203–216.

36
ZEN STORIES TO INSPIRE IMAGINATION IN A CLIENT WITH VASCULAR DEMENTIA

Ravindra Ranasinha

Introduction

This chapter aims to highlight the impact of therapeutic storytelling towards symptomatic improvement of a client with post-stroke vascular dementia, in Sri Lanka. First, the reader is introduced to the influential practice of Buddhism, in this island, and how the Christian clergy has become engrossed in Buddha's teachings. Second, the focus is to understand how storytelling has a therapeutic bearing on patients with vascular dementia. Third, the chapter will elaborate on a storytelling intervention, which was launched in Sri Lanka, as a pilot project, to support a Christian priest with post-stroke vascular dementia. Fourth, an analysis of the efficacy of the project is provided, to understand how Zen Buddhist stories and the storytelling process supported the client, towards his recovery. The chapter concludes, underscoring the therapeutic value of storytelling, to enhance the quality of life of people living with vascular dementia.

Sri Lanka is a country with a majority population belonging to the Buddhist faith, and its influence is felt across all communities in Sri Lanka. Stories from Buddha's life and Zen Buddhist stories are always read and listened to, as they are considered the sources of wisdom, for the past two thousand five hundred years, in this country. In particular, Zen Buddhist stories are valued for their life-enriching messages of mindfulness.

In Sri Lanka, there are Christian priests who have shown a keen interest in studying Buddhism, utilizing Buddhist concepts to support their 'flock'. Since the Christian clergy in this country always witness Buddhistic practices, they have shown a tendency to absorb Buddhist tenets into their lives. They engage in inter-faith discourses, conduct comparative studies on Buddhism and Christianity, and practice vidarshana, or mindfulness meditation. Their understanding about Buddhism has inevitably made them adopt a holistic approach towards living.

Buddhism relates to the philosophical teachings of Buddha, whose mission was to show that 'transformation' is inevitable (Bai & Cohen, 2014). It is about a philosophy of an endless change in all phenomena. This 'truth' makes Buddhist philosophy unique, and its objective view towards life differs from other faiths that refer to an 'Almighty Creator', or a God (McCoy et al., 2016).

The Christian priests in this island, who were keen in adopting a balanced view regarding both the religions, were cautious not to disturb the Christian belief about the Almighty. They were engrossed in treading a path that erases this difference between objectivity and subjectivity.

Zen Buddhist stories were of immense value to achieve this balance, since Zen speaks a universal language of compassion (ibid).

Zen stories create optimal learning conditions within which a person can recognize and begin to realize their enlightened mind-heart (bodhicitta), and can work on transforming what has obstructed the emergence, or manifestation of this enlightened nature (ibid). The metaphors and symbols pertaining to Zen stories create an unconscious discourse to make the practitioner mindful of obstructions, nurture present moment awareness, eradicate non-judgmental behavior, and enhance spiritual growth. These stories are adored for their strength to investigate and dismantle the ego that creates chaos and illusion in man, paving the way for a transformational experience in life (ibid).

Storytelling as therapy

Storytelling is a common and everyday part of human existence, and emerges early in life and is a social activity that occurs across cultures (Fels & Astell, 2011). Stories take different forms, such as, myths, folk tales, legends, fictional, autobiographical, and self-narratives (Kim et al., 2020; Lugmayr et al., 2016). "The reasons people tell stories are manifold: to entertain, to transfer knowledge between generations, to maintain cultural heritage, or to warn others of dangers" (Kim et al., 2020). Therapists have used storytelling as an intervention, or a treatment technique in therapy to support people with dementia (Fels & Astell, 2011; Kim et al., 2020).

The power of story as a transformative teaching tool presents to the reader or listener a virtual world populated not only by human action, but also by intention, desire, emotion, perception, volition, and sensations (Bai & Cohen, 2014). According to Bai and Cohen (2014),

> By virtue of entering and participating in an imaginative story-world, a person lets go of, or at least may hold more loosely, his or her old patterns and meanings, and thus is open and receptive to trying out vicariously patterns of thinking and ways of looking and feeling that are unfamiliar and fresh. Story listening has the potential to facilitate a different state of consciousness in the listener, at least temporarily, and in that altered state an openness may emerge that allows for new possibilities of being – possibilities that are predisposed to be in line with the experience of awakening and seeing the world non-dually.

People with dementia seem to engage in the same storytelling processes that they likely did before they had dementia (Fels & Astell, 2011). While people with dementia have difficulty recalling and discussing current events, they find it easier to speak about memories from earlier in their lives (ibid). Several pieces of research show the benefits of implementing reminiscence programs for people with a dementia diagnosis (Astell et al., 2010; Brooker & Duce, 2000). Fels and Astell concluded that a reminiscence program, with the application of a normative model of storytelling, is an effective way to enhance the cognitive capacity of people with dementia, "even when dementia severity is quite advanced" (Fels & Astell, 2011). Other studies have reported that establishing a way to connect with past memories can help to reestablish a link to the present (Siriaraya & Ang, 2014; Schjavland, 2017).

Vascular dementia

Vascular dementia is better understood as a heterogeneous syndrome in which the underlying etiology is cerebrovascular disease manifesting as dementia (Gorelick et al., 2011). A study states that stroke remains a notorious risk factor for dementia, increasing risk about two-fold (Kuźma et al., 2018). Gorelick and colleagues state that "vascular dementia should be characterized by evidence of clinical stroke or subclinical vascular brain injury affecting at least two cognitive domains and causing sufficient decline to affect the activities of daily living" (Gorelick et al., 2011).

Retrospective, or autobiographical memory

Retrospective memory involves remembering previous events, or previously learned information (Livener, 2009). Therefore, these memories become the autobiographical memory of the person. This important feature of memory system enables recollection of personally experienced past happenings (Bose et al., 2016). According to Bose and others (2016), autobiographical memory helps in developing one's self, or individual identity, and to remain oriented in the world, and to follow goals effectively in the light of past problem solving and interpersonal goals. As an outcome in that study, it is mentioned that patients with vascular dementia have significant impairment in both personal semantic and personal autobiographical incident memory. The researchers have concluded that patients with vascular dementia mostly have problems in expressing their thoughts in a consistent manner (ibid).

Pilot project

A pilot project on therapeutic storytelling was designed to support a client with vascular dementia. We name the client as M. He is a Christian priest, aged 75 years, who experienced his second stroke, resulting in vascular dementia. M. faced challenges due to cognitive impairment, language disability, disorientation, loss of attention, loss of gait, and loss of balance. This client has an immense liking towards Zen Buddhist stories, and had a large collection of Buddhist literature.

A group of six elders, who were M.'s friends, were recruited as a support group, to implement the storytelling intervention. Zen stories that M. was quite familiar with were selected for the sessions. The duration of the storytelling intervention was six (06) months. Every week M. received three sessions of storytelling (Monday, Wednesday, and Friday), with each session lasting 40 minutes.

During the intervention, the facilitator used a reflective diary, to make notes on his observations. A post-intervention semi-structured interview with the client helped in gathering data related to his improvement. The data was analyzed thematically, and the findings have been presented under three themes, namely, 'Embodied memory – bridging the past and the present', 'Expressiveness – Improving language ability, creativity, and imagination', and 'Zen storytellers – caring readers and actors'.

Embodied memory – bridging the past and the present

At the beginning, M. was silent. There was no response from him. "He was just sitting, keeping his eyes closed, or gazing at something else", I observed. He preferred to look down and wait. I wondered whether M. was tired, or was not keen on what we were doing. It was a test on my patience. Uncertainty made me write, "So, will this effort go waste?" Another entry says, "I wonder whether I'm too hasty in trying to see a change in M".

Every time I read a story, I tried to maintain eye contact with him, but it was difficult, since he turned his eyes at some other direction. When there was no response from M., it was quite hard for me as the facilitator. 'Keep calm', I said to myself many times. It was not only me, but the support group, too, was in my situation. I was prepared to accept any result with M., as that will be a 'great learning'. A diary note says, "Any outcome will explain what this ailment is about, and how it should be tackled".

The group was a great strength for M. They were the society around him, reading the lines of those Zen stories that M. liked so much. Reading was done giving a lot of color to the words – in other words, the tone and the speed of reading mattered a lot, to magnify the essence of the story, and make them impressive for M. I wanted my client to recall how he spent time with Zen stories.

In a diary note, I have mentioned the reasons for selecting Zen stories: "I believe that M. was much connected to Zen stories. I can recall how he spoke to me many times about the essence of Zen stories. His attachment to them is very strong. Using Zen stories can stimulate his thinking, and help him to return to who he was". Zen stories were energy suppliers, as I thought, for reminiscence purposes.

In the first four weeks, there was no visible result. There were studies that encouraged me. They mentioned that the symptoms can be improved through immersion. It was a training to M., to listen to stories. He was a spectator for a couple of months. "I cannot tell whether he was a passive spectator, or an active one. This puzzles me", I have written as a reflection. "He can hear us, and he can see us"; that was our only hope.

In the fifth week, "M. had tears in his eyes. I do not know why". It was difficult for me to guess why he had tears. "Can it be that he was tired of listening to the stories? Or, was he tired being seated for forty minutes?" I was in an uncertain state, not knowing how I should handle the situation. I also had the thought that since he could not oppose our activities, perhaps a sense of helplessness crept into him. I kept guessing, but as I had no solution, I consulted a physician who pacified me saying not to worry. I remembered how I faced similar situations, while conducting dramatherapy sessions in elders' homes. Most of those elders having dementia cried when reminiscing about their past. That experience taught me to bear with this situation.

"It was so unexpected", I made an entry in the sixth week. "All were happy to see a slight smile on his face". That smile changed the whole atmosphere. I was overjoyed. A ray of hope appeared. The support group, too, felt relieved. "The tears projected his connectivity to the stories. It was an emotional welcome. He showed his interest, but the tears may have resulted as he was yearning to verbalize. Zen stories touched him. Tears were a positive response". I entered this note after seeing the smile on his face, receiving an assurance of his change.

It was very clear that he had been listening to every story reading, for six weeks. My opinion was that the reading had touched his memory, and also had tapped his unconscious. Zen stories might have caused brain stimulation, to reminisce, and respond through tears, and smiles.

"Storytelling becomes a performance for brain activation", a diary entry states. The support group helped M. to return to the past, and recall what he has read. The capacity for retrospection, I noted, "can be a result of the cognitive reserves, if there is something to that effect".

In one of the sessions, I observed that he was moving his fingers, tapping his knee. That day the support group started sculpting some of the metaphors, while reading the Zen stories. M. was very attentive to what the group created. He had bright cheeks, and tears were rolling down. These physical cues were, as I noted in my diary, "Important data in relation to his improvement".

At the beginning, his keenness to attend storytelling sessions was not visible. Gradually, there was increased interest to attend the sessions. He came walking to the circle without anyone's help. His interest was visible in the manner he walked and sat himself. He sat and bent forward to listen to the reading. There is no doubt that he loved to see the way the support group read, discussed, and performed the Zen stories.

I noted his keenness to listen to the story about the man who stumbled upon a tiger. M. giggled while watching the story being played. Also, the group sculpted the story before him, towards which he raised his right hand and waved, signaling his approval. At this moment, I noted that he was attempting to verbalize what he felt, but the sound was not heard. He closed his mouth, realizing speech was not possible. There was no look of disappointment, but he went on smiling and nodding his head, approving the performance.

Expressiveness – improving language ability, creativity, and imagination

The Zen stories were a great inspiration for M. to verbalize. As my diary notes reveal, it took three months for M. to utter a word. He began by attempting to say a single word from a story. "The group was reading the story about Great Master Chuang Tzu. In that story, the master dreamt that he was a butterfly fluttering here and there. When M. heard the word 'butterfly', he started to utter the word. I saw the difficulty he had in managing the sound. His tongue was not steady, and I saw him struggling to get the right sound", states my diary entry. I observed how he took courage, to complete the word. There was stuttering. "As an intellectual, he showed that he cannot fail in making the correct pronunciation. He struggled, but he accomplished", I noted. The group clapped, encouraging him, and expressing their joy.

M. kept repeating the word 'butterfly'. He was trying to grasp the speech sound correctly. I felt that mirroring of the word was important. The support group joined him, echoing the word. They improvised in creating a butterfly, using demy paper. The word 'butterfly' was written on paper, so that, M. could see the word and visualize. There was a performance built around this word, to inspire M.

Storytelling, sculpting, scene work, role play, and improvisation helped M. to imagine, and be creative. "M. attempts to say at least four to five words", I have noted in my diary. It was the fourth month of our intervention, and I planned to continue with that story about the 'Great Master'. Repetition of the story, and performing it, made M. capture more words. He was able to say the words, 'master', 'butterfly', 'dream', 'person', and 'man'. Repetition, sculpting, and role play reinforced M.'s capacity to verbalize.

"M. learnt new words, and that was a sign of his improvement", I noted as a reflection. I suggested that we read sentences, helping M. to repeat them. Short sentences were devised from the Zen story about the Great Master. Each person in the group read a sentence, and then helped M. to join that person by repeating the sentence. It was a kind of a game, and M. liked it, as he had to interact with each member. "This mirroring practice made him conscious of the lines. His eyes gleamed with that effort he made to utter a sentence", my diary says. One day M. spoke about the Great Master: "He was only a butterfly". I noted that M. was quite conscious of his achievement. "With less faltering, he could utter the line", I have noted in the diary.

The group selected two short Zen stories, to help M. with his short-term memory. One was about the man who did not know where he was going on his horse. The other one was about the thief who entered the Zen master's hut. M. selected the first one. The group wrote the story on demy sheets, so that M. could look and read aloud.

> It was interesting to see how M. made progress in reading what was written on paper. We asked him to repeat the story without looking at the paper, and he, in fact,

summarized it this way: "A man came on a horse. He was going somewhere. Another man asked where he was going. He said to ask the horse".

In this summary, I noted that M. dropped details, but was able to capture the gist of the story.

The other story was re-told in this manner: "A rogue came to a teacher's house. There was nothing to take. The teacher returned, and saw the rogue. The teacher gave his clothes to the rogue. He was naked". M. chuckled at this point. The group wrote the story the way M. told it, and helped him to read. He was happy to read it, and say it aloud. The group performed this story, helping M. to adopt the teacher's role.

At two separate sessions, M. was asked to repeat the two stories. He could remember them, and did not ask for any support from the group. While M. read the stories, the group got an opportunity to perform. The support group was always a motivational factor for M., to improve his skills.

The Zen stories created a play space for all in the circle. They passed a story, each one taking a single line. At times, randomly they picked a word and pointed at someone who was supposed to read a line from a story. "Such energizers bring M. to his earlier state", I wrote in my diary. "His improvement was remarkable", was a note of assurance, in my reflections.

M. achieved a speech time of 30 to 45 minutes, at the final sessions. He had the enthusiasm to speak. At times, he used a considerable time for short discourses, and then I noticed, he faced speech difficulties. He was comfortable with informal conversations, and could continue for 60 minutes.

Zen storytellers – caring readers and actors

The group and I were the storytellers. I observed that the group made an impact on M., being there always, motivating him. The group was his social capital. They assured him of their presence. They spoke softly, tried to keep eye contact, always faced him, had a slow pace when talking, helped him with a touch, never failed to call him by his name, tried to listen to him even if his utterances were not clear, tried to understand M.'s non-verbal behavior, had an amazing patience, never interfered when M. wanted to say something, every time showing their presence and availability, active, and very loving. "The group was a lively entity", I have noted in my diary.

The tone of voice was very important for storytelling. I gave a lot of variance to the tone, thinking that M. would be able to recall his memory on metaphors, symbols, or incidences. The group, too, adopted this pattern telling the stories. When a story was read in the circle, each person took a line, and gave color to the story, making it as true and lively as possible. The members of the group enjoyed storytelling, and encouraged M. to join in.

In fact, the group was more determined to bring in more activities to the circle. They drew pictures of the characters appearing in the stories. Brought costumes and props. Soft music was used. "Every reading was a performance", I noted.

When M. started to utter single words, there came a time of teaching. The group wrote words in large letters, on demy paper. They were holding papers in front of him, to see, and then to read. In some sessions, a storyboard was created, so that M. could visualize, and express what he feels about the story.

"Group helped M. in every possible manner, to retrieve his ability to remember, speak, narrate, and perform", I reflected the progress. An accelerated input from M. was visible in the latter part of the intervention. He was emerging at an increased rate, encouraging the group.

I saw myself in the role of the facilitator, steering the whole mission, guiding the group, and becoming innovative during the process. The facilitator should always equip themselves with related skills and knowledge. Their talents as a story reader, vocalist, and actor, matter a lot, to make them innovative. These help them to overcome risks when conducting interventions, especially for a population with dementia.

When I selected the Zen stories, I used my previous experiences with M., having informal conversations, or attending his discourses. They guided me amply to plan the intervention, selecting the most inspiring and attractive stories for him. I knew his eagerness to speak about them.

I have been associating M. for more than three decades, but after the stroke, to my bewilderment, he could not recognize me. The group members were his friends, but M. did not recognize them, either, until he came to a stage of emerging from his disorientated state. I wrote, "When M. noted that all of us were his friends, his joy was enormous. He felt so secure and confident on recognizing us. It was comfortable for him to stay in the circle, as he realized that he belongs to this group".

Getting to know the group of storytellers was an encouraging experience for M. He came to join the circle, first, with a smile, and then he was able to call each one by their first name. "I noticed that he was improving, since he was happy to be with the team". He was eager to connect with the group, at every session. It was his inner need, as I observed.

The role played by the support group made a drastic change in M. Their multiple roles were healing, as they contained him. They developed a collective experience throughout the intervention. The collective embodiment encouraged M. to return to his earlier patterns of living, gradually.

The group was an inspiring audience for him. At the final interview, M. said:

- "My friends were amazing. I didn't know that they can act. I found them very helpful. They were an encouraging team".
- "My friends have big hearts. I am thankful for their patience".
- "They are good people. I love them so much".
- "They helped me to change. I am thankful to them".
- "I am sure you all had a difficult time with me".
- "We are all about Zen".

Making sense of therapeutic storytelling
Embodied memory

Therapeutic storytelling is an aid for reminiscence for a person with vascular dementia. This intervention utilized Zen stories to assist M. to build connectivity to his history. The post-stroke vascular dementia state impaired his memory, disabling him in remembering his earlier roles and activities. Storytelling can be treated as a stimulative process that helps a client with vascular dementia to bridge their past and the present.

Zen story sessions were a journey to the past, enabling M. to delve into his memories. This excursion to the past comprised of four main steps: careful selection of the Zen story, reading the story, appreciation of metaphors and symbols, and dramatic presentation of the story. The voyage was an indirect approach that resonated a theatrical experience, towards motivation, retrospection, and reconnection.

A play space created in storytelling sessions supported M. to engage with his past memories. The storyteller's tone of voice, facial expressions, and bodily gestures were important performing elements that created the play space, galvanizing M.'s retrospective memory. As the storytellers were the inspiring players of M.'s embodied memories, the play space transformed into a collective experience. It assured him that his treasured experience with Zen is at his disposal.

In patients with vascular dementia, cognitive dysfunction has been identified as a serious pathological condition (Gorelick et al., 2011; Pendlebury & Rothwell, 2019), and its impact on the creative faculties of a person is detrimental. Storytelling is a creative process that invites the participant's imagination. The intervention assisted M. to re-connect with Zen stories, as Zen was an inspirational teaching, towards creative imagination, and living. Creativity is an integral part of the person's memory, and therefore, storytelling can help a person with vascular dementia to transcend the isolation they may be feeling, work through issues still troubling them, and enjoy the pleasure and satisfaction of the process of creative work (Baines, 2007).

M.'s spiritual discourses were the embodiment of his creativity, prior to the stroke. The therapeutic storytelling intervention aimed in restoring this power of creativity, within the group, in order to enhance his social interactions. This implies a shift from the decontextualized individual to an interaction with other participants in the storytelling situation (Hyden, 2013). Creativity enables interpersonal engagement that contributes to overall quality of life for the patient. The continuation of imagination and engagement provides intervals of good feeling in the face of overwhelming adversity (Cohen, 2006).

Zen stories made M. conscious of his creativity. During his earlier life period, he preferred to discuss the metaphors and symbols in Zen stories, projecting his intellectual power. The stories had an unusually good staying power with him, then. It can be ascribed to his 'level of education' (Gorelick et al., 2011), which was an aspect aimed at in this study, to re-construct his life narrative. Therefore, these stories told well and used judiciously stand out as special for M. Storytelling sessions caused a stimulating environment for M. to cherish his memories about Zen.

M.'s emotional and behavioral responses towards storytelling sessions, through tears, smiles, and finger tapping, aptly reflected his passion towards Zen stories. His delayed response to the stories could be due to the severity of damage caused to his brain, due to the stroke. More importantly, the delayed responses inform that the frequency of the intervention had a prospective influence in leveraging the functionality of his retrospective memory. Thus, storytelling sessions thrice a week inspired M.'s cognition, re-connecting him with his previous experiences, and his way of life.

Recalling past experiences become meaningful for M., since the memory with Zen stories contains an emotional aspect. Emotion influences memory at several levels, from recognition (Estes & Adelman, 2008) to recollection (Doerksen & Shimamura, 2001). Nostalgic reverie often revolves around momentous life events and reflects more positive than negative emotions, contains more desirable than undesirable features, and leads to a more positive than negative mood (Tietyen, 2012). Research attributes emotional memory enhancement to arousal (Adelman & Estes, 2013), with the underlying assumption being that our limited memory resources are preferentially allocated to significant stimuli, especially if they are emotionally oriented (Nummenmaa et al., 2006). Memories can be explored in many creative ways to connect to the past events which can bring new awareness to the present, and can serve as a source of positive experience, either by encouraging self-esteem, or by generating enjoyment and pleasure (Subramaniam et al., 2014).

Creative activities are valuable media to serve reminiscence (Tietyen, 2012). Past events and experiences can be stimulated in the person with vascular dementia, and that reminiscence can contribute to the quality of life of that person (Dempsey et al., 2014). Zen stories, as reminiscence-related therapeutic stories, facilitated understanding and respect of M.'s past. Reminiscence is more than just revisiting a person's history. It can be a metaphor, or a storyline which can help the person with dementia to express themselves, and restore personhood and dignity.

Storytelling sessions enabled M. to reminisce through Zen stories, and discover his history. The Zen stories had the potential to capture M.'s past, since they were primarily connected to his intuitive and unconscious parts of the mind. Their influence, as embodied material, had a subtle effect in restoring his memory function. "My whole life is about Zen", he said, subsequent to his return as an abled person.

Storytellers

Zen storytellers comprised the facilitator and the support group. In particular, the facilitator was the chief storyteller, who acted as the 'holding container' for M. The facilitator's key role was to create a safe environment so that M. would have a smooth engagement during the storytelling sessions. A 'safe psychological space', as seen in storytelling sessions, reduces anxiety and low motivation in the listener, and makes the person active and engaged.

The group of narrators had the role of inspiring M., to immerse in a training that can improve his clarity of utterance, language learning, interaction, storytelling, and performance. They utilized their vocal skills, as well as art, movement, and sculpting to inspire M. Initially, he refrained from mirroring the group activities; however, with gradual improvement, he not only mirrored the group, but also made the group mirror him. The emergence of an interactive environment supported him to improve in responsive behavior, enabling him to take charge of his lost narrative.

Friends who joined as a support network performed the roles of narrators and actors, to stimulate M.'s memory. His severed life narrative received reparation through the group's collective engagement in storytelling. Their performative presentations enhanced the value of M.'s life story. The dramatic renderings of Zen stories influenced him to re-connect with his past, and reunite with his self, in order to complete his story. The group embodied memories, narratives, experiences, and interconnections with Zen stories, to re-build his life story.

Storytellers can be treated as an auxiliary ego for M, as they were encouraging, animating, reassuring, cheering, and supporting. One of the main purposes of the auxiliary is to help the protagonist see their experiences more insightfully and clearly (Kaur, 2006). The storytellers utilized the stories to illumine the invisible, say the unsaid, and amplify the implied, to help the protagonist to witness what was demonstrated, and gain insight. They were a group that was willing to learn, and open to the thoughts, feelings, and actions of the protagonist. As the auxiliary, the storytellers were helping to portray M.'s world, before his own eyes, to cause the expected shift. Hence, the role of the storyteller, as the auxiliary, becomes very crucial.

The storytellers were a caring team, containing M. Their playful aspects portrayed an air of casualness and warmth. They created an interactive atmosphere, offering a feeling of belongingness, not only to M., but also for all members in the group. As social and interactive beings, they were able to foster a sense of self-worth in everyone in the group. This social capital created a friendly, educative, and creative environment, enabling M. to exercise freedom, and independence. The storytellers were a stimulating milieu, generating a passion in M., to make him functional.

Gentleness and patience are decisive traits of a caring facilitation group. They are the social and emotional skills that enabled the group of storytellers to ensure the wellbeing of both the client and themselves. Their gentleness and kindness created a caring environment, enabling both parties to experience mental and emotional ease. Interaction with M., whether by speech, or behavior, was gentle. Also, the group demonstrated an inconceivable breadth of patience towards M. For storytellers, patience was an essential quality, to engage in a challenging process of supporting a client with vascular dementia. "They have big hearts", said M. responding to the group's caring nature. They provided the dignity, love, and comfort to M. The significance of the carers' adoption of such qualities becomes a motivating factor for the patient with vascular dementia. The group understood the vitality of sustaining patience, to continually move forward, look for solutions, and work toward their goal.

It was imperative for the group to have appropriate communication skills to nurture rapport, and sustain a productive therapeutic relationship with M. Difficulty in communication is a core effect of vascular dementia (Riachi, 2017). The interpersonal communication with M. needed to blend verbal, behavioral, cultural, and social aspects. Communication for vascular dementia care is a crucial skill, and therefore, the group had to develop new skills, to communicate with M. They were helpful ways to keep M. in a positive frame of mind. As a good communication skill, attention to how one relates to the client is important. Storytellers utilized specific communication skills, such as use of simple spoken language, facial expressions, eye contact, smile, and hand gestures. They reflect an understanding about gentle care for people with vascular dementia. A good level of communication is key to reminiscence and to an individual's retaining a clear sense of personal identity (Dempsey et al., 2014).

The role of storytellers was emotionally and physically demanding; however, they persisted in empowering M. to rely more on his strengths, sensing the personal value, and the capacity for improvement, and wellbeing. Group interaction nurtured confidence and joy in him, and the increased strength enabled him to be a witness towards his own improvement. Every member of the group had a shared understanding that M.'s wellbeing depended on their recognition of his personhood. Hence, they ensured that he felt safe and comfortable throughout the storytelling intervention, to augment his self-esteem.

Conclusion

Storytelling makes a contribution to the quality of life of people living with vascular dementia. It inspires retrospective memory, re-connects with the person's earlier life experiences, brings pleasure to the person, and contributes towards symptomatic improvement, offering an imaginative frame to enable processing of personal psychological material. The client's spiritual relationship with Zen stories inspired developments in memory, language ability, creativity, social communication, and social interaction. It built a continued sense of identity and personhood in the client, to help maintain a sense of self. The stories and metaphors enabled a narrative reconstruction, enhancing self-worth in the person.

Among human activities, storytelling affords enriching experiences for people with a diagnosis of vascular dementia, and prompts the expression of a wide range of emotions. And, it's where the psychosocial wellbeing of an individual living with vascular dementia can be naturally and readily observed and measured. Stories and metaphors, when carefully utilized during treatment, drive change through non-cognitive, sensory, and emotional processing. The listener is invited to identify with characters and story themes that facilitate them towards a better understanding of self and others, cognitive restructuring, and behavioral change.

The storytellers become carers with a stronger sense of purpose, resolve, and commitment, showing the wider community to become more compassionate and aware towards people with vascular dementia. Storytellers bear a responsible role, to support the client, who needs to be held and seen, to be affirmed and welcomed by the group, and the storytelling process. The facilitator's primary role is to activate 'new pathways', through listening to the 'heavy silence', taking into account the needs of the participant. It is the role of the facilitator to offer 'art as a respite, a momentary pause in an awful reality' (Allen, 2006).

In Sri Lanka, an apparent lack of understanding towards the efficacy of arts-based interventions for vascular dementia care has led people to ignore their importance. Hence, opportunities for arts-based research in dementia-specific healthcare settings are very few. Storytelling, as a psychosocial intervention, has been widely researched in dementia-care settings, with positive outcomes. The current reliance on pharmacotherapy for dementia care has hindered the humane support the people with dementia deserve, and shrouds psychosocial interventions in unnecessary mystery. These circumstances will do nothing to progress the quality and humane disposition of the aged care sector, nor will they serve the best interests of the neediest recipients of care in our society (McAdam, 2013).

References

Adelman, J. S., & Estes, Z. (2013). Emotion and memory: a recognition advantage for positive and negative words independent of arousal. *Cognition*, 129(3), 530–535. DOI:10.1016/j.cognition.2013.08.014.

Allen, P. (2006). Wielding the shield: the art therapist as conscious witness in the realm of social action. In F. Kaplan (Ed) *Art therapy and social action: Treating the world's wounds*. Philadelphia: Jessica Kingsley Publishers, 72–88.

Astell, A. J., Ellis, M. P., Alm, N., Dye, R., & Gowans, G. (2010). Stimulating people with dementia to reminisce using personal and generic photographs. *International Journal of Computers in Health*, 1(2), 177–198.

Bai, H., & Cohen, A. (2014). Zen and the art of storytelling. Studies in Philosophy and Education, 33(3). DOI 10.1007/s11217-014-9413-8.

Baines, P. (2007). Nurturing the heart: creativity, art therapy, and dementia. *Quality Dementia Care*, 3, 5–45. www.dementia.org.au/files/20070900_Nat_QDC_QDC3NurturingHeart.pdf

Bose, P., Biswas, A., Pal, S., Basu, J., & Das, S. K. (2016). Autobiographical memory impairment in Alzheimer disease and vascular dementia. *Journal of Alzheimer's Parkinsonism & Dementia*, 1(2), 1–7. www.researchgate.net/publication/312289030

Brooker, D., & Duce, L. (2000). Wellbeing and activity in dementia: a comparison of group reminiscence therapy, structured goal-directed group activity and unstructured time. *Aging and Mental Health*, 4(4), 354–358.

Cohen, G. (2006). Research on creativity and aging: the positive impact of the arts on health and illness. Generations, 30(1), 7–15.

Dempsey, L., Murphy, K., Cooney, A., Casey, D., O'Shea, E., Devane, D., Jordan, F., & Hunter, A. (2014). Reminiscence in dementia: a concept analysis. *Dementia*, 13(2), 176–192. DOI: 10.1177/1471301212456277.

Doerksen, S., & Shimamura, A. P. (2001). Source memory enhancement for emotional words. *Emotion*, 1(1), 5–11.

Estes, Z., & Adelman, J. S. (2008). Automatic vigilance for negative words in lexical decision and naming: comment on Larsen, Mercer, and Balota (2006). *Emotion*, 8(4), 441–444. DOI:10.1037/1528-3542.8.4.441.

Fels, D. I., & Astell, A. J. (2011). Storytelling as a model of conversation for people with dementia and caregivers. *American Journal of Alzheimer's Disease & Other Dementias*, 26(7), 535–541. DOI: 10.1177/1533317511429324.

Gorelick, P. B., Scuteri, A., Black, S. E., et al. (2011). Vascular contributions to cognitive impairment and dementia: a statement for healthcare professionals from the American heart association/American stroke association. *Stroke*, 42, 2672–713.

Gregory, H. (2011). Using poetry to improve the quality of life and care for people with dementia: a qualitative analysis of the Try to Remember programme. *Arts & Health*, 3(2), 160–172.

Hannemann B. T. (2006). Creativity with dementia patients. *Gerontology*, 52, 59–65

Hyden, L. C. (2013). Storytelling in dementia: embodiment as a resource. *Dementia*, 12(3), 359–367. DOI: 10.1177/1471301213476290.

Jaaniste, J. (2011). Dramatherapy and spirituality in dementia care. *Dramatherapy*, 33(1), 16–27. DOI: 10.1080/02630672.2011.558355.

Kaur, B. (2006). Exploring the therapeutic potential of skilled auxiliary work. *ANZPA Journal*. https://aanzpa.org/wp-content/uploads/ANZPA_Journal_15_art05.pdf

Kim, S., Chee, K. H., & Gerhart, O. (2020). Generativity in creative storytelling: evidence from a dementia care community. *Innovation in Aging*, 4(2), 1–7. DOI:10.1093/geroni/igaa002.

Kuźma, E., Lourida, I., Moore, S. F., Levine, D. A., Ukoumunne, O. C., & Llewellyn, D. J. (2018). Stroke and dementia risk: a systematic review and meta-analysis. Alzheimer's and Dementia, 14, 1416–1426. DOI: 10.1016/j.jalz.2018.06.3061.

Livener, A. (2009). *Prospective and Retrospective Memory in Normal and Pathological Aging*. Aging Research Centre, Karolinska Institutet, Sweden.

Lugmayr, A., Sutinen, E., Suhonen, J., Sedano, C. I., Hlavacs, H., & Montero, C. S. (2016). Serious storytelling – a first definition and review. *Multimedia Tools Applications*. DOI 10.1007/s11042-016-3865-5.

Matthews, S. (2015). Dementia and the power of music therapy. *Bioethics*, Vol. 29(8): 573–579. DOI:10.1111/bioe.12148.

McAdam, J. G. (2013). Conducting art-based research in dementia-specific healthcare in Australia. *UNESCO Observatory Multi-Disciplinary Journal in the Arts*, Vol. 3, Issue 3, 1–20. Australia: The University of Melbourne.

McCoy, D., Corduan, W. & Stoker, H. (2016). Christian and Buddhist approach to religious exclusivity. Do interfaith scholars have it right? *HTS Teologiese Studies/Theological Studies*, 72(3), a3266. http://dx.doi.org/10.4102/hts.v72i3.3266

Nummenmaa, L., Hyona, J., & Calvo, M. G. (2006). Eye movement assessment of selective attentional capture by emotional pictures. *Emotion*, 6(2), 257–268. DOI:10.1037/1528-3542.6.2.257.

Pendlebury, S. T., & Rothwell, P. M. (2019). Oxford Vascular Study. Incidence and prevalence of dementia associated with transient ischaemic attack and stroke: analysis of the population-based oxford vascular study. *Lancet Neurology*, 18, 248–258. DOI: 10.1016/S1474-4422(18)30442-3.

Riachi, R. (2017): Person-centred communication in dementia care: a qualitative study of the use of the SPECAL™ method by care workers in the UK, *Journal of Social Work Practice*, DOI: 10.1080/02650533.2017.1381948.

Schjavland, E. (2017). *Heart and Soul: A Phenomenology of Dementia Spouse Caregivers' Relationship Closeness* (Doctoral Thesis). University of Connecticut Graduate School. https://opencommons.uconn.edu/dissertations/1405

Siriaraya, P., & Ang, C. S. (May, 2014). Recreating living experiences from past memories through virtual worlds for people with dementia. In *Proceedings of the SIGCHI Conference on Human Factors in Computing Systems (CHI '14)*. Association for Computing Machinery, New York, NY, USA, 3977–3986. DOI: https://doi.org/10.1145/2556288.2557035.

Subramaniam, P., Woods, B., & Whitaker, C. (2014). Life review and life story books for people with mild to moderate dementia: a randomized controlled trial. *Aging & Mental Health*, 18(3), 363–375, http://dx.doi.org/10.1080/13607863.2013.837144

Swinnen, A. M. C. (2016). Healing words: a study of poetry interventions in dementia care. *Dementia*, 15(6), 1377–1404. DOI: 10.1177/1471301214560378.

Tietyen, A. C. (2012). *Applying Specific Arts Activities to Improve the Quality Of Life for Individuals with Alzheimer's disease And Dementia*. (Master's Thesis, University of Kentucky). https://uknowledge.uky.edu/art_etds/3

Wang, Q. Y., & Li, D. M. (2016). Advances in art therapy for patients with dementia. *Chinese Nursing Research*, 3, 2–9. DOI: 10.1016/j.cnre.2016.06.011.

PART V

Stories

In one sense Part V needs little introduction as the authors adequately introduce their work in a clear and succinct way. Indeed they are not really chapters at all, but we have kept this convention to keep a coherent flow to the whole book.

We felt it very important that in a book about Therapeutic Stories and Storytelling there needed to be a practical aspect, something that the reader could take away and use. Part V offers that.

In Chapter 37 Sharon Jacksties offers a series of 7 stories from around the world that the reader can ponder on and use as appropriate within their own work. Four of these are fuller versions of those referred to in her chapter, which readers may choose to read alongside that account of her practice. Otherwise, as Sharon Jacksties suggests 'It is not for me to explain the meanings of the following stories or how and when they might be used.' Therefore we welcome you to use these stories as you see fit in your own way or in your own practice.

Finally, in Chapter 38, introduced by Alenka Vidrih, we are reminded clearly that Katja Gorečan's therapeutic story, like all stories, has the potential to explore dark difficult subjects. In this case she returns to one of the themes in Part IV, that of dementia. Katja Gorečan's story takes us on a complex winding narrative that allows Lisa, the 6-year-old protagonist, a chance to begin to come to terms with her Grandpa's failing memory. The story reiterates the main theme of the book – that stories and therapeutic storytelling allow us to make sense of not only our own stories but also the stories of others, and is in that sense a fitting end to this volume.

37
AN INTERNATIONAL STORY ANTHOLOGY

Sharon Jacksties

Introduction

In this brief anthology you will find some of the stories that I have used in my therapeutic practice. The first four are ones that I have specifically referred to in Chapter 25 'The Body Politic,' and those readers who may be interested in why I selected them for my work with torture survivors may choose to read them alongside that chapter.

It is not for me to explain the meanings of the following stories or how and when they might be used. To some readers their relevance will be obvious, themes and issues will jump out at them. Others may appreciate them as wonderful stories per se, worth listening to for their own sakes without conditions or contexts being applied to them – just as they often were in those traditional settings where they were first told so very many years ago. That is the magic of traditional narratives: like an onion there seems to be no limit to their layers – only with story onions each layer reveals another meaning. And as with any onions, they may make our mouths water if properly prepared, but they can also make our eyes water!

Such is the richness of the material stored in traditional tales, encapsulating as they do, all human experience, that this anthology could have been much longer. Perhaps this thinnest of layers on this vast body of world heritage will be a starting point for the reader to explore further. Perhaps we may all come to know that the sharing of this priceless wealth can also become a path to health.

Red Hat, Green Hat (East Africa)

Two families lived in a remote place where there were no other neighbours. Their farms were divided by a long road which was lost to sight in either direction. Nobody from the farms could remember having walked that road and travellers were seldom seen. The families sometimes intermarried, the children played together and they helped each other with their work when it was needed. Surplus was shared, there were few disagreements and these were soon settled – until the day when a stranger passed by. It happened like this.

Everyone was outside because it was harvest time. Even though they were all bent over their work, just as the traveller walked between them, that extra sense that comes when something different is about to happen made them all look up. The neighbours on one side of the road saw a man wearing a red hat. The neighbours on the other side of the road saw a man wearing a green hat. What they couldn't see was that the man's hat was made of two colours – red on one side and green on the other – so of course each family could only see the colour that was nearest to them. The sun was setting and in seconds the stranger became a dwindling silhouette.

That evening all the neighbours gathered to discuss the marvel of having seen a stranger.

'Did you see how tall he was?'
'Did you see how fast he walked?'
'I would like a red hat like that!'
'What red hat? It was a green hat!'
'Green hat? Of course it wasn't; it was red!'
'No it wasn't red; it was green!'
'If you think it was green you must be colour blind!'
'Who are you calling colour blind? It was a red hat!'

And so it went on, from raised voices, to insults, to threatening gestures. No-one remembered who struck the first blow, but when that happened it was easy for others to follow. These became more violent as people were injured and others rushed to protect and avenge. Soon farm implements became weapons in that place where no weapons had been before. These were used on both people and property. It seemed that nothing could appease the fire of anger except perhaps fire itself. Dwellings, barns and stores were burned down. Animals perished or fled. Possessions and food stocks went up in smoke. At last people stopped fighting. They were either too weak or too wounded or there was nothing left to fight with.

The destruction had lasted throughout the night and in the dawn light everyone could see what they had been reduced to. They looked round with horror and shock. Nobody had the strength to start clearing up and there was nothing left that could be used for rebuilding. They sat back where this had all started, on opposite sides of the road, paralysed with helplessness. At last that same instinct came upon them again and they looked up to see the stranger returning. This time, because he was walking in the other direction, those who had first seen a green hat, now saw a red one, and those who had seen a red hat now saw a green one. Some people say that in spite of all the destruction they took to arguing again, because each of the survivors knew for sure what they had seen. Some people say that now, because of this second sighting, they realised that they had made a mistake despite feeling in the right before.

What do you think happened? There are some who do not think that this was the ending of the story at all. They say that when the stranger returned, walking towards the light in the stillness that follows tragedy, everyone heard his footsteps on the road. They looked up to watch his approach and everyone could clearly see that his hat was both green and red. His hat was both red and green.

Amina and the Silent City (Iraq)

Amina's family was going through a time of sadness. Her father was ill and everyone knew that this would be his final illness. Shortly before he died, he summoned his wife and children to tell them that he had left them all an equal share of any wealth he still possessed. Several heaps of coins had been placed on a table. Amina took her share and put it in a pouch that hung from a leather belt she always wore. Soon after, her father died. When the forty days of mourning had passed, Amina said to her mother,

We have all been through such a time of sorrow and grief. Now there is nothing to keep us here and we have never travelled. Let us go on a voyage and see something of the world, a change will lift our spirits.

Her mother agreed and soon the family had paid their passage on a ship that was to call in at the ports of neighbouring countries. But their time of trouble was not yet over. Not long into their voyage they were struck by a terrible storm. The ship was wrecked and everyone was washed into the sea. In the darkness Amina felt something solid beneath her – it was a piece of the broken mast and she clung onto it with all her strength. She never knew how long she held on for – night passed into day and back into night before she was washed up unconscious onto a distant shore. It was the beating sun that roused her and for a moment she relished its warmth after the cold sea. How good it felt to feel the solid ground beneath her and to be still at last. However, she soon noticed how thirsty she was and forced herself to raise her dizzy head and open her stinging eyes. It was only then that she forced herself to accept that she had been washed up in a strange land with no sign of her family. She was quite alone.

As she had had enough of the sea, she turned inland to see if she could find help. But it seemed that she had left a sea of salty waves for a sea of sand dunes. Beneath her were miles of sloping sands and above her was the blue scorching sky. She had walked too far in the desert to turn back – her only hope was to continue and find someone or something to help her. At last in the low light of afternoon she thought she saw something different on the horizon. There, ahead, seemed to be a glittering white city. Amina hardly dared let herself believe that it was real – she had heard of the mirages in the desert that tricked weary travellers. Oh how cruel hope could be! But every time she crested a dune, that glittering city remained in sight and now she could make out towers and domes, minarets and walls.

The whiteness of the marble was so bright she could barely look at it, but at last she had stumbled right up to the huge surrounding wall.

There was a gate, and beside it two sentries. To her surprise they did not react to her arrival, staring past her into the desert. Amina was too parched to speak, her tongue was swollen and her throat felt as though she had been swallowing sand. She drew closer and still they did not acknowledge her. As still as stone they stood. She went to pass them, but when she noticed that their eyes didn't follow her, she waved her hand over their faces. They didn't even blink, and it was then that she understood that something was very wrong in this place. Passing into the first courtyard she knew what it was. Here was a huge and magnificent city and it was completely silent. Amina walked past people who were frozen in motion: a silent face cracked open with unheard laughter, silent children playing with their ball that had become suspended in mid-air. Two fighting dogs had leaped at each other, their fangs buried in the other's neck, but had not regained the ground. Money dropped in the hand from a customer had not reached the stall holder's palm.

The first thing Amina did was to go to a fountain whose water was a mist of droplets that had not fallen. She licked and scooped them out of the air as though she would never have enough to drink. Going like this from fountain to fountain, she walked through the streets, squares and markets of the Silent City until at last she came to its centre. There she found a building that could only be a palace. She ran up white marble stairs past silent servants trapped in time. Galleries and audience chambers flashed by as Amina raced to the heart of the building. There were more dazzling steps leading to a dais and, on that, a white silken bed. Above the silk glittered a silver mist. When she saw it, Amina knew why she had come this far. Slowly, as silent as all in that bewitched city, she approached the bed. Now she could see that behind the mist there lay a young man sleeping. Amina sighed at his beauty, sighed with relief that he seemed to feel no pain – for now she could see that the silver mist was made up of the thousands upon thousands of finest needles that pierced every part of his body. Amina knew that she was here to gently, tenderly remove all of those needles while he slept. She was too tired to see how her hand trembled as it reached for the nearest needle. Her eyes were so heavy that she barely noticed how it didn't fall when she dropped it. There it hung in the air, a silver sliver until she plucked at it again and placed it beneath the bed. She didn't remember how she stretched out on that silken platform and fell into a sleep as deep as her companion's.

As she awoke, memories fought with dreams, fought with nightmares. There was the young man still sleeping beside her, still covered in that shimmering haze of needles. Amina refreshed herself at another fountain, fed from the market stalls and began her work. However clever her fingers became, there still seemed to be as many needles. She didn't want to go any faster in case she scratched that beautiful skin, and she could hardly bear to leave him to hurriedly grab some food or a drink. The task went on for many days and nights, with Amina snatching sleep when she could. Then one day she thought she must have dozed off, because in her dream she heard music – but she was awake and the music was getting nearer. She ran to a window and saw a young woman dancing towards her, playing a whistle and beating a drum. She too must be a recent arrival in the city! Amina called down to her,

'Hey, you down there, will you come and help me?'
'Help you? What will you pay me?'

Amina felt hope turn to dismay. She had lost everything in the shipwreck. But then she remembered the pouch strapped to her belt. It was still there. She took it up and shook it. The newcomer smiled up at the sound of jingling coins.

So it was that Amina parted with her money – all that was left of her family. She had help at last, but asked the girl to only watch that no further harm come to the young man while she slept or went to find food. At last all the needles except for one had been removed. This time Amina noticed how her hand trembled as it reached to pluck the last needle from the man's right eye. She couldn't risk scratching him – he might lose his sight! She turned to her helper and told her not to touch him, to only watch whilst she refreshed herself. Fatigue and excitement made her clumsy. She stumbled at the fountain. As she lifted a hand to scoop water from the air, her movement stopped because water was pouring into her palm, splashing her face, hissing and gurgling in the bowl. Her ears were bursting with the sounds of a bustling city – the creaking of carts, market calls, children shouting and the cries of birds. Amina knew what must have happened and rushed back to the palace.

She stopped when she entered the chamber; there was Prince Kareem kissing the girl she had paid to help her. She had removed the last needle as soon as Amina had left the room. The Prince looked quizzically at the dishevelled young woman who had just entered so abruptly. He didn't recognise her as one of the palace servants. Ever gracious, he asked his new love,

'Is this lady with you my dear?'
'Not at all; I've never seen her before in my life. But now that you are here, I have work for you to do. There is soon to be a royal wedding and much to be done. Get downstairs, report to the cook and start making yourself useful.'

Amina stared. Now it was her turn to be paralysed, but this from shock at being betrayed by one to whom she had shown such generosity. She had survived the sad fortunes of fate – the death of her father was eventually to be expected, but the shipwreck was so unlucky and the loss of all her family a sorrow that she could not bear to go near. She was struck dumb with misery, and with an absolute loss of hope at the very moment when her fortune might have improved. Silently she turned, found the bustling kitchen and reported to the cook.

All was in uproar with preparations for the wedding. When the cook asked Amina what she could do, the girl just shrugged her shoulders and hung her head. Well, what better use than to put her to work at a job that nobody else wanted to do, as she didn't seem to have a voice to protest with – so let her go and wash the pots. And that is just what Amina did all day and half the night, dragging herself up to a mean little room at the top of a cold tower if she had the strength to reach her bed. Her clothes became stiff with grease, her hair was matted so thickly with the stuff that you couldn't tell where her hair ended and her clothes began. She smelled of rancid leftovers and she scrubbed those pots until there was no skin left on her fingers. She scrubbed those pots until she was scrubbing on bare bones.

Some time after the wedding, Prince Kareem needed to go on a long voyage. Being as kind as the meaning of his name, he asked all the people who worked for him in the palace what gift he might bring them on his return. In doing this he came upon parts of his home that he had never been in before. He was shocked at the heat and dark of the kitchen – the lack of fresh air and daylight. Nevertheless he forced himself to remain and ask each person who worked there what they would like as a present. At last it seemed that his task was over. He was just about to leave when he thought he saw a movement in the darkest part of the kitchen. There seemed to be the shape of a person in the shadows.

'Is that everyone, now?' he asked the cook.
'Yes, Highness, that is everyone.'

Just then the shape lurched nearer and the prince could see that underneath that matted filth there was a person.

'What about him – her?' He hardly knew how to finish the question. The cook thought to come to his rescue:
'Oh! You don't need to worry about her, Highness, she never speaks anyway.'

Was it courtesy or pity that made him hesitate? The shape shuffled closer. The prince's nose wrinkled. Then he saw something pale stretching towards him in the gloom – it was fingers of bone held out in supplication. Then in a voice rough with disuse he heard,

'Bring me the Doll of Sorrows!' Then Amina turned and shuffled off back to her scrubbing.

All during his voyage, the prince did not forget that miserable encounter. His business accomplished, he enjoyed buying the simple gifts his servants had requested, but he never came across the Doll of Sorrows. No matter where he asked, no-one had heard of such a thing. He needed to return to his own country, but was reluctant to leave without it. After all, a promise is a promise, especially if you are a prince. The sound of that sad, husky voice and the glimpse of those bare-boned hands, haunted him. At last he could delay his return no longer. That evening he watched his crew taking on stores from the quay. Then, restless and troubled, he wandered into a disused part of the harbour where all the boats and buildings seemed abandoned and derelict. He leaned against a filthy shop window, which alone amongst its neighbours still seemed to have glass in its windows. Idly he rubbed at a pane with his robe. The setting sun lit up the interior and he saw that it had been a toy shop – its dolls lying tumbled and broken on the shelves. If ever the Doll of Sorrows were to be found, it had to be here in this forsaken place. He pushed open the door and asked the shopkeeper who had crept out of the back room with a lantern. When the gift was mentioned, the shopkeeper held the lantern closer to his customer's face and swept the light along his body and the prince could see that the hand that held it trembled with shock.

> Forgive me, Sir, I can see that you are a person of rank and fortune and that you are also in good health, God be praised. Whatever could a man as fortunate as yourself be wanting with the Doll of Sorrows?

So Prince Kareem told him. He was surprised at how expensive this ordinary-looking wooden doll was. When he had bought it, the shopkeeper then told him what to do with it. The prince made a speedy voyage home with a clear conscience and distributed his gifts. He saved the Doll of Sorrows for the last and handed it to that pathetic creature in the kitchen. Amina clutched it with a whispered 'thank you' and shuffled out of the kitchen. The prince waited for a moment before following secretly. He was surprised at how quickly she could move and only just managed to see her disappearing up a narrow spiral of stairs. Now it was easier not to be seen and he sped silently after her. He heard a door slam at the top. There was an empty keyhole and he peered through it.

In his line of vision the doll had been placed on a rickety table in a tiny room. He couldn't see the woman, but he could hear her rough voice clearly as she spoke to the doll.

> 'First, my father died. It was a sad time, but every child must expect to grieve over their parents. Soon after that I barely survived a shipwreck…'

It seemed to the watcher at the keyhole that as the woman's words poured over the doll, it began to swell and grow.

> 'I was the only survivor – all my family was washed away and drowned. I never even found their bodies…'

The prince knew that he was not imagining things. The Doll of Sorrows was sitting there now as large as a child.

> 'When I came to this place I was all alone and so tired but still I worked hard to free the prince from the spell of enchantment that had fallen on him and his whole city…'

The doll was now so huge that it blocked all of his vision.

> 'I gave the last thing I had left from my father to a girl who then betrayed me, pretending it was she who had broken…'

Prince Kareem dared wait no longer. He had seen the pattern of the doll's wooden grain expanding like ripples on water. There wasn't a second to lose. He tore open the door, grabbed the young woman and dragged her from the room. Flinging her down outside, he wedged his back against the door just as, with a great roar, the Doll of Sorrows exploded. They listened to the final tinkling of glass as the last of the window pane shattered in the courtyard below. In the silence that followed, the prince knelt before Amina and held her bony hands.

> 'I would like to ask you two things, but I may only have the right to ask one of them. Unknowingly I once made a terrible mistake. Please would you forgive me?'
> 'Of course I forgive you'. Came the husky voice.
> 'Then as you can forgive me, please will you do me the honour of becoming my wife?'

Tears of happiness streamed from two pairs of eyes and covered those bare-boned fingers. Hand in hand they descended and entered the audience chamber where his wife was seated on one of the thrones. Prince Kareem's hand was quite steady when he pointed to her, and his voice was strong,

> 'And as for you, there is going to be a royal wedding and there will be a great deal of work to do. So go down to the kitchen and start scrubbing the pots.'

That is exactly what happened, but not any sooner than Amina and Kareem were already living happily ever after.

Chasing the Sun (Native American tradition)

In the community where this girl lived, everyone would meet regularly to share a meal and listen to music. Then the dancing would begin. One night, not long into the dancing, a strange wind entered the building and blew out the fire and all the lamps. The room was suddenly in utter darkness. It was then that a young woman felt powerful arms around her, pinning her to a wall. The weight of his body held her in place whilst one hand stifled her breath and silenced her cries for help. Despite her struggles his other hand tore apart her clothes and he was inside her, taking what he would never have been invited to take, taking what would never be his.

The fire and lamps were relit. The dancing went on as before. All seemed the same, but it would never be the same for that young woman again. She searched the faces of all the strong men, she ran her eyes over their hands, their bodies, to see if she could pick up any clue as to which one had attacked her. But looking was not recognising, searching was not knowing.

Time passed. She went to the next dance, but this time she was ready. She waited for that strange wind to come again, and so it did. As soon as it had blown out fire and lamps, again she was seized. But before she could be pinned against a wall, she clasped her assailant tightly, wrapping her arms around him to hold fast onto his back. Maybe her embrace surprised him – he soon stumbled away into the crowd. When the lamps and fire were relit, the young woman did not look at the men's faces or hands, she looked at their backs. Then she did know him: there were the black prints of her hands on his shirt, those hands that she had blackened with soot before coming to the dance. Now she knew who her attacker was.

Time passed. She went to the next dance carrying a basket. People drew away from her because of the smell of what she was carrying. They made a path down the room and watched. She strode towards her attacker and stopped some distance from him so that she would need to say what she needed to say loudly – loudly so that everyone would hear it.

> 'Since you have such a taste for my body, you must also enjoy tasting how you have treated it!'

She drew back the cover from her basket which was packed with her own faeces and began to fling them at him.

'Here are my shits. I have saved them all for you!'

Then she rushed to the fire, seized a brand and ran out into the night. The man grabbed another brand and ran after her. Everyone followed and that strange wind came again. This time it did not put out the flames; instead all the people saw how it blew the young woman up into the sky. Before dying away, it blew the man into the sky too. Since then, Moon has always followed Sun across the heavens. Moon's light is not as bright as Sun's because in his haste he had seized a smaller firebrand. You can still see the marks of Sun's shits on Moon's face. Sun remained as radiantly lovely as ever and we now know why she always tries to leave the sky before Moon appears.

The Snake and the King's Dream (Caucasus)

A long time ago, but not so long ago that we can't remember, there lived a king, who, although a powerful ruler, feared his enemies. He slept alone at the top of a well-defended tall tower. One night he had a terrible dream in which he saw, hanging from the ceiling in his own bed chamber, a dead fox with a rope tied around its neck and its tongue hanging out of its mouth. He woke with a shout of alarm.

When his body guards had rushed up the twisting tower stairs, they found their king sweating and shaking with fear. Somehow he knew that although it was only a dream, it was very important. He was determined to discover the meaning of his dream and summoned all his advisors, even though it was the middle of the night. None of his advisors could tell him what the dream meant, so the increasingly anxious king questioned all the palace servants. Nobody could give him the answer he was looking for. The king decreed that every adult in the land had to come to the palace to explain his dream, but no-one could do so.

So it came to be that soldiers were sent to the furthest reaches of the kingdom to round up distant citizens and order them to the palace. At last they crossed the mountains and reached their country's border, where they found a remote farm. The farmer was ordered to go to the palace to be questioned like all his countrymen. He had never crossed the mountains before and had never even seen a town, let alone a palace. He knew that he would fail in the task just as thousands before him had done and was most reluctant to go. However, the soldiers were insistent and, as he feared their punishment more than the journey, he set off in the direction of the palace.

When he was on a narrow path in the midst of the mountains, a huge snake suddenly reared up before him. The farmer leaped back in terror but his fright was soon forgotten in astonishment when the snake began to speak:

> I know where you are going, farmer, and the reason for your journey. When you reach the palace, you must tell the king that his dream means that there is treachery close at hand. The fox is a cunning and sneaking animal. He represents the hidden enemy spying in the king's court. His tongue was flapping because of all the state secrets that he gave away and the false rumours that he spread. The king must hunt him out and hang him as an example to others. Tell this to the king and he will reward you with a bag of gold.

'How do you know all this?' stammered the farmer.

'Because my name is Wisdom and I know all things,' came the reply.

The farmer was now eager to get to the palace and claim his reward, but as he stepped past the snake, he was asked,

'What will you give me for the help that I have given you?'

The farmer promised to repay the snake by giving him half his reward, and went on his way.

When at last he reached the palace the king was delighted at this explanation of what the dream meant. Just as the snake had said, he rewarded the farmer with a sack of gold and the farmer made his way home with it. However, on leaving the town, he decided to go home by a different route. He wanted to avoid meeting the snake as he was no longer willing to share the reward with him. Instead he went the long way round, through the desert, and it was a long time before he got home safely with the gold.

Meanwhile, alone at the top of his tower, the king had another dream, even more frightening than the first. In this dream he saw, hanging from his own ceiling, a sword dangling on a rope with the point poised above his throat. Again his shout of alarm brought his bodyguards running, again no-one was able to tell him the dream's meaning, again the soldiers were sent throughout the land. Remembering who had been able to satisfy the king before, they went straight back to the farmer. This time he knew who could help him, but he was frightened to seek out the snake as he had cheated him out of his reward.

The farmer decided to go back to the palace through the mountains, half hoping to meet the snake and half hoping that he wouldn't. However, as soon as he was back on that narrow twisting path, the snake reared up in front of him again.

'I know why you are back; it is because the king has had another dream. You were frightened to come this way because you had cheated me out of my share of the reward, but nevertheless you still need my help. The sword in the king's dream represents a weapon of war. Tell the king that his enemies abroad are plotting to join forces and attack his country. He should take them by surprise and attack them first; that way victory will be his. He will be so pleased to hear this that he will offer you two bags of gold this time. Give me half your reward for the help that I have given you.'

The farmer promised not to fail the snake again, thanked him for being given a second chance and went on his way. All passed as the snake had foretold and the farmer was given two sacks of gold. Yet again he decided to break his promise to the snake and keep all the gold for himself. He dragged those heavy sacks the long way round via the desert. When at last he reached his distant home, he buried all his gold underneath the farmhouse.

During that journey, the king mustered his army, attacked his enemies abroad, took them by surprise and gained a great victory.

For a while the farmer lived quietly – until the king had a third dream. This time he saw, hanging from the roof of the tower where he slept, a fat sheep with a rope tied around its middle. Again the king insisted on being told the meaning of this dream and sent the soldiers to summon the farmer. This time the farmer was in a real panic – he couldn't manage without the snake but he had betrayed him twice. Because the snake had already been so kind to him, he decided to throw himself on the snake's mercy and beg his forgiveness. As soon as he was back in the mountains the snake reappeared. The farmer threw himself onto the ground weeping and saying how sorry he was. The snake said,

'The meaning of the king's latest dream is this: the sheep, being a gentle animal, is a sign of peace. There will be no more war for a time. The king will stop taking money from the people to pay for war, and everyone will be able to plant crops and have enough to eat. That is why the sheep in his dream was so fat. The king will be so pleased to hear this that he will give you three sacks of gold this time.'

Then the farmer thanked the snake and once more promised to share his reward. He made his way to the palace, where again everything happened just as the snake had said. Now the farmer had too much gold to carry so he bought a donkey and heaped the gold on its back. This time he decided to share his reward as promised. He made his way directly to the mountains and was calling out for the snake. Before even reaching the path, the snake was already waiting for him,

'I have come to give you a share of my reward,' cried the farmer.
'I am a snake,' came the reply, 'what need have I for gold? Can I feed on it?
Will it keep me warm in the winter? I think not.'
'But I was even going to give you all three bags to make up for those times I cheated you.'

At that, the snake laughed,

'Still you do not understand, you foolish man. When you first thought to cheat me of your share of the reward, it was when the king had dreamed about the fox – a time of cunning and deceit. People were cheating and scheming, just as you were. The second time you cheated me was when the king had dreamed of the sword – a time of war. People are not generous in times of conflict. They hang onto what they have, just as you did when you buried the treasure. Now that the king has dreamed about the fat sheep we are in a time of peace. People feel that they can afford to be generous, they ask forgiveness from those they have wronged and honour old bargains, just as you are trying to do now. I am a snake, what use have I for gold? I do not want your gold; I do not need your gold. Keep it, spend it or give it away, it matters not to me, but I doubt that it will bring you wisdom.'

And with that, the snake disappeared.

The Best Hunters (West Africa)

There was once a hunter, famed in the region for his skill. He would disappear into the forest for long periods, returning at last with his kills. His work was difficult and dangerous. His standing in the village was high and his wife respected him. As she was often alone, her brother came to stay to keep her company. He longed to be a hunter too, but his brother-in-law refused to let him accompany him into the forest because he was blind. It didn't matter how often he pleaded, the answer was always the same:

'What is the point of taking you? The game would flee and I would spend all my time looking after you. Stay at home where you won't be a danger to yourself and let others get on with their work.'

So he would stay sadly at home, helping his sister with the chores, milking goats or pounding meal. But every so often he would still ask to be taken into the forest. One day his sister took her husband aside,

> 'Husband, surely you could take Brother just once so that his longing would be satisfied. It pains me to hear him asking the same thing again and again. Let him go with you just once – maybe he will learn for himself what you have been telling him.'
>
> 'And maybe he won't,' said her husband.

Nevertheless he told his brother-in-law to be ready before dawn for their trip. That night Brother taught himself to weave a net for the first time and was ready to leave even before the hunter, and so they set off together at last. The hunter was surprised at how quietly Brother moved. There was no sound of footfall, no rustling of branches as he crept through bushes, no stumbles as he glided over fallen trunks. If he kept still in the forest gloom, the hunter sometimes found it hard to see where he was. As they were skirting a pool, Brother suddenly laid a swift hand on his arm.

'Go another way; I hear a snake slithering down a branch towards us.'

The hunter, looking ahead, was astonished to see the coiled silhouette of a mamba swaying its head to seek them out. Another time Brother paused,

> 'We should wait a while,' he said in that voice that is quieter than a whisper, 'I can smell elephant ahead of us. She is just finishing stripping a branch. Let her move on so we don't disturb her.'

The hunter knew how hard it is to see elephant in the forest for all her size, and how dangerous it is not to give her space to pass. As the day passed, he marvelled at how his brother-in-law was able to tell him things that were happening before he could know them himself – perhaps he had even saved his life.

At last they came to a place which was ideal for spreading nets to catch birds for the bird market. People would pay a high price for ones that sang or those that had beautiful plumage. Although he had never done it before, Brother spread his own net as deftly as any girl stringing shells. They slept in their blankets, waiting for dawn to stir the birds into their trap. Tired out with the extra exercise, Brother was later to wake, and the hunter had already gone to see what they had caught. In the hunter's own net was a rather ordinary bird which would not find a good price, but in his brother-in-law's net was a rare and gorgeous bird that would fetch a high price. Quickly, the hunter swapped them over. When Brother appeared, each disentangled the birds, put them in their game baskets and turned back.

On their journey home, the brother-in-law was silent and barely responded to the hunter's attempts at conversation. The silence became more uncomfortable until, at last, the hunter blurted out:

> 'You are so quiet and it is so unlike you, I feel that there is something wrong. What is the matter?'
>
> 'Yes indeed there is something wrong. I grow sad when I think that men are always so ready to be dishonest and to cheat each other whenever they have the chance.'

Now it was the hunter who remained silent and the tension increased as they neared home.

'Rather than return home dirty from my trip, I would first like to bathe in this pool. I can smell that the water is sweet and fresh.'
'As you wish, that is a good idea,' replied the hunter, who had not yet noticed the inviting water.

When his brother-in-law was splashing in the pool, the hunter quickly swapped the birds around, so each had in his basket the bird that had originally been caught in his own net. For the rest of their journey, Brother chatted and laughed and even broke into song when they were too near the village to disturb any game. This change of mood cheered the hunter who ventured to ask,

'You seem to be so much happier now. What is it that has lifted your spirits?'
'Yes, I am happier. My spirits lift at the knowledge that sometimes people realise that they have done wrong and take action to make amends.'

There were three happy people in that hut that night. Often the brothers would go hunting together. If anyone expressed surprise at a blind hunter, the husband would say,

'I don't know how I ever managed without him. We make the perfect team.'

If the women asked whether the wife was not too lonely with both husband and brother away in the forest, she would say,

'Yes, I am sometimes lonely. But at least I know that my husband will always return safely because he has my brother to protect him.'

The Worst Potter (China)

Every year the emperor would preside over a national pottery competition. As China is an enormous country, and potting is a national craft, you can imagine how many competitors there were even amongst the master potters. If women had been allowed to compete the event would never have finished. But as it was, each year, the pots that were offered up for the emperor's inspection were a marvel of beauty and inventiveness: there would be teapots shaped like unicorns which poured through their horns, vessels shaped like peacocks displaying, glazes that held the blooming colours of dawn if you held them one way and the melting colours of sunset if you held them another. Truly it was the most important event in the calendar for displaying the greatest and the best that mighty country had to offer. The winner would be given a bag of gold with the emperor's own hands, and even more valued was the reputation afforded to that lucky man.

Each year, however, there came amongst them a potter whose work was truly dreadful: solid but shapeless, worked but crude, as unpleasing to the eye and touch as a pile of vegetable peelings. Nobody knew why he came or why his work didn't improve over the years. At last the coterie of master potters lost patience and requested an audience with the emperor.

'Celestial Majesty, his work is an insult to our profession!'
'How dare he come amongst us to show off his disgraceful mockeries year after year?'
'He must be punished!'

The cry of '... He must be punished...' was taken up by them all, so that the emperor was confronted by a furious chorus demanding revenge. At last he held up his hand for silence.

> 'This is my decree: the man shall be warned that his work must improve. If it has not improved by the next competition, only then will he be punished.'

The emperor's order was given, and the worst potter was rather surprised to hear it. Didn't he always try his hardest to produce something wonderful? Wasn't each creation better than the last? However, gratified at His Celestial Majesty's interest in him, he vowed to redouble his efforts. For a whole year he worked on his new pot every day, rising earlier and finishing later. At last it was ready in time for the competition.

He waited impatiently for his turn as potter after potter climbed the one hundred and one marble steps to the emperor's dais to show off his pot. There on a platform below the throne, were seated the master potters. Each one of whom had at some point been winner of the competition, each one of whom was now a judge. The worst potter knew how hard he had worked on this latest pot, how he had cherished it, how proud of it he was. To display it for maximum effect, he ascended those steps with his cloak wrapped around it – to reveal it at the top with a flourish. Halfway up, he lost his footing. He had become entangled in his awkwardly held cloak. You will probably already have realised that he was a rather clumsy man, but at that moment he felt that his feet belonged to somebody else as he struggled and stumbled on those treacherous steps. He was terrified that he would drop his pot. To give himself more time to sort his feet out, he threw the pot high into the air, hoping to gain extra seconds to attend to his lower half before catching it.

Higher and higher the pot soared. Everyone's eye was upon it. As it descended there was a great gasp – but not of wonder; of horror! That lumpen, misshapen object resembled nothing so much as a pile of elephant poo. You couldn't even tell that it was supposed to be a pot. It was by far the most hideous creation that anybody had ever seen. The worst potter tried to catch his beloved pot as it fell towards him, but his clumsiness betrayed him again. He lunged at it and missed. Appalled, he watched it bounce down the one hundred and one marble steps and shatter into many pieces. The master potters could hardly wait for the competition to be over and for the emperor's punishment to be inflicted. They eagerly surrounded his throne, reminding him of his promise.

> 'It is true that I said he should be punished if his work did not improve. But as it is you who are so keen for him to be punished, I decree that it is you who should decide upon a fitting punishment for him.'

This only delighted the master potters further. All their creativity was now bent towards devising a suitable punishment. At last it was decided that the worst potter would be made to gather up every one of those broken pieces and for those shards to be strung on wires. He would be forced to wear them as a heavy, ugly collar on top of his clothes wherever he went. That way he would never be able to forget how he had disgraced such a noble craft and everyone would bear witness to his humiliation. However, one of their number had an even better idea:

> 'Friends, you remember how it was that this miscreant tried to save his abomination by throwing it up in the air to give himself more time to rescue it. That gesture ensured that even more people were able to see and be horrified by that disgraceful object. Let

the punishment further fit the crime; let it be also remembered how he did that. I propose that when he has been made to gather up the broken pieces, and has strung them on wire, it should all be made into a headdress. That would be a far better way to record this appalling event. Just as even more people had to see his abominable creation from afar, so will more people be able to witness his humiliation.'

If icing had been invented in those days, this would have been the icing on the cake! The punishment was announced and the worst potter began to collect up the broken pieces of his beloved creation. His eyes were so blinded with tears that he could barely see what he was doing, but you may be sure that there was always a master potter on hand to point out if he had missed a bit.

At last the task was done and as he was far too clumsy to be entrusted with the making of the headdress; it was done for him. Soon he was sent out amongst the crowd wearing this ridiculous contraption dangling above his head.

The master potters craned forward from their platform to see the people's reaction to this spectacle. The emperor on his throne was looking puzzled. He too tried to follow the worst potter's progress through the crowd. He expected to hear laughter, perhaps jeers, to see the ripple of movement as people pointed – but there were none of these. Mystified, he rose from his throne and descended the one hundred and one marble steps. For the first time in living memory, His Celestial Majesty walked amongst the people to see for himself what was going on. He could just about make out that headdress above the crowd, but wherever it went it was met by a river of silence, not laughter. People made way for the emperor as he tried to draw closer. At last he was near enough to understand the quiet that grew amongst the crowd.

Into that awed silence, swelled the most beautiful sound that the emperor had ever heard. The breeze was moving through the headdress, and as those shards were blown together they emitted the sweetest chiming sound. Quite by accident, the worst potter had become the means for making the first musical instrument that had ever been heard in China. Until then there had been no music, and now there was! The emperor was delighted, he hauled the man back up those one hundred and one marble steps. In front of the master potters he placed a bag of gold in his hands.

> 'This is my royal command: that you return to your home and make as many pots as you can. When you have made them you are to smash them up and arrange for their pieces to be hung on wires so that this wonderful instrument, which would not have been invented without you, can be distributed throughout China. And let it be named wind chimes!'

The delighted man hurried home as fast as he could. Nobody had ever paid him to make pots before; nobody had ever praised his work before. How he loved rising early to make his pots; what a relief it was not to have to worry about what everybody thought of them. He was so eager to seize them from the kiln that he was in danger of burning himself. He bought extra thick boots so that he could dance on them with joy before they cooled. When he looked up from smashing them it was always to see a queue of people waiting to buy the shards so that they could have their own wind chimes made.

So it was that music first came to China. Wherever you go today, throughout that mighty land, you will find wind chimes everywhere. The worst potter had also started a new trend in the Imperial City. Suddenly all the courtiers were commissioning headdresses made of broken pieces of pottery strung on wires. If you look at ancient Chinese scrolls and works of art you can see pictures of everyone wearing what had become the very height of fashion.

The Shadow of Shame (Korea)

A weary traveller had walked a long way. At last this stranger had entered a village in a strange land. All he could think of was that he needed to rest. There on the village green was an ancient chestnut tree. Its huge branches spread wide, the broad leaves casting a pool of deliciously inviting shade against the beating heat of the day. Soon he was stretched out in the shade and fast asleep.

His blissful rest did not last long, however, as he was awakened by a voice shouting at him.

'Hey You! Who do you think you are? Did I give you permission to sleep in my shade?'

The stranger was confused – not just dazed from having been so abruptly woken from his much-needed sleep, but because, if he was understanding this foreign language correctly, it seemed that it was possible to own shade. Own a shadow? Now that was a new idea. How different the world was when you travelled, how unexpected the customs. He got to his feet and bowed, but not before he had noticed that this man was very angry and that from his clothes he must also be very wealthy.

'Sir, forgive me, I am not from these parts,' began the stranger haltingly in this unfamiliar tongue. But he was interrupted,
'Don't you think I can see that? Do you take me for a fool? What are you doing sleeping in my shade?'
'I was tired, I have travelled far. I did not realise that this shade belonged to anybody.'

This reply seemed to make the rich man even angrier, if that were possible. He almost danced with rage as he shouted,

'I'll have you know this is my tree, planted by my great grandfather, and everything about this tree now belongs to me, including its shade. You have no right to set a foot in it!'

His shouting had by now attracted a small crowd as the villagers arrived to see what all the noise was about this time, being used to the rich man's temper.

'If this is your shade, Sir, then it must also be yours to sell. Will you sell it to me?'

The villagers were astonished. The rich man was delighted. Here was one of those foreign fools that he could make some fast money out of – coins that would soon join all the rest of the wealth that weighed in his treasure chest. He named his price. It just so happened that the traveller had exactly that amount of money on him. There were disapproving murmurs amongst some of the villagers. Was this the way to treat a stranger? Was this a fitting welcome for a visitor? What tales would he tell of this place when he returned home? The people gaped, and the rich man gloated as the sum was handed over. Most returned to work and the rich man went inside his house, which was the largest in the whole district.

The stranger returned to the shade and rested. The sun began to sink and the chestnut tree's shadow became longer. It was now in the rich man's garden, so its new owner followed it. The garden was huge and had once held many fine plants, but was now neglected. The rich man was as mean as he was rich and didn't want to spend any money on maintaining it. Just then he looked out of his window and noticed the vagrant in his garden. His furious shouting alerted all the neighbours that this drama was not yet finished, and they drifted over for another instalment.

'How dare you loiter in my garden, you fool; this is private property!'
'It may be your garden, but it is also my shade. You sold it to me yourself and these good people are witnesses to the deed. I shall continue to exercise my right to sit in the shade that I have paid for.'

Many in the crowd began to titter. The rich man had never been laughed at in public before. He threw himself back into the house and slammed the door. By now most people had guessed what would happen next. As the sun sank lower towards the horizon, the shadows continued to lengthen. The chestnut tree's shadow had reached the rich man's veranda and there the stranger now sat. The rich man emerged again, purple-faced, roaring with fury. The crowd roared with laughter. Then he raised his hand to strike the stranger. Enough was enough. Someone in the crowd went to fetch the police, who could hear the aggressive shouts and threats long before they reached the scene. They realised that with everyone's opinion united against just the one man, they had better side with the villagers. The whole story came out and the police accused the rich man of being a swindler. They threatened to fine him the same sum that he had received for the sale. The rich man began to panic – the police had always let him get away with everything before. What was happening? He rushed back into the house, hurriedly packed a bag and scurried away down the village street to the jeers of the people. The drama was over and people went home.

Night had fallen; there were no longer any shadows. But the large house, with all its rich possessions, had been left empty and unsecured. Anybody could come along and take advantage. Perhaps the stranger should stay overnight just to make sure that nothing was stolen. In the morning light, he noticed that although the house had once been lovely, it was now neglected and in a state of disrepair. What a shame to let such a magnificent building fall into decay. It wouldn't take much effort to put things right before they got any worse. Gradually the stranger made repairs here and there. The villagers heard him at his work, enjoyed his strange songs in a language they didn't understand, admired his handiwork from afar. Soon the house regained its dignity under his care.

Now it was time for the garden. The tide of neglect was turned there too. Because he was working outside, he spoke to the villagers more often. They watched him full of curiosity as he sometimes used different cultivating skills from theirs. As he was always friendly, and they were eager to learn, he explained his methods as he went along. Soon he was inviting them into the garden to try things out his way. They marvelled at the seeds he showed them that had never been seen in that place before, and at the new vegetables and flowers that grew from them. It was such a large space that there was plenty of land for everyone. Soon it was a thriving, buzzing hive of activity, laughter and produce. It became everyone's favourite place in the village.

Time passed and Autumn was painting Nature with beautiful glowing colours. There was so much to do in the garden that people spent most of their time working there. It was then that the rich man decided to come back to his home, hoping that the previous incident would by now be forgotten. As he approached the village he heard, for the first time, the glad sounds of happy people, like a flock of starlings, as they called and shrilled to each other. He walked right past his house because he didn't recognise it. At last he looked over his garden fence and marvelled at the transformation. Just then the stranger, who was no longer really a stranger, looked up and recognised him.

> 'There you are at last. I was wondering what had happened to you, when you would finally come home!'

The rich man was astonished, he had never felt this feeling before – that of being welcomed. He looked around at the garden, the busy people, the restored house and appreciated everything he saw. He was so pleased that he begged the stranger to stay and work for him.

> 'Thank you for your offer, but I cannot stay. My work here is done and I am needed elsewhere. Now that you have returned and I have had the chance to share my skills, it is time for me to move on.'

He said goodbye to his new friends, and walked away. Nobody knew where he went, and nobody knows where he is now. Perhaps he is far away or perhaps he is closer than we think.

38
EVERYTHING THAT WE CAN REMEMBER

How to create a safe environment through a poetic story – an introduction to *Forest of Lost Memories*

Alenka Vidrih

Literary texts that focus on the field of dementia intertwined with a child's imagination are rare. As J.R. Baker states, introducing children to the topic of dementia is essential for removing the stigma of dementia and laying the foundations for dementia-friendly communities (Baker, et al. 2018). In the text *The Forest of Lost Memories*, the author Katja Gorečan in a dialogical way (with the help of a poetic drama structure) deals with the problem of Grandpa losing his memories and his granddaughter, a girl named Lisa. Dementia appears as a shadow on Lisa's journey with her Grandpa through the woods. This shadow accompanies them as a problem that appears suddenly and is incomprehensible at first, but as the girl develops empathy for her Grandpa and wants to help him, she develops the story to the point of first getting to know the problem through poetic and subtle language, and then later she confronts the problem, accepts it, and continues the story with her courage and acceptance that the time has come to look back at the memories she created with her Grandpa, which leads to the reconstruction of Grandpa's memories through the eyes of the Other. The forest in the story first represents a safe environment which changes with Grandpa's sudden mood change. The forest is thus a space that expresses his psychological state and consequently also acquires the role of projection.

How the natural environment affects emotions is explained by Schroeder in his article *The spiritual aspect of nature* (1992), where he says that when archetypes are projected onto the natural environment, these environments evoke strong emotions and gain deep meaning for the individual. For nature lovers, trees and other natural entities can evoke awe and fascination. The forest or wilderness may seem like a paradise on earth, a magical place of eternal mystery and perfection, far from the everyday life.

In this way, Lisa finds the inner strength to take her Grandpa out of the forest along the path she remembers from previous trips. Lisa doesn't judge him for his orientation loss, despite being scared at first because he doesn't know anyone's name. After a phase of confusion and disorientation, however, Lisa accepts the situation as a part of life without retreating, running away, hiding, or suppressing. She is helped by a tree that, according to ancestral tradition, is said to be healing for all the diseases and problems of this world. This tree is the Ash Tree (Fraxinus excelsior), which through the function of personification turns into a kind and magical creature that helps her with advice for coping with the situation and above all gives her the strength to take her Grandpa by the hand and bring him home safely (Schroeder, 1992).

References

Baker, J. R., Jeon, Y. H., Goodenough, B., Low, L. F., Bryden, C., Hutchinson, K., & Richards, L. (2018). What do children need to know about dementia? The perspectives of children and people with personal experience of dementia. *International Psychogeriatrics*, *30*(5), 673–684.

Schroeder, H. W. (1992). *The spiritual aspect of nature: A perspective from depth psychology*. In proceedings of Northeastern Recreation Research Symposium (p. 25–30), April 7–9, 1991, Saratoga Springs, NY.

39
THE FOREST OF LOST MEMORIES©

Katja Gorečan

CHARACTERS

- LISA, a 6-year-old girl
- GRANDPA, a gray-haired gentleman, but still vital / 70–80 years of age
- THE GREAT ASH TREE, a mighty tree

Lisa on Grandpa

It is night and there are dark trees all around. The trees are spiral in shape; on the screen we see their shadows moving in slow motion as if a gentle wind is blowing. Only here and there does a lonely firefly light up. We also see the shadow of Grandpa wandering through the woods and moving as if he doesn't know where he is. As if he is completely lost. Lisa steps in front of us.

LISA
Grandpa doesn't know (she addresses us)
what is our name.
Grandpa doesn't know
who we are.
Grandpa is hiding in closets and
Grandpa is wandering elsewhere every day.
We're looking for him in the woods,
on meadows,
around town and around the village.
Grandpa, why did you forget (she addresses Grandpa),
that it is no longer wartime?
Grandpa, you're not a soldier anymore and
you don't have to fight.
Why do you think there are enemies all around you?
Grandpa,
wait for me!

Lisa doesn't want to get out of the bed

Lisa is bouncing around the bed. By no means does she intend to get up. Grandpa is standing by the bed and waiting for her, already a little impatient, but still lovingly calm, as only grandpas can be.

GRANDPA
Come on, Lisa,
let's go to the forest.

LISA
Grandpa, I really don't feel like it,
I would rather sleep a little more.
What should I do outside?

GRANDPA
Lisa, let's go,
I'll show you how
the tree got sick
and now it can no longer stand.
The tree was attacked by small monsters.

LISA
Come on, Grandpa,
the tree can't get sick,
because the tree is not a man.
(she stubbornly turns her back on Grandpa, acts childish)

GRANDPA
You can't know that,
if you just lie in your room.
(the image of the river and the bridge appears on the screen, Lisa gets up and pretends to walk on the bridge with her grandfather)
Let's go by the river and I'll hold your hand
as we cross the bridge.

LISA
Will you to tell the river to stop?
If we fall, we'll not drown.

GRANDPA
Lisa, you know I can't do this,
the river goes its own way. Just like us,
come on, let's go!

LISA
Only if you promise me this time we won't play
that game, who am I and where are we?
That's when I really get scared.

GRANDPA
I promise, Lisa.
You know, I'm already a bit old,
and sometimes I forget things.

LISA
I know, Grandpa, I'm not angry,
I just don't want it to happen again,
our last walk
through the dark night when you got lost.

GRANDPA
This only happened once, and
see – we're still alive,
we just wandered a little aside.
Don't be afraid, Lisa,
we'll follow the path where we know all the trees,
and it won't be a problem to get back home.
Give me your hand and I'll take you –
see how beautiful the day is outside!

Lisa and Grandpa in the forest

Lisa and Grandpa are walking hand in hand through the forest. Lisa is muttering a tune.

GRANDPA
So, Lisa,
now look
how much resin
is on that spruce.

LISA
Yikes,
that poor spruce looks like it is dying,
as if the resin is eating it.

GRANDPA
What are you talking about, my little Lisa!
This resin is not a joke,
it heals all the wounds.
We'll pick some up,
so that Grandma will make
resinous ointment out of it
for the most urgent case,
because you know, Lisa,
the forest can heal any pain.

LISA
Oh, Grandpa, look how that giant tree
is smiling at us in the distance!

GRANDPA
That tree is called the Great Ash Tree,
it will help anyone who is feeling angry,
it will cure every disease
and destroy any mold that you please.

LISA
Wow, this forest must be magic,
but to me from afar
always seemed so gloomy and tragic.

GRANDPA
That's because you were always hiding in your room
and waiting for someone to take you out.
Now you know you can do it alone.

LISA
(shadows of the trees as we see them when we look down at the sky)
I wasn't waiting, I was just scared of those trees,
because they are so high,
almost to the sky,
and even higher and higher and higher.
(Lisa spins, spins, and spins, until she falls to the floor, then looks around)

LISA
Grandpa, are we lost?

GRANDPA
Lisa, don't panic, take a rest,
these are familiar parts of the forest.

LISA
No, Grandpa,
we've never been here before.

GRANDPA
See that spruce?
You hid behind it the last time.

LISA
Grandpa, this is not our forest,
the trees here are different.
This is not our bridge
and I see strange shadows and on the ground there are bird feathers.

GRANDPA
Wait a minute, you're right.
Tell me little girl, what is your name?

LISA

Grandpa, please tell me you're joking.
I'm Lisa.
Lisa, your granddaughter.

GRANDPA

Lisa, my granddaughter? I don't know any Lisa.
You must be one of those girls,
who like hiding under large tables.
How did we get here
and where the heck are we?

LISA

Grandpa, you said you know
this forest and these shadows and that
the barking of the neighbor's dog
is nearby.

GRANDPA

I don't remember,
when did we talk about that?

LISA

When the clock struck noon,
you said we were going to the woods.

GRANDPA

What time is it today?

LISA

I don't know, it's probably late. There are stars and the Big Dipper in the sky.
(dark screen slowly turns into a large sky with stars, which changes according to Lisa's narration of the Big Dipper)

GRANDPA

What is the Big Dipper?

LISA

The Big Dipper consists of seven stars;
two wheels, two as a side and three in the handle.
It will lead us to the Northern Star,
and so we will know where we are.

GRANDPA

But I would like to know your name …
… little girl.

LISA

Grandpa, stop it, it's not funny
and I will start crying
if you don't stop asking me that.

The Forest Of Lost Memories©

GRANDPA

I want to know who I got lost with
and with whom I will walk home now.
Although I don't know where my home is
and who I live with,
what time of year it is and what month.

LISA

Grandpa, stop fooling around,
you live with us
and it is spring, the month of May.

GRANDPA

But now I'm really confused,
I don't even know what spring is.
Why am I walking here with you?
Do you want to take me somewhere?

LISA

Grandpa, don't be silly,
it was you who took me to the woods.

GRANDPA

Why are you telling me
that I am your grandfather?
Where are my parents?

LISA

Grandpa, your parents are long gone,
you are my Grandpa, you are the father of my mother.
Why are you asking me that?

GRANDPA

I think I'm gonna walk away now.

LISA

Where are you going? You can't leave me here all alone.

GRANDPA

I'm going to the forest.

LISA

But we are already in the forest,
and I'm getting afraid of this darkness.

GRANDPA

I'm walking away,
you can go with me
if you want,
but I'm going to look for my family.

LISA
But, Grandpa,
I am your family.
Which other family do you want to go to?

GRANDPA
(wants to walk away, the shadows are changing, escalation, it gets a little creepy)
I'm going to look for my parents.

LISA
Grandpa, please stop,
your parents are gone.
Why are you telling me this,
that you wanna walk away?
Please, let's go home.

GRANDPA
Leave me alone,
I will go home with whoever I want.
Right now I wanna go home alone,
and not with someone who I even don't know.

LISA
I've had it with you, Grandpa!
Walk alone, then!

GRANDPA
So I'll go!
(Grandpa is leaving angrily, Lisa is going after him)

LISA
Grandpa, wait for me,
you can't leave me here alone
in the middle of this horrible, dark forest.
I'm afraid!

GRANDPA
I'm going to look for people that I know.
Ok, I'm sorry, we can go together,
but you will have to tell me something more about yourself.

LISA
If this helps you to remember ...
I like to dance and sing,
I also draw a lot, especially with chalk on the streets
or with brush on the walls.
But you already know that ...
We also painted the wall together once, remember?
For my fifth birthday, you bought me big paints and we squeezed them into a palette,
then you picked me up and I drew the sun around the lights on the wall.

GRANDPA
I remember that a little …
then we both fell to the ground together.

LISA
Yeessss, well you see you remember.
We fell to the ground and then Mom came
and she scolded us both
that we are naughty,
and then we both laughed at her
and she was so angry at us.

GRANDPA
That day was truly a nice day!

LISA
But Grandpa, what is happening to you?
You look like you are falling in and out of a dream.
Just remember who you care about.

GRANDPA
Lisa! This is you!
And your curly hair …

LISA
But where did your memory stop,
where did you lose it?
You were like a tree without roots
and I saw fear in your eyes.

GRANDPA
Fear dusted my memory.
I could feel the shadows inside me and your face
was like the face of someone I first met.

LISA
Grandpa, everything will be fine,
I wanna see your face shine with a smile.
I know we'll find a way out of the forest
and the river path and the bridge at its side.
I will lead you, all right?
Take my hand,
so that the wind blowing wide,
doesn't take you away.
Hold my hand
and I will hold the riverbed
to stop its flow,
when fear will lead you astray.

GRANDPA
You say that Lisa is your name?
And you will take me along the way?

I don't know if I would believe you.
I knew too many people
and I forgot you again.
Let's sit on this stump
and think about where else we can go.
The paths of the world are boundless,
I realized this too late.
I've always been afraid to leave home,
now I would just keep walking on and on.

LISA
Where would you go?
We don't see anything in this deep darkness,
in this deep silence owls croak,
the trees are looking for cannons
to fill all the air with leaves.

GRANDPA
Let's go to a place where we've never been before,
that I may fall asleep, and when I wake up,
my memory will come back.

LISA
Then we have to go to the Great Ash Tree,
it has an airy crown, hardwood and its leaves are feathery,
to protect you and grant your plea.

Lisa takes Grandpa to the Great Ash Tree

Liza takes Grandpa by the hand, determined to solve the problem with his memory.

LISA
And we arrived in a holy place
and the devil
who steals your memory in front of your face,
will now vanish into space.

THE GREAT ASH TREE
Hello, Lisa, and hello, Grandpa,
why have you come here so late,
what is so unsolvable and awful that needs my help?

LISA
Dear Ash Tree, we really need your help.
Grandpa took me into the woods and forgot the way back.
He also forgets the names of all of us
and does not even know the right time.

GRANDPA
Sometimes I remember, sometimes I forget
but the worst are those moments in between,

when I know I'm forgetting but I don't know
where am I going and I'm feeling so slow.

LISA
Dear Ash Tree, can you change this,
fold your leafy wings in my Grandpa's memory,
enable him with the power of your invincible wooden trunk,
magical night breath and mighty wind
and turn him into a man who knows people
he shares his life with?

THE GREAT ASH TREE
Lisa, Lisa, I can't change this,
your grandfather is losing his memory
and you will have to accept that.
We trees also accept that every fall
our leaves fall off,
just like every day darkness
falls through your Grandpa's eyes,
because the leaves that build his memories
they disappear into eternal melodies.
This memory has been preserved somewhere,
it stayed with you, Lisa,
with your Mom,
with your Grandma
and with all the people who know Grandpa.

LISA
So you say Grandpa's memory
is never coming back?
That it is a disease and it remains so?
But are there no spells, no miracles
or magic juices?
I don't believe this is the end of memory.

THE GREAT ASH TREE
It is the end of memory as much as you will allow yourself to be. If all the moments you experienced with your Grandpa become an old rubbish, and not a golden blanket that will protect the mysterious events and
overgrown paths where your grandfather can't
go alone anymore.

GRANDPA
Of course I can go anywhere alone!

LISA
But you don't remember the way back home.

THE GREAT ASH TREE
Lisa, from now on you will have to lead your Grandpa (See Figure 39.1).

Figure 39.1 'Forest of Lost Memories': image created in a workshop of the story by Korina Ferčec from Gimnazija Celje – Center, with the support of her teacher Andreja Džakušič

LISA
But how can I lead him all by myself?

THE GREAT ASH TREE
You still have a lot of memory space.
You know where that mill stands,
which you two walked past,
and where deer graze at night,
so that the world does not hear them.
Lisa, now is the time for you to become your Grandpa's memory.

LISA
So you are saying I take Grandpa home
along the path I think I know?

THE GREAT ASH TREE
That's right, Lisa.
This path is right,
and be sure
even when the thicket appears on your track.

GRANDPA
Let's just go home,
I want to fall asleep, I'm tired and
confused.

THE GREAT ASH TREE
Lisa, trust yourself on the way.
You are nowhere alone –
not in the dark
not in solitude
not in the void
in a form of a large dried-up plateau,
where all seems lost and futile.

LISA
Thank you, dear Ash Tree.
My memory will from now on lead my Grandpa
to the sea dunes he had never seen
and to places he had never been.

THE END

References

Monographs

Gorečan, K. (2012). *Trpljenje mlade Hane*. Ljubljana: Center za slovensko književnost.
Gorečan, K. (2017). *Neke noči neke deklice nekje umirajo*. Ljubljana: Hiša poezije Poetikon.
Gorečan, K. (2018). Cierpienia młodej Hany. Krakow: Korporacja Ha!art.

AFTERWORD

Readers of this book will have been on a journey, one that describes the journeys of so many others. Our constant companions have been stories – the stories of how practitioners from all over the world have used this most ancient and human form of communication. The **act** of telling is our main way of sharing experience; the **art** of telling is our earliest form of literature. This uniquely human gift for oracy imbues what we share with a depth of feeling and interpretation that surpasses the mere events of what happened. It unfolds into the richness of other art forms, whether it is amongst our most ancient forms of visual art such as the narrative cave paintings left by our ancestors or the linguistically sophisticated plays of Shakespeare, the subtleties of Chekhov or the spectacular narrative Balinese dances depicting episodes from the Ramayana.

In my practices as applied, community and performance storyteller, I am often asked, 'What is a story?' Implicit in that query is the interest in distinguishing story from any other kind of speech or writing. My reply is, 'A story is a meaningful sequence of events.' Moreover, every story contains some kind of journey – whether the traveller is discovering the wonders of the 'somewhere else' or whether that changing landscape is a metaphor for the discovery of internal truths and insights. In this volume, contributors from all over the world have shared how, through their work with narrative, in all its glorious forms of oral or written literature and personal testimony, their journeys with stories have been a quest for meaning. These practitioners have generously invited us to become their companions upon their own reflective journeys. We accompany them as they revisit their story travels amongst their varied therapeutic and educational contexts. Their own insights, informed by their patients', clients' and students' journeys towards growth and healing, enrich our understanding of what can be achieved through what we, as the human race, are best at.

Another aspect to this international work is the richness that comes from sharing the different cultures expressed as they are through their traditional stories – and the varied and adaptive approaches in working with those in need according to cultural context. As someone whose main language is English, I am humbled by those who have shared their experiences in what may even be their 3rd or 4th language, rather than their 2nd – I am grateful to them for including us all in the worldwide language that is storytelling.

Not so long ago, when I was on the other side of the world, I came across a story that had also crossed continents.

Afterword

There was once a man who was as poor as he was good and as good as he was poor. So loved was he, that people called him 'The Living Saint'. He would give his last crust and the last rag on his body to anyone needier than himself. One evening, he stood in the last slanting rays of the sun, too tired and hungry to walk any further. A poor peasant came to him, begging for money with which to buy medicines to save the life of his sick mother. 'My dear boy, I am sorry that I have nothing to give you. As you can see I am even more destitute than yourself.' He walked on, tears blinding him because he couldn't help, and did not notice the little green lizard that scurried across his foot. But then the lizard stopped, because on touching the saint's foot he had turned to stone. However, the peasant did notice, and, not quite believing what he had seen, picked the lizard up. It had indeed been turned to stone – it was now an emerald.

The emerald was sold and medicines were bought. The peasant invested the rest of the money wisely and well. From its profits he caused a hospital to be built which was free for the poor. Eventually he made so much money with his investments that he was able to buy back the emerald from the jeweller who had bought it from him many years before. At last he found the saint still walking the dusty roads. He placed the emerald in the old man's hands and thanked him for the loan. The saint had no memory of the jewel. 'It can't be mine, dear boy', he said wonderingly. Nevertheless, the younger curled the old man's fingers around it. But then there was a movement between the fingers, a flick of forked tongue, a flash of pointed tail. The jewel had become a lizard once more and it slithered away.

Not all things go unnoticed. The angels in heaven got to know of the poor man's exploits and went to tell God about them. Surely this was joyous news – that there was someone so very good on Earth? It was joyous news indeed, and God ordered that an angel find the man and grant him a wish as a reward, as long as the wish was for himself and himself only. At first the man refused the gift, saying that he was perfectly content. The angel became anxious – he had been given an order by the Most High and needed to carry it out. At last, taking pity on the angel, he agreed to make his wish: 'If ever I do a good deed may I never look upon it, may I never dwell upon it, may it always be behind me.' That is why, if you ever meet this man yourself, he never looks where his shadow falls and he is always walking towards the light.

Sharon Jacksties

APPENDIX

(to accompany Chapter 4, Storytelling for Disability in Covid-19)

Health Care Professionals Survey

We ask you to answer the following questions thinking about the past few weeks (from March 9 to March 30)

1. Are you working now?
   ○ Yes
   ○ No

2. Lately has your mood changed?

   | Not at all | 1 ○ | 2 ○ | 3 ○ | 4 ○ | Very much |

During the last few weeks, to what extent have you found yourself in the following conditions in your work environment?

3. Do you feel angry?

   | Never | 1 ○ | 2 ○ | 3 ○ | 4 ○ | Always |

4. Have you ever had episodes of aggressiveness and nervousness?

   | Never | 1 ○ | 2 ○ | 3 ○ | 4 ○ | Always |

Appendix

5. Do you have the feeling of doing unnecessary things if you don't work?

   Never 1 ○ 2 ○ 3 ○ 4 ○ Always

6. Did you have trouble falling asleep, insomnia?

   Never 1 ○ 2 ○ 3 ○ 4 ○ Always

7. Are you afraid?

   Never 1 ○ 2 ○ 3 ○ 4 ○ Always

8. Do you have a lack of ideas, an absence of initiative?

   Never 1 ○ 2 ○ 3 ○ 4 ○ Always

9. Do you feel anxiety and worry?

   Never 1 ○ 2 ○ 3 ○ 4 ○ Always

10. Do you feel tired or stressed?

    Never 1 ○ 2 ○ 3 ○ 4 ○ Always

During the past few weeks, have you ever had:

11. Want to go to work:

    Never 1 ○ 2 ○ 3 ○ 4 ○ Always

Appendix

12. Desire to meet and interact with colleagues:

    Never   1   2   3   4   Always

13. Desire to meet and talk to friends outside work:

    Never   1   2   3   4   Always

14. Desire and propensity to stay at home:

    Never   1   2   3   4   Always

15. Desire to meet your patients:

    Never   1   2   3   4   Always

16. Desire to share your own work with colleagues:

    Never   1   2   3   4   Always

17. Desire to be able to confide or tell one's own experience with someone:

    Never   1   2   3   4   Always

18. Desire to take time out for conversations with parents:

    Never   1   2   3   4   Always

Appendix

19. You did your own work as best you could:

   Never 1 ○ 2 ○ 3 ○ 4 ○ 5 ○ Always

During the past few weeks, to what extent have you implemented the following behaviors:

20. You went to work as often as you were allowed?

   Never 1 ○ 2 ○ 3 ○ 4 ○ 5 ○ Always

21. Did you pay particular attention to what the parents told you?

   Never 1 ○ 2 ○ 3 ○ 4 ○ 5 ○ Always

22. Did you keep a diary of your personal experience?

   Never 1 ○ 2 ○ 3 ○ 4 ○ 5 ○ Always

23. You avoided going to work?

   Never 1 ○ 2 ○ 3 ○ 4 ○ 5 ○ Always

24. You carried out your work in a confused and chaotic way?

   Never 1 ○ 2 ○ 3 ○ 4 ○ 5 ○ Always

25. Did you confide in someone or tell someone about your feelings?

   Never 1 ○ 2 ○ 3 ○ 4 ○ 5 ○ Always

Appendix

26. You maintained the relationship you had previously established with patients?

    Never 1 ○ 2 ○ 3 ○ 4 ○ 5 ○ Always

27. You tried to contact patients you haven't met in person?

    Never 1 ○ 2 ○ 3 ○ 4 ○ 5 ○ Always

28. Have you dealt with patients remotely through calls or messages?

    Never 1 ○ 2 ○ 3 ○ 4 ○ 5 ○ Always

29. Did you take a space and time to talk to the parents of your patients?

    Never 1 ○ 2 ○ 3 ○ 4 ○ 5 ○ Always

30. How did you manage to deal with patients remotely?
    - [ ] Calling to greet and warn of the interruption of the activity in the ward
    - [ ] Suggesting activities to do at home
    - [ ] Speaking with parents regularly several times a week
    - [ ] Welcoming parents' concerns
    - [ ] Following the family in carrying out specific activities from home
    - [ ] I didn't worry about it
    - [ ] Other: _____

31. To which patients (or families) did you manage to dedicate your attention?
    - [ ] I have not paid particular attention to anyone
    - [ ] To all without distinction
    - [ ] I talked to everyone, but there were a few I followed the more
    - [ ] I have followed more those patients whom I believe are in need the most
    - [ ] I have followed more patients with whom I have established a good relationship
    - [ ] I have followed only the patients with whom I have established a good relationship
    - [ ] I have followed the nicest patients the most
    - [ ] I followed more patients that it was easier for me to manage remotely
    - [ ] Other: _____

32. How satisfied are you with the work you've done during the past few weeks?

| Not at all | 1 ○ | 2 ○ | 3 ○ | 4 ○ | 5 ○ | Very much |

33. Finally, we ask you to leave us a little personal statement on your experience of these weeks, also in relation to your work, and the relationship with the patients

_____
_____
_____
_____
_____

Parents' Survey

We ask you to take a few minutes to answer these short questions, in relation to the last three weeks (from March 9 to March 30). In this particular emergency period, our purpose is to observe the situation of the families we care about, and understand any kind of difficulties that families may be dealing with, also in relation to the changes that have occurred in the modalities of the therapeutic service provided to your children by health care professionals (HCP).

1. Year of birth:
   _____

2. Gender:
   ○ Male
   ○ Female
   ○ Other:_____

3. Instruction:
   ○ Elementary school
   ○ Superior
   ○ Graduation
   ○ Other:_____

4. Profession:
   ○ Employee
   ○ Retiree
   ○ Freelance
   ○ Unemployed
   ○ Other:_____

Appendix

Answer the following questions in relation to your experiences during the past three weeks (From March 9 to March 30)

5. Current working situation:
   - ○ Regularly work
   - ○ Smart working (works from home)
   - ○ Redundancy fund
   - ○ Unemployed
   - ○ Other:_____

6. If you went to work, how much did you feel at risk during work?

   Not at all 1 ○ 2 ○ 3 ○ 4 ○ 5 ○ Very much

7. How many times did you bring your son or daughter to the IRC?

   Never 1 ○ 2 ○ 3 ○ 4 ○ 5 ○ Always

8. When you were at IRC in the past few weeks, were you satisfied with the HCP's work?

   Not at all 1 ○ 2 ○ 3 ○ 4 ○ 5 ○ Very much

9. Do you think that the needs of your child have been met?

   Not at all 1 ○ 2 ○ 3 ○ 4 ○ 5 ○ Very much

10. Have you received clear information regarding the organization of IRC activities in the previous weeks?

    Not at all 1 ○ 2 ○ 3 ○ 4 ○ 5 ○ Very much

Appendix

11. Was it difficult living at home during these weeks?

    Not at all 1 ○ 2 ○ 3 ○ 4 ○ 5 ○ Very much

12. Was it difficult being with your son or daughter during these weeks?

    Not at all 1 ○ 2 ○ 3 ○ 4 ○ 5 ○ Very much

13. Have you been given advice on activities to do at home with your child?

    Not at all 1 ○ 2 ○ 3 ○ 4 ○ 5 ○ Very much

14. Have there been any moments during these weeks when you needed help?

    Not at all 1 ○ 2 ○ 3 ○ 4 ○ 5 ○ Very much

15. Did you need to confide in someone?

    Not at all 1 ○ 2 ○ 3 ○ 4 ○ 5 ○ Very much

16. Would you like to be able to tell someone about your experience?

    Not at all 1 ○ 2 ○ 3 ○ 4 ○ 5 ○ Very much

17. Lately has your mood changed?

    Never 1 ○ 2 ○ 3 ○ 4 ○ Always

Appendix

18. Have you ever had episodes of aggressiveness and nervousness?

    Never 1 2 3 4 Always

19. Did you have trouble falling asleep, insomnia?

    Never 1 2 3 4 Always

20. Do you have a lack of ideas, an absence of initiative?

    Never 1 2 3 4 Always

21. Do you feel anxiety and worry?

    Never 1 2 3 4 Always

22. Do you feel tired or stressed?

    Never 1 2 3 4 Always

23. Did you keep a diary of your personal experience?

    Not at all 1 2 3 4 Very much

24. Did you confide in someone or tell someone about your feelings?

    Never 1 2 3 4 Always

Appendix

25. Do you think that the support from the IRC during this period is sufficient?

    Not at all 1 ○ 2 ○ 3 ○ 4 ○ 5 ○ Very much

26. Did you find it necessary to contact the HCP of the IRC?

    Not at all 1 ○ 2 ○ 3 ○ 4 ○ 5 ○ Very much

27. Have you tried to contact the HCP of the IRC?

    Not at all 1 ○ 2 ○ 3 ○ 4 ○ 5 ○ Very much

28. Were you able to organize the time and activities to do at home with your child?

    Not at all 1 ○ 2 ○ 3 ○ 4 ○ 5 ○ Very much

29. Have you managed to keep in touch with the HCP of the IRC for continuity of therapy?

    Not at all 1 ○ 2 ○ 3 ○ 4 ○ 5 ○ Very much

30. Have you had the opportunity to speak to the HCP of the IRC to establish a goal and a treatment modality during these weeks?

    Not at all 1 ○ 2 ○ 3 ○ 4 ○ 5 ○ Very much

31. If you managed to do activities with your child, how did you feel about these moments?
    - ☐ Struggling
    - ☐ Bored
    - ☐ Satisfied
    - ☐ Full of energy and ideas
    - ☐ Indifferent
    - ☐ Other:_____

Appendix

32. Finally, we ask you to leave us a little personal statement on your experience of these weeks, also in relation to your child, and the work of the IRC HCP.

INDEX

Note: Page numbers in **bold** indicate tables; those in *italics* indicate figures.

Abramovic, M. 126
Acropolis 270
adapting oral tales 231–232; reasons for 232; *Yomandene and the Stubborn Son* 232–239
adolescents *see* children and young people
Adoption Support Fund (UK) 304
adoptive foster and kinship families 304–313
Adults in the Room (film) 123
Adventures and Misadventures of Fanny Fust, The 187
Aeschylus 127
aesthetic distance 284
aesthetics of learning disability performance 184–185
Agamben, G. 132
aggression: against people with learning difficulties 299; social healing 210
Alsawy, S. 340
Amina and the Silent City 250, 366–371
Amnesty International 243
amygdala 48, 49, 278
Anansi 293
anchor words 196
Andersen, H.C. 172; *The Emperor and the Nightingale* 64–66
anecdotal stories: English language teaching and learning 144, 146–147, *147*; healthcare settings 288
anger: City Mission Boston, Public Voice Project 200, 202; crisis intervention team 281; foster families 318–320; learning disabilities, people with 297; social healing 210; *Yomandene and the Stubborn Son* 238
Animals in the Forest 282–283
anxiety: adopted children 311, 312; City Mission Boston, Public Voice Project 194; Covid-19 pandemic 7, 9, 14, 37, 41; dementia, people living with 326, 358; Drimmo story 168; English language teaching and learning 145, 148; fostered children 318; Irpinian culture 224; learning disabilities, people with 188; Narrative Medicine 37, 41; pitfalls in story-work 71; trauma, adult survivors of 305
archetypal stories: Covid-19 pandemic 13, 15; healthcare settings 287, 291, 294; Mahabharata 102, 105–107; multiple meanings 63; myths 122, 125; Trickster-Fool 130–132
Archytas of Tarentum 65
Aristotle 124; catharsis 8, 159, 271; tragedy 271, 273
Armstrong, J. 181
art, storytelling as 142
art therapy: learning disabilities, people with 181; multi-sensory storytelling 118; sand tray 114
Arthurian legend 303
Artists in Healthcare Manitoba (AIHM) 287
arts in health movement 111, 113, 114
Ashmolean Museum 271
assertiveness, adopted children 310
Astell, A.J. 351
asylum seekers 243–245, 247, 250, 253
Atellan Farce 218
attachment: adopted children 305–307; Burnett's *The Secret Garden* 48, 50, 51; and culture 305–306; foster families 316–324; limbic system 48; Neuro Dramatic Play 166; Theatre of Attachment model 304, 307–313; Through the Fairy Door to the Land of Stories 51
Auden, W.H. 181
Austen, J. 172

authenticity: English language teaching and learning 147; English theatre 161; learning disabilities, people with 183, 184, 185; 'Metamyth: Therapy through the Arts in Museums'© 273
autistic spectrum disorder: case studies 298–299, 300–301; *I believe in unicorns* 254, 256
autobiographical memory 352, 357, 359
autonomy: dementia, people living with 327, 328; English language teachers 147, 148; learning disabilities, people with 188; prisoners 95, 98
Awomgalema 187
Ayalon, O. 278

Babych, M. 162
Bai, H. 351
Baker, J.R. 382
Bakweri people 231, 233
balloon exercise for people living with dementia 328
Bamber, H. 243, 244, 247
Barnett, M., Jr 158
Barnett, M., Sr 158–159
Barrie, J.M. 171
Barthes, R. 126
Bartlett, F.C. 142
Barton, D. 146
Basile, G. 214
Bateson, G. 12
bearing witness: clay stories 267; healthcare settings 292; social healing 210–211; Sophocles' *King Oedipus* 79–80, 82
Beckett, S. 132, 156; *Waiting for Godot* 121, 156
Beloved story 25–26
Benjamin, W.A. 63, 68
bereavement *see* death and bereavement
Best Hunters, The 374–376
Bhagavatha Purana 109
Bible: burning bush 265; missionaries 232; sower parable 12–13, 15
bibliotherapy 278
Big Wave, The 279–280
Black Lives Matter 83, 252
Blake, W. 130
Blowsnake, S. 131
Boal, A. 107
Bohanek, J.G. 307
Booker, C. 112
Bose, P. 352
Boston Public Voice Project (PVP) 191–203
Bowlby, J. 50
Bowyer, S. 304
brain 48–49, 55–56; corpus callosum 52, 55; cortex activity 49–50; dementia 353, 357; dopamine 49; dreams 278; everyday reality and dramatic reality pairing 52; mirror neurons 49; multi-sensory storytelling 118; neural coupling 49; psychotrauma 284; stroke 357
Branch, K. 186
breathing exercises 196
Brecht, B. 132
Breuer, J. 277
Brexit 123
Brooker, D. 327
Bruner, J. 307
Buchbinder, D. 208
Buck, S.P. 279
Buddha 350; and Covid-19 pandemic 12, 13–14, 16–17
Buddhism 350–351; Zen stories and vascular dementia 350, 352–360
bullying: foster families 319; *I believe in unicorns* 254; learning disabilities, people with 187
Burnard, P. 148
Burnett, F.H., *The Secret Garden* 48, 50–51
Butake, B. 232

Calvert, D. 183, 184
Calvino, I. 133, 226
Cameroon, *Yomandene and the Stubborn Son* 231–239
Campbell, J. 13, 102, 112, 121, 122, 278
caporaballo 214, 218, 220–221, *220*, 228
Capossela, V. 229
Caps for Sale 294
Capstick, A. 344
Captain Tom Moore 15, 17
Carmichael, A., *Camina Gadelica: Hymns and Incantation* 69–70
Carroll, L.: *Humpty Dumpty* 280; *Through the Looking Glass* 289
Carstensen, J.G. 65, 66
Carter, A., 'Twelve Wild Ducks' 90n1
Castaño, E. 344
Casula, C.C. 41
Catannach, A. 121
catharsis: drama 8; English theatre 159; Mahabharata 106, 108; museums 271
cave drawings 275–276, 396
Caw, J. 306
ceremonies, adoptive foster and kinship families 308, 309, 313
Charon, R. 30, 33
Chasing the Sun 251, 371–372
check-ins, City Mission Boston, Public Voice Project 197, 201, 202
Chekhov, A. 396
children and young people: adopted 304–313; brain function 49; with challenges 254–260; clay stories 261–268; dementia (*The Forest of Lost Memories*) 382–395; developmental disability 30–42, 398–408; Drimmo story 166–168; fostered 316–324; Jungle Theatre

Company 152–155; learning disabilities 180, 300–301; moral transformation 231–239; Neuro Dramatic Play 47, 111–119; protection 323; rights 47, 304; second language learning 146; Through the Fairy Door to the Land of Stories 48, 51; traumatic situations, stories in 278

Chippewa Cree people 246, 296

Chukchi people 294

Churchill (film) 123

Cinderella 319, 323

City Mission Boston, Public Voice Project (PVP) 191–203

Clandinin, D.J. 344

Clark, R. 158–159

clay stories 261–268; adopted children 309, 312

Clever Mountain Girl, The 170; story 172–174; workshop 171–178

Cohen, A. 351

collaboration: adoptive foster and kinship families 313; dementia, people living with 337, 339, 341, 343, 347

collective unconscious 112; clay 261; Covid-19 pandemic 8, 9; myths 122, 125; Rosen and Oxenbury's *We're Going on a Bear Hunt* 114

colonialism 252

Colton, C.C. 172

Commedia dell'Arte 132

communication: clay stories 262; Covid-19 pandemic 12, 15, 30–33; dementia, people living with 327–329, 331, 337, 340, 354–355, 359; developmental disability 30–33, 40–41; difficulties 296–303, 354–355, 359; English language teaching and learning 144–146, 148, 149; families 232; foster families 319; healing 313; learning disabilities, people with 183; pitfalls in story-work 66, 67, 68; prisoners 91; social healing 208

community: Bakweri 231; City Mission Boston, Public Voice Project 192–193, 198, 202–203; English language teaching and learning 145; English theatre 156–163; healthcare settings 287; Irpinia, Italy 222, 226; learning disabilities, people with 181; oral storytelling 86, 87; prisoners 93, 95, 96, 98; social healing 207, 209; torture survivors and their families 246

compassion: adoptive foster and kinship families 307, 313; City Mission Boston, Public Voice Project 193, 203; dementia, people living with 359; torture survivors and their families 249, 253; Zen Buddhism 351

compassion fatigue 281

confidence: adopted children 313; children and young people with challenges 256; City Mission Boston, Public Voice Project 193, 194; dementia, people living with 327, 329, 345, 359; Drimmo story 166; foster families 318; Jungle Theatre Company 154; learning disabilities, people with 183, 184, 185; prisoners 96, 98

connection: adoptive foster and kinship families 306; City Mission Boston, Public Voice Project 195, 198, 199; Covid-19 pandemic 12–17; dementia, people living with 327–329, 331, 339, 343, 346, 347, 356; healthcare settings 295; 'Metamyth: Therapy through the Arts in Museums'© 272; social healing 208

Connelly, F.M. 344

Contact, Theory of 262

container, therapist as 79, 82

Convention on the Rights of the Child 47, 304

corpus callosum 52, 55

Corrao, F. 135

cortex activity 49–50

counselling people with learning disabilities 181

counter-transference 74

courage: City Mission Boston, Public Voice Project 192, 194, 203; dementia, people living with 354; social healing 207, 211; torture survivors and their families 250, 251; *Yomandene and the Stubborn Son* 238

Covid-19 pandemic 2; The Deathlands 20, 26–27; developmental disability 30–42, 398–408; dramatic perspective 7–11; learning disabilities, people with 183, 189n4; multiple stories 43–44; Narrative Medicine 30–42, 398–408; Siddhartha and Captain Tom stories 12–17

Cracked Pot, The 321

Craft, A. 143

creation myths 251, 261

creativity: adapting oral tales 237; adopted children 307, 310, 312; as a basic need 275; children and young people with challenges 256; *The Clever Mountain Girl* workshop 175, 177; dementia, people living with 328, 346, 354–355, 357–359; dramatherapy 175, 177; English language teaching and learning 141, 147–149; foster families 316; healthcare settings 294–295; 'Metamyth/Dramatherapy'© 272; 'Metamyth: Therapy through the Arts in Museums'© 272, 273; myths 121; Neuro Dramatic Play 114; physical and mental health 111; prisoners 92, 94, 95; social healing 204, 207–209; storytelling as stimulus for 143

Creed, R. 156–157, 158, 161, 162

Crimmens, P., *Storymaking and Creative Groupwork with Older People* 334

crisis intervention team 280–281

Csapo, E. 8

culture 396; adapting oral tales 232; adoptive foster and kinship families 305–308, 313; and attachment 305–306; blackberries 265; children and young people with challenges 257; Chippewa Cree nation 246; Cypriot stories

164; dementia, people living with 341, 343, 347; English language teaching and learning 144–146, 149; English theatre 157; foster families 316; healthcare settings 291; heritage maintained through stories 351; and identity 306; institutional 252; Irpinia, Italy 212, 215, 218; Jungle Theatre Company 152–153, 155; learning disabilities day centre 302; 'Metamyth: Therapy through the Arts in Museums'© 272, 273; social healing 205–207; stories 317; storytelling as 142; torture survivors and their families 245–250

Cypriot stories 164; Drimmo 164–168; Neuro Dramatic Play 166–168

Cyrulnik, B. 312

Dancing through the Shadows (Vergette) 160–163
Daoguang Emperor 65
Darkest Hour (film) 123
Davies, S.L. 159
Day of the Dead ritual 21, 22
Daykin, N. 113
De Bono, E. 143
De Botton, A. 181
De Martino, E. 220, 221
De Simone, R. 220
Dear Paul McCartney (Sproxton) 159
death and bereavement: adoptive foster and kinship families 309; *Big Wave* 279–280; Buddhism 17; clay stories 266–268; Covid-19 pandemic 9, 14, 15, 21, 27; crisis intervention team 281; The Deathlands 19–28; fear of, in Post Traumatic Stress Disorder 277; foster families 320, 323; Near Death Experience 283; oral storytelling 83–84; preparation for death 287–295; ritual 21; therapist–client relationship 78

Death Café movement 21
Deathlands, The 19–20, 28; Bereavement shire 25–26; Diagnosis shire 22–23; Dying Process shire 23–24; Grace 26–27; Peripherality shire 24–25; stories and ritual in 22

Declaration of Human Rights 245
dementia, people living with: *The Forest of Lost Memories* 382–395; power of storytelling 326–336; sharing experiences of living dementia 337–347; Zen stories 350–360
depression: dementia, people living with 329; healing stories 281; social healing 208, 210
destructiveness, Covid-19 pandemic 9–10
developmental disability 30–42, 398–408
Dewey, J. 148
Dia de Muertos ritual 21, 22
Diasporic Genius 208–209
Diné people, *Mountain Chant* 69–70
Discepolo, E.S. 228
Disney, W. 84

dissociation 283
Djoha 135
Doh, G. 232
Dokter, D. 9
Donne, J., *A Valediction Forbidding Mourning* 74
dopamine 49
Doran, G. 157
Downs, H. 172
Down's syndrome: case studies 297–298, 301–302; life expectations 180
drama: Covid-19 pandemic 7–11; meanings of 7–8; story and therapy, connection between 112; and the three-legged stool 1, 2; *see also* Neuro Dramatic Play

dramatherapy 8; *The Clever Mountain Girl* workshop 170–178; Covid-19 pandemic 9; dementia, people living with 326–328, 353; everyday reality and dramatic reality pairing 52; Grace 27–28; 'Metamyth/Dramatherapy'© 272; multi-sensory storytelling 118; myths 120–124, 126–128; Neuro Dramatic Play 112; pitfalls 61, 62; safety and intimacy 176–177; sand play 114; therapist–client relationship 73–82

dramatic irony 10
dreamcatchers 277–278
Drimmo story 164–168
Drumm, M. 148, 343
drumming exercise for people living with dementia 328, 331–335
Dunkirk (film) 123
Durkheim, E. 126
Dying Matters 21
dyslexia 256

East, H., *The Singing Sack* 329, 331, 332
Eden is West (film) 123
Edgar, D. 158
education: English language teaching and learning 141, 143–149; prisoners 91–92
Einstein, A. 171
Elam, K. 7, 8, 10
Elijah and the Wish 293
Eliot, T.S., *Four Quartets* 82
Elizabeth II 10–11
embodied memory 352–354, 356–358
Embodiment–Projection–Role (EPR) model 167, 170; children and young people with challenges 255–260, **258–259**; multi-sensory approach 111, 113–118; safety and intimacy 176–177
Emergency Shakespeare 98
emotional intelligence: City Mission Boston, Public Voice Project 193; learning disabilities, people with 303
emotional literacy, foster carers 317–324
emotions: adoptive foster and kinship families 305–308; children and young people with challenges 256; City Mission Boston, Public

Voice Project 194, 197, 200, 203; clay stories 267; dementia, people living with 328, 329, 342, 346, 357, 359; English theatre 157; fostered children 317, 318; healthcare settings 291; Mahabharata 103; 'Metamyth: Therapy through the Arts in Museums'© 272; and natural environment 382; prisoners 94; social healing 210; traumatic situations 277, 284

empathy 296; adoptive foster and kinship families 305, 306, 307, 313; bereaved people 281; Burnett's *The Secret Garden* 51; City Mission Boston, Public Voice Project 193, 199; dementia, people living with 340; developmental disability 40; English language teaching and learning 144, 146, 148; foster families 318, 319; learning disabilities, people with 187, 297; oral storytelling 83, 86; prisoners 93, 97, 98; response-tasks 68; social healing 206, 208; Sophocles' *King Oedipus* 76–79, 82; traumatic situations 278, 281

empowerment: adopted children 313; City Mission Boston, Public Voice Project 193, 196, 199–203; creativity 143; dementia, people living with 340, 359; Drimmo story 166, 168; learning disabilities, people with 189; SEE FAR CBT 284; torture survivors and their families 247

Enchanted Blackberry, The 262, 264–266, 268

engagement: City Mission Boston, Public Voice Project 199; clay stories 267; dementia, people living with 339–344, 346–347, 353–354, 357, 358; English language teaching and learning 145, 149; English theatre 156; foster families 320; learning disabilities, people with 184, 303; Neuro Dramatic Play 114; prisoners 93, 98

English for Speakers of Other Languages (ESOL) learners 141, 144–149

English theatre 156–163

Entertaining Strangers (Edgar) 158, 162

ethical conduct: Indian thought (*dharma*) 103, 104, 108; torture perpetrators 253

Euripides 127

European Court of Human Rights 244

Every Time it Rains (Creed) 158, 162

evolution 276–277, *276*; play's role 306

Fairy Door 48, 51–55, *53*, *54*

fairy tales: *The Clever Mountain Girl* 170–178; Covid-19 pandemic 20, 21; cultural aspects 142; foster families 319, 321; Italian 133; and myths, difference between 122; traumatic situations 278

Fantasia (film) 217

fear: adopted children 305–308; City Mission Boston, Public Voice Project 194, 200, 202; Covid-19 pandemic 7, 14, 15; dementia, people living with 328; fostered children 318, 319; healthcare settings 290, 294; moral teaching 103; prisoners 97; Sophocles' *King Oedipus* 77; trauma, adult survivors of 305; traumatic situations 275–278, 283; *Yomandene and the Stubborn Son* 231–233, 239

Fels, D.I. 351

Fesenko, P. 218

Festival at the Edge 185

Finders Keepers (Davies) 159

First Nations people 246

Fivush, R. 307

Floyd, G. 83

Fo, D. 130, 132

folk tales: *Awomgalema* 187; Basile 214; cultural aspects 142; dementia, people living with 329; healthcare settings 287–290, 293–294; Italian 133

Folke Bernadotte Academy (FBA) 204, 206

Fool archetype 130, 132; Giufà 130, 132–138

Forest of Lost Memories, The 382–395

Forget-me-not-pot; Not the Witch's Pot, The 262–264, 268

Forster, E.M. 60

foster families: attachment and emotional literacy 316–324; life story therapy 304–313

Fostering Network 317

Foucault, M. 221, 272

Frazer, J. 124, 126

Freedom from Torture 243–253

Freud, S. 9, 125, 126, 277

Frog Wife, The 290

Frohlich, D.M. 342

Fudduni, P. 130, 135–136, 137

Fulani people 306

Fust, F. 187

Gaelic people: *Carmina Gadelica: Hymns and Incantation* (Carmichael) 69–70; Samhain 48

Gallowfield Players 95–97

Gareth of Orkney 303

Gavras, C. 123

Gawhâ 135

Gazzaniga, M. 55

Genette, G. 60

Georgousopoulos, K. 124

Gersie, A. 2, 112, 114

Gilgamesh 294

Giufà 130, 132–4; avatars in Sicily 135–136; being and appearing 137–138; in the Mediterranean world 134–135

Godber, J. 159

Goldsilver, P.M. 344

Gonzenbach, L. 133

Gorečan, K., *The Forest of Lost Memories* 382–395

Gorelick, P.B. 352

Gotami, K. 16–17

Gottschall, J. 278

Grace 21; The Deathlands 22, 25, 26–27; dramatherapy 27–28
Great Greedy Beast story 27
Greek mythology 120–125, 127–128; 'Metamyth: Therapy through the Arts in Museums'© 270, 273; Trickster archetype 132
Gridley, K. 341
grief *see* death and bereavement
Grimm, J. and W., *Cinderella* 319, 323
Grinberger, I. 284
Grove, N. 302, 324
Gruneir, M.R.B. 344
Guhâ 130, 135
Guhi 135
guilds 157
guitar 300

Haen, A. 307
Hamilton, M. 146
Hammel, S. 112
Hardy, B. 179
Hargrave, M. 184
Harrison, J. 126
Harry Potter stories 319
Harry's Luck (Vergette) 159–160
Harvard Centre for Child Development 66
Haven, K.F. 59
healing 281–283; City Mission Boston, Public Voice Project 192–203; clay stories 268; communication 313; dementia, people living with 356; Mahabharata 107–110; 'Metamyth: Therapy through the Arts in Museums'© 273–274; myths 122; social 204–211; torture perpetrators 252–253; torture survivors and their families 246–247; traumatic situations, stories in 276–277
health care professionals (HCP) 30–42, *35, 36, 37,* 398–403
health care settings, storytelling in 287–295
Healthfield, D. 144
Henley, D. 94
Henriksen, D. 147
Hermes myth 132
hidden histories, people with learning disabilities 186–187
Hillman, J. 13, 16
historic stories, people with learning disabilities 186–187
Holland, K.C. 181
Holmwood, C. 1–3, 5, 7–11, 45, 111–119
Homer: Hermes hymn 132; *Iliad* 122, 127; *Odyssey* 127
hope: City Mission Boston, Public Voice Project 201; clay stories 266; Covid-19 pandemic 15; Cypriot stories 164; healing stories 281
hospitals and hospices, storytelling in 287–295
How to Train your Dragon (film) 324

Howe, D. 305
Hughes, D. 322
Hull Truck Theatre 158–162
humanity: Earth, bond with 268; social healing 204, 207; torture survivors and their families 253; *Yomandene and the Stubborn Son* 234
humour: City Mission Boston, Public Voice Project 196, 200; dementia, people living with 332, 338, 344, 346; foster families 321; learning disabilities, people with 301; oral storytelling 86
Humpty Dumpty 280–281
Hyde, L. 131–132
Hydén, L.-C. 339, 341, 346

I believe in unicorns (Morpurgo) 254–260
identity: adoptive foster and kinship families 306–308, 310, 313; autobiographical identity 352; children in care 304; and culture 306; dementia, people living with 327–329, 337, 342, 344, 345, 359; Irpinia, Italy 212–214; learning disabilities, people with 184–185; names 205; social healing 205, 209
ill people, storytelling for 287–295
imagery, in healthcare settings 287, 291, 294–295
imagination: children and young people with challenges 255, 260; clay stories 264, 266; dementia, people living with 328, 354–355, 357, 359; English language teachers 141, 147, 148; English theatre 157; foster families 317, 318, 322; healthcare settings 294–295; myths 124; oral storytelling 87, 89; psychotrauma 283; social healing 204, 207, 209
individualism 206–207
intellectual disabilities *see* learning disabilities, people with
interrogative questions as pitfall 61–63
intimacy, Embodiment Projection Role (EPR) model 176–177
Ionesco, E. 156
Iraqi oil situation 204–205
Irpinia, Italy 212–229
Ishiguro, K. 212
isiXhosa people 153
İslamoğlu, M. 164
isolationism, and Covid-19 pandemic 9–10
Israel, bibliotherapy 278
Italy: Atellan Farce 218; Irpinia 212–229

Jacksties, S. 2, 189, 241, 243–253, 326, 363, 365, 396–397
janare 214, 216–217, 221
Jeffrey, B. 143
Jellicoe, A. 158
Jennings, S. 1, 61, 272, 308, 313, 328: attachment and culture 306; drama as ritual 8, 9–10; Embodiment Projection Role (EPR) model 111, 113, 114, 116, 118, 167, 170, 176,

255–257, 260; healing 313; myths 120, 121, 122; Neuro Dramatic Play 111, 112–113, 166–167; Through the Fairy Door 45, 47–56
Johnson, M. 70
joy, people living with dementia 328, 329, 332, 356, 359
Joyce, J. 124; *Ulysses* 229
Jung, C.G.: collective unconscious 8, 9, 112, 114, 125, 261; earth 261; neuroticism 13; sand play 114; Wakdjŭnkaga myth 131, 132
Jungle Book (film) 84
Jungle Jive (Jungle Theatre Company) 153–154
Jungle Theatre Company (JTC) 152–155

Kalff, D.M. 114
Kaplansky, N. 283
Keady, J. 345
Kearney, R. 340
Keats, J. 209
Kerenyi, K. 122, 125, 132
Killick, S. 307, 321
Kim, S. 351
Kipling, R., Six Honest Men 60
Korkut and the Music of Death story 22–23
Kottler, J. 338–340, 343
Kytna's Story 294

Labov, W. 143
Lacher, D. 317, 323
Lahad, M. 121, 278
Lakoff, G. 70
Lanchester, W. 51
Lancy, D. 306
Landy, M. 284
Landy, R. 121
Lane, N. 159, 161
language skills 142–143; dementia, people living with 338–339, 341, 345, 347, 354–355, 358, 359; English language teaching and learning 141, 144–149; fostered children 324; Neuro Dramatic Play 114, 115
Laurel and Hardy 301
learning disabilities, people with 180, 296–297, 300; case studies 297–303; *I believe in unicorns* 254; OpenStoryTellers' work 179–189
legends: Arthurian cycle 303; Irpinia, Italy 216; learning disabilities, people with 185–186
Leszcz, M. 15, 16
Levi-Strauss, C. 125
Liebling, M. 143
life story therapy: adoptive foster and kinship families 304–313; dementia, people living with 342, 358; foster families 316; validation 341
lifelong learning 337–338, 341, 343, 345
limbic system 48–49, 278
Linguistic Inquiry and Word Count (LIWC) 41
linguistic scheme theory 142

listening: active 193, 198, 199, 338, 340–341, 347; altered consciousness 351; careless, as story-work pitfall 66–68; children 113; City Mission Boston, Public Voice Project 193, 198–199, 202, 203; dementia, people living with 338–341, 344, 347; English language teaching and learning 143, 146; foster families 317, 319–320, 322; healthcare settings 288–289, 291–295; learning disabilities, people with 188; Mahabharata 103, 104; oral storytelling 84, 86; social healing 205, 208, 210–211; torture survivors and their families 246, 247
literacy skills 145–146, 149
Lonebird story 23–24
Lonely Mermaid, The 329–331
Louvre 271
Love 83–84
Ludwin, L. 344
Luma, F. 233
Lynn, V. 10

Magic Drum, The 293
Magic Fish, The 292
Mahabharata 101–104; healing 107–110; Immersion 104–107
Malinovski, B. 123
Mallows, D. 144
Mandela, N. 171
Mann, T. 124–125
Maori people 153
Marin, K.A. 307
Marshall, B. 181
Martin, L.S. 344
Maruna, S. 92
Maslow's Hierarchy of Needs 275, 327; prisoners 95
Mathura, A. 304
Matthews, W. 69
May, J. 317
May, R. 13
Maybe Good, Maybe Bad 291
McCaffrey, T. 183, 184
McCulloch, E. 304
McMurray, I. 304
McNiff, S. 288
Meader, R. 189
meaning, and people living with dementia 328
mediating role of therapist 80–81, 82
Medical Foundation for the Care of Victims of Torture and their Families (later Freedom from Torture) 243–253
Meldrum, B. 124
memories: adoptive foster and kinship families 305, 307–309; children and young people with challenges 255; clay stories 267; dementia, people living with 326–328, 337–340,

345–347, 351–359; foster families 317, 320, 322; healthcare settings 294; 'Metamyth: Therapy through the Arts in Museums'© 272; oral storytelling 87, 89; Post Traumatic Stress Disorder 283, 284; prisoners 95; retrospective/autobiographical 352, 357, 359; SEE FAR CBT 284; theatre performance 201; torture perpetrators 253; torture survivors and their families 246; traumatic 277, 283, 284

Mercier, M. 156
Meringoff, L. 255
Messia, A. 133
Metamorphosis (Jungle Theatre Company) 154
'Metamyth'© 272, 273
'Metamyth/Dramatherapy'© 272
'Metamyth: Therapy through the Arts in Museums'© 270–274

metaphors and symbols 396; adoptive foster and kinship families 309, 312; City Mission Boston, Public Voice Project 197; clay stories 266; dementia, people living with 338, 344–345, 347, 353, 355–359, 359; foster families 318, 319; healthcare settings 287, 288, 291, 294–295; myths 124; orientational 68–71; SEE FAR CBT 284; social healing 207, 209; Zen Buddhism 351, 353

Miller, A. 161–162
Miller, M. C. 8
mime 183
Minde, A. 122
mindfulness: City Mission Boston, Public Voice Project 196, 197; foster families 324; Zen Buddhist stories 350, 351
mirror neurons 49
Mishra, P. 147
Mitchell, S. 121
modelling behavioural interventions 301
Monty Python and the Holy Grail (film) 298
Moore, Captain Tom 15, 17
Moore, J. 306
moral transformation of children and youths 231
Morgan, M. 148
Morpurgo, M., *I believe in unicorns* 254–260
multi-sensory storytelling **118**; children 111–119; dementia, people living with 326, 329, 331, 334; learning disabilities, people with 188
museums 270–274
Mussolini, B. 136
Mussorgsky, M., *A night on the Mount Calvo* 216–217
Mystery Plays 157, 162
myths 120–125; blackberries 265; clay stories 261; Covid-19 pandemic 13, 15, 17, 20, 21; creation 251, 261; dramatherapy 120–124, 126–128; forms 126; Greek *see* Greek mythology; healing energies of Earth 268; healthcare settings 287–288, 290, 293–294; Irpinian culture 228; Mahabharata 108; 'Metamyth: Therapy through the Arts in Museums'© 270–274; New Mythologies 126; Philoctetes 127–128; psyche 125, 126, 131; respect for original 153; saviour 280–281; traumatic situations 277; Wakdjŭnkaga 131; wisdom 102

Nair, R. 142
Narrative Medicine 30–42
narrative scaffolding 338–340, 346, 347
narratives and stories, differences between 141
Nasreddin Hodja/Hoca 130, 135; Streetlight Effect 59–60
National Coalition of Creative Arts Therapies Associations (NCCATA) 181
National Institute for Health and Care Excellence (NICE) 304
National Storytelling Network 141
National Theatre 158
natural world: clay 261, 266, 268; and emotions 382; Jungle Theatre Company 152–155; storytelling by animals 296
Navajo people, *Mountain Chant* 69–70
Near Death Experience (NDE) 283
Nelson, O. 145
Nemcova, B., *The Clever Mountain Girl* 170–176
neo-cortex 49
neural coupling 49
neuro-diversity *see* learning disabilities, people with
Neuro Dramatic Play (NDP) 47, 111–113, **118**; Cypriot stories 166–168; Rosen and Oxenbury's *We're Going on a Bear Hunt* 113–119, *116*, *117*
neurological development 118
Nichols, T. 317
Nicolas II, Tzar 218
Nietzsche, F. 41
nightmares 277–278
Northern Trawl, The (Creed) 159, 162

Oatley, K. 319
Ojibwe people 277–278
Old Woman Who Cheated Death, The 293
Olsen-Morrison, D. 307
OpenStoryTellers 179, 188–189, 302–303; nature of the company 181–183; performance storytelling 183–185; purpose and history 180–181; stories 185–188
oral storytelling 83–90; cultural aspects 142; English language teaching and learning 145; performance 143
orientational metaphors 68–71
Oromo people 245
Oscan Games 218

Oxenbury, H. and Rosen, M., *We're Going on a Bear Hunt* 111, 113–119; developmental themes **112**
Ozer, E.J. 283
Öznur, Ş. 164, 165

Page, S. 345
palliative care centres, storytelling in 287–295
paranoia 125
parents: adapting *Yomandene and the Stubborn Son* 233; adoptive 304–313; communication with children 232; developmental disability 30–42, 37, 38, 403–408; Drimmo story 168; foster 316–324
participation: City Mission Boston, Public Voice Project 198; dementia, people living with 329–333, 335, 346, 355; Drimmo story 168; English language learning and teaching 143–145; foster families 320–321; Jungle Theatre Company 152, 154–155; learning disabilities, people with 183, 301–302; 'Metamyth: Therapy through the Arts in Museums'© 273
Paulme, D. 235
Pearson, J. 8, 9
Pennebaker, J.W. 41
performance: dementia, people living with 354, 355, 357, 358; dramatherapy 177; learning disabilities, people with 183–185, 187, 301–302; oral storytelling 143
Perry, B.D. 304, 305
person-centred therapy 327, 335–336
personal stories, Covid-19 pandemic 12, 15–16
Peter the 'Wild Boy' 186–187
Philoctetes myth 127–128
photography 337–339
physical disability 226–227
Pignatelli, M. 217
Pintalgato story 24–25
Pinter, H. 156
pitfalls in story-work 58–59, 71; careless listening and the neglect of response-tasks 66–68; ignoring the healing potential of orientational metaphors 68–71; interrogative questions and unwelcome feelings 61–63; neglecting a traditional story's multiple meanings 63–66; Streetlight Effect 59–60; unclear and underprepared for story-work 60–61
Pitrè, G. 133
play and play therapy: adoptive foster and kinship families 306–313; dementia, people living with 328, 355–357, 358; Drimmo story 166; fostered children 316–318, 321–324; learning disabilities, people with 296–303; multi-sensory storytelling 118; myths 124; sand tray 114; three-legged stool 1, 2; *see also* Neuro Dramatic Play

Playfulness, Acceptance, Curiosity and Empathy (PACE) approach 322–323
plays *see* theatre
poetry: and mythology 124; oral culture 123
Polyvagal theory 305
Pomme, C. 56
Porges, S.W. 305
Post Traumatic Stress Disorder 89, 277; pitfalls in story work 62; use of storymaking in 283–284
Poulton, M. 157
prejudice 180, 181, 187
Prenkti, T. 132
prevention model 278
Price, The (Miller) 161–162
prisoners: released 191; Shakespeare 91–98
projection 74, 80, 167; children and young people with challenges 256; myths 125; Neuro Dramatic Play 113, 114, 115; Sophocles' *King Oedipus* 75
projective identification 74, 80
Propp, V. 142
Proust, M. 171, 272
psyche: myths 125, 126, 131; psychotrauma 283; sense, quest for 278
psychotherapy: group 15, 16, 125; hope 15; learning disabilities, people with 181; myths 120, 121, 125; sand play 114
psychotrauma *see* traumatic situations, stories in
Pulcinella 132, 135
Pullman, P. 144
puppetry 51

Quilla Bung 331–332

race, and City Mission Boston, Public Voice Project 192–203
racism, and adoptive foster and kinship families 311–312
Radin, P. 131, 132
Ramayana 108–109, 396
Rand, A. 172
Rank, O. 124
rape survivors and their families 248, 250–251
rapport: learning disabilities, people with 301; Neuro Dramatic Play 114
Rapunzel 324
Read, H. 126
reading skills: dementia, people living with 354, 355; English language teaching and learning 143
Reason, M. 180, 184, 185
Red Hat, Green Hat 249–250, 365–366
reductionism, Covid-19 pandemic 9–10
refugees 243, 244, 247, 252, 253
relaxation activities, children and young people with challenges 255

reminiscence, people living with dementia 351, 353, 356–359
Remould Theatre Company 156–157
resilience: City Mission Boston, Public Voice Project 194; clay stories 267, 268; Covid-19 pandemic 36, 41, 43–44; Drimmo story 166; Embodiment Projection Role model 167; learning disabilities, people with 187, 188; multiple stories 43–44; Rosen and Oxenbury's *We're Going on a Bear Hunt* 114; social healing 207
response-tasks, neglect of as story-work pitfall 66–68
Resurrection 83–84
retrospective memory 352, 357, 359
Reynolds, R. 97
Richardson, R. 148, 149
Rinvolucri, M. 148
rituals: adoptive foster and kinship families 308, 313; Atellan Farce 218; cave drawings 276; children and young people with challenges 257; City Mission Boston, Public Voice Project 197, 198; clay stories 262, 263; death 21–22; dementia, people living with 328; drama as 8, 10; food 262; Indian culture 104–107; Irpinian culture 214, 218–220, 226, 228; Jungle Theatre Company 154–155; theatre 308
role-playing, by people with dementia 329
Romanoff, B.D. 288
Rose, H.J. 125
Rosen, M. and Oxenbury, H., *We're Going on a Bear Hunt* 111, 113–119; developmental themes **112**
Rossi, A. 220
Rowling, J.K., *Harry Potter* stories 319
Royal Tomb; Afterlife and Togetherness, A 262, 266–268
Royle, R. 157
Rumi 20, 135
Ryan, E.B. 344

safeguarding foster children 323
safety: adopted children 304–307, 310, 313; City Mission Boston, Public Voice Project 193, 195–197, 199; dementia, people living with 326, 327, 358, 359; dramatherapy 176–177; Embodiment Projection Role (EPR) model 176–177; foster families 316–320, 322–324; healing from trauma 192; learning disabilities, people with 298, 300; SEE FAR CBT 284
Saint Anthony's pig 224–226, 228
Salas, J. 15
Salt of the Earth (Godber) 159
Samhain, Festival of 48
Sami people 209–211
Samudra Manthan story 103–104

sand play: adopted children 309, 312; Neuro Dramatic Play 114–117, *116*, *117*
saviour myth 280–281
Savvidou, C. 146
Scheidt, R.J. 342
Schelling, F.W.J. 123
Scheub, H. 130, 131
Schiera, G. 130, 136
Schlegel, F. 124, 126
Schroeder, H.W. 382
Scott, J.-A. 343
Sea Shall Not Have Them, The (Remould Theatre Company) 156–157
Sebba, J. 306
second language learning 141, 144–149
security *see* safety
SEE FAR CBT 283–284, *285*
self-confidence *see* confidence
self-esteem: adopted children 305, 310–312; culture and identity 306; dementia, people living with 329, 357, 359; foster children 321; *I believe in unicorns* 254; learning disabilities, people with 296, 301, 302
Seven Circle Story Structure 52
sexual assault: institutional culture 252; torture survivors and their families 248, 250–251
Shadow of Shame, The 379–381
Shafted (Godber) 159
Shakespeare, W. 73, 396; continued relevance 13; Fools 132; *Hamlet* 156, 179; *Julius Caesar* 96–97; *Macbeth* 93–96, 156; *The Merchant of Venice* 97; *A Midsummer Night's Dream* 48, 51; myths 125; *Othello* 98; prisoner programmes 91–98; *Romeo and Juliet* 10, 94
shame: attachment theory 306; City Mission Boston, Public Voice Project 194, 201; Irpinian culture 224, 226; social healing 210; torture survivors and their families 251
Shelley, P.B. 16
Shonkoffield, J.P. 232
Short, D. 41
Sicilian folklore 130, 132–138
Siddhartha (Buddha) 350; and Covid-19 pandemic 12, 13–14, 16–17
Sills, B. 171
Simmons, R. 143, 148
single story issue, Covid-19 pandemic 43
Sioux Winnebago tribe 131
six degrees of separation 63
Six Honest Men (Kipling) 60
Slade, P. 8
small-world phenomenon 63
Smith, J.A. 92
Snake and the King's Dream, The 253, 372–374
Snow-Tiger's Whisker, The 320
social healing 204–211
social model of disability 181, 186

Index

Social Practice Theory 146
social skills: adopted children 306; fostered children 319
socialisation, English language teaching and learning 145–146
softball exercise for people living with dementia 328
Sophocles: *King Oedipus* 73–82; Philoctetes myth 127
Souter-Anderson, L. 262
South Africa: theatre 152–155; Truth and Reconciliation Commission 210
spatial orientation metaphors 68–71
speaking skills: dementia, people living with 328, 354–355; English language teaching and learning 143, 145, 146, 149; Neuro Dramatic Play 115, 117
special educational needs, prisoners 91
Spencer, M.M. 246, 249
Spider Drummer 332–334
Spiller, B. 96–97
Spiro, J. 144
Sproxton, M. 159
Sri Lanka, Zen Buddhist stories 350–360
stage directions, *Yomandene and the Stubborn Son* 234–235
stage plays *see* theatre
Stella Maris Scientific Institute Foundation, Calambrone Institute for Rehabilitation (IRC) 30–39; assessment method 33–34; research participants 32, **32**; research results 34–39; survey 398–408; training 33
Stenhouse, R. 341
stereotypes, people with learning disabilities 185, 186
Stevens, W. 124
Stevenson, R.L., *Fables* 124
stigma, people with learning disabilities 185, 186, 187
Stone of Vishnu 207–208
Stone Soup 188, 289
Stoppard, T., *Rosencrantz and Guildenstern Are Dead* 121
stories: drama and therapy, connection between 112; as lower education 20–21; nature of 141–142, 288, 396; notion of 112; and the three-legged stool 1, *2*
Storm, The (Lane) 159
Story Circles 204–211
storytelling: as art and culture 142; constructs 338–340; as creativity and participation stimulus 143–145; functions 289–290; language learning 142–143; nature of 141–142; pedagogic tool in the ESOL classroom 145–149
Streetlight Effect 59–60
stress: adoptive foster and kinship families 310; prevention 278; social healing 208

stroke 352, 356
Sufism 59–60
Sunderland, M. 112
swanee whistle 300
symbols *see* metaphors and symbols
Syrian Dialogue Meetings 206
Szalavitz, M. 305
Szifris, K. 93
Tala, K.I. 235
Talen model 318
Talking Tortoise, The 321
tango 228
tarantella 214, 219, 220, 228
Taylor, D. 87
Temiar tribe 48, 120
Thacker, D. 161
Thanatos 9
theatre: adapting oral tales 231–239; England 156–163; learning disabilities, people with 184–185; memorisation 201; 'Metamyth: Therapy through the Arts in Museums' 272; rituals 308; South Africa 152–155
Theatre of Attachment model 304, 307–313
Theory of Contact 262
therapeutic relationship 73–74; clay stories 264; dementia, people living with 359; developmental disability 31–32, 41; 'Metamyth: Therapy through the Arts in Museums' 271; Sophocles' *King Oedipus* 74–82
Thomas, T. 321
Thompson, B.E. 288
Thompson, R. 143, 148
Thoreau, H.D. 172
three-legged stool 1, *2*
Through the Fairy Door to the Land of Stories 48, 51–55, *53*, *54*
Tiepolo, G. 132
Toronto, Diasporic Genius 208–209
torture perpetrators 252–253
torture survivors and their families 243–247; aims and objectives of therapeutic group 247–248; practice of therapeutic group 248–249; stories 249–253
traditional stories, multiple meanings of 63–66
trance 48
transference 74, 80; Sophocles' *King Oedipus* 75
transitional space, museums as 271, 272, 273
transitional storytelling 288–290
trauma: adopted children 305–307, 317; fostered children 316, 318, 321
traumatic situations, stories in 275–278; *Big Wave* 279–280; crisis intervention team 280–281; healing story 281–283; prevention model 278; psychotrauma 283–285
Trickster archetype 130–132

trust: adoptive foster and kinship families 307, 310; children and young people with challenges 256; City Mission Boston, Public Voice Project 192–193, 195, 197–198, 202; dementia, people living with 327, 342; dramatherapy 176; English language teaching and learning 148; 'Metamyth: Therapy through the Arts in Museums'© 272; oral storytelling 86; social healing 207, 211; therapeutic relationship 271; torture survivors and their families 246
Turner, V. 8
Tutu, D. 210

Umlambo Wobomi – River of Life (Jungle Theatre Company) 152–153
uncertainty, and Covid-19 pandemic 9, 14, 17
unclear story-work pitfall 60–61
underprepared story-work pitfall 60–61
United Nations Convention on the Rights of the Child 47, 304
unwelcome feelings as pitfall 61–63
Up 'n' Under (Godber) 159, 162

Valery, P. 272
vascular dementia, people living with 350–352; Zen stories 350, 352–360
Vaucanson, J. de 65
Vergette, R. 159–163
Vickers, S., *The Other Side of You* 82n1
Vico, G. 124
Vishnu, Stone of 207–208
visual cortex 284
visualisation: City Mission Boston, Public Voice Project 196; dementia, people living with 354, 355; foster families 322
Voltaire 124, 171
vulnerability: adopted children 313; City Mission Boston, Public Voice Project 194, 195, 199; Covid-19 pandemic 12, 14–17, 26; healthcare settings 292

Wakdjūnkaga myth 131, 132
Watts, P. 13
We're Going on a Bear Hunt (Rosen and Oxenbury) 111, 113–119
Weber, C. 307
wellbeing: dementia, people living with 329, 359; domains of 327, 327–328; social healing 207
White, J. 148
White Stone, The 290
Wilkinson, J. 304
Wilshire, B. 80
Wilson, J.A. 146
Winnebago tribe 131, 132
Winnicott, D.W. 271, 273
wisdom: *caporaballo* 218; clay stories 261; Giufà 137–138; healthcare settings 288; myths 102; social healing 204, 206–208, 211; Zen Buddhist stories 350
witnessing *see* bearing witness
Wittgenstein, L. 126
Woolf, V. 66
Worsley, L. 186
Worst Potter, The 376–379
writing skills, and English language teaching and learning 143, 149

Yaaba 334–335
Yalom, I.D. 15, 16
Yalom, Y. 212
Yashinsky, D. 183
Yomandene and the Stubborn Son 231–239
Yorke, J. 156
Yoruba people 263
Young, E. 172
young people *see* children and young people

Z (film) 123
Zen Buddhism 350–351; vascular dementia 350, 352–360
Zha 135
Zipes, J. 65, 320

Printed in the United States
by Baker & Taylor Publisher Services